MEDIEVAL CIVILISATION

MEDIEVAL CIVILISATION

Kay Slocum

Laurence King Publishing

In Memoriam Coburn V. Graves

LAURENCE KING

Published in 2005 by Laurence King Publishing Ltd
71 Great Russell Street
London WC1B 3BP
United Kingdom
Tel: + 44 20 7430 8850
Fax: + 44 20 7430 8880
e-mail: enquiries@laurenceking.co.uk
www.laurenceking.co.uk

A catalogue record for this book is available
from the British Library

ISBN 1 85669 444 5

Commissioning: Editors Damian Thompson, Melanie White
Editor: Jessica Spencer
Designer: Karen Stafford
Picture Researcher: Emma Brown
Cover Design: Price Watkins
Maps: Advanced Illustration

Printed in Singapore

Front cover: "The Garden of Love" from *Roman de la Rose*,
Bruges, *c.* 1490. British Library, MS Harley 4425.
Back cover: Illustration from *Lancelot* by Chrétien de Troyes,
c. 1350. Bibliothèque Nationale de France.
Frontispiece: Blanche of Castile and Louis IX, from
the *Bible abregée.* © 2001, Photo Scala, Florence.

CONTENTS

PREFACE AND ACKNOWLEDGMENTS

The thousand-year period known as the Middle Ages was long thought to be a time of extreme stagnation and decline—a "dark age" in which social and intellectual progress ceased, only to begin again during the era known as the Renaissance. Although this view is no longer held by scholars, the medieval era is not yet fully appreciated for its diversity, its cultural legacy in the areas of art, architecture, music, literature, and philosophy, and its fundamental contributions to contemporary institutions such as the university and the church. In order to offer a modest remedy for this lack of recognition, this book undertakes a virtually impossible task—the integration and presentation of the many and varied facets of medieval culture and civilization. It is, of necessity, a highly selective introductory survey; many important events and personalities have been omitted or given somewhat limited treatment in order to include discussions of peripheral areas and their influence on social and cultural developments. As a result, detailed analysis has been sacrificed to breadth of coverage.

In addition to providing information about political and social developments, the book includes extensive material on art, literature, philosophy and music in medieval Europe; these analyses show the vibrant nature of medieval life and offer a path toward a richer perception of the medieval world. It is my hope that the student and general reader will come away from the book with a deeper understanding and appreciation of this multifaceted historical epoch.

I was first introduced to serious study of the Middle Ages in a class taught several decades ago by Dr. Leslie Domonkos (Professor Emeritus, Youngstown State University, Ohio). His enthusiasm and erudition stimulated my interest in this fascinating era, and I decided to pursue a doctoral degree in Medieval History at Kent State University. My work there was guided by Dr. Coburn V. Graves (Professor of History and Department Chair, now deceased), whose brilliant lectures on medieval topics provided fascinating sources of information. These, in addition to serving as models for my own classroom teaching, formed my understanding of the Middle Ages as presented in this book. As a result of the influence of Dr. Graves, I think of this text as his as much as my own, and I dedicate the work to his memory, in the hope that he would have been pleased by the result of his labors.

Appreciation is also due to the many friends and colleagues who have offered advice and support in the preparation of this book. These include Harry Jebsen (Capital University), Nigel Hiscock (Oxford Brookes University), Thomas Maroukis (Capital University), Susan Nash (Capital University), Virginia Newes (Professor Emeritus, Eastman School of Music), Alexander Pantsov (Capital University), Leslie Ross (Dominican University), Morris Slavin (Professor Emeritus, Youngstown State University), Jane Snyder (Emeritus Professor, The Ohio State University), and Cassandra Tellier (Capital University). Thanks are also due to Michael Aradas, Suzanne Balch-Lindsay, Douglas Bisson, and several anonymous reviewers who read parts of the manuscript.

The staff at Laurence King Publishing, including Melanie White and Damian Thompson (commissioning editors), Jessica Spencer (senior editor), Emma Brown (picture researcher) and Lee Greenfield (publishing director), provided gracious and helpful guidance and assistance in the preparation of this book. I am grateful for their encouragement and enthusiasm. I also wish to thank Clark Baxter (Publisher) at Wadsworth Publishing, who offered useful and supportive help at several crucial stages in the writing of the text.

My husband, Dieter Droste, drafted several of the graphs and drawings included in the text. In addition, he spent countless hours carefully reading and commenting upon the manuscript during the various stages of preparation; his helpful suggestions rescued me from many infelicities and several errors of translation. Finally, the students in my Western Civilization and Medieval History classes have played an active role in the creation of this book by reading and commenting on the primary source excerpts embedded in the text; I offer them my sincere appreciation for helping me to make choices that have appeal as well as significance.

INTRODUCTION

Why study the Middle Ages? First of all, there is the inherent fascination of the era between the Roman Empire and the Italian Renaissance—that thousand-year period when many of the important nations and institutions of our modern world were born. Developing an understanding of the foundations and early evolution of these varied and unique entities makes possible a deeper comprehension of our contemporary experience. For example, studying the birth of Islam and the subsequent Crusades leads to a more informed comprehension of issues confronting the world of the twenty-first century.

Equally fascinating is the cultural world of the Middle Ages. This book introduces the reader to many exciting personalities and medieval artworks, focusing on the development of art (brilliant manuscript illuminations, sculpture, glistening stained-glass, and mosaic ornamentation); architecture (the awe-inspiring Romanesque and Gothic cathedrals); music (the songs of the troubadours and the emergence of complex polyphony); and literature (including the marvelous epic poems and the tales of Chaucer and Boccaccio). The discussions of these cultural artifacts illustrate various influences, showing the interactions of western european artists and writers with their Byzantine and Islamic counterparts. This analysis shows that medieval people viewed the world as hierarchical, harmonious, and highly integrated. It becomes evident that there exists among these various genres a connective tissue which makes possible concrete comparison as well as depth of understanding. Hence, another purpose of this book is to investigate these connections, and to show what one scholar has called "the medieval concept of order," thereby offering a unique opportunity for study.

In order to clearly present the complicated details of medieval political, cultural, and religious development, the book follows a chronological pattern. This structure enables the reader to contextualize the materials discussed in the text, and to form a clear understanding of the social, artistic, and geographical interactions. Part I (*c.* 476–1000) describes the political transition of western Europe from a broken Roman Empire to a centralized government under the leadership of Charlemagne. Along the way, we see the establishment of Germanic tribal kingdoms and the emergence of two great religions—Christianity and Islam. A sub-theme traces the cultural roots of medieval civilization from their tripartite origins in the Greco-Roman tradition, Germanic tribal customs and practices, and Christianity, and shows the influence of Islamic culture on the emerging Europe.

Part II (*c.* 1000–*c.* 1200) continues the political story with the establishment of strong monarchies in western Europe, and the conflict between religious and secular power. During this period western europeans began to reach out toward the eastern Mediterranean area, enlarging their horizons by participating in pilgrimages and Crusades. In addition, this section of the book analyzes the cultural evolution of the artistic style known as Romanesque, and discusses the artistic and intellectual movement known as the Renaissance of the Twelfth Century.

Part III (*c.* 1200–*c.* 1400) describes the reigns of several important kings in England, France, and the Holy Roman Empire, and their participation in the later Crusades. The High Gothic era, with its hallmarks—the cathedral and the university—is discussed in detail. The story closes with a description of the traumatic fourteenth century and a discussion of the gradual demise of many of the institutions of medieval Europe—conditions which led ultimately to the birth of the Renaissance.

Although the book deals with customary themes such as the political development of the feudal monarchies and the history of the church in the Middle Ages, it integrates social research and cultural history with this more traditional material. An important aspect of this book is the inclusion of the histories of women and hitherto less-studied groups in the medieval world. Exciting personalities such as Eleanor of Aquitaine and Hildegard von Bingen and female religious groups such as the Beguines are introduced as an integral part of the general topics so as to provide a more comprehensive view of life in the Middle Ages. The role of women in the Christianization of Europe and the British Isles, and the function of women as patrons of culture, is discussed as part of the narrative, so that women are viewed as actual participants in the making of history, rather than being isolated from the general historical context, as is often the case.

The book also includes material concerning the Islamic world and the Byzantine Empire, and discusses the roles of these important entities in the political developments of the medieval world. There are, in addition, discussions of the brilliant intellectual and cultural influences of the Byzantine and Islamic traditions within the art and philosophy of the Central and High Middle Ages.

A significant pedagogical feature of the book is the inclusion of brief excerpts from primary sources; these have been carefully chosen to fulfill several purposes. First, the sources clarify and expand the meaning of the narrative in the text by presenting the actual thoughts and words of medieval people. In addition, the selections provide an opportunity for the instructor to demonstrate to the students the purpose of utilizing primary sources in historical research.

The book is extensively illustrated and includes examples of cultural artifacts from the Merovingian period and the Islamic world in addition to art from the Romanesque and Gothic periods of western European history. Also included are discussions of the evolution of music, presented in non-technical language so as to be accessible to a wide variety of students. Maps and genealogical charts clarify geographical and chronological material. Each chapter concludes with a summary emphasizing the primary points of the narrative, and also suggestions for further reading.

Although the book is designed primarily for use in upper-level undergraduate history courses, it is also appropriate for use in humanities courses that focus on the Middle Ages, and as general background reading for literature, art history, and music history courses.

The medieval world may be thought of as a brilliant tapestry, composed of fascinating strands drawn from the infinite variety and complexity of human experience. Although it is impossible to discuss and analyze more than a few of these strands in an introductory book such as this, it is my hope that the reader will come away with a basic appreciation of the beauty, vigor, and complexity of medieval civilization.

	Politics	Culture	Religion
250–500	284–305 r. of Diocletian 312 Battle at the Milvian Bridge 324 Founding of Constantinople 350 Germanic tribal migration 378 Battle of Adrianople 410 Visigoths attack Rome 475–526 r. of Theodoric the Ostrogoth 476 Fall of Rome c.485–511 r. of Clovis 497–711 Visigoth kingdom in Spain c.497–548 llife of Theodora	250 Plotinus and Neo-Platonism c.300 Catacomb paintings in Rome: Christ as "Good Shepherd" c.330 Old St. Peter's Basilica in Rome completed c.480–524 life of Boethius c.485–c.580 life of Cassiodorus	after 250 "Mystery cults" gain popularity 251–356 life of St. Antony (eremitic monasticism) 313 Edict of Milan; Constantine legalizes Christianity 325 Council of Nicea establishes the Nicene Creed c.340–397 life of St. Ambrose (hymns) 345–420 life of St. Jerome ("Vulgate" Bi... 354–430 life of St. Augustine (Confession... c.431 St. Patrick's mission to Ireland
500–750	527–565 r. of Justinian 632–661 era of the Rashidun caliphs 661–750 era of the Umayyad caliphs c.688–741 life of Charles Martel 711–716 Muslim conquest of Spain c.714–768 life of Pepin the Short 718 Leo III defeats the Muslims at Constantinople 732 Battle of Tours	532 Hagia Sophia begun 533 Justinian (Corpus juris civilis) c.535 San Vitale at Ravenna completed c.570–636 life of Isidore of Seville c.660 Sutton Hoo treasures buried c.672–735 life of St. Bede "The Venerable" 691 Dome of the Rock completed 705–715 Great Mosque at Damascus built c.725 Lindisfarne Gospels produced 727–843 Iconoclastic Controversy c.732–804 life of Alcuin	c.530 St. Benedict of Nursia develops his monastic Rule 540–604 life of Pope Gregory the Great c.570–632 life of Muhammad after 632 text of the Qur'an collected and recorded
750–1000	768–814 r. of Charlemagne 787–c.886 Viking invasion of France and England 827 Muslims invade Sicily 843 Treaty of Verdun 871–899 r. of Alfred the Great 895–955 Magyar invasions 955 Battle of Lechfeld	c.770–840 life of Einhard c.770–877 Carolingian Renaissance 784 Great Mosque of Córdoba begun 790–805 Chapel at Aachen built c.800 Coronation Gospels 802 Abbey Church at Fulda rebuilt c.840–912 life of Notker, the monk of St. Gall c.870 Codex Aureus 878–950 life of al-Farabi before 900 The Arabian Nights written down 980–1037 life of Avicenna	

PART I

THE EARLY MIDDLE AGES

c. 476–c. 1000

1 THE FOUNDATIONS OF MEDIEVAL CIVILIZATION

EUROPEAN CIVILIZATION during the Middle Ages was enormously complex, and the study of its numerous facets is a source of endless fascination. It is impossible to trace all of the historical threads from which the fabric of medieval culture was woven, but it is possible, in broad terms, to isolate and examine some aspects of the civilization of the late antique period that were particularly influential in this vibrant era. Three sources in particular combined to create the medieval synthesis: the Classical legacy of imperial Rome; the rise of Christianity; and the traditions of the Germanic tribes, or peoples of northern Europe, who migrated into the Roman Empire in the early centuries of the Christian era. Each of these had a decisive impact on the society, culture, and government of medieval Europe, and on its intellectual and artistic life. Though scholars argue about the relative importance of these three sources on the formation of the medieval experience, it is vital to examine the contributions of each, beginning with the heritage of Rome.

The Classical Legacy

The late Roman Empire

In the first century AD, Rome was at the pinnacle of power. Its hegemony extended as far as Britain in the west, beyond the Alps in the north, to the Euphrates River in the east, and across North Africa in the south (**Map 1**). Rome's possessions in the west included Britain, Spain, Gaul, and Italy; to the north it controlled part of what is now western Germany; to the east were Greece, Dacia, Turkey, Syria, and Judea; and on the southern coast of the Mediterranean, the Romans controlled Egypt, Libya, Nubia, and the remaining land as far as the Atlantic.

Because the empire extended over such a vast area, it was inevitable that each of its regions had its own identity and character. Most importantly, the eastern and western parts of the empire differed from one another in many respects, and these differences

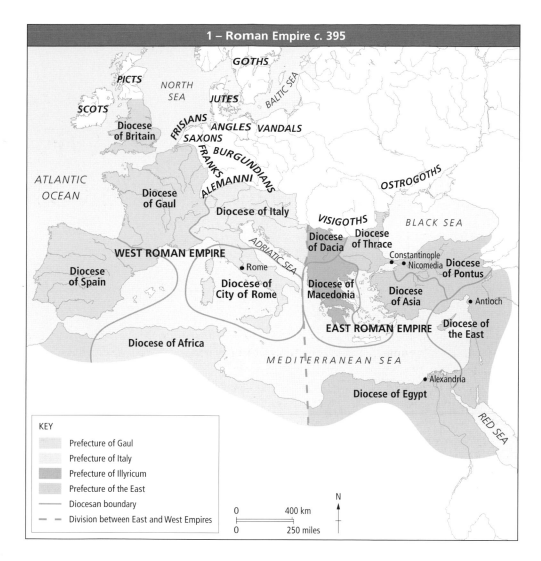

1 – Roman Empire c. 395

GOTHS

PICTS

NORTH SEA

JUTES

BALTIC SEA

SCOTS

Diocese of Britain

FRISIANS

ANGLES VANDALS

SAXONS

FRANKS BURGUNDIANS

ALEMANNI

OSTROGOTHS

ATLANTIC OCEAN

Diocese of Gaul

Diocese of Italy

VISIGOTHS

BLACK SEA

Diocese of Dacia

Diocese of Thrace

WEST ROMAN EMPIRE

ADRIATIC SEA

Constantinople
Nicomedia

Diocese of Pontus

Diocese of Spain

• Rome

Diocese of City of Rome

Diocese of Macedonia

Diocese of Asia

• Antioch

EAST ROMAN EMPIRE

Diocese of the East

Diocese of Africa

MEDITERRANEAN SEA

• Alexandria

Diocese of Egypt

RED SEA

KEY

Prefecture of Gaul
Prefecture of Italy
Prefecture of Illyricum
Prefecture of the East
Diocesan boundary
Division between East and West Empires

0   400 km
0   250 miles

N

continued to characterize the two halves of the former empire during the entire Middle Ages. When the Romans conquered the western part of Europe, they encountered an unsophisticated rural population that had a limited legal and cultural heritage. In the course of time, however, the native peoples here adopted Roman law, religion, culture, and even language. They also began speaking their own vernacular forms of Latin, from which modern French and Spanish eventually evolved. And in the lands they conquered to the west, the Romans built cities, **civitates** (sing. **civitas**), which recreated their own urban architectural traditions, with temples to the Roman gods and amphitheaters for public games.

In the east, however, there were civilizations more ancient than Rome itself, such as those in Egypt, Mesopotamia, and Greece. These areas already had their own highly sophisticated cultures, characterized by art, literature, and philosophy of lasting value. Indeed, the drama, literature, and art of the Roman world were themselves based

1 The tetrarchy created by Diocletian to govern the newly divided empire is portrayed in this porphyry sculpture, of c. 305, now on the exterior of St. Mark's Cathedral, Venice. The sculptor has emphasized the unity of this system of governance by representing the four rulers—the two bearded *augusti*, or senior emperors, and their younger, clean-shaven *caesars*—as close associates. In battle dress, they can be seen as supporting one another against the problems of a society in decline.

primarily on Greek models. Most eastern areas of the empire continued to speak Greek, although the area of modern Romania, where the inhabitants conversed in Latin, was an exception. Latin was also the language of law and government.

The differences between east and west were solidified when the empire was divided during the reign of the emperor Diocletian (r. 284–305). Diocletian saw that the empire was too large to be governed successfully by one person and thus split the vast lands into two parts, east and west. He ruled the eastern half himself, and his colleague, Maximian, governed the western part. Diocletian was regarded as the senior emperor, or *augustus*, and most legislation was instituted by him and followed by his co-ruler (see Map 1).

Yet the sheer size of its empire was not the only factor undermining the stability of Rome. Like most other third-century emperors, Diocletian, a highly skilled soldier, had seized the throne by military force. This was, in fact, the usual method of transferring power upon the death of an emperor, whether by natural or "artificial" causes. Needless to say, the seizure of power, which occurred more than twenty times during the third century, created a situation of instability that severely undermined the well-being of the state.

Diocletian attempted to solve the problem of succession to the throne by creating the office of *caesar*—a junior emperor who would automatically assume power when the *augustus* retired at the end of a twenty-year reign. Thus, future emperors would be co-holders of the office for two decades, during which they could prepare themselves to rule effectively. Since the empire was now split into two parts, east and west, each with its own *augustus* and *caesar*, this new system was known as a tetrarchy—a government in which power was shared among four men. It is depicted in sculptural form in **fig. 1**.

Another problem that Diocletian attempted to resolve stemmed primarily from a failure to collect sufficient tax revenue. The collection of taxes was the responsibility of men of the **curial class**, who were committed to producing a certain amount of revenue. If they did not extract the required sum from the taxpayers, they were obligated to make up the difference themselves. This became an increasing problem, as taxpayers in many professions, including farming, refused to pay the high taxes and simply left their positions. The collectors themselves ultimately abdicated their responsibilities, forfeiting what was a privileged status in society. The result of this mass resignation was severe economic dislocation, with many of the basic social services and needs remaining unfulfilled.

Diocletian attempted to deal with this difficulty by making the professions hereditary; that is, a son would be forced to follow the occupation of his father, regardless of his own wishes. However, this policy had unforeseen consequences in the agricultural system. If farmers were unable to pay the high taxes, their land was either seized by the state or absorbed into the vast estates held by aristocrats. They became "tenant farmers," known as **coloni** (sing. **colonus**), and paid rent for their holdings in money, service, or produce. In this system, which some scholars have viewed as the harbinger of medieval serfdom, agricultural service was mandatory; to leave the land was a crime against the government. The result of Diocletian's policies was the creation of an economic caste system in which people were frozen into specific occupations. Their economic futures were thus completely predetermined.

An additional problem that beset the empire during the course of the century before Diocletian's rule was that of inflation. Earlier emperors had tried to solve this difficulty by debasing the coinage. Diocletian, however, decided to issue new silver coinage throughout the empire, thus establishing a more stable currency.

On a more general level, Diocletian "orientalized" the office of emperor, greatly increasing the ceremonial aspects of court life. He demanded that his subjects prostrate themselves in his presence, and sponsored an ideology that emphasized the divinely ordained position of the emperors: the ruler was a sacred person, far above the status of an ordinary mortal. Many historians have seen Diocletian's actions as a perversion of traditional Roman society, and although he did succeed in establishing policies that prolonged the empire, he transformed it into a state that was no longer truly "Roman."

Unfortunately, Diocletian's carefully thought-out plan for succession to the throne was not successful. When he and his co-emperor Maximian resigned in 305, as planned, there was again a civil war. The two appointed successors or *caesars*, Constantius in the west and Galerius in the east, were named as emperors or *augusti*. Constantius was in residence at York, in England, when the abdication took place, but he became ill shortly afterwards, and sent for his son, Constantine, who joined him in his military camp. Constantius died within months, and his soldiers hailed his son Constantine as the new *augustus*. The situation was complicated when Maximian's son, Maxentius, declared himself *augustus*. Soon there were two more competing *augusti*, and the civil wars of the previous century began again.

In 311, Galerius died, and Constantine moved against Maxentius to protect his claim to the throne. He marched to Italy in 312, and as he approached Rome he engaged the forces of Maxentius at the Milvian Bridge, which crossed the Tiber River. Constantine won a great victory, and, as his biographer Eusebius reported, "Maxentius and the soldiers and guards with him, went down into the depths [of the river] like stone." As proof of Constantine's triumph, when Maxentius's body washed ashore the next day, his head was cut off and carried into Rome on a spear.

The Battle at the Milvian Bridge was of great importance, and not only because it established Constantine as *augustus* in the west (a co-ruler, Licinius, was *augustus* in the east until his death in 324). Even more significant was the fact that Constantine pledged to convert to Christianity immediately prior to battle, despite the fact that, at this time, it was illegal to worship the Christian God. The only contemporaneous account of Constantine's conversion is from the *Life of Constantine*, by Eusebius of Caesarea (*c.* 260–*c.* 340), a friend of the emperor who was employed at his court. Eusebius was anxious to highlight Constantine's role as the first Christian leader. He claimed that Constantine, having lost confidence in pagan deities, and believing that divine assistance was necessary, sought the protection of the Christian God:

> Accordingly he called on Him with earnest prayer and supplication that he would reveal to him who He was, and stretch forth his right hand to help him in his present difficulties. And while he was thus praying with fervent entreaty, a most marvelous sign appeared to him from heaven . . . he saw with his own eyes the trophy of a cross of light in the heavens, above the sun, and bearing the inscription, Conquer by This . . . and while he continued to ponder and reason on its meaning, night suddenly came on; then in his sleep the Christ of God appeared to him with the same sign which he had seen in the heavens, and commanded him to make a likeness of that sign which he had seen in the heavens, and to use it as a safeguard in all engagements with his enemies.

The sign that Constantine saw was the Chi-Rho, the first two letters of Christ's name in the Greek alphabet, with the letter *P* being intersected by *X* in its center (**fig. 2**). Constantine had the symbol painted on the shields of his soldiers, and commissioned a banner that incorporated the design. According to Eusebius, he "constantly made use of this sign of salvation as a safeguard against every adverse and hostile power, and commanded that others similar to it should be carried at the head of all his armies."

The veracity of Constantine's conversion experience has been the topic of scholarly debate for centuries. However, regardless of his motivations, and of the brutality of some of his subsequent behavior, the emperor's "conversion" dramatically changed the circumstances of the emerging religion (**fig. 3**). In the Edict of Milan, issued in 313, Constantine and his co-ruler Licinius boldly proclaimed that Christian worship was from now on to be tolerated: "[Anyone] who freely and sincerely carries out the purpose of observing the Christian religion may endeavor to practice its precepts without any fear or danger . . . we have given free and absolute permission to practice their religion to the Christians." The new religion began to flourish, and the legalization of Christianity provided a cohesive force, except during the brief reign of Julian the Apostate (r. 361–363), an emperor who attempted to return the people to pagan ways. Eventually, in the reign of Theodosius (r. 379–395), Christianity became the sole religion of the empire.

Constantine's policy of religious tolerance was designed to increase the stability for which Diocletian had worked so hard. The emperor further stabilized the currency and developed a more efficient system of tax collection. He guaranteed his position through the creation of a large field army, and disbanded the praetorian guard (an elite force whose primary responsibility was the protection of the emperor), replacing them with a bodyguard drawn from the Germanic population. This measure is indicative of the degree to which "barbarians" were being assimilated into the empire by this time.

2 The Chi-Rho, representing the first two letters of Christ's name in the Greek alphabet, became a symbol of Christian belief in the late Roman Empire. Following his vision before the Battle at the Milvian Bridge, the emperor Constantine (r. 306–337) ordered his soldiers to paint the sign on their shields as a gesture of allegiance to the Christian God and as an emblem of solidarity.

3 This head, from a colossal statue of Constantine dating from *c.* 313, shows the emperor with eyes raised to God, reflecting his mission as the first Roman ruler to embrace and tolerate Christianity. Although he did not officially convert to Christianity or receive baptism until he was dying, Constantine's policies created a receptive environment for the growth and practice of the new religion.

One of Constantine's lasting contributions to civilization was the founding of a new imperial capital on the site of the old city of Byzantium, which had a fine defensive location on the shores of the Bosporus. The emperor said that he acted "on the command of God" in establishing the new capital for the entire empire, one that had never been sullied by pagan rites. The foundation of the city—later called Constantinople—was thus designed to symbolize a break with the pagan past and the beginning of a new Christian empire. Nonetheless, by centralizing the rich economy of the eastern empire, Constantine's action probably hastened the eventual collapse of the empire in the west; Constantinople became a thriving commercial city that was the religious and economic heart of the Byzantine Empire.

In analyzing the demise of the Roman Empire, scholars have pointed to many possible causes and given widely varying accounts. Early scholars tended to conceive of a sharp division between the ancient and medieval worlds, which they placed at AD 476, when the last Roman emperor in the west, Romulus Augustus, was deposed. Modern historians, however, prefer to talk of a gradual transformation of social and political structures in the fifth, sixth, and seventh centuries. The most famous work concerning the end of the empire is *The Decline and Fall of the Roman Empire,* by the eighteenth-century British historian Edward Gibbon. Among other forces, Gibbon cited Christianity itself as a potent influence in the decline. Gibbon believed that the ethos of Christianity, which advocated acceptance of prevailing conditions, led to a passive state of mind; this mental outlook, which Gibbon characterized as a "loss of nerve," ultimately prevented the populace from solving the problems of the late empire. It is not possible to discuss in detail all the other theories that have been put forward; however, some historians have attributed the decline to lack of manpower, moral corruption, soil erosion, economic distress, or increasing loyalty to local constituencies, rather than allegiance to the central government. The shift of the capital to Constantinople certainly weakened the west in economic terms, and, even more devastatingly, it was impossible for the Romans to guard the vast frontier of the empire effectively. All of these difficulties were exacerbated by the migrations of the Germanic tribes (see below).

Language and literature

One of the most enduring legacies of the Roman empire was its language. As we saw earlier, Latin was spoken by the native populations in Spain and Gaul, as well as Italy, and was eventually transformed into the languages we know as Spanish, French, and Italian. In a religious context, the ancient language was kept alive even longer. Classical Latin, with minor alterations, remained the language of the western church until the convocation of Vatican II in the 1960s, when the celebration of the Mass in the vernacular languages was approved. There was an important secular revival by Renaissance scholars in the fifteenth and sixteenth centuries, which emphasized a return to Classical linguistic traditions, and Latin remained the language of scholarship until the eighteenth century. Furthermore, in some areas of eastern Europe, dissertations concerning medieval topics were being written in Latin as late as the twentieth century.

The literary heritage of the Romans was, as noted earlier, based on Classical Greek models, and this Greco-Roman tradition proved to be influential in the development of medieval literature. Beginning with Homer, the tradition of the epic poem was a significant Classical legacy. In Roman culture, the poet Vergil's great work, *The Aeneid,* remained an important model, and influenced such medieval works as *The Song of Roland* (see Chapter 8). However, the literary works with the most pervasive influence were devoted to education: two books on Latin grammar by Donatus, the *Ars minor* and the *Ars major,* as well as the *Institutes* by Priscian, were used in schools throughout the Middle Ages. Another work, the *Nuptials of Mercury and Philology,* by Martianus Capella, is of interest because of its classification of educational fields into the **Trivium** and the **Quadrivium** (see Chapter 2 for a detailed discussion of this tradition).

Philosophy in the late Roman Empire developed its own individual character, especially in the works of the **Stoics**, such as the emperor Marcus Aurelius, and the **Epicureans**, most notably Lucretius. Although Marcus Aurelius died in 180, his *Meditations* clearly reflects the attitude of Stoicism:

> What, then, is that which is able to conduct a man? One thing, and only one— philosophy. But, this consists in keeping the demon within a man free from violence and unharmed, superior to pains and pleasures, doing nothing without a purpose, not yet falsely and with hypocrisy, not feeling the need of another man's doing or not doing anything; and besides, accepting all that happens, and all that is allotted, as coming from thence, wherever it is, from whence he himself came; and, finally, waiting for death with a cheerful mind, as being nothing else than a dissolution of the elements of which every living being is compounded.

Scholars have often seen the works of these philosophical schools as indicative of the problematic nature of the late Roman Empire, since they, like Christianity, emphasize the cultivation of a passive and non-reactive attitude.

The Roman literary tradition was often preserved during the late empire by aristocrats living in luxury on vast rural estates, who spent much of their time studying Classical works, and writing letters to one another about their literary interests. One such writer, whose letters reflect this pastime, was Sidonius Apollinaris. In a communication to a friend, he described his stay as a house guest in fifth-century Gaul in glowing terms:

> Well, I was hurried from bliss to bliss. Hardly had I entered one vestibule or the other when behold! I found on one side opposing ball-players bending low amid the whirling evolutions of the **catastrophae**; in another quarter I would hear the clatter of rattling dice-boxes and of dice mingled with the rival shouts of the gamesters; in another part were books in any number ready to hand; you might have imagined yourself looking at the shelves of a professional scholar, or at the tiers in the Athenaeum, or at the towering presses of the booksellers. The arrangement was such that the manuscripts near the ladies' seats were of a devotional type, while those among the gentlemen's benches were works distinguished by the grandeur of Latin eloquence; the latter, however, included certain writings of particular authors which preserve a similarity of style though their doctrines are different; for it was a frequent practice to read writers whose artistry was of a similar kind: here Augustine, there Varro, here Horace, there Prudentius . . .

The writings of aristocrats such as Apollinaris clearly reveal an indifference to the changes brewing in Roman society, since these literary enthusiasts lived away from the urban environment and devoted themselves to gaming and intellectual pursuits. This indifference might be cited as another factor contributing to the demise of the empire. But the passage quoted above also indicates another important development: how Christian writers such as Augustine had assimilated the Classical heritage of Latin eloquence into their elucidations of Christian thought. A parallel amalgamation may be seen in the adoption of a Roman architectural form—the basilica—for the purposes of Christian worship.

Architecture

One of the most important architectural forms of late antiquity and the early Middle Ages was the Roman **basilica**. The basilica form provided the basic ground plan for the great cathedrals of medieval Europe. It also clearly demonstrates one of the ways in which the early Christians incorporated Roman architectural sources as they developed their own environment for worship.

The basilica was a rectangular structure, with an **atrium** at its narrower end. The atrium was generally square, and as wide as the front of the basilica itself. The interior of the basilica consisted of a central **nave** with side aisles, separated from each other by rows of columns parallel to the longer main axis of the building. Above the columns there was a wall, which contained a row of windows. The purpose of these windows, or **clerestory**, was to provide light and air for the long central nave; this was covered by a wooden roof, whose supporting trusses were often hidden by an elaborately coffered ceiling (see the ground plan and elevation in **fig. 4**). Although scholars have suggested different theories concerning the original purpose of the Roman basilica, the most plausible idea asserts that it was a structure originally attached to the **forum** as a shelter for businessmen and the general public; eventually it functioned as a law court.

After the conversion of Constantine, the Christian community was faced with the task of creating a new monumental architecture to serve the needs of a growing community. Prior to Constantine's reign, Christians met in the homes of wealthy members of the sect; however, for liturgical ceremonies attended by large numbers of people, the Christian community needed a new form of cult edifice. Constantine saw the need for an architectural expression in which ideological features and practical elements were inextricably woven together—one that would reflect the new dignity of the Church and of its imperial patron. It was probably inevitable that Constantine's architects

4 Old St. Peter's Basilica, Rome, was built in the 320s with funds supplied by Constantine. Containing an apse, and a long nave and side aisles separated by columns, it provided the ground plan for the development of Christian architecture in the Middle Ages. The interior of the basilica was approximately 208 x 355 feet (63 x 108 m), with the height of the nave being 105 feet (32 m).

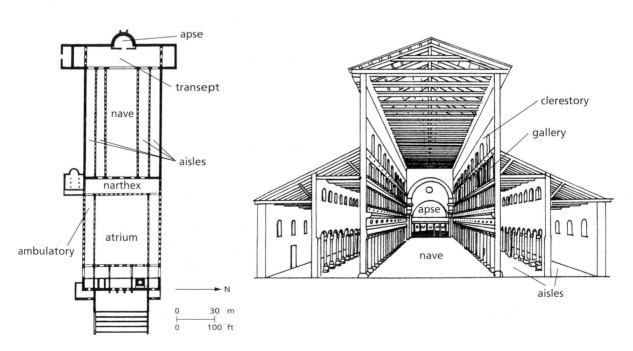

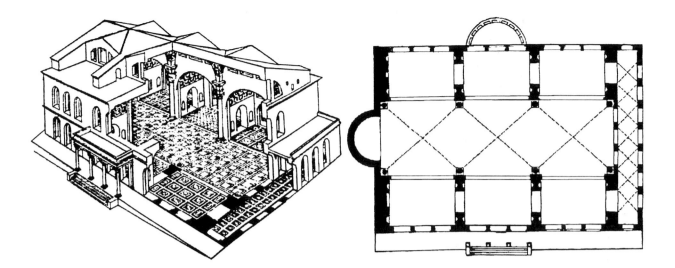

would draw inspiration from public, official architecture, and excavations have established that early church foundations under Constantine consisted of an atrium, a rectangular basilical hall with a nave and four side aisles, and, at the eastern end of the basilica, a sanctuary or **apse**.

The apse was a semicircle projecting from one end of the nave and covered with a half-dome. The floor of the apse, together with the area directly in front, was raised to a height of three or more steps to form the **bema**, a space reserved for the higher clergy, and lined with a series of seats towards the back. In the center of the bema was the episcopal throne, or bishop's chair, known as the **cathedra**. The apse was probably derived from the audience halls of the imperial palaces in Rome (**fig. 5**) and the provinces during the late empire, such as those at Split and Trier. These were also known as basilicas, and seem to have been longitudinally colonnaded halls, with clerestory lighting, and at one end of the long axis an area reserved for an imperial throne or statue. In the early Christian basilica, this area became the apse, and served as the sanctuary, with the altar replacing the throne or statue. Some scholars have interpreted this as a deliberate attempt to present Christ as the true emperor.

Most early Christian basilicas were constructed according to a definite system of orientation. This was a departure from Roman religious custom, wherein the temples faced as often in one direction as in another. The main facade of the Christian basilica, which incorporated the columns leading from the atrium, usually faced to the west. Thus, the longer axis of the nave extended towards the east and generally culminated in the apse at the eastern end of the building.

In some basilicas there was a **transept** at the eastern end of the nave. In essence, this was a single-aisled nave at right angles to the main axis of the basilica. Ordinarily, the roof of the transept was the same height as the nave, so that the area where the transept intersected the nave (the "crossing") became an impressive open space in front of the apse. Medieval architects generally used a transept in their churches, probably recognizing that the resulting form mirrored the shape of a cross, a design often referred to as "cruciform."

5 The Basilica of Maxentius, Rome (completed by Constantine after 312), was a rectangular structure with the interior divided into a nave and side aisles. It was originally used as a place for commercial and legal enterprises, and provided the ideal model for buildings where large crowds of worshipers could gather.

The crossing—the square formed by the intersection of the nave and transept—was the holiest place in the entire basilica. At its center was the altar, which became the focus of the whole interior. The artistic and liturgical significance of the crossing was often enhanced by an elaborately decorated architectural canopy supported by four columns, known as the **ciborium** or **baldacchino**. Attention was centered on the altar even more directly by a broad arch, called the triumphal arch, which extended across the eastern end of the nave, linking the two ranges of columns and framing the view of the altar. This arch was frequently decorated with frescoes or mosaics, thus adding to the aesthetic quality of the sanctuary.

The most famous of the early churches was the great martyr-shrine that Constantine built over the tomb of St. Peter in Rome (see the ground plan in fig. 4). St. Peter's was one of the first basilicas to incorporate a transept, but so great was its influence that the transept became a common feature in western European church architecture, in contrast to the plan of ecclesiastical buildings in the Byzantine Empire, such as Hagia Sophia (see Chapter 2).

Under Constantine's policy of toleration and patronage, Christianity gained an increasing number of converts. They joined a religion that had been developing, mostly in secret, during the previous 300 years, as various emperors subjected them to persecution.

Christianity

Origins

The origins of Christianity are to be found within the traditional Jewish religion, Judaism; indeed, the first people to believe that Jesus was the long-promised Messiah of the Old Testament were a group of Jews. Dissension arose among the early adherents of the new religion, however, as questions involving new converts emerged. The followers of Jesus believed that their mission was to extend his message to all people, whereas many Jewish converts thought that non-Jews should not be accepted as members of the developing religion. Soon, however, Christianity was established as a cult distinct from Judaism. Converts began to infuse the new religion with ideas brought from the multitude of "mystery cults" and competing philosophies that characterized the religious atmosphere of first-century Roman life.

As Christianity evolved and began to attract followers throughout the Roman Empire, it absorbed many of the external features of the cults of Mithras, Cybele, Isis, and other deities, which had been assimilated by the Romans. Many of these cults focused on a divine being whose birth and death were characterized by miraculous circumstances, often coinciding with the winter solstice and spring equinox. The symbolism of light was a prevalent feature in many of these groups, as was the use of blood and wine in initiation services. The aspect that set Christianity apart from these "mystery cults" was its focus on a once-living historical person—the crucified Jesus.

The Roman government felt that, as a general rule, it was sensible and effective to allow the people they conquered to continue to worship their own gods, in accordance with their own precepts; hence, they usually extended a policy of toleration to members of the cults. They did require that adherents of other sects sacrifice to the Roman gods and participate in the cult of the emperor, but as the Romans were polytheistic, they had little difficulty in accepting additions to their panoply of gods. Believers in Jesus as the Christ, however, were monotheistic, believing their god to be the only true deity, and so they would not conform to Roman religious demands. This refusal was especially problematic because it constituted treason against the state. Furthermore, being pacifists, Christians resisted serving in the army.

But these were not the only reasons the Christians were regarded as a threat to the empire. The doctrine of Christianity concerning the afterlife had great appeal for people of the lower classes, who were able now to anticipate a better life after death, and might prove more difficult to control. Furthermore, since they met in secret, and participated in secret rites, they were regarded with suspicion, and became targets for blame. As early as AD 64, when there was a fire in Rome, the emperor Nero found it convenient to make the Christians into scapegoats. According to the Roman historian Tacitus:

> To put an end to the rumor that he [himself] had ordered the fire, Nero invented charges of guilt and inflicted the most exquisite tortures on a group of people whom the Roman mob called "Christians" and hated because of their shameless activities. During the reign of Tiberius, Christus, who gave his name to this group, had suffered crucifixion under the procurator Pontius Pilatus; and a dangerous cult, which had been kept in check for the moment, burst forth again, not only throughout Judea, the origin of the evil, but even in Rome, where all the hideous and shameful things from all over the world flow together and swarm. Therefore, first of all, people who admitted their belief were arrested, and then later, through their information, a huge crowd was convicted not so much of the crime of setting the fire, as of hating humankind. Mockery was heaped upon them as they were killed. Wrapped in skins of wild animals, they were torn apart by dogs, or nailed to crosses, or set on fire and burned alive to provide light at night, when the daylight had faded.
>
> Nero offered his gardens for this spectacle and provided . . . entertainment [in the Circus] where he put on a chariot driver's outfit and mingled with the crowd or stood in a chariot. And so pity arose, even for those who were guilty and deserved the most extreme punishment, since they seemed to have been slaughtered not for public good but to satisfy the cruelty of one man.

However, this early persecution did not immediately lead to widespread killing of Christians. What persecution there was during the next two centuries was sporadic and took place only in certain parts of the empire. The most intense persecutions occurred in the third century, during the reigns of the emperors Septimus Severus (r. 193–211) and Decius (r. 249–251). But, as some observers noted at the time, these violent actions against the Christians served only to increase interest in their religion. According to the early Christian writer Tertullian, "the blood of the martyrs is the seed of the Church." Martyrdom was seen as a heroic achievement, and onlookers were attracted by the evident conviction of Christians that their religious belief was more important than life itself.

One famous example of early Christian martyrdom concerns a twenty-two-year-old woman, Vibia Perpetua, who was killed during the Severan persecution in 203, along with her maidservant Felicitas. The narrator of *The Martyrdoms of Perpetua and Felicitas* describes the scene of their execution:

> For the young women the Devil had prepared a mad heifer. This was an unusual animal, but it was chosen that their sex might be matched with that of the beast. So they were stripped naked, placed in nets and thus brought out into the arena. Even the crowd was horrified when they saw that one was a delicate young girl and the other was a woman fresh from childbirth with the milk still dripping from her breasts. And so they were brought back again and dressed in unbelted tunics.
>
> First the heifer tossed Perpetua and she fell on her back. Then sitting up she pulled down the tunic that was ripped along the side so that it covered her thighs, thinking more of her modesty than of her pain. Next she asked for a pin to fasten her untidy hair: for it was not right that a martyr should die with her hair in disorder, lest she might seem to be mourning in her hour of triumph.

Perpetua got up, and, seeing that Felicitas had been thrown to the ground, she helped her to her feet. Since "the cruelty of the mob was by now appeased," the women were taken back into their cells, where the gladiators would cut their throats.

> But the mob asked that their bodies be brought out into the open that their eyes might be the guilty witnesses of the sword that pierced their flesh. And so the martyrs got up and went to the spot of their own accord as the people wanted them to, and kissing one another they sealed their martyrdom with the ritual kiss of peace . . . Perpetua screamed as she was struck on the bone; then she took the trembling hand of the young gladiator and guided it to her throat. It was as though so great a woman, feared as she was by the unclean spirit, could not be dispatched unless she herself were willing.

The martyrdom of Perpetua and Felicitas is one of the most dramatic and memorable accounts of Christian persecution, but it is also indicative of the widespread participation of women in early Christianity. According to **hagiographical** accounts, letters written by churchmen, and early Christian theologians such as Irenaeus of Lyons and Clement of Alexandria, women comprised a large proportion of adherents during the first three centuries of the Christian era. They were often agents of conversion, stimulating their husbands and children to adopt the religion. And although they were generally not allowed to function as pastors or religious leaders, they were frequent participants in ritual ceremonies. Furthermore, wealthy women used their money and power to endow churches and to influence pastoral appointments. This intense interest of women in Christianity has been seen by some scholars as a way for them to break free of the traditional constraints of the Greek and Roman family, and to assert their individuality and equality with men in a male-dominated society.

There was a final and brutal persecution of the Christians during the reign of the emperor Diocletian (r. 284–305). By this time, however, the new religion was so firmly established that measures to eradicate it failed. And by the time Diocletian's successor, Constantine, legalized the practice of Christianity in the fourth century, the early Church had already assumed a hierarchical structure and an embryonic governance system.

Development of the early Church

Initially, Christians met privately in small groups at individual homes, and there was no formal distinction between clergy and laity. By the second century, however, some members had assumed teaching and preaching functions, and had become leaders of the religious community. The most important person was the bishop, and his advisers or assistants were known as priests and elders. Officials called deacons were responsible for the distribution of charity. The priests ultimately became the rectors of the communities, and administered the assets of the groups. Women were generally excluded from the priesthood, but they were able to serve in other official positions.

As the Christian Church grew, it began to be divided into separate geographical units, and its administrative divisions mirrored the existing administrative units of the state. The diocese, governed by a bishop, was a unit corresponding to the Roman *civitas* (pl. *civitates*) established during the reign of Diocletian. Each diocese was divided into parishes, with each parish being served by a priest, who was subject to the authority of the bishop. The choice of bishops was determined by the needs of the community.

Both bishops and priests were entitled to administer the holy **sacraments**, such as baptism and communion, but only a bishop could ordain men into the priesthood. Furthermore, the bishop was responsible for defining religious practice for the diocese, establishing approved doctrine and standard rules.

Dioceses were grouped into archdioceses, under the jurisdiction of an archbishop. Like the dioceses, these corresponded to existing Roman geographical divisions but covered much larger areas—for example, whole provinces such as Spain or Gaul. These became very important since representatives to the early church councils were determined by provincial boundaries.

The bishops of centers where the early apostles were active—Jerusalem, Antioch, Alexandria, and Rome—were thought to be more important and were given special distinction, as was Constantinople after its dedication in 330. Thus, by the fourth century, the Church had assumed a highly developed system of organization in which powerful men could exert significant leadership.

By 325, Constantine had become aware of sources of disagreement within the Church, and he felt that a clear statement of belief was necessary for proper development of the religion. The greatest source of strife was an argument between the bishop Athanasius of Alexandria and a priest, Arius, concerning the nature of the Godhead. Was Christ wholly divine and co-equal with the Father? Or did God create Christ, establishing him in an inferior position? And was co-equality the true nature of the Trinity: Father, Son, and Holy Spirit? Arius claimed that Christ had not existed for all eternity, but had been created by God the Father, who alone was eternal. Hence, Christ was not of the same divine essence as the Father, but neither was he an ordinary man. Athanasius, however, saw Christ as co-equal and co-eternal with God the Father.

In order to resolve this strife, which was threatening to split the Church, Constantine called together the Council of Nicea, which met in 325. The emperor instructed the delegates to produce a clear doctrinal statement, which they did after much debate; later, it was slightly amended at a subsequent council in 385, but the essential components were established at Nicea. The statement of belief produced there, known as the Nicene Creed, remains the fundamental declaration accepted today by Roman Catholic,

Greek Orthodox, Anglican, and some other Protestant churches; it defines the position of Athanasius, and states that:

> We believe in one God, the Father All-Governing, creator of all things visible and invisible. And in one Lord Jesus Christ . . . begotten not created, of the same essence as the Father . . . but those who say, Once he was not, or he was not before his generation, or he came to be out of nothing, or who assert that he, the Son of God, is of a different substance, or that he is a creature, or changeable, or mutable, the Catholic and Apostolic Church condemns them.

Thus, the Council of Nicea confirmed the position of Athanasius. However, Arius, though defeated at the council, refused to conform to the principles of belief as defined in the new creed, and continued to preach his form of Christianity. As Christianity spread, Arianism was ultimately adopted by several of the Germanic tribes, including the Visigoths, Ostrogoths, Vandals, Burgundians, and Lombards. Other groups—Angles, Saxons, Jutes, Alemanni, Franks, and Bavarians—were converted to the Athanasian belief.

The Council of Nicea was of great importance in establishing lasting Christian doctrine. Perhaps of equal significance, though, were the contributions of the four men now regarded as the ideological pioneers of medieval Christianity, or the four "Fathers of the Church": saints Ambrose, Jerome, Augustine, and Pope Gregory the Great.

The Fathers of the Church

Ambrose (c. 340–397) was the bishop of Milan. He was highly skilled as a Roman administrator, and, though he was not a priest, he was acclaimed by the people of Milan as their choice for bishop. He was ordained in 370, and served the Church effectively until his death in 397, strengthening the Christian position against paganism and heresy. He was, in addition, one of the first clergymen to assert the power of the Church against the claims of secular authority.

In addition to his work as bishop, Ambrose was a prolific author who wrote an important series of treatises, including the *Heptameron*, *De officiis ministrorum*, and *De virginitate*. His work concerning virginity was based on the teachings of St. Paul, and was an attempt to reconcile attitudes towards the spiritual and physical elements of life. Ambrose recognized the contest in Christian thought between the eternal quest of the soul and the compelling needs of the body, and he intended in this treatise to balance these demands and provide a prescription for appropriate behavior. Ultimately, the practices of virginity and celibacy were adopted by monks, nuns, and, after 1049, the priesthood. Chastity, which led to the denial of the life of the body and the exaltation of the life of the soul, was considered to be a common ideal throughout the Middle Ages; it was an extraordinary "talent" of the spiritual elite.

Ambrose was also deeply interested in music and liturgical practice. He composed hymns, and although only four of the many ascribed to him are now considered to be authentic, they confirm his reputation as the originator of the Latin hymn tradition. According to Augustine, Ambrose also introduced into the liturgy of the western church the eastern practice of the antiphonal singing of psalms, in which two choirs chant the verses alternately.

Augustine (354–430), another of the Church Fathers, was somewhat younger than Ambrose. He was born in Thagaste, North Africa (modern Souk Ahras, in Algeria). His father, Patricius, was pagan, but his mother, Monica, was a Christian. Augustine received an excellent education in the liberal arts, which trained him for public life, and he became a teacher of rhetoric in Milan.

In late adolescence and early adulthood, Augustine explored a variety of religious and philosophical traditions, including **Manicheanism**, **Neoplatonism**, **Gnosticism**, and several of the mystery religions. While he was in Milan, he heard some of Ambrose's sermons and these were instrumental, along with the influence of his mother, in his conversion to the Christianity of Athanasius and the ever-more powerful followers of the Nicene Creed. The account of his struggle to find truth and to understand the origins of evil is beautifully recorded in his famous *Confessions*. In Chapter 8 of the *Confessions*, he movingly describes how certainty concerning the God of the Christians came to him as he sat in a garden with his friend Alypius:

> Suddenly a voice reaches my ears from a nearby house. It is the voice of a boy or a girl (I don't know which) and in a kind of singsong, the words are constantly repeated: "Take it and read it. Take it and read it." At once my face changed, and I began to think carefully of whether the singing of words like these came into any kind of game which children play, and I could not remember that I had ever heard anything like it before. I checked the force of my tears and rose to my feet, being quite certain that I must interpret this as a divine command to me to open the book and read the first passage which I should come upon. For I had heard this about Antony: he had happened to come in when the Gospel was being read, and as though the words read were spoken directly to himself, had received the admonition: *Go, sell all that you have, and give to the poor, and you shall have treasure in heaven, and come and follow me.* [Matthew 19:21]. And by such an oracle he had been immediately converted to you.
>
> So I went eagerly back to the place where Alypius was sitting, since it was there that I had left the book of the Apostle when I rose to my feet. I snatched up the book, opened it, and read in silence the passage upon which my eyes first fell: *Not in rioting and drunkenness, not in chambering and wantonness, not in strife and envying: but put you on the Lord Jesus Christ, and make not provision for the flesh in concupiscence.* [Romans 13:13–14]. I had no wish to read further; there was no need to. For immediately I had reached the end of this sentence it was as though my heart was filled with a light of confidence and all the shadows of my doubt were swept away . . .

Soon after this experience, Augustine resigned his position as professor of rhetoric and formally accepted Christianity as dictated by the Council of Nicea. He was baptized in Milan by Ambrose on Easter Sunday, April 25, 387. In 388, he returned to Thagaste and established a religious community, where he began writing treatises on various religious topics. His fame began to spread as a result, and early in 391 he moved to the ancient seaport of Hippo (present-day Annaba, in Algeria), near to Thagaste, where he was ordained as a priest, and began his demanding career as an administrator. In 396, he became bishop of Hippo, and he remained in that position until his death in 430.

The years that Augustine spent as priest and bishop were years of intense activity and prolific writing. During this time, he formulated a philosophical and religious tradition that lasted for the entire Middle Ages and beyond. He was primarily concerned with interpreting Christian scriptures and doctrine, and it is this legacy that profoundly influenced the development of medieval theology. Augustine based his theological views on the scriptural vision of God as a pure, omnipotent, eternal, infinite Being; in this sense he was the initiator of a specifically Christian philosophy. But his broad intellectual heritage also enabled him to conceptualize Christianity in terms of the philosophical framework established by the ancient Greek philosopher Plato—and, most importantly, to relate it to Plato's vision of reality. He was able to synthesize the Platonic world of Ideas or Forms with the concepts of the philosopher Plotinus concerning the Divine Mind, and to present this as corresponding to the mind of the Christian God. Thus Christianity was related to this particular ancient philosophical tradition which therefore became a founding principle of medieval Christian philosophy. (See the discussions in Chapters 10 and 13.)

The ultimate aim of Augustine's theology was to lead the Christian mind upwards to God. He described this path as an ascent of the soul in which the first level was the knowledge of creatures through science, the second was the knowledge of scripture and theology through wisdom, and the third was the knowledge of the supreme truth through intuition. The final achievement was a mystical union with God. The development of the soul towards this spiritual goal became a key element in religious teaching in western civilization for centuries.

Augustine was interested in Christian debates taking place in his own lifetime, as well as in relating Christianity to other philosophies. Among his many important works was *The City of God*, which discussed current religious controversies and defined the relative positions of the state and society. His writings earned him a distinguished reputation during his lifetime, and his influence was vast. The inscription on an anonymous early image of Augustine bears witness to his fame: "Various fathers have said many things, but this man has said everything with Roman eloquence, thundering forth mystical meanings."

An equally important contribution to medieval religious life was made by Jerome (345–420), whose special concern was the adaptation of Latin literature to the teachings of Christianity. He was torn between his love for Classical, pre-Christian, and hence technically pagan, literature and a need for Christian **asceticism**. We know of this struggle from his many *Letters*. One particularly fascinating epistle describes a dream in which Jerome, having died, appeared at the gates of heaven:

> Suddenly I was caught up in the spirit and dragged before the judgment seat of the Judge; and here the light was so bright, and those who stood around were so radiant, that I cast myself upon the ground and did not dare to look up. Asked who and what I was, I replied: "I am a Christian." But He who presided said: "Thou liest, thou art a follower of Cicero and not of Christ. For 'where thy treasure is, there will thy heart be also.'" Instantly I became dumb, and amid the strokes of the lash (for He had ordered me to be scourged) I was tortured more severely still by the fire of conscience, considering with myself that verse, "In the grave who shall give thee thanks?" Yet for all that I began to cry and to bewail myself, saying: "Have mercy upon me, O Lord: have mercy upon me."

Jerome struggled to find a way to reconcile his beloved Classical literature with Christian teaching, and at last he came upon a passage in the letters of St. Paul that described how women taken as prisoners could be "purified" in order to become acceptable as wives:

> He read in Deuteronomy the command given by the voice of the Lord that when a captive woman had had her head shaved, her eyebrows and all her hair cut off, and her nails pared, she might then be taken to wife. Is it surprising that I too, admiring the fairness of her form and the grace of her eloquence, desire to make that secular wisdom which is my captive and my handmaid, a matron of the true Israel? Or that shaving off and cutting away all in her that is dead, whether this be idolatry, pleasure, error, or lust, I take her to myself clean and pure and beget by her servants for the lord of Sabaoth? My efforts promote the advantage of Christ's family, my so-called defilement with an alien increases the number of my fellow-servants.

Jerome had his answer. By paring away all of the licentious and irreverent passages in pagan literature, not only would it become acceptable to Christians, it might, in fact, increase the flock.

In 382, Jerome went to Rome as secretary to Pope Damasus, and he began to write letters and treatises concerning worldly vices such as greed and an appetite for power which he believed were poisoning religious life in the city. This did not endear him to the powerful leaders of Roman society, and when Pope Damasus died in 385, Jerome moved to Bethlehem, where he devoted himself for the next thirty years to the major accomplishment of his life, the translation of the Bible from Greek and Hebrew (the Old Testament) and Greek (parts of the New Testament) into Latin. This had previously been attempted unsuccessfully, but Jerome's version, albeit incomplete, became the standard text of the Bible, known as the "Vulgate" (from Latin *vulgata*, meaning "common version"), and was universally used throughout the western, or Latin-speaking, church. Jerome's work defined the Christian vocabulary and set the framework for Christian thought; his translation was influenced by his deep knowledge of Latin literature, and his work provided a bridge between the literary tradition of antiquity and that of the Middle Ages. In addition, his attitudes towards asceticism and celibacy provided inspiration for the growing movement known as monasticism (see below).

Gregory I (Gregory the Great) was an effective leader and a gifted administrator. He was pope from 590 to 604 and became the virtual ruler of Rome at a time when there was a breakdown of political authority, as the city was threatened by the Lombards, and the citizens of Rome were starving. His solutions to these problems were masterful; he was able to negotiate a truce with the Lombards, and he reorganized the extensive lands of the Church in southern Italy in order to provide food for the hungry mobs. He also vastly improved the economy of Italy by establishing new markets for export products.

One of Gregory's most important contributions, however, was his action to promote the conversion of the British Isles. As will be discussed in Chapter 2, the success of his emissary, a missionary also named Augustine, was to have far-reaching consequences, not only for Britain, but for Continental Europe as well.

Gregory was also instrumental in establishing a pattern for ideal priestly behavior in his *Book of Pastoral Care*, a treatise that bore witness to his own understanding of

6 This ivory carving from the tenth century illustrates Pope Gregory the Great writing down the words and melodies of Gregorian chant as the Holy Spirit (in the form of a dove) whispers them into his ear. Since the chant was thus said to have come directly from God, it was considered to be perfect, and could not be altered.

the problems involved in ministering to the bishop's flock. But perhaps even more important was his codification of the chant that had been sung in liturgical services since the earliest days of Christianity. Prior to Gregory's time there were several varieties of chant melody, with no ecclesiastical guidance as to which were acceptable or preferable. Gregory commissioned an examination and codification of these melodies. Although modern scholars view his role in systematizing liturgical practice as organizational rather than artistic, the form of chant approved by his commission has been known since his time as "Gregorian chant." A ninth-century legend asserted, moreover, that the Gregorian chant form had been whispered directly into Gregory's ear by the Holy Spirit in the form of a dove, and was therefore a gift from God that was perfect and unchangeable (**fig. 6**). This view of chant had profound implications for the future development of music, as subsequent chapters will demonstrate.

Realizing the importance of music in the Church, Gregory established a *schola cantorum*—a school for singers in which the methods of proper chant singing were taught. This was of great benefit, since a system for writing music down had not been developed. Melodies were passed from generation to generation by memory, and Gregory's school helped immeasurably to ensure the proper transmission.

Perhaps Gregory's greatest contribution to the development of the Church, however, was his active promotion of the role of the pope. Gregory asserted the equality of the pope to his rival, the patriarch of Constantinople, and confirmed the primacy of the pope over the western church.

The papacy

In the early period of Christianity, all bishops were considered to possess equal authority; the early bishoprics were significant population centers, and their bishops were pious men from within the **apostolic tradition**. That is, they could claim that their authority derived from direct contact with one of the apostles or their close associates. The first references to the bishop of Rome having primacy over all other bishops date to the second century and appear in religious correspondence such as the letters of St. Ignatius (AD 110) and St. Irenaeus (*c.* 185). Nonetheless, the evolution of the theory of papal preeminence—a theory that provided the foundation for the thoughts and actions of the medieval popes—was a slow process and took place over a long period of time. The fifth century marked a crucial stage in this evolution, for this was when the first arguments for the preeminence of the bishop of Rome began to be put forward. The justifications given for this view were derived from various sources, and the synthesis of these arguments was eventually known as the **Petrine theory**.

Supporters of the theory argued that Rome was the capital of the ancient world; it was wealthy, and was the center of commerce. It had special distinction in Christian teaching because both St. Peter and St. Paul were martyred there. Furthermore, the bishops of

Rome, historically, provided excellent leadership; in the early councils of the Church they always provided effective answers, so much so that St. Augustine remarked, *Roma dixit; causa finita est* ("Rome speaks; the issue is closed"). Indeed, the primacy of the bishop of Rome was formally acknowledged by the Council of Sardica (343).

Another key factor was the stipulation by the Roman emperor that all bishops in the western part of the empire were subordinate to the bishop at Rome. This occurred in an edict issued by Emperor Valentinian III in 445:

> Inasmuch as the preeminence of the Apostolic See is assured by the merit of St. Peter, the first of the bishops, by the leading position of the city of Rome and also by the authority of the holy synod, let not presumption strive to attempt anything contrary to the authority of that See . . . Whatsoever the authority of the Apostolic See has enacted, or shall enact, let that be held as law for all.

And in addition to this imperial sanction, there was a scriptural foundation for Roman primacy. Matthew recounted that Christ had said to Peter:

> Thou art Peter; and upon this rock I will build my Church. And I will give unto thee the keys of the kingdom of heaven. And whatsoever thou shalt bind on earth, shall be bound in heaven; and whatsoever thou shalt loose on earth, shall be loosed also in heaven. [Matthew 16:18]

This reference was the subject for an important sermon by Pope Leo I (r. 440–461), who asserted that Peter,

> . . . [who] was ordained before the rest in such a way that from his being called the Rock, from his being pronounced the Foundation, from his being constituted the Doorkeeper on the kingdom of heaven, from his being set as the Umpire to bind and to loose, whose judgments shall retain their validity in heaven, from all these mystical titles we might know the nature of his association with Christ.

Furthermore, the preeminence of the bishop of Rome was supported by the doctrine of **apostolic succession**, which stated that all future bishops of Rome inherited the power and authority of Peter.

However, the pope was not the only person with influence in establishing Church doctrine. By the sixth century, monasticism had become an integral element in the Church, with monks and nuns exerting a powerful force on its development. Indeed, Pope Gregory the Great was himself a monk.

Monasticism

As discussed above, during the first century following the birth of Christ, the new religion was practiced in small communities of believers in which there was no distinction concerning authority. By the second century, however, a hierarchical administration had developed, and Christianity was directed by chosen leaders. Although this systematization was appealing to some Christians, others saw it as a perversion of the original values and truths as taught and practiced by Christ and the apostles. These dissidents came to believe that it was impossible to practice the Christian religion properly within society, and they withdrew to the fringes of society, often to the desert, in order to pursue a pure and ascetic life and to establish direct contact with the divine. This movement, which is considered to be the beginning of monasticism, is known as **eremitic monasticism**.

The eremitic experience began in the near east, probably in Egypt. The individuals who chose to pursue truth in this way, known as hermits, divested themselves of all possessions and lived simply, praying constantly and often subjecting their bodies to extreme deprivation and challenge. Not only did they exist on a very small diet of food, some sat on pillars for extended periods of time, perhaps as long as twenty years; others ate only grass, and are known in the hagiographical tradition as "grazing saints;" many never bathed, and wore hair shirts that constantly rubbed their bare flesh, ultimately inducing painful and maggot-infested sores. These individuals are sometimes described as "spiritual athletes" because of the rigors of their disciplined existence. By the fourth century, tales of these heroic individuals were circulating widely throughout the Christian community, rivaling accounts of the Christian martyrs; further, as persecution ended, ascetic monasticism provided an alternative way for pious Christians, both male and female, to express their devotion.

The most important account of the "flight to the desert" may be found in the *Life of St. Antony*, by the fourth-century bishop Athanasius of Alexandria, who also formulated the fundamental statement of Christian belief endorsed by the Council of Nicea. St. Antony (251–356) was a famous example of the so-called "desert saints," and as Athanasius described his life of ascetic contemplation, he remarked that "many marveled at him, but he bore the life easily."

> The zeal that had pervaded his soul over a long time had effected a good frame of mind in him, with the result that even a slight inspiration received from others caused him to respond with great enthusiasm. For instance, he kept nocturnal vigil with such determination that he often spent the entire night sleepless, and this not only once, but many times, to their admiration. Again, he ate but once a day, after sunset; indeed, sometimes only every other day, and frequently only every fourth day did he partake of food. His food was bread and salt; his drink, water only. Meat and wine we need not even mention, for no such thing could be found with the other ascetics either. He was content to sleep on a rush mat, though as a rule he lay down on the bare ground. He deprecated the use of oil for the skin, saying that young men should practice asceticism in real earnest and not go for the things that enervate the body; rather they should accustom it to hard work, bearing in mind the words of the Apostle: *When I am weak, then am I powerful* [2 Corinthians 12:10]. It was a dictum of his that the soul's energy thrives when the body's desires are feeblest.

St. Antony, like other hermits, was subjected to repeated incidents of temptation by the Devil:

> The Enemy would suggest filthy thoughts, but the other [Antony] would dissipate them by his prayers; he would try to incite him to lust, but Antony, sensing shame,

would gird his body with his faith, with his prayers and his fasting. The wretched Devil even dared to masquerade as a woman by night and to impersonate such in every possible way, merely in order to deceive Antony. But he filled his thoughts with Christ and reflected upon the nobility of the soul that comes from Him, and its spirituality, and thus quenched the glowing coal of temptation. And again the Enemy suggested pleasure's seductive charm. But Antony, angered, of course, and grieved, kept his thoughts upon the threat of fire and the pain of the worm. Holding these up as his shield, he came through unscathed.

After emerging unsullied from this struggle, Antony continued his quest for salvation. Athanasius recounted that, after he had spent more than twenty years in self-imposed isolation, people interested in emulating his holy life approached his shack and broke down the door. "Antony came forth as out of a shrine, as one initiated into sacred mysteries and filled with the spirit of God, and the onlookers were amazed at his appearance, which was neither obese from want of exercise, nor emaciated from his fastings and struggles with demons." He looked just as he did before he had enclosed himself in his cell.

Antony became a model for the ascetic life, and stood as an icon of the eremitic experience. His example was emulated by women as well as men. Accounts of desert monasticism include many legends of females, often prostitutes who sought to cleanse themselves of their former sins through ascetic practices. A typical tale concerns Mary of Egypt, a courtesan who was turned away from church on a feast day. She fled to the desert to redeem herself, and spent many years in deprivation, growing old and blackened through exposure to the sun. When sought out by a hermit, she was so thin as a result of fasting that he first thought she was a shadow, and then a wild beast. Covering her nakedness with men's clothing, she then instructed the visitor in the practices of eremitism.

Obviously, however, not everyone could emulate the rigors of such a life. Not only were the physical hardships beyond the ability of most people to bear, but the extreme isolation for years at a time was possible for only the most dedicated "spiritual athletes." As the fourth century progressed, while leaders of the Church such as Athanasius, Jerome, Ambrose, and Augustine endorsed the monastic experience in principle, people began to experiment with other modes of monastic life. These new patterns of monasticism placed less rigorous demands upon the body and the psyche, and were thus more appealing to a wide variety of men and women. In addition, they provided ways in which monasticism could be accommodated within the organizational structure of the Church.

It was St. Pachomius (c. 290–346) who first suggested solving the problem of social isolation through group eremitic life. Each monk or nun would live in his or her own separate quarters or cell within a larger community, whose members would come together for common prayer and liturgy, although they would not speak to one another. This pattern of life was later taken up by several monastic orders, including the Carthusians, founded in the late eleventh century. Pachomius was also the first to suggest that manual labor should be a part of monastic life. Nevertheless, for all who joined the religious life, the primary mission was to save their own souls; other activities were secondary to this main purpose.

As the monastic movement developed, a form of community life known as **cenobitic monasticism** became popular. It was initially proposed in the second half of the fourth century by St. Basil, who suggested that the monks should eat and work together in addition to worshiping as a community. Cenobitic monasticism became the predominant form in the west, while the model of community eremitism was more popular in the east.

In the sixth century, St. Benedict of Nursia (*c.* 480–543), after attempting to live an eremitic existence, gathered a community and provided a Rule for them, which set out regulations for a monastic community. This proved to be so viable that it became the basic guide for monasticism in the west. Benedict's Rule is traditionally dated at 529, though some scholars now believe 540 is a more accurate estimate. From it grew Benedictine monasticism, which was the predominant form for religious communities in the west, both male and female, until the eleventh century; it is still prevalent in the twenty-first century.

The Rule of St. Benedict was characterized by reason, moderation, discipline, and excellent principles of organization. It proposed "nothing harsh nor burdensome," but clearly set forth the monastic precepts of poverty, chastity, stability, and obedience. The leader of the monastery was a monk known as the abbot, and the members of the community were subject to his authority. A new monastery was established by a grant, usually from the Church, but often from a nobleman or noblewoman, which endowed the monks with enough land to sustain the members of the community; it was thus a self-supporting agricultural establishment. The monks lived together, slept in a common dormitory, ate together in a refectory, worked together, and prayed together. They could not leave the confines of the monastery without the permission of the abbot.

According to the Rule, the monks were given a moderate amount of food:

> For the daily refection of the sixth as well as the ninth hour, two cooked dishes . . .
> and, if it is possible to obtain apples or growing vegetables, a third may be added.
> One full pound of bread shall suffice for a day, whether there be one refection, or a
> breakfast and a supper . . . But if, perchance, some greater labor shall have been
> performed, it shall be in the will and power of the abbot, if it is expedient, to increase
> anything; surfeiting above all things being guarded against, so that indigestion may
> never seize a monk . . . moderation being observed in all things.

Each monk was granted a *hemina* (about a pint) of wine a day, but those who could abstain completely "shall know that they will have their own reward." The monks were given clothing suitable to the climate of the monastery, and shoes and boots to cover their feet. Each one had a cowl, or hood, and a gown, and "a working garment, on account of their labors."

One of Benedict's provisions in the Rule was the requirement for manual labor. This was to be coupled with reading of the sacred text, and both activities were to be supervised by senior members of the community:

> Idleness is the enemy of the soul. And therefore, at fixed times, the brothers ought
> to be occupied in manual labour; and again, at fixed times, in sacred reading . . .
> there shall certainly be appointed one or two elders, who shall go round the

monastery at the hours in which the brothers are engaged in reading, and see to it that no troublesome brother chance to be found who is open to idleness and trifling, and is not intent on his reading; being not only of no use to himself, but also stirring up others.

The most important part of the Rule stipulated the practice of community prayer, which occurred seven times during each twenty-four-hour period. "Let nothing be preferred to the service of God," Benedict wrote, and it is evident that, in his view, performance of the liturgy took precedence over all other monastic activity.

Because Benedict's Rule was characterized by moderation, it made monasticism a more realistic option for a wider segment of the population. The demands made on the individual were reasonable; Benedictine monks and nuns were given adequate clothing, adequate nourishment, and the reassuring routine of prayer, reading, and manual labor within the framework of a community.

Women were active in all phases of the development of monasticism. Although women's establishments were generally smaller and less wealthy, many were founded during the fourth and fifth centuries, often by aristocratic women (see the discussion in Chapter 2). Although the search for salvation and contact with the divine characterized both male and female religious communities, scholars have suggested several reasons why the monastic life may have been particularly appealing to women. The convent offered an escape for a woman trapped in an unsatisfactory, or violent marriage, and provided protection for widows against forced remarriage. Furthermore, the convent established an atmosphere in which women, free of male control except for visitations by the bishop, could develop their own intellectual capabilities and guide and control their own existence.

Early Christian art

Although, as we saw earlier, Pope Gregory was particularly interested in the religious significance of music, this was not the only art form used by the early Christians to enhance the emotional and spiritual effect of the liturgy. The architecture of the basilicas, the liturgical garments of the celebrants, the elaborate censers and altar vessels, and the wall paintings that graced their places of worship, all contributed to the religious experience of the worshipers. Beauty was seen as a gift of God, and its presence in the music, the architectural surroundings, the vestments, and the incense that represented the prayers of the saints, led the human soul into closer contact with the divine.

Just as the early Christians borrowed the Roman basilica form to create a suitable place for congregational worship, so the artists of the third and fourth centuries used techniques derived from Roman wall painting, adapting the subject matter to Christian themes and symbols. The best examples of early Christian wall painting are found in the **catacombs** of Rome, where it is possible to view the transition from Roman themes to those of Christianity. In one prominent example, Christ is seen as Orpheus, a figure from Roman mythology, with the legendary ability to calm wild beasts. In another painting, he has been fully transformed into the "Good Shepherd." Many of the paintings use themes drawn from the Old Testament, as well as scenes from the life of Christ as recounted in the New Testament. By the mid-fourth century, the image of the adult, bearded Christ was fully developed, in **fig. 7**, where Christ is depicted flanked by the Alpha and Omega.

There are also images of daily life, such as workers harvesting grain, picking olives, and making wine. Several paintings show praying figures, such as the one in **fig. 8**. This posture, with the hands outstretched in receptivity, is known as the *orans* gesture (*orans* is Latin for "praying"), and symbolizes the spirit in prayer. It is thought by scholars to have been an innovation of early Christian artists; it does not seem to have been drawn from pre-Christian Roman art. The *orans* is associated with women in several paintings, indicating the participation of females in the early Christian community.

The tradition of Christianity and the legacy of Classical Rome were two significant sources from which the civilization of the Middle Ages developed. In order to understand the third of the powerful influences present in medieval culture and society, it is important to explore the traditions and contributions of the Germanic tribes who were never fully absorbed into the Roman Empire but did have a major impact on it.

7 In the early centuries of Christian belief, Christ was frequently portrayed as a graceful young man, often modeled after Classical images of the Greek god Apollo. Later he was shown as a bearded adult, as in this mid-fourth-century wall painting from the Catacomb of Commodilla in Rome. On either side are the first and last letters of the Greek alphabet—Alpha and Omega—signifying the biblical reference that Christ is the "beginning and the end" of Christian belief.

8 The worshiping figure of a Christian woman shown in this wall painting from the late third century is holding her arms in the *orans* (literally "praying") gesture, symbolizing the human spirit in prayer and supplication. The painting, in the catacomb of Maius, Rome, reflects the large proportion of early Christians who were women.

The Germanic Tribal Tradition

The people the Romans referred to as "barbarians" had been migrating into the empire since the first century AD. It is evident that they were known to the Romans at an even earlier time, however, since Julius Caesar described his conflicts with them in his history of the Gallic Wars. By the third century, there were many Germanic people living within the boundaries of the Roman Empire; in the fifth century, these Germanic tribes had a decisive influence on that empire.

Our sources for information concerning the early Germanic peoples are scant, however, and our understanding of them is based primarily on the works of the Roman historian Tacitus, who lived at the end of the first century AD. It is important to remember that Tacitus was writing from a biased viewpoint; for him, all Germanic peoples were barbarians—uncivilized and uncultured nomads. Nonetheless, his works provide a great deal of valuable information about tribal practices and customs, and it is possible to ascertain from these early writings certain features of Germanic life that deeply influenced the development of medieval society, especially with regard to the system known as **vassalage** (see Chapter 5).

Tacitus claimed in his *Germania* that each of the tribes, regardless of location, was led by a chieftain, elected by his warriors. Each chief gathered around him a band of warriors, called a ***comitatus***: a "companionship."

> The companions have different ranks in the company, according to the opinion of the chief; there is a great rivalry among the companions for first place with the chief, as there is among the chiefs for the possession of the largest and bravest band of followers. It is a source of dignity and of power to be surrounded by a large body of young warriors, who sustain the rank of the chief in peace and defend him in war. The fame of such a chief and his band is not confined to their own tribe, but is known among foreign peoples; they are sought out and honored with gifts in order to secure their alliance, for the reputation of such a band may decide a whole war.

It is possible to see within this practice the seeds of medieval vassalage, often called feudalism—a system based on bonds of loyalty among military associates. By providing his men with the spoils of battle, the chieftain guaranteed their allegiance:

> In battle it is shameful for the chief to allow any one of his followers to excel him in courage, and for the followers not to equal their chief in deeds of valor. But the greatest shame of all, and one that renders a man forever infamous, is to return alive from the fight in which his chief has fallen. It is a sacred obligation of the followers to defend and protect their chief and add to his fame by their bravery, for the chief fights for victory and the companions for the chief. . . . Glory is to be gained only among perils, and a chief can maintain a band only by war, for the companions expect to receive their warhorse and arms from the leader, . . . and the means of liberality are best obtained from the booty of war.

In this passage, it is evident that the virtues of loyalty and bravery were preeminent among the Germanic peoples. A warrior was distinguished by his bravery, and his chieftain became famous as a result of the valor he demonstrated in battle. A man's loyalty to his leader implied disregard for his own life; it was a "sacred obligation" to defend the chief. These qualities and values were also praised in medieval literature, as will be discussed in Chapters 2 and 8. The resonance of the Germanic *comitatus* is evident, for example, in the tales of King Arthur and his Knights of the Round Table, and the poems *Beowulf* and *The Song of Roland*.

Other elements of medieval feudalism were also described in embryonic form by Tacitus. The following account, for example, refers to a practice quite like the "knighting" of a young warrior in the Middle Ages:

> They go armed all the time, but no one is permitted to wear arms until he has satisfied the tribe of his fitness to do so. Then, at the general assembly, the youth is given a shield and a sword by his chief or his father or one of his relatives. This is the token of manhood, as the receiving of the toga is with us.

According to Tacitus, the war leaders led "by example rather than command, winning great admiration if they are energetic and fight in plain sight in front of the line." The greatest incitements to courage and valor, however, came from the families of the warriors, who accompanied them to battle:

> . . . their dear ones are close at hand so that the wailings of the women and the crying of the children can be heard during the battle. These are for each warrior the most sacred witnesses of his bravery, these his dearest applauders. They carry their wounds to their mothers and their wives, nor do the latter fear to count and examine their wounds while they bring them food and urge them to deeds of valor . . . it is said that on more than one occasion broken and fleeing ranks have been turned back to the fight by the prayers of the women, who feared captivity above everything else . . . They believe that women are specially gifted by the gods, and do not disdain to take council with them and heed their advice.

Women thus had a position in tribal society quite different from that of contemporaneous Roman wives, who may have had some political influence, but certainly did not join their husbands on the battlefield.

Kinship and the bonds of clan membership were characteristic of Germanic society, and the laws adjudicated in their courts seem to have been observed primarily to prevent the blood-feuds generated by quarreling kinship groups (see Chapter 2). Justice was administered in courts consisting of assemblies of the warriors, with their chiefs officiating. The courts also tried criminal cases, and although the death penalty could be assigned, there were other penalties for different crimes: "traitors and deserters are hanged on trees, cowards and base criminals are sunk in the swamps or bogs, under wicker hurdles . . ."

Laws and customs such as these seem to have been prevalent among the many different tribes that migrated from the east into western Europe in the early centuries of the Christian era. The following discussion will deal with the four largest and most influential of the tribes: the Visigoths, Vandals, Ostrogoths, and Franks.

As these tribes pressed westward, their relations with the Roman Empire consisted of periods of peaceful trading interspersed with occasional warlike raids along the frontier. Many German men even served in the Roman military, and several rose to positions of great power. The Vandal general Stilicho, for example, virtually ruled the empire during the fourth century.

In 375 the Visigoths, or "West Goths," requested permission from the emperor Valens (r. 364–378) to move across the Danube River and establish a settlement. This was the first example of an entire tribe migrating into the empire. In 378, however, the Visigoths, complaining that they were being unfairly treated by provincial officials, began a revolt against the Roman authority. They engaged the Roman forces at Adrianople, and won a stunning victory, killing the emperor. Theodosius, who was next to rule, was able to pacify the Visigoths, who remained content to live peacefully for several decades.

The situation grew more complex in the early part of the fifth century, when the Huns from the steppes of Asia began to move westward, for reasons that remain unclear. Their migrations placed pressure on the various tribes in the areas east of the Rhine, and large groups of them began to move into the empire (**Map 2**). In 406, a huge horde composed primarily of Vandals stormed the frontier, ravaged Gaul, and moved into Spain. Four years later, Alaric, the leader of the Visigoths, invaded Rome and looted it—an occurrence that sent shock waves throughout the empire. (Augustine devoted part

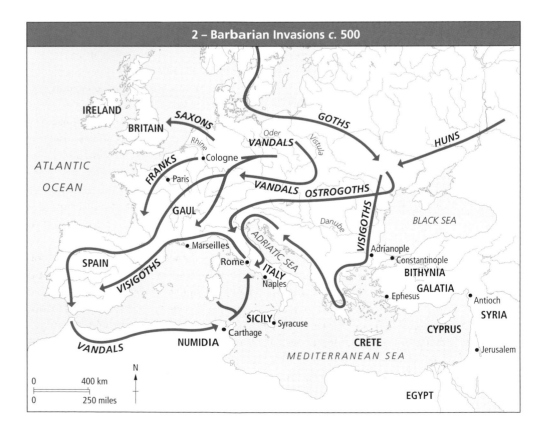

2 – Barbarian Invasions c. 500

of his *City of God* to an attempt to explain the significance of the event.) The Visigoths pushed on, pressuring the Vandals, who left Spain and moved on to North Africa, while the Visigoths remained in Spain to create their own kingdom.

Italy continued to be subject to invasion and plundering, and the weak emperors of the fifth century were unable to stave off the attacks. Several were assassinated, and others were mere puppet rulers controlled by Germanic generals. The last of these generals, Odoacar, deposed Romulus Augustulus, the final titular emperor, in 476, and did not bother to replace him. Thus, in a rather undramatic way, the western part of the Roman Empire drew to a close.

Two more invasions with lasting effect in Gaul and Italy occurred during the fifth century. The tribal peoples responsible for these invasions—the Franks and the Ostrogoths, or "East Goths"—were able to establish two of the most important and powerful "successor states" discussed in Chapter 2. The leader of the Ostrogoths, Theodoric, defeated Odoacar in Italy and built a kingdom that incorporated many Roman customs and traditions. The king of the Franks, Clovis, was able to lay the foundation for a kingdom that ultimately became the Carolingian Empire.

Summary

The fascinating complexity of medieval civilization was derived from three major sources: the heritage of Rome, the precepts of the Christian religion, and the customs of the Germanic tribes. Each possessed unique qualities that interacted with the other two in producing a new culture—one that became characteristic of the new civilization.

From Rome came geographical determination, language, literature, art, and the architectural form of the basilica. Christianity provided a belief system that became universal in medieval "Christendom," and the Church preserved literary and organizational skills that enabled the Germanic monarchs of the sixth century to establish relatively cultured and sophisticated kingdoms. The Germanic tribal tradition contributed the seeds of vassalage—a system founded on bonds of loyalty between warriors, which became the basis of governance in the Middle Ages. It was the synthesis of these three traditions that produced the distinctive and intricate civilization of medieval Europe.

Suggestions for Further Reading

Primary sources

A helpful collection of sources concerning early Christianity is contained in *The New Testament Background: Writings from Ancient Greece and the Roman Empire that Illuminate Christian Origins*, by Charles Kingsley Barrett (London: SPCK, 1956). Another excellent

volume of readings has been compiled by Karl F. Morrison in *The Church in the Roman Empire* (Chicago: University of Chicago Press, 1986).

The first volume of *Papal Letters in the Early Middle Ages*, by Detlev Jasper and Horst Fuhrmann (3 vols., Washington, D.C.: Catholic University of America, 2001)

contains material pertaining to this chapter. *The Confessions of St. Augustine*, translated by James J. O'Donnell (3 vols., Oxford: Oxford University Press, 1992) is an excellent new edition of the classic work, with a fine commentary and analysis. Augustine's *City of God* is available in several translations. One of the most recent is by R.W.

Dyson (Cambridge: Cambridge University Press, 1998). Several works of Tacitus are available in *Tacitus: Dialogus, Agricola, Germania*, translated by M. Hutton, revised by E.H. Warmington (Cambridge: Harvard University Press, 1946).

A widely available translation of *The History of the Church from Christ to Constantine*, by Eusebius, is by Geoffrey A. Williamson (Harmondsworth: Penguin, revised ed., 1989).

The Life of Saint Antony and *The Letter to Marcellinus*, by St. Athanasius, have both been translated by Robert C. Gregg (New York: Paulist Press, 1980). *The Rule of St. Benedict* is available in many editions. Two of the most recent translations are by David Parry (London: Darton, Longman, & Todd, 1984) and Timothy Fry, Imogene Baker, *et al.* (New York: Vintage Books, 1998).

Writings concerning the experiences of early Christian women may be found in *Handmaids of the Lord: Contemporary Descriptions of Feminine Asceticism in the First Six Centuries*, translated and edited by Joan M. Peterson (Kalamazoo, MI: Cistercian Publications, 1996).

Secondary sources

Diocletian's reign is analyzed in *Diocletian and the Roman Recovery*, by Stephen Williams (New York: Routledge, 1997). An excellent study of the first Christian emperor is *Constantine*, by Ramsay MacMullen (London, New York: Croom Helm, 1969). See also his study, *Corruption and the Decline of Rome* (New Haven: Yale University Press, 1988).

A classic analysis of the late Roman Empire is *The World of Late Antiquity*, by Peter Brown (New York: W.W. Norton, 1971). It is a beautifully illustrated book, which provides a fine introduction to European culture from 150 to 750. See also his *Society and the Holy in Late Antiquity* (London: Faber, 1982) and *The Body and Society: Men, Women, and Sexual Renunciation in Early Christianity* (London: Faber, 1989). *Christianity and Paganism in the Fourth to Eighth Centuries*, by Ramsey MacMullen (New Haven: Yale University Press, 1997), is an important study of religious and cultural relations in the early Middle Ages.

A splendid biography, also by Peter Brown, is *Augustine of Hippo: A Biography* (Berkeley: University of California Press, 1969), which provides a comprehensive analysis of the life of Augustine and his era.

Two groundbreaking works by Caroline Walker Bynum are *Holy Feast and Holy Fast: The Religious Significance of Food to Medieval Women* (Berkeley: University of California Press, 1987) and *The Resurrection of the Body in Western Christianity, 200–1336* (New York: Columbia University Press, 1995).

JoAnn Kay MacNamara's *Sisters in Arms: Catholic Nuns Through Two Millennia* (Cambridge, MA: Harvard University Press, 1996) is a fine study of women's monastic life. Chapters 1–4 provide an excellent overview of the development of female monasticism prior to the seventh century. *The Desert Fathers*, by Helen Waddell (Ann Arbor, MI: University of Michigan Press, 1951), is a fascinating description of eremitic monasticism. *Medieval Monasticism: Forms of Religious Life in Western Europe in the Middle Ages*, by Clifford Hugh Lawrence (3rd ed., London: Longman, 2000), contains a fine discussion of the development of monasticism from its earliest days through the late Middle Ages.

The history of the papacy during the era pertaining to this chapter is analyzed in *The Popes and the Papacy in the Early Middle Ages (476–752)*, by Jeffrey Richards (London: Routledge & Kegan Paul, 1979).

2 THE SUCCESSORS OF ROME

WITHIN ITALY, the Ostrogothic king, Theodoric, was determined to preserve Classical Roman culture, and, though his kingdom did not endure much beyond his lifetime, his patronage provided a lasting cultural legacy. In the eastern empire, meanwhile, Justinian struggled with the grand dream of reuniting the ancient Roman world, spending lavishly on magnificent buildings such as Hagia Sophia. The Germanic tribes that entered western Europe in the fifth and sixth centuries established kingdoms in which each had their own distinct identity in terms of religion, law, culture, and society. Each tribe, however, was influential in the development of medieval Europe. In Gaul, the Franks created a kingdom that was closely associated with the papacy and provided the foundation for the great Carolingian Empire. In the British Isles, the Angles and Saxons were eventually able to create a unified monarchy, and were converted to Christianity by papal missionaries. And in Spain, the Visigoths established themselves as overlords to the native population, by whom they were eventually assimilated.

Theodoric and the Preservation of Classical Roman Culture

When the Ostrogoths invaded Italy in 489, they encountered a well-preserved system of Roman government. The bureaucratic mechanism of the provinces and *civitates* had survived, and the Ostrogothic king, Theodoric (r. 475–526), was determined to perpetuate the functioning apparatus of Roman statecraft (see Map 1). As a boy, Theodoric had spent several years as a hostage at the court of Constantinople, and he had been deeply influenced by the culture and governance system of the Roman world. Under his leadership, a program of civil governance called ***civilitas*** was instigated, which aimed to preserve the Roman administrative system, economy, and culture. As a result, the Roman tradition of orderly governance was maintained more successfully by the Ostrogoths than in any of the other Germanic successor states.

Theodoric's determination to impart Roman values to the Ostrogoths, and eventually to other Germanic tribes, is clearly demonstrated in the following letter, which was written to the southern provinces in Gaul:

Obey the Roman customs. You are now by God's blessing restored to your ancient freedom; put off the barbarian; clothe yourselves with the morals of the toga; unlearn cruelty, that you may not be unworthy to be our subjects . . . Do not dislike the reign of law because it is new to you, after the aimless seethings of barbarism.

In order to achieve his goal of orderly rule, Theodoric retained Roman administrators to continue the preexisting system, rather than entrusting the offices of civil administration to his tribesmen. The Ostrogothic warriors had a purely military role, furnishing armies that proved to be adequate for the defense of Italy during Theodoric's lifetime. They were supported by revenues from lands provided by wealthy Italian landowners, who were required to set aside portions of their large estates for the use of the invaders.

The Ostrogothic people lived alongside the Romans but separately from them, under the leadership of their own chieftains and governed according to their own customs and traditions. They also practiced their own religion—the Arian form of Christianity. (See Chapter 1 for a discussion of the Arian and Athanasian forms of Christianity.) Theodoric, who was himself an Arian Christian, was nevertheless prepared to tolerate the faith of the Italian population, declaring that "We cannot command the religion of our subjects, since no one can be forced to believe against his will." Theodoric governed his subjects impartially, though he expected that all people living in his realm would conform to the law. His tolerant attitudes extended to the Jews, as may be seen in his letter to the Jews of Genoa:

> . . . all the privileges which the foresight of antiquity conferred upon the Jewish customs shall be renewed to you, for in truth it is our great desire that the laws of the ancients shall be kept in force to secure the reverence due to us. Everything which has been found to conduce to *civilitas* should be held fast with enduring devotion.

In addition to maintaining the religious and governmental traditions of Rome, including a functioning Senate, Theodoric hoped to rebuild the city of Rome after the ravages it had suffered throughout the fifth century. He saw this process of reconstruction as one of "adornment in time of peace, [and] a precaution for time of war." As he remarked in a letter to Maximian and Andreas, officials in his court:

> The wandering birds love their own nests; the beasts haste to their own lodgings in the brake [thicket]; the voluptuous fish, roaming the fields of ocean, returns to its own well-known cavern. How much more should Rome be loved by her children!

The ultimate ambition of the Ostrogothic king was to blend Roman and Germanic traditions, and to provide a peaceful environment for the growth of culture. He viewed peace as "the fair mother of all liberal arts, the softener of manners, the replenisher of the generations of humanity. Peace ought certainly to be an object of desire to every kingdom."

An important aspect of Theodoric's goal of establishing peace was a foreign policy that made extensive use of marriage diplomacy. For example, he fostered peaceful relations with his most threatening enemies, the Vandals, a tribe that had settled in northern Africa, by arranging a marriage between the Vandal king and his own sister, and Theodoric himself married the sister of the Frankish king, Clovis. One of Theodoric's daughters married the king of the Burgundians, and another married the Visigothic king. In this way, he created an intricate system of alliances that involved the leaders of most of the Germanic tribes, while carefully maintaining the Ostrogothic kingdom at the center.

Under Theodoric's leadership, much of the Italian peninsula prospered. In addition to providing peace and security, the king controlled food prices and changed the tax laws so that the lower classes would pay less than they had under Roman rule. The wealthy and the poor alike benefited from his measures.

Theodoric's legacy of good governance was short-lived. Soon after his death in 526, the forces of Justinian, the eastern emperor, besieged Italy; a few decades later they were followed by another Germanic tribe, the Lombards. Theodoric's cultural patronage, however, resulted in the preservation of the Roman system of education—the Seven Liberal Arts, consisting of the *Trivium* (logic, grammar, and rhetoric) and the *Quadrivium* (arithmetic, geometry, astronomy, and music). Two men in particular were responsible for this extraordinary heritage: Boethius and Cassiodorus, both of whom were Roman aristocrats employed at the court of Theodoric.

Boethius

Anicius Manlius Severinus Boethius (*c.* 480–524) was a scholar who aspired to translate into Latin the complete works of the ancient Greek philosophers Plato and Aristotle. He hoped ultimately to interpret the writings of both men, and to harmonize Platonic and Aristotelian thought. Unfortunately, he was implicated in a plot against Theodoric, which resulted in his imprisonment and ultimate execution in 524; and his ambitious program was never completed. Only his translation of Aristotle's four treatises on logic, known collectively as the *Organon*, remains today. However, Boethius also wrote "textbooks" for the four subjects of the *Quadrivium*; of these, the works on arithmetic and music have survived. Probably the most influential of these two is *De institutione musica* (*The Fundamentals of Music*), a treatise that was used as the basis for teaching music theory during the entire medieval period; indeed, it remained part of the curriculum at Oxford University until the middle of the eighteenth century, and continues to be studied by musicologists and music theorists today.

Boethius viewed music as an object of knowledge, something to be intellectually appreciated rather than a form of self-expression or creative activity. Music, he wrote, is the discipline of examining carefully the diversity of high and low sounds by means of reason and the senses. Just as learned men are not content to behold colors and forms without investigating their properties, so they should not be delighted by melodies without knowing how the sounds are proportionately interrelated. Therefore, the true musician is neither the singer or the instrumentalist, nor one who only composes by instinct without knowing the meaning of what he does, but the philosopher, the theorist, or the critic, whose judgments are formed on the basis of intellectual apprehension or reason.

Much of *De institutione musica* was thus derived from Classical Greek musical theory and philosophy. The first three parts drew on the philosophies of Plato and Pythagoras; the fourth reflected the works of Euclid and Aristoxenus; and the fifth was based on Ptolemy (**fig. 9**). The most original and important sections of *De institutione musica* were those that defined music itself and the nature of musicianship.

Boethius envisioned music as being of three kinds: *musica mundana*, *musica humana*, and *musica instrumentalis*. *Musica mundana* referred to the harmony of the macrocosm, or celestial spheres, and was to be studied in the orderly mathematical relationships of the stars and planets that were observed in the heavens. *Musica humana* referred to the ways in which these harmonious relations were exemplified in the microcosm—the soul and body of man; there could be no doubt, Boethius stated, that man's soul and body seemed to be combined according to the same proportions that linked the modulations of harmony. The third category, *musica instrumentalis*, described harmonic proportions and modulations as they occur and take audible form when musical sounds are actually produced; it represented all natural and artificial means by which human beings produce music, thus including both vocal music and music played on instruments. Boethius saw the three kinds of music as inextricably related to each other, so that,

for example, audible music was ideally a reflection of the ratios that exist between planets; thus, music received its meaning from *musica mundana*. This concept of cosmic harmony had a significant influence on the development of music in subsequent centuries—an influence that was extended during the later Middle Ages to include architecture and literature (see Chapter 13).

During the imprisonment Boethius suffered prior to his execution, he wrote his most celebrated work, *The Consolation of Philosophy*, which became one of the most widely read works of the Middle Ages and the Renaissance. Its long-lasting popularity is demonstrated by the fact that the work was translated into English by King Alfred the Great (in the ninth century), Geoffrey Chaucer (fourteenth century), and Queen Elizabeth I (sixteenth century). The *Consolation* is a long dialogue between the author and Lady Philosophy, in which they discuss, among many other issues, the illusory nature of wealth and fame:

9 This twelfth-century manuscript illumination shows Boethius discussing the meaning and practice of music with the Greek philosopher Plato and the theorists Pythagoras and Nichomachus. Boethius's treatise *De institutione musica* (*The Fundamentals of Music*) was a basic "textbook" for the study of music during the Middle Ages.

Though fame may be wide scattered and find its way through distant lands, and set the tongues there talking; though a splendid house may draw brilliance from famous names and tales; yet death regards not any glory, howsoever great. Alike he overwhelms the lowly and the lofty head, and levels high with low.

The Consolation of Philosophy has been called a "prison work," exploring the thoughts and emotions of a human being in an extreme circumstance. Another of Theodoric's officials, who also provided a legacy that influenced the educational tradition of the Middle Ages, managed to escape the malicious plots of court life. This was Cassiodorus.

Cassiodorus

Theodoric's program of *civilitas*, or civil governance, is clearly set out in the edicts and letters written to various individuals and groups, such as the Roman Senate. Since the king was illiterate, the letters were composed on his behalf by his chief minister, Cassiodorus (*c.* 485–*c.* 580). They provide a major source of information about the period. The lasting influence of Cassiodorus himself, however, extended beyond the purely practical realm.

Before entering political life, Cassiodorus had dreamed of founding a school that would provide a Christian education as competently as the old pagan academies had taught Classical literature and philosophy. However, after Theodoric's death, with Italy once again subjected to war and turmoil, the realization of this project was impossible. Thus, in about 537, Cassiodorus retired from public life and returned to his family estates in southern Italy, where he established the famous monastery of Vivarium and collected the finest library of his time. He envisioned monastic life as providing the atmosphere most conducive to Christian education and learning; he was thus the first to appreciate the potential of the "vast leisure of the convent for the preservation of divine and human learning and for its transmission to posterity."

Cassiodorus defined his purpose in a handbook for monastic scholars, which he called *An Introduction to Divine and Human Readings*:

> . . . [since] my ardent desire could in no way have been fulfilled because of the struggles that seethed and raged excessively in the Italian realm, inasmuch as a peaceful affair has no place in anxious times, I was driven by divine charity to this device, namely, in the place of a teacher to prepare for you under the Lord's guidance these introductory books; through which, in my opinion, the unbroken line of the Divine Scriptures and the compendious knowledge of secular letters might with the Lord's beneficence be related—books not at all fluent, perhaps, since in them is found, not studied eloquence, but indispensable narration; to be sure, they are extremely useful, since through them one learns the indicated origin of both the salvation of the soul and secular knowledge. In them I commit to you, not my own learning, but the words of men of former times, which it is right to praise and glorious to proclaim for future generations.

Cassiodorus urged a synthesis of secular knowledge and Holy Scripture, and this, together with the works of Boethius, provided a framework for scholarly education in the medieval period. By the middle of the eighth century, his program of preserving and transmitting the texts of the ancient world within the educational curriculum of the monastic school had been widely adopted, initially in England and Ireland, and then in the kingdom of the Franks.

Intellectual life in the Germanic kingdoms of the west was carried forward by the efforts of a very few privileged men. In the eastern empire, however, extensive patronage from the emperor continued to foster artistic and intellectual culture on a broad scale.

Justinian and the Survival of the Empire in the East

After Romulus Augustus, the last Roman emperor in the west, had been deposed in 476, the empire in the east continued to exist as a rich and vibrant society; indeed, it was a powerful state for much of the Middle Ages, and was not conquered until 1453, when the Turkish armies sacked Constantinople. Thus, the eastern, or Byzantine, empire lasted almost a millennium after the "fall" of the west. This was due partially to geographical location, since the eastern provinces were not directly subject to the Germanic migrations of the fifth century (see Map 1). The empire was characterized, for the most part, by a common religion, deeply rooted and shared by almost all classes of society. At its heart, the capital city of Constantinople provided a psychological symbol of this unity and a practical center for commerce. As such, it was a testament to the ambitions of the emperor, Constantine, who in the fourth century had intended to replace the corrupt and jaded Rome with a pure and vibrant Christian city.

Constantinople functioned as the center of a sophisticated government with an extensive bureaucracy supported by a well-trained and thoroughly equipped army. Unlike the empire in the west, the rulers of the east who followed Constantine had solved the problem of taxation; they taxed the everyday necessities of life, placed a government monopoly on high-priced commodities, and controlled the modes of transportation. These revenues allowed the emperor to establish a complex and efficient administration and to undertake bold new projects.

The wealth of the empire was generated, in part, by thriving agricultural production; equally important, however, were numerous cities that were centers of industry and commerce. The industries were carried on by guilds or corporations strictly controlled by the state. The most important items of manufacture were luxury goods such as silk, high-quality wool, and jewelry. Agricultural and industrial products were exchanged in a flourishing network of commerce, of which Constantinople was the center; in the early Middle Ages it was the greatest market in the world.

At the apex of this rich society stood the emperor, viewed by his subjects as a sacred person appointed by God to rule over them. His was an absolute monarchy; he controlled all aspects of life, and his authority was supreme.

As Justinian remarked in a letter sent to Demosthenes, his prefect: "The Emperor shall justly be regarded as the sole maker and interpreter of the laws . . ." Imperial authority extended to questions of religion as well, since it was the emperor who appointed the patriarch of Constantinople: the leader of the ecclesiastical organization. This pattern had been established in the Roman world during the reign of Augustus (r. 27BC–AD 14), who was *pontifex maximus*, or high priest, as well as emperor, but Augustus had not been a Christian. Now, however, in the Byzantine Empire, Christian doctrine and liturgy were assimilated in the old pattern. The emperor was anointed with holy oils, and his position was sanctified by doctrine. He was solicitous of the priesthood, but held the power to discipline clergy who did not conform to his wishes.

> For all things terminate happily where the beginning is proper and agreeable to God. We think that this will take place if the sacred rules of the Church which the just, praiseworthy, and adorable Apostles, the inspectors and ministers of the Work of God, and the Holy Fathers have explained and preserved for Us, are obeyed . . .
> We grant permission to everyone, no matter what may be his office or to what order he may belong, when he becomes aware of any of these breaches of discipline, to notify Us, or the government; so that We, who have established the said rules, in accordance with the sacred apostolic canons of the Church, may inflict the proper penalty upon those who are guilty.

These words were written by the most important emperor of the early medieval period, Justinian (r. 527–565). At the beginning of his reign, Justinian had the largest treasury since Alexander the Great, its wealth based on government intervention in the economy. At the time of his death, however, the state coffers were empty as a result of vast expenditures for Justinian's grandiose plans to reunite the western and eastern empires.

Justinian believed that it was his mission to re-establish the Roman Empire as it had been during the time of Augustus. In 527 his armies attacked the Ostrogoths in Italy, with limited success. The initial invasion began a struggle that lasted some twenty-five years, during which time the Byzantines established a fragile hegemony. Following Justinian's death, however, the Italian peninsula was overrun by the Lombards, who defeated the resident forces; the emperor's grand dream thus remained forever unfulfilled.

Nevertheless, the extravagant Justinian did make several lasting contributions to the history of western civilization. One of these came in the form of his legal system, the *Corpus juris civilis*.

The *Corpus juris civilis*
The legal system of the Romans had evolved slowly throughout their long history, beginning with the *Laws of the Twelve Tables* in 450 BC. As a result, the legacy of Roman law was hopelessly confused, rather than being systematic and well ordered. For one who believed, as Justinian did, that "there is nothing to be found in all things so worthy of attention as the authority of the law, which properly regulates all affairs both divine and human, and expels all injustice," this was a disastrous state of affairs. Hence, in a letter to his *quaestor*, an official in charge of his treasury, he decreed that:

> We have found the entire arrangement of the law which has come down to Us from the foundation of the City of Rome and the times of Romulus, to be so confused that it is extended to an infinite length and is not within the grasp of human capacity; and hence We were first induced to begin by examining what had been enacted by former most venerated princes, to correct their constitutions, and make them more easily understood; to the end that, being included in a single Code, and

having had removed all that is superfluous in resemblance and all iniquitous discord, they may afford to all men the ready assistance of their true meaning.

Justinian found many problems in the empire's legal inheritance. First, the body of law had been interpreted and reinterpreted in different ways throughout the years of Roman dominance, resulting in a mass of sometimes differing opinions. Further, many enactments had been duplicated, some of which contradicted one another, and some of which contained anachronisms. Also, new laws had been passed that needed to be collected. Justinian's solution was to sponsor legal scholars to produce the *Corpus juris civilis*, a summary of the empire's laws, ultimately consisting of four parts. The first was the *Codex Justinianus*, or "Justinian's Code," which was a codification of statute law. The second was the *Digesta* ("Digest," also known as the *Pandects*), which consisted of a summary of the legal opinions of Roman jurists concerning civil and criminal cases. The third was the *Institutiones* ("Institutes"), which functioned as a textbook for the study of law. And finally, the *Novellae leges* ("New Laws"), which provided a collection of laws enacted during the previous 150 years.

The *Corpus juris civilis* was perhaps the greatest work of legal scholarship in western civilization. It was not widely known in western Europe during the early part of the Middle Ages, although it continued to provide the foundation for law in the Byzantine Empire. By the end of the eleventh century, it was being intensively studied in the west; by the fourteenth century it had become the basis of legal doctrine throughout the European world.

Another lasting, and more visible, monument was built during Justinian's reign. This was the great cathedral in Constantinople, Hagia Sophia, now converted into a mosque.

Hagia Sophia

The magnificent building known as Hagia Sophia expressed through its scale and complexity all the power and majesty of empire and Church. Just one of the many structures in Justinian's extensive construction program in Constantinople, it rises on the highest ground of the peninsula separating the Bosporus from the Sea of Marmara, on the site of a previous basilica constructed during the reign of the emperor Theodosius. It was begun in 532 and dedicated on Christmas Day, 537.

The building's ground plan combines the longitudinal three-aisled form of the basilica (see p. 20) with a domed centralized core. It thus amalgamates the longitudinal axis of the Latin-cross plan with the square axis of the Greek-cross plan. (See the ground plan in **fig. 10** and the interior view in **fig. 11**). The walls, arcades, and dome contain numerous windows that provide a luminous effect. More than forty windows at the base of the dome cause the massive structure to project a floating, almost miraculous appearance. According to Justinian's historian, Procopius:

[It] seems somehow to float in the air on no firm basis, but to be poised aloft to the peril of those inside it . . . Yet [the dome] seems not to rest upon solid masonry, but to cover the space with its golden dome suspended from Heaven . . . And whenever anyone enters this church to pray, he understands at once that it is not by any human power or skill, but by the influence of God that this work has been so finely

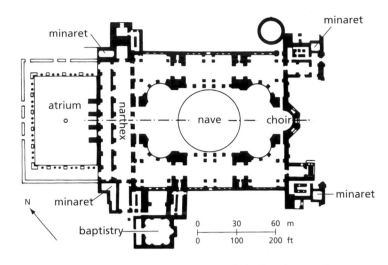

10 and 11 The ground plan *(right)* of Hagia Sophia (constructed 532–537) combines the longitudinal three-aisled form of the basilica with the Greek cross plan, thereby addressing the liturgical and symbolic requirements of the Byzantine liturgy. The structure is crowned with a centralized dome, symbolizing the canopy of heaven. The numerous windows *(below)* contained in the walls, arcades, and dome allow the dramatic passage of light, creating a miraculous, floating effect, and lifting the mind towards God.

turned. And so his mind is lifted up toward God and exalted, feeling that He cannot be far away, but must especially love to dwell in this place which He had chosen.

The magical effect was heightened by the mosaics and colored marble surfaces that once adorned the inside of the building. After the Turkish invasion of 1453, however, when the church became a mosque, the mosaics were whitewashed to conform to the Islamic prohibition against images. It is nevertheless still possible to form some idea of the brilliance of the original artwork by observing the mosaic surfaces in another building dating from the era of Justinian, the church of San Vitale at the emperor's provincial capital of Ravenna, in northeastern Italy.

The interior of San Vitale is sheathed in marble and decorated with mosaic. On one side of the altar is a depiction of Justinian and his courtiers (**fig. 12**); on the other is his queen, Theodora, with her retinue.

12 A mosaic (c. 547) from the church of San Vitale at Ravenna depicts the emperor Justinian with his courtiers and ecclesiastical councillors, symbolizing the emperor's vision of the unity of spiritual and worldly power. His halo emphasizes his nearly divine status, and indicates that he is Christ's representative on earth. Justinian holds a bowl to be dedicated as a donation to God, emulating royal offerings to the gods from ancient monarchs as diverse as Roman rulers and Egyptian pharaohs.

The iconography symbolizes the Byzantine concept of sacred kingship. By offering a bowl and chalice to the apse and altar, the monarchs reenact the ancient role of royal patronage, as practiced much earlier by Egyptian pharaohs and near-eastern rulers. The presentation of gifts by the emperor and empress signified the eternal participation of the imperial presence in the liturgy of the Church. Justinian is accompanied on his right by soldiers, who bear shields adorned with the Chi-Rho, thereby asserting that they are defenders of Christ. To his left is a group of priests celebrating the Mass, carrying liturgical objects: the crucifix, the scripture, and the incense vessel. The mosaic thus presents in iconographic form Justinian's belief in the unity of temporal and spiritual power, embodied in the person of the emperor, whose semi-divine status is underscored by the halo surrounding the imperial head.

The other mosaic depicts Justinian's powerful queen, Theodora, who is accompanied by her courtiers and handmaidens. The concept of royal patronage is emphasized by the image of the Three Magi that appears on the border of her cloak. She, too, is portrayed with a halo, and this powerful image of her role as queen makes a provocative statement about female power within the Byzantine world.

Although Theodora was by no means typical, her life and career are strikingly indicative of the ability of women in the Byzantine world to advance their positions in society. Theodora was not an aristocrat; she was born into a family of circus performers, and spent her childhood as a circus entertainer. (It is important to realize that the circus in sixth-century Byzantium was not simply a display of animals and pyrotechnical acrobatics; it was, rather, an erotic combination of gymnastic entertainment and pornography.) Our best source for information about Theodora is the *Secret Histories* of Procopius, and it is certainly less than flattering to the empress. One recent historian has even described it as a "vicious attack on the imperial couple." Procopius no doubt exaggerated Theodora's depravity, but there is general agreement among historians that she was, indeed, a prostitute before her marriage to Justinian. As empress, however, she proved herself to be a woman of intelligence, practicality, and strong will.

Her courage was demonstrated early in Justinian's reign, when the royal couple was confronted by rioting citizens. The emperor was inclined to abdicate, but Theodora rallied him by saying, "For one who has been an emperor it is unendurable to be a fugitive . . . may I not live that day on which those who meet me shall not address me as mistress." Justinian responded by ordering his troops to attack the rebels, and his throne was preserved.

Procopius also makes clear in his writings that imperial policy was determined jointly by the emperor and empress—"neither did anything without the consent of the other." And Theodora's influence was eagerly sought by powerful people:

> To the Queen's presence even the highest officials could not enter without great delay and trouble; like slaves they had to wait all day in a small and stuffy antechamber, for to absent himself was a risk no official dared to take. So they stood there on their tiptoes, each straining to keep his face above his neighbor's, so that eunuchs, as they came out from the audience room, would see them. Some would be called, perhaps, after several days; and when they did enter to her presence in great fear, they were quickly dismissed as soon as they had made obeisance and kissed her feet. For to speak or make any request, unless she commanded, was not permitted.

No one dared to cross the empress, for "neither length of time, fullness of punishment, artifice of prayer, nor threat of death, whose vengeance sent by heaven is feared by all mankind, could persuade her to abate her wrath." Theodora had thoroughly absorbed the qualities and prerogatives of imperial power. The *Secret Histories* also contains much information about women in Theodora's entourage, indicating that, although the authority of the empress was paramount, the influence of other females was not insignificant. Furthermore, power and control such as those wielded by Theodora were not uncommon among her successors.

When Theodora died in 548, Justinian was left disconsolate and demoralized. In addition, he was burdened by his inability to deal with the problems caused by a devastating plague that had raged through Byzantium and western Europe in 541–543. The effects of the pestilence were profound, causing a lack of manpower for the armies as well as a crippled economy. Byzantium was not able to hold the territories it had conquered in the west, and in 561 the eastern empire found itself threatened by a nomadic tribe from the north, the Avars, who had subjugated the Slavs and Bulgars. In addition, it was now endangered by the Persian Empire to the east.

The eastern empire after Justinian

Justinian's successors were forced to turn their attention away from grandiose dreams of world empire to deal with more immediate problems. The greatest crisis occurred during the reign of the emperor Heraclius (r. 610–641), when Persian armies conquered Byzantine territories in Syria, Palestine, and Egypt in their quest for imperial expansion;

a further threat came in 626, when Constantinople was besieged by the combined forces of the Persians and Avars. The Byzantine forces were able to withstand the onslaught, however, and under the leadership of Heraclius, an able soldier, they drove the Persians from the empire and recovered the lands they had lost. In 627, the Byzantine armies entered Persian territory and crushed the Persian forces in a great battle near the site of ancient Nineveh, thus ending forever the threat of Persian domination.

A new crisis soon occurred when, as part of the rapid expansion of Islam in the seventh century (see Chapter 3), the Muslims conquered Syria, Palestine, and Egypt (633–644), and advanced to conquer Constantinople. The city was threatened several times during the last part of the seventh century, and faced imminent destruction in 717–718. However, Emperor Leo III was able to turn back the forces of Islam. This action, along with the Battle of Tours/Poitiers (732/33), when the forces of Charles Martel defeated the Muslims (see p. 103), has long been regarded as one of the decisive battles of history, although some modern scholars have questioned its importance. Nonetheless, these conflicts firmly established the division of medieval Europe into the three great societies of Byzantium, western Christendom, and the emerging Islam.

The Iconoclastic Controversy

The Byzantine rulers, as we have seen, viewed themselves as divinely appointed by God to govern the Christian world, while the popes in Rome also claimed, by virtue of the Petrine theory (see p. 30), that they had been given the right to rule the Church by Christ himself. This rivalry between the two powers inevitably led to friction between them, which was aggravated by various theological disputes that emerged in the fifth and sixth centuries. The Council of Nicea, in the fourth century, had issued a statement concerning the nature of the Godhead (see p. 25), but this had not succeeded in quelling all the arguments, especially among Byzantine prelates and theologians, who attached great importance to such discussion. The churchmen of the west, by contrast, seem to have been much less eager to devote time and energy to questions that they saw as unimportant, preferring to solve more practical issues of organization and governance.

The most important of these theological arguments arose during the reign of the Byzantine Emperor Leo III (r. 717–741), and is known as the Iconoclastic Controversy. Although the dispute had social and political dimensions, it essentially grew out of an intense preoccupation with questions of theological doctrine, in which people on all levels of society were caught up. According to one early Byzantine writer, this obsession with theology was so pronounced that it actually interfered with the activities of daily life. For example, when he asked a baker for a piece of bread, the man responded, "The Father is greater than the Son," and when he asked his servant if his bath was ready, he was told that "The Son proceeds from nothing." Such obsessive zeal was a potent factor in the conduct of a government intimately connected to religious issues. During an era of religious concord it could provide a powerful sense of confidence and mission, but in times of religious dissension it caused difficulty. The emperors themselves naturally took an active role in any theological controversies, and had great influence because of the Byzantine concept of divine rulership.

The most significant controversy of the early medieval period concerned questions of **icon** worship. The quarrel arose between two groups: the "iconoclasts," who wished to prohibit the worship of icons (images of Christ, the Virgin Mary, and the Saints), and the "iconophiles," who saw such veneration as an enhancement to devotion. The discussion was begun in the eighth century by the Emperor Leo III.

The iconoclasts advanced a series of theological views to support their position. First, they believed that the worship of images was pagan, rather than Christian. In addition, they thought that nothing made by human beings should be worshiped by them. Further, Christ was so divine that he could not be conceived of in terms of human art, and scripture had presented a prohibition against the worshiping of "graven images" in the Old Testament (Exodus 20:4). This seemed to place the matter beyond dispute.

There were other reasons as well to support the iconoclasts' arguments. Leo III had led the forces that saved Constantinople from the onslaught of Islam, whose adherents zealously shunned religious images on the grounds that they were "the work of Satan" (see Chapter 3). Adopting the iconoclastic policy might undermine one of the main Islamic criticisms of Christianity and thus deprive Islam itself of some of its appeal.

Political and financial motives may have provided another impetus to support the iconoclasts. By proclaiming a new religious movement, the emperors may have wished to reassert their control over the Church, and especially to combat the growing influence of the monasteries, which promoted the cause of the iconophiles. Constantine V (the son of Leo III), for example, bitterly persecuted the monasteries as a result, but also took the opportunity to appropriate much monastic wealth.

In 843, the question was finally resolved by an imperial decree from Empress Theodora II (r. 836–856), who advocated a return to the use of images in worship. This was a typical example of how a religious question was decided in the Byzantine world by the word of the ruler, rather than the patriarch of the church. The results of the controversy were less than positive, however; in the process, much splendid religious art had been destroyed, and a serious breach between the eastern and western churches had been opened, since the pope had supported the iconophiles.

Before the emergence of the Iconoclastic Controversy, the pope had given respect and honor to the Byzantine ruler; however, the threat to abolish images met with severe denunciation by the head of the western church. In 727, Pope Gregory II had written to Leo III warning him that he should not "meddle in ecclesiastical affairs." If the emperor threatened to "destroy the statue of St. Peter [at Rome] . . . the people of the west are ready and they will avenge the injuries you have inflicted on the people of the east . . . we protest to you that we shall be innocent of the blood that will be shed. The responsibility will fall on your head." The "injuries inflicted on the people of the east" probably refers to the brutally suppressed revolts in Greece that followed the issuing of the first iconoclastic decree in 726, or to the spiritual damage inflicted by the decree.

The pope's implicit threat to turn to the barbarian kings for support would soon become a reality, for the Frankish kings had already formed an alliance with the papacy, and this was strengthened in the ninth century by their successors, the Carolingian monarchs.

Clovis and the Merovingian Dynasty

The Franks were a large group of Germanic tribes who had extended their territory from the area of the Rhine into Gaul during the fifth century. They subsequently established a kingdom that was more powerful and endured for longer than those of the Ostrogoths, Visigoths, and Vandals. There were many reasons for their success, even though the practice of dividing the realm among the king's sons at his death caused problems of disunity. Yet there was one other important factor in the success of the Franks: the fact that they were led by ambitious and powerful chieftains.

The first significant king of the Franks was Clovis (r. 485–411), the leader of the Salian Franks, a tribe from near the North Sea. His initial task was to gain the loyalty of the fierce Frankish war chieftains. In 486, he occupied the kingdom of Syagrius, in northern France, which was the one remaining Roman stronghold. This triumph increased his prestige among his fellow warriors and spurred him on to other campaigns; in 496, 501, and 507 he waged war against other tribes, which led to the unification of the kingdom of the Franks (**Map 3**).

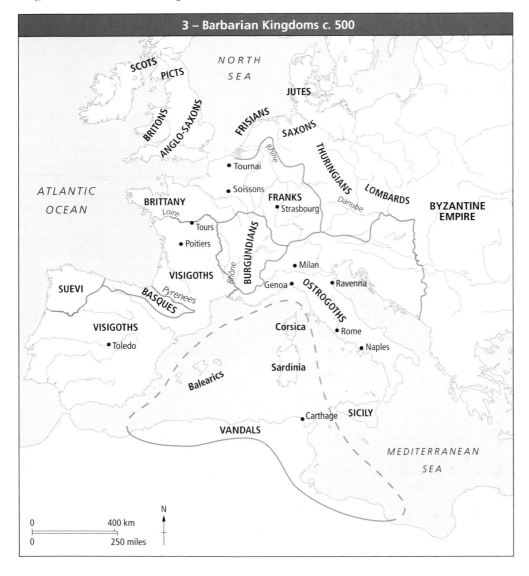

3 – Barbarian Kingdoms c. 500

In 496, during the campaign against another tribe, the Alemanni, Clovis was converted to the Athanasian form of Christianity. This was a significant event for the future of both the Frankish kingdom and the Roman Catholic Church. At this time, none of the major rulers in the Christian world was associated with the pope; the east German kings were Arians, and the Byzantine emperor was quarreling with the pontiff. Thus, the conversion and subsequent close connection between the papacy and Clovis proved of great advantage to both.

Evidence concerning the subsequent behavior of Clovis indicates that his acceptance of Christianity was only nominal. Indeed, judging by ensuing events, it seems that it may have been a move of purely political expediency. The actual conversion experience was described by the historian Gregory of Tours, who, it is important to note, was determined to establish the Franks as the saviors of Athanasian Christianity. His account suggests that the king's conversion was genuine:

> Now the queen without ceasing urged the king to confess the true God, and forsake his idols; but in no way could she move him to this belief, until at length he made war against the Alemanni, when he was driven of necessity to confess what of his free will he had denied. It happened that when the two armies joined battle there was grievous slaughter, and the army of Clovis was being swept to utter ruin. When the king saw this he lifted up his eyes to heaven, and knew compunction in his heart, and, moved to tears, cried aloud: "Jesus Christ, Thou that art proclaimed by Clotilde [Clovis's wife] Son of the living God, Thou that art said to give aid to those in stress, and to grant victory to those that hope in Thee, I entreat from a devout heart the glory of Thy aid. If Thou grant me victory over these enemies, and experience confirm that power which the people dedicated to Thy name claim to have proved, then will I also believe in Thee and be baptized in Thy name. I have called upon my own gods, but here is proof that they have withdrawn themselves from helping me; wherefore I believe that they have no power, since they come not to the aid of their servants. Thee do I now invoke, on Thee am I inclined to believe, if I may be plucked out of the hands of my adversaries." And as he said this, lo, the Alemanni turned their backs, and began to flee. And when they saw that their king was slain, they yielded themselves to Clovis, saying: "No longer, we entreat you, let the people perish; we are now your men." Then the king put an end to the war, and having admonished the people, returned in peace, relating to the queen how he had called upon the name of Christ and had been found worthy to obtain the victory. This happened in the fifteenth year of his reign.

From this time, Clovis developed a close relationship with the Church. He received high praise for his Christian leadership in a letter written to him by Bishop Avitus:

> The ray of truth has shone forth even among present shadows. Divine Providence has found the arbiter of our age . . . Your Faith is our victory . . . Your ancestors have prepared a great destiny for you; you willed to prepare better things [for those who will follow you]. You follow your ancestors in reigning in this world; you have opened the way to your descendants to a heavenly reign. Let Greece indeed rejoice it has

elected an emperor who shares our Faith; it is no longer alone in deserving such a favor. Your sphere also burns with its own brilliance, and, in the person of a king, the light of a rising sun shines over the western lands.

The conversion of Clovis to Athanasian Christianity allowed him to gain the support of the native Gallo-Roman population, since he now shared their religion. He could present himself as the savior of the people, who were no longer threatened with forced conversion by Arian tribal leaders.

In the process of establishing his rule, Clovis sought to integrate Church and state. The old Roman *civitates*, which coincided geographically with the ecclesiastical bishoprics, survived, and the king made convenient use of the preexisting structure. Clovis appointed a **comes** (or count) to govern these units, and these secular officials often shared their power with the bishops. The new kingdom was, in essence, a primitive Germanic monarchy, and the Roman political order gradually disappeared; at the same time, however, the Franks were slowly being assimilated into the Church of the late Roman Empire.

Much of the land that formed the kingdom of the Franks was gained through war; for example, early in the sixth century, Clovis drove the Visigoths out of southern Gaul, thereby extending his hegemony to the Pyrenees. But Clovis also used crafty and cunning diplomacy to establish his control. In the following passage from *The History of the Franks*, by Gregory of Tours, we learn how he persuaded the son of a rival king to kill his own father:

While Clovis was sojourning at Paris, he sent secretly to the son of Sigibert, saying: "Your father has grown old, and is lame in one foot. If he were to die, his kingdom would be yours by right, together with our friendship." The prince, seduced by his ambition, plotted his father's death. One day Sigibert left Cologne and crossed the Rhine, to walk in the forest of Buchau. He was enjoying a midday repose in his tent when his son caused his death by sending assassins against him, intending to get possession of the kingdom. But by the judgment of God he himself fell into the pit which he had treacherously dug for his father. He sent messengers to King Clovis announcing his father's death in these terms: "My father has perished, and his kingdom and treasure are in my power. Come to me, and gladly will I hand over to you whatever things may please you from his treasure." Clovis answered: "I thank you for your good will, and request of you that you show all to my envoys; but you shall keep the whole." On the arrival of the envoys, the prince displayed his father's treasure, and while they were inspecting its various contents, said to them: "In this coffer my father used to amass pieces of gold." They answered: "Plunge in your hand to the bottom, to make sure of all." He did so; but as he was stooping, one of them raised his two-edged axe and buried it in his brain; so was his guilt towards his father requited on himself. When Clovis heard that Sigibert was slain, and his son also, he came to Cologne and called all the people together, addressing them in these words: "Hear what has happened. While I was sailing the Scheldt [River], Chloderic, son of my cousin, was harassing his father, and telling him that I desired his death. When his father fled through the forest of Buchau, he set bandits upon him, delivering him over to death. But he in his turn has perished, struck I know not

by whom, while he was showing his father's treasure. To all these deeds I was i
n no wise privy; for I could not bear to shed the blood of my kindred, holding it
an impious deed. But since things have so fallen out, I offer you this counsel, which
you should take, if it seems good to you: turn to me, and live under my protection."
At these words the clash of shields vied with their applause; they raised Clovis upon
a shield, and recognized him as their king. Thus he became possessed of the
kingdom of Sigibert and of his treasures, and submitted the people also to his
dominion. For daily the Lord laid his enemies low under his hand, and increased his
kingdom, because he walked before Him with an upright heart, and did that which
was pleasing in His sight.

Gregory's *History* implies that the author was willing to accept these vicious acts
as acceptable in a leader whom he saw as determined to further Athanasian Christianity. From a more objective point of view, it is obvious that Clovis was not an exemplary
Christian in his dealings with his fellow tribal leaders. Nonetheless, through a combination of force and "diplomacy" he was able to extend his power, and eventually ruled
an area that extended from the Rhine to the Pyrenees. In the process he laid the foundations of the Merovingian dynasty, named for a legendary ancestor known as Merovech
(sometimes Latinized to Meroveus).

As part of his program of state-building, Clovis recognized the need for written laws.
Until now, the Germanic tribes had lived according to customary law, passed from generation to generation through memory. Perhaps as a result of encountering Roman
institutions, a code of written legal measures, known collectively as the **Salic Law**,
was established during the reign of Clovis, probably about the year 500. It was presumably codified and written down by Gallo-Romans who had been trained in the Roman
legal tradition, but it reflects Germanic customary law dating from as early as the
fourth century.

The code consists of sixty-five "titles" or chapters, most of which contain subsections.
For the most part, these deal with private law, rather than public or administrative law.
Contained in the code are provisions for the penalties for injury, damage, and theft. As
may be seen in the following selections from the code, specific fines are given for each
infraction, so as to settle disputes between individuals and prevent personal reprisals. The
code contained many provisions regarding wounds, insults, false accusations, assault and
robbery, thefts of animal stock, housebreaking, and summonses to court, an institution
known as the *Thing*. A man summoned to court who did not appear, for example, was
assessed a fine of 15 *solidi*.

The Salic Law, like other Germanic law codes, provide for the payment of the wergeld
(literally, "man-money"), an amount to be paid to the kinsmen of a slain man or woman;
the acceptance of this payment signified that a blood feud would not be pursued. According to the code, the sons of the murdered man would receive half of the money, and
the other half would be divided among the nearest relatives, on the mother's side of
the family as well as the father's. If there were no relatives, the *wergeld* would be paid into
the public treasury (the *fisc*).

Title XLI contains provisions concerning the murder of free men:

1. If anyone is convicted of killing a free Frank or a barbarian living by the Salic Law, he shall pay 8,000 **denarii**, which make 200 *solidi*.
2. If he has put the body in a well, or under water, or has covered it with branches or other things for the purpose of hiding it, he shall pay 24,000 *denarii*, which make 600 *solidi*.
3. If anyone kills a man in the king's trust [service], or a free woman, he shall pay 24,000 *denarii*, which make 600 *solidi*.
4. If he kills a Roman who was a table-companion of the king, he shall pay 12,000 *denarii*, which make 300 *solidi*.
5. If the slain man was a Roman landowner, and not a table-companion of the king, he who slew him shall pay 4,000 *denarii*, which make 100 *solidi*.
6. If anyone kills a Roman **tributarius**, he shall pay 63 *solidi*.

It is evident that status and position in royal service brought increased value, and age and gender were also factors. A free woman, because of her potential for bearing children, was as valuable as a man "in the king's trust," that is, in the service of the king and probably bound to him by an oath. The killing of a woman past child-bearing age carried a penalty of only 200 *solidi*, whereas the fine for slaying a boy younger than ten years was 600 *solidi*.

Title XIII, which contains provisions concerning rape "committed by free men," clearly shows the lack of equality in the treatment of persons of differing status.

1. If three men carry off a free-born girl, they shall be compelled to pay 30 *solidi*.
2. If there are more than three, each one shall pay 8 *solidi*.
3. But those who commit rape shall be compelled to pay 2,500 *denarii*, which makes 63 *solidi*.
4. But if they have carried off that girl from behind lock and key, or from the spinning room, they shall be sentenced to the above price and penalty.
5. But if the girl who is carried off be under the king's protection, then the **frith** [peace-money] shall be 2,500 *denarii*, which make 63 *solidi*.
6. But if a bondsman of the king, or a **lete**, should carry off a free woman, he shall be sentenced to death.
7. But if a free woman has followed a slave of her own will, she shall lose her freedom.

These laws indicate much about the position of women in Merovingian society. Women were highly valued for their childbearing potential—as shown by the fact that the *wergeld* of a woman of childbearing age was three times that of a man of the same rank—and this has been interpreted as evidence of significant appreciation of women generally. However, a closer analysis indicates that this emphasis on reproductive function probably fostered feminine attitudes of passivity and dependence. Although their Germanic ancestors had actually carried arms into battle, defending themselves and their tribes, women in Merovingian society, especially aristocratic women, were confined to what we would regard as more traditional gender roles. The stereotypical view of women as helpless creatures provided justification for subjection to male authority and the prevailing sexual double standards.

Merovingian women were among the first Germanic people to adopt Christianity, and there are many accounts of women being instrumental in the conversion of their husbands and children. Examples include references to Clotilde, the wife of Clovis. Women were also noted for founding monasteries, endowing churches, and dispensing alms. Little evidence exists, however, to indicate that women were accorded recognition as assertive individuals who could participate in political and economic activity alongside their male relatives. Instead, the chroniclers encouraged behavior patterns in which women were nurturing and obedient. The biographer of St. Balthild, the wife of Clovis II (r. 639–657), praised her in these terms:

> She obeyed her husband as her ruler, was like a mother towards her stepchildren, a daughter toward priests, and a pious nurse towards infants and adolescents. Being amicable with all, she loved priests as fathers, monks as brothers, the poor as members of her household, and the pilgrims as her sons.

Although the ideal Merovingian woman seems to have been completely subjected to the will of her husband, she was not without some legal rights, especially when compared with the rights of Roman women. Indeed, it was in the area of marital law that the fusion of Germanic and Roman law occurred most rapidly. Under Merovingian rule, for example, a widow assumed full responsibility for her household. When her husband died, she assumed all of his rights, and gained control of his property and his rights of guardianship over minor daughters and sons. She retained these rights unless she remarried.

The rights of an unmarried woman, however, remained with her father, who could decide the matrimonial arrangements for both his sons and daughters. When a young woman married, her father gave his right of protection (*mundium*) to her husband. In return for this right, the groom provided his bride with a bride-gift (*dos*), which would provide sustenance for her in the event she was rejected.

Marriage did provide the opportunity for women to free themselves from parental control, and to improve their social standing. Under the Merovingians, laws were enacted that permitted women of the lower classes, even former slaves and concubines, to marry men of the ruling elite, and aristocratic women could enjoy the power that resulted from marital alliances with other families of wealth and influence.

The rapid fusion of Roman and Frankish legal measures was undoubtedly one reason for the stability of the Frankish kingdom, which, in contrast to the Ostrogoths, the Vandals, and the Visigoths, survived for centuries. Although the Merovingian practice of dividing the realm among the king's sons at his death resulted in serious problems of disunity, there were other factors that contributed to the longevity of the kingdom. First, in contrast to the Germanic tribes in the east, the Franks could draw on a vast number of men in their lands west of the Rhine to provide military strength. Second, their center of power was far north of the Mediterranean, and was thus protected from the Muslim invasions (see Chapter 3). Furthermore, there was no religious division between the Franks and the native Gallo-Roman population. As a result, during the sixth century the society of the Franks and the Gallo-Romans became a fusion of traditions from both; the Roman heritage dominated in religion, language, and aspects of economic organization, while the laws of the Franks replaced those of the Romans. Eventually this rich mixture produced a new nation and a new culture.

Merovingian culture

By the seventh century, Merovingian society was an amalgam of Germanic and Gallo-Roman traditions. This fusion was evident in the social, economic, and religious dimensions of life, and in the artistic products of the Merovingian world. For example, when the Merovingians built churches, they borrowed architectural techniques and structural forms from the Romans. The church of St. Martin at Tours, built between 466 and 470, resembled an early Christian basilica. The Merovingian architects, however, no doubt bowing to the necessity of the times, placed a defense tower over the western entrance, and a bell tower over the crossing of the transept and nave. The addition of the towers gave a new vertical accent to the horizontal form of the building, and this feature was to have a significant influence in the later development of Romanesque and Gothic architecture.

The Merovingians also borrowed structural features such as the use of columns with capitals reminiscent of Roman style. One example may be seen in the Crypt of St. Paul at the abbey of Notre Dame, Jouarre, France, which dates to the seventh century. Some of the columns may have been taken from local Gallo-Roman buildings, to which the builders added capitals made in workshops in southern France. As may be seen in **fig. 13**, the stonecarvers in this area had never stopped using Classical forms and techniques of carving.

The use of Classical traditions is even more evident in the Sarcophagus of Theodochilde, located in the crypt on the right of this photograph. The sides are decorated with rows of scallop shells, and the top with vine scrolls and leaves and grapes, suggesting contact with Byzantine artisans. This assumption is reinforced by another sarcophagus in the same crypt, thought to be that of Bishop Agilbert. On the end panel there is a carving of Christ in majesty, surrounded by the symbols of the Four Evangelists. The youthful, beardless Christ faces the viewer, while the Evangelists look away from the Lord. This positioning, together with the fantastic floral decoration, is characteristic of Byzantine art, indicating that the carver of the sarcophagus had seen eastern models. It seems that Classical tradition may have traveled to the Merovingians through the intermediary of Byzantine art.

13 The seventh-century Merovingian Crypt of St. Paul, at the Abbey of Notre Dame, Jouarre, France, reflects the common use of columns and capitals based on Roman models. Located in the crypt is the Sarcophagus of Theodochilde, which is carved with scallop shells and vine scrolls reflective of Byzantine style. The combination of eastern and western motifs demonstrates that artists from western Europe probably had contact with Byzantine craftsmen.

Germanic style is clearly evident in the work of Merovingian goldsmiths, whose jewelry and weapons reflect the use of polychrome and animal forms characteristic of tribal traditions. The craftsmen had ample opportunity to see the metalwork of other tribal peoples, since weaponry and jewelry, as favorite forms of booty, were constantly being passed back and forth between warring tribesmen.

The zoomorphic (animal) forms were probably derived from the small figures of quadrupeds or bird heads that decorated the bronze pins and brooches worn on some late Roman and Gothic clothing. As the forms evolved in the Germanic tradition, their naturalistic character was lost, and the realistic images were deformed to emphasize the strongest features, such as beaked heads, sinews, or talons.

Another characteristic of Germanic style was derived from Classical decorative tradition known as interlace (often referred to as "Celtic interlace" or "knotwork"). In the Roman period, this was a regular and simple decorative motif suggested by the work of basketmakers. The Germanic artists abandoned the regularity of the earlier style, working instead with irregular, asymmetrical windings and knots to create motifs known as "dynamic" interlace. The expressive patterns may be seen in the art of various Germanic tribes, as well as that of the Merovingian culture, whose artistic traditions

14 The famous Sutton Hoo excavation in Britain has provided much information about the Anglo-Saxon world. This gold buckle once worn by a chieftain is a fine example of the intricate patterning known as "dynamic" interlace, and demonstrates the close connection between English goldsmiths and Scandinavian artists. There are thirteen fantastic animals and birds incorporated into the swirling design, interlocked and attacking one another.

15 Another example of interlace is the Matthew "carpet page" from the Lindisfarne Gospels—so called because of its resemblance to an oriental rug. Composed of twisting, knotted shapes, the page is dominated by a cross, which stands out from the background because of its varying coloration. This magnificent manuscript from the early eighth century was produced at the monastery of Lindisfarne, one of the centers of monastic culture in northern England.

were influenced by other migrating peoples through trade and the exchange of booty. Two particularly clear and famous examples in differing media are the Anglo-Saxon gold buckle from treasure excavated at Sutton Hoo in East Anglia, England, probably buried *c*. 660 (**fig. 14**) and the so-called "carpet page" from the Lindisfarne Gospels (**fig. 15**).

One of the most popular Germanic metalworking techniques was that of cloisonné, in which gold wires forming patterns were soldered to a solid metal plate made of silver or copper, and then filled with colored glass. The object was fired at a high temperature, melting the glass, and the result when cooled was a luminous, gem-like surface. Merovingian artists working in cloisonné used simplified forms and brilliant colors, and the glittering quality of the glass lessened the need for precious or semi-precious gems.

These metalworking skills were soon employed in producing objects that reflected the Merovingian conversion to Christianity. A brilliantly colored cloisonné plaque pictures Christ holding the Bible, with the Alpha and Omega on either side (**fig. 16**). He is placed above the arc of the heavens, and flanked by animalistic heads. A design such as this satisfied both the need for Christian expression and the Germanic love of animal forms.

Merovingian artistic expression also found an outlet in manuscript illumination. Scribes in the ***scriptoria*** of monasteries such as that at Jouarre adopted traditional Germanic motifs in decorating the manuscripts of the Bible and the writings of the Church Fathers. Their work reflects the tribal fascination with animal forms, birds, and fish, combining them with Christian symbolism and Roman architectural forms to produce a unique and brilliant synthesis. Similar techniques were popular in the culture that developed in the British Isles, as Germanic people settled in England.

16 This cloisonné medallion showing Christ holding the Bible reflects the Merovingian conversion to Christianity, and yet the animalistic forms with which he is surrounded indicate the survival of pagan artistic traditions.

Anglo-Saxon and Celtic Culture in the British Isles

Angles, Saxons, and Jutes

Roman civilization came to an end in the British Isles with a series of incursions by the Angles, Saxons, and Jutes, who came from Denmark and the area around the North Sea. Although these tribes were not the only ones to migrate to Britain, it has become traditional and convenient to refer to them collectively as the Anglo-Saxons. Between 450 and 650, they sailed up the rivers of England, cleared the forests, settled on the land, built villages, and made England their home. The Roman roads and the walls of the towns remained, as did the native Celtic population, which was largely reduced to slavery. In the west—in Wales, Ireland, and western Scotland—Celtic kingdoms kept alive the language, learning, literature, and religion of the Celts. Over the course of many centuries, the Celtic civilization also influenced English traditions, but the roots of English civilization itself lay in the laws, customs, language, and institutions of the Anglo-Saxons.

The Anglo-Saxons came to England first as pirates, then as mercenaries, and finally as colonists. As early as 287, Saxon pirates plundered the coasts of Britain; by the year 429 they had penetrated inland. The permanent conquest of Britain, however, was carried out not by pirates, but by mercenaries brought into the land to protect it. A Welsh monk named Gildas wrote about the invitation, which came from King Vortigern, the ruler of southeastern Britain. He called in the Saxons, led by two brothers, Hengest and Horsa, who may once have served in the Roman army. They came in about 449, served Vortigern for six years, and ultimately quarreled with him over pay. When the dispute could not be resolved, they left his service and established a kingdom in the southeastern part of the country, in what is now Kent. According to Gildas,

> They [the invaders] first landed on the eastern side of the island, by the invitation of the unlucky king, and there fixed their sharp talons, apparently to fight in favor of the island, but alas! more truly against it. Their motherland, finding her first brood thus successful, sends forth a larger company of her wolfish offspring, which sailing over, join themselves to their bastard-born comrades. From that time the germ of iniquity and the root of contention planted their poison amongst us, as we deserved, and shot forth into leaves and branches. The barbarians being thus introduced as soldiers into the island, to encounter as they falsely said, any dangers in defense of their hospitable entertainers, obtain an allowance of provisions, which, for some time being plentifully bestowed, stopped their doggish mouths. Yet they complain that their monthly supplies are not furnished in sufficient abundance, and they industriously aggravate each occasion of quarrel, saying that unless more liberality is shown them, they will break the treaty and plunder the whole island. In a short time, they follow up their threats with deeds.

The native population fought to resist the Saxons, often without success. They did win a stunning victory at the Battle of Mount Badon (c.516), but this, as Gildas remarked, was "almost the last great slaughter inflicted upon the rascally crew." Although the Britons were able to restrain the Saxon advance for the next forty years, from about 550 the Saxons and the Angles resumed their drive westward. Not limiting themselves to a seizure of power followed by military occupation, the Germanic tribesmen colonized the land. They arrived in boats measuring about 75 feet (23 m) in length, and rowed up the Thames to the Trent River, then up the Trent to the midlands. The small bands of warriors were followed by wives and children. The Angles settled in the north of England, the Saxons in the south, and the Jutes in Kent, the Isle of Wight, and Hampshire.

Between 450 and the reign of Alfred the Great (r. 871–899), the boundaries of large regions known as shires were formed, as was the diocesan organization of the church. Also determined were the location of smaller units called boroughs, the names of villages, the existence of open fields and manors, the division of England into parishes, the institution of monarchy, and the beginnings of the English language.

The society of these Germanic tribespeople was based on the values of aristocratic warriors—a society described later in the famous Old English poem known as *Beowulf*. A product of the tradition of oral performance, *Beowulf* was probably written down in the eighth century, though it recounts the folk history of an earlier period.

It was written in Old English, the language spoken in England between the fifth and the eleventh centuries, and consists of three episodes: Beowulf's battle with the monster Grendel, his slaying of Grendel's mother, and his attempt to kill the fire-breathing dragon that is threatening his people. The poem, which memorializes the mythic origins of the Germanic tribespeople, clearly expresses the values held by the Anglo-Saxon warrior society. The following passage is from the third episode:

> I paid back the treasures which he [Hygelac] had given me, in battle, by my gleaming sword, as was permitted me. He gave me land, a dwelling place, a glad possession. There was no need for him that he should have to seek among the Gepidae or Spear-Danes, or in the Swedish realm, a less good warrior—to purchase him with treasure. For him I would always be to the fore in the host—by myself at the front. And so through life shall do battle, while this sword lasts, which has often done me service, early and late, since by valor I became the slayer of Daeghrefn, champion of the Hugas. He could not bring the adornments, the breast-decoration, to the Frisian king; but he, the standard-bearer, sank in battle, a noble in prowess. Nor was the sword his slayer, but my unfriendly grasp crushed his body, the surgings of his heart.

It is evident that the strongest bond among the Germanic nobility was that which existed between a man and his lord. This was a society in which every chief and every king was surrounded by a company of warriors or attendants, later called **thegns**. The thegns owed loyal service to their chief; in turn, he rewarded them with treasure, arms, gold, and land. The ability of a kingdom to survive depended on the ability of the king to win battles, thereby gaining the treasure and land to provide booty for his men. The greatest virtues in this society were courage, honor, endurance, generosity, prowess in battle, boasting at table, and drinking at a feast.

Also admired in this rugged culture was splendor in dress. The Anglo-Saxons were fond of elaborate ornaments, as demonstrated by the treasure from Sutton Hoo. The gold buckle from the hoard (shown above in fig. 14) exhibits the Germanic predilection for interlacing forms, both organic and abstract, in art.

The Anglo-Saxon warriors were successful in conquering much of England, and by 650, seven English kingdoms had come into existence. The native population was reduced to a condition of servitude; indeed, the Anglo-Saxon word for a "Briton" came to denote a slave. Crucially, however, these seven kingdoms were eventually unified into a single kingdom of "Angla-land," or England.

The unification of the Anglo-Saxon monarchy was achieved in several steps. First, lesser kingdoms were consolidated into three large ones: Northumbria, Mercia, and Wessex. This was eventually followed by the triumph of Wessex over the other two (**Map 4**). During the seventh century, it seemed that Northumbria, under kings Edwin, Oswald, and Oswy (also known as Oswin or Oswio), would unify all England, and indeed Oswy did briefly extend his authority from the Firth of Forth to the borders of Wessex. The Northumbrian kings ultimately failed, however, since they were unable to defend two widely separate frontiers, against the Mercians in the south, and against the Picts and the Scots in the north. Indeed, the final unification of England occurred only after the **Danelaw** was conquered c. 950 (see Chapter 6).

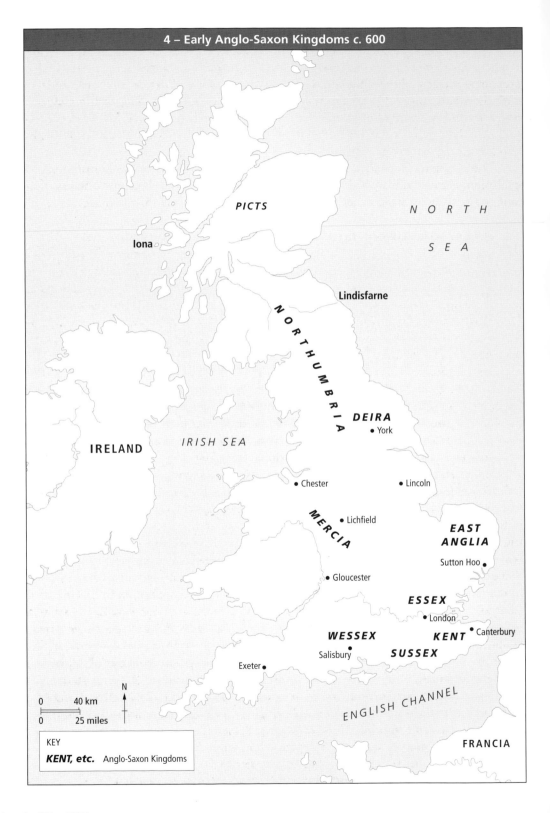

4 – Early Anglo-Saxon Kingdoms *c.* 600

PICTS

Iona

N O R T H

S E A

Lindisfarne

N O R T H U M B R I A

DEIRA

• York

IRELAND

IRISH SEA

• Chester

• Lincoln

MERCIA

• Lichfield

EAST ANGLIA

Sutton Hoo •

• Gloucester

ESSEX

• London

WESSEX

KENT

• Canterbury

Salisbury •

SUSSEX

Exeter •

ENGLISH CHANNEL

N

0   40 km

0   25 miles

FRANCIA

KEY

KENT, etc.   Anglo-Saxon Kingdoms

In the eighth century, supremacy passed to Mercia, whose greatest king was Offa (r. 757–796). Offa was able to extend Mercian power through all England south of the Humber River; other accomplishments during his reign included the establishment of an archbishopric at Lichfield, the minting of a silver penny, and the development of trade with the Continent. Offa's assumption of the title *Rex Anglorum* ("king of the English") was not merely an idle boast. His work of unification did not last, however, as two forces in the ninth century destroyed his achievement: the rise of the house of Wessex and the Viking incursions into England.

The creation of a unified monarchy was certainly a significant development in the evolution of English history. Equally important, however, was the conversion of England to Christianity, which occurred during the seventh and eighth centuries.

Christian missionaries and the Christianization of the British Isles

Although direct evidence is scanty, it is generally thought that some small Christian communities existed in the frontier areas of Britain as early as the fourth century. The first "definite" information regarding missionaries to the British Isles comes from a chronicler named Prosper of Aquitaine, in southwestern France, who reported that a priest named Palladius was sent from Gaul in 431 to minister to a Christian community in Ireland. We know very little about Palladius, however, and in any case he has been completely overshadowed by the most famous of the early missionaries to Ireland: St. Patrick.

The chronology of Patrick's life is disputed by scholars, but it is generally agreed that he lived during the fifth century, and his mission to Ireland occurred after 431. Patrick, the son of Romano-British Christians, recounted in his autobiography that he was kidnapped at approximately age sixteen and held in Ireland as a slave for several years. He eventually escaped and traveled to Gaul, where he studied in monasteries that had been influenced by the Egyptian ascetic tradition (see Chapter 1). In a later vision, Patrick wrote, he heard the Irish people pleading for his return, and soon he traveled back to Ireland, where he began the conversion of the pagans to Christianity. The details of Patrick's mission are not clear, but it seems likely that his activity was centered in the northern half of the island. He claimed in his writings that he converted thousands of people, including individuals of every social level from aristocrats to slaves, and scholars see no reason to doubt his assertions. There is some evidence that he divided the land into dioceses served by bishops and priests according to the Continental pattern. Because of the lack of an urban substructure, however, the diocesan system did not take hold. Instead, as Christianity grew in Ireland, monasteries became the centers of ecclesiastical governance, with the abbots as leaders; bishops, who elsewhere had administrative responsibilities, were subordinated to sacramental roles within the Irish monastic community. Perhaps as a result of the prominence of the monastic establishments, Irish Christianity was traditionally characterized by a reverence for asceticism—a life of austerity.

Irish monasticism became one of the great forces of the medieval church, and was instrumental in the development of scholarship, the creation of illuminated manuscripts, and the promulgation of highly successful missionary activities. One of the most prominent missionaries was St. Columba, who died in 597. He founded a monastery on the island of Iona (see Map 4) that was significant in the conversion of the Picts of Scotland and the English of Northumbria. St. Columbanus (c. 530–615), a rigorously ascetic missionary, was even more influential, traveling to the Continent and establishing monasteries in Burgundy and Italy that survived as prominent centers of learning throughout the medieval period. These Continental monasteries became important centers of evangelization for the conversion of the population of rural areas (see Chapter 7).

Another significant influence in the conversion of Britain was Gregory the Great. About 585 Gregory—who had not yet become pope—saw several boys with fair hair and fair complexions for sale in the slave market in Rome. When he inquired as to whether they were Christian or pagan, he was told that they were pagan. "Alas," he remarked, "how sad that such handsome folk are still in the grasp of the author of darkness, and that faces of such beauty conceal minds ignorant of God's grace!" He then asked about their origin, and was told they were Angles. "That is appropriate," he said, "for they have angelic faces, and it is right that they should become fellow-heirs with the angels in heaven." Gregory asked the pope to send him to Britain to convert the English, but the pontiff refused to allow him to leave Rome, since he was a skilled administrator. After he became pope in 590, he was able to initiate his long-cherished project.

Gregory directed a monk named Augustine to go to England as a missionary, and in 597 Augustine and forty companions arrived at Canterbury, in Kent. It was a propitious time, since Ethelbert, the pagan king of Kent, had married Bertha, a Christian princess from Gaul. Within a year Ethelbert received baptism, and his nephew, the king of Essex, did the same shortly thereafter. The result was that the English generally became receptive to the new religion.

The conversion of Kent and Essex established a pattern that was later followed elsewhere. The king would accept Christianity and baptism, and his thegns would follow his example. Missionaries were then sent to preach to the general population. Although the death of a monarch might result in a reversion to paganism, the missionaries were tenacious in delivering their message; by 663, Christianity was permanently established in the southeastern part of England.

When King Ethelbert died in 616, his son returned to pagan forms of worship, and the influence of Christianity in the south was reduced. However, the marriage of Ethelburga, one of Ethelbert's daughters, to Edwin, the pagan king of Northumbria, provided an opportunity for Christian missionaries to proselytize (that is, seek to make converts) in the north. It was a condition of the marriage contract that the princess from Kent and her attendants be allowed to practice their Christian religion, and Edwin himself had expressed a willingness to adopt his wife's beliefs if his councillors agreed.

The bride was accompanied to Northumbria by Paulinus, who had been consecrated bishop of Canterbury in 625. During the first year, the missionary had little success in securing converts, but in 626, Edwin agreed that his infant daughter could be baptized, along with several other members of the royal family. The following Easter, Edwin himself was baptized in a small wooden chapel built especially for the purpose at York.

At the time of his baptism, Edwin was the most powerful ruler in the country, and his example was quickly followed by many members of the nobility and others among his subjects. Paulinus took full advantage of the opportunity, traveling widely throughout Northumbria, visiting the estates of the nobility, and preaching to crowds from the rural areas, later baptizing them in nearby rivers.

The conversion of the north was proceeding rapidly when Edwin was killed in battle in 633. The queen and the royal family escaped with Paulinus to Kent, but the warriors who defeated Edwin were cruel in their treatment of the native population, both Christian and pagan, "sparing neither women nor innocent children, [and] putting them to death with ruthless savagery." The conquerors were soon subdued, however, by another member of the royal house: Oswald, who became king.

The new king had spent some time in exile on Iona, where he had been converted by Irish monks. By 635, King Oswald had secured his position, and he sent to Iona for help in re-establishing Christianity. His request was answered by a monk named Aidan, who settled on the island of Lindisfarne and founded a monastery from which missionary work could be continued on the mainland. Other missionaries followed, and within a generation the kingdom of Northumbria had become almost entirely Christian.

With both Celtic and Roman monks working in Northumbria, a major conflict developed between the two different forms of Christianity. As mentioned earlier, the government of the Roman church was based on the bishop and the diocese, whereas the Celtic church was centered on the abbot and his monastery. The Roman monk shaved his head in the form of a circle, in imitation of Christ's crown of thorns, whereas the Celtic monk followed the Druid custom of shaving a broad strip from ear to ear. In addition, the two churches disagreed about the date of Easter. More important, however, were their spiritual differences: the Roman church emphasized order and discipline, and possessed wealth and power; in contrast, the Celtic church relied on evangelical fervor and praised the ascetic life. The monk Aidan exemplified this life as he walked the roads of Northumbria, preaching the Gospel and helping the poor. With the constant support of King Oswald, Aidan and his fellow missionaries rescued Northumbria from heathenism. But when Oswald's successor, Oswy, married a princess from Kent who followed Roman usage, this presented a practical and urgent problem. How could the king be celebrating Easter when the queen was observing Lent? King Oswy decided to seek a resolution to the problem by calling a church council—the Synod of Whitby (664). According to the "Venerable" Bede, writing in the following century (see below), King Oswy opened the conference by observing that "all who served the One God should observe one rule of life, and since they all hoped for one kingdom in heaven, they should not differ in celebrating the sacraments of heaven." He gave the bishops of both traditions an opportunity to speak, and each gave his reasons for establishing the Easter customs. When a spokesman for the Roman position argued that the pope was the successor to St. Peter, and the Celtic representatives conceded the truth of this assertion, the king ruled that the English church would henceforth follow Roman usage.

Northumbria eventually developed a flourishing intellectual and artistic culture, often referred to as the "Northumbrian Renaissance." This was especially vibrant at Lindisfarne, and at the monasteries of Jarrow and Wearmouth. From this milieu came the most famous writer of eighth-century England: the "Venerable" Bede (c. 672–735). Bede, a follower of Roman, rather than Celtic, Christianity, spent his entire career at Jarrow as a teacher of young monks, and most of his writings were pedagogical in nature. His most important work was the *Ecclesiastical History of the English People*, which he completed in 731 and which provides much information about the development of monarchy and Christianity in England. In addition to providing a rich intellectual tradition, Northumbria was also a site of sophisticated manuscript illumination, such as the "carpet page" from the Lindisfarne Gospels (see p. 62, fig. 15), which shows the influence of "dynamic" (often referred to as "Celtic") interlace.

There were many reasons for England's successful conversion to Christianity. The most important was undoubtedly the zeal of the missionaries, who were determined to bring the word of the Christian God to the pagans. Furthermore, Christianity offered, in contrast to the Germanic belief in spirits and magic, an ethical system with a promise of eternal life. The teachings of Christianity also provided precepts for social discipline that were useful to a settled agrarian society; the Church opposed violence, condemned sexual promiscuity, defended marriage, and urged acceptance of one's lot in the world.

Another factor in the conversion of Anglo-Saxon England was the influence exerted by aristocratic women. Bede's *Ecclesiastical History of the English People* contains several accounts of queens who influenced their royal husbands to accept Christianity, including Ethelburga, the wife of Edwin. A letter to her from Pope Boniface clearly shows the expectations of the pontiff concerning her role:

> We have been greatly encouraged by God's goodness in granting you, through your own profession of faith, an opportunity to kindle a spark of the true religion in your husband; for in this way He will more swiftly inspire not only the mind of your illustrious Consort to love of Him, but the minds of your subjects as well . . . We also know that you carefully shun idol-worship and the allurements of temples and divinations; and that, having given your allegiance to Christ, you are unshakably devoted to the love of our Redeemer and labor constantly to propagate the Christian Faith . . . My illustrious daughter, persevere in using every effort to soften his [the King's] heart by teaching him the commandments of God . . . If you do this, the witness of the Holy Spirit will most certainly be fulfilled in you, that "the unbelieving husband shall be saved through the believing wife."

Boniface asked the Queen to send a messenger informing him of her progress "in the conversion of your husband and the people over whom you reign." It is obvious that the pope regarded her as a powerful ally in his mission to convert the English people.

Another queen, Etheldreda of Northumbria, was renowned for her chastity; according to Bede she "preserved the glory of perpetual virginity" during her twelve-year marriage to King Egfrid. After much pleading, she eventually convinced the king to allow her to retire from "worldly affairs," and to enter a convent at Coldingham. Etheldreda eventually became the abbess of a convent she founded at Ely, near Cambridge, where she "became the virgin mother of many virgins vowed to God and displayed the pattern of a heavenly life in word and deed."

The monastic life had great appeal for many women in the Anglo-Saxon world, including both commoners and aristocrats, because the world of the convent offered not only spiritual solace, but also the possibility for independent and influential action. Bede's *History* recounts the founding of several "double monasteries," for both men and women, such as the one at Barking, near London. These monastic establishments were placed under the guidance of the abbess, rather than an abbot; although this privilege was withdrawn from women in the ninth century, following the invasions of England by the Vikings, the custom indicates that some women held significant power in the ecclesiastical world of the Anglo-Saxons.

There are few sources of information about the lives of ordinary women in Anglo-Saxon England. The early law codes, such as that of King Ethelbert of Kent, are similar to other Germanic codes, and are concerned primarily with compensation in case of injury or death. Some of the clauses pertain to women, especially to cases of abduction, with the amount of compensation being dependent on rank. Casual sexual encounters were also subject to fines, with 50 shillings due for sleeping "with a maiden belonging to the king," but 25 shillings for sleeping with a woman from the class of slaves employed to grind grain, and 20 if the woman was the cup-bearer of a nobleman.

Some women held positions of responsibility on an estate, such as supervising the communal oven, but most ordinary women were probably dairymaids or domestic servants, engaged in household tasks, sewing, and weaving. The presence of sewing implements such as thread boxes, spindles, and weaving batons in the graves of Anglo-Saxon women indicates the importance of their role as cloth producers. Small sickles among the grave goods bear witness to female participation in agriculture, and women no doubt helped their husbands in family farm duties.

Anglo-Saxon men and women thus created a productive and relatively prosperous Christian society. It was not to last, however, for during the ninth century, England, along with the rest of western Europe, faced an onslaught by the Vikings that would shatter this fragile stability. The kingdom established by the Visigoths in Spain, however, was even more short-lived.

Visigothic Spain

The Visigothic migration into Spain began in the fifth century, when a force numbering approximately 200,000 moved across the border from Aquitaine, in southwestern France. By 497, the migrants, who included peasants as well as soldiers and clergy, were able to establish themselves as overlords without much opposition from the native Hispano-Roman population. The native landowners were compelled to give up two-thirds of their cultivated land, but the invaders did not undertake a general expropriation. By the reign of King Leovigild (r. 568–586), a Visigothic capital had been established at Toledo.

Several factors prevented the Visigoths from being easily assimilated by the native population. First, like the Ostrogoths, the Visigoths practiced Arianism, while the Hispano-Romans were Athanasian Christians. Leovigild attempted to convert the Athanasian bishops to Arianism, but succeeded only in provoking rebellion. His son Recared (r. 586–601) decided to solve the problem by converting to Athanasian Christianity, and he was able to persuade his Arian bishops to follow him. A council at Toledo proclaimed the conversion of the entire kingdom in 589, thus removing the source of tension that had been prevalent throughout the history of the Ostrogothic kingdom.

Initially, intermarriage between the native population and the Visigoths had been prohibited, but the conversion of the Visigothic population removed the religious obstacle. By the latter sixth century, integration of the Germanic tribespeople with the Hispano-Roman natives was proceeding rapidly.

At first, the Visigoths governed themselves according to their own laws, but beginning with the reign of Leovigild, Visigothic kings passed laws that were binding for the entire population. A collection of new laws combining both Roman and Gothic measures, known as the *Book of Judgments*, was drawn up during the reign of King Recceswinth (r. 649–672). This code provided a common law for all of the Spanish people, and remained an important feature of legal process in Spain during the entire medieval period.

The primary source of instability in the Visigothic kingdom was the principle of elective monarchy, which resulted in a bloody struggle for the crown each time a king died. Moreover, sometimes an ambitious noble would become restive and simply assassinate the king. An indication of the volatile nature of the situation is given by the fact that four kings were murdered between 531 and 555. This lack of a stable succession to the throne led to the ultimate disappearance of the Visigoths as a separate, identifiable people. In 711, when the Muslims arrived in Spain from north Africa, various local factions were feuding over the succession to the kingship, and the invaders were able to establish themselves without serious opposition (see Chapter 3). Thus, although the Visigothic kingdom in Spain survived longer than the Ostrogothic monarchy in Italy, it, too, ultimately vanished.

Although the Visigoths did not make a concerted effort to preserve Roman institutions, they did use the administrative units of the Romans in ways that resembled the Ostrogoths. In addition, their intellectual culture produced Isidore of Seville (c. 570–636) who had lasting influence in the Middle Ages.

Like Boethius and Cassiodorus, Isidore of Seville was interested in preserving the intellectual heritage of the past. Although he was not an original thinker, his zeal for compiling historical detail in every area of human endeavor resulted in a twenty-volume encyclopedia known as the *Etymologiae*. His scholarly technique took the form of explaining the meaning and derivation of Latin words ("etymologies"). Although his work seems archaic and obscure to modern scholars, it did preserve a vast amount of information from the ancient world.

Thus, Roman culture and governance were preserved to one degree or another in the kingdoms formed by the Germanic tribal peoples, including the Ostrogoths, the Franks, and the Visigoths. The Ostrogoths were conquered by another tribe, the Lombards; the Franks endured and prospered, ultimately forming the Holy Roman Empire; and the Visigothic kingdom was destroyed by a new force that emerged in the early seventh century—the Muslims, or adherents of Islam.

Summary

During the fifth and sixth centuries, the Germanic people who migrated into the lands of the Roman Empire established several different kinds of kingdoms. The Ostrogoths, who entered Italy at the end of the fifth century, found strong remnants of Roman government and culture, which they worked to preserve. Although their kingdom did not endure beyond the reign of Theodoric, their cultural legacy provided a fruitful link between the ancient world and the newly emerging western societies.

The eastern, or Byzantine, empire, continued to be powerful and productive for almost a millennium after the "fall" of Rome. It was led by several charismatic emperors, who viewed themselves as semi-divine representatives of God. One of the most famous was Justinian, who attempted unsuccessfully to unite the eastern and western parts of the former Roman Empire. Justinian's lasting contribution was a compilation of laws known as the *Corpus juris civilis*—a work that was highly influential in western Europe during the twelfth and thirteenth centuries.

The Visigoths, who created a kingdom in Spain, did not find extensive remains of Roman governance. Instead, they superimposed their own traditions on the native population. However, the Visigothic kingdom, like that of the Ostrogoths, was of brief duration, destroyed in the eighth century by a new invading force: the Muslims.

Both the Ostrogoths and the Visigoths continued to practice Arian Christianity. In Gaul, however, the Franks adopted the Athanasian version practiced by the native inhabitants, thus providing a more complete fusion of cultures. This may have been one reason for the longevity of the Frankish realm, although the establishment of Salic Law and the great supply of Frankish manpower were equally important.

The Angles and Saxons who invaded England eventually united the tribal units and formed a stable monarchy; they were converted to Christianity through missions sent from the pope, and their monastic establishments fostered a vibrant intellectual and artistic life. Thus, the seeds of a new Europe emerged alongside the eastern empire, which, not having been subjected to the same stresses, had survived the demise of the empire in the west.

Suggestions for Further Reading

Primary sources

An extensive collection of primary source material may also be found in *From Roman to Merovingian Gaul: A Reader*, edited and translated by Alexander Callander Murray (Peterborough, Canada: Broadview Press, 2000). A major source for Merovingian history is *The History of the Franks*, by Gregory of Tours, translated by Lewis Thorpe (Harmondsworth: Penguin Books, 1977) is . See also *Late Merovingian France: History and Hagiography, 640–720*, edited by Paul Fouracre and Richard A. Gerberding, (Manchester: Manchester University Press, 1996).

The most important source for Anglo-Saxon history is Bede's *History of the English Church and People*, translated by Leo Sherley-Price, (Harmondsworth: Penguin, 1968). Additional materials are contained in *English Historical Documents c. 500–1042*, vol. 1, 2nd ed., edited by Dorothy Whitelock (London: Eyre Methuen, 1979). *Early Sources of Scottish History: AD 500–1286*, by Alan Orr Anderson, reprint ed. (2 vols., Stamford: Paul Watkins, 1990) is a massive collection of sources concerning political and religious life in Scotland.

The Consolation of Philosophy, by Boethius, translated by Victor Watts, is available in a revised edition (London: Penguin, 1999) and Boethius's *De institutione musica* has been translated by Calvin Bower, edited by Claude V. Palisca (New Haven: Yale University Press, 1989). Writings by Cassiodorus are published in *Variae of Magnus Aurelius Cassiodorus*, translated by S.J.B. Barnish (Liverpool: Liverpool University Press, 1992).

The *Digesta* of Justinian is available in a translation by C.F. Kolbert (Harmondsworth: Penguin, 1979, reprint ed. 1985) and his *Institutes* have been translated by Peter Birks and Grant McLeod (London: Duckworth, 1987). *The Secret History* by Procopius, translated by G.A. Williamson (Harmondsworth, UK: Penguin Books, 1966), contains a series of anecdotes by Justinian's courtier. *Social and Political Thought in Byzantium: From Justinian I to the Last Palaeologus*, by Ernest Barker (Oxford: Clarendon Press, 1957), consists of documents and passages from Byzantine writers (c. 527–c. 1450).

Secondary sources

A Concise History of Byzantium, by Warren Treadgold (Houndmills, UK: Palgrave, 2001), provides an excellent introduction to Byzantine civilization. Another helpful introductory work is Michael Angold's *Byzantium: The Bridge from Antiquity to the Middle Ages* (London: Phoenix Press, 2002).

A more comprehensive work, which covers the entire period discussed in this text, is *The Byzantine Commonwealth: Eastern Europe 500–1453*, by Dimitri Obolensky (London: Phoenix Press, reprint ed., 2000). *Justinian*, by John Moorhead (London: Longman, 1994), is an excellent biography of the emperor. See also Robert Browning's study *Justinian and Theodora* (London: Thames and Hudson, revised ed., 1987).

A fascinating discussion of the role of empresses in the Byzantine empire is contained in *Empresses and Power in Early Byzantium*, by Liz James (New York: Leicester University Press, 2001).

A fine analysis of the historians of the age of migration is presented in *The Narrators of Barbarian History* (AD 550–800), by Walter Goffart (Princeton: Princeton University Press, 1988). In addition to the works of Bede and Gregory of Tours, his study includes the writings of Jordanes, the author of a sixth-century account of the Goths, and Paul the Deacon, an eighth-century monk whose *History of the Lombards*

is a source of human interest as well as political information.

The development of the Frankish kingdom from the era prior to Clovis through the sixth century is analyzed in an absorbing study, *The Franks*, by Edward James (Oxford: Basil Blackwell, 1988). See also *Before France and Germany: The Creation and Transformation of the Merovingian World*, by Patrick J. Geary (Oxford: Oxford University Press, 1988), and *The Merovingian Kingdoms: 450–751*, by Ian Wood (London: Longman, 1994).

The Barbarian Conversion: From Paganism to Christianity, by Richard Fletcher (Berkeley, CA: University of California Press, 1997), is a comprehensive investigation of the adoption of Christianity by much of Europe between the fourth century and the fourteenth.

Chapters 1–3 of *Women in Frankish Society: Marriage and the Cloister: 500 to 900*, by Suzanne Fonay Wemple (Philadelphia: University of Pennsylvania Press, 1985), offer an interesting survey of women's life in the Merovingian and Carolingian kingdoms.

The Making of England, 6th ed., by Warren C. Hollister, is a good overview of early English history. (Lexington, MA: D.C. Heath & Co., 1992). The third edition of a classic study, *Anglo-Saxon England*, by Frank Stenton, has been reissued recently (Oxford: Oxford University Press, 2001). The Anglo-Saxon monarchy is the subject of an excellent work by Barbara Yorke, *Kings and Kingdoms of Early Anglo-Saxon England* (London: Seaby, 1990).

Henrietta Leyser's *Medieval*

Women: A Social History of Women in England: 450–1500 (London: Butler and Tanner, Ltd, 1995) provides information concerning women during the early Middle Ages in Chapters 1–4.

The Coming of Christianity to Anglo-Saxon England, by Henry Mayr-Harting (London: Batsford, 3rd ed., 1991), is the best introduction to the Christianization of England. Women's participation in religious life is discussed in *Anglo-Saxon Women and the Church: Sharing a Common Fate*, by Stephanie Hollis (Woodbridge: Boydell Press, 1992).

James J. O'Donnell's *Cassiodorus* (Berkeley: University of California Press, 1979) is a fine analysis of the life and works of the late antique author.

An excellent introduction to Visigothic Spain is included in *Early Medieval Spain: Unity in Diversity, 400–1000*, 2nd ed., by Roger Collins (New York: St Martin's Press, 1995)

Medieval Architecture in Western Europe: From AD 300 to 1500, by Robert Calkins (Oxford: Oxford University Press, 1998), contains an excellent description and analysis of the basilica in Chapter 3.

Rowland J. Mainstone's *Hagia Sophia: Architecture, Structure and Liturgy of Justinian's Great Church* (London: Thames and Hudson, 1988) is a comprehensive analysis of the famous Byzantine monument. The Iconoclastic Controversy is the topic of a fascinating study by Jaroslav Pelikan, *Imago Dei: The Byzantine Apologia for Icons* (New Haven: Yale University Press, 1990).

THE EMERGENCE OF ISLAM

3

DURING THE SEVENTH CENTURY, as the Merovingian rulers were struggling to maintain their dominance in western Europe, there arose in the Arabian peninsula what could arguably be classed as the medieval world's third great monotheistic religion (after Judaism and Christianity): Islam. The new religion swept rapidly through northern Africa and the Near East, with its adherents gaining territory as far east as India. The forces of Islam entered Spain in the eighth century, where they remained to create a vibrant culture during the next 750 years. The political, intellectual, and artistic influence of this culture on western Europe was profound. Indeed, the evolution of the Carolingian Empire has been seen by some scholars as the direct result of the Islamic domination of the Mediterranean Sea.

As with Christianity, the religion of Islam began with the birth of an exceptional individual. Unlike Christ, however, Muhammad is not himself considered to be divine. Instead, he is viewed as the human prophet of a supreme being called Allah, sent to spread His word in a new revelation.

Muhammad and the Birth of Islam

The cradle of Islam—the Arabian peninsula—was, until the seventh century, a relatively insignificant area situated between the Persian and the Byzantine empires. Both of these great powers had attempted to establish authority in the peninsula, but had failed in their efforts to control the fierce, nomadic Bedouin tribesmen who inhabited the arid interior desert. The Bedouins lived in a tribal society where the principal sources of livelihood were trade, herding, and raiding. They were polytheistic, and worshiped some 300 nature deities.

Bedouin social organization was based on the extended family, with several families grouped together to comprise a clan, and several clans forming a tribe. The resulting tribal ties and group loyalty were foremost in the legal structure of the society, with the *lex talionis*, or "eye for an eye" concept of retaliation, establishing the basis for legal action, just as it had in the communities of the ancient Near East. Tribal affiliation and group allegiance thus provided the framework for protection as well as identity. But the influence of such ties was not limited to those leading a nomadic existence; tribal allegiance was also a prominent feature in the societies of agricultural and trading settlements such as Mecca, a center of commercial activity, and Medina, an important agricultural community.

Tension and hostility often existed among neighboring tribes, and it became essential to establish some place of neutrality where tribal members could meet safely, to exchange goods and resolve disputes. This need was met with the creation of the institution called the **haram**. The *haram* was originally an area declared by a holy man to be neutral ground. There was usually a shrine built on it, often a very simple structure. Violence was forbidden in this neutral area, and enemies could meet there, assured of their security. The holy man could be consulted, and he often acted as judge in resolving disputes. The people who used the *haram* and the services of the holy man were obliged to pay him, and he, in turn, fed and entertained the tribesmen. Since there was no centralized law enforcement system, the holy men often became persons of great power and influence. Their positions tended to become hereditary, with their roles and responsibilities being passed from generation to generation within one family.

The foundation of the *haram* at Mecca is attributed by Muslims (believers in Islam) to Abraham—the same Abraham as in the Christian Old Testament—and is thought to have been administered by a series of holy families or holy lineages. In the first half of the sixth century, the existing guardians of the *haram* at Mecca were replaced by a holy man, Qusayy, and his tribe, the Quraysh. Qusayy's descendants became the new holy family, and one of his direct descendants was Muhammad ibn Abd Allah, which means "Muhammad the Prophet of God." Although the Quraysh had lost some power by the time of Muhammad's birth, it is important to remember his tribal affiliation in order to understand his life and mission.

Muhammad was born in Mecca *c.* 570, into the prosperous clan of Hashim, of the Quraysh tribe. According to traditional accounts, Muhammad's father died on a trading expedition before his birth, and his mother, Amina, passed away when he was six. He was then raised by his uncle, Abu Talib, who was a powerful member of the clan of Hashim. Not many details are known concerning Muhammad's early life, although as a young man he seems to have made a career in the rapidly expanding trading network that developed as a result of Mecca's prosperity. In his twenties he was employed as business manager for a wealthy widow, Khadija, who soon became his wife. Their marriage seems to have been one of close companionship, and Khadija gave Muhammad comfort and moral support during difficult periods. They had two sons and four daughters, including Fatima, whose descendants became very important in later Islamic history (see below, p. 87).

When he was forty years old, in about 610 (the exact chronology is not certain), Muhammad began to receive revelations from Allah. The circumstances were later recorded in several sources, which indicate that he had gone from Mecca to the nearby mountain of Hira for a period of meditation and reflection, as was his custom. On the night that Muslims refer to as "The Night of Power and Excellence," he received the first of the revelations. A heavenly visitor, identified by tradition as the angel Gabriel, commanded him to recite. Frightened and bewildered, he responded that he had nothing to say. The angel persisted, and finally the words came to Muhammad:

Recite: In the name of thy Lord who created,

created man out of a blood-clot.
Recite: And thy Lord is the Most Generous,

who taught by the Pen,
Taught man that he knew not.

Muhammad continued to receive revelations from Allah over the next twenty-two years, and these 114 messages were collected and recorded after Muhammad's death in the **Qur'an** ("The Recitation"), the sacred book of Islamic scripture, which Muslims believe to be the transcript of a tablet preserved in heaven. It is organized by length rather than chronologically, with the longest revelations appearing first. Thus, the earliest revelations, as the shortest, appear towards the end of the loosely collected verses. For example, the verses, or **ayat** (sing. **aya**), from the **sura** (pl. **suwar**), or "chapter" above, are numbered as 96: 1–5.

Muhammad viewed himself as the final messenger in a line of prophets that extended from Abraham through Moses and Jesus. He considered his god (Allah) to be the one true God, just as the Jews and the Christians viewed their own Supreme Beings. Muhammad himself was the human prophet of Allah, whose teachings about Islam, meaning "submission to God's will," completed God's revelation to all "People of the Book." Islam was thus the culmination of revealed religious truth, fulfilling the Judeo-Christian tradition of deliverance:

God! There is no god but Him, the Living, the Ever-existent One. He has revealed to you the Book with the Truth, confirming the scriptures which preceded it; for He has already revealed the Torah and the Gospel for the guidance of mankind, and the distinction between right and wrong. (3: 1–2)

For Muslims, the Qur'an is the literal, eternal Book of God, revealed to the Prophet Muhammad as a guide for human beings. The powerful verses stress the majesty and glory of Allah, as in *sura* 16: 1–3:

The judgment of Allah will surely come to pass: do not seek to hurry it on. Glory be to Him! Exalted be He above their idols!

By His will He sends down the angels with the Spirit to those among His servants whom He chooses, bidding them proclaim: "There is no god but Me: therefore fear Me."

The Qur'an also emphasizes the importance of doing good, especially the obligations of the wealthy towards the poor, and the *suwar* stress the inevitability of the Day of Judgment and Resurrection:

But of all creatures, those that embrace the Faith and do good works are the noblest. Their reward, in their Lord's presence, shall be the gardens of Eden, gardens watered by running streams, where they shall dwell for ever. (98: 8–9)

The Qur'an deals with all aspects of human life and society, including the position of women. Although it has been pointed out by many scholars that the Qur'an's exhortations to protect and help women and children demonstrate a vast improvement over earlier conditions, it is made clear that women are inferior to, and subject to, men:

Men have authority over women because Allah has made the one superior to the other, and because they spend their wealth to maintain them. Good women are obedient. They guard their unseen parts because God has guarded them. As for those from whom you fear disobedience, admonish them, forsake them in beds apart, and beat them. Then if they obey you, take no further action against them. Surely Allah is high, supreme. (4:34)

The Qur'an instructs men to marry no more than four wives, and admonishes them to treat their wives equally: "If you fear that you cannot maintain equality among them, marry one only . . . this will make it easier for you to avoid injustice" (4: 3). These provisions are followed by instructions about the inheritances of women, which represent a great improvement over conditions in pre-Islamic Arabia. Nevertheless, women's inheritances are obviously not equal to those of men—indeed, they are worth only half as much (4: 11).

Another important concept in the Qur'an is that of the **jihad**, or "Holy War." In a general sense, *jihad* refers to the individual, personal struggle of a Muslim to follow the will of Allah. More specifically, the Qur'an urges:

Fight for the sake of Allah those that fight against you, but do not attack them first. Allah does not love aggressors.

Slay them wherever you find them. Drive them out of the places from which they drove you . . . But do not fight them within the precincts of the Holy Mosque unless they attack you there; if they attack you put them to the sword. Thus shall the unbelievers be rewarded: but if they mend their ways, know that Allah is forgiving and merciful. (2: 190)

The psychological message delivered by the Qur'an is powerful. Those who fight and die in the cause of Allah will be given rich rewards in the afterlife:

The believers who stay at home—apart from those that suffer from a grave disability—are not the equals of those who fight for the cause of Allah with their goods and their persons. God has exalted the men who fight with their goods and their persons above those who stay at home. Allah has promised all a good reward; but far richer is the recompense of those who fight for Him. (4: 96)

Further,

Let those who would exchange the life of this world for the hereafter, fight for the cause of Allah; whoever fights for the cause of Allah, whether he dies or triumphs, on him We shall bestow a rich recompense . . . The true believers fight for the cause of Allah, but the infidels fight for the Devil. Fight then against the friends of Satan. Satan's cunning is weak indeed. (4: 76)

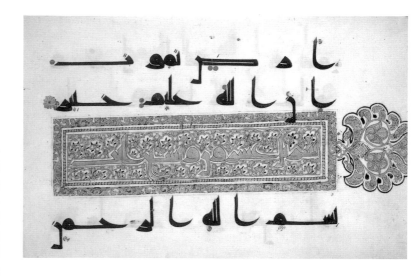

In addition to providing the scriptural text and canon of ethical and moral life for followers of Islam, the Qur'an was central to the development of the grammar, vocabulary, and syntax of the Arabic language. It was the first prose book in Arabic, and established the linguistic style for future writings. And as will be discussed below (see p. 90), the highly decorative Arabic calligraphy that provided the script in which the Qur'an was written also came to be used to ornament buildings, glassware, and porcelain products (**fig. 17**).

17 This exquisitely colored leaf from the Qur'an was probably created in ninth-century Iraq. Sacred calligraphy such as this became a prominent aspect of Islamic manuscript art, assuming an almost iconic status. The *sura* (chapter) heading is in gold, with red dots indicating the placement of vowels and thin black marks specifying diacritical marks.

In the year following the first heavenly visitation, Muhammad began preaching in public. His wife and his close relatives became his first converts, but initially there were few others. This may have been because his teaching was strongly opposed by the prosperous oligarchs of Mecca. Muhammad's exclusive monotheism was a challenge to the traditional polytheistic religion, and his advocacy of social equality threatened the economic and political interests of the establishment. The powerful Umayyad clan, in particular, saw his ministry as dangerous.

Like the clan of Hashim, of which Muhammad was a member, the Umayyads belonged to the tribe of Quraysh, who were then the custodians of the **Ka'ba**. This was a cube-shaped religious shrine that housed the 360 idols of the tribal deities, and functioned as the central sanctuary of the tribal religion. According to traditional Muslim teaching, the Ka'ba was built by the prophet Abraham and his son Ismail to contain a sacred black stone given to Abraham by the angel Gabriel; it is thus a symbol of the covenant made with Ismail by Allah. The Ka'ba was (and still is) the site of an annual pilgrimage and festival that produced significant revenues (**fig. 18**). The Umayyad leaders feared the potential economic loss that might occur if Muhammad's ministry resulted in their losing control of access to the shrine. Even more alarming was Muhammad's concept of society as a single universal community (**umma**), to which all true believers (i.e., Muslims) belonged. Such an idea threatened the ancient tribal affiliations.

Given these circumstances, the first ten years of Muhammad's ministry were extremely problematic. He did establish a small group of followers, but life was made even more difficult by the deaths of his wife and uncle in 619. Furthermore, the political opposition in Mecca became more threatening, with verbal insult developing into active persecution.

Things changed dramatically in the next year, when Muhammad was invited by a delegation from Medina to act as judge in a tribal feud. The prophet and seventy of his followers, known later as *muhajirin* or emigrants, went to Medina in 622. This

18 The Ka'ba in the Masjid al-Haram at Mecca is the most important Islamic shrine. It contains the Black Stone, which is covered, according to medieval poets, "like a bride," with a silken veil, now black in color but originally multicolored. The stone indicates to Muslims throughout the world the direction towards which they must pray. The shrine is the goal of the *hajj* (pilgrimage) —the journey required of Muslims at least once in a lifetime.

migration, or ***hijra*** (or ***hegira***), marked a significant moment in the history of Islam, because it was in Medina that an Islamic community was first established. The importance of the *hijra* is indicated by the fact that the Muslims date their history from this creation of the Islamic community, the *umma*, at Medina, rather than from the birth of Muhammad or the date of his initial revelation. It was through the community that Allah's will on earth would be realized.

In Medina, Muhammad was free from the oppression of the ruling clans of Mecca, and he was able to preach and worship openly. However, even though he had been invited to Medina, it was necessary to come to an agreement with the townspeople concerning the new form of social organization practiced by the *muhajirin*, who no longer adhered to tribal or clannish bonds. A series of agreements was drawn up during the next two or three years, collectively known as the "Constitution of Medina." In this document, the believers in Islam were described as forming a community, an *umma*, separate from the surrounding pagan society. Living according to a bond that transcended other allegiances, they were to defend themselves as one body. If any Muslim was killed fighting "in the way of God," the members of the *umma* were to seek revenge. If one Muslim killed another, however, the traditional rules of retaliation applied.

Mecca did not diminish in religious importance during the *hijra*. Indeed, the significance of the city for Islam grew as a result of the designation of Mecca as the direction for prayer (*qibla*) and the site for the Muslim pilgrimage (*hajj*) to the Ka'ba. The traditional establishment of Mecca, however, viewed the Muslims as traitors and secessionists, and this situation served to heighten the tensions between the followers of the prophet and the local authorities.

During the early years of the *hijra*, Muhammad and his followers (the *muhajirin* who had emigrated from Mecca, and new converts known as **ansar**, who had been raised in Medina) worked to establish his authority within Medina, and to secure the allegiance of the surrounding tribes. These alliances were vital in Muhammad's struggle against Mecca. Unless the prophet subdued and won over the powerful Meccan Quraysh tribe, Islam would never be more than a local cult. Attacking the city of Mecca itself, however, would have been imprudent, and so Muhammad's strategy was to assault the trade caravans traveling from Mecca to Syria, which passed close to Medina. This action would destroy his adversaries' economic base and eventually starve the city into submission, since it depended on imported food for survival.

There had been raids by small groups of Muslims during the initial eighteen months of the *hijra*, but the first significant confrontation took place in 624, when a valuable caravan set out from Gaza to Mecca. It was led by one of the most influential men in Meccan politics, Abu Sufyan, of the Umayyad clan. Fearing Muhammad's attack, the Meccans sent a force of 950 men led by Abu Jahl, leader of the city, to protect the caravan. The caravan took a coastal route, and arrived safely in Meccan territory. Part of the force continued to advance, however, intending to annihilate Muhammad's troops. The Prophet, with his group of about 300 followers, was waiting for them by the wells at Badr; although inferior in numbers, they possessed the advantage of having a water source, and were able to defeat the Meccans decisively. According to the Qur'an, Muhammad's army was aided by a band of invisible angels. Abu Jahl was killed, and numerous prisoners and animals were taken. The battle at Badr was a complete triumph for Muhammad, and marked a decisive turning point in the struggle against Mecca. Furthermore, those who were willing to risk their lives for Allah and his Prophet at Badr were immortalized in the subsequent tradition as early warriors for Islam.

There were several practical results of this victory. Economically, Muhammad was able to provide for the needs of his followers and those Muslims who were in distress. Certainly the Bedouin tribal chiefs lost respect for the Meccan leaders, and the Quraysh suffered diminished prestige. But the most important result was the enhancement and consolidation of Muhammad's position in Medina. Many of his critics were silenced by his success, and new converts were won over to Islam.

Soon after the triumph at Badr, Muhammad moved against the Jews in Medina. He saw the Jews as a potent threat to his authority because, unlike the pagans, they provided a genuine ideological challenge. Several of the Jewish clans in the city had been urged to convert to Islam, but few of them had agreed. For them to accept Muhammad's political authority would mean acknowledging his claims to being the Prophet of Allah. Since the Jews refused to recognize this, their coexistence with Muslims in Medina threatened to undermine his position.

Muhammad initially moved against the Jewish silversmiths, who controlled much of the town's commercial activity. In addition to their enviable economic prosperity, they were allied with Allah ibn Ubayy, a man whom Muhammad viewed as a rival in terms of political power. Using as a pretext a market quarrel in which one Jew and one Muslim had died, Muhammad ordered the execution of an entire clan. Ubayy, despite his powerful position, was able to secure only a commutation of the sentence to banishment and confiscation of property.

The sense of triumph after Badr ended when the Meccans narrowly defeated the Muslims at the Battle of Uhud (625), in which the Prophet himself was slightly wounded. The battle was not decisive, but Muhammad's position in Medina became less secure; moreover, both sides realized that further armed conflict was inevitable.

With the Prophet now in a weakened position, his enemies, especially Ubayy and the Jews, were anxious to challenge him. Muhammad realized that he had to reassert his authority. Believing that the primary obstacle to his control was the inherent opposition of the Jewish religious view, he accused the Jews of plotting treachery against him. Muhammad and his followers besieged the Jewish clan in its fortresses, and with their own allies, including Ubayy, refusing to provide help, the Jews eventually agreed to leave Medina, taking with them everything they could carry except arms. They set out for Khaybar, a town 95 miles (153 km) from Medina, where there was a large Jewish population, and their lands were divided among the *muhajirin*, the followers of the Prophet, many of whom became landowners for the first time.

In the two years following the conflict at Uhud, both the Meccans and the Muslims tried to win the support of the Bedouin nomads of the neighboring areas. The results became evident in the spring of 627, when the Meccans, with an impressive coalition of some 10,000 men, attempted to take Medina from the north. Muhammad, with only 3,000 men, could not prudently engage in open confrontation, and his solution was to have a trench (***khandaq***) dug to prevent troops from entering the city. The attackers, who had come prepared for battle, did not have equipment or supplies for a siege or a war of attrition; after three weeks and some sporadic hostilities, they retreated. The Battle of the Khandaq established Medina as a rival force equal to Mecca, but at this point neither city was in a position to overcome the other by military power.

The final phase in the struggle between the two communities demonstrates the diplomatic skill of Muhammad, as the Prophet sought to incorporate his opponents into the *umma*, rather than seeking military victory. In 628, a truce was established with the Meccans, which permitted the Muslims to make their pilgrimage to Mecca in the following year. The pilgrimage, led by Muhammad, took place peacefully in 629, but in 630 Muhammad accused the Quraysh of breaking the treaty. Using this as a pretext, some 10,000 Muslims marched on Mecca. The Meccans surrendered, and Muhammad granted them amnesty rather than extracting vengeance. As a result, many of the defeated people accepted Muhammad as leader, converting to Islam and becoming part of the Muslim community. It is believed that the Prophet also cleansed the Ka'ba of the ancient tribal idols at this time, thereby restoring the shrine to worship of the one true God.

During the next two years, Muhammad managed to extend his authority to most of the Arabian peninsula through a combination of military victory and diplomacy. The Bedouin tribes that resisted were defeated militarily, but many communities sent delegations to establish alliances with the new leader of Mecca. A proportion of the new allies converted to Islam, although not the entire population. Representatives were sent from Medina to instruct the new converts in the tenets of the religion, and to collect the taxes due to the new ruling establishment. Those who remained Christian were obliged to pay the *jizya* or poll tax, thereby establishing a secure, if inferior, position for themselves in the new regime.

In the spring of 632 Muhammad led an expedition to the Ka'ba in Mecca, making his final pilgrimage to that holy site, during which he preached his "Farewell Sermon." His message incorporated in succinct form the basic expectations of Muslim religious practice:

> O People, listen to me in earnest. Worship Allah, say your five daily prayers, fast during the month of Ramadhan, and give your wealth in *zakat*. Perform *hajj* if you can afford to. You know that every Muslim is the brother of another Muslim. You are all equal. Nobody has superiority over any other except by piety and good action. Remember, one day you will appear before Allah and answer for your deeds. So beware, do not stray from the path of righteousness after I am gone.

Within a relatively brief period of time, study of the Qur'an and the **sunna** (or actions) of Muhammad led to the codification of these Islamic practices and beliefs, which became known as the "Five Pillars of Islam." These directives, which continue to be practiced by all Muslims today, consist of the following precepts:

> I. The initial requirement is the profession of faith, in which the Muslim believer affirms his or her faith by the repetition of the phrase, "There is no god but Allah and Muhammad is the messenger of God." It is repeated during prayer, and bears continuing witness to the Muslim belief in monotheism.

> II. Five times each day, the call to prayer (**salat**) is issued from the **minaret** of a **mosque** by the **muezzin**. The followers of Islam, either alone or in a group, face Mecca and offer their prayers. It is not necessary for them to be in a mosque; they may be anywhere—at home, at work, or traveling. Their ritual action recalls the revelation of the Qur'an and strengthens a sense of participation in a universal community of believers. The times for prayer, which were not defined in the Qur'an, were established by Muhammad.

> III. During one month of the year Muslims are expected to fast from sunrise to sunset, refraining from taking either food or drink. Known as **Ramadhan**, it is a time for spiritual renewal, and for expressing gratitude for the guidance of Allah, as well as for reflecting on and responding to the needs of the poor and hungry.

> IV. All adult Muslims are expected to pay a tax annually, which amounts to a percentage (usually 2½ percent) of their total assets. This tax, known as *zakat*, is used to support the poor, especially orphans and widows, and to advance the cause of Islam. *Zakat* is not considered to be charity, since it is not voluntary; it is regarded as a means through which the rich share their God-given wealth with those who are less fortunate.

V. The pilgrimage season occurs after Ramadhan, and every adult Muslim who can afford the cost is expected to perform the pilgrimage (*hajj*) at least once during a lifetime. The goal of the pilgrimage is the Ka'ba, which, as mentioned above, originally contained the tribal gods of the Meccans; it was cleansed by Muhammad, who restored it to the worship of the one true God, Allah.

Muhammad's final sermon emphasized two further precepts that became fundamental to the practice of Islam: strict egalitarianism within the Muslim community, and the belief in a Day of Judgment when all people will answer to Allah for their deeds.

By the time of Muhammad's death in 632, the Muslim community, or *umma*, had expanded throughout the Arabian peninsula. In the next forty years, the new religion swept through northern Africa with astonishing rapidity, bringing vast new territories under the control of Muhammad's successors. This is in strong contrast to Christianity, which, as discussed in Chapter 1, did not become a religion of state until nearly four centuries after the death of Christ.

The Spread of Islam

Following the death of Muhammad, there was a struggle to determine how the Prophet's successor was to be chosen. Three main factions vied for control. The first consisted of the early companions who had accompanied the Prophet on the *hijra*. The second group comprised the important men in Medina who had made the original pact with Muhammad. Finally, there were the members of leading Meccan families, many of whom were recent converts. A meeting was held, and it was determined that Muhammad's successor (*khalifa*, or **caliph**) would be Abu Bakr, a companion from the early days of Islam who was related to the Prophet by marriage (his daughter was one of Muhammad's wives). According to the historian Al-Tabari (839–923), two of Abu Bakr's rivals for the position withdrew from consideration, saying:

> We shall not accept this authority above you, for you are the worthiest of the emigrants and the second of the two who were in the cave and the deputy [*khalifa*] of the Prophet of God in prayer, and prayer is the noblest part of the religion of the Muslims. Who then would be fit to take precedence over you or to accept this authority above you? Stretch out your hand so that we may swear allegiance to you . . . [and] people came from every side to swear allegiance to Abu Bakr.

Abu Bakr's response set forth a program for Muslim action:

> Then Abu Bakr spoke and praised and lauded Allah as is fitting, and then he said: "O people, I have been appointed to rule over you, though I am not the best among you. If I do well, help me, and if I do ill, correct me. Truth is loyalty and falsehood is treachery; the weak among you is strong in my eyes until I get justice for him, please Allah, and the strong among you is weak in my eyes until I exact justice from him, please Allah. If any people holds back from fighting the holy war for Allah, Allah

strikes them with degradation. If weakness spreads among a people, Allah brings disaster upon all of them. Obey me as long as I obey Allah and his Prophet. And if I disobey Allah and His Prophet, you do not owe me obedience. Come to prayer, and may Allah have mercy on you."

Abu Bakr reigned from 632 to 634, and was followed as caliph by three other early companions of the Prophet: Umar ibn al-Khattab (r. 634–644), Uthman ibn Affan (r. 644–656), and Ali ibn Abi Talib (r. 656–661). This era of the first four caliphs, which was roughly contemporaneous with the rule of the Merovingians in western Europe, is known as the time of the Rashidun ("rightly guided") caliphs. Although the state was wracked with internal strife—three of the four rulers were assassinated by dissidents—it is regarded by Muslims as a formative period. During this time the fundamental tenets of the religion were established, the Islamic community was founded, and the pattern for legal process was determined. Furthermore, a common religious identity and purpose developed in the Muslim *umma*, and for believers it remains a time to be remembered and emulated; all subsequent Islamic revival and reform movements have used the doctrines and teachings of this period as a reference point. Muslims further believe that the message and purpose of Islam were validated during this era by successful geographical expansion—an expansion accomplished through astonishing military victories.

Although the caliphs were not prophets or messengers from God, an aura of holiness surrounded them, and they claimed to have religious authority. However, they also held political power, and were soon faced with dissension in the areas controlled by Islam. Initially, some of the alliances made by Muhammad threatened to dissolve, and Abu Bakr and his successors were challenged with revolt; the response of the caliph was military action undertaken to affirm his authority in the so-called wars of the **Ridda**. In the process of facing these uprisings, an army was formed, and once the revolts were subdued, the momentum of military action carried the force beyond the original borders of Islamic control into the frontier regions of the neighboring empires. By the end of the reign of the second caliph in 644, the religious–political movement of Islam had spread throughout Arabia, part of the Persian Empire, Syria, and Egypt (**Map 5**).

The rapid expansion was a result of a variety of factors. First, the Islamic Arabs were an organized army with developed military skills. Their use of camel transport provided an advantage when fighting campaigns over broad areas, and they were motivated by the promise of land and wealth. Furthermore, religious zeal inspired them with added enthusiasm. In addition, the areas they entered—the Byzantine and Persian empires—had been weakened by long wars and epidemics of plague. Moreover, Mediterranean trade had been declining since the Germanic invasions, and economic prosperity suffered as a result, further debilitating the European powers.

Another possible explanation is that many of the conquered peoples did not care whether they were ruled by Persians, Greeks, or Arabs as long as they were secure, at peace, and taxed at a reasonable rate. Furthermore, in parts of Syria and Iraq already occupied by people of Arabian descent and language, it was not difficult for the new conquerors to establish themselves.

The newly subdued areas were ruled from armed camps of Arabian soldiers. In Syria these were located in existing cities, but in Egypt and Iraq new settlements were created.

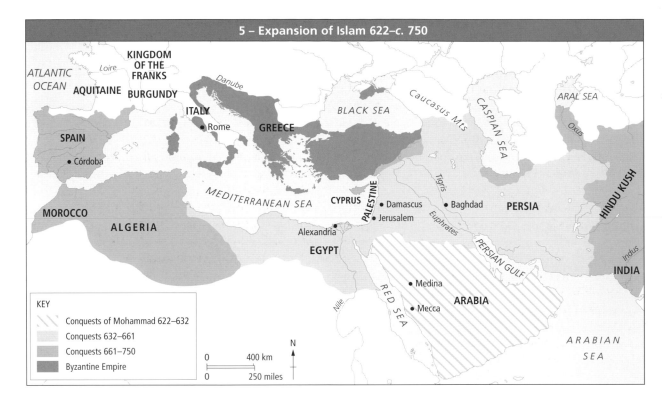

5 – Expansion of Islam 622–c. 750

KEY

- Conquests of Mohammad 622–632
- Conquests 632–661
- Conquests 661–750
- Byzantine Empire

The power and economic opportunity of these villages appealed to migrants from the rural areas and they eventually grew into cities, with the mosque, the place of public assembly for prayer, at the center.

The new rulers held power in the old areas of control, such as Medina, as well as the new camp-cities, which were linked to the older urban areas by inland routes. Some of the new ruling elite had been companions of Muhammad, but many of its leaders were drawn from the powerful Meccan families, chosen for their political and military skills. Indeed, the third caliph, Uthman ibn Affan, was a member of the Umayyad clan that had earlier opposed Muhammad.

Uthman was chosen by a new process that had been initiated by his predecessor, Umar, as he lay dying, stabbed by a Christian slave. Umar appointed a selection committee (*shura*) to choose the next caliph. The choice of Uthman was confirmed by a clasping of hands, the sign of allegiance (*baya*). Thus, a pattern of selection was established, consisting of consultation followed by the oath and symbol of allegiance.

The selection of Uthman resulted in great resentment among the family members of Muhammad, as well as in the leadership of Medina. The early companions of the Prophet recalled that Uthman's family had openly opposed Muhammad, and they resented the growing wealth, power, and prestige of Uthman's kin. It was true that Uthman also lacked the military and political skills of the first two caliphs, and this weakness ultimately led to political intrigue. In 656, Uthman was assassinated—another example of the tribal fratricides and internal rebellions that prevented stability and hampered the political development of the Muslim community.

The fourth caliph was Ali, a cousin of Muhammad who was married to his daughter, Fatima. Ali seems to have been a charismatic leader who inspired great loyalty and commitment. His supporters (**Alids**) strongly believed that succession to the caliphate should remain within the Prophet's family, and that Ali had been unlawfully deprived of his rightful inheritance by the first three caliphs. Muslims who hold this view became known as **Shi'a** (or *shiat-u-Ali*, the party of Ali), in contrast to the **Sunni**, who believe that the traditional *sunna*, or actions of the Prophet, are of primary importance in guiding the Muslim community.

The reign of Ali did not produce peace and harmony; his brief term as "Commander of the Faithful" was plagued by civil war. The first conflict was initiated by a coalition led by Muhammad's widow Aisha and the second by Muawiyah, a nephew of Uthman who was a governor of Syria. The first uprising culminated in the so-called "Battle of the Camel," which takes its name from the fact that the battle took place around a camel that Aisha was riding; Ali's forces were able to quell the revolt with ease.

Muawiyah's revolt was of more lasting consequence. Muawiyah was firmly established in Syria, holding control through his strong army. When he refused to accept Ali as successor to Uthman, the caliph led his forces into Syria in an attempt to establish his authority. The battle was inconclusive, and Muawiyah continued to govern Syria during Ali's reign, extending his control to Egypt as well. When Ali was assassinated by a dissident group in 662, Muawiyah was able to assert his own claim to the caliphate, despite the protestation of the Alids that the leader of the Muslim community should be chosen from the descendants of Muhammad.

Muawiyah's reign initiated the Umayyad caliphate, during which the capital was moved from the Arabian peninsula to Damascus, in Syria, and what had been an Arab sheikhdom was transformed into an Islamic empire. The Umayyad era, like the age of the First Four Caliphs, proved to be one of extensive territorial and economic expansion. In addition to establishing Islamic hegemony in new areas, the Umayyads also initiated patronage of art, architecture, and scholarship, ultimately providing a foundation for the sophisticated artistic and intellectual culture of the Islamic world.

The Umayyad Caliphate

The establishment of an Islamic empire that took place during the Umayyad caliphate was accomplished through a combination of religious authoritarianism and military might. By the time that Muawiyah seized the caliphate, Islam had spread throughout Egypt, Libya, the Tigris–Euphrates river valley, Syria, Iraq, Persia, Armenia, and to the borders of Afghanistan. During the Umayyad dynasty, the Muslims further extended their hegemony through northern Africa, Spain, and Portugal, and attempted to take France, where they were stopped by the forces of Charles Martel at the Battle of Tours in 732 (see Chapter 4). In the east the empire was extended as far as the Oxus (Amu) valley in present-day northern Afghanistan, and the first Muslim advances were made into northwestern India (see Map 5).

The vast new empire required a different style of government, and the Umayyad caliphs were able to meet the challenge. First of all, they saw to it that the position of caliph would be virtually hereditary. Although in theory they maintained the traditional method whereby the caliph was chosen, or at least formally recognized by the leaders of the community, the reality was that Muawiyah was succeeded by his son, who was followed by his own son. Then, after a period of civil war, the caliphate was taken over in 684 by another branch of the same family.

The Umayyads have been criticized by later generations as being dedicated to worldly concerns, as opposed to the "rightly guided" caliphs who were devoted to religion. However, the reality is probably that the Umayyad dynasty was forced by circumstance to develop a more sophisticated governance mechanism, and to make the political and moral compromises which that entailed. They gradually adopted the attitudes and policies of the Near Eastern rulers with whom they came into contact, and began to receive guests, envoys, and subjects in the ceremonial style of the Byzantine emperor, demanding absolute subjection to the royal will.

In order to maintain political control, they replaced the first, volunteer armies with paid forces, and a new elite class of society was formed from the Syrian military officers. The old Meccan and Medinan families ceased to be important and influential, and the new dynasty relied on armed force to sustain its power. The cities of Mecca and Medina, far from the seat of power in Damascus, revolted more than once, but the insurrections were quelled by the armies of the caliph. The cities in Iraq were also restive under the Umayyad yoke, and had to be controlled by governors loyal to the central government. An incident from the late seventh century (694–695), in which a new governor sent to Iraq by the Umayyad caliph addressed his subjects, clearly demonstrates the tough, uncompromising attitudes and methods of the rulers:

> By God, O people of Iraq, people of discord and dissembling and evil character! I cannot be squeezed like a fig or scared like a camel with old water skins. My powers have been tested and my experience proved, and I pursue my aim to the end. The Commander of the Faithful emptied his quiver and bit his arrows and found me the bitterest and hardest of them all. Therefore he aimed me at you. For a long time now you have been swift to sedition; you have lain in the lairs of error and have made a rule of transgression. By God, I shall strip you like bark, I shall truss you like a bundle of twigs, I shall beat you like stray camels. Indeed, you are like the people of "a village which was safe and calm, its sustenance coming in plenty from every side, and they denied the grace of God, and God let them taste the garment of hunger and of fear for what they had done" [Qur'an, 16: 112]. By God, what I promise, I fulfill; what I purpose, I accomplish; what I measure, I cut off. Enough of these gatherings and this gossip and "he said" and "it is said!" I swear by God that you will keep strictly to the true path, or I shall punish every man of you in his body. If after three days I find any member of Muhallab's expedition, I shall shed his blood and seize his possessions."

Coupled with intimidation and armed power was the financial administration, which continued as before. Secretaries and tax collectors were drawn from among the people who had served previous rulers. At first these officials used the Greek language in the western part of the empire, and Pahlavi in the east. In the 690s, the language of governance was changed to Arabic, and a new style of coinage—carrying Arabic words rather than human portraits—was introduced.

The governors sent by the Ummayad caliph established themselves in the cities and on crown lands in the countryside, maintaining the systems of irrigation and cultivation they encountered there. Huge palaces were built and decorated in the style of the Near Eastern rulers they replaced, with impressive audience halls, mosaic floors, and sculptured entrances.

Even more significant was the creation of great monumental buildings, beginning with the Dome of the Rock in Jerusalem. Completed in 691 after a turbulent decade in which the Umayyad caliphate had briefly lost control of the **Hijaz** (the region including Mecca and Medina), the building asserted clearly that Islam was a distinct and powerful religion. Some scholars have suggested that it was a victory monument designed to proclaim the power of the Umayyads, while others see it as a purely religious shrine, intended to supplement, or even supplant, Mecca as the most important goal for pilgrimage. The dome was built on the site of the ancient Temple of Solomon in Jerusalem, sacred to Jews, which had been destroyed by the Romans in AD 70 during the reign of the emperor Titus. The site, shunned by Christians and Jews alike since that time, had become a Muslim *haram*, or holy site. The building contained an ambulatory for pilgrims around the rock where Adam was created, and where, according to Jewish rabbinical tradition, Abraham was called by God to sacrifice Isaac (**figs. 19** and **20**). The rock was also believed to be the location of Muhammad's Ascent to the Seven Heavens (the "Night Journey"), a visionary voyage described in the Qur'an (*sura* 17), during which the prophet traveled from Mecca to Jerusalem and then to the throne of God, accompanied by the angel Gabriel. The choice of this site for the Dome of the Rock thus served as a symbolic link between Islam and the earlier tradition of Judaism and Christianity, while asserting its own distinct character.

To decorate the interior and exterior walls of the dome the builders used mosaic, featuring images of jeweled plants, trees, and vases. These have been variously interpreted as symbols of the victory of Islam, the Temple of Solomon, or Paradise itself.

19 and **20** The Dome of the Rock *(below left)* was built on the prominent site of the Temple of Solomon in Jerusalem. Since the location was believed by Muslims to have been the place of Muhammad's "Night Journey," it was a sacred area for adherents of Islam as well as Christians, and served to link Islam with the earlier religion. It was built on a geometric plan *(below right)*, with its domed octagon containing a double ambulatory that functions as a passageway for pilgrims.

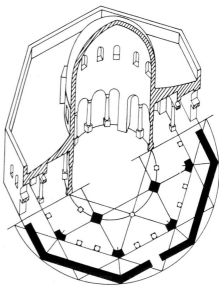

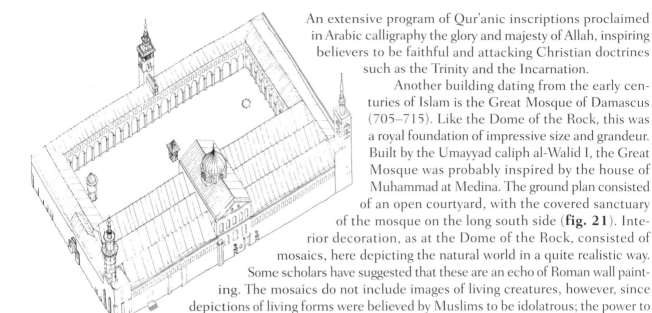

An extensive program of Qur'anic inscriptions proclaimed in Arabic calligraphy the glory and majesty of Allah, inspiring believers to be faithful and attacking Christian doctrines such as the Trinity and the Incarnation.

Another building dating from the early centuries of Islam is the Great Mosque of Damascus (705–715). Like the Dome of the Rock, this was a royal foundation of impressive size and grandeur. Built by the Umayyad caliph al-Walid I, the Great Mosque was probably inspired by the house of Muhammad at Medina. The ground plan consisted of an open courtyard, with the covered sanctuary of the mosque on the long south side (**fig. 21**). Interior decoration, as at the Dome of the Rock, consisted of mosaics, here depicting the natural world in a quite realistic way. Some scholars have suggested that these are an echo of Roman wall painting. The mosaics do not include images of living creatures, however, since depictions of living forms were believed by Muslims to be idolatrous; the power to create life belonged to Allah alone.

21 This isometric drawing of the Great Mosque at Damascus (constructed 705–715) shows the open courtyard and covered sanctuary on the long south side. The house of Muhammad at Medina may have inspired the plan for this building, the grandeur of which reinforced the political and religious strength of the Umayyad caliphate.

Buildings such as the Dome of the Rock and the Great Mosque at Damascus were a testament to the power of the Umayyads, but the growing size and strength of the Muslim community ultimately proved to be more than the ruling dynasty could control. Syria, the Umayyads' primary base of operations, was weak in comparison with the rapidly developing area of Iraq, with its new cities and burgeoning wealth. Whereas the cities of Syria were old establishments with a non-Arabic heritage and tradition, the cities of Iraq were more fully Arabic, and attracted immigrants from Iran and the Arabian peninsula. A new and powerful class arose in this area that was later able successfully to challenge the ruling dynasty.

Another factor that contributed to the disintegration of the Umayyad dynasty seems to have been poor leadership. In discussing the late Umayyad rulers, the historian Al-Masudi observed:

Abd al-Malik was a tyrant who took no thought of what he did. Sulayman cared only for his belly and his private parts. Umar ibn Abd al-Aziz was a one-eyed man among the blind. The best man of that family was Hisham. The Umayyads kept a firm grip on the authority that had been prepared for them, containing it, defending it, and preserving what God had given them, while keeping to the highest and rejecting the lowest of things. This continued until their authority passed to their pampered sons, whose only care was the pursuit of passion and the quest for pleasure in those things which are forbidden by Almighty God, unaware of God's stealthy retribution and lulled by His cunning. So they discarded the preservation of the Caliphate, made light of the right of Almighty God and the duties of sovereignty, and became too feeble to govern. Then God deprived them of power, covered them with shame, and withdrew His grace from them.

Weak leadership was compounded by internal dissent, especially among those who viewed the Umayyad policies as being contrary to the egalitarian principles of the Islamic faith. One of the most important areas of contention was the practice of taxation. Arab Muslims were given special tax privileges, and were exempted from the higher taxes paid by non-Arab Muslims (**mawali**) and non-Muslims. These policies created great resentment, especially among the *mawali*, and became another contributing factor to the fall of the Umayyad dynasty.

By the eighth century, the sentiment against the Umayyad rulers was growing in intensity. In addition to the discontent among the wealthy families of Mecca, Medina, and Iraq, who resented the privileged status of the Syrian aristocracy, the old dissenting groups, such as the *Shi'a*, who supported the descendants of Muhammad, were actively criticizing the Umayyads. Further, pious Muslims, both Arab and non-Arab, saw the lavish and luxurious lifestyle of the caliph as being contrary to the fundamental, established way of life taught and exemplified by the Prophet. Reformers called for a return to the purity described by the Qur'an and practiced by Muhammad and the early *umma* in Medina.

This opposition movement gained momentum, and in 750, with substantial *Shi'a* support, Abu al-Abbas, a descendant of the Prophet's uncle al-Abbas, was proclaimed caliph. His assumption of the throne initiated the Abbasid dynasty, which lasted until 1258, though its effective rule ended before that date. The Abbasids moved the capital to Baghdad, known in Arabic as the "City of Peace," and a new era of strong, centralized government and great economic prosperity began. Before turning to the accomplishments of the Abbasid dynasty, however, it is important to discuss one of the great events of the Umayyad era: the Islamic conquest of Spain.

Islamic Spain

The Islamic conquest of Spain occurred with astonishing rapidity between 711 and 716. During that time, in the course of a few poorly coordinated expeditions, it seems that a relatively small force of Muslim soldiers, perhaps as few as 25,000 in all, was able to conquer all of the Spanish peninsula, with the exception of the most mountainous northern areas. For generations, the reigning Visigothic monarchy in Spain had been weakened through family rivalries, and it now proved unable to resist the Muslim onslaught. According to one legendary account, the invaders, under their leader Tariq ibn Ziyad, were actually invited into Spain by Aquila, a rival claimant to the throne. Tariq was a general serving Musa ibn Musayr, the Muslim conqueror of Morocco, who sent Tariq to Spain with a small army. There, supported by persecuted Jews and some members of the Christian aristocracy, he defeated the Visigothic king Rodrigo in 711. The Muslims used terror tactics, as well as more traditional methods of war. One example, related by the eastern Arabic chronicler Ibn Abd al-Hakam, gives the following account of the Muslim journey to the Iberian peninsula:

> Tariq set out on his way. With his men, he crossed a bridge which led from the
> mountain to a village called Qartajanna [Carteia]. Then, advancing towards Córdoba,
> he passed near an island in the sea . . . When the Muslims landed on this island,

they found some wine growers and no one else. They made them prisoners. Then they picked on one of the wine growers, killed him, cut him to pieces, and cooked him while his surviving companions watched. Now the Muslims had already prepared meat in other pots. When this meat was ready, they threw away the cooked human flesh unbeknown to the Spaniards, and substituted and ate the meat which they had previously cooked. The surviving wine growers saw this and had no doubt but that they were eating the flesh of their friend. Then they released them, and they told the Spaniards that they ate human flesh and told them what had happened to the wine grower.

Although the gruesome details of such stories no doubt spread quickly, when Tariq had crossed the straits of Gibraltar, his meager forces were met by the army of Córdoba, whose members were encouraged when they saw the limited size of Tariq's retinue. They engaged in battle, but after a fierce fight the Córdobans fled. Tariq pursued them, killing them as he overtook them, all the way to Córdoba.

Rodrigo, the Visigothic king of Toledo, heard about the defeat and led an army against the invaders. They fought fiercely, and, according to Arabic chronicles, "Almighty God caused Rodrigo and his men to perish." Tariq then proceeded to Toledo, which he entered. The chronicler recounts that Tariq's immediate concern was to find a table that had belonged to Solomon, the son of David, "according to what the People of the Book claim." Tariq was given the table by a nephew of Rodrigo:

It was adorned with gold and jewels, the like of which had never been seen. Tariq tore off one of the legs, with its gold and jewels [apparently to keep it for himself when the booty was given to Musa, his commander], and put another leg in its place. This table, because of its jewels, was assessed at 200,000 dinars. Tariq seized whatever there was of jewels, arms, gold, silver, and vessels, as well as other property, the like of which has never been seen. Having put all this together, he went to Córdoba and stayed there. He wrote to Musa ibn Musayr, informing him of the conquest of Spain and of the booty he had gathered.

These reports of rich rewards encouraged many more Muslims to go to Spain. Although the accounts of treasure are no doubt exaggerated, they are numerous, and tell of circumstances such as one in which the soldiers broke into a treasure house "and were flooded with topaz and rubies such as they had never seen before."

In Spain the Muslim invaders encountered a population that had been, for the most part, Romanized and Christianized. The earliest royal convert to Christianity, the Visigothic king Recared, had accepted Arian Christianity in 587 (see Chapter 2). Although the country had officially been converted to the Athanasian form of Christianity during the seventh century, the influence of Arian thought remained prominent, because it was associated with the national heritage of the Visigoths.

Several factors contributed to the seemingly widespread acceptance of Muslim rule. First, the governance structure of the Visigoths had been weakened through its dependence on the administrative organization supplied by the bishops and church councils. This administration, however, was driven by the personal ambitions of its members, quite apart from those of the Visigothic rulers. Another divisive factor seems to have been the increased persecution of the Jews that occurred at this time; since the Jews formed a major part of the merchant and artisan classes, their economic influence was significant. Further, neither the urban nor the rural population felt great loyalty either to a united monarchy or a strongly unified religion.

The new rulers made little attempt to alter the existing society, either politically or religiously. The lands of the supporters of the defeated King Rodrigo were expropriated and distributed to the Islamic war chieftains, but members of the Visigothic aristocracy who had supported the Muslim invasion were allowed to retain their estates. The Muslims did not make changes in the style of agriculture and seem to have appeased the local population by making improvements in sharecropping. Since the Hispano-Roman towns, although in a state of relative decay, were more prosperous than those of North Africa, they were encouraged to continue their economic enterprises. And there seems to have been little direct attempt, either through proselytizing propaganda or force, to convert the population to Islam. Furthermore, the Muslim leaders were specifically tolerant of all "People of the Book," (Christians and Jews), whose religions were viewed as forerunners of the revelation of Muhammad.

Christians residing in the area of Spain controlled by the Muslims—known as *al-Andalus*, now Andalucía—began to adopt the customs and habits of their rulers, imitating them in dress and in some elements of language. Some Christian women veiled their faces in public, and many Christians ceased to eat pork, no longer raising pigs. The Christians also grew fond of Arabic literature and music, and Christian scholars eventually began to write in Arabic, rather than Latin. This period of peaceful coexistence did not endure, however, as more militant Muslims gained control in Spain.

The Islamic conquerors were not a united group. They were made up of warriors from the Arabian peninsula, Syrians, and Egyptians, who were suspicious of each other, and none of them could trust their armies, which were largely made up of Berbers from North Africa. As a result, the era immediately following the conquest was fraught with conflict between the numerous war leaders, and a fierce spirit of local autonomy developed in the various areas of control. Between 732 and 755, no fewer than twenty-three governors of Spain were appointed by the caliph.

The demise of the Umayyad caliphate and the establishment of the Abbasids led indirectly to a somewhat more stable political system in Spain. In 756 Abd-al-Rahman I, a young Umayyad prince, or **emir**, who had managed to survive when the rest of his family in Syria was slaughtered in the Abbasid uprising, sought refuge in Spain. The prince must have had great personal charisma and political skill; by promising virtual independence from the Abbasid caliph to various factions, he was able to establish the **emirate** of Córdoba, a regional province of the caliphate, under the virtually independent control of the Umayyads. In the tenth century it became an autonomous caliphate. Abd-al-Rahman chose the city of Córdoba, in the center of Andalusia, as his capital because of its geographical advantages, but perhaps also because relatively few Christians lived there.

Abd-al-Rahman was able to establish a central administration that lasted for two and a half centuries, despite many local revolts during his reign. When he died in 788, the emirate extended throughout eastern Spain south of the Pyrenees (with the exception of Navarre). It also included all the western land to the south of the Duero River

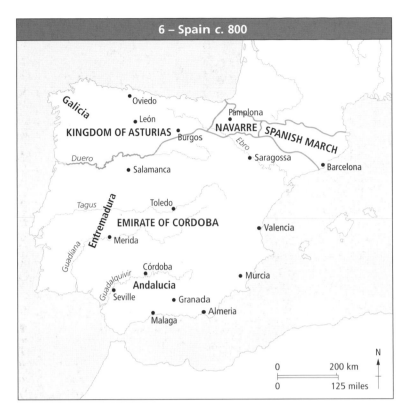

6 – Spain c. 800

Galicia
Oviedo
León
KINGDOM OF ASTURIAS
Burgos
Pamplona
NAVARRE
SPANISH MARCH
Ebro
Saragossa
Barcelona
Duero
Salamanca
Tagus
Toledo
Entremadura
EMIRATE OF CORDOBA
Valencia
Merida
Guadiana
Córdoba
Guadalquivir
Andalucia
Murcia
Seville
Granada
Malaga
Almeria

0   200 km
0   125 miles
N

(**Map 6**). He extended toleration to the various religious and ethnic groups in his realm, and attempted to make peace with those who had been in power before his arrival in Spain. When necessary, however, he demonstrated that he could be ruthless in dealing with his enemies. In 763, for example, when an attempt at conciliation with some Abbasid rebels failed, he sent the salted and camphored heads of the executed leaders to the caliph in Damascus, who responded that he was grateful for the broad expanse of sea between Syria and Spain.

Abd-al-Rahman was able to establish a large professional army, drawn from Berbers from North Africa and Slavs from eastern Europe, and led by Syrian and Berber officers. His economic measures served to reinforce his independence from Damascus, since he coined his own dinars and used a system of weights and measures based on the old Roman practice. Although trade statistics from his reign do not exist, the importance of his commercial dealings with Europeans is reflected in the fact that the Carolingian financial reform undertaken by Charlemagne to standardize currency was based on a coin weighing exactly half the Córdoban dinar.

Abd-al-Rahman I was instrumental in initiating the building of the Great Mosque at Córdoba (784), which within a year had the capacity to contain a congregation of 5,500. Over the next 300 years the mosque was enlarged, ultimately being converted into a cathedral in the sixteenth century, after the Muslims had been expelled from Spain (see Chapter 7). The interior of the building consists of more than 500 double-tiered columns, which originally supported a wooden roof. There are horseshoe-shaped arches spanning the spaces between the pillars, which were constructed from alternating wedges of white marble and red sandstone (**fig. 22**)—a typically Moorish technique. The ground plan (**fig. 22a**) shows an "unfocused" interior, quite unlike the plan of an early Christian basilica, in which the worshiper is directed visually and physically from the basilica entrance to the altar—from sin to salvation. Mosques are essentially places for prayer, with the **_mihrab_** (niche) indicating the _qibla_ (direction of Mecca), whereas basilicas developed as an architectural response to the complex needs of the Christian liturgy.

From the time of the Muslim conquest until the end of the eighth century, Christian rule was confined to two small areas in the north of Spain: a rural kingdom in the Asturian mountains, and a Basque kingdom near to Pamplona. These kingdoms were ruled by war chieftains, without an established administration or army. The Carolingian monarchy in France attempted to extend its authority across the Pyrenees in 778, but the

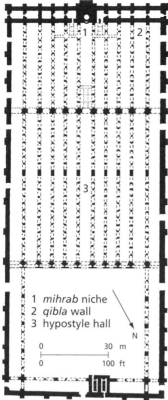

1 *mihrab* niche
2 *qibla* wall
3 hypostyle hall

N

| 0 | | 30 m |
| 0 | | 100 ft |

expedition proved to be a disaster (see Chapter 4). During the following two decades the Franks were able to establish small domains in the valleys of the Pyrenees, creating an area of control known as the Spanish March, but most of Spain and Portugal remained under Muslim control (see Map 6).

The emirate (after 929 renamed the caliphate) of Córdoba was the dominant society of Spain during the Middle Ages. It was characterized by great economic prosperity, which was fueled by successful agriculture, industry, and trade. The government was ably administered, and the regime was known for its religious and racial tolerance. The emirs, and after them the caliphs, were great patrons of art and scholarship, and the culture they fostered was one of the most vibrant of the High Middle Ages (see Chapter 9).

The Early Centuries of the Abbasid Dynasty

As mentioned above, the Umayyad dynasty was replaced in 750 by the Abbasids—descendants of the Prophet's uncle, al-Abbas (see p. 90). The first Abbasid caliph, Abu al-Abbas, whose reign was contemporaneous with that of Pepin the Short in western Europe (see Chapter 4), soon demonstrated that he could be as ruthless and determined as any of his predecessors. He began his reign by executing his opponents as well as his *Shi'a* supporters, who he believed were growing too powerful. In the process

22 The ground plan (*above right*) of the Great Mosque at Córdoba (constructed 784–787, with additions in 832–848, 961, and 987) demonstrates a path for worship that is not directional, unlike the groundplan of an early Christian basilica. The forest of columns and colored arches (*above left*) emphasizes the unfocused nature of the interior of the mosque. As in all mosques, however, the location of the *mihrab* (niche) and the *qibla* wall are prominent.

he earned the title "the blood shedder" (*al-Saffah*)—in fact, he is known in history as Abu al-Saffah. His betrayal of the *Shi'a* served to alienate them further from the traditional *Sunni* majority, thus compounding the problem of dissident activity during the reign of the Abbasids.

The rulers of the new dynasty had come to power by promising a return to the foundations of Islam, and their seizure of control and continuing reign depended on acceptance by the Islamic community. Hence, they were careful to align their government with fundamental Islamic principles. In order to achieve this goal, they became great patrons of a new religious class, the **ulama**, or religious scholars. They also contributed to the developing Muslim culture by fostering scholarship, building mosques, and establishing schools.

One of the most important contributions of the Abbasids resulted from their patronage of legal experts who developed the **sharia**, or "Body of Law." Literally "the road to the watering hole," *sharia* came to mean the divinely mandated path: the straight path of Islam, to be followed by Muslim believers. Since the Qur'an did not contain an exhaustive and specific body of prescribed laws, the necessity arose for a comprehensive and consistent science of law, or jurisprudence: the **fiqh**. The *fiqh* (literally "understanding") is the resulting discipline which sought to ascertain and interpret God's will and to apply it to all aspects of life.

The Abbasids were not, however, committed to a return to the simple lifestyle of the early Muslims. Deeply influenced by the ritualistic court practices and concepts of power held by the Persian rulers, the Abbasid caliphs emphasized the theoretical premise of their divine right to rule. The title "Deputy of the Prophet" was changed to "Deputy of God," and another designation for the Abbasid rulers, borrowed from Persian practice, was "Shadow of God on Earth." The caliph's exalted status was proclaimed by magnificent residences, vast retinues of attendants, and a court etiquette that demanded that subjects bow before the caliph and kiss the ground.

Non-Arab influence was also evident in changes in the previously Syrian-dominated military, as powerful Persians became leaders in a new salaried army and bureaucracy. The Abbasids proclaimed that this was a result of their adherence to principles of Islamic egalitarianism, though their actions did not match their rhetoric; obedience to royal dictate was often the result of fear, symbolized by the royal executioner, who appeared at the side of the caliph.

The Abbasids began diplomatic relations with the European powers as early as the reign of Pepin (see Chapter 4), and caliph Harun al-Rashid (r. 786–809) sent an ambassador to the court of the emperor Charlemagne in 797. Legendary accounts claim that the Carolingian ruler received sumptuous gifts from the caliph, including an elephant and a clock with an elaborate mechanism. Although there is no proof of this largesse, it is evident that the emperor and the caliph communicated; one result was the granting of a church in Jerusalem to the Latin clergy.

The success and economic prosperity of the Abbasid dynasty were achieved by trade, commerce, and agriculture, whereas the regimes of the past had prospered mainly through conquest. The caliphs were able to accumulate enormous wealth, which they used to foster a glittering cultural life, immortalized in the many works of art and literature proclaiming Islamic creativity and originality.

Islamic Culture

One of the most famous prose works of the era, *The Arabian Nights* (also known as *The Thousand and One Nights*), describes in sumptuous detail the luxurious and magical world of the caliphates. This collection of stories, which derived from Persian, Arabic, and Indian sources, consists of four categories of folk tales, namely fables, fairy tales, romances, and historical anecdotes. Some of the stories describe the reign of the exemplary caliph, Harun al-Rashid, who founded the city of Baghdad. The success and enduring popularity of the tales is due to the intrinsic fascination created by the interweaving of the extraordinary and the supernatural into the fabric of daily life.

The stories were disseminated orally before they were compiled and written down in Arabic between the eighth and tenth centuries, circulating in various manuscript copies (no longer extant) before they were finally copied in definite form during the thirteenth century. The foreword to the collection explains its purpose:

> It provides [its readers] with the opportunity to learn the art of discourse, as well as what happened to kings from the beginnings of time. This book, which I have called *The Thousand and One Nights*, abounds also with splendid biographies that teach the reader to detect deception and to protect himself from it, as well as delight and divert him whenever he is burdened with the cares of life and the ills of this world. It is the Supreme God who is the True Guide.

The tales give evidence of the rich and elegant culture created by the Abbasid caliphs, whose wealth enabled them to patronize artists and musicians as well as storytellers. The splendor of the Abbasid court was described by the historian al-Khatib al-Baghdadi in the eleventh century, in an account of the reception of an embassy from Byzantium. The envoys received an audience with the caliph, who commanded that they be shown the palace. After touring the reception halls, the courts and parks, and the treasures in the storerooms, they saw, in the Room of the Tree,

> ... a tree, standing in the midst of a great circular tank filled with clear water. The tree had eighteen branches, every branch having numerous twigs, on which sit all sorts of gold and silver birds, both large and small. Most of the branches of this tree are of silver, but some are of gold, and they spread into the air carrying leaves of different colors. The leaves of the tree move as the wind blows, while the birds pipe and sing.

Then the ambassadors were led into the presence of the caliph:

> He was arrayed in clothes . . . embroidered in gold, being seated on an ebony throne . . . to the right of the throne hung nine collars of gems . . . and to the left were the like, all of famous jewels . . .

The enormous wealth of the Abbasids was not only employed in the display of opulence of this sort. A vitally important aspect of the cultural legacy of the Abbasids was the encouragement of the Arabization of the Muslim territories, begun under the Umayyads. By the end of the ninth century, the Arabic language had displaced local languages—Syriac, Aramaic, Coptic, and Greek—in the conquered areas, and had become the language of government, law, literature, and public discourse throughout the multiethnic empire. Many scholars believe that the dominance of the Arabic language played a key role in the success of Islam, and that the use of Arabic in all dimensions of public life aided in the establishment of the new religion and new community—a community that was able to retain its identity and separateness in a society characterized by many ancient and highly evolved religious traditions.

The most significant result of this Arabization with regard to intellectual culture was the creation of centers of translation. Between the seventh and ninth centuries, important manuscripts were collected from all areas of the empire and translated into Arabic from their original languages (Sanskrit, Greek, Latin, Syriac, Coptic, and Persian). As a result, the works of Plato, Aristotle, Galen, Hippocrates, Euclid, Ptolemy, and other philosophers, scientists, and even music theorists were accessible to Muslim scholars. This translation program held great importance for the intellectual history of the west, since the Arabic translations preserved the works of the ancient world at a time when European civilization was under siege by the Magyars, Vikings, and Muslims, and many centers of scholarship were destroyed (see Chapter 4). These translations provided the conduit through which European scholars were able to rediscover the works of the ancient philosophers in the thirteenth century.

The period during which the Muslim world assimilated the cultures of conquered peoples provided the foundation for an era of exceptional artistic and intellectual creativity. The Arabic language and the Islamic faith combined with the absorption of ancient knowledge to foster innovation in many fields: philosophy and literature, science and medicine, algebra and geometry, and art and architecture. Important scholars included al-Razi (865–925), al-Farabi (878–950), who worked under the patronage of Abd al-Rahman III, ibn Sina, known as Avicenna (980–1037), and ibn Rushd, known as Averroes (1126–1198). The influence of these thinkers in the European intellectual tradition of the thirteenth century is discussed in Chapter 13.

One area of Islamic culture in which the practice of translating the ancient treatises seems to have been particularly influential is the development of music. Like the ancient Greeks, Muslim philosophers and theorists of music believed that music was one of the sciences, and that the ordering of musical sounds could be explained by mathematical principles. They adopted the Greek view of musical sounds as reflecting the music of the spheres, a concept also found in the works of the philosopher Boethius, who was active at the court of Theodoric the Ostrogoth (see Chapter 2).

In addition to theoretical principles, some of the works of the philosopher Avicenna provide information about musical performance practice in the Muslim world in the eleventh century. In courtly life, music, played on stringed instruments, flutes, and percussion, was used to accompany the singing of poetry. It also provided musical accompaniment for professional female dancers who entertained in the sumptuous palaces and private residences. A musical performance at court is described in a famous anthology, *Kitab al-aghani*, in which the ruler keeps his distance from the musicians by concealing himself behind a curtain. According to the composer of a song:

I was led into a large and splendid saloon, at the end of which there hung a gorgeous silk curtain. In the middle of the room were several seats facing the curtain, and four of these seats had already been taken by four musicians, three female and one male, with lutes in their hands. I was placed next to the man, and the command was given for the concert to commence. After these four had sung, I turned to my companion and asked him to accompany me with his instrument . . . I then sang a melody of my own composition . . . Finally the door opened; Fadl ibn Rabi cried, "The Commander of the Faithful," and Harun appeared.

Musical performances such as the one described above were associated with the worldliness of court life, and the religious men (**imams**) of Islam disapproved of its use, echoing the beliefs of some of the early leaders of the Christian Church, including Augustine (see Chapter 1). They could not disallow music entirely, however, since it was used in religious ceremony, and furthermore, the call to prayer—and indeed the Qur'an—was chanted in formal ways. They believed, however, that it was important to define the circumstances under which music might be permitted. Musical theorists and theologians ultimately decreed that music might be used to stimulate the desire

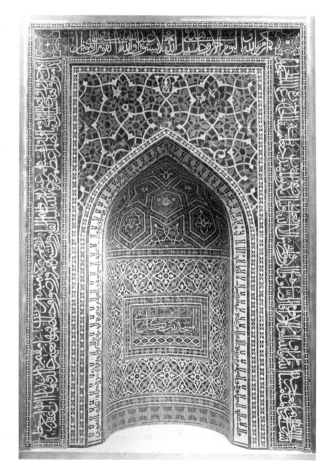

23 A mosaic *mihrab* (niche) originally from a mosque in Iran indicates the direction of Mecca. This magnificent example, several feet high, incorporates intensely colored geometric design and calligraphy that Muslims hold sacred as revealing the Word of Allah.

for a pilgrimage, or call men to war when war was legitimate, or to relieve sorrow, or to express the love of God. But, like their Christian counterparts, they believed that music should be forbidden if its style aroused the listener to temptation, or if the song was obscene or blasphemous or incited lust. Furthermore, string instruments and pipes should not be played because they were traditionally associated with drunkards and those who were effeminate.

The religious leaders of the Muslim community also held strict views concerning visual expression. Eschewing the portrayal of human and animal forms, the walls of mosques were typically covered with decoration, including designs of plants and flowers, as in the Dome of the Rock and the Great Mosque. **Fig. 23** provides a typical example, featuring a *mihrab* from Iran.

Beginning in the Umayyad dynasty, calligraphy became one of the most important Islamic arts, appearing as decoration and religious message on coins, textiles, carpets, ivories, pottery, and glassware. Calligraphy had special meaning for Muslims, who believed that Allah revealed Himself through his Word. The writing of the language was developed by calligraphers in ways that lent themselves to architectural decoration, and words were either repeated again and again or blended with plant forms or geometric figures.

The music, literature, and art of this golden age of Islamic civilization were the results of a synthesis of influences from many sources—tribal, ethnic, and religious. In assimilating these traditions, the Muslims proceeded from a sense of mission, fueled by a belief in their power and superiority. They absorbed the customs and practices of other cultures, but they did so in a controlled manner, maintaining their autonomy and identity, and avoiding the threat of political or cultural domination. Muslims look back upon this period of brilliant success as evidence of Allah's favor, and of the divine validation of their universal message and mission.

Summary

One of the most important events of the seventh century was the emergence of a third great monotheistic religion. Islam began *c.* 610 with the first of many revelations from Allah to his prophet, Muhammad. These revelations were codified and set down after Muhammad's death in the Islamic book of sacred scripture, the Qur'an. Together with Muhammad's actions and statements (his *sunna*), the Qur'an provided the basis for worship of Allah as well as directives for human behavior and interaction in the Muslim community, the *umma*.

After beginning his ministry, Muhammad met with opposition in his native city of Mecca, and when antagonism to his activities intensified, he migrated to Medina—a period in his life known as the *hijra*. When the Prophet first arrived in Medina, he led a small group of companions, the *muhajirin*. After a number of years that were characterized by struggle with the political forces of Mecca, Muhammad returned to his place of birth, now as the leader of a large contingent of believers in Islam. The religion gained adherents rapidly, and by the time of the Prophet's death in 632, much of the population of the Arabian peninsula had become Islamic.

Following Muhammad's death, there was a struggle for power among his early companions. Abu Bakr was finally selected to lead the community as caliph, or successor to the Prophet. His reign began the period known as the era of the Rashidun caliphs, which lasted from 632 to 661. During this time the territorial boundaries of countries embracing Islam grew dramatically, ultimately including much of North Africa, Syria, and Persia.

The Rashidun caliphs were followed by rulers from the Umayyad family, who established a dynasty lasting from 661 to 750. During this period, territorial expansion continued, as the Muslims conquered most of Spain and lands to the east as far as India. The Umayyads, in addition to establishing strong governmental control throughout their realm, became great patrons of art, architecture, and scholarship.

Weakened by internal dissension and ineffective leadership, however, the Umayyad caliphate gave way in 750 to the Abbasid dynasty. Building on the economic, political, and cultural foundations inherited from the previous rulers, the new caliphs strengthened the financial base of the empire through expanded trade and industry. They used the resulting wealth to further the process of Arabization of the Muslim world that the Umayyads had begun. By the year 1000, the Muslims had established a vital and vibrant society that would have significant influence on the political life and intellectual culture of the High Middle Ages.

Suggestions for Further Reading

Primary sources

There are many editions of the Qu'ran. Among them are *The Glorious Qur'an*, by Abdul Majid Daryabadi (Leicester, UK: The Islamic Foundation, 2001), and *The Holy Qur'an*, by Abdullah Yusuf Ali (Birmingham, UK: Islamic Vision, 1934, reprinted 2000). A widely available translation is Arthur J. Arberry's *The Koran Interpreted* (Oxford: Oxford University Press, 1964, reprint ed. 1983).

Islam: from the Prophet Muhammad to the Capture of Constantinople, by Bernard Lewis (2 vols., Oxford: Oxford University Press, 1987), offers a comprehensive collection of documents concerning Islamic history. A massive compilation of sources is presented in *Judaism, Christianity, and Islam: The Classical Texts and Their Interpretation*, by F.E. Peters (Princeton: Princeton University Press, 1990). The selections are organized topically, comparing the teachings of the three religions concerning specific issues.

Secondary sources

The Oxford History of Islam, by John Esposito (Oxford: Oxford University Press, 1999), offers a comprehensive study of Islamic civilization. A concise work by the same author, *Islam: The Straight Path* (Oxford: Oxford University Press, 1988), provides an excellent introduction. Part I of *The Cambridge History of Islam*, edited by P.M. Holt, Ann K.S. Lambton, and Bernard Lewis (Cambridge: Cambridge University Press, 1970), provides several articles pertaining to the subject of this chapter. Albert Hourani's *A History of the Arab Peoples* (Cambridge: Harvard University Press, 1991) is a fine survey of the Islamic world.

Two excellent studies of early Islam are *The Prophet and the Age of the Caliphates*, by Hugh Kennedy (London: Longman, 1986), and *Muhammad and the Origins of Islam*, by F.E. Peters (Ithaca, NY: State University of New York, 1994). The latter uses many quotations from primary sources to support the narrative. The first conquests of the Muslims are analyzed in the detailed but highly readable work by Fred McGraw Donner, *The Early Islamic Conquests* (Princeton: Princeton University Press, 1981).

Loyalty and Leadership in an Early Islamic Society, by Roy P. Mottahedeh (Princeton: Princeton University Press, 1980), is a detailed study of the social structure of western Iran and southern Iraq in the tenth and eleventh centuries. A number of helpful articles concerning Muslim politics and society by W. Montgomery Watt have been collected in *Early Islam* (Edinburgh: Edinburgh University Press, 1990). *Byzantium and the Early Islamic Conquests*, by Walter E. Kaegi (Cambridge: Cambridge University Press, 1992), is a detailed study of the military incursions of the Muslims into Byzantine territory.

A splendidly illustrated collection of articles is contained in *The World of Islam: Faith, People, Culture*, edited by Bernard Lewis (London: Thames and Hudson, 1976, reprint ed. 1992). The subjects range from political analysis to religion, art, literature, and music. Islamic art is the subject of two fine surveys: *Islamic Art and Architecture*, by Robert Hillenbrand (London: Thames and Hudson, 1999), and *Islamic Art*, by Barbara Brend (Cambridge, MA: Harvard University Press, 1980). The intellectual life of the Islamic world is analyzed in Charles M. Stanton's *Higher Learning in Islam: The Classical Period, 700 AD to 1300 AD* (Langham, MD: Rowman and Littlefield, 1990).

Children of Abraham: Judaism/Christianity/Islam, by F.E. Peters (Princeton: Princeton University Press, 1982), is an interesting comparative study of the three religions. Richard A. Fletcher's *Moorish Spain* (London: Weidenfeld and Nicolson, 1992) provides a readable overview of the history of the Muslims in Spain from 711 through the final expulsion in the fifteenth century.

Women in the Qur'an: Traditions and Interpretation (Oxford: Oxford University Press, 1994) offers information concerning women in the Muslim world. See also *Writing the Feminine: Women in Arab Sources*, edited by Manuel Marin and Randi Deguilhem (London: I.B. Tauris, 2002).

4 THE CAROLINGIAN EMPIRE

UILDING ON THE ACHIEVEMENTS of the earlier Frankish kings, most notably Clovis and the early Merovingian dynasty, the rulers of the Carolingian dynasty (the name derives from the large number of family members who bore the name Charles, most notably Charlemagne) extended their power and authority throughout western Europe in the eighth and ninth centuries, establishing a new western empire that scholars frequently identify as the "First Europe." In addition to consolidating their territorial control, the Carolingians also continued to solidify the close relationship with the papacy and the western church initiated by Clovis—a relationship symbolized by the coronation of Charlemagne as Holy Roman Emperor by Pope Leo III on Christmas Day, 800. A further accomplishment of the Carolingians was the patronage of a cultural and educational program, often referred to as the "Carolingian Renaissance." This movement was significant both for its preservation of the Classical past and its intellectual and artistic contribution to the cultural life of the following centuries. Although the empire dissolved within three decades of Charlemagne's death, the religious and cultural institutions and trends established during his reign endured in the following centuries, providing a basic foundation for the development of medieval civilization, despite the disruptive invasions of the Vikings and other groups in the ninth century.

The Rise of the Mayor of the Palace

During the seventh century, the power of the Merovingian kings waned significantly. Their policies of dividing the realm among the successors to the throne and of parceling out lands to their supporters had severely weakened their control. As a result, the members of the regional nobility had increased their power, to the detriment of the monarch, and real authority now lay with an official known as the Mayor of the Palace, who had made the office hereditary in his own family. As Charlemagne's contemporaneous biographer Einhard remarked, looking back at the previous era, "All that was left to the [Merovingian] King was that . . . he should sit on the throne, with his hair long and his beard flowing," enjoying the royal title and acting the part of the ruler. Although Einhard was guilty of painting the Merovingians as do-nothing kings in order to enhance the glory of Charlemagne, there is much truth in his statement that "Beyond this empty title of King, and a precarious living wage which the Mayor of the Palace allowed him at his own discretion, the King possessed nothing at all of his own, except a single estate with an extremely small revenue." The Mayor of the Palace "took responsibility for the administration of the realm and all matters which had to be done or planned at home or abroad." The lack of a royal title did not disturb one celebrated holder of the office, Charles Martel (c. 688–741), who had inherited it from his father, Pepin of Héristal, in 714.

Martel's most famous, though historically controversial, action was his military leadership in halting the northward advance of the Muslims at the Battle of Tours/Poitiers in 732/33. Responding to a request from the Duke of Aquitaine for help against the invaders, Martel amassed a formidable army, and was able to crush the Muslim forces. Although some historians have questioned the importance of this battle, recent scholars have pointed out that Martel's achievement in blocking the Muslim advance was a necessary step towards accomplishing his long-term objectives. It is important to note that he did not take advantage of his victory at Tours to lead his troops into Spain in search of rich plunder, and this restraint reveals his dedication to the strategic aim of establishing control over the kingdom of the Franks.

In addition to protecting the realm against Muslim incursions, Charles Martel strengthened the office of Mayor of the Palace and added to the territory under his authority by imposing his own rule on provinces that the weak Merovingian kings were no longer able to govern. When the Merovingian king Theodoric IV died in 737, Martel went on ruling as Mayor of the Palace until his death in 741 without bothering to find a new king. However, Martel's son Pepin the Short (c. 714–768) was troubled by the situation and he found a distant relative of the late king, whom he placed on the throne as King Childeric. After this situation proved impractical, since the man who wore the crown had no authority, and real control was in the hands of the Mayor of the Palace, Pepin decided that he himself should ascend the throne in place of Childeric. It was necessary, however, for Pepin to obtain divine sanction for the new royal line in order to effect a secure transfer of authority. Hence, in 751 he sent two emissaries to Pope Zachary to inquire whether one man should bear the title of king while another actually ruled. According to a contemporary chronicle,

> Pope Zachary replied that it was better for the man who had power to be called king rather than one who remained without royal power, and, to avoid a disturbance of the right ordering of things, he commanded by apostolic authority that Pepin should become king.

Therefore, Zachary named Pepin king of the Franks and sent his emissary, Boniface, to anoint him, thus granting divine sanction to the new monarch. The pope had his own motives for supporting Pepin's claim to the throne. He was seeking a powerful ally whom he could enlist to support him against the Byzantines and the Lombards, who had been contending for political supremacy in Italy. So, in 754, the pope himself traveled to the kingdom of the Franks to crown and anoint Pepin in person at the royal monastery of St. Denis, thus reinforcing the spiritual authority of the new Carolingian monarchy. In the same year, Zachary asked for Pepin's direct intervention against the Lombards.

The king of the Franks obliged by leading his armies into Italy, where he defeated the Lombards and then granted a large portion of central Italy to the papacy. This so-called "Donation of Pepin" was of lasting historical significance. Not only did it rid the pope of the Lombard threat, but the grant of land also formed the nucleus of what later became the Papal States, an area that retained political influence well into the nineteenth century.

Pepin ruled for another fourteen years, during which time he continued to protect Aquitaine from the Muslims and added to the possessions of the Frankish realm. When he died in 768, he bequeathed a strong and powerful kingdom to his two sons, Charles and Carloman. The brothers ruled together, none too happily it would appear, until Carloman died in 771. Charles, known in history as Charles the Great, or Charlemagne (r. 768–814), then ignored the rights of Carloman's infant son and quickly took possession of the entire Frankish kingdom.

Charlemagne and the Creation of the Empire

Charlemagne's biographer, Einhard, patterned his *Life of Charlemagne* after *Lives of the Caesars* by the Classical Roman historian Suetonius (in particular the "Life of Augustus") as well as the orations of Cicero, and he presumably used these models to present the emperor in glowing terms. Scholars have engaged in extensive debate concerning the date of the work, which was written ten to fifteen years after Charlemagne's death in 814, and they have pointed out various references to the reign of Charlemagne's son Louis the Pious (r. 814–840), which no doubt influenced the tone of the biography.

Many of the facts presented by Einhard do not agree with events as we now know them, perhaps a product of hazy memory or lack of archival sources. Furthermore, some recent historians have seen his work as being responsible for creating an impression of Charlemagne that is merely a figment of unrealistic hero worship; he became a figurehead, whose image was proclaimed as a unifying force by generations of Europeans. These scholars prefer to view Charlemagne as a product of his age, rather than a personality who shaped the destiny of an empire. Nonetheless, Einhard's biography provides a rich portrait of Charlemagne, which remains a fascinating, if controversial, account of his court and reign.

According to Einhard, Charlemagne was "strong and well built . . . tall in stature . . . and he always appeared masterful and dignified." He loved the outdoors, and spent much of his time hunting and riding horseback. He ate and drank moderately, and "hated to see drunkenness in any man, and even more so in himself and his friends." The emperor "practiced the Christian religion with great devotion and piety," and "went to church morning and evening with great regularity, and also for early morning Mass, and the late-night hours." He was, however, aggressive and ambitious, and determined to achieve his own ends, even when ruthless action was required. Although some recent historians have viewed his accomplishments as mere "logical conclusions" to the territorial expansion and religious consolidation of the reigns of his father and grandfather, Charlemagne's role as a military leader was remarkably influential, as was his devotion to the cultural advancement of his realm. Even more important was his vision of the Christian mission entrusted to him; he was determined to convert those of his subjects who were still heathens and to establish a vast Christian realm (**fig. 24**).

Charlemagne's most significant achievement was the creation of the empire. Beginning with the lands of his inheritance, he expanded the Frankish holdings in all directions (**Map 7**). By the end of his reign, the Franks controlled all of western Europe with the exception of the British Isles, most of Spain, and southern Italy. Following Charlemagne's coronation in 800, this initially loose confederation was known as the Holy Roman Empire. As Einhard recounted:

> These are the wars which this powerful King Charlemagne waged with such prudence and success in various parts of the world throughout a period of forty-seven years, that is during the whole of his reign. The Frankish kingdom which he had inherited from his father, Pepin, was already far-flung and powerful. By these wars of his he increased it to such an extent that he added to it almost as much again. Originally no more land was occupied by the Eastern Franks, as they were called, than the region of Gaul which lies between the Rhine, the Loire, the Atlantic Ocean and the sea round the Balearic Islands, together with the part of Germany which is situated between Saxony, the Danube, the Rhine and the Saal, which last river divides the Thuringians and the Sorabians. To this must be added, too, the fact that the Alemanni and the Bavarians formed part of the Frankish kingdom. By the campaigns which I have described, Charlemagne annexed Aquitaine, Gascony, the whole mountain range of the Pyrenees, and land stretching as far south as the River Ebro, which rises in Navarre, flows through the most fertile plains of Spain and then enters the Balearic Sea beneath the walls of the city of Tortosa. He added the whole of Italy, which stretches for a thousand miles and more in length from Aosta to southern Calabria, at the point where the frontiers between the Greeks and the men of Benevento are to be found. To this he joined Saxony, which forms a very considerable part of Germany and is considered to be twice as wide as the territory occupied by the Franks, while it is just about as long; then both provinces of Pannonia, the part of Dacia which is beyond the Danube, Istria, Liburnia, and Dalmatia, with the exception of its maritime cities, which Charlemagne allowed the Emperor of Constantinople to keep, in view of his friendship with him and the treaty which he had made. Finally he tamed and forced to pay tribute all the wild and barbarous nations which inhabit Germany between the rivers Rhine and Vistula, the Atlantic Ocean and the Danube, peoples who are almost identical in their language, although they differ greatly in habit and customs. Among these last the most notable are the Welatabi, the Sorabians, the Abodrites, and the Bohemians, against all of whom he waged war; the others, by far the greater number, surrendered without a struggle.

24 Albrecht Dürer painted this portrait of Charlemagne in the late fifteenth century, long after the emperor's death. It preserves the belief in Charlemagne's mission as a powerful Christian emperor, depicting him with a cross on his crown and on the orb in his left hand, and wielding an awe-inspiring sword. Contemporaneous images do not survive, with the possible exception of a small equestrian sculpture, although this may in fact portray a successor, rather than Charlemagne himself.

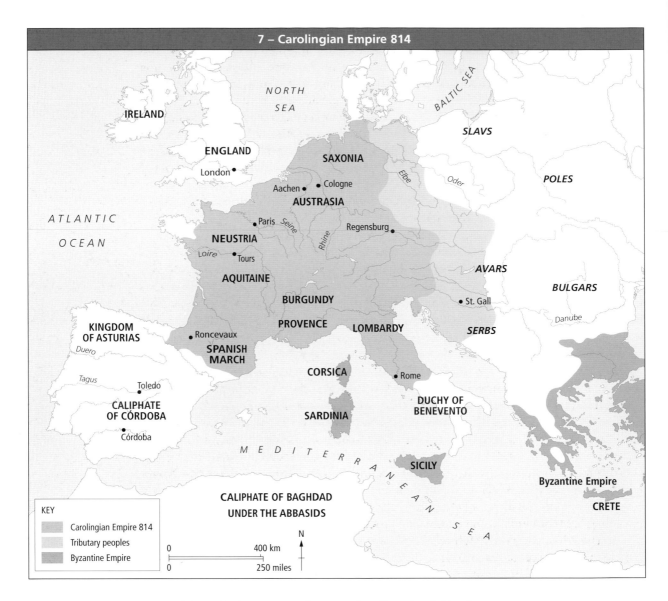

7 – Carolingian Empire 814

NORTH SEA

BALTIC SEA

IRELAND

ENGLAND

SAXONIA

SLAVS

London

Aachen • Cologne

Elbe

Oder

POLES

AUSTRASIA

ATLANTIC

OCEAN

Paris • Seine

Rhine

Regensburg

NEUSTRIA

Loire • Tours

AVARS

BULGARS

AQUITAINE

BURGUNDY

• St. Gall

Danube

PROVENCE

KINGDOM OF ASTURIAS

Duero

• Roncevaux

LOMBARDY

SERBS

SPANISH MARCH

CORSICA

• Rome

Tagus

• Toledo

CALIPHATE OF CÓRDOBA

• Córdoba

SARDINIA

DUCHY OF BENEVENTO

M E D I T E R R A N E A N

SICILY

Byzantine Empire

CRETE

CALIPHATE OF BAGHDAD
UNDER THE ABBASIDS

S E A

N

KEY

Carolingian Empire 814

Tributary peoples

Byzantine Empire

0   400 km

0   250 miles

Although this excerpt from Einhard's *Life of Charlemagne* contains inaccuracies undoubtedly designed to enhance the king's reputation (for example, he did not conquer Tortosa or Calabria and his reign was forty-six, not forty-seven years long), it is evident that Charlemagne devoted much energy to expanding his frontiers, beginning with an assault on the Lombards in 773. It had become apparent that the territory Pepin the Short had acquired in Italy was not stable, and the papal state would not be safe as long as there was a strong Lombard kingdom. Furthermore, Charlemagne's relationship with the Lombard king, Desiderius, was troubled. He and his brother Carloman had both married daughters of Desiderius, but Charlemagne had subsequently rejected his wife and taken the inheritances of her sister's children. In retaliation, Desiderius began to plot rebellions against Charlemagne with the support of some hostile Frankish nobles.

Charlemagne marched on the Lombards, captured the Lombard capital city, Pavia, and placed Desiderius in a monastery. He assumed the title of king of the Lombards, and remained the actual ruler of the Lombard state for his lifetime, although he had his son, another Pepin, crowned king of Italy in 780, probably for administrative purposes.

Charlemagne also moved to extend his control into Spain, leading his troops against the Spanish Muslims in 778. Although this campaign did not meet with notable success, Charlemagne's armies were able to establish a protective border district on the Spanish side of the Pyrenees, known as the "Spanish March." A minor incident from this campaign provided the basis for the twelfth-century epic poem, *The Song of Roland* (see Chapter 8).

Charlemagne also undertook major campaigns to solidify the eastern frontier of his empire. These required several decades, from about 772 to 804, during which time his armies conquered and assimilated Bavaria, Pannonia (present-day Hungary), and Dacia (present-day Romania), and created the border region known as the East March (Ost-mark), which became the nucleus of present-day Austria. In the 770s and 780s, Charlemagne's forces were engaged in wars against the Saxons, a fierce tribe of pagan barbarians based in an area along the western side of the River Elbe, who required his most concerted military efforts. Again and again the Saxon warriors surrendered, only to revolt as soon as the king's forces had left. Furthermore, the Saxons were stubbornly loyal to their own gods, and they frequently returned to their own religion, an offense equal to rebellion in Charlemagne's view. He was able to convert them to Christianity only through brutal coercion. For example, the *Frankish Royal Annals*, the chronicle of royal activities, tells us that he executed 4,500 Saxons on a single day. Further, another source, the *Capitulary for Saxony*, which was a legal code dealing primarily with religious misdeeds, stipulates capital sentences for persons who continued to practice their pagan religions. In 785, Widukind, the Saxon leader, finally surrendered to Charlemagne and converted to Christianity. Widukind's conversion symbolized the end of intense Saxon resistance, although several revolts had to be suppressed during the next twenty years. By 804, Frankish control of Saxony was well established and Charlemagne's efforts towards Christianization of the pagans had produced significant results.

In the 790s, the Frankish forces conquered and subjugated the Avars, a wealthy Asiatic tribe that had been terrorizing the inhabitants of the eastern section of Charlemagne's kingdom. The Franks were able to confiscate a substantial part of the Avar treasure. As Einhard remarked, "These Franks, who until then had seemed almost paupers, now discovered so much gold and silver in the [Avar] palace and captured so much precious booty in their battles, that it could rightly be maintained that they had in all justice taken from the [Avars] what these last had unjustly stolen from other nations." The plundered wealth of the Avars greatly facilitated the advancement of the kingdom, not only in military terms, but also relative to cultural development.

This brief recounting of Charlemagne's military victories does not do justice to his astonishing martial achievements. He had to muster the forces of the Frankish kingdom almost yearly, and supplying the armies during their forays along the border was extremely difficult. The fact that this could be accomplished is a tribute to Charlemagne's military skill, his intelligence, and his absolute determination to achieve his objective of creating a unified Christian realm.

Although the creation of the empire was a brilliant achievement, Charlemagne's governmental administration was perhaps an even greater accomplishment. He used all of the usual means of control, including the building of fortresses to guarantee permanent garrisons to be used against insurrections. He also depended on the Church to establish his authority, and created episcopal sees throughout the conquered lands. These sees served as missionary centers from which the clergy encouraged the creation of obedient and reliable subjects.

Charlemagne was also extraordinarily astute in his establishment of strong bonds of loyalty with the Frankish nobility. Since land was the king's greatest resource, he granted lifetime tenure of sections of the royal holdings to nobles known as **Grafen** (counts). These men functioned as military commanders, judges, provincial governors, and royal representatives. They had assistants, including viscounts and officials known as *scabini*, or *judices*, who were trained in the law. Courts were to be held by the counts every four months, and the emperor directed that at least one person who could read and write Latin must be in attendance. The counts became **vassals** of the king, and were obligated to Charlemagne through vows of **fealty**, in which they pledged loyalty and fidelity. As shown in eighth- and ninth-century documents, there was constant emphasis on personal loyalty to the king, and, indeed, this was the primary source of unity in the empire. Charlemagne, who had to rely on the loyalty of powerful local lords and their networks of clients, encouraged his counts to require the noblemen of their areas to pledge vassalage to them. This practice, as we shall see in Chapter 5, became a prominent feature of the political structure of Europe in the following centuries.

At the top of the governmental hierarchy, Charlemagne's sons were named kings of various parts of the realm. The interior areas of the empire, which tended to be peaceful, were ruled by the *Grafen* (counts), while the border regions, which required more defense, were governed by **Markgrafen** (margraves), who had more military authority than the counts (the title was taken from the German words *Mark* and *Graf*, meaning "border district" and "count," respectively). Ranked above these officials were representatives of the king who safeguarded his interests. Because there was a constant threat of intrigue on the part of many of these administrators, Charlemagne created a system whereby teams of two men, known as **missi dominici** ("messengers of the lord"), traveled the kingdom, inspecting the activities of the officials, transmitting the orders of the king, and conducting judicial **assizes**. As an extension of the royal mandate, they had authority to judge any case submitted to them. One member of the team was a clergyman, and the other was a lay noble, and the pairs were shifted to different regions on a regular basis so that no one person would repeatedly visit the same area. The system worked well during Charlemagne's reign largely because the *missi* were supported by the emperor's military power. The weaker rulers who followed him, however, were unable to control the *missi* successfully, and therefore lacked the administrative apparatus necessary to govern such a vast realm.

The different ethnic groups of the empire were allowed to live according to their own time-honored laws, although Charlemagne had these various local laws recorded in order to clarify and preserve them. This practice, which the emperor endorsed throughout his reign, did not cause problems for Charlemagne, because he possessed the military strength to maintain control. The resulting lack of cohesion, however, was naturally divisive later, when his weaker successors were attempting to preserve the unity of the empire.

In addition to the myriad local laws, Charlemagne instituted a number of new decrees that applied to everyone. These new imperial laws were known as capitularies, and the local counts were expected to register and enforce them. They dealt with many issues, including military service and the system of *missi* described above, as well as the conduct and duties of clergymen and bishops. A capitulary regarding military obligation from the year 812 demands *Of a free man summoned to the host* [that is, army]:

> Any free man whatever, who should be summoned to the host, and who should refuse to come, shall pay the full army-tax [*heribannum*], that is, 60 *solidi*. And if he cannot pay, he shall place himself in the service of the Prince, with his own person as guarantor, until such time as he shall have paid off the debt [*bannus*]. And then he shall return again to his free status. And if that man who placed himself in [the royal] service because of the army-tax should die in that service, [nevertheless] his heirs shall not lose the inheritance which belongs to them, nor their liberty, nor shall they be liable to pay army-tax.

Certain capitularies regulated the behavior of the soldiers, as, for example, *Prohibition of drinking challenges in the host*:

> Let no one in the host challenge his equal or any other man to drink. Whoever shall be found drunken in the army shall be so ostracized that he shall drink only water, until he realizes the evil he has done.

Charlemagne was determined to control the activities of the clergy as well, and he issued capitularies that referred to proper behavior for the clergy, as in this stipulation addressed *To the priests alone*:

> Priests and deacons and all who are among the clergy are prohibited from having women in their dwellings because of the suspicion this would cause; unless they be either their mother, sister, or other such women who do not give rise to suspicions.

The decrees also made clear that the clergy were to be tried in courts under the jurisdiction of the Church, as in the following capitulary, addressed to all clergy:

> It is ordered that no bishop nor any cleric without consent or written authorization of the bishops or metropolitans, presume to demand that his legal cases be brought before the royal dignity, but they ought to be examined in the common council of the bishops.

The capitularies provided a means of control for Charlemagne, who was determined to centralize and standardize the various dimensions of activity in his realm—military, religious, and intellectual. The emperor's success in accomplishing the creation and centralization of the empire was symbolized by his coronation on Christmas Day in the year 800.

The Coronation of Charlemagne

On April 25, 799, a rebellion against Pope Leo III occurred, and the pope was attacked by the citizens of Rome while he was walking in a procession. The assailers beat him brutally and imprisoned him for a time, but he escaped and fled to a palace of Charlemagne's at Paderborn, now in Germany. He appealed to the emperor for aid, and Charlemagne agreed to travel to Rome to hear the charges brought against the pope by his attackers. As Notker Balbulus ("the Stammerer," c. 840–912), a monk of the abbey of St. Gall in Switzerland thought by many to have been the author of another *Life of Charlemagne*, reported:

> Thereupon his Holiness invited the unconquered Charlemagne to come to Rome. In this he followed God's will: for, since Charlemagne was already ruler and emperor of so many people in his own right, he should now in his glory be granted the title of Emperor and Caesar Augustus by the authority of the Apostolic See. Charlemagne was always ready at a moment's notice to set out in full martial array. Although he was completely ignorant of the reason for the summons [a disingenuous statement, since Leo had requested aid directly at Paderborn] he, the head of the world, set out immediately for the city which had hitherto held that position. When the wicked people of Rome learned of his unexpected coming, they took flight and concealed themselves in various hideouts, cellars, and lurking-places just as little birds hide when they hear the voice of their master. Nowhere under heaven could they escape from his energetic and shrewd search: and they were captured and brought in chains to the cathedral of St. Peter. There Leo, this incorrupt Pope, took the gospel of our Lord Jesus Christ, held it above his head, and in the hearing not only of Charlemagne and his soldiers but also of those who had persecuted him, swore the following oath: "As I hope on the great Judgment Day to have my share in this gospel, I am guiltless of the crime of which these men have falsely accused me." Many of the prisoners begged that they might be allowed to swear on the tomb of St. Peter that they too were guiltless of the crime imputed to them. The Pope was quite aware of their dishonesty. "I beg you, unconquered servant of God," said he to Charlemagne, "not to be deceived by their cunning. They know very well that St.Peter is always willing to forgive. Look among the tombs of the martyrs for the stone on which is written the name of the thirteen-year-old boy St. Pancras. If they swear to you by his name, then you may be sure of them." What the Pope had ordered was done. A crowd of people came forward to take their oath on this stone, but some of them fell down dead and the others were seized by the Devil and went mad. Then Charlemagne in his mighty power said to his men: "Do not let one of them escape." They were all seized and condemned to a variety of deaths, or else imprisoned for life.

Notker's colorful report, written some seventy years after the event, embroiders the accepted version of the incident, which states that the pope asserted his innocence at a council of senior clergy and lay nobles, where the assembled dignitaries accepted his claim. It does, however, provide a view of the practice of oath-giving and the subsequent divine punishment, which was a potent aspect of the mental and religious conviction of the people of the Carolingian world.

Notker's account goes on to say that Charlemagne stayed in Rome for a few more days, and that, when he went to St. Peter's Basilica to worship on Christmas Day,

> The Bishop of the Apostolic See [that is, the pope] called together such people as he could from the neighboring districts and then, in their presence and that of all the unconquered comrades-in-arms of the glorious Charlemagne, who, himself, of course, expected nothing of the kind, Leo pronounced him Emperor and Defender of the Church of Rome. Charlemagne could not refuse what was offered, the more so as he believed that it was pre-ordained by God, but he did not receive his new titles with any great pleasure.

Einhard, like Notker, emphasized the modesty of the king in accepting the title of emperor: "At first he was far from wanting this. He made it clear that he would not have entered the cathedral that day at all, although it was the greatest of all the festivals of the Church, if he had known in advance what the Pope was planning to do."

Generations of scholars have devoted much energy to research and debate concerning this incident. It seems unlikely that Charlemagne was totally unaware of the pope's intentions, and it is probable that his own men arranged the coronation, as he had been in Rome with his entourage since early November. Various points have been raised in an attempt to determine the source of the action. Certainly the ritual acclamation that Charlemagne received from the assembled congregation, "To Charles Augustus, crowned by God, great and peace-giving emperor, life and victory," was well rehearsed. Further, the *Frankish Royal Annals* record that Charlemagne had been persuaded to accept the title during the preceding week by the assembled prelates and nobles who heard the case against the pope.

It is generally agreed that Charlemagne was less than enthusiastic about the new title. It did, however, enable him to assert a position of equality with the Byzantine emperor. Einhard claimed that Charlemagne overcame the jealousy on the part of the ruler in Constantinople, "by the sheer strength of his personality." However, in subsequent correspondence with the Byzantine emperor he continued to be addressed as a sub-king, while, until 813, the ruler of Constantinople was referred to as both emperor and **basileus**. Whatever the source of the action, papal or Frankish, the anointing of Charlemagne as Holy Roman Emperor symbolized the creation of a new empire, devoted to Christ and the preservation of the Christian religion. The coronation gave a sacred aura to the Carolingian monarchy, and emphasized the religious unity of purpose that characterized the relations between Church and state during the remainder of the Carolingian era and beyond.

Carolingian Society

The aristocracy

Noblemen in the Carolingian Empire were trained from boyhood to enter into ties of vassalage, and to function as officials and representatives of the emperor. Sons of aristocratic families also assumed positions of power and authority in the Church.

As discussed in Chapter 2, women in the Merovingian era had achieved considerable legal and social rights when compared to women in antiquity and primitive Germanic societies. Female roles had been expanded and women were given opportunities for personal fulfillment in a variety of ways; it seems clear, however, that the direct political and economic power of ordinary women had lessened during Charlemagne's reign.

With regard to Carolingian royal and aristocratic women, ninth-century sources indicate that the queen had the duty of managing the royal estates. She was responsible for administering the finances and domestic affairs of the kingdom in order to allow the king to pursue matters that he considered to be more crucial to the well-being of the realm. The queen was specifically endowed with this power in the capitulary *De villis*, issued by an unknown king (probably Charlemagne): "We wish that everything ordered by us or by the queen to one of our judges, or anything ordered to the ministers, seneschals [stewards], or cupbearers . . . be carried out to the last word." Thus, although female power had long been a reality in the Byzantine Empire, the Carolingians were the first in the west to give official sanction to a practice that became common: the active participation of crowned and anointed women in royal administration.

The aristocracy followed this royal pattern, and competent and trained wives were expected to administer and manage the affairs of their households. Thus, although women were never appointed to official positions such as *missi dominici*, they were often extremely influential in the economic life of the empire.

Women also had an increased opportunity for economic independence. The Germanic custom of bride purchase, in which the groom gave the family of the bride a sum of money, had begun to disappear during the Merovingian era. By the time of the Carolingians it was replaced by a practice whereby the groom endowed the bride with a "bride gift," usually a piece of land over which she held full rights. Women also had an increased share in the rights of inheritance. Although they had always been eligible to receive movable property from their own relatives or their husbands, laws established by the ninth century allowed women to inherit immovables. This increased economic power enabled women to live independent lives as widows.

Laws were also enacted to ensure that marriages would be virtually indissoluble. The position of the early Church was that divorce was possible only when the wife was guilty of adultery; infertility or illness did not provide sufficient cause. These principles had not been enforced in the centuries before the reign of Charlemagne, and, as part of his zeal in securing the support of the Church, the emperor enacted legislation that conformed to canon, or church, law. This was the beginning of a body of legislation that extended the principle of marital indissolubility to common-law marriages and betrothals. The new laws obviously increased marital stability; however, since women were offered security within the domestic structure, they may have been encouraged to pursue lives of nurturing and housekeeping rather than active political and cultural participation outside the domestic sphere.

There is strong evidence that Carolingian women were at least partially responsible for the education of their children. A well-known example is the noblewoman Dhuoda, who lived near Nimes, in southern France. She wrote a *Handbook* for her son, William, when he was sent, at age sixteen, to serve at the court of Charlemagne's grandson Charles the Bald. Dhuoda's work reflects a level of education thought by scholars to be indicative of a general literacy among women of her class in the late Carolingian world—a standard that would not be widely achieved in the following century. Her treatise is one of moral instruction, replete with the aristocratic ideals of honor, fidelity to one's lord, and Christian doctrine. In one section, "Direction on your comportment toward your lord," she counsels:

> You have Charles ["the Bald"] as your lord; you have him as lord because, as I believe, God and your father, Bernard, have chosen him for you to serve at the beginning of your career, in the flower of your youth. Remember that he comes from a great and noble lineage on both sides of his family. Serve him not only so that you please him in obvious ways, but also as one clearheaded in matters of both body and soul. Be steadfastly and completely loyal to him in all things . . . I urge you to keep this loyalty as long as you live, in your body and in your mind. For the advancement that it brings you will be of great value both to you and to those who in turn serve you. May the madness of treachery never, not once, make you offer an angry insult. May it never give rise in your heart to the idea of being disloyal to your lord. There is harsh and shameful talk about men who act in this fashion. I do not think that such will befall you or those who fight alongside you because such an attitude has never shown itself among your ancestors. It has not been seen among them, it is not seen now, and it will not be seen in the future.

Through such clear and direct advice, Dhuoda asserted her right to influence her son's moral behavior and his activity as a noble warrior. She seemed to view maternal authority as supportive of patriarchal organization, and was probably typical of the Carolingian noblewoman in this belief.

It was common for aristocratic women, especially those who had been widowed, to seek refuge in a convent. As discussed in Chapter 2, during the Merovingian and Anglo-Saxon eras women were able to participate actively in the life of the Church as strong and powerful abbesses. This tradition did not disappear entirely in the Carolingian era; Charlemagne's sister Gisela was Abbess of Chelles (near Paris) and functioned as one of his advisers. However, many laws were enacted in the Carolingian period that reinforced the idea prevalent in the early Church that "the weakness of her sex and the instability of her sex and the instability of her mind forbid that [a woman] should hold the leadership over men in teaching and preaching." Nuns and canonesses were to be strictly cloistered; they could no longer assist priests in the celebration of the Mass and the administration of the sacraments, and abbesses were placed under the direction of bishops. In the *General Capitulary* for the *missi* from 802, it was stipulated that:

> Monasteries for women shall be firmly ruled, and the women shall not be permitted to wander about at all, but they shall be guarded with all diligence, and they shall not presume to arouse litigations or strife among themselves, nor shall they dare to be disobedient or refractory in any way toward their rulers and abbesses. Where, moreover, they have a rule, let them observe it in every respect; let them not be given to fornication or drunkenness or lust, but let them live justly and soberly in every respect. And into their cloisters or monasteries let no man enter, except when the priest enters with a witness to visit the sick, or for the Mass alone; and let him immediately go forth. And let no one from another place enroll his daughter in the

congregation of the nuns without the knowledge and consideration of the bishop to whose diocese that place pertains; and the latter shall diligently inquire why she desires to remain in the holy service of God, and shall confirm her residence or profession in that place. . . . If the abbesses wish to send any nuns out of the cloisters, they shall not do this without the consent and advice of their bishops. Likewise, also, when there ought to be any ordinations or receptions in the monasteries, they shall previously discuss these fully with their bishops; and the bishops shall announce to the archbishop what seems the safer or more useful way, and with his advice they shall perform what ought to be done.

Furthermore, nuns were now forbidden to teach boys in their convents, a ruling that proved more detrimental to laymen than to laywomen. Whereas girls continued to be taught until they reached marriageable age, boys who were not entering the religious life often received no literary education at all. The young girls continued to be trained in the writings of the Classical era and the works of the Fathers of the Church (see Chapter 1).

The peasantry

There is limited surviving information about the lives of ordinary people in the Carolingian period. It seems clear, however, that they, like the women of the aristocracy, functioned primarily as parts of family units. The new laws regarding divorce were beneficial to them as well as to the elite. Such familial ties were especially important in an environment where each member was preoccupied with obtaining the necessities of life, and survival depended on the labor of each family member. The manorial records specifically list the status of each man and woman on the manor with the precise obligations owed by each person to the lord. Thus, in addition to familial responsibilities, women owed certain services to the lord.

The records indicate that one primary responsibility of peasant women, besides family duties, was the making of cloth. The capitulary *De villis* made provisions to ensure the production of household linens and clothes needed by the emperor and his retainers. Women on the royal estates worked in "women's workshops," which the capitulary specified should be "well ordered, with houses, heated rooms, and cottages; and let them be enclosed by good fences and strong doors, such that they may do our work well." The stewards were to supply women working in the *gynaeceum* (women's workshop) with "linen, wool, woad [blue dye], vermilion and madder (red dyes), wool-combs, teazles, soap, oil, vessels, and any other small items that are necessary for their work." The women worked individually or in teams, carding and washing the wool and presumably weaving it, and they were obviously dyeing the cloth. The recognized quality of their work is reflected in the fact that when he received a fine chess set and an elephant from the caliph Harun Al-Rashid, Charlemagne sent in return a cape made from vermilion-dyed Frankish wool—the finest present he could offer.

According to a "General Admonition" issued by Charlemagne in 789, women could not do textile work on Sunday, and men were also prohibited from doing "servile work" on the sabbath. Nor could they undertake "rural labors" on a Sunday—that is, cultivate vines, plow fields, plant hedges, clear woods, cut trees, quarry stones, or build houses. Also forbidden were hunting and public assemblies. They could, however, carry three cartloads of supplies for the army and, if necessary, bury the dead.

The aspirations of women in the Carolingian Empire, like those of men, were limited by class. The rights of women, however, had been strengthened within the family. The enforcement of the principle of marital indissolubility and the right to share in their patrimonial inheritance gave them a measure of personal and economic security that would endure following the collapse of the Carolingian Empire in the late ninth century.

The Carolingian Renaissance

Charlemagne was, without question, a great warrior and a consummate politician. As we have seen, he was able to consolidate his inheritance, expand his realm, and contribute to the Christianization of his empire, thereby providing a unified system that has been called, with justification, "the first Europe." Equally important, however, was Charlemagne's cultural legacy, his role in the establishment of monasteries and schools, the improvement of educational standards, and the preservation of the heritage of the Classical past.

This era of cultural activity is most often referred to as the "Carolingian Renaissance," although some scholars have disputed the accuracy of the term, on the basis that this was not a period of creative innovation. The fact remains, however, that the work of the monks and scholars supported by Charlemagne produced some 8,000 manuscripts that are still extant today. These comprise approximately 90 percent of our inheritance from the Classical literary tradition of Rome, and form the basis for most modern editions. The Carolingian Renaissance was not, however, an attempt to revive the forms and standards of antiquity. It was, rather, an attempt to recreate what the people of the Carolingian era believed to have been the golden age of early Christian Rome. Contemporaries called it a *renovatio*: that is, a renewal of education, literature, art, liturgy, calligraphy, and architecture.

Alcuin and educational reform

Because of the practical need for a literate clergy and bureaucracy, Charlemagne was devoted to the task of improving the intellectual standards of his empire. According to Einhard,

> [Charlemagne] paid the greatest attention to the Liberal Arts; and he had great respect for men who taught them, bestowing high honors upon them. When he was learning the rules of grammar he received tuition from Peter the Deacon of Pisa, who by then was an old man, but for all other subjects he was taught by Alcuin, surnamed Albinus, another Deacon, a man of the Saxon race who came from Britain and was the most learned man anywhere to be found. Under him the Emperor spent much time and effort in studying rhetoric, dialectic, and especially astrology. He applied himself to mathematics and traced the course of the stars with great attention and care. He also tried to learn to write. With this object in view he used to keep writing-tablets and notebooks under the pillows on his bed, so that he could try his hand at forming letters during his leisure moments; but, although he tried

very hard, he had begun too late in life and he made little progress. [Einhard is probably referring here to Charlemagne's efforts to master the new style of writing, Carolingian minuscule, see fig. 25.]

It is evident that Charlemagne himself was genuinely devoted to study of the Liberal Arts, and that he made every effort, under the tutelage of Alcuin, to improve his own standard of literacy and capability in mathematics. Notker, the Monk of St. Gall, describes the relationship between Charlemagne and Alcuin in the following way:

> Alcuin, a man more skilled in all branches of knowledge than any other person of modern times, was, moreover, a pupil of Bede, that priest of great learning, himself the most accomplished interpreter of the Scriptures since St. Gregory. Charlemagne received Alcuin with great kindness and kept him close at his side as long as he lived, except on the frequent occasions when he set out with his armies on mighty wars. The Emperor went so far as to have himself called Alcuin's pupil, and to call Alcuin his master. He gave Alcuin the rule of the Abbey of St. Martin, near the city of Tours, so that, when he himself was away, Alcuin could rest there and continue to instruct all those who flocked to him. His teaching bore such fruit among his pupils that the modern Gauls or Franks came to equal the Romans and the Athenians.

In addition to Alcuin, Charlemagne brought scholars from throughout Europe to his court at Aachen, near the modern German border with Belgium and the Netherlands. From Italy came the grammarian Peter of Pisa and Paul the Deacon, who wrote a history of the Lombards. Einhard, the royal biographer, was a Frank. Other scholars came from Visigothic Spain, from Ireland, and from Germany. All of them brought manuscripts from their native lands, and these volumes formed the basis for much of the systematic hand-copying that took place during the Carolingian era. Other teachers and students were attracted to Aachen by the fame of these scholars, and Charlemagne was able to provide a livelihood for them by granting bishoprics and clerical positions.

For fifteen years Alcuin conducted a school at Charlemagne's palace at Aachen, where the curriculum was based upon the Liberal Arts—the *Trivium* (grammar, rhetoric, logic) and the *Quadrivium* (music, arithmetic, geometry, and astronomy), inherited from the Roman educational system. In reality, most students, for whom it was a great challenge simply to read and write Latin properly, probably concentrated on grammar—the first subject of the *Trivium*. According to Einhard, in the palace school, Charlemagne's "daughters just as much as his sons were given a proper training in the Liberal Arts." They were also taught to "spin and weave wool, use the distaff and spindle, and acquire every womanly accomplishment rather than fritter away their time in sheer idleness."

Schools were also established in monasteries and cathedrals throughout the empire, and the pupils, according to Notker, were "chosen not only from the noblest families but also from middle-class and poor homes; and he [Charlemagne] made sure that food should be provided and that accommodation suitable for study should be made available."

Charlemagne himself, in a letter written between 780 and 800, detailed his views on the educational process. In addition to cultivating the monastic life in the bishoprics and monasteries under his control, he wrote that the monks

. . . ought also to be zealous in the cultivation of learning and in teaching those who by the gift of God are able to learn, according to the capacity of each individual . . . therefore, we exhort you not only to avoid neglecting the study of literature, but also with most humble mind, pleasing to God, to study earnestly in order that you may be able more easily and more correctly to penetrate the mysteries of the divine scriptures.

Charlemagne's educational reforms were designed to create a clerical elite that was literate in Latin, knowledgeable in theology, and familiar with the Roman liturgy. However, since women did not participate in sacerdotal functions and did not preach, there was no reason for convent schools to absorb the new learning. Nor was female scholarship encouraged. Nevertheless, by improving the level of reading and writing in the monastic and cathedral schools and creating a literate class of officials, the program led to a vibrant literary culture during the reign of Charlemagne's grandson Charles the Bald (see below).

Manuscripts and manuscript illumination

The building of churches, monasteries, and schools meant there was a need for correct scriptural and liturgical texts, the production of Gospel books, new collections of sermons, revised forms of Gregorian chant, and a means of knowing that the movable feasts of the Church—that is, feasts with no fixed date, such as Easter—were celebrated on the correct day. The manuscripts produced for these purposes were copied by monks in special rooms of the monasteries called *scriptoria*, using a new form of script known as Caroline or Carolingian minuscule. This introduced for the first time the letters that became the lowercase symbols of modern handwriting and typefaces. (This was probably the style of writing that Einhard described Charlemagne as trying to learn, quoted above) As may be seen in **fig. 25**, the letters are elegantly formed and there are spaces between words in the new script, a feature not present in the previous Merovingian form of writing, known as Merovingian majuscule, in which letters and words ran into one another. Copies made from these almost illegible manuscripts were inevitably corrupt; thus, the new Carolingian script had great practical as well as aesthetic value.

The manuscripts were sometimes lavishly illustrated with beautifully colored illuminations and covered with sumptuous plates of gold set with precious gems, or with ivory panels. For inspiration, the court painters and workers in metal and ivory turned either to the art of late antique Rome, or to comparatively recent works—the mosaics, frescoes, panel paintings, and illuminated manuscripts of the seventh and eighth centuries produced both in the west and in the Byzantine Empire. One example, the ivory bookcover illustrating Christ treading on the beasts and scenes from the life of Christ, originally covered a collection of **pericopes**, short

25 Merovingian majuscule (*example "a," below*), was replaced by Carolingian minuscule (*example "b," below*), which provided the medieval world with a far more legible form of writing. The letters are neatly formed, and spaces between the words provide clarity. Carolingian style has continued in use, forming the basis for our present-day lowercase letters.

(a) Merovingian

(b) Carolingian

passages, usually of Scripture, for public worship, for the convent at Chelles near Paris, and relies heavily on models dating from about 430 (**fig. 26**). Of the eleven scenes portraying episodes from the life of Christ (excluding the Annunciation above his head), six can be traced to a fifth-century ivory prototype. This book cover is typical of the ivories of the court school of Charlemagne, which frequently made use of Christological scenes. Further, the intricate carving bears testament to the highly developed skills of the artisans in Charlemagne's workshop.

From later in the ninth century comes an example of a gold book cover, the *Codex Aureus* (*Golden Codex*) of St. Emmeram, which shows Christ in Majesty, the Four Evangelists, and scenes from the life of Christ, set within a border of gold filigree and precious gems (**fig. 27**). The figures here are considerably more elongated than in the ivory cover of Christ treading the beasts, and less reminiscent of the

26 During the Carolingian era, manuscripts were often enclosed in elaborately carved ivory covers, as in this example originally created for the convent at Chelles, in France, where Charlemagne's sister was abbess. Carvings for manuscript coverings typically portrayed scenes from the life of Christ, such as this image of Jesus "treading the beasts."

27 The *Codex Aureus* (*Golden Codex*) of St. Emmeram (*c.* 870) is a manuscript created during the reign of Charles the Bald. On the gold cover, Christ, enthroned, is surrounded by jewels, as well as images of the Four Evangelists and scenes from his life. The internal folios, with purple ground and acanthus-leaf borders, are covered with golden calligraphy.

Classically influenced art of the early Christian era. These images reflect the evolution of a style that incorporated the influence of the artistic schools that had grown up in the towns of Reims and Tours, in which perspective was more marked and the forms more clearly asserted. There are, moreover, no precise models for the pictorial forms on the cover of the codex, leading art historians to emphasize the wide eclecticism and high degree of originality in the works created under the patronage of Charlemagne's grandson Charles the Bald (r. 843–877).

Like the St. Emmeram cover, a great portion of the Carolingian manuscript illuminations portray the Evangelists, either in the act of writing or drawing inspiration while in the process of writing. The portrait of St. Mark seen in **fig. 28** shows the Evangelist seated in an apse in an almost regal manner, framed by Corinthian columns and sitting against a pink bolster on a throne-like structure. The awkward position of the hand dipping the pen into the inkstand implies that the artist did not intend a naturalistic representation. The Gospel balanced on the Evangelist's knee is ritually displayed, and the clumsy gesture of dipping the pen is not a commonly used motion in the writing of calligraphy. The magnificent setting suggests that the artist may have intended to present Mark as an imperial force; the Evangelist composing his gospel could be compared to an emperor, perhaps Theodosius or Justinian writing a law code. Gold is used in the lettering, and in details such as the draping of his robe, but it is not used for the background, a feature that, by contrast, was typical of Byzantine illumination.

The influence of Byzantine art was, however, a significant feature of some of the works produced at the court of Charlemagne. In 796, when Alcuin retired to become abbot of the monastery of St. Martin at Tours, Einhard became head of the palace *scriptorium*. During his tenure, the manuscript painters were influenced by Byzantine style, which had preserved the illusionistic painting of ancient Rome. Furthermore, there is evidence that one or more Greek illuminators may have come to Aachen to work in the *scriptorium*; the Greek name *Demetrius presbyter* (Demetrius the priest) appears on the first page of the Gospel according to Luke in the Coronation Gospels. The influence of

28 St. Mark is portrayed in this manuscript illumination in a regal architectural setting, which the artist has drawn using Classical motifs, such as the apse and the rust-colored Corinthian capitals. Scholars have suggested that the artist probably intended to project an image of the Evangelist as an individual of power and influence, comparable to a king or emperor.

Byzantine style is evident in **fig. 29**, taken from a Gospel book produced at Aachen and still in the cathedral treasury there. It shows all four Evangelists writing in a rocky landscape—an image of the concentration and purpose that Charlemagne wished to have implemented in the *scriptoria* of his empire. The Evangelists are dressed in simple togas, in contrast to the elaborate costume of the portrait of Mark in fig. 28, and they are seated in a naturalistic landscape, as opposed to an architectural setting. Behind each of them is the outline of a rocky hill which contains a small recess for the symbolic attribute, or symbol, associated with each Evangelist. There are Byzantine stylistic elements in the sense of space, and the concentration of substantial human shapes in an impressionistic vista is reminiscent of the style favored by Byzantine painters. Some art historians have suggested that the artist was probably an Italian working at Charlemagne's court who had come under the Greek influence; the same image of the white-clad Evangelists in a blue and rocky landscape appears in the mosaic design at San Vitale, Ravenna, which was a frequently used source of inspiration for Carolingian artists. The image also carries a theological message: the Evangelists are working together to produce four Gospels that will provide an account of the life of Christ. Furthermore, it reflects the interest of Carolingian scholars in a text *De consensu Evangelistarum* (*Concerning the Consensus of the Evangelists*) by St. Augustine.

29 In this illumination from a Gospel book produced at Aachen in the early ninth century, the Four Evangelists are situated in a rocky, naturalistic setting. Matthew, Mark, Luke, and John are shown here in the act of writing—a characteristic pose for paintings of these apostles during the Carolingian era.

The scholarly manuscripts that preserved the heritage of the past, the glorious illuminations, and the sumptuous book covers of ivory and gold were made possible by the patronage of an emperor who believed that his Christian mission and the glorification of God were served through the cultivation of art and scholarship. Charlemagne was equally devoted, moreover, to the construction of sacred buildings in his empire for the services of laypeople as well as for monastic purposes.

Architecture

After 794, Charlemagne made Aachen his chief and permanent place of residence. He desired a "sacred place" like the *sacrum palatium*, the chapel in the palace at Constantinople, but he wished it to reflect Rome as well; indeed, he envisioned that his complex of court buildings at Aachen would comprise a *Roma secunda* ("a second Rome"). Presumably, Charlemagne's chief architect, Odo of Metz, and his assistants studied earlier buildings in Rome, Ravenna, Milan, Trier, and perhaps even in England as they were designing the complex.

The most famous of these Carolingian buildings at Aachen is the chapel, built between 790 and 805. It has often been compared to the church of San Vitale at Ravenna, but recent historians of architecture believe that the pattern for the chapel was in fact the Chrysotriclinion (golden dining hall) built by the emperor Justin II (r. 565–578) as a reception area within the precincts of the Great Palace at Constantinople. That building, no longer extant, was octagonal in design, with niches opening from the sides. It was ornamented with vibrant mosaics, which included a representation of Christ enthroned set above the emperor's throne.

Charlemagne's chapel at Aachen—known as the Palatine Chapel (**figs. 30** and **31**)—is a sixteen-sided structure with a central octagon surrounded by an **ambulatory**, which is divided into alternating rectangular and triangular bays. The most important architectural contribution of the chapel is its aggressive verticality, which became an essential feature of Gothic cathedrals. In contrast to the light brick vault construction of San Vitale, the chapel features heavy tunnel and groin vaults. Roman ruins were dismantled to obtain some of the stone, and marble was brought from Ravenna by permission of the pope. The building was decorated,

30 and **31**
(*fig. 30, left*) This image shows the interior of Charlemagne's Palatine, or Palace, Chapel (constructed 790–805), crowned by a soaring dome symbolizing heaven. His biographer, Einhard, implies that the emperor's throne occupied a commanding position on the second level above the west door (*fig. 31, below*), from which he could survey both the altar to the east and his subjects.

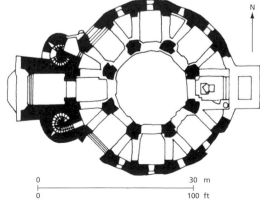

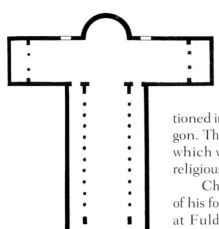

according to Einhard, with "gold and silver, with lamps, and with lattices and doors of solid bronze." Reminiscent of the Chrysotriclinion at Constantinople, the imperial cult was emphasized, with mosaics (no longer extant), picturing Christ enthroned, surrounded by the Four Evangelists and the Twenty-four Elders of the Church, mentioned in the biblical book of Revelation, placed inside the **cupola** over the octagon. The imperial throne was placed underneath. Unlike the Chrysotriclinion, which was essentially a secular building, the Palatine Chapel was built for religious purposes, and as such was a specifically Carolingian creation.

Charlemagne also sponsored many other building projects, the outgrowth of his founding of churches and monasteries. One of these was the Abbey Church at Fulda, east of Aachen, which was rebuilt from 802 with the deliberate intention of providing a replica of St. Peter's Basilica in Rome.

32 The Abbey Church at Fulda was rebuilt beginning in 802 with the intent of replicating, as much as possible, St. Peter's Basilica in Rome. The extensive dimensions of the new building, which featured an apse on both ends of the nave, made it the largest northern church of the ninth century. It was designed by Abbot Rutger's architects to provide a magnificent setting for the remains of St. Boniface, apostle to the Germans.

33 and **34** The plan for an ideal monastery from St. Gall (c. 820) shows a church with a double apse similar in shape to that of the Abbey Church at Fulda. Other buildings, such as the abbot's house, the school, the guest house, the infirmary, and the refectory, are clearly evident in the modern drawing (*fig. 34, opposite*) based on an original manuscript (*fig. 33, right*). The plan shows that the monastery was fully self-sufficient, with livestock, a bakery, a mill, and a garden to provide for the needs of the monks.

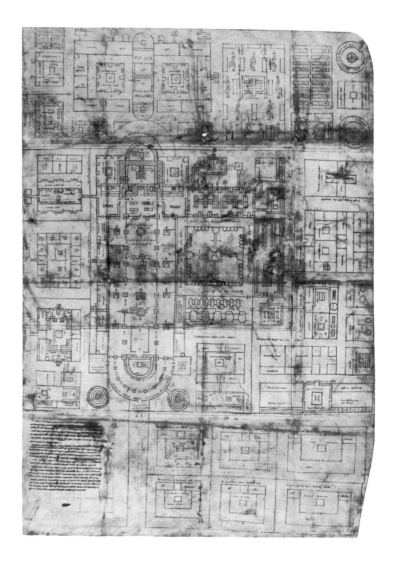

The original church was a simple rectangular building, terminating in an eastern apse. Abbot Rutger, in order to provide a worthy setting for the body of the martyred St. Boniface (which belonged to the abbey), designed a transept and apse west of the nave that were similar to the western transept of St. Peter's, thus creating a structure with two apses (**fig. 32**). He also requested that the dimensions replicate the great length of the church at Rome, with the result that the Abbey Church of Fulda was the largest of all of the churches in the north of Charlemagne's empire. The structure was begun in about 802 and was dedicated in 819, in spite of a petition from the monks to Charlemagne in 812 asking him to stop the abbot from continuing the "enormous and superfluous buildings and all that other nonsense by which the brethren are unduly tired and the peasants are ruined."

Other major architectural projects from the Carolingian Renaissance include the Church of St. Riquier at the monastery at Centula in northern France; the Abbey Church at St. Denis (begun by Pepin around 754) just north of Paris, Cologne Cathedral in northern Germany, and many monasteries. One celebrated project was a plan for an ideal monastic complex, details of which appear in a manuscript at the famous monastery of St. Gall (c. 820) (**figs. 33** and **34**). The manuscript shows an abbey church with a double apse similar in shape to the Abbey Church at Fulda.

The idealized church in the plan of St. Gall was part of a large establishment designed to house people who had chosen to follow the religious life by living in a community sworn to poverty, chastity, and obedience, and to provide them with a center where they could worship together according to the Rule of St. Benedict. The plan for this ideal monastery was probably drawn in 817, at the direction of a synod convened by Charlemagne's son and successor, Louis the Pious. As may be seen in the illustration, the monastery was designed in a systematic way, with the administrative buildings on one side of the church and the monks' lodgings on the other. Since the activities within the church were the center of life in the monastery, it provided the central core of the architectural plan. The *scriptorium* and library adjoined the church, whereas auxiliary structures such as the kitchen, bakery, baths and latrines, shops, stables, barns, and gardens were placed farthest from the cloister. The layout, which reflected a common pattern for

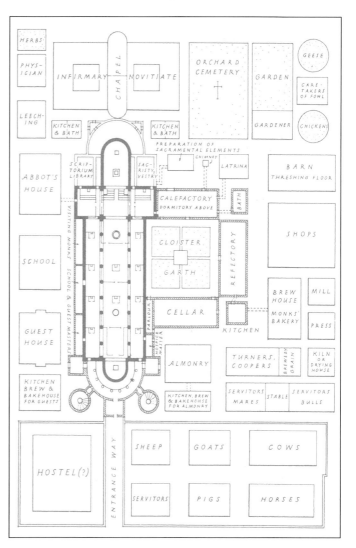

monasteries, was beautifully and logically designed to fulfill the needs of the residents. The monks entered the church either from the cloister or the dormitory, using stairs that led directly into the choir. This was, of course, the sacred space where the monks fulfilled St. Benedict's regulations concerning prayer and chant.

At St. Gall, as in all other Benedictine monasteries, music was an integral part of worship, and the monks devoted much effort and energy to the proper understanding and performance of the chant.

Music

A significant part of Charlemagne's reform movement in the monasteries and churches involved an effort to standardize and centralize musical practice in the services. St. Benedict had specified in his Rule that the liturgy be celebrated with chant for both the Mass and the Divine Office: the services for prayer and sacred readings that took place eight times each day. As discussed in Chapter 1, St. Gregory had codified the chant in the sixth century, and it was his liturgy, known as the Roman liturgy, that was adopted in the Frankish kingdom. Both Pepin and Charlemagne seem genuinely to have preferred the Roman to the Gallican liturgy, which had been in use during Clovis's reign, perhaps because of the growing respect for the authority and prestige of Rome as the center of western Christendom. Liturgical books were imported from Rome, which provided the texts for the services; musical notation, however, was only just beginning to be used during the Carolingian era. Hence, for the most part, the chant had to be taught to each new generation by rote. To this end, Charlemagne characteristically gave attention to establishing the schools and methods that would accomplish this task.

Although the impetus towards standardization of the chant using Roman models was strong, it appears to have been impossible to prevent some local, Gallican elements being incorporated into the Roman melodies. For example, in 785–786 Pope Hadrian sent a **sacramentary**, or liturgical book, to Charlemagne that did not contain the usual Sunday masses, but only included the liturgy for special festivals. Alcuin was given the task of supplementing and completing this sacramentary, and he incorporated elements from the locally practiced **Gallican chant**. It is interesting to note that this Frankish version of the sacramentary eventually displaced the local liturgy in Rome, ultimately providing a degree of musical unity.

The problem of teaching the melodies of the liturgy prompted at least one interesting solution. Notker, the monk of St. Gall mentioned earlier, described how, when discouraged by the difficulty of remembering long melodies, he "invented" a new form

35 In this manuscript illumination, Notker Balbulus ("the Stammerer"), a monk of St. Gall, struggles to memorize the long melodies of the liturgical chant as they escape from his "poor little head." In order to aid in the process of recollection, he eventually devised a new musical form called a *sequence* or *prosa*, with one syllable being sung for each note of the melody.

S. NOTKERVS.

56.

called a **sequence** or ***prosa*** when he began to write words syllabically under long melodies in order to aid in their memorization (**fig. 35**):

> When I was still young, and very long melodies—repeatedly entrusted to memory—escaped from my poor little head, I began to reason with myself how I could bind them fast.
>
> In the meantime it happened that a certain priest from Jumieges [a village in northwestern France] (recently laid waste by the Normans) came to us; bringing with him his antiphonary, in which some verses had been set to sequences; but they were in a very corrupt state. Upon closer inspection I was as bitterly disappointed in them as I had been delighted at first glance.
>
> Nevertheless, in imitation of them I began to write *Laudes Deo concinat orbis universus, qui gratis est redemptus* [*Let the Entire Universe, which has been Redeemed by Grace, Sound Praises to God*] and further on *Coluber Adae deceptor* [*The Serpent, Deceiver of Adam*]. When I took these lines to my teacher Iso, he, commending my industry while taking pity on my lack of experience, praised what was pleasing, and what was not he set about to improve, saying, "The individual motions of the melody should receive separate syllables." Hearing that, I immediately corrected those which fell under ia; those under le or lu, however, I left as too difficult; but later, with practice, I managed it easily—for example in *Dominus in Sina* and *Mater*. Instructed in this manner, I soon composed my second piece, *Psallat ecclesia mater illibata* [*Let the Immaculate Mother Church Sing Psalms*].
>
> When I showed these little verses to my teacher Marcellus, he, filled with joy, had them copied as a group on a roll; and he gave out different pieces to different boys to be sung. And when he told me that I should collect them in a book and offer them as a gift to some eminent person, I shrank back in shame, thinking I would never be able to do that.

The problem of memorizing a vast body of liturgical melody was formidable, and the first step towards establishing notation of the melodies came when various signs were written above the chant texts (**fig. 36**). These signs, known as ***neumes***, did not specify a pitch for each syllable, nor did they contain any indication of rhythm. Hence, for all practical purposes, the signs functioned merely as rough aids to the singer, who already knew the melody and needed only a reminder of melodic direction. Gradually the *neumes* began to be carefully placed in terms of vertical relationship to the text, and eventually lines were drawn to indicate specific notes, thus defining the pitch relationships more accurately. These lines were the genesis of the staff system used today, though a four-line, rather than a five-line, staff was used for medieval chant notation. The development of the four-line staff is credited to Guido d'Arezzo in the eleventh century (see Chapter 8).

36 In an early attempt to notate melodies, signs called *neumes* were placed above the syllables of the text. These indications probably functioned as reminders to singers who already knew the melody, since they did not indicate either rhythm or specific pitches. This example is taken from a tenth-century manuscript from Limoges.

The cultural achievements of the Carolingian period, while not remarkably original, provided the most important link between the tradition of Classical Greece and Rome and the artistic, architectural, literary, and musical accomplishments of western Europe in the following centuries. Without the painstaking work of the monks in their *scriptoria*, the artists and craftsmen in their workshops, and the musicians in their cathedrals and monasteries, there would have been no foundation for the cultural advancement of the High Middle Ages. First, however, the educational traditions and artistic accomplishments of the Carolingian era had to survive the devastation of the ninth-century invasions.

The Decline of the Carolingian Empire

When Charlemagne died in 814, he left his kingdom to his one surviving son, Louis the Pious, who ruled until 840. Louis was a well-educated and civilized man, but he lacked the military skills of his father, and he failed to control not only the recalcitrant Frankish nobility, but also his own sons. In order to preserve the unity of the empire, he tried to establish a line of succession through a decree (*Ordinatio Imperii*) that would give the royal title and most of the land of the empire to his eldest son, Lothair I (see table, below), leaving his other two sons with small sub-kingdoms. Needless to say, this plan was unacceptable to Lothair's younger siblings, and from 829 on they fought incessantly against Lothair and their father. After Louis's death in 840, Charles the Bald and Louis the German, united forces against their brother, and a final battle was fought at Fontenoy in 843.

Although the battle was not completely decisive, the brothers agreed to divide the empire into three parts, as stipulated in the Treaty of Verdun. Charles the Bald took the western territories, which would later become France; Louis the German received the eastern portion; and Lothair was granted the imperial title, together with the "Middle Kingdom," consisting of a narrow band of land extending from the North Sea to the

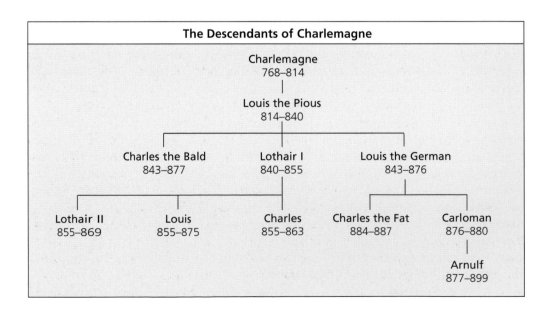

The Descendants of Charlemagne

Charlemagne
768–814

Louis the Pious
814–840

Charles the Bald
843–877

Lothair I
840–855

Louis the German
843–876

Lothair II
855–869

Louis
855–875

Charles
855–863

Charles the Fat
884–887

Carloman
876–880

Arnulf
877–899

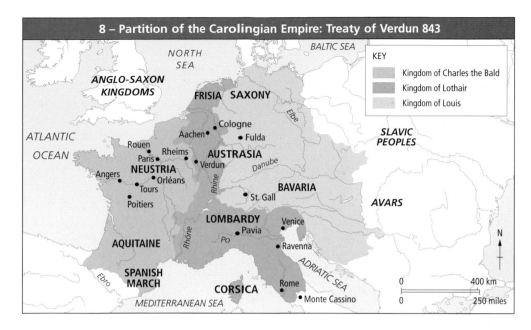

8 – Partition of the Carolingian Empire: Treaty of Verdun 843

KEY
- Kingdom of Charles the Bald
- Kingdom of Lothair
- Kingdom of Louis

Adriatic. Its boundaries included the Netherlands, the Rhineland, the Rhône valley, and northern Italy (**Map 8**). The *Annals of Fulda* described the compromise in the following way:

> The kingdom [of Francia] having been sketched out by the magnates and having been divided into three, the three kings, coming together in the month of August at Verdun, a city in Gaul, divided the kingdom among themselves. Louis received the eastern part, Charles held the western, [and] Lothair, who was the eldest, chose the middle portion among them. And peace having been agreed upon between them and confirmed with an oath, each returned to arrange and protect the lands of his kingdom.

This tripartite division was to be short-lived, however, because Lothair died in 855, and his realm was parceled out among his three sons, further fragmenting the initial division of the great Carolingian Empire.

Many scholars have pointed to other factors contributing to the dissolution of the empire, some of which began before Charlemagne's death, and were a product of his own style of government. As mentioned above, the empire contained a variety of ethnic groups, each with its own language and customs. Furthermore, each group was allowed to retain its individual customary laws. The linguistic divisions had been profoundly demonstrated in 842, when the alliance between Charles's West Franks and Louis's East Franks was established by the Oath of Strasbourg; Charles spoke his oath in the German vernacular so that Louis's army could understand him, whereas Louis swore his loyalty in the Romance language of Charles's men, the precursor of modern French. It is evident that, with such strongly marked linguistic and cultural differences, the various peoples of the empire were forged into a unified state through Charlemagne's power and personality. When he died, there was a natural, and perhaps inevitable, drift into fragmentation.

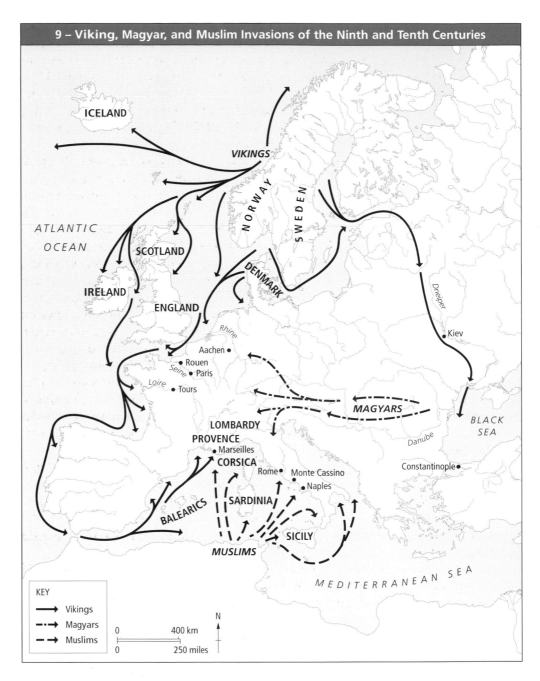

9 – Viking, Magyar, and Muslim Invasions of the Ninth and Tenth Centuries

ICELAND

VIKINGS

NORWAY

SWEDEN

ATLANTIC
OCEAN

SCOTLAND

DENMARK

Dneiper

IRELAND

ENGLAND

• Kiev

Rhine

Aachen •
• Rouen
Seine • Paris
Loire • Tours

MAGYARS

LOMBARDY
PROVENCE

Danube

BLACK
SEA

• Marseilles

CORSICA

Rome •

Monte Cassino

Constantinople •

• Naples

SARDINIA

BALEARICS

SICILY

MUSLIMS

MEDITERRANEAN SEA

KEY

→ Vikings

–·–► Magyars

– –► Muslims

N

0   400 km

0   250 miles

During and shortly after the period of civil war among Charlemagne's successors, the old Carolingian empire was subjected to incursions by various non-Christian groups that surrounded it. The political instability of the empire itself may have attracted some, but other invaders were pressured by forces at work in their own lands (**Map 9**).

The Magyars, originally from the steppes of Asia, were attacked by another Asiatic tribe, the Pechenegs, and fled west into central Europe, reaching the Carpathian

Basin in 895. There they allied themselves with the Avars, another Asiatic tribe that had been subjugated by the Franks in the 790s (see p. 107). During the next decade they plundered Bavaria, Saxony, and Thuringia, ultimately raiding throughout Germany and into the regions of Alsace and the Rhine valley, reaching as far as Reims in 937. In 955, they were defeated by King Otto the Great at the Battle of Lechfeld, and thereafter settled in the region now known as Hungary. Within fifty years they had adopted Christianity, and by the High Middle Ages (1200–1400) their kingdom had become one of the strongest in eastern Europe (see Chapter 11).

The ninth century also witnessed new attacks from the Muslims of North Africa. In 827 they invaded Sicily, and by mid-century, through a series of assaults, they had conquered the whole island. Rome itself was raided in 843, and Muslim invaders also occupied Corsica, Sardinia, and the delta of the Rhône in southern France. They did not establish any permanent settlements on the mainland of Italy, but they maintained bases there until they were driven out by Byzantine forces in 915. The Muslims remained in Sicily during the next century, however, and established a flourishing culture there.

The invasions with the most lasting effect, however, came from the Vikings, referred to by their contemporaries as "the Northmen." In the early years of the invasions, these Scandinavians lived in a patchwork of insignificant states which gradually coalesced into three groups: Danes, Swedes, and Norwegians. For reasons that are not entirely clear, they began the final movement of Germanic migration in the last years of the eighth century. The impetus may have been a sudden increase in population in a land of limited resources; as a result, peasants without land to farm, as well as nobles in search of new lands to rule, took to the sea in quest of adventure, plunder, and possible colonization. Some scholars have suggested that the more adventurous people migrated to other lands when orderly government was established. Whatever the reason, they came in ever-increasing hordes.

An important factor in the assault on Europe was the development of the Viking ships, powered by both oars and sails, and capable of carrying forces of between forty and one hundred warriors at speeds of up to ten knots. These ships could successfully navigate rivers as well as the open sea, and this maneuverability enabled the Viking forces to sail far into the interior of France and England, where they plundered monasteries, villages, and cities.

Charlemagne himself saw the Viking ships in the English Channel, and was said to have shed tears as he thought of the plight of future generations. By the mid-ninth century, the incursions were so frightening that a Frankish chronicler described them thus:

> The number of ships grows larger and larger; the great host of Northmen continually increases; on every hand Christians are the victims of massacres, looting, and arson—clear proof of which will remain as long as the world itself endures. The Northmen capture every city they pass through, and none can withstand them.

All three of the Scandinavian tribes participated in these migrations, but only the Danes and the Norwegians entered western Europe. The Swedes traveled east, traversing the Baltic Sea to invade the Slavic lands. They arrived at Novgorod in the middle of the ninth century, and traveled from there to Kiev, where they established a permanent settlement. Fortified posts were founded throughout the Slavic lands by these Varangians, as the Swedish Vikings were called, and the native population was forced to submit to their rule.

Among these Viking invaders were merchants as well as warriors, and they began to establish trade routes along the Black Sea as far as Constantinople, to which they brought the products of the Russian forests: furs and honey. As was typical, Viking raiders also assaulted the Byzantine capital, launching several attacks on the city. This harassment ultimately resulted in the granting of trading privileges from the emperor. As the tenth century progressed, the Varangians consolidated their holdings into a unified state, ruled by the prince of Kiev.

In the west, the North Sea and the Atlantic Ocean proved to be highways for the Norwegian and Danish adventurers. The Vikings first attacked England in 787, and within seven years the northern monasteries of Jarrow and Lindisfarne were burned. The monastery on the island of Noirmoutier, off the west coast of France, met a similar fate in 814.

For some decades the Vikings confined their forays to summer raids, returning to their homelands in winter. However, in 843 after an assault on Nantes, on the Atlantic coast of France, the Vikings spent the winter encamped on nearby Noirmoutier instead of returning to Scandinavia. From this vantage point they were able to intensify their forays into France and Spain, where they eventually sacked Seville. The attacks continued over the next two decades, with Bordeaux, Tours, Blois, Orléans, Poitiers, and Paris all being targeted at least once, and in some cases twice. In 859, the Vikings assaulted the coasts of Spain, raided Morocco and the Balearic Islands, and made camp for the winter in the delta of the Rhône. From there they launched raids on the towns of the Rhône valley. By 880 they were looking for new areas to conquer, and they sailed up the Seine. This foray resulted in a two-year siege of Paris, which eventually ended when the emperor Charles the Fat (r. 884–887) arrived with a powerful army. Rather than defeating the Vikings militarily, however, he paid them to travel south to plunder the Gascons, with whom he was at odds.

The Viking assault on France was countered at last by Charles the Simple, king of the West Franks (r. 893–923), whose solution was to grant land in northern France to the Viking leader Rollo. This was the region that was later known as Normandy. Rollo became the vassal of the king, married his daughter, and accepted Christianity. The establishment of a permanent Viking settlement was quite effective in providing an ally to help the Frankish kings ward off future Viking raids.

England suffered even more than the Carolingian Empire as a result of the Viking incursions. In 851, winter quarters were established by the Danes on the island of Thanet, in the estuary of the Thames. In 870 they conquered most of East Anglia; in 876 they occupied Northumbria; and in 877 they took most of Mercia. These were not mere raids, but serious attempts to conquer and rule the countryside. The Anglo-Saxon resistance was organized and led by Alfred, King of Wessex (r. 871–899), whose forces defeated the Danes at the Battle of Edington in 878. They initially refused to accept his terms, but in 886 Alfred forced the Danes to accede to a treaty whereby he continued to rule Wessex, the area south of the Thames, and Mercia became an Anglo-Saxon duchy allied to Wessex. The Danes remained in an area that included East Anglia, eastern Mercia, and the regions of Lincolnshire and Yorkshire, an area that subsequently became known as the Danelaw. The Danes accepted Christianity as part of the peace settlement, and this in addition to inter-marriage with the Anglo-Saxon people, made possible their eventual assimilation into a more or less united kingdom.

In addition to their settlements in England, France, and Russia, the Vikings also ventured across the Atlantic Ocean, where, between 875 and 930, they reached Iceland and remained to found a community. The Norse culture that emerged there remained untouched by European influences for several centuries. Here the Norse saga, an oral tradition at first, was eventually written down, providing epic tales of great heroes. The Vikings also ventured to Greenland in the tenth century, and in the eleventh century they founded temporary settlements on the coast of North America which lasted almost until the time of Columbus's voyage.

Although the monastic chroniclers of the ninth and tenth centuries may have exaggerated the scale of the Viking raids, it is understandable that, accustomed to a peaceful existence within their cloistered walls, they were terrified by the assaults. And the warrior class of Europe, though accustomed to fighting on land, was not able to cope successfully with invaders who arrived by sea. The threat gradually diminished, however, and by the eleventh century it had virtually disappeared. By the year 1000, the Scandinavian kings had successfully discouraged the bands of raiders, and instead enlisted their warriors into royal armies. Further, the efforts to Christianize Scandinavia had produced many converts, and the ethos of less warlike behavior began to have an effect on the raiding mentality of the marauders.

Europe was, however, profoundly changed by both the invasions from the outside and the internal warfare of the ninth and tenth centuries. Recovery from the onslaught was slow, and the collapse of central government in the old Carolingian Empire, coupled with the need for protection on a routine basis, led to new forms of social and political organization, to be discussed in the following chapter.

Summary

The Frankish kings, beginning with Clovis, built an extensive and powerful empire that extended over much of Europe. In addition to establishing their territorial control, they initiated bonds with the papacy and the western church. These actions, carried on under the leadership of Charles Martel and his son Pepin the Short, reached their fruition during the reign of Pepin's son Charles the Great, or Charlemagne.

Making use of the foundation laid by his father and grandfather, Charlemagne extended the boundaries of Frankish rule in all directions, defeating the Lombards in Italy, establishing protective districts on the Spanish side of the Pyrenees Mountains and along the eastern borders of the empire, and bringing the Saxons and the peoples on the eastern frontier of his kingdom under his control.

Charlemagne was dedicated to the Christianization of the pagan nonbelievers, and envisioned that his mission was to create a great Christian empire; he aimed to be "the pastor and shield of [his] Christian flock." The realization of this goal was symbolized by his coronation as Holy Roman Emperor on Christmas Day, 800.

He was able to govern his vast realm through a system whereby he established ties with the warrior nobility based on bonds of loyalty and fidelity. In order to ensure this total allegiance, Charlemagne instituted the office of *missi dominici*—"messengers of the lord," who would inspect the activities of the counts and margraves and report back to the emperor. The *missi* also carried royal orders throughout the realm. Further, although he allowed the conquered peoples to keep their own customary laws, he issued new laws known as capitularies, which were designed to produce uniformity of legal practice, and, to some extent, behavior within his realm. Among other issues, the capitularies regulated matters concerning women. For example, laws were enacted to ensure that marriages would be virtually indissoluble, and that women could inherit immovables, such as estates and property. This provided them with a new measure of economic stability.

Another major aspect of the reign of Charlemagne was the "Carolingian Renaissance." Bringing the greatest scholars of the time to his court, the emperor patronized the development of scholarship, education, art, architecture, and liturgical music. The court scholars, under the leadership of Alcuin, advanced a program of study for the clergy that raised intellectual standards. In addition, they instituted a procedure for copying manuscripts that resulted in some 8,000 manuscripts extant today. These form the basis for many modern editions of the works of the Classical literary tradition.

The extraordinary accomplishments of Charlemagne with regard to the creation of the Holy Roman Empire were not to last, however. His only surviving son, Louis the Pious, could not control the rebellious nobility or even his own sons, who were caught up in vicious internecine warfare. By 843, approximately forty years after the death of Charlemagne, his great empire was divided into three parts, and two years later it was split still further, into five kingdoms.

In addition, Europe was by this time under attack from all sides, facing an onslaught by the Magyars from the east, by the Muslims from the south, and by the Vikings from the north. The mid-ninth century was a time of devastation and suffering; the collapse of centralized government, coupled with the need for protection, gave rise to new forms of social and political organization.

Suggestions for Further Reading

Primary sources

There are several good collections of primary source materials, including: P. Dutton, ed., *Carolingian Civilization, A Reader* (Peterborough, Ontario, 1993); B. Scholz and B. Rogers, trans. *Carolingian Chronicles: Royal Frankish Annals* and *Nithard's Histories*; E. Amt, ed., *Women's Lives in Medieval Europe* (New York, 1993); and *The Reign of Charlemagne: Documents on Carolingian Government and Administration*, by H.R. Loyn and John Percival (London: Edward Arnold, 1975). The biographies of Charlemagne by Einhard and Notker are available in several editions, including *Two Lives of Charlemagne*, trans. Lewis Thorpe (Middlesex, 1969), and A.J. Grant, *Early Lives of Charlemagne, by Eginhard* [sic] *and the Monk of St. Gall* (New York, 1966). There is an excellent new edition of Einhard's works, edited and translated by Paul Edward Dutton: *Charlemagne's Courtier: The Complete Einhard* (Peterborough, Canada: Broadview Press, 1998). The introduction to Dutton's edition presents an informative synthesis of recent scholarship.

Dhouda's *Handbook for William: A Carolingian Woman's Counsel for her Son* is available in a translation by Carol Neel (Lincoln: University of Nebraska Press, 1991).

Secondary sources

The most thorough and detailed

study of this period is Rosamond McKitterick, ed. *The New Cambridge Medieval History*, vol. II, *c. 700–c. 900* (Cambridge, 1995). Shorter works include Geoffrey Barraclough, *The Crucible of Europe* (Berkeley, 1976), and Heinrich Fichtenau, trans. Peter Munz, *The Carolingian Empire* (New York, 1964). Rosamond McKitterick's *The Frankish Kingdoms under the Carolingians: 751–987* (London: Longman, 1983) is an excellent and highly readable narrative and analysis of the reigns of all the Carolingian kings. Another good introduction to the period is *The Frankish World, 750–950*, by J.L. Nelson (London, 1996). Also useful is Nelson's *Charles the Bald* (London, New York: Longman, 1992).

For a discussion of the Carolingians and the Church, see Rosamond McKitterick, *The Frankish Church and the Carolingian Reforms, 789–895* (London: Royal Historical Society, 1977). The coronation of Charlemagne is discussed in articles by several different scholars in R.E. Sullivan, ed., *The Coronation of Charlemagne: What Did It Signify?* (Boston: Heath, 1959). A recent study by Bernard S. Bachrach, *Early Carolingian Warfare: Prelude to Empire* (Philadelphia: University of Pennsylvania Press, 2001), traces the methods by which the early Carolingians created the military machine that made it possible for Charlemagne to establish his empire.

For social history and the history of women see: Pierre Riche, trans. Jo Ann McNamara, *Daily Life in the World of Charlemagne* (Philadelphia: University of Pennsylvania Press, 1978); Suzanne F. Wemple, *Women in Frankish Society: Marriage and the Cloister: 500–900* (Philadelphia: University of Pennsylvania Press, 1985); Patricia Ranft, *Women and the Religious Life in Premodern Europe* (New York: St Martin's Press, 1998), especially Chapter 2; and David Herlihy, *Opera Muliebria: Women and Work In Medieval Europe* (New York: McGraw-Hill, 1990), especially Chapter 2.

For the Carolingian Renaissance see: D.A. Bullough, *Carolingian Renewal: Sources and Heritage* (Manchester: Manchester University Press, 1991), which contains an interesting collection of articles on subjects ranging from education to liturgy. Two excellent works by Rosamond McKitterick dealing with Carolingian culture are *The Frankish Kings and Culture in the Early Middle Ages* (Aldershot, UK: Variorum, 1995) and *The Carolingians and the Written Word* (Cambridge: Cambridge University Press, 1989). She has also edited several collections of articles, including *The Uses of Literacy in Early Mediaeval Europe* (Cambridge: Cambridge University Press, 1992) and *Carolingian Culture: Emulation and Innovation* (Cambridge: Cambridge University Press, 1994). See also Richard Sullivan, ed., *The Gentle Voices of Teachers: Aspects of Learning in the Carolingian Age* (Columbus, OH: Ohio State University Press, 1995).

Information concerning art in the Carolingian world may be found in: Jean Hubert, Jean Porcher, and Wolfgang Fritz Volbach, *Carolingian Art* (London: Thames & Hudson, 1970); J. Beckwith, *Early Medieval Art* (New York: Praeger, 1965); Marilyn Stokstad, *Medieval Art* (New York: Harper & Row, 1986), especially Chapter 5; and Genevra Kornbluth, *Engraved Gems of the Carolingian Empire* (University Park, PA: Pennsylvania State University Press, 1995). For Carolingian liturgical and devotional objects see Peter Lasko, *Ars Sacra: 800–1200*, 2nd ed. (New Haven: Yale University Press, 1994).

On music in the Carolingian world see Richard Hoppin, *Medieval Music* (New York: W.W. Norton, 1978), especially Chapter 6; Donald J. Grout and Claude V. Palisca, *A History of Western Music*, 4th ed. (New York: Norton, 1988), especially Chapter 2; Kenneth Levy, *Gregorian Chant and the Carolingians* (Princeton: Princeton University Press, 1998); and articles on the Carolingian period in James McKinnon, ed., *Antiquity and the Middle Ages: from Ancient Greece to the Fifteenth Century*, reprint ed. (Englewood Cliffs, NJ: Prentice Hall, 1991). For a detailed discussion of the sequence and Notker's contribution, see Richard L. Crocker, *The Early Medieval Sequence* (Berkeley: University of California Press, 1977).

For information concerning the Vikings see Peter Sawyer, *The Age of the Vikings* (New York: St Martin's Press, 1972), and *Kings and Vikings: Scandinavia and Europe*, AD *700–1100* (London, New York: Routledge, 1989).

Politics

ENGLAND/FRANCE
987–996	r. of Hugh Capet
1042–1066	r. of Edward the Confessor
1066–1087	r. of William the Conqueror
1086	Domesday Book
1087–1100	r. of William Rufus

HOLY ROMAN EMPIRE
936–973	r. of Otto I ("the Great")
973–983	r. of Otto II
983–1002	r. of Otto III
1002–1024	r. of Henry II
1024–1039	r. of Conrad II
1039–1056	r. of Henry III
1056–1106	r. of Henry IV

HUNGARY/POLAND
972–997	r. of Prince Geza
992–1025	r. of Boleslav the Great
997–1038	r. of Stephen of Hungary
1077–1095	r. of Laszlo I
1095–1116	r. of Kalman

SCANDINAVIA
c.940–c.985	r. of Harold Bluetooth
990–1022	r. of Olaf "the Taxgatherer"
995–1000	r. of Olaf Tryggvason

SPAIN
1063–1094	r. of Sancho "the Great"
1065–1109	r. of Alfonso VI

BYZANTIUM/KIEV
976–1025	r. of Basil II
1015–1054	r. of Yaroslav "the Wise"
1081–1118	r. of Alexius Comnenus

Culture

c.1000–1050	life of Guido of Arezzo
c.1025	Speyer Cathedral begun
c.1060	St.-Sernin at Toulouse
1071–1127	r. of William IX, Duke of Aquitaine
1079–1142	life of Peter Abelard
c.1082	Bayeux Tapestry made
c.1093	Durham Cathedral begun
c.1096	Enlargement of Church of Ste.-Madelaine at Vézelay begun
c.1100	*The Song of Roland*

Religion

863	Cyril and Methodius begin mission to Slavs
910	Cluny founded
1049–1054	r. of Pope Leo IX
1073–1085	r. of Pope Gregory VII
1090–1153	life of Bernard of Clairvaux
1095–1099	First Crusade
1096–1141	life of Hugh of St. Victor
1098–1179	life of Hildegard of Bingen
1098	Cistercian Order founded
1099	Hospitallers founded

ENGLAND/FRANCE
1100–1135	r. of Henry I
1108–1137	r. of Louis VI ("the Fat")
c.1122–1204	life of Eleanor of Aquitaine
1135–1154	r. of Stephen
1137–1180	r. of Louis VII
1154–1189	r. of Henry II
1180–1223	r. of Philip II "Augustus"
1189–1199	r. of Richard I
1199–1216	r. of John

HOLY ROMAN EMPIRE
1152–1190	r. of Frederick Barbarossa
1190–1197	r. of Henry VI

SICILY
c.1015–1085	life of Robert Guiscard
1061–1101	r. of Roger I
c.1113–1154	r. of Roger II
1154–1166	r. of William I
1166–1189	r. of William II

OTHERS
1169–1193	r. of Saladin
1172–1196	r. of Bela III

Culture (after 1100)

after 1100	Troubadours, *trouvères*, and *Minnesänger* traditions become established
1100–1155	life of Geoffrey of Monmouth
c.1120–1130	St.-Lazare at Autun built
c.1120	Church at Souillac begun
1122–1151	Suger is Abbot of St.-Denis
1135–1140	Additions to St.-Denis under Abbot Suger
1160–1191	life of Chrétien de Troyes
c.1160–1215	life of Marie de France

Religion (after 1100)

1119	Templars founded
1120–1170	life of Thomas Becket
1135–1204	life of Maimonides
c.1140–1160	*Codex Calixtinus*
1145–1153	r. of Pope Eugenius III
1147–1149	Second Crusade
1154–1159	r. of Pope Adrian IV
1158	Order of Calatrava founded
1175	Order of Santiago founded
1189–1192	Third Crusade

PART II

THE CENTRAL MIDDLE AGES

c. 1000–*c.* 1200

5 THE AGRICULTURAL REVOLUTION AND THE RISE OF FEUDAL SOCIETY

THE ELEVENTH CENTURY was a time of great importance in the history of medieval civilization, during which the material and political foundations were established that made possible the cultural and economic developments of the High Middle Ages.

Although our sources for the period under discussion are relatively limited, we do know that the years following 1000 witnessed a significant growth in the population of Europe, which resulted from a more benign political atmosphere, changes in the climate, and technological and dietary improvements. In addition, a new political system developed in response to the collapse of centralized government at the end of the Carolingian era. This political system rested on an agricultural base that remained in place until the disastrous plague, wars, and famine of the fourteenth century. The political and economic patterns of vassalage and the seignorial system, often identified as feudalism and manorialism, defined the social parameters of the central years of the Middle Ages. This chapter will explore first the demographic and technological changes, and then the political developments and their effect on the daily existence of the people of medieval Europe.

Population Increase and Distribution

During the eleventh century, medieval Europe witnessed a dramatic increase in population. This was due to several factors: the climate had been warming significantly since the ninth century, existing food sources were enriched by the addition of protein in the form of legumes, and there were a number of important technological inventions. In addition, the birth rate had increased since the eighth century, and the death rate fell after the cessation of the plague that had raged throughout Europe in the seventh

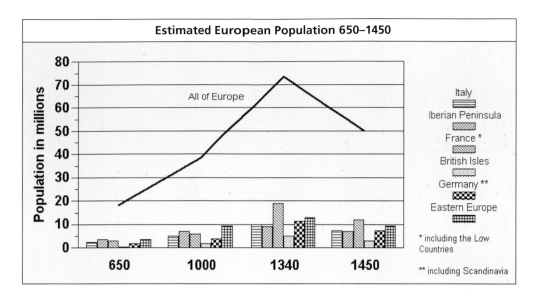

Estimated European Population 650–1450

Legend: Italy, Iberian Peninsula, France *, British Isles, Germany **, Eastern Europe

* including the Low Countries

** including Scandinavia

century. The disease did not recur on a widespread continental basis until the fourteenth century (see Chapter 14).

Also of great benefit was the warmer climate. From about 750 until about 1215, Europe was warmer and drier than it had been in the previous three and a half centuries. Although it is difficult to measure the exact results of the more temperate climate in this period, it has been demonstrated that the rate of expansion of European forests decreased, thus easing the way for land clearance. Moreover, the longer growing seasons were a decisive factor in raising the level of agricultural production.

Another reason for the growth in population was the fact that a more peaceful political environment had developed. The Viking invasions of the ninth and tenth centuries were the last incursions from outside the continent to be endured by Europe during the Middle Ages. Furthermore, the civil wars among the successors of Charlemagne had ended by the late ninth century, and this cessation contributed to a less violent atmosphere. Although warfare continued to be an endemic reality throughout the Middle Ages, armed conflict inside Europe was waged only in limited areas and for relatively brief periods.

Looking at the medieval period as a whole, the population of Europe increased from approximately 25 million around the year 700 to over 70 million by 1300. The graph above provides estimates for growth in the European population from 650 to 1450, and shows the largest increase occurring around the year 1200. The greatest rise occurred in the British Isles and France, where the increase was more rapid than in other countries. Statistical data for the British Isles (comprising England, Scotland, Wales, and Ireland) demonstrates that its population nearly tripled between 1068 and 1348, when it reached a total of between 5 and 6 million. Even more remarkable are the statistics from France, where the population reached almost 20 million by the beginning of the fourteenth century, a figure half as great as the country's population in 1940. This suggests a possible reason why France was such a significant influence in the medieval period; her population amounted to nearly one-third of the total population of Europe.

The increased population, aided by new technological inventions, led to the establishment of many new agricultural settlements, the development of cities, and the continuing expansion of arable land surrounding the existing villages. This active, vigorous peasant society provided the economic means for the great achievements of the High Middle Ages: the splendid cathedrals, universities, and institutions of government, as well as the traditions of feudal chivalry, which will be explored later in this chapter.

Technological Innovations

The robust expansion of the European economy could not have been achieved without the development of several important inventions, coupled with improved agricultural techniques. Together, these produced what some recent scholars have referred to as a "technological complex," or "package." Perhaps the most significant of these technical advances was the harnessing of water power through the development of the watermill, the most widely employed type of machinery in the Middle Ages. The mill was used, among other purposes, for crushing wheat, grinding corn, pulverizing olives, fulling cloth (i.e., making it thicker and thinner by pressing, moistening, etc.), and tanning leather. **Fig. 37** shows the mechanical details of a twelfth-century watermill.

It is documented that the mill was used as early as the sixth century in the Italian peninsula, and was employed on an extensive basis throughout northwestern Europe by the ninth century. For example, records from the monastery of Montier-en-Der in eastern France show that there were eleven watermills on the River Voire which flowed through their domain, with three of them within a stretch of less than 4 miles (6 km). And in the monastery of St. Germain-des-Prés there were no fewer than fifty-nine watermills, the majority of them built on small streams.

The rate of expansion in the construction of mills in the following centuries was substantial. On the banks of the Robec, which joins the Seine at Rouen in northern France, there were two mills in the tenth century, four in the eleventh century, ten in the thirteenth century, and twelve at the beginning of the fourteenth century. In the Aube region of central France, there are records mentioning fourteen watermills in the eleventh century, sixty in the twelfth, and over 200 in the thirteenth century.

37 Watermills were essential to manorial life in medieval Europe, especially before the twelfth century. They were used for crushing and grinding grain, fulling cloth, and tanning leather, among other purposes. This drawing shows the gearing details of a twelfth-century vertical undershot watermill.

The *Domesday Book*, the important land survey produced in England in the late eleventh century (see Chapter 6), gives a detailed view of water power in England at that time. In all, 5,624 watermills were recorded on 9,250 manors, and more than one-third of these manors (3,463) had more than one mill. These were widely spread throughout England, although the counties with the best natural river systems typically possessed more mills. On rivers such as the Wylye in Wiltshire, for example, there were thirty mills within about 10 miles (16 km) of water, or three mills for every mile.

In the twelfth century, a method of harnessing wind power was developed. Windmills of various types were

38 The popularity of windmills grew rapidly during the twelfth century, as waterwheels were replaced by sails driven by the wind. The machinery of the windmill—a mechanism that had an advantage over the watermill in that it was not subject to freezing in cold weather—was contained in a framed wooden body, which also supported the sails. As can be seen in this early drawing of a raised windmill, the box was mounted on a large post which turned freely in the wind.

invented in different parts of Europe, and some scholars have claimed that the new technology originated in an arid, windy area of the Muslim world or in the southern part of the Continent, while others claim that it was first found along the south and east coasts of England and on the shores of the English Channel.

A typical windmill was adapted from the mechanism of the watermill; the waterwheels, driven by hydraulic power, were replaced by sails driven by the wind. The framed wooden body of the mill, which contained the machinery and supported the sails, was mounted on a massive upright oak post which was free to turn with the wind (**fig. 38**). The use of windmills increased rapidly, partly because they could be built almost anywhere at moderate cost. Furthermore, their use had an obvious advantage in areas that lacked fast-flowing streams; in addition, they could operate in freezing weather conditions, and were thus built in large numbers throughout northern Europe.

Mills were a source of significant financial benefit for their owners, who were determined to protect their priceless assets. The following document from the abbey of Corbie, in Picardy, demonstrates the importance of the mills and their operators:

> Every miller shall have a holding of six ***bonniers*** of land, to enable him to do what is required of him and pay his proper toll of flour. He must have oxen and all he needs for plowing, so that he and his family will be able to live, keep pigs, geese, and hens, look after the mill, cart the materials for the repair of the mill, cart the millstones, and keep the mill and its **leat** in repair. We do not want him to perform any other services, neither carting, nor plowing, nor sowing, nor harvesting, nor haymaking, nor brewing, nor delivering hops or wood, nor doing anything else for the master, so that he can devote himself entirely to his mill.

Serfs—unfree tenants, bound to the land—were required to use the lord's mill on the manor, and wealthy landowners jealously guarded their prerogatives. Records indicate that, when a person built a windmill near one owned by someone else, the initial owner would often bring the intruder before a court, or might even employ violence in order to have the new owner's mill destroyed. The English chronicler Jocelin of Brakelond, for example, tells of the anger of Samson, abbot of Bury St. Edmunds, Suffolk, when he heard that Herbert, the dean, had built a windmill for his own use:

> Herbert the Dean set up a windmill on Habardun; and when the Abbot heard this, he grew so hot with anger that he would scarcely eat or speak a single word. On the morrow, after hearing mass, he ordered the Sacrist to send his carpenters thither without delay, pull everything down, and place the timber under safe custody. Hearing this, the Dean came and said that he had the right to do this . . . and that free benefit of the wind ought not to be denied to any man; he said he also wished to grind his own corn there and not the corn of others, lest perchance he might be thought to do this to the detriment of neighboring mills. To this the Abbot, still angry, made answer: "I thank you as I should thank you if you had cut off both my feet. By God's face, I will never eat bread till that building be thrown down. You are an old man, and you ought to know that neither the King nor his Justiciar can change or set up anything within the liberties of this town without the assent of the Abbot and the Convent. Why have you then presumed to do such a thing? Nor is this thing done without detriment to my mills, as you assert. For the burgesses will throng to your mill and grind their corn to their hearts' content, nor should I have the lawful right to punish them, since they are free men. I would not even allow the Cellarer's mill which was built of late, to stand, had it not been built before I was Abbot. Go away," he said, "go away; before you reach your house, you shall hear what will be done with your mill." But the Dean, shrinking in fear from before the face of the Abbot, by the advice of his son Master Stephen, anticipated the servants of the Abbot and caused the mill which he had built to be pulled down by his own servants without delay, so that when the servants of the Sacrist came, they found nothing left to demolish.

Accounts such as this show that the large income to be derived from the fees charged for using the mills provided an impetus for owners to act in oppressive ways to protect their local business monopolies.

In addition to the watermills and windmills that supplied the amplified sources of energy available in the eleventh century, there were other factors that contributed to increased agricultural production.

The most important of these were improvements in agricultural techniques, such as the introduction of the three-field system of farming (**fig. 39**). The Romans had used only a two-field system, in which one field would be left unsown every other year to let the earth rest. Animals were kept on the unsown or fallow land to fertilize it with manure. In the three-field system, which scholars believe was first employed in the eighth century, the plot of land was divided into three portions. The first field was planted with a winter crop, such as wheat, the second with a spring crop, such as oats, and the third was left fallow. The second year the fallow field was planted with a winter crop, the original first field was planted with a spring crop, and the second field was left fallow. The third year, the first field was left fallow, the second was planted with a winter crop,

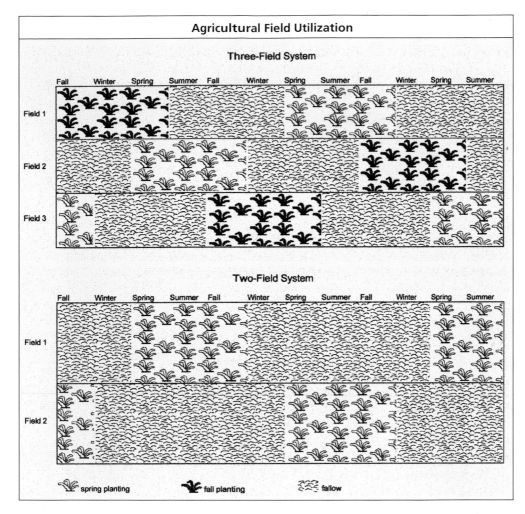

Agricultural Field Utilization

Three-Field System

| | Fall | Winter | Spring | Summer | Fall | Winter | Spring | Summer | Fall | Winter | Spring | Summer |

Field 1
Field 2
Field 3

Two-Field System

| | Fall | Winter | Spring | Summer | Fall | Winter | Spring | Summer | Fall | Winter | Spring | Summer |

Field 1
Field 2

spring planting   fall planting   fallow

39 The widespread use of the three-field system of agriculture dramatically increased the food supply of medieval Europe. In this procedure, two fields were planted (one with a winter crop, and one with a spring crop), while the third lay fallow. In the next year, one of the originally planted fields was left fallow, and in the following year the third was not planted. This system of field rotation enhanced the productivity of the land.

and the third with a spring crop. The three-year cycle was then repeated, beginning in the fourth year.

There were obvious advantages to this system, which was gradually adopted throughout Europe. First, only 33 percent of the land lay fallow in any given year, as opposed to 50 percent in the two-field system. Further, the fact that two different crops were sown at different times of the year spread the plowing more evenly throughout the year and offered some protection against a failing crop. In addition, the system enabled farmers to grow a spring crop of oats, which provided fodder for their horses.

A technological innovation that had a significant effect on agricultural production in northern Europe was the adoption of the heavy plow. This replaced the light scratch-plow used by the Romans, although the scratch-plow continued to be employed in the south, where the soil was lighter. The new implement, whose design had many local variations, was more suited to the dense soil of the north, since it was equipped with a blade that cut vertically into the sod, a flat plowshare that sliced the grass horizontally at the roots, and a moldboard that turned the slice of turf. Some plows had two wheels,

40 The heavy-wheeled plow, equipped with a blade which cut vertically into the sod, was much more effective in cultivating the heavy earth of northern Europe than the light scratch-plow suited to the more sandy soil of the south. The wheels made it possible for the farmer to move from furrow to furrow more easily—a great advantage in fields customarily plowed in long strips.

which served as a fulcrum, so that the farmer could put more pressure on the share, allowing him to move more easily from field to field and aiding him in regulating the depth of the furrows (**fig. 40**). Other heavy plows had a swing mechanism, in which the direction and depth of the furrow were totally governed by the skill of the operator.

Use of these heavy plows brought some vital changes to the agricultural practices of Europe. In order to till the heavy soils, the farmers had to use larger teams of animals for plowing, such as eight oxen, or a combination of six oxen and two horses (primarily in England) or four horses (primarily in France). Since it was difficult to turn these long teams when they reached the end of the furrow, the fields were made as long as possible. Thus, the use of the heavy-wheeled plow tended to change the shape of the fields from a square form to an oblong area in which long strips could be cultivated with greater efficiency. (**Fig. 41** shows an

41 The system of plowing fields in long strips, commonly used in the Middle Ages, endures to this day as is shown in this mid-twentieth-century photograph of the village of Padbury, England. The hedges seen here are not a medieval feature, but rather a development of the late eighteenth century.

aerial view of English fields plowed in strips, a pattern typical of the medieval period.) The use of the heavy plow also led to the adoption of another agricultural implement, the harrow, which leveled the earth and helped blend the seeds with the soil.

The new technique of plowing greatly increased the production of grain. Calculations indicate that the average yield at harvest for each measure of grain sown increased from approximately 2.5 to 4. According to some estimates, it was not until the eighteenth century that yields rose beyond the level attained in the thirteenth and early fourteenth centuries.

Other developments of great importance in the increase of agricultural production in the eleventh century were the invention of the horse collar and the increased use of iron horseshoes, both of which made possible a more efficient use of horsepower. The Greeks and the Romans had never learned the proper way to harness a horse. Instead, they had adapted the yoke harness commonly used for oxen, apparently not realizing that when the horses began to pull, the neck straps of the harnesses pressed on the animals' jugular veins and windpipes, partially strangling them. As a twentieth-century French historian, Lefebvre des Noettes, pointed out, the horses that adorn many ancient mon-

42 The month of October in the *Fécamp Psalter* (c. 1180) is represented by images of plowing and sowing. A rigid collar rests on the shoulder blades of the horse, and onto it is attached a harrow. The development of this harness and the use of horseshoes made horsepower more practical, although the animals were expensive to acquire and maintain.

uments may have assumed the graceful pose shown, with their heads raised and thrown back, in order to avoid strangulation. Des Noettes discovered from experiments with live animals that horses harnessed in the ancient way had a difficult time pulling loads heavier than 1,100 pounds (500 kilograms).

Medieval farmers began to use rigid padded collars which lay on the shoulder blades of the animal and did not hamper its breathing. These collars, originally designed for camels, seem to have been used initially in the steppes which separate China from Siberia. By 800 they were being used in Europe, and Norwegian documents from the late ninth century mention the employment of horses for plowing, no doubt with the new collars. After the eleventh century, illustrations of horses plowing with the modern harness appear with increasing frequency, and it may be noted that the horses no longer raise their heads. An example of horses working the fields is to be found in the *Fécamp Psalter* (c. 1180) (**fig. 41**), where a horse pulls a harrow.

The efficiency of horses was further enhanced by the nailing of iron shoes to their hooves as protection and support, an especially necessary aid in moist climates. This practice was probably initiated by the nomadic riders of Siberia, as indicated by archeological remains from the ninth and tenth centuries. They were used in Byzantium soon afterwards, and by the eleventh century horseshoes were common in Europe. The *Domesday Book*, a survey of England in the late eleventh century, records that six smiths in Hereford were obliged to make 120 horseshoes for the king each year, and by the twelfth century the mass production of horseshoes was common. They became a vital necessity for war and transportation, as well as for agriculture.

Medieval farmers were slow, however, to adopt the use of horsepower. Although horses were considerably more efficient than oxen, because of their greater speed and agility, they were more expensive to acquire and maintain. Further, horses were fed oats, which had to be specially grown. While the adoption of the three-field system aided in accommodating this need, this still represented a substantial investment, and horses were initially used only by the wealthy and enterprising landowners. They were employed first in densely populated areas because horses, particularly when used with the heavy plow and the three-field system, led to a very great increase in productivity. In areas of sparse population, agricultural innovation such as this occurred slowly.

These technological developments also had a significant social influence. Since few small landowners could afford to acquire and maintain the expensive machines and the animals necessary to pull them, they turned to communal effort. As a consequence, the cultivated area was extended, and the nucleated village emerged as a distinctive form of settlement. The result was the dramatic growth of a rich agricultural economy. This in turn made possible the development of the manorial (or seignorial) and political system that characterized the medieval world—a system often referred to as "feudalism."

Vassalage and the Manorial Economy

The dominant political structure of the medieval period, a structure built on ties of loyalty, is frequently defined as a system of vassalage. Although this system used to be described by the term feudalism, some historians now believe that that term should be abolished. Their argument stems from research which has demonstrated that there was great variation in the practice of vassalage in different areas; it is therefore impossible, they argue, or at least inappropriate, to see all of these practices as examples of a single, universal theoretical model. The issue is made more complicated by the fact that Marxist historians have used the term "feudalism" to apply to any form of economic exploitation, rather than to describe a specific political system. Hence, many historians feel that the term has become so imprecise as to be meaningless.

Nonetheless, while it is certainly true that the concept presented in textbooks of a single feudal system is oversimplified, and that the term is not frequently found in documentary sources without some form of qualification, some of the features traditionally associated with feudalism are common throughout European society of the Middle Ages. Furthermore, it is impossible to begin to understand such concepts as "chivalry," for example, or "manorialism," if one lacks familiarity with the general premises of the feudal system. Hence, the description that follows presents the basic ideas and practices—practices that can be substantiated in documents, both legal and literary—on which society was built between the ninth and fifteenth centuries.

Vassalage

The Carolingian rulers, as noted in Chapter 4, established relationships with their nobility that were based on bonds of loyalty. These bonds had their origins in the pledges or ties of allegiance exemplified by the practices of the *comitatus* of the Germanic tribal tradition (see Chapter 1). By the time of the Carolingians, these vows had been formalized, and the nobility became ***vassi dominici***, or vassals of the lord. In order to establish a force of expert cavalry, the Carolingians then developed a system usually described as "feudal tenure" by associating vassalage with the holding of parcels of land or **fiefs**. These grants of land included organized agricultural settlements known as **manors**, which were worked by the native peasants according to a customary routine of labor. Within his fief, the royal vassal raised military forces, administered justice, collected fines and local taxes, and exacted services from the peasants for the upkeep of roads, bridges, and fortifications.

These practices then spread rapidly from the Carolingian Empire to other areas of Europe. When that empire disintegrated, the system evolved to become the mainstay of a society that had no centralized government. The feudal institutions continued to thrive because they provided a simple and practical means of stabilizing a community that was under assault. Thus, in its evolved form, feudal practices provided military protection in a time of great upheaval.

By the eleventh century, the association of vassalage with the holding of fiefs had become institutionalized, and specific rituals that confirmed the bonds between the grantor and the holder of the fief were mandatory. It is important to remember that the system of vassalage applied only to individuals of one social class: the nobility. Although the vassal was technically in an inferior position to his lord, both were members of the warrior aristocracy. The system was not confined, however, to laypeople. Men and women of high rank in the clergy could, and often did, enter into the feudal relationship of vassalage, holding fiefs of secular lords. Their military responsibilities were either performed by substitutes or commuted to a money payment (see below, p. 149).

Lord and vassal were bound to one another by a ceremony known as **homage**. The details of the homage ritual are exemplified in a description from 1127. The vassal, bareheaded and unarmed, knelt before the lord.

> First, they did homage in the following way. The count asked if he [the vassal] would become completely his man, and the other replied "I am willing"; and with the clasped hands [of the vassal] surrounded by the hands of the count, they were bound together by a kiss.

Another account from a French digest of feudal practice by Boutillier gives a similar description:

> The man should put his hands together as a sign of humility, and place them between the two hands of his lord as a token that he vows everything to him and promises faith to him; and the lord should receive him and promise to keep faith with him. Then the man should say: "Sir, I enter your homage and faith and become your man by mouth and hands [that is, by taking the oath and placing his hands

43 The "mixing of hands" (*immixtio manuum*) was an essential part of the homage ceremony, symbolizing the pledging of one nobleman to another. In the almost "cartoon-like" gestures seen in this manuscript from Heidelberg, the vassal also points to himself, meaning that he is willing to "be the man" of his lord, and he indicates stalks of grain growing around him—symbols of the fief he will receive.

between those of the lord], and I swear and promise to keep faith and loyalty to you against all others, and to guard your rights with all my strength."

As may be observed in these accounts, the homage ceremony consisted of three parts. First the clasped hands of the vassal were surrounded by the hands of the lord; this was the ***immixtio manuum*** or "mixing of hands." This was followed by a declaration of intention to serve, the ***volo*** (literally "I am willing"), and the ceremony was completed by a kiss.

Fig. 43 pictures the *immixtio manuum*, by which one man pledged himself to another. Contemporaneous texts speak of "commending oneself into vassalage by one's hands," and this act formed an essential part of the ceremony. According to an English digest of feudal law by Bracton, it signified "on the part of the lord, protection, defense, and guarantee; on the part of the vassal, reverence and subjection." In the illustration the vassal has three additional hands; with one he points to himself as the person desiring to enter the relationship, and with the other two he points to stalks of corn, which symbolize the fief for which he is doing homage.

44 After the pledge and the "mixing of hands," the ritual of homage was "sealed" with a kiss, as shown on this tile from Chertsey Abbey, England (c. 1250–70). In this, as well as other components of the ceremony, the rites of homage and fealty resemble a present-day wedding service.

The feudal kiss, seen in **fig. 44**, was described in an ordinance on homage and fealty in the following way. After receiving homage from the vassal and performing the *immixtio manuum*, "The Lord should immediately reply to him: 'And I receive you and take you as my man, and give you this kiss as a sign of faith.'"

The homage ceremony was followed by the swearing of **fealty**, in which the vassal pledged his faith to the lord. He then confirmed this oath while resting his hand on the Bible or on a casket of holy relics. One digest of feudal practice recounts that the man who had done homage gave his fealty to the representative of the count with these words: "I promise on my faith that I will in future be faithful to Count William, and will observe [the obligations of] my homage to him completely, against all persons, in good faith and without deceit." He then took his oath to this on the relics of the saints. Afterwards, with a little rod that the count held in his hand, the count granted fiefs to all who by this agreement had given their security and homage and sworn the necessary oath.

The oath of fealty was described in more detail in another document ("The Grant of a Fief," c. 1200):

> When a free tenant shall swear fealty to his lord, let him place his right hand on the book and speak thus: "Hear thou this, my lord, that I will be faithful and loyal to you and will keep my pledges to you for the lands which I claim to hold of you, and that I will loyally perform for you the services specified, so help me God and the saints." Then he shall kiss the book [the Bible]; but he shall not kneel when he swears fealty, nor take so humble a posture as is required in homage.

Following the rituals of homage and fealty, the lord invested the vassal with a symbol of the fief, which could take the form of a stalk of grain, a clod of earth, or a standard, as in **fig. 45**. Here the lord is handing standards to his vassals who are laymen, while he gives a scepter to two other vassals, a bishop and an abbess.

These actions of public ritual—homage and fealty—confirmed the relationship between lord and vassal but also implied a series of obligations or responsibilities between them. The primary responsibility of the lord was to provide protection and maintenance. He was bound to come to his vassal's aid in the event of unjustified attack, and he was obliged to shield the vassal against his enemies. He was also expected to defend him in a court of law. The lord guaranteed the vassal's possession of the fief, and would guard against any attempts to deprive him of it. The granting of the fief, on the other hand, enabled the vassal to provide the military service that he owed to his lord.

Vassalage implied a personal obligation on the part of the vassal to fight for the lord as a heavy-armed cavalryman, or knight. In addition, the holder of a valuable fief was expected to bring with him a mounted company of his own vassals. The army of every feudal prince was gathered in this way. In the early stages of feudalism the quota of knights and length of time required in the field was not fixed, but by the twelfth century the usual span was forty days.

45 This manuscript from Heidelberg illustrates vividly the bestowing of the symbols of the fief. Here, the vassals (on the right) who are laymen receive a battle standard from the lord, and the bishop and abbess are given a scepter.

It is interesting to note that the period of fine weather just before the harvest season tended also generally to last about forty days, and that it was probably the most common time for combat. A document from the thirteenth century defines military service in the following way:

> The baron and the vassals of the king ought to appear in his army when they are summoned, and ought to serve at their own expense for forty days and forty nights, with whatever number of knights they owe. And he [the king] possesses the right to exact from them these services when he wishes and when he has need of them. If, however, the king wishes to keep them more than forty days and forty nights at their own expense, they need not remain unless they so desire. But if he wishes to retain them at his cost for the defense of the kingdom, they ought lawfully to remain. But if he proposes to lead them outside of the kingdom, they need not go unless they are willing, for they have already served their forty days and forty nights.

In order to fulfill his quota of knights, the vassal often employed a process that became known as **subinfeudation**. This feudal arrangement was by no means universal, and the precise details varied from place to place. However, as an example, let us assume that a nobleman gave a large and valuable fief to a vassal, and that the fief consisted of land with twenty-five manors to be held in exchange for the service of ten knights. The vassal had the option of retaining all twenty-five manors in his own possession, or he could subinfeudate some of them to meet his feudal obligation. If he wanted to retain the manors for his own use, or in **demesne**, he would need either to hire or to maintain ten knights in his own household. But if he found this difficult or impractical, he could grant some of his holdings as fiefs to vassals of his own. For example, he might grant five of the manors to another man, who would promise him, in exchange, the service of five knights. He could also grant one manor each to four more knights, thus achieving the requisite number of ten knights, including himself, to fulfill his own obligation.

The system of subinfeudation became very complex, since many vassals committed themselves to more than one lord. In theory, however, and in practice, the vassal's primary allegiance was to the first lord to whom he had pledged his loyalty. This man was his **liege lord**. The process may be seen in operation in France, in the grant of Thiebault, count of Troyes, to Jocelyn d'Avalon, in which the order of allegiance is clearly specified:

> I, Thiebault, **count palatine** of Troyes, make known to those present and to come, that I have given in fee [a fief] to Jocelyn d'Avalon and his heirs the manor which is called Gillencourt, which is of the castellany of La Ferte sur Aube; and whatever the same Jocelyn shall be able to acquire in the same manor I have granted to him and his heirs in augmentation of that fief . . . The same Jocelyn, moreover, on account of this has become my liegeman, saving, however, his allegiance to Gerard d'Arcy, and to the lord duke of Burgundy and to Peter, count of Auxerre.

> Done at Chouaude, by my own witness, in the year of the Incarnation of our Lord 1200, in the month of January. Given by the hand of Walter, my chancellor.

Jocelyn, in accordance with typical feudal practice, has become the vassal of Thiebault, and will be his liegeman, with the exception of his commitments to Gerard d'Arcy and Peter, count of Auxerre.

An obvious problem might occur if two lords of the same vassal declared war on each other. Sometimes provision was made in the original pledge to deal with such an event, as in the following document:

> I, John of Toul, make known that I am the liege man of the lady Beatrice, countess of Troyes, and of her son, Theobald, count of Champagne, against every creature, living or dead, saving my allegiance to lord Enjorand of Coucy, lord John of Arcis, and the count of Grandpré. If it should happen that the count of Grandpré should be at war with the countess and count of Champagne on his own quarrel, I will aid the count of Grandpré in my own person, and will send to the count and the countess of Champagne the knights whose service I owe to them for the fief which I hold of them. But if the count of Grandpré shall make war on the countess and the count of Champagne on behalf of his friends and not in his own quarrel, I will aid in my own person the countess and count of Champagne, and will send one knight to the count of Grandpré for the service which I owe him for the fief which I hold of him, but I will not go myself into the territory of the count of Grandpré to make war on him.

In this case, John pledged himself to four lords, and owed allegiance and military service to all of them. It was the usual practice, as documented here, for the vassal to do liege homage to one of the lords whom he would serve in person. He would send the required contingent of knights to his other lords.

Another responsibility of the vassal was his obligation to serve on the lord's court, which he was expected to attend at his own expense when summoned. This service was known as **suit to court**. The occasion might be ceremonial, such as a wedding or a festival. More frequently, however, the vassals were expected to give advice to the lord concerning war or governance, or to take part in a trial. The law under which vassals lived was subject to interpretation, and when one of them was accused of a misdeed, he was entitled to be judged by his peers. Thus the vassal was expected to participate in deciding disputes that arose between the lord and a vassal, or between two vassals. He would also help to adjudicate disputes arising from questions concerning rights of inheritance. In addition, the vassal provided counsel—that is, he gave advice to the lord concerning matters such as the advisability of going on a crusade, or making war on his neighbors. Since the lord technically required the service of his vassals in these enterprises, it became a practical necessity as well as a feudal custom to seek counsel from his men.

In the Carolingian period the fief, and the obligations deriving from it, were not hereditary. Over the following centuries, however, the nobility established the practice of passing the lands and power they had accumulated to their heirs. By the eleventh century, it was customary for the heir to inherit the fief as well as the responsibility for holding it, and to do homage and swear fealty to his lord on taking up possession. Indeed, the repetition of the original ceremony of homage and fealty was mandatory.

The practice of passing the fief and its obligations to the next generation carried with it potential problems. What would happen if the heir was not yet an adult, or if she was a woman? In the first instance, the child became the ward of his lord, who was obliged to give the fief to the child when the latter reached maturity, and who was pledged not to give away any portion of the fief and to maintain it satisfactorily. The lord had the same commitment to maintain the fief if the heir were a girl, and also possessed the right to choose a husband for the young woman when she reached marriageable age. According to a source from Normandy:

> When a female ward reaches the proper age to marry, she should be married by the advice and consent of her lord, and by the advice and consent of her relatives and friends, according as the nobility of her ancestry and the value of her fief may require; and upon her marriage the fief which has been held in guardianship should be given over to her. A woman cannot be freed from wardship except by marriage; and let it not be said that she is of age until she is twenty years old. But if she be married at the age at which it is allowable for a woman to marry, the fact of her marriage makes her of age and delivers her fief from wardship.
>
> The fiefs of those who are under wardship should be cared for attentively by their lords, who are entitled to receive the produce and profits. And in this connection let it be known that the lord ought to preserve in their former condition the buildings, the manor houses, the forests and meadows, the gardens, the ponds, the mills, the fisheries, and the other things of which he has the profits. And he should not sell, destroy, or remove the woods, the houses, or the trees.

If a childless widow inherited the fief, the lord had the right to choose a new husband for her, although it was possible in some circumstances for her to pay a fee to avoid remarriage. The English *Exchequer Rolls* offer evidence concerning several women who were able to do this:

> Alice, countess of Warwick, renders account of 1,000 pounds and 10 palfreys [horses] to be allowed to remain a widow as long as she pleases, and not to be forced to marry by the king. And if perchance she should wish to marry, she shall not marry except with the assent and on the grant of the king, where the king shall be satisfied; and to have the custody of her sons whom she has from the earl of Warwick her late husband.
>
> Hawisa, who was wife of William Fitz Robert, renders account of 130 marks and 4 palfreys that she may have peace from Peter of Borough, to whom the king has given permission to marry her; and that she may not be compelled to marry.

Furthermore, just as in the case of the female ward, the lord could not disparage a widow, that is, force her to marry anyone below her social rank.

Heirs were obliged on taking possession of the fief to pay an inheritance "tax" called a **relief**. The amount was arbitrary at first, but by the twelfth century there were some fixed standards. Extracts from English treasury records show that, for example, John of Venetia rendered an account of 300 marks for the fine (fee) of his land and for the relief of the land that was his father's, which he held from the king by direct royal grant (*in capite*), and Peter de Bruce rendered an account of 100 pounds for his relief for the barony that he inherited from his father.

Other feudal responsibilities were known as **feudal aids**. These were irregular and exceptional expenses incurred by the lord to which the vassals were obliged to contribute. The custom in Normandy, for example, was "to pay three aids . . . first, for the knighting of the lord's oldest son; second, for the marriage of the lord's oldest daughter; third, for the ransom of the lord." As may be seen in the following excerpt from the Poiton region in western France, the expected aids eventually included, in addition to these three, the payment of relief on inheritance of the fief and the provision of resources, either personal or monetary, when the lord went on crusade.

> In the chatelainerie [territory dependent on a castle] of Poitou and that region, according to the custom of the land, those who hold fiefs pay five aids to the lord: for the knighting of the lord's son, for the marriage of the lord's oldest daughter, for the rachat [relief] of the lord's fief, for the crusade, and for the ransom of the lord from the hands of the Saracens.

As well as these expenditures, the vassal owed hospitality to his lord; this consisted of providing food, shelter, and entertainment for the lord and his entire retinue when he came to visit. As these expenses could become quite onerous, they were eventually very clearly defined, and were sometimes commuted to a money payment.

In addition to material obligations, there was a code of personal behavior expected of the vassal, commonly defined as honor. The vassal was required to be completely loyal to his lord, and to make certain that he would come to no harm. The worst violation on the part of the vassal was allowing his lord to be wounded or slain, but an almost equal offense was the seduction of his lord's wife or his eldest daughter. Although younger daughters were not specified in feudal law codes, it was probably also considered socially unacceptable to seduce them.

As long as both parties in the feudal contract, the lord and the vassal, met their respective obligations, the fief remained in the possession of the vassal. If the vassal died without heirs and without leaving a will, fief reverted to the lord by a custom known as **escheat**. This also occurred when the vassal committed treason or a felony, or if he failed to fulfill his feudal responsibilities. In common practice, however, warfare often broke out in such a situation, as one lord attempted to retain possession of the fief while the other fought to reclaim it.

The nature of these feudal obligations and arrangements makes clear that military action was an endemic part of the medieval world. Feudal lords fought one another in order to gain territory, and dominated their immediate environs through the use of force, employing their knights to subjugate the local villages and plunder the lands of the Church. They used their castles as strongholds from which to prey upon traveling merchants and to hold hostages for ransom; such acts of violence were common and devastating to society.

In an attempt to establish a more peaceful atmosphere, the Church eventually enacted a series of measures known as the **Peace of God** and the **Truce of God**. The Peace of God, initially proclaimed by Church councils between 989 and 1050, stipulated that anyone who used violence towards women, peasants, merchants, or members of the clergy should be excommunicated. The Truce of God, initiated by Pope John XV in 958 and first enacted in 1027, proclaimed that men should abstain from warfare and violence for part of each week, and during specified church festivals and holy seasons. Extended periods, such as Lent, were eventually incorporated, until only eighty days remained in the entire year during which it was permissible to fight. The following decree, from about 1065, contains provisions of both the Peace and the Truce:

> 1. This Peace has been confirmed by the bishops, by the abbots, by the counts and viscounts and the other God-fearing nobles in this bishopric, to the effect that in the future, beginning with this day, no man may commit an act of violence in a church, or in the space which surrounds it and which is covered by its privileges, or in the burying-ground, or in the dwelling-houses which are, or may be, within thirty paces of it.

> 2. Furthermore, it is forbidden to despoil or pillage the communities of canons, monks, and religious persons, the ecclesiastical lands which are under the protection of the Church, or the clergy, who do not bear arms; and if any one shall do such a thing, let him pay a double fine.

> 3. Let no one burn or destroy the dwellings of the peasants and the clergy, the dovecotes and the granaries. Let no man dare to kill, to beat, or to wound a peasant or serf, or the wife of either, or to seize them and carry them off, except for misdemeanors which they may have committed; but it is not forbidden to lay hold of them in order to bring them to justice, and it is allowable to do this even before they shall have been summoned to appear. Let not the raiment of the peasants be stolen; let not their ploughs, or their hoes, or their olive fields be burned.

> 4. The bishops of whom we have spoken have solemnly confirmed the Truce of God, which has been enjoined upon all Christians, from the setting of the sun of the fourth day of the week, that is to say, Wednesday, until the rising of the sun on Monday, the second day . . . When the bishop and the chapter shall have pronounced sentences to recall men to the observance of the Peace and the Truce of God, the sureties and hostages who show themselves hostile to the bishop and the chapter shall be excommunicated by the chapter and the bishop, with their protectors and partisans, as guilty of violating the Peace and the Truce of the Lord; they and their possessions shall be excluded from the Peace and the Truce of the Lord.

The Peace of God and the Truce of God provide examples of the way in which the Church encouraged the aristocratic warrior class gradually to adopt less aggressive, more civilized, and more genteel forms of behavior. By the end of the eleventh century, other aspects of this change were evident, as various texts begin to mention a religious ceremony that took place for the purpose of "making a knight," or "dubbing to knighthood."

Knighthood and the development of chivalry

A male of the aristocratic class, the son of a knight, usually was groomed to be knighted. While still a young boy, he began his apprenticeship as a squire, often in the household of his father's lord, where he cleaned stables, curried horses, cleaned armor, and served at table while he was learning the knightly accomplishments of riding a horse and wielding a sword and lance. When he was deemed ready, he participated in the "dubbing" ritual associated with entering into knighthood.

During the night before the ceremony, the candidate kept a vigil in the castle chapel. The next morning he dressed in new clothing, usually made of white silk, and appeared for the dubbing ceremony. First he was given the arms symbolic of his new status by an older sponsor, often his father or his father's lord. Then the sponsor laid a heavy blow with the flat of his hand on the young man's neck or cheek, accompanied by the words, "Be *preux*" (i.e., be a knight possessing prowess, or the ability to defeat opponents in battle). This blow, called the *paumée* or *colée* in French documents, was very like the blow bestowed by the bishop on a clerk being ordained as a priest during the confirmation ceremony, and seems to have symbolized a similar relationship between the sponsor and the newly established knight (**fig. 46**). An essential part of the ceremony was the blessing of the sword. The aspiring knight laid his sword on the altar, a gesture that was accompanied or followed by prayers. A specific liturgy eventually developed which comprised similar prayers for the other arms or insignia—banner, lance, and shield—and the officiating priest did the arming himself. The sword was girded on by the bishop, while the delivery of the spurs was reserved for a layman. The ceremony often ended with a display of knightly prowess by the new initiate, as he jumped onto his horse and with a blow of his lance demolished a suit of armor attached to a post (the *quintaine*).

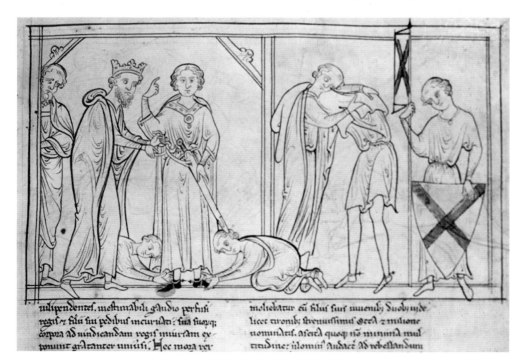

46 In this drawing from the *Historia de Offa Rege* (*Life of King Offa*) by the twelfth-century writer Matthew Paris, the young Offa receives his arms from King Wermund, who girds the new knight with his sword as courtiers attach spurs to his boots. In the center he receives a cloak, and at the right he is seen with his shield and battle standard.

In addition to his prowess with weaponry, the knight was expected to be accomplished in various aristocratic pursuits, such as hunting and falconry. Later in the medieval period he was also expected to compose poetry and music, and to be versed in the arts of courtly love (see Chapter 10).

The peasantry and the manorial system

Just as the relationships between members of the nobility were defined and circumscribed by a set of customs, so the relationships between the nobles and their peasants were governed by a set of practices, which may be subsumed under the term **manorialism**. As mentioned earlier, each fief held by a vassal contained within it one or more manors, and wealthy noblemen frequently held several fiefs with several manors in each. These agricultural settlements were worked by the peasants in order to provide sustenance for the feudal nobility. Manors differed significantly in terms of size and complexity, and there was great variety in the political, social, and legal status of the inhabitants, with some being free peasants and others unfree serfs. The *Domesday Book*, for example, includes five main categories of peasants, although the distinctions are not consistently applied. These are **freemen**, **socmen**, **cottagers**, **bordars**, and **villeins**. The freemen and socmen seem to have been bound to their lords by payment of rents, and the bordar probably possessed a smallholding. The villeins (serfs) were typical peasants under bondage. Slaves are also mentioned in the survey, although slavery seems to have been rare by the end of the eleventh century.

The living conditions of the free peasants were quite similar to those of the unfree serfs or villeins. The main distinction between the two groups was the right to own and inherit property (see below). The difference in status seems to have been an outgrowth of the gradations of subordination to a chieftain that characterized early medieval society, and the customs regarding actual "freedom" varied widely in the different regions of Europe. Agricultural practices, however, were quite similar in England, northern France, and most of Germany. The following discussion provides a description of these common elements, as found in manors throughout northern Europe.

The medieval manor was a self-contained agricultural settlement which grew up around a large establishment such as a castle, an abbey, or a bishop's residence. It was generally under the control of a single lord, who was supported by his tenants, both free and unfree, in exchange for his protection. The manor included a village (sometimes more than one) where the peasants and unfree serfs lived, and a small church. A stream with one or more ponds and a forested or wooded area were typical geographical features (**fig. 47**). The arable land on the manor was divided into portions; the greater part, usually between a third and a half, comprised the demesne of the lord; another portion (the **glebe** land) was cultivated for the use of the Church; and the remainder was apportioned into tenants' holdings and common lands. The demesne land consisted of strips interspersed with those of the tenants. Also found on the manor were utilities, called **banalities**, owned by the lord, which the serfs were required to use. These included a mill, an oven, and a wine press (and/or brewery).

The daily management of the manor was generally entrusted to a steward or bailiff, who supervised planting, cultivating, and harvesting, and collected the lord's revenues, which consisted of both rents and services. A description of an English manor held by the

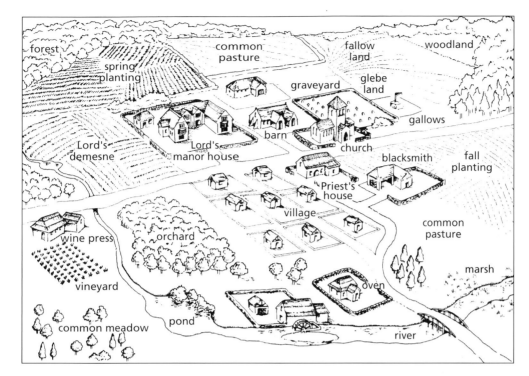

Abbot of Peterborough illustrates typical obligations in goods and labor:

> In Wermington are 7 **hides** at the taxation of the king. And of this land 20 full villeins and 29 half-villeins hold 34 **virgates** and a half; and for these the full villeins work 3 days a week through the year; and the half-tenants as much as corresponds to their tenancies. And these men have in all 16 plows, and they plow 68 acres and a half and besides this they do 3 boon-works with their plows, and they ought to bring from the woods 34 wagonloads of wood. And all these men pay 4 pounds, 11 shillings, 4 pence; and at the love feast of St. Peter, 10 rams and 400 loaves and 40 platters and 34 hens and 260 eggs. And there are 8 socmen who have 6 plows. In the demesne of the court are 4 plows and 32 oxen and 9 cows and 5 calves and 1 riding horse and 129 sheep and 61 swine and 1 draught horse and 1 colt. And there is 1 mill with 1 virgate of land, and 6 acres which pays 60 shillings and 500 eels. And Ascelin, the clerk, holds the church with 2 virgates of land, from the altar of St. Peter of Borough. Robert, son of Richard, has 2 virgates and a half. In this vill 100 sheep can be placed.

This document delineates an arrangement through which the lord exploited the labor of his peasants and unfree serfs, generally called the manorial or seignorial system. As may be seen, the landlord was due three days of work each week during the year, with a commensurate commitment from the half-tenants. The peasants were also obligated to work an extra three days (boon-works) with their plows, and required to gather 34 wagonloads of wood. In addition, they paid rent both in money and in animal produce.

As noted above, the peasants and serfs worked the demesne for the lord, who was also entitled to a share of the hay that the peasants harvested from the meadow. The lord's livestock grazed in the pasture, under the watchful eye of the village shepherds. Peasants provided labor at the times of the year when crops were planted and harvested, and if a bridge needed to be repaired, or if the lord wanted to have a ditch dug or a barn built.

Besides performing these services, the tenants were obliged to pay a variety of rents in kind; in the example above, the peasants owed hens and eggs. They were also expected to give a portion of the wood they gathered to the lord, and to pay him in pork if they allowed their pigs to feed in the forested area, a practice known as *pannage*. If the tenant fished in the stream on the manor, he owed a portion of his catch to the lord. The women of the village assisted in the field, and they were also expected to work in the lord's house on tasks such as spinning, weaving, or combing wool. In addition to all of these rents and taxes, the peasants were required to pay a **tithe** (a tenth of their produce) to the Church.

Besides the aforementioned rents, goods, and services owed to the lord by his peasants, he had some additional rights over his unfree tenants, who were known as serfs.

Although outright slavery was known in the early medieval period, it was rare by the eleventh century. Serfs, in contrast to slaves, were personally free; that is, they had the right to own and inherit property, and to bring suit in the manorial court. The primary restriction on their freedom was that they were not allowed to leave the manor where they were born; they were "bound to the soil," and this was the main distinction between serfs and free peasants. One obligation, usually considered to be a hallmark of the unfree, was the payment of the *merchet*, a fee owed to the lord for permission for a serf's daughter to marry. The fee was higher if the woman married a man from another manor, since the lord would then lose the labor of her offspring.

The serf was also subject to the jurisdiction of the lord. Disputes among the villagers as well as cases of petty crime were settled in the manorial courts, and the fines levied became an additional source of revenue for the lord. The bailiff of the manor generally presided over the court, and judgments were rendered according to the customs of the individual manor—a body of community regulations established and transmitted by generations of peasants. The following excerpt provides an example of the type of case tried in a manorial court:

If anyone cuts another's wood, or mows his grass, or fishes in his streams, he shall pay a fine of three shillings and make good the damage besides. If he fishes in another's fish-pond, or cuts down trees which have been planted, or fruit trees, or if he takes the fruit from a tree, or cuts down trees which mark boundaries, or removes stones which have been set up to mark boundaries, he shall pay a fine of thirty shillings . . . Whoever by night steals wood that has been cut, or grass that has been mown, shall be hung. If he steals them by day, he shall be punished in his "hair and skin." [This involved flogging the guilty party and winding his hair around a stick, which was turned round and round until the hair was pulled out.]

In deciding the verdict for more serious crimes such as rape and murder, the lord possessed rights of jurisdiction over the persons and property of his peasants. In

France and western Germany, this often constituted the power of life and death; in England and Normandy such "high justice" was restricted to duke and king.

The life of a medieval peasant, whether freeman or unfree serf, was therefore highly restricted and very onerous. He did, however, have a voice in the governance of his village community, and, most important, he had stability and security, knowing that he possessed the right to hold his own land and to pass it on to his heirs.

Domestic Life

Families in the eleventh century, in both the aristocratic and peasant classes, were based on the conjugal unit, and women of both economic levels participated in a variety of activities, within the family and outside the home. The lives of peasant women on the manor will be discussed later in this chapter; at this point let us turn to an examination of the duties and responsibilities of the women of the aristocratic world.

Recent research has shown that the once popular view of women as purely passive, as mere appendages to their husbands, is not completely authenticated by the sources. It is true that restrictions existed concerning marriage and the inheritance of land, as shown by the quotations earlier in this chapter, but it has become evident that women were not confined to the inner chambers of castles, only to be displayed on ceremonial occasions in order to enhance the status of their husbands. Instead, they were regarded as full members of their natal and marital families, and were not entirely excluded from inheriting and controlling property, although their prerogatives varied from region to region. In many areas of western Europe their rights to fiefs, titles, and wardship over minor heirs drew them into the network of vassalage. Although it was generally only men who performed the military service required of vassals, women, especially in France, took part in the customary oath-giving ceremonies and those who possessed a fief assumed the responsibilities for providing knights. Sometimes women garrisoned and fortified castles, amassed and commanded troops, and even rode into battle.

One fascinating example was Sichelgaita, a Lombard princess who became the wife of Robert Guiscard, the Norman conqueror of southern Italy (see Chapter 9). She often rode out to battle with her husband, clad in armor like his knights. Once, when their forces were retreating from an attack, Sichelgaita rode after them, her sword held high above her head. She must have been a ferocious sight, since she was highly effective at rallying the troops back into battle. Records indicate that she also managed the kingdom when her husband was traveling. (In addition, she bore ten children!)

Within the family, aristocratic women engaged in the expected activities. They bore children and supervised their educations and marriages, and they provided hospitality for visiting dignitaries, participated in courtly activities, performed lordly functions when their husbands were away, served as guardians and regents, and dispensed patronage and gifts.

A girl's education in an aristocratic household was often quite extensive (see, for example, the case of Heloise, discussed in Chapter 10), and most noble women seem to have achieved at least rudimentary literacy. Typically, however, literary accomplishment was second to the skill of needlework. There is also evidence that many women knew how to sing and perhaps played musical instruments.

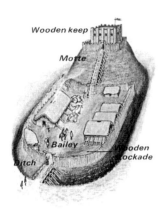

Wooden keep

Motte

Bailey

Wooden Stockade

Ditch

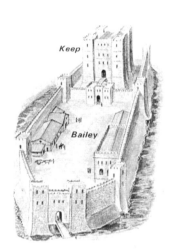

Keep

Bailey

48 Motte and bailey castles were inexpensive and quick to construct. Earth was excavated and piled into a mound, called the "motte," which rose over a flat area known as the "bailey." The ditch that resulted from the excavation was often filled with water, providing an effective line of defense. The central tower, called the "citadel" or "keep" was made of wood or, less often, stone.

In the eleventh century, the knight and his family, while certainly living more comfortably than the peasants, did not inhabit a grand establishment. The era of the handsome and spacious castle was in the future, and aristocrats lived in relatively primitive fortified buildings known as motte and bailey castles, one of the building styles widely used in England by William the Conqueror after 1066 (**fig. 48**) (before that time there were only half a dozen such castles in all of England). Most of these were of timber and earthwork, like the Continental castles of the eleventh century. A typical northern French castle in this style was described by Jean de Colmieu in the following way:

> It is the custom of the nobles of the neighborhood to make a mound of earth as high as they can and then encircle it with a ditch as wide and deep as possible. They enclose the space on top of the mound with a palisade of very strong hewn logs firmly fixed together, strengthened at intervals by as many towers as they have means for. Within the enclosure is a house, a central citadel or keep which commands the whole circuit of the defense. The entrance to the fortress is across a bridge . . . supported on pairs of posts . . . crossing the ditch and reaching the upper level of the mound at the level of the entrance gate [to the enclosure].

Since they required little specialized labor, motte and bailey castles were easy and inexpensive to build. Most were constructed of timber and earthwork, and, since the design was such that the structure was not dependent upon a specific type of terrain, a castle could be built wherever a fortification was needed. The motte, or mound, was sometimes natural, or partly natural, and sometimes partially or wholly artificial, having been created with the soil from the encircling ditch. The motte was circular, and was usually between about 100 and 300 feet (30–90 m) in diameter at the base. It varied in height from 10 to almost 100 feet (3–30 m), and had a wooden palisade at the top. The central part, called the "citadel" or the "keep," was usually made of wood, and was not much more extensive than a blockhouse or tower.

In areas where stone was plentiful, such as the French regions of Normandy and Anjou, the tower was sometimes of masonry construction. The tower was only large enough to accommodate the lord and his immediate family, and the entire space of the motte was too limited to house the garrison with its animals and supplies except in times of emergency. In order to solve this problem, a large space was cleared below the motte, called the bailey. This was circular or oval in shape, and also had a ditch and a palisade. The bailey was connected to the upper motte by an inclined trestle with a drawbridge. Sometimes two, or even three, baileys were constructed, depending on need. The entire garrison could use the bailey for everyday living, and in times of serious danger, they could crowd into the motte.

The living arrangements in these early castles were primitive by modern standards. The chronicler Lambert of Ardres gives the following description of a castle hall constructed on a motte in Flanders, in the twelfth century:

The first story was on the ground level, where there were cellars and granaries and great boxes, barrels, casks, and other household utensils. In the story above were the dwelling and common rooms of the residents, including the larders, pantry, and buttery and the great chamber in which the lord and lady slept. Adjoining this was . . . the dormitory of the ladies in waiting and children . . . In the upper story of the house were attic rooms in which on the one side the sons of the lord of the house, when they so desired, and on the other side the daughters, because they were obliged, were accustomed to sleep. In this story also the watchmen and the servants appointed to keep the house slept at various times. High up on the east side of the house, in a convenient place, was the chapel, decorated like the tabernacle of Solomon . . . There were stairs and passages from story to story, from the house into the [separate] kitchen, from room to room, and from the house into the gallery, where they used to entertain themselves with conversation, and again from the gallery into the chapel.

Such elaborate architecture must have been rare in the motte and bailey castle. In a typical castle the lord's family ate and slept in a building on top of the motte, while the outbuildings such as the kitchen, servants' quarters, barracks, smithy, stables, barns, and storehouses were located in the bailey. In another arrangement, the lord's family lived in a hall in the bailey, while the motte served as a watchtower and refuge.

The primary architectural feature of the living quarters in either of these styles was the hall. This was a large, one-room structure with a high ceiling, which was usually situated on the first floor; sometimes it was placed on the second story, a location that provided greater security. Initially the halls had aisles, similar to a church, with rows of wooden posts or stone pillars that supported the timber roof. Soon carpenters developed a method of roof construction with triangular supports that made it possible to eliminate the aisles and to have a large open space. In the eleventh and twelfth centuries, the windows were rarely set with glass, but were equipped with wooden shutters fastened by an iron bar. By the thirteenth century, however, kings and great noblemen often had white glass in some of the windows, and by the fourteenth century, glazed windows were unexceptional.

If the hall was located on the first story, the floor was of earth, stone, or plaster; if it was elevated to the second level, the floor was almost always made of timber, supported either by a row of wooden pillars or by stone vaulting. Carpets, which provided decoration as well as warmth, were placed on walls, tables, and benches, but they were not used on floors in England and northwestern Europe until the fourteenth century. Floor surfaces were covered with rushes, and sometimes with herbs such as basil, balm, chamomile, lavender, violets, and winter savory. The rushes and herbs were replaced occasionally, and the floor was swept.

The hall was usually entered through a door in a side wall. When the hall was on the second level, there was an outside stairway leading to the entrance. In some castles the staircase was enclosed in a building that guarded the entry to the keep; in others it was provided with a roof.

The great hall was the location for meals and festivities. A raised dais of wood or stone provided seating for the lord and his family. This platform was located at the opposite end of the hall from the entrance, thus providing shelter from drafts and intruders. The lord, and perhaps his wife, sat in huge chairs which were sometimes surmounted by a canopy to emphasize their status. The other occupants of the castle, as well as the guests, sat on benches below. The dining tables were usually set on trestles which could be disassembled between meals; a permanent table was another indication of prestige, and only the greatest lords possessed them. All of the tables were covered with cloths.

The hall was lit with rushlights or candles; oil lamps were sometimes used, which provided better lighting. It was heated by a log fire, a relatively efficient source of warmth. The fireplace was square, circular, or octagonal, and was surrounded by stone, tile, brick, or stone. Smoke poured out through a louver, a lantern-shaped structure in the roof with side openings. In order to provide protection against rain and snow, the openings were covered with sloping boards which could be closed by pulling strings.

In early castles, the lord and his family slept at the end of the hall, in sleeping quarters at the back of the dais, which was separated by a curtain or a screen. Eventually a permanent wooden partition was substituted for this temporary arrangement.

Water was generally available for washing and drinking on each floor. Castles such as Chepstow, on the Welsh border, or Restormel in Cornwall, had a cistern on an upper level from which pipes carried water to the floors below, with the flow controlled by valves with bronze or copper taps and spouts. Servants filled this tank, and waste water was carried away by lead pipes.

The lord and his family took baths in a wooden tub which was padded with cloth and situated under a tent or canopy. In winter, the tub was placed near the fireplace, and in summer it was often moved out into the garden. When the family traveled, the tub was taken along, and baths were prepared by a bathman. Some important thirteenth-century castles had permanent bathrooms, and the English king Henry III (r. 1216–1272) even had hot and cold running water in his bath house.

Eleventh-century castles did not provide an exceptionally luxurious environment for the aristocracy. As might be expected, however, the living circumstances of the aristocratic class were a good deal more comfortable than those of the peasants who worked their lands.

The peasant dwelling was a simple hovel, consisting of one room. It was a cottage constructed by establishing a frame made from two pairs of branches joined together at the top to support a ridge pole. The ridge pole provided support for other timbers, fixed either in the ground, a low wall of mud, or a solid foundation plank, which created a rectangular floor space. The roof timbers were stabilized and made watertight with a covering of mud or thatch. Building techniques gradually improved throughout the medieval period, and a long structure was eventually developed that contained a **wattle-and-daub** partition; this created two chambers, one for the family and the second for the cattle and other animals. The dwelling had a dirt floor, and heat was provided by the fire. Since there was no chimney, smoke escaped through the doorway and chinks in the roof. The only furniture available was built by the family, and straw or rushes provided the bedding.

By modern standards, the daily routine of the medieval peasant was grim and difficult. Peasants did not receive an education, although they would have gained a practical knowledge of the natural world as a result of their agricultural duties. The reality of daily existence is reflected in the following response from a plowman to his master:

O my lord, I work very hard: I go out at dawn, driving the cattle to the field, and
I yoke them to the plow. Nor is the weather so bad in winter that I dare to stay at
home, for fear of my lord: but when the oxen are yoked, and the plowshare and
coulter attached to the plow, I must plow one whole field a day, or more.

The men rose before daybreak to begin their work in the fields, or in their special
occupations on the manor, such as carpenter, blacksmith, shepherd, beekeeper, swine-
herd, or cowherd. Women did not usually drive the plow, but they were often enlisted
in the work of harvesting; although they probably were not given heavy tasks, they participated as gleaners, picking up stalks and kernels left behind by the harvesters. They
also weeded and cleaned the fields. Generally women were closely tied to the hearth—
cooking, weaving, and looking after the children.

The care of animals belonging to the family or peasant community was also a significant responsibility of women, as records from all over Europe indicate. They worked
as shepherdesses and milkmaids, milking the cows and ewes and making cheese. The
women prepared breakfast, which consisted of coarse rye bread, washed down with some
watery ale. No doubt they also cooked the evening meal—a meatless soup accompanied by more bread and a ration of cheese. Meat was available for food only in the autumn,
when the animals that were not needed for breeding or ploughing were slaughtered, owing
to the scarcity of winter fodder for them. If there was a quantity of meat, it would be salted
to preserve it for consumption at winter feasts; if there was no salt, it was hung in the
rafters of the cottage so it could be preserved by the smoke from the fire. Either fresh
or salted, it was probably tough because of the age of the slaughtered animals, and
more suited to boiling than roasting.

The children of serfs learned the tasks of manorial life in early childhood, undoubtedly by copying their elders. When they were younger than seven, both boys and girls were
expected to help with household tasks, and in later childhood they were sent to gather
fruit and nuts, to fish in the stream, and to gather firewood. As they approached adolescence, the girls were taught to cook and weave, while boys followed their fathers in
working with tools and performing agricultural duties.

The manorial villages were, for the most part, self-supporting. Certain articles, however, were purchased if they were not produced locally. Salt, tar, iron, and millstones were
examples of some of these. Salt was an especially necessary commodity, and when the
king and the lords who were fortunate to possess the rights in the great salt "**wiches**" had
taken enough for their needs, the "salter" arrived and filled his wagon with salt blocks,
to be sold in the villages and market towns. The blocks were stored and then ground
for general use.

During the winter, when people could not work in the fields, both men and women
devoted themselves to domestic chores. They worked in unpleasant conditions—dark,
smoky, and odorous—with artificial light provided by the fire and the rushlights made
by the women from peeled rushes, soaked in fat. The men constructed crude furniture
and made wooden platters and spoons for domestic equipment and scythes as well as
rakes and other rough tools used in cultivation. They also braided reed baskets and
traps for catching fish. The women spun and wove the wool sheared from the family sheep
and made linen from hemp or nettles as well as sewing thread from nettles. Although

women were, for the most part, confined to the domestic sphere, there was one specialized occupation in which they represented a majority—that of brewer. There was an alehouse in each village, run by an alewife. A recent study of the manor of Brigstock in Northamptonshire during the fourteenth century shows that at that period almost all the brewers were female.

The social life of the peasants probably consisted of dancing and merrymaking on the village green, and the church provided a focus for the spiritual life of the inhabitants. Here the rituals and sacraments essential to medieval society took place: baptism, marriage, and burial. The villagers were expected to attend Mass every Sunday, as well as services on the many feast days. Seats were not provided, so the parishioners stood throughout the long ceremonies. Since the peasantry was illiterate, what they knew of the Bible came from the priest (often not highly educated himself), and from the paintings of biblical stories and lives of the saints on the walls of the church. Promising boys from the community were chosen as acolytes by the priest, and some of these applied in the manor court for permission to enter the priesthood. This seems to have been the only route for advancement available to the son of a villein.

It is difficult to ascertain the true level of religiosity in medieval peasant society. Since their daily existence was so onerous and without any expectation for change or improvement, one can speculate that following religious doctrine was their only hope for a better life hereafter. In many areas, "folk Christianity" was a mixture of pagan magical custom and early Christian practice. Most people were probably pious, in that they attended church services regularly, and participated in rituals that bound them ever more closely to the Church. However, verifiable evidence of true religious devotion in eleventh-century peasant society does not exist, since the population was largely illiterate.

The church and churchyard also served other purposes besides those of a purely religious nature. Village meetings were held in the church, and the churchyard was often used as a marketplace, although this was more common in towns than in small villages. Thus, the church did provide a "center" for medieval life, in a real, as well as a metaphorical sense.

Summary

Europe in the eleventh century was in a state of recovery and transition. The Carolingian Empire had dissolved, leaving the population without a centralized government; further, Europe was being assaulted on all sides. Drawing on traditions established in the Carolingian period, a new political system emerged that provided protection in limited geographical areas. This new order was based on bonds of loyalty between noblemen, and was predicated on a set of rights and duties, primarily military and judicial, by which a vassal was bound to his lord. This practice, formalized in rituals known as "homage" and "fealty," is often referred to by the somewhat loose terms "feudalism" or "vassalage." In exchange for vows of commitment, the vassal received a grant of land known as a "fief," which incorporated one or more self-contained agricultural settlements known as "manors." In this way, the feudal system was supported by an economy based on agriculture and the labor of an increasing peasant population tied to the land by the manorial or seignorial system.

This period was marked by major agricultural and technological improvements, such as the introduction of the "three-field system" and the adoption of the heavy plow, in addition to the increasing use of watermills and windmills. Developments such as these, along with favorable climate change, resulted in rapid population growth and improved living conditions for people of all classes.

In the eleventh century, aristocrats lived in relatively primitive dwellings known as "motte and bailey" castles, which were designed primarily for defense, rather than comfort. A woman in an aristocratic family fulfilled many responsibilities, including the garrisoning of the castle in the absence of her husband.

The peasants lived in simple hovels, usually consisting of one room with a dirt floor and inadequate ventilation for smoke from the open fire which provided heat. Women joined their husbands in cultivating and harvesting the fields, and, in addition, were generally responsible for cooking and the care of whatever animals the family possessed. Children were expected to help their parents with daily tasks as soon as they were able.

Thus, the hard work of a growing population and the relative stability of Europe in the eleventh century made possible the political and cultural developments that characterized the history of the following era.

Suggestions for Further Reading

Primary sources

The Chronicle of Jocelin of Brakelond Concerning the Acts of Samson, Abbot of the Monastery of St. Edmund, translated by H.E. Butler (London: Thomas Neslon, 1949), offers interesting views of the workings of monastic life. *The Art of Courtly Love*, by Andreas Capellanus, translated by John Jay Parry (New York: Columbia University Press, 1990) provides a contemporary view of the relationship between knights and ladies. *The Peace of God: Social Violence and Religious Response around the Year 1000*, edited by Thomas Head and R. Landes (Ithaca, NY: Cornell University Press, 1992), is a useful compilation of documents concerning the problems of controlling feudal conflict.

The Medieval Warfare Source Book, vol. 1, *Warfare in Western Christendom*, by David Nicolle (London: Arms and Armour, 1995), contains much fascinating information about feudal warfare. Peter Speed has edited two volumes of sources, titled *Those Who Worked: An Anthology of Medieval Sources* (New York: Italica Press, 1997) and *Those Who Fought: An Anthology of Medieval Sources* (New York: Italica Press, 1996), which provide a comprehensive view of life in the Middle Ages from the Romans to the fifteenth century. (A third volume is forthcoming.)

Secondary sources

The debate surrounding the use of the term "feudalism" is discussed in detail in the article "The Tyranny of a Construct: Feudalism and Historians of Medieval Europe," by Elizabeth A.R. Brown, published in *Debating the Middle Ages: Issues and Readings*, by Lester K. Little and Barbara H. Rosenwein (Oxford: Blackwell Publishers, 1998). The classic studies of feudalism are Marc Bloch, *Feudal Society*, 2 vols., trans. L.A. Manyon (Chicago: University of Chicago Press, 1961), and F.L. Ganshof, *Feudalism*, 3rd English ed., translated by Philip Grierson (Toronto: University of Toronto Press, 1996). Other works that see feudalism as a political system are Joseph R. Strayer's *Feudalism* (Princeton: D. van Nostrand Co., 1965), and Carl Stephenson's *Mediaeval Feudalism* (Ithaca, NY: Cornell University Press, 1942). Their paradigms have been challenged by many recent historians. Among the most prominent is Susan Reynolds, whose works include *Fiefs and Vassals: The Medieval Evidence Reinterpreted* (Oxford: Oxford University Press, 1994) and *Kingdoms and Communities in Western Europe: 900–1300*, 2nd ed. (Oxford: Clarendon Press, 1997).

Chivalry and knighthood have been popular fields of scholarly research during the past two decades, generating a large bibliography. A limited representation includes a fascinating recent work, *Chivalry and Violence in Medieval Europe*, by Richard W. Kaeuper (Oxford: Oxford University Press, 1999), which draws on documentary and literary evidence to analyze the connections between warlike violence, high social status, honour, and piety. See also *Chivalry*, by Maurice Keen (New Haven: Yale University Press, 1984), which contains some lovely illustrations, and by the same author, *Medieval Warfare: A History* (Oxford: Oxford University Press, 1999). *The Knight and Chivalry*, by Richard W. Barber, revised ed. (Woodbridge,UK: Boydell Press, 1995) is another comprehensive study based upon literary as well as historical sources.

An excellent analysis of medieval warfare from the age of Charlemagne through the High Middle Ages is Hans Delbrück's *Medieval Warfare*, translated by Walter J. Renfroe, Jr. (Lincoln, Nebraska: University of Nebraska Press, reprint ed., 1990). See also *War in the Middle Ages*, by Philippe Contamine, translated by Michael Jones (London: Basil Blackwell, 1984). Knighthood in France is discussed in *The Chivalrous Society*, by Georges Duby, translated by Cynthia Postan (London: Edward Arnold, 1977), and in an excellent recent work by Constance Brittain Bouchard, *Strong of Body, Brave & Noble: Chivalry and Society in Medieval France* (Ithaca: Cornell University Press, 1998).

A reassessment of the development of Europe from the late tenth century to the thirteenth is presented in R.I. Moore's *The First European Revolution, c. 970–1215* (Oxford: Blackwell Publishers, 2000).

The development of agricultural communities and the evolution of trade are the primary topics of a clear and readable study by Robert S. Lopez, *The Commercial Revolution of the Middle Ages: 950–1350* (Cambridge: Cambridge University Press, 1976). Two works by Edward Miller and John Hatcher that analyze English medieval society, both rural and urban, are *Medieval England—Rural Society and Economic Change: 1086–1348* (London: Longman, 1978) and *Medieval England—Towns, Commerce and Crafts: 1086–1348* (London: Longman, 1995).

Life in the Middle Ages from the Seventh to the Thirteenth Century, by Hans-Werner Goetz, translated by Albert Wimmer (Notre Dame: University of Notre Dame Press, 1993), is a comprehensive work dealing with monastic life as well as peasant and aristocratic existence. Another work, based primarily on German sources, is *Peasants in the Middle Ages*, by Werner Rösener, translated by Alexander Stützer (Cambridge: Polity Press, 1992).

Two classic works that discuss technological innovation are *Medieval Technology and Social Change*, by Lynn White, Jr. (Oxford: Oxford University Press, 1962), and Jean Gimpel, *The Medieval Machine: The Industrial Revolution of the Middle Ages*, 2nd ed. (London: Pimlico, 1992). Some of White's concepts have been qualified in a group of articles published in *Technology and Resource Use in Medieval Europe: Cathedrals, Mills, and Mines*, edited by Elizabeth Bradford Smith and Michael Wolfe (Aldershot, UK: Ashgate, 1997). Information concerning medieval warfare and weaponry may be found in Kelly DeVries, *Medieval Military Technology* (Peterborough, Ontario, 1992).

The lives of medieval English women are described in several recent books, including Judith M. Bennett, *Women in the Medieval English Countryside: Gender and Household in Brigstock Before the Plague* (Oxford: Oxford University Press, 1987), and Henrietta Leyser, *Medieval Women: A Social History of Women in England 450–1500* (London: Weidenfeld & Nicolson, 1995). *Aristocratic Women in Medieval France*, edited by Theodore Evergates (Philadelphia: University of Pennsylvania Press, 1999), examines the experience of French noblewomen.

The subject of marriage is analyzed in detail in Georges Duby's *The Knight, The Lady, and the Priest: The Making of Modern Marriage in Medieval France*, translated by Barbara Bray (Harmondsworth, UK: Penguin Books, 1983).

EAST AND WEST: THE CONSOLIDATION OF POWER FROM THE TENTH TO THE TWELFTH CENTURY

6

THE ERA FOLLOWING the disintegration of the Carolingian Empire was characterized by extensive political fragmentation. Eastern Francia, which became Germany, extended from the Rhine River to the Elbe, the Saale, and the Danube rivers in the East. Western Francia, which became France, comprised the area between the Scheldt and the Rhône rivers, stretching to the Mediterranean in the south and the Atlantic Ocean in the west. The so-called "Middle Kingdom" of Lothair had been divided into Lotharingia, which was incorporated into Germany in 925, and Burgundy and Provence. The Italian peninsula consisted of the kingdom of Italy, the Papal States, several independent Lombard principalities, Naples, Amalfi, Venice, and the Byzantine territories in the extreme south (see Map 7).

During the tenth, eleventh, and twelfth centuries, powerful men in each of these areas began to develop strong governments. In France, the Capetians laid the foundation for a stable centralized monarchy which lasted until the fourteenth century. Germany, by contrast, was not united by a single long-lasting dynasty. The German kings, who often bore the title "Holy Roman Emperor," sought to establish their hegemony over northern Italy, claiming the old "Middle Kingdom" of Lothair rather than consolidating their power in their homeland. The emperor Henry IV became embroiled in a dispute with the pope—often called the "Investiture Controversy"—that had far-reaching implications for the relationship of Church and state in the High Middle Ages.

The unity of Anglo-Saxon England had been re-established by the successors of Alfred the Great, and the country was linked to the northern world through regular trading relations that the inhabitants of the eastern regions, mostly Danish, maintained with the Scandinavian countries. In the eleventh century, Britain was invaded once again, this time by the Normans under the leadership of William the Conqueror, who was able to establish a strong, authoritative monarchy.

As Europe was recovering from the onslaught of the Vikings, Magyars, and Muslims, Byzantium was experiencing a "Golden Age," characterized by the development of artistic and intellectual progress. The eastern empire's cultural accomplishments ultimately provided a fertile source of inspiration for its western European neighbors.

This chapter will deal with the consolidation of power in western European countries from the tenth century to the twelfth, exploring the development of centralized monarchies and their relationships with the Byzantine Empire, the Scandinvian countries, Russia, and eastern Europe.

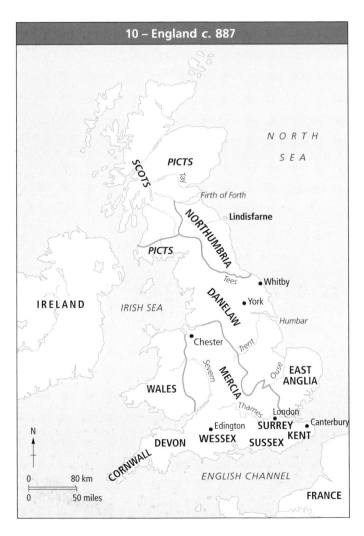

10 – England c. 887

NORTH SEA

PICTS

SCOTS

Tay

Firth of Forth

Lindisfarne

NORTHUMBRIA

PICTS

Tees

Whitby

IRELAND

IRISH SEA

DANELAW

York

Humbar

Chester

Trent

Severn

Ouse

EAST ANGLIA

MERCIA

WALES

Thames

London

Edington

SURREY

Canterbury

DEVON

WESSEX

SUSSEX

KENT

CORNWALL

N

0   80 km
0   50 miles

ENGLISH CHANNEL

FRANCE

England and the Development of the Norman Monarchy

As discussed in Chapter 4, the Danish invasion of England was halted by Alfred the Great, who eventually managed to negotiate a treaty that allowed him to rule over most of southern and southwestern England (see p. 130). Much of England, the Danelaw, was governed by the Danes (**Map 10**). Alfred and his successors on the throne of Wessex continued their efforts to reconquer the Danish territories, however, and by 954 they had accomplished their goal; England was under the control of the king of Wessex. Although many Danish settlers remained in the northern and eastern parts of England, political unity had been established. The Danes were not, however, totally committed to the English monarchy.

In 978, a child, Ethelred "the Unready," ascended the throne (in Anglo-Saxon *unred* meant "uncounseled" or "poorly advised"). Seizing their opportunity, the Danes took advantage of the weak monarchy to resume their invasions. The Anglo-Saxon forces were unable to stave off the assaults, and the king agreed to pay a tribute to the Danes, known as the *danegeld*. The payment was not only a symbol of weakness; during the course of Ethelred's long reign it resulted in a tremendous loss of English wealth.

When Ethelred died in 1016, England was again assaulted by the Danes. Ethelred's son, Edmund Ironside, came to an agreement with the invaders: their king could have half the kingdom of England, and when either he or the Danish king died, the survivor would rule over the whole country. Edmund lived only a few months, and the Danish ruler Canute, known as "Canute the Great," became king of the entire realm, reigning from 1016 to 1035. After Canute's death, his sons, who were fighting over the Danish monarchy, could not maintain control of England, and the country was plunged into a period of anarchy. Finally, in 1042, following the Anglo-Saxon custom by which the monarchy was, in theory, elective, the nobles selected an English king, Edward the Confessor, who was the younger brother of Edmund Ironside.

The reign of Edward the Confessor (r. 1042–1066) was not a happy one; the Danes wished to regain control of England, and the Anglo-Saxon nobility was restive. For much of his reign Edward was dominated by Godwin, the powerful Earl of Wessex, whose daughter he married. When Godwin died, his ambitious son Harold succeeded him as earl. Edward the Confessor had no children, and it became clear that Harold intended to be his successor on the throne.

There were, in addition, other contenders for the monarchy. Edward's cousin William, duke of Normandy, later to become known as "William the Conqueror," believed that he had the strongest claim to the title, and furthermore, he asserted that Edward had promised the throne to him.

The situation became more complicated in 1064, when Harold of Wessex was shipwrecked while sailing in the English Channel and was captured by a vassal of Duke William. Later Norman chronicles, as well as the celebrated eleventh-century embroidery, the Bayeux Tapestry, claim that Harold swore fealty or allegiance to William as the price of his freedom, and promised to help him to become king of England after the death of Edward. In a panel from the Bayeux Tapestry, shown in **fig. 49**, Harold stands with his hands on caskets of sacred relics; he utters a solemn vow that he will be William's man, and will serve and obey him in everything.

When Edward died in 1066, Harold was elected king by the council of Anglo-Saxon nobles, the **Witan**. William viewed this as treachery of the most base kind, and

49 The Bayeux Tapestry, embroidered in the eleventh century, takes its name from the northern French town where it is displayed. The 20-inch(50 cm)-high panel is over 230 feet (70 m) long, and recounts in dramatic pictures and captions the events leading up to the Battle of Hastings, and the bloody battle itself. In this illustration, taken from an early part of the tapestry, Harold of Wessex swears fealty to William the Conqueror on two reliquary caskets.

he appealed to the papacy for support. The pope, aware that the English church was sub-stantially controlled by the king, and eager to establish an alliance with William, gave his blessing for an invasion of England. The duke summoned his vassals for the expe-dition, but many refused to accompany him, believing that they did not owe military service outside France. William then extended a general invitation to anyone interested in gaining booty and grants of land, and the response was quite gratifying. A few of the Norman lords who were close personal friends of the duke, as well as younger sons of the nobility, joined the host, and a force of about 5,000 soldiers gathered to cross the English Channel.

In addition to the threat from Normandy, King Harold faced insurrection at home. His elder brother Tostig, who was envious of his success, joined in a conspiracy with another Harold, the king of Norway, for an invasion of England. Further, several of the Anglo-Saxon noblemen wavered in providing support, and he could depend only on his other brothers and the nobility of Wessex. As he was gathering his army to travel south to meet William, he learned of an invasion in the north by Tostig and Harold of Norway. The English king was warned by a dire portent in the sky. As the *Anglo-Saxon Chronicle*, a collection of monastic annals begun during the reign of Alfred the Great, reported: [On April 16] "over all England there was seen a sign in the skies such as had never been seen before. Some said it was the star 'comet' which some call the star with hair." Certainly no one doubted that the omen was negative.

Harold marched north to meet the invading force and, again in the words of the *Anglo-Saxon Chronicle*:

> Then Harold our king came upon the Northmen by surprise and met them beyond York at Stamford Bridge with a large force of the English people; and that day there was a very fierce fight on both sides. There were killed Harold of the Fair Hair [Harold of Norway] and Earl Tostig, and the Northmen who survived were put to flight; and the English attacked them fiercely from behind until some of them came to ship, some drowned, and some also burned, and thus variously perished, so that there were few survivors, and the English had possession of the place of slaughter.

Three days after Harold won his great victory, however, Duke William landed on the southern coast of England with his army. On October 14, 1066, William engaged the exhausted forces of Harold, who had marched south to meet the Normans. The *Anglo-Saxon Chronicle*, which was obviously biased in favor of the Anglo-Saxons, claimed that:

> William came against him by surprise before his army was drawn up in battle array. But the king nevertheless fought hard against him, with the men who were willing to support him, and there were heavy casualties on both sides. There King Harold was killed and Earl Leofwine his brother, . . . and many good men, and the French remained masters of the field, even as God granted it to them because of the sins of the people.

The outcome was probably the result of a stroke of good luck. Had Harold's army not been exhausted from the earlier battle with Tostig and Harold of Norway, and from the long

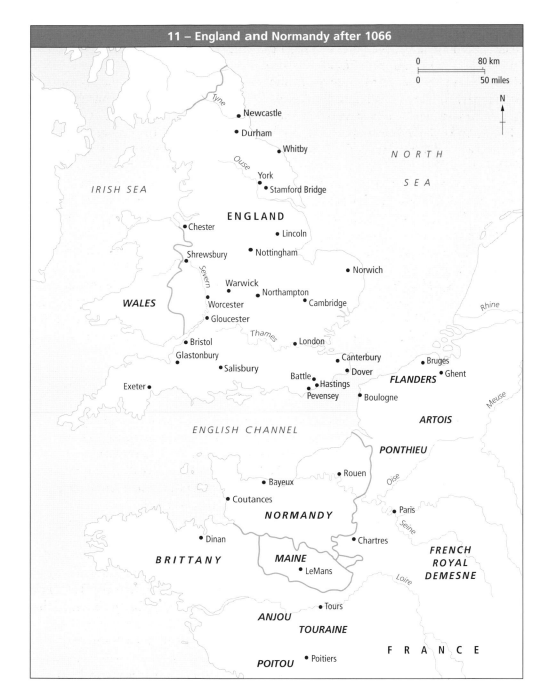

11 – England and Normandy after 1066

and difficult march of some 300 miles (480 km) from Stamford Bridge, the Anglo-Saxons might well have defeated the Normans (**Map 11**).

Following his victory, William was faced with the task of securing his newly won realm. As he moved through the country he erected a motte and bailey castle in each borough, the most famous of which is the White Tower in London, built after his coronation

on Christmas Day, 1066 (**fig. 50**). This was one of the first buildings in a vast program of castle construction that resulted in a total of more than 500 castles in England by the beginning of the twelfth century. William's actions were not appreciated by the native population, however. As the *Anglo-Saxon Chronicle* reported, he "built castles here far and wide throughout this country, and distressed the wretched fold, and always after that it grew much worse. May the end be good when God wills!"

Thus, William was forced to deal with a restive population, an unhappy nobility, and difficulties with his own people, who were dissatisfied with their booty. He needed to make provision for an army, and to do this he maintained the *fyrd*, a force that had originally been gathered to fight the Danes. Further, in order to ensure the loyalty of his nobles, he had them swear direct personal allegiance to him in the "Oath of Salisbury."

William may have initially intended to allow the Anglo-Saxon aristocracy to share some aspects of power. However, a series of revolts by the Anglo-Saxon nobles

50 The White Tower in London was built following the coronation of William the Conqueror on Christmas Day, 1066. It features strongly fortified walls, capped with crenellations. William moved quickly to secure the country under Norman rule, partly through the erection of numerous castles similar to this one.

between 1066 and 1071 resulted in a royal policy of thorough Normanization, and the Anglo-Saxon aristocrats had their property seized. Furthermore, the secular nobility were not the only victims; most of the great abbeys and bishoprics were given to Norman prelates.

When William was crowned, he swore that "he would be a gracious liege lord . . . [and] . . . rule all this people as well as the best of the kings before him, if they would be loyal to him," but, as the *Chronicle* reports, "all the same he laid taxes on people very severely."

In order to institute a thorough system of taxation, William ordered, in 1086, a survey of all of the land and inhabitants of England, known as the *Domesday Book*. According to the *Anglo-Saxon Chronicle*:

> The king had much thought and very deep discussion with his council about this country—how it was occupied or with what sort of people. Then he sent his men over all England into every shire and had them find out how many hundred hides there were in the shire, or what land and cattle the king himself had in the country, or what dues he ought to have in twelve months from the shire. Also he had a record made of how much land his archbishops had, and his bishops and his abbots and his earls—and though I relate it at too great length—what or how much everybody had who was occupying land in England, in land or cattle, and how much money it was worth. So very narrowly did he have it investigated, that there was no single hide nor a yard of land, nor indeed (it is a shame to relate but it seemed no shame to him to do) one ox nor one cow nor one pig was there left out, and not put down in his record: and all these records were brought to him afterwards.

The bishop of Hereford recounted the general dissatisfaction when the first surveyors were followed by others, "in order that they might be given the opportunity of checking the first survey and, if necessary, of denouncing its authors as guilty to the king. And the land was vexed with much violence arising from the collection of the royal taxes."

A brief example from the *Domesday Book* demonstrates the content and style of the survey:

> A manor. In Godmanchester King Edward had 14 hides assessed to the **geld**. There is land for 57 plows. There are 2 plows now on the king's demesne on 2 hides of this land; and 80 villeins and 16 bordars have 24 plows. There is a priest and a church; 3 mills rendering 100 shillings; 160 acres of meadow; and 50 acres of woodland for pannage. From the pasture come 20 shillings. From the meadows come 70 shillings. T.R.E. [Time of King Edward] it was worth 40 pounds; now it is worth the same "by tale" [by count].

In the survey the "hides" are units of assessment, not measures of land. A statement that there is land for so many "plows" indicates the amount of arable land capable of being plowed each year by a plow team of eight oxen. Villeins were serfs subject to labor services and servile payments, and bordars probably possessed a smallholding (see Chapter 5). The survey also indicates that there was great variety in the English social structure of the eleventh century.

Historians have debated for centuries about the impact of the Norman conquest on Anglo-Saxon society. Some scholars have viewed the events of 1066 as marking a radical break with the past, while others see English history as essentially continuous, with little real change taking place as a result of the Norman invasion. Although it is evident that the Anglo-Saxon aristocracy was replaced by a new French-speaking nobility that was well schooled in cavalry warfare, some historians assert that many aspects of daily life remained virtually unaffected. The routines of peasants and townspeople were altered very little by the dynastic upheaval, and the economic growth that took place in eleventh-century England had already been set in motion by the time of the conquest. Furthermore, the passage just quoted from the *Domesday Book* demonstrates that property values changed very little. Thus, although some things were altered, much remained the same, and the ultimate result of the conquest was the development of an Anglo-Norman synthesis in the twelfth century.

The career of William the Conqueror, a vassal of the king of France, provides an excellent example of the strength of the nobility of France in relation to that of the crown.

The Capetian Dynasty in France

The two largest fragments of the Carolingian Empire were the West and East Frankish kingdoms, which ultimately became France and Germany. These two regions were remarkably different in origin and political development. France had been part of the Roman Empire and had been ruled since the fifth century by the Merovingians and the Carolingians. As a result, it displayed considerable cultural homogeneity; indeed, there were no groups of inhabitants in France who regarded themselves as having their own ethnic customs and traditions, with the possible exceptions of Brittany and Aquitaine. Much of Germany, by contrast, had been newly conquered by Charlemagne, and had not been completely assimilated into the empire.

The counties of the West Frankish kingdom were based on the old Roman *civitates*, which provided the foundation for the geographical divisions. The most powerful magnates in the political structure were the counts, who, although they were technically vassals of the king, became increasingly independent. Some of these counts extended their power throughout several counties. One notable example was Robert the Strong, who became count of Angers, Tours, Blois, Orléans, Chartres, and Paris.

Many of the successors of Charlemagne's grandson Charles the Bald (r. 843–877) in the West Frankish kingdom were weak and ineffectual, making it inevitable that some of the great lords would attempt to gain the throne. Although the Carolingians had passed the crown from father to son, in theory the royal office had remained elective. In 888, when the available Carolingian successors were minors and the continuing Viking threat required the leadership of an able soldier, Odo, marquess of Neustria, son of Robert the Strong, was elected king by the magnates.

The subsequent history of the tenth century was marked by bitter struggle between the Carolingian princes and the descendants of Robert the Strong. Altogether there were three kings elected from the Robertian house and four from the Carolingian. Often the rival claimant would make war on his opponent, a situation that was welcomed by the feudal lords, whose chief desire was freedom from effective control. Further, the noble class, bred and trained for warfare, thrived on continued anarchy.

The Church was opposed, on principle and by tradition, to the continual warfare surrounding the succession to the throne. Hence, the clergy preached the sanctity of royal office and the obligation to elect a strong and powerful king who would be duly anointed and crowned by the Church.

In 987, after the death of King Louis V, the election process was repeated and the lords chose as king Hugh Capet (r. 987–996), grandson of Robert the Strong, duke of the Franks and count of Orléans, Paris, and Dreux. The account of his election indicates that they were perhaps swayed in their choice by Adalbero, archbishop of Reims, who was the primate of the West Frankish church and the man who anointed the kings. He urged the election of Capet rather than Charles of Lower Lorraine, uncle of the deceased king:

> We are aware that Charles has his partisans, who claim that the throne belongs to him by right of birth. But if we look into the matter, the throne is not acquired by hereditary right, and no one ought to be placed at the head of the kingdom unless he is distinguished, not only by nobility of body, but also by strength of mind—only such a one as honor and generosity recommend. [Charles] is not guided by honor, nor is he possessed of strength . . . Make a decision, therefore, for the welfare rather than for the injury of the state. If you wish ill to your country, choose Charles to be king; if you have regard for its prosperity, choose Hugh, the illustrious duke . . . Elect, then, the duke, a man who is recommended by his conduct, by his nobility, and by his military following. In him you will find a defender, not only of the state, but also of your private interests.

According to a contemporaneous chronicler named Richer, from whom this account was taken, "This speech was applauded and concurred in by all, and by unanimous consent the duke was raised to the throne."

Unlike the previous kings of the Robertian line, Hugh Capet was determined to make the throne hereditary in his own family. Soon after his coronation he demanded that the magnates elect his son Robert as his associate on the throne, asserting that governing the realm was too great a responsibility for one man. This action effectively assured that Robert would be his father's successor. Obviously this method negated the elective principle, and ensured that a Capetian would remain on the throne of France. It stayed in force as long as the royal family produced male heirs. The Capetian dynasty was remarkably successful in this regard, producing fifteen successive kings, who reigned from 987 to 1328.

The actual influence of the early Capetians was severely limited by the power of the French magnates, who regarded the king as their equal, not their superior. It is remarkable that the Capetians were able to maintain the title of king, even though they were ultimately not able to retain their original power in the royal domain. Between 987 and 1108, Hugh Capet and his immediate successors lost ground steadily to their vassals; they were unable to control even the minor lords in their counties of Paris and Orléans. The fact that the monarchy survived is probably due to two factors: the continuing support of the Church, and the reality that the powerful vassals were neither seriously threatened by the Capetians nor inclined to unite to obstruct royal authority. They needed a titular king, and they preferred that the holder of the throne should be so weak that he could not trouble them; furthermore, the royal holdings were not large enough to stimulate much greed.

The decline in the fortunes of the Capetians was reversed during the reign of Philip I (r. 1060–1108), Hugh Capet's great-grandson. Philip was able not only to halt the shrinkage in the size of the royal lands, but also to stabilize and enlarge the demesne (**Map 12**). However, even though he was much more effective than his predecessors, he was unable to control his powerful vassals effectively, and his newly expanded resources remained much smaller than those held by the feudal magnates. Each of the counties of Flanders, Maine, Anjou, and Blois, and the duchies of Brittany, Burgundy,

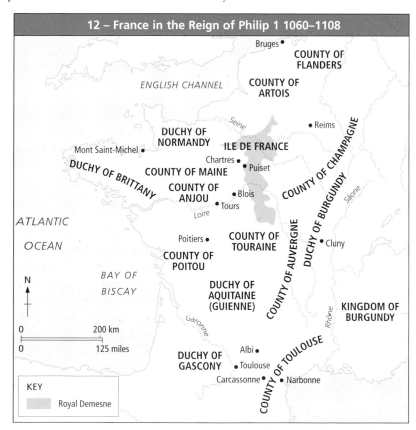

12 – France in the Reign of Philip 1 1060–1108

and Aquitaine exceeded the royal domain in size and wealth. Most of the lords of these areas were more powerful than their king, and none was much weaker. As will be discussed in Chapter 8, during the twelfth century the French monarchy emerged from this unpromising situation to become a significant European power.

Germany

The basic social and political structure of the East Frankish kingdom differed from that of the West Franks in several respects. Except for Lorraine, none of the lands inherited by Charlemagne's grandson Louis the German had been part of the Roman Empire for a significant time, and only Lorraine and Franconia had been permanent components of the Merovingian state. Bavaria, Swabia, and Saxony had been added to the Frankish kingdom by earlier Carolingians (**Map 13**).

In the western part of the East Frankish kingdom, the counts administered districts based on the old Roman *civitates*, but in the eastern section they were not as independent, and functioned as representatives of the king with only vague powers of supervision. There were no stable, organized counties such as those found in the West Frankish state. In general, the East Frankish area was a region of free landholders, noble and peasant, who governed themselves through the popular court under the administration of the counts. In the border areas, which were crucial for defense, large geographical units were administered by margraves.

In many regions, such as Bavaria, Swabia, and Saxony, there remained a measure of local patriotism, deriving from the era before the conquest of these areas by the Carolingians. Here, the king's true power rested on his ability to control the counts, and on his right to choose the bishops and abbots who held vast Church estates.

Charlemagne's grandson Louis the German—who had been ceded the eastern part of the empire by the Treaty of Verdun—died in 876. After his death, Louis's kingdom was divided among his three sons, resulting in years of chaos. Eventually, Arnulf was elected king, and he managed to halt the incursions of the Vikings for a time. The next monarch was Louis the Child, who ruled from 899 to 911, from age six to age eighteen. His reign witnessed disastrous invasions by the Magyars, who had come into Hungary from Central Asia and joined the remnants of the Avars, another Asiatic tribe who had been subdued by the Franks in the 790s. They then proceeded to make serious inroads into Germany, plundering Bavaria in 890, Saxony in 906, and Thuringia in 908. Since there was no strong central government, each region provided its own protection; sectional leadership was undertaken by local families, and duchies, known as Stammesherzogtümer or "stem duchies" emerged, based on old Germanic tribal frontiers. These included Saxony, Franconia, Bavaria, Swabia, and Lorraine, the last of which vacillated between France and Germany for centuries.

The death of Louis the Child in 911 marked the end of the Carolingian dynasty in Germany, and the succession to the throne reverted to the elective principle. So as not to erode their own power, the "stem" dukes elected as king the weakest of their number, Conrad of Franconia, who reigned ineffectually until 918. His years on the throne were plagued with additional Magyar raids as well as rebellions in the duchies. At his death the dukes changed their tactics and elected as king Henry, duke of Saxony, the most powerful of the dukes, known as Henry I ("Henry the Fowler") (r. 919–936). Henry devoted his energies to consolidating his power in the west by annexing Lorraine and making an alliance with its duke. He built fortifications on his eastern border to ward off attacks by the Slavs, and he raised a formidable force of cavalry which proved to be effective against the Magyars. When he died in 936, he left a significant base of power to his son Otto I, who was one of the most important rulers of the central Middle Ages.

Ottonian rule and clerical reform

From the beginning of his reign, Otto I ("Otto the Great") (r. 936–973) was determined to assert his dominance and authority over his fellow "stem" dukes. In order to make this clear, he traveled to Aachen, Charlemagne's capital, to be crowned and anointed. The dukes swore homage to Otto at his coronation, but when they became aware of his true intent to be king in fact as well as name, they began a wave of insurrection. Otto separated the rebels and defeated them one by one. The duke of Franconia died in the fighting, and Otto left the position vacant, ruling Franconia himself in addition to Saxony; he thus had complete control over two of the four stem duchies. This enabled him to reduce the influence of the dukes of Swabia and Bavaria. Moreover, he introduced feudal ideas of vassalage (see Chapter 5) and obliged the dukes to hold their offices as royal vassals.

The support of the Church was another important factor in Otto's assertion of his power over the dukes. In the tenth century, the monarch was theoretically regarded as a sacred figure, and Otto emphasized his divine mandate as much as possible. Further, he chose the bishops and abbots of his kingdom and rewarded them with wealth and power, but he insisted on their complete support and allegiance. Thus, in Germany, even more than in England and France, the Church became the mainstay of the monarchy.

At the beginning of his reign, Otto was primarily a northern magnate whose power base was in Saxony and Franconia. Eventually, however, he began to expand, first conquering the region between the Elbe and the Oder rivers and securing it with well-garrisoned fortresses. He then extended his control over Bohemia, forcing the Bohemians to pay tribute to him (see Map 13).

Otto worked closely with the clergy in subduing and converting the Slavic peoples to the east. When he defeated a tribe, he required its members to pay tithes to the Church. New bishoprics were founded in the conquered territory and endowed by Otto with large grants of land. In 962, he established the archbishopric of Magdeburg and arranged with the pope that the new see would have no eastern boundary, so that any more lands conquered in that area could be assimilated with ease. Such actions indicate that Otto was beginning to pattern his policies after those of Charlemagne, and to think of himself as the direct successor to the great emperor.

Another area of primary concern was the old inheritance of Lothair—the "Middle Kingdom"—which comprised, in addition to Lorraine, the kingdom of Burgundy, Provence, and some areas of the Italian peninsula. In 937, Otto managed to assert his authority over Burgundy, placing the king under his protection. Fourteen years later he invaded Lombardy. He organized this new acquisition according to the system that had been successful in Germany: he gave bishops both secular and ecclesiastical control in their dioceses, thus binding them to his own interests.

It seems clear that Otto intended to assume the imperial crown when he conquered Lombardy in 951, but he was recalled to Germany because of insurrections by the nobility and new raids by the Magyars. In 955, he put an end to the Magyar threat with a stunning victory at the Battle of Lechfeld. The Magyars subsequently settled in the area known today as Hungary, and ultimately developed a strong monarchy (see p. 90).

Otto returned to Italy in 962 and was crowned Holy Roman Emperor, now becoming literally the successor to Charlemagne. He tried to bring southern Italy under his control, but this created conflict with the Byzantine Empire, which held the major cities there. Following a series of indecisive campaigns, he was able to negotiate a peace settlement. The Byzantines acknowledged his imperial title, and agreed to a marriage between his son, the future Otto II, and a Byzantine princess, Theophano.

Otto I has been criticized by historians for failing to concentrate on the consolidation of his power in Germany, allowing himself to be diverted by the invasion of Italy. It seems probable, however, that he believed that the security of the German kingdom depended on the control of the Middle Kingdom once ruled by Lothair. Since Lothair had been emperor, it seemed logical that Otto would assume that title to indicate his hegemony and to assert his royal power. He also extended his policy of close alliance with the Church by making important grants of land to the bishops of northern Italy in order to secure their loyalty.

Otto II (r. 973–983) was a less successful monarch than his father. In 978, he was faced with a major rebellion led by the duke of Bavaria, which he managed to quell. In 980 he was crowned emperor in Rome, and two years later he led a force to southern Italy to fight off an invasion by the Muslims. He suffered a devastating defeat and, having lost a major portion of his army, returned to Rome, where he died within a few months. When word of his death reached Germany, there was a revolt by the Slavic peoples living between the Elbe and the Oder rivers, who had been conquered and Christianized by

Otto I. Colonists and missionaries from Germany were killed, and the Saxon forces were barely able to hold the old Elbe frontier. As a result, the colonization of the area by the Germans was interrupted for two centuries.

Otto II left a three-year-old son as his heir, who was raised in the custody of his mother, the former Byzantine princess Theophano. As king, Otto III (r. 983–1002) developed ideas of monarchy that had a significant Byzantine cast, probably as a result of the influence of his mother. He envisioned Rome as the capital of his empire, and built a palace on the Aventine Hill there. The entire imperial design was impractical since Otto's only real strength was the Saxon army, and he was never accepted by the Roman aristocratic factions. However, since he died at the age of twenty-one, a true test of his imperial mission never took place.

Just as the Ottonian rulers wished to emulate Charlemagne in expanding the Christian empire and assuming the imperial dignity, so they also revived Charlemagne's policy of patronizing scholarship and the arts, using the Carolingian symbols of power and the artistic styles developed during the previous century. **Fig. 51** depicts an ivory carving of the royal family adoring Christ between the Virgin and St. Maurice, who were patrons especially favored by the Ottonian dynasty. The inscription reads *Otto Imperator* ("Emperor Otto"), and the emperor (Otto II), empress, and young prince are crowned with Germanic diadems. Images such as this served to emphasize the Christian role of the emperor and his family.

An illumination from a Gospel book of Otto III stresses the imperial dignity of the emperor (**fig. 52**). Otto is enthroned, with Church prelates on his right side and soldiers on his left. He is receiving the homage of the four sections of the empire: Slavinia, Germania, Gallia, and Roma. The work probably dates from the period immediately after Otto's victory over the Slavs in 997 and reflects the words of Gerbert of Aurillac, an archbishop of Reims who became Pope Sylvester II in 999. As Gerbert wrote in December, 997:

> Ours, ours is the Roman Empire. Italy, fertile in fruits, Lorraine and Germany, fertile in men, offer their resources, and even the strong kingdoms of the Slavs are not lacking to us. Our august emperor of the Romans art thou, Caesar, who, sprung from the noblest blood of the Greeks, surpass the Greeks in Empire and govern the Romans by hereditary right, but both you surpass in genius and eloquence.

51 The Ottonian concept of Christian kingship is portrayed in this splendid tenth-century ivory carving. Christ, enthroned between the Virgin Mary and St. Maurice and flanked by angels, is worshiped by Otto II, his wife Theophano, and their son, the future Otto III. The image vividly promotes the idea that Otto's secular rule was divinely sanctioned.

52 This pair of colorful images from a Gospel book of Otto III (produced between 997 and 1000) shows the emperor seated on a splendid throne in a stylized architectural setting, between two soldiers (on the left), and two ecclesiastical prelates, representing the army and the Church. The emperor is receiving homage from female figures who personify four parts of the empire: Slavinia (the Slavic lands), Germania (Germany), Gallia (roughly present-day France), and Roma (Rome).

A second Gospel book of Otto III, produced probably about 990, shows an even more lofty concept of the divine right of kingship. The text on the page portraying the emperor refers to St. Augustine's commentary on Psalm 90—the "imperial" psalm—and the illumination shows Otto being crowned by the hand of God, raised up by Earth, and attended by two subject kings and the representatives of church and state (**fig. 53**). Furthermore, his image is set in an almond-shaped frame known as a ***mandorla***, often used to represent Christ in majesty, surrounded by the symbols of the Evangelists.

Whereas Charlemagne had always been pragmatic about his position, in spite of the hyperbole of his biographers, Otto had a more mystical vision of his entitlement. He saw himself as truly *christomimetes*, the "actor" or "impersonator" of Christ. Invisible in heaven, Christ was made manifest in the anointed one on earth; the emperor was therefore Christ on earth. The idea of *christomimetes* is Byzantine, and can be traced to the writings of Eusebius, the contemporaneous biographer of the fourth-century Roman emperor Constantine. But no Byzantine emperor would have been portrayed in the manner of Otto III, since the Byzantine court would have found such a conflation of the real world with the supernatural an unacceptable image. This illumination (fig. 53) was a purely western visual interpretation of the Byzantine concept.

The grand design of Otto III ended with his early death. He left no heir, and was succeeded on the throne by the head of a younger branch of the Saxon house, Henry II (r. 1002–1024). Although Henry was a Saxon, his land holdings and political power were in Bavaria; he was thus occupied during his entire reign with attempting to secure the loyalty of the Saxons and with maintaining his position.

When Henry died in 1024, the magnates of Germany elected Conrad II of Franconia as their king. He was the first monarch of the **Salian** dynasty, so-called because Franconia was the homeland of the Frankish tribe, the Salians. Conrad was a hard, tough soldier who was quite able to cope with the problems of maintaining his royal authority. By the time of his election, the great magnates of Germany, called *Fürsten* by German historians and "princes" by English-speaking scholars, had increased their power in significant ways. Many members of the nobility who were not dukes held **allodial lands**—that is, lands held directly by them rather than in feudal tenure. They might also have fiefs granted by the emperor or one of the powerful nobles. Their allodial lands could be passed on to their descendants, but their feudal holdings were not hereditary in Germany. One of the important goals of these noblemen was to make their offices and fiefs inheritable.

Conrad was able to maintain his position within this structure; for example, when the throne of Burgundy became vacant, he asserted his claim to the kingship, and added Burgundy to the holdings of the German crown. His campaigns outside Germany were also successful; he was able to win victories over the Poles, and forced them to acknowledge his overlordship. Internally, Conrad saw the wisdom of building a class of civil servants who would not be linked by family ties or common interest to the nobility or the clergy. These men, known as *ministeriales*, were drawn from the peasant class, and were trained to be administrators or warriors.

Conrad's policies were continued by his son Henry III (r. 1039–1056). Henry realized the importance of creating a center of power, and built castles in Thuringia and southern Saxony, garrisoning them with *ministeriales* in order to extend the area of royal control. These measures were troubling to the duke of Saxony, and to the Saxon nobles, who had been virtually free of royal control for years.

Henry III was also concerned with the growing corruption in the Church, and was an ardent proponent of the monastic reform movement (see Chapter 7), as long as the new measures did not interfere with royal authority. He strongly championed proposals that advocated abolishing clerical marriage, nepotism (conferring privileges or offices on one's own family), and simony, the sale of Church offices.

53 An illumination from this gospel book (Aachen, c. 990) presents Otto III as *christomimetes*. In a *mandorla* and surrounded by symbols of the Evangelists, he is clearly emulating Christ in majesty: crowned figures bow to him, and soldiers and prelates appear beneath him. The blank scroll appearing across the emperor's chest probably refers to an inscription on a facing page: *Hoc Auguste Libro Tibi Cor Deus Induat Otto* ("With this book, Otto Augustus, may God invest thy heart").

The practice of simony was widespread, with high offices, such as bishoprics, archbishoprics, and abbacies commanding exorbitant prices. This custom resulted in a Church hierarchy drawn from the wealthy classes, where appropriate spirituality was generally of limited concern. Henry strongly encouraged the members of the papal court who wished to bring the reform measures to fruition in the Church as a whole, and in 1049, in spite of the implication of nepotism, he appointed as pope his cousin Bishop Bruno of Toul—an ardent reformer—who took the name Leo IX (r. 1049–1054).

Leo is generally considered to be the first pope seriously to advocate clerical reform by eliminating abuses such as simony, nepotism, and pluralism (holding more than one office at a time). In order to achieve his goals, he appointed vociferous reformers from throughout Europe as cardinals, and held a series of synods to establish rules against simony and clerical marriage. Furthermore, he realized the importance of freeing the papacy from secular control, and distanced himself from the Roman magnates who considered the pope to be their pawn. In addition, Leo was aware of the significance of being an actual presence for the faithful, and spent much of his time traveling throughout Europe. He presented himself in spectacular processions with much fanfare, preceded by trumpeters, banners, and ecclesiastical prelates in their gorgeous vestments. During his journeys he was greeted by enormous crowds of followers, the first pope to have been seen by large segments of the general European population, beyond those with the means and opportunity to make the pilgrimage to Rome.

As he traveled, Leo arranged for opportunities for the faithful to express their unhappiness with their priests and bishops. Any clergyman who was seriously compromised was required to confess publicly and to take an oath to uphold the precepts of the reformed Church. This practice had several important results. First, the people were able to witness their own clergymen confessing to the pope. Second, the pope was able to establish his authority openly over the bishops and priests. As a result, people were now aware that the clergy functioned because they had been confirmed in office by the pope.

The pontificate of Leo IX represented a serious turn towards change in the Church. Reforming efforts continued during the reigns of his successors, and the issue of ecclesiastical regeneration became a primary focus of Church–state relations during the pontificate of Gregory VII (r. 1073–1085), who became pope during the reign of the German emperor Henry IV (r. 1056–1106).

Henry IV and the papal revolution

Henry IV had inherited the throne as an infant, and when he began to rule in his own right he was faced with the many difficulties that had developed during his childhood and adolescence. The nobles of Germany had gained in strength during his long minority, and they resented his attempts to assert royal power. Northern Italy was restive under the overlordship of Germany, and the native population deeply resented the German nobles and the Italian bishops who were allied with the Germans. An additional source of stress presented itself when Norman warriors seized Sicily and began to expand to the north. Furthermore, the reform movement in the Church that had been encouraged by Henry III and Pope Leo IX had gathered momentum; it became a source of great conflict between Henry IV and Pope Gregory VII.

During the reigns of Henry's predecessors, the administration of Church government had been carried out under royal control. As discussed above, in the Ottonian period the emperors were viewed as theocratic monarchs, representatives of God on Earth, and indeed this concept had actually been formulated by the Church as the only practical solution to establishing order during the chaotic ninth and tenth centuries. Henry II had appointed bishops and other clerics who served him as vassals and ruled over secular provinces. While he generally made responsible and reasonable choices, his successor, Conrad II, had not been as careful to appoint men who were spiritual leaders. Further, it was not only customary for the king to choose his prelates; he actually conferred their offices on them in a ceremony known as **lay investiture**, in which they were "invested" or consecrated with the ring and pastoral staff. These objects symbolized the candidate's marriage to the Church and his responsibility to be a good shepherd to his flock. The reformers in the Church wished to eliminate lay investiture because the appointees were often not morally fit for high ecclesiastical office, and furthermore, the practice implied lay authority over churchmen. Thus, inherent in the desire to abolish the practice of lay investiture was a challenge to the rights and prerogatives of royal authority.

In order to eliminate interference by the laity in the election of popes, the College of Cardinals was created in 1059. The college was composed of clergymen from Rome, who met in a secret conclave after the death of the pope to elect his successor without outside influence. Once the election was decided, it was expected that the Holy Roman Emperor would agree to the choice.

In 1073, an ardent reformer, the papal secretary Hildebrand, was elected to the papacy, taking the name Gregory VII. He was convinced that God had chosen him to save mankind through the Church, which he must purify in order to establish the perfect instrument for saving souls. He believed that the Church was superior to the secular world, and further, that the pope was the head of all society. His struggle with secular authority, most notably with the German emperor Henry IV, was long known as the "Investiture Controversy," or "Contest"; more recent scholars have preferred to identify the conflict as the "Papal Revolution," since it did, indeed, pose a threat to the existing hierarchy of European institutions.

Gregory's ideas of papal power were codified in 1075, when the following propositions, known as the *Dictatus Papae* (the "Dictate of the Pope") were included in the pope's official register.

1. That the Roman Church was founded by God alone.
2. That the Roman pontiff alone is rightly called universal.
3. That he alone has the power to depose and reinstate bishops.
4. That, in a council, his legate, even if he is of lower ecclesiastical rank, presides over bishops in council, and has the power to give sentence of deposition against them.
5. That the pope may depose the absent [that is, without giving them a hearing].
6. That, among other things, we ought not to remain in the same house with those excommunicated by him.
7. That for him alone is it lawful, according to the needs of the time, to make new laws, to assemble together new congregations, to

make an abbey of a canonry; and, on the other hand, to divide a rich bishopric and unite the poor ones.

8. That he alone may use the imperial insignia.

9. That all princes shall kiss the foot of the pope alone.

10. That his name alone shall be spoken in the churches.

11. That this is the only name in the world.

12. That he has the power to depose emperors.

13. That he has the right to transfer bishops from one see to another when it becomes necessary.

14. That he has power to ordain as a cleric anyone from any part of the Church whatsoever.

15. That anyone ordained by him may preside [as bishop] over another church, but may not hold a subordinate position [as priest] in it; and that such a cleric may not receive a higher rank from any other bishop.

16. That no general synod may be called without his order.

17. That no action of a synod and no book shall be considered canonical without his authority.

18. That his decree can be annulled by no one, and that he can annul the decrees of anyone.

19. That he himself may be judged by no one.

20. That no one shall dare to condemn one who has appealed to the apostolic seat.

21. That the important cases of any church whatsoever shall be referred to the Roman Church [in other words, to the pope].

22. That the Roman Church has never erred; nor will it err to all eternity, according to the testimony of the Holy Scriptures.

23. That the Roman pontiff who has been canonically ordained, is undoubtedly made a saint by the merits of St. Peter, according to the testimony of St. Ennodius, bishop of Pavia, which is confirmed by many of the holy fathers, as is shown by the decrees of the blessed pope St. Symmachus.

24. That by his command or permission subjects may accuse their rulers.

25. That he may depose and reinstate bishops without assembling a synod.

26. That he who does not agree with the Roman Church shall not be considered Catholic.

27. That he has the power to absolve subjects from their fealty to wicked rulers.

It is evident that Gregory's declarations presented a challenge to the established institutions of the Christian world, as may be seen in propositions 9 and 12, in which the pope asserts his power over secular rulers. Further, proposition 24 extends this authority by allowing subjects to accuse their rulers by papal command or permission, and proposition 27 gives the pope the power to sever the feudal bonds of fealty. It should also be noted that many of the remaining statements deal with papal control of the bishops and the right of the pope to convene synods and approve their actions. Scholars are not certain of Gregory's exact intention—the document may have been only the outline of a program of action—but certainly the emperor Henry IV saw it as a challenge to imperial supremacy.

In keeping with Gregory's philosophy, a papal decree was promulgated in 1075 that forbade Church prelates to receive their churches from lay rulers: "We decree that no one of the clergy shall receive the investiture with a bishopric or abbey or church from the hand of an emperor or king or of any lay person, male or female."

Henry IV had no intention of recognizing the decree. He and Gregory were already at odds over the appointment of the bishop of Milan. Henry had been supporting a different candidate from the pope for the position, since he was eager to have a personal ally in his quest to control northern Italy. In 1075, Gregory wrote a letter to Henry threatening to depose and excommunicate him. The salutation alone indicates the tone of the letter: "Gregory, bishop, servant of the servants of God, to Henry, the king, greeting and apostolic benediction—that is, if he shall prove obedient to the apostolic see as a Christian king should." Henry reacted by convening a synod of German bishops which declared Gregory a usurper, and asserted that he had shown himself to be unworthy of the papacy because he had challenged Henry's royal authority. These claims were reflected in a letter from Henry to Gregory in 1076:

Henry, king not by usurpation, but by the holy ordination of God, to Hildebrand, not pope, but false monk:

This is the salutation you deserve, for you have never held any office in the Church without making it a source of confusion and a curse to Christian men instead of an honor and a blessing . . . from the seat of peace you have expelled peace . . . You have attacked me, who, unworthy as I am, have yet been anointed to rule among the anointed of God, and who, according to the teaching of the fathers, can be judged by no one save God alone, and can be deposed for no crime except infidelity . . . St. Peter himself said: "Fear God, honor the king." But you, who fear not God, have dishonored me, whom He hath established . . . Come down, then, from that apostolic seat which you have obtained by violence . . . let another ascend the throne of St. Peter, one who will not use religion as a cloak of violence, but will teach the life-giving doctrine of that prince of the apostles. I, Henry, king by the grace of God, with all my bishops, say unto you: "Come down, come down, and be accursed through all the ages."

This caused Gregory to carry out his initial threat, and, invoking the authority to "bind and loose," the pope declared Henry to be excommunicated and deposed from his position as king:

Confident of my integrity and authority, I now declare in the name of the omnipotent God, the Father, Son, and Holy Spirit, that Henry, son of the emperor Henry, is deprived of his kingdom of Germany and Italy; I do this by thy authority and in defence of the honor of thy church, because he has rebelled against it.

The reaction in Germany was immediate. The princes, who had become alarmed at Henry's growing power, welcomed the excuse for rebellion, and even the bishops who had originally supported Henry were swayed by the pope's sentence of excommunication. Henry, abandoned by all of his supporters, was forced to accede to the demands of the princes. It was agreed that a **diet**, or assembly, of bishops and nobles would be

54 In an image from the *Life of Countess Matilda* (of Canossa), the emperor Henry IV, appearing barefoot as a humble supplicant, requests that Matilda and the abbot intercede on his behalf with Pope Gregory VII, who had excommunicated him. After he had confessed his sins, begged for absolution, and waited three days, the pope finally granted his petition. The inscription, *Rex rogat abbatem Mathildim supplicat atque*, means "The king asks the abbot and Matilda to intercede."

called at Augsburg in 1077, with the pope presiding, and the assembled dignitaries would decide whether Henry should be restored to his throne.

Henry then undertook an action that caused considerable personal humiliation, but which was politically astute. Knowing that the pope would travel through northern Italy on his way to the assembly, Henry decided to meet him at the town of Canossa in order to beg his forgiveness. Appearing barefoot, as a humble penitent, the king confessed his sins and asked for absolution (**fig. 54**). After a delay of three days, during which the king waited outside the castle, Gregory granted his petition. The pope described the display of penitence in a letter to the German princes:

> Once arrived, [Henry] presented himself at the gate of the castle, barefoot and clad only in wretched woolen garments, beseeching us with tears to grant him absolution and forgiveness. This he continued to do for three days, until all those about us were moved to compassion at his plight

and interceded for him with tears and prayers . . . At length his persistent declarations of repentance and the supplications of all who were there with us overcame our reluctance, and we removed the excommunication from him and received him again into the bosom of the Holy Mother Church.

Henry, taking a vow to satisfy the grievances of his bishops and nobles "within the time set by Pope Gregory and in accordance with his conditions," returned to Germany to rebuild his damaged authority. After some three years of civil war, he was able to regain control. He disregarded the promises he had made at Canossa, ultimately provoking another sentence of excommunication from the pope. By this time, however, his political position was more secure, and he could afford to disregard the papal action. He soon returned to Italy, taking an army with him, and in 1084 occupied the city of Rome. The pope took refuge in the fortress of St. Angelo, and appealed to the Normans who now occupied southern Italy for aid. As the Normans moved towards Rome, the imperial armies withdrew. Although the pope was rescued, the Normans took advantage of the chaotic situation and looted the city. They eventually returned to the south, taking Gregory with them; he died a few months later, a desolate and bitter man. The "victory" of Henry was a hollow one, however, since the prolonged struggle had damaged the feudal relationship between the crown and the nobility. The emperor spent the last years of his reign attempting to quell various rebellions and to regain royal authority in his domain.

The Investiture Controversy was not officially settled until 1122, when the emperor Henry V (r. 1106–1125) and Pope Calixtus II (r. 1119–1124) signed the Concordat of Worms. The emperor agreed to give up lay investiture, but the pope conceded to Henry the right to bestow on a new prelate the symbols of his feudal lands and secular administration. Bishops and abbots were to be elected according to the precepts of canon law, but the emperor had the right to be present during the election. There was no immediate victor in the struggle; the Church had achieved the abolition of lay investiture, but the monarch still had considerable control over the clergy in his domain. Over the long term, however, the German emperors had lost a significant component of their power.

A recurring theme in this book has been the relationship of the western kingdoms to the Byzantine Empire. In order to understand more fully the interactions between these medieval states, it is important to explore various aspects of the history and culture of this wealthy and powerful neighbor to the east.

The Golden Age of Byzantium

The Byzantine Empire, which developed from the eastern half of the Roman Empire, was a wealthy and sophisticated society during the sixth and seventh centuries, as discussed in Chapter 2. The power of the emperor was absolute, as demonstrated by Justinian (r. 527–565), and confirmed by his legal code, the *Corpus juris civilis*. The imperial rights were reaffirmed in the Greek version of that text, the *Basilika*, issued in 888, which asserted: "That which pleases the emperor is law," and "God has sent the emperor to earth as animate law." In addition to legal sanction, the control of the Byzantine ruler was a direct result of his support by the Church, the army, and the elaborate bureaucracy of the empire.

As mentioned earlier, the Orthodox church, in addition to providing a common religion for the people of the empire, also furnished an ideology that established the divine right of the emperor to guide the people of his realm; he had been chosen by God especially for this role. The position of the emperor was constantly reinforced and emphasized by elaborate and magnificent ceremonies. In the tenth century, reports were sent back to the court of the Holy Roman Emperor Otto I in the west by Otto's ambassador to Byzantium, Liudprand of Cremona (c. 920–c. 972). He colorfully described the court ceremonies in which Otto's Byzantine counterpart was presented:

> Before the emperor's seat stood a tree, made of bronze gilded over, whose branches were filled with birds, also made of gilded bronze, which uttered different cries, each according to its various species. The throne itself was so marvelously fashioned that at one moment it seemed a low structure, and at another it rose high into the air. It was of immense size and guarded by lions, made either of bronze or of wood covered over with gold, who beat the ground with their tails and gave a dreadful roar with open mouth and quivering tongue. Leaning upon the shoulders of two eunuchs, I was brought to the emperor's presence. At my approach the lions began to roar and the birds to cry out, each according to its kind . . . So after I had three times made obeisance to the emperor with my face on the ground, I lifted my head, and behold! the man who just before I had seen sitting on a moderately elevated seat had now changed his raiment and was sitting on the level of the ceiling. I could not imagine how it was done, unless he was lifted there by the hydraulic pressure that raises the beams of wine presses.

Such ceremony was not limited to the court, but was an important feature of the ecclesiastical, bureaucratic, and military facets of Byzantine society. Indeed, the entire existence of a Byzantine citizen was marked by ceremony, which the Church and state viewed as providing unity and homogeneity to life.

The bureaucracy of the Byzantine Empire was intricate and extensive. The most highly educated people served as government officials, and supervised diplomatic relations with foreign countries in addition to the administration of domestic concerns, such as the collection of taxes. They were part of an elaborate hierarchy in which each individual was supervised by a higher authority. A handbook from 899 lists the most important civilian and military officials invited to the banquet table at the palace; it included fifty-nine high officials and some 500 lesser bureaucrats. The full number of provincial officials no doubt numbered several thousand, all of whom were subject to the man at the apex of the pyramid—the emperor, or *basileus*, as he was known.

This relationship is evident in **fig. 55**, which shows the emperor Nikephoros III (r. 1078–1081) on a throne, flanked by the personifications of Truth and Justice. Two officials stand on either side of the emperor; they are depicted as much smaller than their ruler, thereby emphasizing his importance. The illumination represents the emperor as the light shining on the high officials of his court, who turn their eyes and faces towards him. It echoes the words of a contemporary courtier, Michael Psellos (1018–c. 1096), who described the relationship of the emperor to his officials and his subjects, remarking: "What the creator is in relation to you, this you may be in relation to us."

Such reverence for the emperor had been a prominent feature in the so-called Macedonian dynasty inaugurated by the emperor Basil I (r. 867–886), which brought cultural renewal and geographical expansion to the Byzantine state. Basil was initially faced with threats from the Vikings, who sailed down the Dnieper River to assault Constantinople. They were defeated at the walls of the city, however, supposedly as a result of the intervention of the Virgin Mary. Another attack on the empire was launched by Oleg, prince of Kiev, in 907, who was willing to negotiate a commercial treaty when his military ventures proved ineffectual. As a result of the ensuing trading enterprises and marriage diplomacy, a close association developed between the Byzantine Empire and the people of Kiev (see below).

Another threat to the empire came during the reign of the son of Basil I, Leo VI (r. 886–912), when King Symeon of Bulgaria launched an attack in 894. His troops proved victorious after two years of warfare, and the imperial Byzantine government agreed to pay him an annual subsidy. In 913, the subsidy was discontinued, and Symeon renewed the war; he continued to besiege the borders of the empire until his death in 927.

The Bulgarians were finally defeated in 1014, when Emperor Basil II (r. 976–1025) led his forces against Samuel, their leader. Basil was so successful in this campaign that he was given the title of *Bulgaroctonus*—"Bulgar-slayer." His fame resulted from his capture of 14,000 prisoners and his directive to blind all of them except for every hundredth man, whom he left with one eye so that he could lead the others back to their ruler. Samuel was so shocked by the grisly sight of his returning army that he died of a stroke.

Beginning in the 930s and continuing through the reign of Basil II, the Byzantine armies also fought against the Muslims, recapturing the city of Antioch and almost all of Syria and Palestine from them, as well as reclaiming the island of Crete, which had provided a convenient launching area for Muslim expansion in the Mediterranean. Futhermore, by conquering Armenia, the Byzantines completed a vast empire that extended from Azerbaijan to the Adriatic Sea (see Map 21).

A time of great cultural development, which some historians identify as a "Byzantine renaissance," began during the reign of Basil II and continued under the patronage of his successors, especially Nikephoros III. It was an era when scholars devoted themselves to the study of ancient manuscripts, and their work preserved nearly all of the Classical Greek poetry, drama, and philosophy known today. A school of philosophy was established under the direction of the courtier and scholar Michael Psellos, where commentaries on the works of Plato and Aristotle were prepared. Scholars also wrote histories, secular poetry, and manuals concerning law, veterinary science, military tactics, and other practical matters.

Despite all the political and cultural accomplishments of the era, serious political and social problems were becoming evident throughout the empire within fifty years of the death of Basil II. The difficulties first appeared in the provinces of the empire, known as *themes* (sing. *thema*), which had long been administered by an intricate bureaucracy under the command of the high military officers, the magnate-generals. Each territorial unit was controlled by a general (*strategos*), who held ultimate authority in both administrative and military concerns, with the exception of finance. Over time, these magnates became owners of vast hereditary estates which generated immense agricultural incomes; during the course of the tenth and eleventh centuries, these military leaders gradually increased their control over the local peasants, often forcing them into a condition of serfdom. The Byzantine state was ultimately weakened by this suppression, since it was more difficult to force the magnates to pay taxes than it had been to extract payment from the peasants.

Furthermore, the army had previously been recruited from the free peasantry, and the dwindling supply of soldiers led to diminished military resources. The government attempted to solve the problem by hiring mercenaries, but, according to an eleventh-century Byzantine historian, John Skylitzes, "the bravest part of the army had been removed from the military rolls." Soon, new threats appeared on the borders, and in addition, the state was convulsed by civil war. The situation was dire, for, as an official warned, "the army is the glory of the emperor, the strength of the palace, and if there is no army, there is no longer any government." In the last part of the eleventh century, the empire was threatened by the Seljuk Turks, a tribe that had migrated into western Asia in the previous century. In their quest to establish themselves as an independent state, they had defeated the Byzantine forces in a number of battles, most notably at Manzikert in 1071, when they destroyed a large segment of the Byzantine army. The threat of the Seljuk Turks' invasion caused the Byzantine emperor to take an unprecedented step—he appealed to the pope for aid, thereby providing impetus for the First Crusade.

Russia and Eastern Europe

As we have seen, the pagan inhabitants of the regions to the east and north of the old Carolingian Empire lived by plundering and raiding. Indeed, high status in these communities was conferred on the men who were most successful in stealing cattle and goods from their neighbors, and who were able to bring back the most booty from the areas they attacked. During the tenth and eleventh centuries, however, two major developments in these regions altered this violent and nomadic way of life and led to the establishment of a unitary political order. The first of these was the gradual spread of Christianity to the pagan peoples; the second was the subsequent foundation of Christian monarchies that in many ways resembled the kingdoms of western Europe (**Map 14**).

As we saw earlier, Otto I viewed the Christianization of the pagans as an important facet of his imperial mission. Hence, in addition to supporting missionary activity, he established the bishopric of Magdeburg without a fixed eastern border, so that newly Christianized lands could be incorporated with ease (see above, p. 176). It was his intention that the new bishopric should serve as a center from which missionaries could be sent to convert the Slavic peoples of Poland.

Although missionaries from the Greek Orthodox church had come to Poland early in the tenth century, the most important period of Christian conversion occurred during the reign of Prince Mieszko (r. c. 960–992), when western Christianity was established. In a manner reminiscent of the conversion of the Anglo-Saxon nobility of an earlier era (see Chapter 2), Mieszko married a Christian princess, in this case from the Czech royal family, and accepted Christian baptism. His choice had an important influence on future developments; by adopting the Roman Church—in other words, western Christianity—rather than the Greek Orthodox form, he could turn to the pope for support. His desire for independence from German ecclesiastical control was made evident in 990, when, not wishing to accept supervision by the bishop of Magdeburg, he put his land under the direct protection of the Roman Church, holding it as a vassal of the pope. Ten years later, the pope established an independent Polish bishopric at Gniezno, with the approval of Otto III.

Mieszko's son, Boleslav the Great (r. 992–1025), organized the Polish church into dioceses, and made the city of Giezno the center of ecclesiastical power. It is possible that Boleslav received his title from Otto III, but he later crowned himself in order to establish his independence from the Holy Roman Empire. Boleslav extended his kingdom from the Baltic to the Carpathian Mountains, but, lacking natural boundaries, it was

KEY

Christian by 900

Converted by c. 1000

Boundary between Latin and Eastern Orthodox Churches

0   400 km

0   250 miles

N

Nidaros

Uppsala

BALTIC SEA

Novgorod

RUSSIA

Lund

Bremen

Magdeburg

Gniezno

POLAND

Kiev

Prague

Regensburg

MORAVIA

BOHEMIA

Salzburg

HUNGARY

Venice

CROATIA

Ravenna

SERBIA

BULGARIA

Rome

Constantinople

BLACK SEA

ANATOLIA

Antioch

CYPRUS

Damascus

CRETE

Jerusalem

MEDITERRANEAN SEA

Alexandria

Cairo

always prone to invasion. At his death, the kingdom became a virtual fiefdom of the Holy Roman Empire.

Boleslav's successors, Boleslav II and III, were able to take advantage of the preoccupation of Henry IV with the Investiture Controversy to rebuild some of the former royal authority. At the death of Boleslav III, the Polish kingdom was divided into four parts, creating a series of small principalities that were unable to maintain themselves against the encroachments of neighboring peoples.

Christianity also spread in the ninth century to Bohemia, where the dukes converted to it as early as 894; by the 920s, the Czechs had proclaimed their first martyr, St. Ludmila. The episcopal see established at Prague was initially governed by German bishops, but by the time of Otto III, the bishopric was held by Adalbert (born Vojtech), who was canonized in 999. He was the first bishop of Prague to be of Czech origin, and became a close associate of the emperor. Influenced, perhaps by Adalbert, Otto III was more willing than the previous Ottonians to support the foundation of national churches that functioned without the supervision of German prelates.

After their crushing defeat by Otto the Great at the Battle of Lechfeld in 955, the Magyars settled to the east of the Holy Roman Empire, establishing the nucleus of the Hungarian kingdom. The Magyar leaders soon realized that they would need to adapt to European ways in order to survive, which essentially meant adopting Christianity.

Missionary work and Christianization in Hungary began under Prince Geza (r. 972–997), who accepted German missionaries, primarily from Regensburg and Salzburg. It was his son Stephen (r. 997–1038), however, who achieved the conversion of the Hungarians to Christianity. In recognition of the new Christian monarchy, Pope Sylvester II sent a crown to Hungary, and granted its ruler the title of "Apostolic King." These actions were confirmed in a letter written by Sylvester to Stephen in the year 1000:

> Because you have fulfilled the office of the apostles in preaching Christ and propagating his faith, and have tried to do in your realm the work of us and of our clergy, and because you have honored the same prince of apostles above all others, therefore by this privilege we grant you and your successors, who shall have been legally elected and approved by the Apostolic See, the right to have the cross borne before you as a sign of apostleship, after you have been crowned with the crown which we send and according to the ceremony which we have committed to your ambassadors.

Stephen, who was later canonized, was crowned on Christmas Day, 1000. Thus, the newly formed state entered into an alliance with western Christianity, and a hierarchy directly dependent on Rome was established.

During the four decades of his rule, Stephen organized the former tribal territories into royal counties and appointed administrators for them. He used force to defend himself against internal rebellions, and was able to create a strong centralized government. In addition to adopting Christianity, he was interested in assimilating western European culture into his realm, and invited scholars, priests, and skilled craftsmen to Hungary. As a result, the art of the ancient Magyars was fused there with the dominant western European style of that time, now referred to as Romanesque (see Chapter 8).

Stephen's son, Imre, died at an early age, and Hungary was left without a successor to the throne. Thus, when Stephen died in 1038, various factions struggled for possession of the monarchy, and these conflicts, which lasted for years, seriously weakened the newly established state. Hungary continued to develop during the next two centuries, however, and several strong kings—notably Laszlo I (r. 1077–1095), Kalman (r. 1095–1116), and Bela III (r. 1172–1196)—were able to establish and maintain order. During the interim periods between the reigns of these powerful rulers, struggles for the throne bred instability, and the Byzantine and Holy Roman empires attempted to take advantage of the situation; as a result, there were wars to prevent Hungary being absorbed by one empire or the other.

As discussed in Chapter 4, the vast area of Russia was penetrated by the Swedish Vikings (the Varangians) during the ninth century (see p. 130). An early Viking leader, Rurik, established the town of Novgorod about 860, and another group of Vikings founded a dynasty in Kiev, a settlement that was destined to become an important trading center. Merchants, already known as "Rus," (Russians) also maintained a camp and trading-post at the town of Bulgar, on the Volga River. Their customs and habits were described in a most interesting account from 922 by Ibn Fadlan, who served as secretary to a Muslim ambassador sent by the Baghdad caliph to the Volga Bulgars:

> When they have come from their land and anchored on, or tied up at the shore of, the Volga, which is a great river, they build big houses of wood on the shore, each holding ten to twenty persons more or less. Each man has a couch on which he sits.
>
> With them are pretty slave girls destined for sale to merchants. A man will have sexual intercourse with his slave girl while his companion looks on. Sometimes whole groups will come together in this fashion, each in the presence of the others. A merchant who arrives to buy a slave girl from them may have to wait and look on while a Rus completes the act of intercourse with a slave girl.

Of couse, these merchants also traded in commodities other than slave girls, such as furs, wax, and honey, and apparently carried on a lively commerce with the people of Baghdad.

In the tenth century, the relations between the people of Kiev and the Byzantine Empire took on new meaning when the emperor Basil II appealed to Vladimir, the prince of Kiev (r. 972–1015), for aid in suppressing some rebellions. Vladimir agreed to furnish military assistance and also indicated his willingness to accept Orthodox Christianity, provided that he was given the emperor's sister Anna as his bride. His motives were probably quite similar to those of other early monarchs—he saw that an organized church could be a great advantage in building a strong centralized state. Further, even though he reputedly had several wives and 800 concubines before he married Anna, he knew that a close alliance with the Byzantine emperor would be beneficial. Anna was sent to Kiev, and Vladimir adopted Orthodox Christianity and had his people baptized. As a result of his actions, close cultural and commercial ties developed between Constantinople and Kiev. This may be seen during the reign of Vladimir's son Yaroslav—known as Yaroslav the Wise (r. 1015–1054)—a period of significant artistic and intellectual development.

Yaroslav was a great patron of the arts, and encouraged the building of many churches. These were primarily in the Byzantine style and included the cathedral of St. Sophia in Kiev, which was inspired by Hagia Sophia in Constantinople. The prince imported many Greek craftsmen into Russia, who decorated the churches with mosaics and painted icons, and left the imprint of their style on the work of Russian artists for many generations. Scholars were also supported by Yaroslav, and numerous Byzantine religious writings were translated into the local Slavic language during his reign, including liturgies, saints' lives, sermons, and works on canon law.

After 1037, Kiev had an independent church organization, with its own archbishop. The principality developed into a major power that was oriented towards Byzantium in religious and cultural terms, although its rulers also maintained extensive diplomatic contacts with western kingdoms.

The conversion of the peoples of the Balkan area was initiated in 863, when the Byzantine emperor Michael III sent two brothers, Cyril and Methodius, as missionaries to the Slavs. Before embarking on their mission, the brothers invented a Slavonic alphabet, and translated the Gospels into Slavonic. Then, after they had converted a significant number of people, they created a Slavonic liturgy. In 867, they went to Rome and obtained the approval of the pope for these projects. Within a brief period of time, Cyril and Methodius and the missionaries they trained had converted most of the southern Slavs to Christianity. However, both the pope and the patriarch of Constantinople wished to obtain the allegiance of the new Christians. As a result, the Slavs who lived along the Dalmatian coast (the Croats) embraced western Christianity, while their neighbors to the east (the Serbs) accepted the Orthodox form.

Another area that was converted to Orthodox Christianity was Bulgaria. This alignment was the result of the conversion of Kahn (Tsar) Boris of Bulgaria in 864, who had also been the object of a prolonged struggle between the pope and the patriarch of Constantinople. He converted to the Orthodox form, and the patriarch sent an archbishop and twelve bishops to establish an ecclesiastical hierarchy for his country. In addition, the Bulgarian churches adopted the Slavonic liturgy developed by Cyril and Methodius. Thus, the final result of the Christianization of eastern Europe was that the Poles, Bohemians, Hungarians, and Croats adopted western (Roman) Christianity, and the Serbs, Bulgarians, and Russians converted to eastern Orthodoxy.

Scandinavia

At the height of Viking expansion, the Scandinavian peoples occupied a vast area of northern Europe; in addition to the Scandinavian peninsula and Denmark, they held the Russian states of Novgorod and Kiev, Normandy, Frisia, parts of England and Ireland, and the Faroe, Hebridean, Orkney, and Shetland islands. By the end of the period of migration in the tenth century, they had also colonized in Iceland and Greenland.

The internal history of the Scandinavian states during the eleventh and twelfth centuries consisted of struggle and warfare between the various ruling families. Although direct evidence is limited, it seems that feudal practices did not become widespread in Scandinavia, and the nobility generally lived on allodial lands, rather than fiefs.

The first of the Viking states to accept Christianity was Denmark. This occurred about 960, during the reign of Harold or Harald Bluetooth (r. c. 940–c. 985), grandfather of Canute the Great, king of England and Denmark (see above). Harold's conversion was different from those we have previously encountered; it resulted from a debate at court as to the nature and worship of gods. The Danes were willing to accept Christ as a god, but they claimed he was less powerful than the Norse gods, known as the Aesir. A visiting Christian missionary, Poppo, insisted that there was only one God: the Father, his son Jesus Christ, and the Holy Ghost. Furthermore, the Aesir were nothing but a pack of demons. Harold Bluetooth challenged Poppo to prove his faith by undergoing a test known as the "ordeal of the hot iron," and he agreed. Following the traditional formula for ordeal, Poppo inserted his hand into a white-hot iron glove, and pulled it out unscathed. When the king saw this proof of Christ's divinity, he recognized that Christ must be the one true God, and decreed that Christ alone would be worshiped in his kingdom.

Harold then publicly confirmed his acceptance of Christianity and provided an example for his subjects by accepting baptism from Poppo.

Again, the conversion to Christianity was one factor in the foundation of a strong kingdom, and Harold's action was followed in the last half of the tenth and first part of the eleventh centuries by the conversion of two other great kings, Olaf Tryggvason of Norway (r. c. 995–c. 1000), and Olaf, called Olaf the Taxgatherer, of Sweden (r. 990–1022). All three kings understood that solid church organization was necessary to the formation of a highly structured state.

In many areas of Scandinavia, however, the old folk religion survived tenaciously for two centuries. The religious practices and the Old Norse mythology served as a powerful unifying force—one that set the Vikings apart from the Christians of western Europe. Furthermore, most Scandinavians had long been isolated from Christian influence, and their non-Christianity served as an even greater bond than their common worship of Norse gods such as Odin, Thor, or Freya.

The *Saga of Olaf Tryggvason*, an epic tale written in the late twelfth century, tells of the deeds of the Norwegian king, and describes his struggles when attempting to Christianize his kingdom:

> Olaf called to him his [close relatives], and with the greatest warmth he put before them a matter which they should take up with him and afterwards help on with all their skill, namely, that he intended to have Christianity throughout the whole of his kingdom. He said that he would set out to convert all Norway to Christianity or otherwise die. "I shall make you all great and mighty men, for I trust you most on the grounds of kinship and friendship." All these men agreed to do as he bade and, together with those who would follow their advice, to help him in everything he wished. King Olaf straightway opened the matter with the common folk, that he would ask all men in his kingdom to become Christian. Those who had already promised to do so, agreed first to that behest, and they were the mightiest present: all the others followed them. Thereupon all the men in the east in Viken [southern Norway] were baptized. Now the king went north in Viken and bade all men take up Christianity, and those who spoke against it he dealt with hard; some he slew, some he maimed and some he drove away from the land. So it came about far and wide over all the kingdom which his father King Trygve had formerly ruled and likewise over that which his kinsman Harald Grenske had had, that all the folk took up Christianity as Olaf bade. And in that summer and the following winter the folk in the whole of Viken were all converted to Christianity.

Olaf's activities, undertaken to convert his subjects, included not only the sort of coercion described above but also the sponsoring of Christian missionaries from England.

Another of Olaf's goals was to extend royal authority over the powerful Norse aristocracy. His actions towards this objective led to his early demise in the year 1000, however, when the nobles, supported by the Danish and Swedish kings, killed him. It was not until Olaf's godson assumed the throne as Olaf II in the year 1016 that the tasks of royal centralization and conversion to Christianity were resumed. The greatest center of the old pagan religion was the town of Uppsala, in Sweden, and conflict there continued throughout the eleventh century, but by the early twelfth century Christianity was generally accepted.

The archbishop of Bremen was initially the only **metropolitan** in Scandinavia, and the bishops of all the dioceses in Scandinavia were subject to his authority. However, during the twelfth century, archbishoprics were established in the northern kingdoms: in 1104 at Lund in Denmark; in 1152 at Nidaros in Norway; and in 1164 at Uppsala in Sweden. Although there were occasional quarrels between the ecclesiastical authorities and the monarchy, the Church generally supported the kings in their attempts to unify and centralize their realms. Hence, by the beginning of the thirteenth century, strong Christian kingdoms had developed in the regions in the extreme north of Europe.

Summary

During the eleventh and twelfth centuries, life in much of Europe was affected by monarchal attempts to consolidate power by ecclesiastical reform, and by the widespread Christianization of the border areas. Strong monarchies developed in England, France, and Germany, soon to be followed by the establishment of Christian kingdoms in Hungary, Bulgaria, and the Scandinavian countries.

The Byzantine Empire grew in prosperity during the first part of the eleventh century, but began to decline during the latter decades. Faced with an eroding tax base and a deterioration of his own military strength, the Byzantine emperor ultimately sought the help of the pope in combatting his enemies. This plea had unexpected results, as we shall see in Chapter 7, as the warriors of Christian Europe converged upon the Holy Land in a crusade to regain the sacred sites of Christendom from the Muslims.

Suggestions for Further Reading

Primary Sources
An excellent collection of documents concerning English history during the eleventh and twelfth centuries may be found in *English Historical Documents*, vol. 2, *1042–1189*, edited by David C. Douglas and George W. Greenaway, 2nd ed. (London: Eyre Methuen, 1981). The invasion of William the Conqueror is well documented in *The Norman Conquest of England: Sources and Documents*, by Reginald Allen Brown (Woodbridge: Boydell, 1995). There are many translations of the *Anglo-Saxon Chronicle*. One of the best is by M.J. Swanson

(London: J.M. Dent, 1996).

The Register of Pope Gregory VII (1073–1085) has been translated by H.E.J. Cowdrey (Oxford: Oxford University Press, 2002). A colorful picture of Byzantine civilization may be found in *Liudprand of Cremona: The Embassy to Constantinople and Other Works*, translated by F. A. Wright, edited by John Julius Norwich (London: J.M. Dent, 1993).

Secondary sources
Alfred the Great: War, Kingship and Culture in Anglo-Saxon England, by Richard Abels (London: Longman,

1998), is a fine biography of the famous Anglo-Saxon monarch. *Anglo-Saxon England and the Norman Conquest*, 2nd ed., by H.R. Loyn (London: Longman, 1991), provides an interesting study of economic issues involved in the change from Anglo-Saxon to Norman governance, including a detailed analysis of the *Domesday Book*. Ann Williams, in *The English and the Norman Conquest* (Suffolk: Boydell Press, 1995), is concerned with "the conquered rather than the conquerors," and discusses the gradual intermixture of the Anglo-Saxons and the Normans in the "intermediate classes" that occurred by the end of the twelfth century. *Edward the Confessor*, by Frank Barlow (Berkeley, CA: University of California Press, 1970), is a fine biography of the Anglo-Saxon monarch. Robert Bartlett's *England under the Norman and Angevin Kings* (Oxford: Clarendon Press, 1999) is a stimulating recent study of the period.

The Normans: The History of a Dynasty, by David Crouch (London: Hambledon & London, 2002), is a perceptive analysis of the actions of the Normans in France and England, beginning with Rollo, leader of the Vikings of Rouen, in the ninth century. Political trends, the development of the French monarchy, and aristocratic life are analyzed in detail by Jean Dunbabin in *France in the Making: 843–1180*, 2nd ed. (Oxford: Oxford University Press, 2000), which also includes chapters on sources and an excellent suggested reading list.

Germany in the eleventh through the thirteenth centuries is discussed in *Medieval Germany (1056–1273)*, by Alfred Haverkamp, translated by Helga Braun and Richard Mortimer, 2nd ed. (Oxford: Oxford University Press, 1992). The first part of the book contains an extensive and helpful analysis of the broader European context within which medieval Germany developed. Horst Fuhrmann's *Germany in the High Middle Ages c. 1050–1200*, translated by Timothy Reuter (Cambridge: Cambridge University Press, 1986), is a clear and interesting study of the fundamental political and social history of medieval Germany. A classic work, newly revised, is Geoffrey Barraclough's *Origins of Modern Germany*, 3rd. ed. (Oxford: Oxford University Press, 1988). Parts I and II pertain to the topics of this chapter.

The Papal Monarchy: The Western Church from 1050 to 1250, by Colin Morris (Oxford: Clarendon Press, 1989), provides a fine analysis of the Investiture Controversy and papal authority. Uta-Renate Blumenthal's *The Investiture Controversy* (Philadelphia: University of Pennsylvania Press, 1988) gives a detailed examination of the struggle between Henry IV and Gregory VII. The impact of monastic reform and the Norman Conquest on the English Church is analyzed in *The English Church: 940–1154* by H.R. Loyn (Essex, UK: Longman, 2001). The relevant chapters (14 through 19) of Warren Treadgold's *A History of the Byzantine State and Society* (Stanford, CA: Stanford University Press, 1997) provide a detailed analysis of the political history of the period discussed in this chapter.

A comprehensive study of Viking civilization may be found in *A History of the Vikings*, 2nd ed., by Gwyn Jones (Oxford: Oxford University Press, 1984, reissued 2001). *Chronicles of the Vikings: Records, Memorials and Myths*, by R.I. Page (London: British Museum Press, 1995) is an interesting study of the social history of the Vikings which uses their chronicles as source material.

7 THE EXPANSION OF CHRISTIAN EUROPE: PILGRIMAGE, CRUSADE, AND REFORM

THE ELEVENTH AND TWELFTH CENTURIES IN EUROPE were characterized by rapid economic growth and political development, and by a geographical and spiritual expansion of Christian Europe. With this spiritual awakening came a new religious fervor, exemplified by the popular practice of participating in a pilgrimage. Men and women would undertake a journey to a shrine in order to venerate the relics and memory of a saint, believing that this would provide an expiation of sin and a guarantee of salvation. The most popular destinations for pilgrimage during the Middle Ages were Jerusalem, Rome, Santiago de Compostela, and Canterbury, although there were many less important sites.

Religious fervor, allied to monetary gain, also inspired European knights to undertake a recovery of areas in the eastern Mediterranean that had been lost to the Muslims during the seventh and eighth centuries. In their quest to retake the sacred areas of apostolic Christianity, these knights traveled to the Holy Land in a series of military campaigns known as crusades. Religious faith also led to a campaign to recapture the Muslim areas of Spain—a movement known as the "Reconquista"—which recent historians have recognized as a form of crusade. A horrifying perversion of the prevailing religious enthusiasm that gripped the crusaders resulted not only in the massacre of Muslims in the Holy Land, but also occasionally in the random sacking of Jewish communities, as some Christians viewed the Jews as descendants of the murderers of Christ.

A less militaristic form of religious zeal provided the inspiration for efforts to reform the monastic life. Several new orders were founded during the late eleventh and early twelfth centuries, including the Carthusians and the Cistercians. It was the view of the founders of these new orders that the existing monastic groups had strayed from their roots, and that these new forms of monasticism more closely approximated the spirit of the apostolic life and the dictates of the Rule of St. Benedict.

All of these movements had at least one common motivating factor—the desire to spread Christianity far and wide.

Pilgrimage

Pilgrimage was a favored activity in the Middle Ages for a variety of reasons, the most important of which were spiritual in nature. Men or women undertook a journey to faraway places of particular religious significance, or to shrines closer to home, because they believed that travel to these sites would bring them closer to God, and to ultimate salvation. Often they went in order to make amends for prior sinful behavior, fulfilling a penance either self-imposed or stipulated by a priest or bishop. Some pilgrims were seeking divine intervention in a crisis. Others hoped to be healed by the saint whose shrine was visited; cures were sought by the pilgrim for himself, or for family members who were either present or languishing at home, unable to make the journey. Sometimes a pilgrimage was the fulfillment of a vow; the saint had acted to heal or bring aid in response to a promise that the pilgrim must now honor.

There were other reasons beyond the spiritual, however. Undertaking a pilgrimage provided adventure and excitement, and for many the journey simply furnished an excuse to escape from the boredom of daily existence. Frivolous attitudes were, however, discouraged by the Church. Decrees promulgated in 813 at the Council of Chalons in France warned "laity who think they can sin with impunity simply by frequenting such places of prayer, clergymen who think they can purge their sins by going on a pilgrimage and at the same time escape from their pastor duties, and poor folk whose sole purpose is to have better opportunities for begging" to refrain from embarking on a pilgrimage. The variety of motivations for taking part in a pilgrimage is made abundantly clear by the characters in Geoffrey Chaucer's literary masterpiece, *The Canterbury Tales* (see Chapter 14). Pilgrimage was possible for people at all levels of society. Many of them simply visited shrines that were nearby, but for hardy and adventurous individuals there were the great pilgrimage venues: Jerusalem, Rome, Santiago de Compostela, and Canterbury.

Jerusalem

The initial pilgrimage destination was the Holy Land, where individuals as early as the second century sought spiritual enlightenment, as well as comfort and healing, in visits to Jerusalem and other biblical locations. By the eleventh century, pilgrimage to the Holy Land was being undertaken by a growing number of Christians, perhaps thousands each year. As a result of the rapid territorial expansion of Islam in the seventh and eighth centuries, biblical sites such as Jerusalem were now in Muslim hands, so such a journey involved overcoming substantial difficulties. First, although Christian pilgrimage had been allowed during the Muslim caliphates, there was no guarantee that this privilege would be granted for ever. Indeed, an important reason for the First Crusade was to recover Jerusalem from the Muslims so that pilgrimage would be safer and less

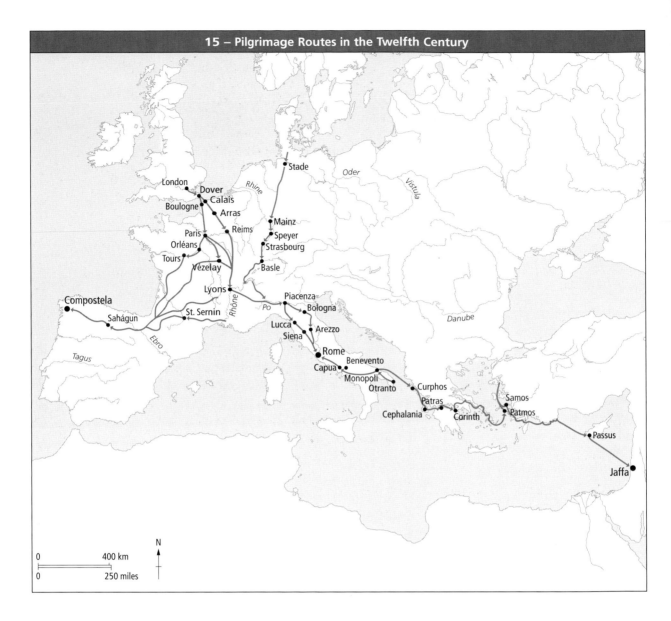

fraught with difficulty (see below). Further, the pilgrims were often subjected to attack by marauders while they were on the road. It was implicit that an arduous journey was to be anticipated as part of the pilgrim's penitence, but it was hoped that the trials would be merely physically demanding rather than life-threatening.

The ultimate pilgrimage destination was Jerusalem, which pilgrims believed was more holy than other places. According to a pilgrim's guide written by a German monk, Theodoric, who made the pilgrimage between 1169 and 1174,

It is holier because it is illuminated by the presence there of our God and Lord Jesus Christ and of his good Mother, and the fact that all the Patriarchs, Prophets, and

Apostles have lived and taught and preached and suffered martyrdom there.

Once they had made a decision to undertake the trip, the pilgrims attended a special Mass, where they received a blessing and were given the insignia of the pilgrim: a staff and a small leather bag called a scrip, to contain money and "letters of recommendation." They were said to be "taking the cross," and their garments were marked with this sign, which became the special badge of pilgrims to Jerusalem. [The scallop shell indicated a pilgrimage to Santiago de Compostela, and later, a tin badge with a portrait of St. Peter signified a journey to Rome.]

It was a long and arduous trip, as one British pilgrim, Saewulf, indicated in his journal, written between 1101 and 1103. The pilgrims left Monopoli on the southeastern coast of Italy, and "after a spell of thirteen weeks . . . during which we had lived sometimes on the waves of the sea, and sometimes in empty huts or cottages . . . with great happiness and gratitude we arrived at the port of Jaffa on a Sunday" (**Map 15**). When Saewulf's ship arrived in port, he was warned by someone ("as I imagine through God") to go ashore immediately, as there was a storm approaching.

> The next morning we heard the sound of the sea, and people shouting, all congregating and telling of new and unheard-of horrors. We were afraid, and running along with the others came to the shore. When we were there we saw the storm, with the height of its waves equal to the hills. We noticed innumerable human bodies of both sexes who had been drowned lying miserably on the shore. We saw too the remains of ships floating nearby. No sound could be heard apart from the noise of the sea, and the sinking ships, for it drowned the shouts of the people and the sound of the crowds . . . of human beings of either sex more than a thousand died that day.

The road from Jaffa to Jerusalem was dangerous, as well:

> The journey lasted two days and it was by a very hard mountain road. It was very dangerous too, because the Saracens [Muslims], who are continually plotting an ambush against Christians, were hiding in the caves of the hills and among rocky caverns. They were awake day and night, always keeping a look-out for someone to attack . . . sometimes the Saracens could be seen everywhere in the neighborhood, and sometimes they disappeared . . .
>
> Anyone who has taken that road can see how many human bodies there are in the road and next to the road, and there are countless corpses which have been torn up by wild beasts. It might be questioned why so many Christian corpses should lie there unburied, but it is in fact no surprise. There is little soil there, and the rocks are not easy to move. Even if the soil were there, who would be stupid enough to leave his brethren and be alone digging a grave! Anybody who did this would dig a grave not for his fellow Christian but for himself! So in that road not only poor and weak people have dangers to face, but also the rich and strong. Many are killed by the Saracens and many of heat and thirst—many through lack of drink and many from drinking too much. But we with all our company arrived at our goal unharmed.

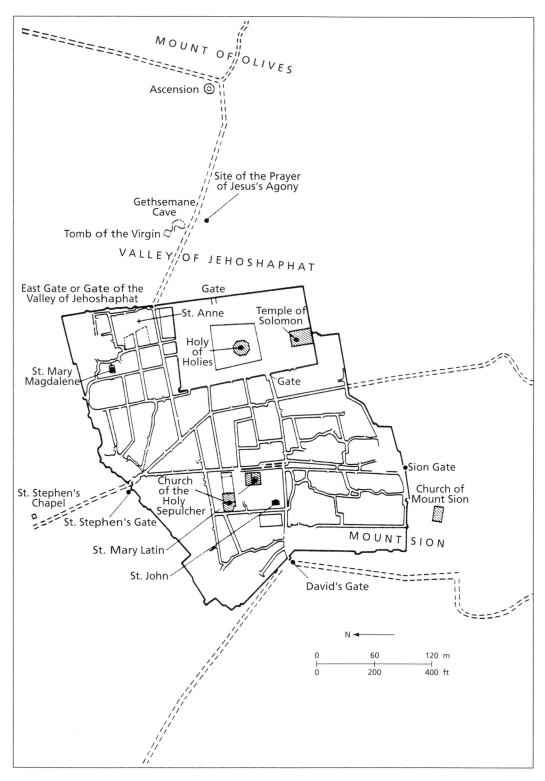

56 This plan details the locations of important pilgrimage sites in Jerusalem during the twelfth century, including the Church of the Holy Sepulche and the Temple of Solomon. The Order of Templars was granted a residence close to the temple by the king of Jerusalem—hence their name, "Knights Templar."

MOUNT OF OLIVES

Ascension ◎

Site of the Prayer
of Jesus's Agony

Gethsemane
Cave

Tomb of the Virgin

VALLEY OF JEHOSHAPHAT

East Gate or Gate of the
Valley of Jehoshaphat

Gate

St. Anne

Temple of
Solomon

Holy
of
Holies

St. Mary
Magdalene

Gate

Sion Gate

Church of
Mount Sion

Church
of the
Holy
Sepulcher

St. Stephen's
Chapel

St. Stephen's Gate

St. Mary Latin

St. John

David's Gate

MOUNT SION

N ◄

0	60	120 m
0	200	400 ft

Those pilgrims who were fortunate enough to finally reach Jerusalem took off their shoes and visited the holy places with their feet bare, declaring their devotion with tears, kisses, and frequent prostrations. They entered the holy area, according to Saewulf, through "David's Gate," and first visited the Church of the Holy Sepulcher, which Christians believed had been built on the site of Christ's resurrection (**fig. 56**). After viewing sites associated with the Passion of Christ, the pilgrims went to Mount Calvary (or Golgotha in Hebrew). Near to the Church of the Holy Sepulcher they visited the monastery of the Holy Trinity, the chapel of St. James, and the Church of St. Mary. The Temple of Solomon and the Church of St. Anne, as well as the Garden of Gethsemane, were other important pilgrim sites.

Ambitious pilgrims visited other places of importance in the life of Jesus, such as Nazareth, Bethlehem, Bethany, and Jericho, and a swim in the Jordan River seems to have been obligatory. After exploring, like Saewulf, "each one of the Holy Places of the city of Jerusalem and the cities near it," the exhausted pilgrims boarded ships for the perilous return journey. On the way home, some individuals of extraordinary stamina might visit another major pilgrimage site, such as the city of Rome.

Rome

Christian pilgrims began traveling to Rome as early as the second century, seeking, as they did in the Holy Land, close contact with the origins of their religion. Rome was a popular site because the apostles Peter and Paul were buried there, along with other martyrs of the early Church. Indeed, pilgrimage to Rome in the Middle Ages was known as a pilgrimage *ad limina apostolorum* ("to the threshold of the apostles").

The city became particularly popular as a pilgrimage site after the seventh century, when the Muslim advance in the Holy Land made the journey to Jerusalem more difficult and dangerous. Although pilgrims were now hindered in their desire to walk in the footsteps of Jesus, they could at least venerate two of his apostles at Rome. As Charlemagne's tutor Alcuin remarked in the *Life of St. Willibald*:

> The city of Rome, the head of the world, rejoices especially in the very glorious triumphs of the apostles Peter and Paul. Daily the races and people flock to this place with devoted heart so that each by compunction of faith might either weep for their crimes or ask in the hope of a more abundant life in heaven, that entry be granted to them.

And Chut, a pilgrim who journeyed to Rome in 1027, spoke of his pilgrimage with similar sentiments:

> Wise men have told me that the apostle Peter has received from God the power of binding and loosing and carries the keys of paradise. I therefore deemed it useful in no ordinary way to seek his patronage before God.

Once the pilgrim had determined to travel to Rome, he received his staff and scrip from a bishop or abbot in the blessing ceremony, and he set out on his journey. As with pilgrimage to the Holy Land, there were established routes to the Eternal City.

See Map 15 for typical itineraries from Britain and northern Europe, as well as the roads taken by pilgrims from southern Italy. For travelers from the north, whose journeys necessitated crossing the Alps, the choice of season was vitally important. Several medieval guidebooks suggest beginning travel in the middle of August, since it was warm, the paths were dry, there was not much danger of flooding, and it was certainly easier to cross the mountains. The roads were treacherous in the winter months, and there are many accounts of people freezing to death in their attempt to traverse the Alps. John, a monk of Canterbury, writing in 1188, described the Great St. Bernard Pass as "a place of torment, where the ground was so slippery that I was unable to stand."

But arrival in Rome during the summer months brought its own form of torment. At this time of year the incidence of malaria was extremely high, and pilgrims remarked on the unhealthy quality of the air in Rome and the resulting infections. Thus, the ideal time for beginning a journey from Britain or northern Europe was well before the snow posed a threat, but late enough to avoid arriving in Rome in the heat of summer.

Natural disasters, weather, and disease were not the only tribulations faced by the pilgrims. Robbery and brigandage were as prevalent on the routes to Rome as on the way to Jerusalem. Furthermore, during much of the twelfth and early thirteenth centuries parts of Italy were subject to warfare, which made the major roads unsafe for travel. In spite of all these deterrents, however, pilgrimage continued to grow in popularity, thereby demonstrating the intense religious piety of medieval people, who possessed a strong conviction that the undertaking of such a journey would ultimately provide a secure place in heaven.

Along the way pilgrims were provided with guarantees of safe passage in some areas, and exemptions from tolls were often granted. The Church was obliged to furnish food and shelter for pilgrims, and to provide medical care for those who fell ill on the journey. As acts of pilgrimage grew in popularity, secular leaders passed laws protecting the pilgrims and establishing fines for people who cheated them, such as unscrupulous innkeepers. Because of these special privileges it was necessary for pilgrims to be easily distinguished, and they were clearly set apart from casual travelers by the staff, the scrip, and the badge.

Once in Rome the pilgrims viewed the catacombs, which contained the remains of early Christians as well as relics of the early martyrs. They also visited numerous churches. One tenth-century list contains twenty-three churches where the pilgrims venerated the relics of saints and martyrs with tender devotion.

By the twelfth century the desire of pilgrims to have contact with relics was a pronounced feature of the journey, reflecting a more general fascination with holy relics then developing in society. One example is the visit in 1191 of King Philip Augustus of France (r. 1180–1223) to Rome as he was returning from the Holy Land. Rather than praying at the tomb of a martyr, Pope Celestine III took his royal visitor to see the heads of Saints Peter and Paul, as well as the Veronica Cloth, a piece of fabric allegedly bearing the imprint of Christ's face.

Pilgrimage to Rome began to become less popular during the twelfth century for several reasons. The capture of Jerusalem by the crusaders provided safer access to the sites of the Holy Land, and it became once again the preferred pilgrimage goal. And, although the bodies of two important apostles could be venerated in Rome, in Jerusalem the pilgrims could "see and touch the places where Christ was present in the body." Furthermore, there were other competing shrines, such as those at Bari, Canterbury, and Cologne, and especially that of St. James (Santiago) at Compostela, in northwestern Spain.

Santiago de Compostela

St. James, one of Christ's most favored apostles, had traveled widely during the years after the crucifixion, preaching the gospel and converting people to the Christian faith. According to legend, Spain was included in his itinerary, although the details of his mission there are obscure. The most significant miracle associated with his visit was the appearance of the Virgin Mary, standing on a column in the town of Zaragoza. A church, known as Our Lady of the Pillar, was built on the site, and it became one of the most important shrines in Spain.

James was martyred at Jerusalem in AD 44, but shortly after his murder, several of his fellow disciples took his head and his body, placed them in a boat, and set sail from the port of Jaffa. In a mere seven days the ship, miraculously driven along by wind and waves, arrived at the coast of Spain. As the ship approached the shore, a horseman who had been riding along the beach was suddenly carried into the sea by his horse; the horse and rider escaped drowning, and emerged from the waves covered with scallop shells. The scallop shell was afterwards recognized as the symbol of St. James and the badge of pilgrimage to his shrine (**fig. 57**).

The apostles came ashore, bringing the remains of the saint. After overcoming obstacles such as a dragon and ferocious oxen, they were provided with a suitable coffin by a Christian woman. When they had buried James, several of the apostles traveled through Spain preaching and teaching, although two remained to guard the tomb. Years passed, and the Christians in Spain were subject to persecution, as in all of the Roman Empire. Veneration of the relics of James was no longer practiced, and his tomb was forgotten.

In 813, during the reign of the Spanish king Alfonso II (r. 791–842), known as "the Chaste," the coffin was discovered by a shepherd in a ruined building located in a remote field in northern Spain. He reported his find to Theodomir, bishop of Iria, who identified the tomb as that of St. James. Theodomir went to the royal court to inform King Alfonso, and they traveled together to visit the site. Alfonso decreed that a church

57 Pilgrims to the famous cathedral at Santiago de Compostela, which contained the tomb of the apostle James, were distinguished by the scallop-shell badge, seen here on the scrip, or leather bag carried by a pilgrim figure on the church of Santa Marta Ide Tera. St. James (or Santiago), was the patron saint of Spain, and Christians believed he was a potent force in helping them to recover the areas controlled by the Muslims.

should be built, dedicated to St. James and containing a shrine for his relics; the place was known afterwards as Santiago de Compostela (meaning "St. James of Compostela"). The cult of the saint was further promoted by King Alfonso III (r. 866–910), who sponsored a new and much larger church at the site.

James became the patron saint of Spain as a result of his early associations with the area, but also because the Christians came to believe that he aided them in the recovery of the areas under Muslim control. According to legend, he appeared at the Battle of Clavijo around 834, where he killed 60,000 Muslims, an achievement that gained him the nickname *Santiago Matamoros* ("St. James the Moor-slayer"). Hoping for more support from the saint, the Spanish army used the words *Santiago Matamoros* as their battle cry.

Pilgrims began to come to Compostela during the reign of Alfonso III, and the first record of a foreign visitor dates from 951. The popularity of this shrine is less easily explained than that of Jerusalem or Rome, but is probably due to its association with the Reconquista and James's role in the recovery of Spain by Christian forces. Furthermore, a journey to Compostela was considered to be a worthy alternative to Rome, because it consisted of many of the same arduous features such as crossing a mountain range (in this case, the Pyrenees), and for many northern European pilgrims the trip was approximately the same length as the road to Rome.

There were several routes across Europe to Santiago (see Map 15). Pilgrims generally began their journeys on one of the smaller paths that eventually converged with the major thoroughfares. The primary roads from northern and southern France met at Puente la Reina, after which most of the pilgrims took a common route to Compostela. Along the way they stopped to venerate relics in various French and Spanish churches and cathedrals; many of these, such as those at Vézelay and Toulouse, both in France, became important sites in the development of medieval architecture, as will be discussed in Chapter 8. The pilgrimage to Compostela was enthusiastically promoted by the Cluniac order of monks, which fostered the building of roads, bridges, and hospices and ensured that the dangerous roads were properly guarded.

Once they were under way, the pilgrims shouted rallying cries, either *Deus adjuva* ("God help us") or *Sancte Jacobe* ("St. James"). As they drew near to Compostela, most of the travelers followed the route contained in a guidebook which forms the fifth part of the *Liber Sancti Jacobi* (*Book of St. James*), often identified as the *Codex Calixtinus*. The table of contents for the section of the manuscript containing the guidebook indicates the route and the sites for the pilgrims' visits:

    I. The Road to Santiago
   II. The Days' Journeys on the Road of the Apostle
  III. The Names of the Towns on His Road
  IV. The Three Good [Religious] Houses of This World
   V. The Names of the Overseers of St. James's Road
  VI. Bitter and Fresh Waters on His Road
 VII. The Characteristics of the Countries and People on His Road
VIII. The Bodies of the Saints to be Visited on the Way and the Passion of St. Eutropius

Praying at tombs and veneration of relics appear not to have been the only activities of the pilgrims. Like modern tourists, they also devoted some time to shopping and looking for souvenirs. A twelfth-century guide to Compostela (Book V, Chapter IX of the *Codex Calixtinus*) provides evidence of the kinds of goods for sale in the nearby markets. "After the fountain there is [a room with a] stone floor, where the pilgrim badges are sold." The pilgrims could also purchase wine, shoes, scrips, straps, belts, cloth, candles, rings, chalices, candelabra, and a variety of other items.

The *Guide* also provided information about proper dietary habits while traveling in Spain:

> Do not eat fish in Spain, or in Galicia, for undoubtedly you will die shortly afterwards, or at least you will become ill. If someone should by chance eat it and not fall sick, he is simply much healthier than others, or, more likely, he has become acclimatized by a long stay in the country. All the fish, beef, and pork in all of Spain and Galicia make foreigners sick.

The three major pilgrimage sites—Jerusalem, Rome, and Santiago de Compostela— had many lesser rivals. The shrines of local saints in various countries drew pilgrims from the surrounding areas, but most memorials remained regional, rather than national or international in character. One exception was the shrine of the English martyr St. Thomas Becket at Canterbury.

Canterbury

The murder of Archbishop Thomas Becket in Canterbury Cathedral on December 29, 1170, profoundly shocked the people of Europe. Becket was killed by four knights who were agents of the English king Henry II; although the king maintained that he was innocent of issuing a clear directive, the murder was the culmination of a quarrel between Becket and the king which had far-reaching implications for Church and state (see Chapter 9). Soon after the murder, the archbishop's tomb in the cathedral became the site of numerous miracles, and, as word of these occurrences spread, pilgrims began to visit in increasing numbers. According to one of Becket's close associates, John of Salisbury, the tomb was visited first by the poor, then by people from the middle classes, and finally by aristocrats, including King Henry himself. Although Canterbury did not rival Jerusalem, Rome, or Santiago de Compostela, it became the most prominent pilgrimage site in England.

Within the first two decades following Becket's martyrdom, his cult had spread throughout the European and Scandinavian countries, and as far away as Iceland. Pilgrims streamed to Canterbury from all of these areas, seeking the healing power of the saint. Many of the miracles attributed to Becket are depicted in the stained-glass windows surrounding the shrine in the apse of the cathedral, which was dedicated in 1220, fifty years after the martyrdom (**fig. 58**).

58 The stained-glass windows of Trinity Chapel, Canterbury Cathedral, where St. Thomas Becket's shrine stood until its destruction by Henry VIII, contain vividly colored images of Becket's miracles and the popular pilgrimage to Canterbury. In this panel, pilgrims travel to Canterbury, some riding on horseback as others trudge along the path.

Like the other main pilgrimage sites, Canterbury had its own special badges, which depicted the head of Becket or the scene of his martyrdom. The murder in the cathedral became a prominent subject for artistic expression in the following century, as will be discussed in Chapter 8.

Pilgrimage was one aspect of the intense religious zeal that characterized the eleventh and twelfth centuries. A further example of spiritual fervor was the phenomenon of "armed pilgrimages" to the Holy Land undertaken by the crusading armies of western Europe to recover land that had been taken by the Muslims during their initial forays into Christian areas.

The First Crusade

The crusades were among the most significant events of the Middle Ages. They took place over a period of 200 years, during which they influenced the lives of most Europeans as well as many people in the lands of the eastern Mediterranean. The term "crusade" was originally used by historians to refer only to the wars in the Holy Land, but it has recently been recognized that warfare against the enemies of the Christian faith in Spain, central Europe, and the Baltic region also shared many of the characteristics of a holy war, and the definition of crusade has therefore been broadened to include religious conflict in these areas.

Scholarly debate concerning the motivation of the crusaders has produced an extensive historiography. Some historians have suggested that the knights of western Europe were more interested in the promise of land and wealth than in spiritual reward. However, recent scholars have advanced the view that the main impetus came from Church reformers in the eleventh century, who, beset by conflict with secular and ecclesiastical authorities, turned to the aristocracy of western Europe for aid. The churchmen were building on extremely close connections between ecclesiastical institutions and the local nobility, and their rhetoric fostered an intense crusading fervor among the knights. Further, it has been shown that there were important crusading traditions within noble families that emphasized duty to God and Church.

A man became a crusader by swearing a public vow, which was akin to the vow to make a pilgrimage; the two were, in fact initially indistinguishable from one another. Crusaders and pilgrims enjoyed the same legal status; both were subject to ecclesiastical courts, rather than those of the secular administration. Furthermore, they were entitled to ecclesiastical protection for their persons, families, and property. In addition, the crusader was responding to a call from the pope, acting in his role as Christ's representative on earth.

The crusading warriors were obviously the most directly involved, but the clergy who traveled with them, the people who supported them monetarily, the farmers whose crops were taken as food for the armies, and the wives and families left behind, were all profoundly affected by the holy war. Although the combination of reasons for the crusades is complicated, the spark that initially ignited the military and religious fervor came from the Byzantine emperor.

By the second half of the eleventh century, the Byzantine Empire had lost a great deal of its former power. Incompetent and weak rulers had wasted vast sums of money in maintaining an extravagant lifestyle while allowing the military network to decay. In addition, the ranks of the army were weakened by the dwindling supply of recruits as an increasing number of peasants were suppressed into serfdom. This situation rendered the empire vulnerable, and during the tenth century it was subjected to attacks from various groups, including the Vikings, the Bulgars, and the Muslims (see Chapter 6). Circumstances became even more precarious with the emergence of the powerful Seljuk Turks in the eleventh century. The Seljuks had settled in the area of the Tigris River valley formerly held by the Abbasids, and were poised to move into the rich Byzantine holdings in Asia Minor. In 1071, the Byzantine emperor Romanus IV (r. 1067–1071) decided to advance into the territory held by the Turks. The armies engaged in battle at Mazikert, in Armenia, where the Turkish forces won an overwhelming victory against the imperial army, and succeeded in capturing the emperor. The defeat was particularly disastrous because the provinces lost to the Turks were among the wealthiest in the empire, and the resulting diminution of revenue placed further strain on the dwindling resources of the state.

In 1081, a new and more effective emperor came to the throne—Alexius Comnenus (r. 1081–1118). Eventually realizing that he could not hope to recover the lost lands with his own forces, Comnenus appealed to the pope for help, and on November 17, 1095, Pope Urban II (r. 1088–1099) issued an urgent appeal to the knights of western Europe to display their valor by joining forces in a crusade. Although there had been much quarreling and dissension between the popes and the Byzantine leaders during the previous two centuries, there seems to have been a prevailing attitude that the Greeks, as fellow Christians, deserved the assistance of the west, particularly when they were facing a common foe—Islam. Furthermore, there was hope that the sources of conflict between Roman and Byzantine Christianity could be resolved, and that the Latin and Greek churches might be reunited. It seems probable that Pope Urban II, in responding to Comnenus, was not primarily interested in helping the emperor to regain his lands; his most important objective was rather to retake the Holy Land in order to recover the sacred sites of Christianity. In addition, it should not be ignored that beyond the religious motivation lay the promise of power and wealth.

Although we do not have the exact words used by Urban in his appeal, there are various versions of his speech recorded somewhat later by eyewitnesses. Thus, there is no shared text, and historians have suspected that writers may have manipulated Urban's supposed words to correlate with the results of the crusade. Nonetheless, certain common themes emerge, and these are well represented in the account of a chronicler known as Robert, a monk of Reims in northeastern France. His words probably preserve the essential spirit of the papal exhortation to the crowd assembled at the Council of Clermont, which had been convened in 1095 to discuss Church reform. Urban's speech emphasizes the spiritual value of Jerusalem and the horror of the pollution of holy places by the infidel, as well as the spiritual (and temporal) rewards of taking up the cross.

> Let the deeds of your ancestors move you and incite your minds to manly achievements; the glory and greatness of King Charles the Great, and of his son Louis, and of your other kings, who have destroyed the kingdoms of the pagans, and have extended in the lands the territory of the Holy Church. Let the Holy Sepulcher of the Lord our Savior, which is possessed by unclean nations, especially incite you, and the holy places which are now treated with ignominy and irreverently polluted with their filthiness. Oh, most valiant soldiers and descendants of invincible ancestors, be not degenerate, but recall the valor of your progenitors.

Urban was able to rouse the emotions of the crowd in attendance by recounting, in gory detail, some of the alleged practices of the Turkish Muslims:

> From the confines of Jerusalem and the city of Constantinople a horrible tale has gone forth and very frequently has been brought to our ears, namely, that a race from the kingdom of the Persians, an accursed race, a race utterly alienated from God, a generation forsooth which has not directed its heart and has not entrusted its spirit to God, has invaded the lands of those Christians and has depopulated them by the sword, pillage, and fire; it has led away a part of the captives into its own country, and a part it has destroyed by cruel tortures; it has either entirely destroyed the churches of God or appropriated them for the rites of its own religion. They destroy the altars, after having defiled them with their uncleanness. They circumcise the Christians, and the blood of the circumcision they either spread upon the altars or pour into the vases of the baptismal font. When they wish to torture people by a base death, they perforate their navels, and dragging forth the extremity of the intestines, bind it to a stake; then with flogging they lead the victim around until the viscera having gushed forth the victim falls prostrate upon the ground. Others they bind to a post and pierce with arrows. Others they compel to extend their necks and then, attacking them with naked swords, attempt to cut through the neck with a

single blow. What shall I say of the abominable rape of the women? To speak of it is worse than to be silent. The kingdom of the Greeks is now dismembered by them and deprived of territory so vast in extent that it can not be traversed in a march of two months. Of whom therefore is the labor of avenging these wrongs and of recovering this territory incumbent, if not upon you? You, upon whom above other nations God has conferred remarkable glory in arms, great courage, bodily activity, and strength to humble the hairy scalp of those who resist you.

After describing the horrors to which the Christians were being subjected, Pope Urban pleaded with the knights to lay aside their own quarrels and to cease their petty warfare. "Enter upon the road to the Holy Sepulcher; wrest that land from the wicked race, and subject it to yourselves." And further, "When an armed attack is made upon the enemy, let this one cry be raised by all the soldiers of God: 'It is the will of God! It is the will of God!'"

Although Urban's description of the actions of Muslims was grossly exaggerated, it is true that episodes of brutality against pilgrims and other Christians had become more widespread during the course of the eleventh century. These incidents were generally not the result of governmental programs, but occurred as a product of spontaneous popular violence. There were, however, examples of political persecution, such as the directives issued during the reign of 'al-Hakim (r. 996–1021), the caliph of the Fatimid dynasty in Egypt, which ordered the persecution of both Christians and Jews. In 1009, 'al-Hakim sent an army to Jerusalem, where the soldiers killed the non-Muslim residents of the city and severely damaged the Church of the Holy Sepulcher. Although incidents such as this were isolated, it was perhaps inevitable that Muslim society, as it developed, established practices and traditions that effectively marginalized the Christian and Jewish inhabitants of areas under Muslim control and created an atmosphere where repression and persecution of the minority were tolerated.

In his speech at Clermont, Urban urged the knights to march to the Holy Land, setting out on a "holy pilgrimage" that would free the sacred sites of Christianity. The Christian warriors should disregard the claims of home, family, and "the alluring charms of your wives." The old and feeble should stay behind, and "women ought not to set out at all, without their husbands or brothers or legal guardians. For such are more of a hindrance than aid, more of a burden than advantage." Each man who set out "shall make his vow to God . . . and shall offer himself to Him as a living sacrifice, holy, acceptable unto God." The pope declared that the crusader should "wear the sign of the cross of the Lord on his forehead or on his breast," and since "God has conferred upon you above all nations great glory in arms . . . [you should] undertake this journey." Furthermore, "Remission of sins will be granted for those going thither, if they end a shackled life either on land or in crossing the sea, or in struggling against the heathen. I, being vested with that gift from God, grant this to those who go." Urban thus granted a **plenary indulgence** to any knight who died in battle—his sins would be forgiven and he would be granted admission into heaven.

Pope Urban's intention was to inspire the knights of Europe—men who possessed enough wealth to equip themselves for such an enterprise. He implied that the nobility, by undertaking the crusade, would be seeking penance for its own warlike brutality and its unfair treatment of the poor. In this sense, his plea was an extension of the Peace of God and the Truce of God, which formed part of the program of the Church designed to provide a more peaceful environment during the previous century (see Chapter 5). Urban's speech also pointed out the relative poverty of western Europe in comparison with the fabled wealth of the eastern Mediterranean lands, which would belong to the victorious Christian forces once they had defeated the infidel.

The pope's exhortation to engage in a holy war also motivated the lower classes, who were neither trained for warfare nor able to acquire the necessary weapons and supplies for the adventure. Because they had no preparations to make, however, they could set out immediately for the Holy Land. In 1096, led by a charismatic preacher with apocalyptic ideas known as Peter the Hermit and a poor knight named Walter Sansavoir, a motley crew, numbering perhaps 50,000, set out from France on an expedition now known as the "Peasants' Crusade." The mob included many pious and dedicated Christians, but also "adulterers, homicides, thieves, perjurers, robbers . . . and even women." Peter animated his followers with dire warnings of the imminence of the end of the world, and promised them that their crusade would result in the successful capture of the Holy Land. As proof of their divine election, Peter carried a letter he claimed to have received directly from heaven, which stated that God had selected the poor citizens of Europe to prepare the way for the Second Coming of Christ. His message was spread far and wide, and he gained adherents from throughout western Europe.

As the peasants passed through Germany, more adventurers joined them, and several extremely militant groups were formed. From these crusading bands evolved serious assaults on European Jewry, especially those in the Rhineland. One group, under the leadership of a local nobleman named Emicho, perpetrated an organized military assault, subjecting the Jews in the German town of Mainz to a dreadful slaughter, supposedly "to avenge the blood of 'the hanged one' [Jesus]." Their actions were characteristic of the prevailing attitude of the time, which viewed both Muslims and Jews as heretical and dangerous.

Rather than being killed by the crusaders, many of the Jews at Mainz committed suicide. According to the historical account written in 1140 by Solomon bar Samson,

> As soon as the enemy came into the courtyard they found some of the very pious there with our brilliant master, Isaac ben Moses. He stretched out his neck, and his head they cut off first. The others, wrapped in their fringed praying-shawls, sat by themselves in the courtyard, eager to do the will of their Creator. They did not care to flee into the chamber to save themselves for this temporal life, but out of love they received upon themselves the sentence of God. The enemy showered stones and arrows upon them, but they did not care to flee; and with the stroke of the sword, and with slaughter, and destruction the foe killed all of those whom they found there. When those in the chambers saw the deed of these righteous ones, how the enemy had already come upon them, they then cried out, all of them: "There is nothing better than for us to offer our lives as a sacrifice."

The less violent members of the crusading group led by Peter the Hermit were themselves the victims of brutality. They had gained permission from Coloman, the Hungarian

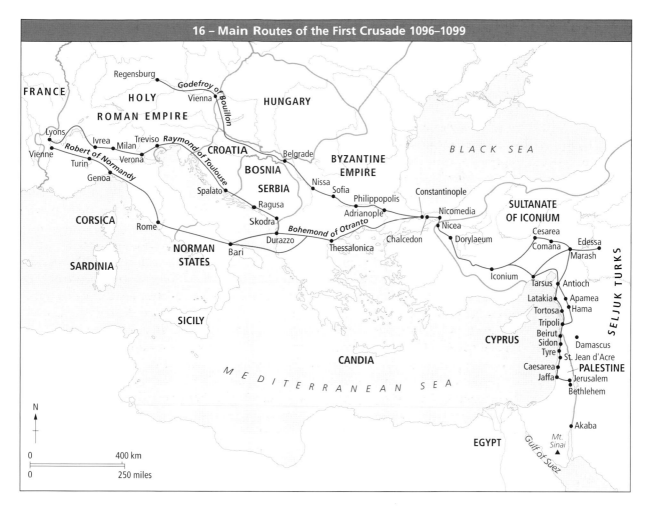

king, for a peaceful transit across Hungary, but some were robbed by Hungarian peasants. Determined to seek revenge, the peasant crusaders attacked the Hungarian forces, killing about 4,000 Hungarians, according to an eyewitness account, while only 100 crusaders died. Some of the crusaders were further harassed as they passed through Bulgaria, and skirmishes occurred between the Bulgarian forces and the peasant throng.

Eventually they reached Constantinople, where the emperor was less than impressed by the undisciplined "army"; he immediately sent them on to Asia Minor, where they were annihilated by the Turks. Although the "Peasants' Crusade" was obviously a mistake and a failure, it remains a testament to the faith of a number of pious individuals who truly believed that God would award them victory in their quest to defeat the infidel.

The first "official" crusading army was led by Adhemar, bishop of Le Puy, who was appointed by Pope Urban II. Although no important king took part in the First Crusade, the force included the brothers of the kings of England and France as well as many famous knights, including Godfrey of Bouillon, Baldwin of Flanders, Bohemond of Otranto, and Robert of Normandy (**Map 16** shows the routes taken by the crusaders).

They reached Constantinople in 1097, and the emperor struck a bargain with the leaders: he would provide food for the army and transportation to Asia Minor in exchange for an oath of allegiance. This was eventually given, although a band of crusaders plundered and burned a suburb of Constantinople before the agreement was finalized.

The Byzantine court viewed the western knights as invading barbarians, and, as their behavior demonstrates, this was not an unfair assessment. The daughter of the emperor, Anna Comnena (1083–c. 1148), described the following episode in the *Alexiad*, a history that she wrote concerning her father's reign:

> When all, including Godfrey [of Bouillon], were assembled and after the oath had been sworn by every count, one nobleman dared to seat himself on the emperor's throne. Alexius endured this without a word, knowing of old the haughty temper of the Latins, but Count Baldwin went up to the man, took him by the hand and made him rise. He gave him a severe reprimand: "You ought never to have done such a thing, especially after promising to be the emperor's liege-man. Roman emperors don't let their subjects sit with them. That's the custom here and sworn liege-men of His Majesty should observe the customs of the country." The man said nothing to Baldwin, but with a bitter glance at Alexius muttered some words to himself in his own language: "What a peasant! He sits alone while generals like these stand beside him!" Alexius saw his lips moving and calling one of the interpreters who understood the language asked what he had said. Being told the words he made no comment to the man at the time, but kept the remark to himself.

When it was time for the knight to leave, the emperor asked him who he was. "I am a Frank," he replied, "of the most high and ancient nobility, . . . and nobody dares to measure swords with me." The emperor did not accept the implicit challenge, instead advising the knight to put himself neither "at the head nor rear of the army, but in the middle." The knight was later killed in battle.

The military skill of the crusading army was not held in high esteem by the Byzantines, as indicated in Anna's history:

> The truth is that the Frankish race, among other characteristics, combines an independent spirit and imprudence, not to mention an absolute refusal to cultivate a disciplined art of war . . . [they] are indomitable in the opening cavalry charge, but afterwards, because of the weight of their armor and their own passionate nature and recklessness, it is actually very easy to beat them.

Nonetheless, when the crusaders attacked Nicea, they won a victory that enabled the emperor Alexius to occupy the city with imperial troops. The crusading army then began its trek towards Palestine.

Although accounts of the strategy against the Turks indicate that the European knights waged a disorganized campaign, they were able to defeat the Turks at the Battle of Dorylaeum, opening the way towards Antioch. Baldwin of Flanders, with a small group of followers, left the army to secure a fief for himself at Edessa, while the remainder of the force moved on. Antioch fell to the crusaders after a siege of several months, and

Bohemond assumed the title of prince of Antioch. He stayed at Antioch as the remaining army marched towards Jerusalem, laying siege to it in June, 1099. They entered the city in July, where they won a stunning victory. The *Chronicle* of Fulcher of Chartres, a French chaplain and historian of the First Crusade, describes the dreadful slaughter of the inhabitants:

> On the top of Solomon's Temple, to which they [the Arabs] had climbed in fleeing, many were shot to death with arrows and cast down headlong from the roof. Within this temple about ten thousand were beheaded. If you had been there, your feet would have been stained up to the ankles with the blood of the slain. What more shall I tell? Not one of them was allowed to live. They did not spare the women and children.

This victory provided the crusaders with the opportunity to establish small kingdoms in the Holy Land. Godfrey de Bouillon, who took the title "Defender of the Holy Sepulcher" rather than "king," became the monarch of Jerusalem, the most important area. The remaining conquered lands were divided among the leaders of the crusade. Baldwin and Bohemond retained their original territories of conquest (Edessa and Antioch), and the county of Tripoli was given to another of the leaders, Raymond of Toulouse. All four of the areas governed by the crusaders became highly organized feudal states.

Soon after the formation of the crusader kingdoms, new monastic orders emerged, known as the Military Orders. These were communities of ascetic warrior monks who were professionally dedicated to fighting the holy war, and in them Christian knight-hood reached its apogee. The first of these orders, founded during the early years of the kingdom of Jerusalem, was the Knights of the Temple, commonly known as "Knights Templar" or "Templars"—a name that derived from the proximity of their headquarters to the Temple of Solomon.

The Templars

The Templars were founded primarily in response to problems of Muslim harassment and brigandage on the pilgrim routes to Jerusalem. One of the crusading nobles, Hugh de Payns, who was residing in that kingdom, suggested the formation of a religious mili-tary organization to provide protection for merchants and travelers.

According to the chronicler William of Tyre,

> In 1119 certain nobles of knightly rank, devout, religious, and God-fearing, devoting themselves to the service of Christ, made their vows to the patriarch [of Jerusalem] and declared that they wished to live forever in chastity, obedience, and poverty, according to the rule of regular canons . . . Since they had neither a church nor a house, the king of Jerusalem gave them a temporary residence in the palace which stands of the west side of the temple [of Solomon]. The canons of the temple granted them, on certain conditions, the open space around the aforesaid palace for the erection of their necessary buildings, and the king, the nobles, the patriarch, and the bishops, each from his own possessions, gave them lands for their support. The

patriarch and bishops ordered that for the forgiveness of their sins their first vow should be to protect the roads and especially the pilgrims against robbers and marauders.

The Templars developed a plan for the order, which was approved by a council at Troyes, France, in 1128. The composition of a Rule was entrusted to a Burgundian nobleman named Bernard of Clairvaux (see below). Based on the Rule of St. Benedict, it stipulated that the knights were to be bound by personal vows of poverty, chastity, and obedience. They were to shun all contact with women, and were directed to wear white robes, "because they have put the dark life behind them." These robes were to be emblazoned with crosses of red cloth. They were also required to cut their hair short:

> All brothers, especially the permanent ones, ought to have their hair so tonsured so that normally they can be considered from front or back as regular and ordained. The same rule is to be observed without fail in respect of their beard and whiskers so that no excess or vice of the face may be noted.

The Rule also restricted the footwear of the knights:

> It is patently obvious that pointed shoes and laces are characteristic of Saracens (*gentili*), and since this is recognized as an abomination by everyone, we forbid and prohibit anyone from having these, indeed he should henceforth jettison them. We do not even allow temporary servants to have pointed shoes and laces and excess hair or immoderately long clothes; in fact we positively forbid them.

The Templars slept in a common dormitory, and were expected to be present at Mass and the office liturgies, though singing was left to the clergy attached to the order. The dietary provisions of Benedict's Rule were amended to provide more meat for the warrior monks, since they faced greater physical demands.

Recruits were drawn from two classes of society: the "knights" were members of the military aristocracy, whereas the "sergeants," or serving men, came from a more humble background. Chaplains were fully incorporated as ordained members of the order, and a number of household workers and servants were employed.

The new monastic vocation had great appeal in an era when men who were trained for military action were motivated by religious fervor. The Templars grew rapidly as a result of successful recruitment, and donations of money and land soon made them a wealthy international order. In 1139, Pope Innocent II approved the Rule and issued a decree that gave privileged status to the order. The Templars were now allowed to own oratories and burial grounds, were exempted from paying tithes, and were made directly responsible to the pope, rather than to local bishops.

By the middle of the twelfth century, the Templars had established an institutional structure. The monks were subject to a "Grand Master," who was elected by a special convocation. The lands and houses of the order were divided into provinces, each of which was under the direction of a master and a commander, and the individual houses were supervised by a preceptor.

In the course of the thirteenth century, the Templars became the protection agency for the bankers of Europe. They regularly transferred money across long distances, and began to make credit arrangements and to lend money to crusaders, travelers, and even the kings of England and France. Their economic power did not engender a positive response, however. Their vast wealth was widely envied, and their arrogance was bitterly resented. Furthermore, since they were responsible only to the pope, they were technically exempt from any form of secular control. They were thus resented by figures such as the French king Philip IV, who managed to persuade Pope Clement V to dissolve the order in 1312 (see Chapter 11).

The crusading fervor of the Middle Ages spawned several other military monastic orders, both in the Holy Land and in Spain, where the Orders of Calatrava and Alcantara were established later in the twelfth century. The most famous, however, was also formed in Jerusalem—the Order of Hospitallers, or Knights of St. John of Jerusalem.

The Hospitallers

About twenty-five years before the first crusaders arrived in the Holy Land, the Benedictine monastery of St. Mary of the Latins was built adjacent to the site of the Holy Sepulcher in Jerusalem (see fig. 56) with funds provided by some merchants from the Italian republic of Amalfi. The monks, seeing the need to care for an increasing number of pilgrims, built a hospice, or hospital, which they dedicated to St. John the Baptist. The hospital was run by a fraternity of Italians who took monastic vows. In 1099, when the warriors of the First Crusade captured Jerusalem, the master of the hospital, an Italian named Gerard, convinced Godfrey de Bouillon, ruler of the crusader kingdom, to endow the hospice with land in the newly conquered areas. The organization was soon extended through the establishment of daughter hospitals in southern France and Italy, particularly in locations where pilgrims set sail for the Holy Land. The fraternity was granted exemptions from tithes and taxes by the patriarch of Jerusalem, and in 1113 Pope Paschal II issued a bull recognizing the Hospitallers as a monastic order, directed by their own master, under papal authority.

At first, the Hospitallers were not a military order, and existed only to provide care for poor and sick pilgrims. In 1118, however, under the direction of their master Raymond du Puy, their mission changed course, apparently in response to military needs in the outlying areas of the Latin kingdoms. A strong army of professional soldiers was required for defense, and the well-endowed Hospitallers could fulfill that role. Their first major campaign was waged in 1123, in response to an invasion by the Fatamid caliphate in Egypt, which was seeking to expand its holdings, and the Hospitallers fought alongside the Templars in subsequent military engagements. They built strategically placed castles, including the *Crak des Chevaliers* (Castle of the Knights), the greatest of the crusader fortresses, which they constructed in Syria, near the border of present-day Lebanon (**fig. 59**). By 1180, the Hospitallers possessed twenty-five castles in the Holy Land.

59 Castles were important to the defense of the Holy Land, where a strong fortress was capable of controlling vast areas. One of the most impressive of these structures is the *Crak des Chevaliers*, situated on the frontier between the Turks and the county of Tripoli. During the twelfth century it was fortified by the Hospitallers: the thick walls and commanding towers are evident in this photograph.

Like the Templars, the order was soon stratified into knights, sergeants, and clergy, with a corps of domestic servants to serve household needs. The Hospitallers took monastic vows of poverty, chastity, and obedience, and lived in a community where they observed the daily round of liturgical ceremonies. Their distinctive symbol was a white cross sewn onto their overcoats, in contrast to the red cross worn by the Templars. By the middle of the thirteenth century they controlled an extensive network of estates in various European areas.

The military orders were products of the crusading fervor of the twelfth and thirteenth centuries, and they embodied the expansive spirit of the western Europeans. Because they were centered in the Holy Land, and found their mission in defending the Christian states against the incursions of the Muslims, the future success of their orders was tied to the fortunes of the crusader kingdoms. The failure of subsequent crusades was thus a source of disillusion and discouragement for the military orders. Unlike the Templars, the Hospitallers, because they had never completely given up their initial responsibility of caring for pilgrims, continued to exist, though in 1308 their headquarters was shifted to the Greek island of Rhodes.

Military orders also developed in Spain during the Reconquista (see Chapter 9). These crusading warriors were actively involved in the mission of Christian Spain to recover the lands conquered by the Muslims in the eighth century, an undertaking that took nearly 500 years to complete.

The Reconquista

At the time of the Muslim conquest of Spain (see Chapter 3), the Christian Visigoths were driven into the northern part of the country, where the war chieftains established the kingdom of Asturias. By the eleventh century, this kingdom had expanded and been divided into two states: Castile and León. As discussed in Chapter 4, in the late eighth century, Charlemagne had established the Spanish March in the border area along the Pyrenees, and by the end of the ninth century the western part of this "buffer zone" had become the kingdom of Navarre. In 1035, the region of Aragón became an independent kingdom, and the eastern portion of the Spanish March was incorporated into it as the county of Barcelona. Thus, by the middle of the eleventh century, the area of northern Spain comprising Castile, León, Navarre, Aragón, and Barcelona formed the nucleus for the "recovery" of Spain by the Christians, a movement commonly known as the Reconquista (**Map 17**).

Before the eleventh century, the Christian kingdoms in the north could not advance against the Muslims to the south because the powerful Ummayad caliphate of Córdoba effectively controlled all of central and southern Spain. After 1009, however, the caliphate was severely weakened by civil war. The result was the political disintegration of centralized authority and the formation of twenty-three separate states known as *taifas*, or "party kingdoms," ruled either by Spanish Muslims or by Berbers from North Africa. Many of the *taifas* proved to be unable to defend themselves against the Christian kingdoms. Furthermore, wars between the various *taifas* were unceasing, and their leaders were willing to pay tribute to their northern neighbors for protection against their Muslim rivals.

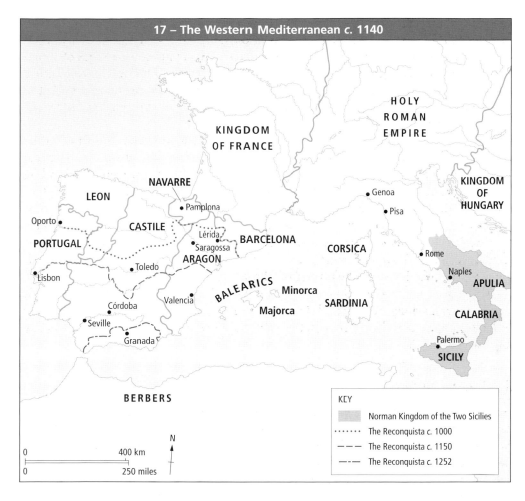

17 – The Western Mediterranean c. 1140

KINGDOM OF FRANCE

HOLY ROMAN EMPIRE

KINGDOM OF HUNGARY

LEON

NAVARRE
• Pamplona

PORTUGAL

CASTILE

Oporto •

• Lérida
Saragossa •
ARAGON

BARCELONA

Genoa •
• Pisa

CORSICA

• Rome

Naples
•

APULIA

Lisbon •
• Toledo

Valencia •

BALEARICS
• Minorca

Majorca

SARDINIA

CALABRIA

Córdoba •

• Seville

Granada •

BERBERS

Palermo
•

SICILY

N

0   400 km
0   250 miles

KEY

   Norman Kingdom of the Two Sicilies

······· The Reconquista c. 1000

– – – The Reconquista c. 1150

–·–·– The Reconquista c. 1252

The weakness of the *taifa* states provided the opportunity for the knights of northern Spain to fulfill the exhortations of the Church prelates to recover the southern region from the infidel. A corollary to this religious impetus was a natural desire to expand the geographical limits of the Christian area. The leaders of the "recovery" movement were Alfonso VI (r. 1065–1109), king of Castile and León, and Sancho "the Great" (r. 1063–1094), king of Aragón and Navarre. These two kings, supported by Norman and Burgundian knights, advanced against the Muslims, and in 1085 Alfonso captured the city of Toledo, in central Spain, ending 374 years of Islamic rule. Alfonso, who identified himself by the title "Emperor of the Two Religions," granted religious freedom to both the Muslims and Mozarabs (Spanish Christians of Arab descent), but he extracted monetary tributes from the residents of Toledo and other newly conquered cities.

One of Alfonso's vassals was the semi-legendary Spanish hero Rodrigo Díaz de Vivar, generally referred to as "El Cid" ("the lord"), whose career typifies the difference in attitude between the French knights and the Spanish warriors. Whereas the Frenchmen saw themselves as fighting for the Christian faith, Spanish knights tended to fight on either side—Christian or Muslim—as the situation dictated. Hence, when El Cid and

King Alfonso were on friendly terms, the vassal fought bravely for his lord, but when they quarreled, El Cid would join forces with the Muslims.

Nonetheless, the forays by the armies of Alfonso and his royal ally, Sancho "the Great" significantly weakened the Muslim *taifas*. The Muslim leaders, facing the reality that they needed assistance in combatting the Christians, sought the aid of the *Almoravides* (meaning "bound to the service of God"), a fundamentalist sect within Islam led by a tribe of Berbers who were then in control of northern Africa.

The *Almoravides* entered Spain in 1086, forcing Alfonso to relinquish much of his newly conquered territory. However, it took the Berber tribe some fifteen years to establish control in the area of the *taifas*, through a combination of terrorism and assassination. They ultimately enjoyed popular support, however, by lowering taxes and creating a stable government, although they treated Mozarabs and Jews harshly, causing a significant number of them to migrate to northern Spain.

Like the phenomenon of the pilgrimage, the crusades and the Reconquista can be seen as examples of the religious fervor of the eleventh and twelfth centuries. A further example of this zeal may be observed in the various reform movements dedicated to purifying monastic practice and renewing the ancient precepts of monasticism. The monastic reformers sought a return to the principles that were in close harmony with the original Rule of St. Benedict.

Monastic Reform

During the reign of Charlemagne, monasticism was practiced according to a variety of local traditions, although it had been the aim of the emperor to create a uniform monastic existence (see Chapter 4). Charlemagne's successor, Louis the Pious, was left with the responsibility of establishing a standard that would become the basic pattern for monasticism throughout the Carolingian realm. Accordingly, the emperor enlisted the expertise of St. Benedict of Aniane (*c.* 750–821), a monk who was devoted to strict interpretation of the Rule of St. Benedict originally set out by Benedict of Nursia in the sixth century (see Chapter 1). Louis summoned Benedict of Aniane to Aachen and instructed him to found an abbey at nearby Inde, which became a model for Benedictine observance. In 816 and 817 Benedict presided over two assemblies of abbots that met at Aachen, during which the principles of the reform program were explained. Furthermore, the plan for an ideal monastery at St. Gall (see Chapter 4) was probably drawn up at these synods. Every abbot was to return to his monastery and read and explain the original Rule of St. Benedict to his monks; he should also require that every monk who was able would memorize the Rule. The **divine office**—the daily routine of prayer for each time of day— was to be celebrated according to the instructions of the assembly, and other details of monastic life were similarly regulated. The purpose was a common code of practice, to be followed by all Benedictine monasteries.

The provisions were not just theoretical. Practical steps were undertaken to ensure that they would be followed. Representatives were sent from each Benedictine house to Benedict's monastery at Inde to be instructed in specific aspects of the observance, and special *missi* from the emperor were directed to inspect the monasteries in order to make certain that regulations were adopted.

Ironically, Benedict's new regulations altered Benedictine life in ways that would ultimately draw criticism. There was a change in the governance structure, with the abbot-general (supported by the secular government) functioning as the highest authority. Before this time, each monastic establishment had been virtually autonomous in the conduct of internal matters.

Even more innovative were the additions to the liturgy. Whereas the original Rule had established seven offices to be celebrated during a twenty-four-hour period, monks were now required to chant additional psalms before the night office, and to walk in elaborate processions. In addition, the Office for the Dead was to be sung daily. Although these measures were not inherently objectionable, the elaboration of liturgical activity in the monastery meant that the monks had much less time available for the manual labor that had been stipulated by the Rule. Thus, because of the new emphasis, servants were now being employed by the monastery to do domestic and agricultural work.

The concept that the primary purpose of a Benedictine monastery was to celebrate the divine liturgy began with the decrees of this "second" Benedict, and it was this emphasis that encouraged noble donors, in hopes of achieving salvation, to endow and patronize Benedictine monastic establishments. A century later, in 910, one such donor, Duke William of Aquitaine, provided the foundation for a new abbey at Cluny in Burgundy; his objective was to put into practice the precepts of Benedict of Aniane.

Cluny

(September 11, 910) To all right thinkers it is clear that the providence of God has so provided for certain rich men that, by means of their transitory possessions, if they use them well, they may be able to merit everlasting rewards. As to which thing, indeed, the Divine Word, showing it to be possible and altogether advising it, says: "The riches of a man are the redemption of his soul" (Proverbs xiii). I, William, count and duke by the grace of God, diligently pondering this, and desiring to provide for my own safety while I am still able, have considered it advisable—nay, most necessary—that from the temporal goods which have been conferred upon me I should give some little portion for the gain of my soul. I do this, indeed, in order that I who have thus increased in wealth may not, perchance, at the last be accused of having spent all in caring for my body, but rather may rejoice, when fate at last shall snatch all things away, in having reserved something for myself . . . and making the act not a temporary but a lasting one, I should support at my own expense a congregation of monks.

Thus William set forth his purpose and his plan in founding Cluny, and he followed with a detailed list of properties to be given to the monastery. He specified that "the monks shall congregate and live according to the Rule of St. Benedict," and that "celestial converse shall be sought and striven after with all desire and with the deepest ardor." Further, "there shall daily, with the greatest zeal, be performed there works of mercy towards the poor, the needy, strangers, and pilgrims."

William also prescribed a procedure for the election of an abbot when his appointee, Berno, died: "Those same monks shall have power and permission to elect any one of their order whom they please as abbot and rector, following the will of God and the rule promulgated by St. Benedict." The monastery was thus free to determine its own leadership.

Over time, other Benedictine monasteries were founded throughout Europe, based on the pattern established at Cluny, and these Cluniac institutions became not only quite numerous but also wealthy. Much property was donated by wealthy laypeople, and since this was the era of feudal development, serfs came with the land to provide labor in order for it to be productive. Hence, the Benedictines became landlords, and were involved in political life. By 1100, there were at least 300 Cluniac houses, and most of the monks were drawn from the aristocracy. Prestige and wealth were hallmarks of these establishments. (**Figs. 60** and **61** show Cluny as it was around 1157.)

The aristocratic families of medieval Europe saw the Benedictine monasteries as places that could offer a career to members of their families who could not be accommodated within the secular feudal structure. Younger sons, for whom there was not enough dynastic land, and daughters for whom suitable marriage alliances could not be found, were sent to monasteries or convents where they would live in dignity, as befitted their position in society. Children were also sometimes given to a monastery through a process of religious donation known as **oblation**, often with an endowment of property. In the ceremony for the acceptance of such children—known as **oblates**—the parents made the vows on the child's behalf and wrapped his or her hand in the cloth used for Mass offerings, symbolizing a donation placed in the offertory plate. A typical pledge was: "I dedicate this boy, in the name of God and his holy saints, to serve our Lord Jesus Christ as a monk, and to remain in this holy life all his days until his final breath." The oblates received a fine education in the monastic school, and often rose to high positions in the hierarchy of the Church, where they were able to influence policy, usually presenting the point of view of their noble families. According to the chronicler of St. Riquier, an abbey in Picardy, "Every high dignitary, wheresoever he was in the kingdom of the Franks, rejoiced that he had a relative in the monastery."

Many monastic communities were unwilling to accept children who were not of aristocratic birth. For example, the abbey of Reichenau, situated on an island in Lake Constance, on the border of Germany, Austria, and Switzerland, claimed in a petition to the pope in 1029 that "in the monastery there have always been, and are, only monks of illustrious and noble birth . . . from its foundation there have been none but the sons of counts and barons." And the nunnery of Monheim in the

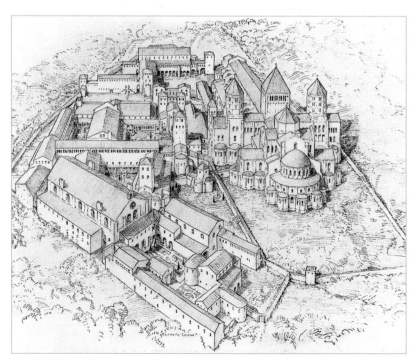

60 This reconstruction drawing of Cluny shows the monastery as it was in the mid-twelfth century. It had grown rapidly since its foundation in 910, as indicated by the many buildings, and especially by the contrast between the large and magnificent church on the right (begun in 1088) and the more modest structure in the center, which was the community's second place of worship (constructed under Abbot Maieul, 948–994).

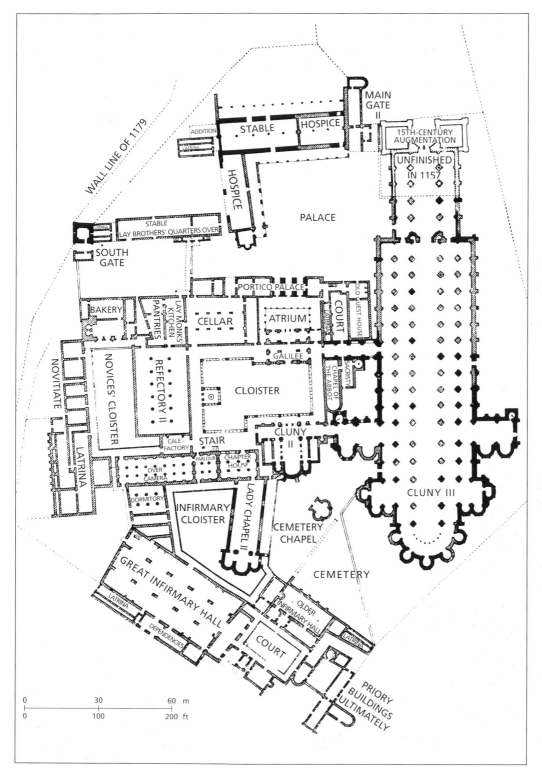

61 The ground plan of the twelfth-century monastery at Cluny shows the function of the many different buildings: the infirmary may be seen at the bottom left; the refectory where the monks ate is on the left side in the center, with the bakery, pantries, and kitchens adjoining; and the hospice (guest house) and stables are situated near the main gate.

WALL LINE OF 1179

MAIN GATE II

ADDITION

STABLE

HOSPICE

LATRINA

HOSPICE

15TH-CENTURY AUGMENTATION

UNFINISHED IN 1157

LATRINA

STABLE
LAY BROTHERS' QUARTERS OVER

PALACE

SOUTH GATE

PORTICO PALACE

OLD GUEST HOUSE

COURT

BAKERY

PANTRIES

LAY MONKS'
KITCHEN

CELLAR

ATRIUM

NOVITIATE

NOVICES' CLOISTER

REFECTORY II

GALILEE

CLOISTER

SACRISTY

CHAPEL OF THE ABBOT

LATRINA

CALE-FACTORY

STAIR

CLUNY II

PARLOUR

CHAPTER HOUSE

CLUNY III

OVER
CAMERA

DORMITORY

INFIRMARY CLOISTER

LADY CHAPEL II

CEMETERY CHAPEL

GREAT INFIRMARY HALL

CEMETERY

LATRINA

DEPENDENCIES

OLDER INFIRMARY HALL

LATRINA

COURT

PRIORY BUILDINGS ULTIMATELY

0	30	60 m
0	100	200 ft

diocese of Eichstatt, southern Germany, was promised by the bishop that "our successors shall see that the abbess has no permission to admit girls of base or ignoble birth to the monastery." Thus, the sources of both secular and ecclesiastical power were controlled by the nobility.

Because the monastic life had become pampered and indulgent since the changes initiated by Benedict of Aniane, a new reform movement emerged from within Benedictine monasticism by the late eleventh century. Not surprisingly, it was an attempt to return to the eremitic life of the desert fathers, according to the pattern originally established in the fourth century by Pachomius (see Chapter 1). The monks who began this movement lived at La Grande Chartreuse, located in a remote mountain valley in the diocese of Grenoble, France, and were known as Carthusians. They chose to reside separately in small one-story houses, and to come together twice a week for worship. Because of the stringent, austere demands, this form of monasticism never became very popular.

Another reform movement, however, which proved to be much more successful, was begun by a monk known as Robert of Molesme, who left his monastery at Molesme, probably in 1098, in order to found a community at Cîteaux, in northern France. Robert envisioned an establishment that would more closely approximate the monastic life as decreed in the original Rule of St. Benedict. His reforming mission did not have immediate results; indeed, after twenty years, only his original company of six monks remained. However, in 1113 he was joined by a Burgundian nobleman who was to become known to history as Bernard of Clairvaux. Bernard was a brilliant spokesman for the community at Cîteaux, which grew into a new monastic order known as the Cistercians.

The Cistercians

The mission of Robert of Molesme and Bernard of Clairvaux began as a reaction against the wealth, worldly political involvement, and elaborate ritual of Cluniac monasticism. In 1124, Bernard published a diatribe directed against Cluny, in which he vehemently criticized the monks' way of life:

> I marvel how monks could grow accustomed to such intemperance in eating and drinking, clothing and bedding, riding abroad and building, that wheresoever these things are wrought most busily and with most pleasure and expense, there Religion is thought to be best kept. For behold! Spare living is taken for covetousness, sobriety for austerity, silence for melancholy; while, on the other hand, men rebaptize laxity as "discretion," waste as "liberality," garrulousness as "affability," giggling as "jollity," effeminacy in clothing and bedding as "neatness." Who, in those first days when the monastic Order began, would have believed that monks would ever come to such sloth? . . . Dish after dish is set on the table; and instead of the mere flesh-meat from which men abstain, they receive twofold in mighty fishes. Though they have eaten their fill of the first course, yet when they come to the second they seem not even to have tasted the first; for all is dressed with such care and art in the kitchen that, though they have swallowed four or five dishes, the first are no hindrance to the last, nor does satiety lessen their appetites.

Bernard went on to castigate the Cluniac manner of dress (too costly), the monks' possession of horses (too much like a secular lord), and their love of beauty in their ecclesiastical establishments.

> I say naught of the vast height of your churches, their immoderate length, their superfluous breadth, the costly polishings, the curious carvings and paintings which attract the worshiper's gaze and hinder his attention, and seem to me in some sort a revival of the ancient Jewish rites. Let this pass, however: say that this is done for God's honor . . . at the very sight of these costly yet marvelous vanities men are more kindled to offer gifts than to pray. Thus wealth is drawn up by ropes of wealth, thus money bringeth money; for I know not how it is that, wheresoever more abundant wealth is seen, there do men offer more freely. Their eyes are feasted with relics cased in gold, and their pursestrings are loosed . . . Hence the church is adorned with gemmed crowns of light—nay, with lustres like cartwheels, girt all round with lamps, but no less brilliant with the precious stones that stud them . . . O vanity of vanities, yet no more vain than insane! The church is resplendent in her walls, beggarly in her poor; she clothes her stones in gold, and leaves her sons naked; the rich man's eye is fed at the expense of the indigent.

The Cistercians were determined to revive the pristine monasticism of the Rule of St. Benedict, based on a literal observance of Benedict's precepts. In part, their mission was an outgrowth of the monastic fervor of the day; devout people wished to live according to the requirements of poverty, chastity, and obedience stipulated in the Rule. This meant a return to corporate poverty, symbolized by manual labor, and a location remote enough to avoid becoming entangled in feudal involvements. Attachment to the aristocracy was limited, since the Cistercians refused to accept child oblates; a person desiring to join the order did not make his or her profession of faith before reaching adulthood. (**Fig. 62** depicts a reluctant child oblate being given to the monastery by his father.) The new order announced their intention, in part, by their garb. Whereas the Cluniacs wore beautifully woven habits that were dyed black (for which they were known as "black monks"), the Cistercians wore undyed habits made of coarse cloth (and hence were called "white monks"). This was merely one reaction against Cluniac practices, which they viewed as frivolous.

The Cistercians were equally determined to display a disregard for wealth in their churches, which were simple, plain,

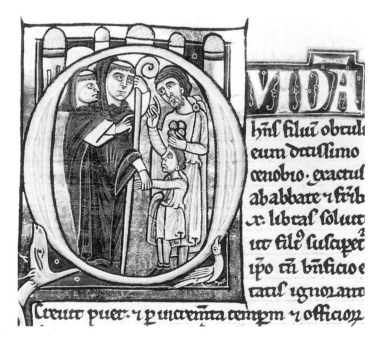

62 In this image, taken from a Cistercian manuscript, a father pledges his reluctant young son to the abbot of a monastery. In depicting the boy's obvious sorrow, the illumination serves as a forcible condemnation of the Cluniac practice of child oblation.

and unadorned with carvings and paintings. They eschewed elaborate vestments and altar vessels, which they made of wood or iron rather than precious metals. This puritanical rejection of aesthetic expression was exemplified by an important quarrel between Bernard and Abbot Suger of St. Denis, discussed below in Chapter 10.

The order soon began to expand, founding new houses in northern France: at La Ferté in 1113, and at Pontigny the following year. In 1115, Bernard was sent to establish a community at Clairvaux, where he remained abbot until his death in 1153. Another abbey was founded at Morimond in 1115, and, as the order grew, these first four "daughter houses" of Cîteaux were given special status and the responsibility of advising the "mother house." In 1118, La Ferté and Clairvaux themselves established "daughter houses," and the order began to increase in size.

In seeking isolation from the world, the Cistercians often founded their monasteries on deserted and uncultivated lands, though recent scholars have pointed out that this pattern was not universally practiced. The policy did encourage donations from benefactors who were willing to give up uncleared waste land, and it ultimately influenced the development of the economy of the Cistercian abbeys. In Britain, for example, where Cistercians settled in the uplands of Wales and Yorkshire, the monks became involved in sheep farming and wool production. In Germany and France, they were instrumental in the clearing of large areas of uncultivated land, which they made agriculturally viable. In the early years of the order they rejected the usual sources of monastic income, such as manorial rents, mills, serfs, altar offerings, and tithes; however, this policy proved impossible to maintain for more than a generation.

As mentioned earlier, the Cistercians advocated a return to manual labor, and they restructured their days to spend their morning hours in the fields. They did not, however, totally abandon the requirements of Benedict's Rule regarding the celebration of the liturgy. The daily office had to be sung, including the Office for the Dead on weekdays, and there were daily masses. Furthermore, the monks were required to spend time in private devotional reading and prayer. It finally became impractical to cultivate land at a distance from the monastery, and the demands on time and energy proved to be too great for a part-time labor force unaccustomed to the difficult outdoor tasks. Hence, the Cistercians decided to employ hired workers and to accept lay brothers, or **conversi**, who would do the agricultural labor. These were men who had not been given the benefit of a clerical education, and they were generally illiterate. The bearded lay brothers took monastic vows and wore the monastic habit, but their duties were different from those of the full-time monks. They attended the liturgies, but did not take part in the singing. Hence the full-time monks became known as "choir monks." The *conversi* were expected instead to spend most of their time doing manual work, participating in the community as farmers, shepherds, carpenters, or masons. They were generally recruited from the peasant class, and they provided a permanent workforce for the monastery while the choir monks were left free to devote themselves to liturgical duties and reading. The practice of accepting lay brothers became extremely popular, and recruitment remained at a high level for the first two centuries of the Cistercian order's existence. This was an era of vibrant devotional activity, and becoming a lay brother allowed an uneducated peasant to participate in the monastic life, which was regarded by medieval people as the principal road to salvation.

The order was governed according to a charter known as the *Carta Caritatis* (*The Charter of Charity*), written by 1165, and the *Institutes of the General Chapter*, a set of regulations collected and compiled in the 1150s. The charter asserted that the bond that united the daughter houses to Cîteaux was one of mutual love, in contrast to the pattern of the centralized Cluniac empire, in which the abbeys and priories were subject to Cluny in a dependent status. The workable method that emerged for the Cistercians after the death of Bernard of Clairvaux in 1153 was a system of mutual supervision, which guaranteed strict observance of the *Rule*. It was the duty of every abbey to oversee the activities of its daughter foundations, and this was achieved through regular visitations. New regulations and the resolution of problems were disseminated by the "general chapter" which was attended annually by all of the abbots or their deputies. At these meetings, which lasted from seven to ten days, the members of the chapter received reports from the abbeys, imposed penalties on disobedient abbots, and authorized new foundations. This kind of assembly, which was international in character and met on a regular basis, was a new phenomenon in medieval Europe. As such, it formed an influential group and constituted a forum for public opinion. The Cistercian model was emulated by the other monastic orders, such as the Carthusians and the Premonstratensians, founded in France in 1120 by St. Norbert, and was also adopted by Cluny in 1200. In 1215, the Cistercian general chapter was authorized as an approved model by Pope Innocent III, who commended it to all monasteries that lacked a similar organization.

In the course of the twelfth century, the Cistercian ideal of apostolic poverty was eroded, and the order became wealthy as it acquired land and demonstrated much acumen in the conduct of business. Indeed, the original ideal had proven incompatible with the process of expansion, and it became virtually impossible to differentiate the Cistercians from the Cluniacs, with the exception of their policy of accepting lay brothers. Gradually the idealistic Cistercian order had adopted the ways of the order they had criticized so vehemently. In the thirteenth century, however, another new monastic movement would emerge, once again devoted to the ideal of poverty (see Chapter 13).

During the eleventh and twelfth centuries, the leaders of Christian Europe had advanced their cause spiritually and geographically. They took part in pilgrimages, they attacked Muslims in Spain and the Holy Land to drive out the infidel, and they instituted reform measures to purify the monastic orders. The same religious zeal also led to pogroms and riots against the Jewish communities in Europe during these centuries, although such outbursts of violence tended to be confined to particular areas and were never systematic.

The Jews in Medieval Europe

During the Middle Ages, the Jews were more numerous in Muslim Spain than in any other European country, and they were able to live there in peace longer than in other areas. In no other medieval kingdom did the Jews comprise more than 1 percent of the population, and in no European city outside Spain did their number exceed 1,500, although most of the cities of England, France, and Germany did have small Jewish communities. It appears that the Jews initially coexisted harmoniously with the Christians, although their insistent loyalty to their Jewish identity constituted a challenge to the Christian population, who believed that they alone possessed religious truth. Furthermore, they were encouraged by their rabbis to live near one another. As one record stipulated: "If they can by any means contrive it, my sons and daughters should live in communities, and not isolated from other Jews, so that their sons and daughters may learn the ways of Judaism." This advice was probably given to facilitate dietary restrictions and ritual observances and to encourage marriage within the Jewish community, but it had unfortunate consequences. One of these was that it was much easier for the Jews to be trapped by angry mobs.

In addition to these communities within towns, which came to be called ghettos, there were "Jew Streets," usually found in the suburbs outside the original fortifications of the cities. Often members of the same profession would occupy a single street, such as "Tanners' Street," or "Furriers' Street."

The Jews of medieval Europe became prosperous initially as a result of long-distance trade, which extended from Spain to China. Since Roman times they had preferred commerce to other professions and, furthermore, there was little competition from Christians, who preserved the lingering Roman stigma against commercial endeavor. The ninth-century Muslim historian Ibn Khordadbeh described the economic trading adventures of the Jews in *The Book of the Roads and the Kingdoms*:

> These merchants speak Arabic, Persian, Roman, the language of the Franks, Andalusians and Slavs. They journey west to east, from east to west, partly on land, partly by sea. They transport from the west eunuchs, female and male slaves, silk, castor, marten and other furs, and swords . . . on their return they carry back musk, aloes, camphor, cinnamon, and other products of the Eastern countries . . .

Many, though certainly not all, Jews became wealthy through these commercial enterprises, and they soon had capital to lend. Christians were not allowed to loan money at interest—this was considered to be the sin of **usury**—whereas Jews, although similarly forbidden to loan money at interest to their own people, could charge interest on loans to outsiders. Hence, moneylending became an important profession for Jews; their clients ranged from small businessmen to kings and Church prelates, and they financed a great variety of ventures, from building shops and palaces to waging war.

The usual interest rate was 2 pence per week for each pound loaned, which represents an exorbitant annual rate of 43 percent. As with modern lending practices, if the debtor failed to repay his debt, he was required to forfeit the goods or land he had pledged as collateral. As might be expected, the lending transactions generated a great deal of animosity against the Jewish moneylenders, and their burgeoning wealth was envied and resented.

The Jews seem to have lost their economic advantage over the Christians during the revival of commercial activity that was fueled by urban development during the eleventh century. This may have been, in part, due to the lessening of the Christian aversion to mercantile enterprise. Many Jews migrated to Italy and England, among other places, expressly to participate in trade and moneylending. They were not motivated purely by profit; although moneylending was lucrative, it was not time-consuming. Jewish lenders valued the repose for scholarship and community leadership activities. Furthermore, lending could be practiced by anyone with free funds, and women, as well as men, took advantage of the opportunity.

As discussed above, the Jews were subject to mob violence in Mainz at the time of the Peasants' Crusade, and this was not an isolated incident. There were, however, attempts by both royal and papal mandate to limit such attacks. For example, the German king Frederick I (Barbarossa) (r. 1152–1190) promulgated the following decree in 1157:

> Be it known . . . that we have confirmed by our royal authority . . . the statutes in favor of the Jews of Worms and their fellow-religionists which were granted to them by our predecessor emperor Henry, in the time of Solomon, rabbi of the Jews.
> 1. The only official who may exercise authority [over the Jews] is the man whom the emperor puts over them in accordance with their choice, because they are entirely under the control of our treasury.
> 2. They shall travel in peace and security throughout the whole kingdom for the purpose of buying and selling and carrying on trade and business . . .
> 3. If anyone takes part in a plan or plot to kill a Jew, both the slayer and his accomplice shall pay twelve pounds of gold to the royal treasury . . . If a serf wounds or slays a Jew . . . he shall suffer the penalty which was visited upon the serf who, in the time of our predecessor emperor Henry, slew the Jew named Vivus; namely, his eyes shall be torn out and his right hand cut off.

The decrees stipulated further privileges that pertained to the Jews, such as the right to change money, the right to erect buildings, and the right to sell spices and medicines to the Christians. Furthermore, Jews could not be forcibly baptized or subjected to trial by ordeal if accused of a crime. These royal decrees were echoed in a letter written by Pope Innocent III (r. 1198–1216) in 1199, which codified the official attitude of the Church towards the Jews:

> No Christian shall do the Jews any personal injury, except in executing the judgments of a judge, or deprive them of their possessions, or change the rights and privileges which they have been accustomed to have. During the celebration of their festivals, no one shall disturb them by beating them with clubs or by throwing stones at them . . . And to prevent the baseness and avarice of wicked men we forbid anyone to deface or damage their cemeteries or to extort money from them by threatening to exhume the bodies of their dead.

However, Innocent's letter probably did little to dispel the reaction against the Jews created by a diatribe delivered as part of a sermon by Bernard of Clairvaux:

> Not the flight of demons, not the obedience of the elements, nor life restored to the dead, was able to expel from their [the Jews'] minds that stupidity bestial, and more than bestial, which caused them, by a blindness as marvelous as it was miserable, to rush headlong into that crime, so enormous and so horrible, of laying impious hands upon the Lord of Glory.

For medieval Christians, it was this conviction that the Jews were responsible for the crucifixion of Christ that made them an obvious target for violence: "The Jews live among us, whose fathers unwarrantedly slew and hanged Him on the cross." This focus allowed other motives, such as envy and greed, to be disguised by religious purpose. Unfortunately, during the thirteenth century, the attitudes of both kings and Church prelates hardened against the Jews, and they were subjected to a series of exclusionary decrees, as well as pogroms, forced removals, and further brutality.

Summary

The lives of European people in the eleventh and twelfth centuries were largely shaped by religion, the dominant force in the society of the time. Many individuals participated in pilgrimages to the Holy Land, Rome, Santiago de Compostela, and Canterbury. Although their journeys were generally motivated by a desire to do penance and to achieve salvation, their travels also provided adventure and an escape from the drudgery of everyday life. The knights of western Europe meanwhile, inspired by religious fervor, waged war on the Muslims in Spain and the Holy Land, and created new kingdoms which expanded the control of the Christian leaders and provided safer routes for trade and pilgrimage.

Another manifestation of religious fervor was a monastic reform movement, which resulted in the creation of several new orders, among them the Carthusians and Cistercians. The founders of the Cistercian order found it necessary to accept lay brothers into the order, thereby opening the monastic experience to a wider segment of society.

The expansion of Christian Europe had a profound effect on future historical development, fueling economic growth and facilitating the exchange of ideas that would characterize the intellectual life of the twelfth and thirteenth centuries.

Suggestions for Further Reading

Primary sources

Jerusalem Pilgrimage: 1099–1185, by John Wilkinson *et al.* (London: Hakluyt Society, 1988), contains translations of primary sources, as well as excellent introductory material and a fine selection of maps and plans. Two works by Edward Peters, *Christian Society and the Crusades, 1198–1229* (Philadelpha: University of Pennsylvania Press, 1971) and *The First Crusade: The Chronicle of Fulcher of Chartres and Other Source Materials* (2nd ed., Philadelphia: University of Pennsylvania Press, 1998), offer sources concerning the crusades,

as does *The Crusades: Idea and Reality: 1095–1274*, by Louise and Jonathan Riley-Smith (London: Edward Arnold Publishers, 1981). Another helpful collection may be found in *Medieval Warfare*, vol. 2, *Christian Europe and its Neighbors*, by David Nicolle (London: Arms and Armour, 1996). The Muslim view of the conflict is presented in *Arab Historians of the Crusades*, translated by Francesco Gabrieli (Berkeley: University of California Press, 1969).

The Jew in the Medieval World: A Sourcebook, 315–1791, by Marcus Jacob (New York: JPS, 1938)

provides an excellent collection of sources. *The Jews and the Crusaders*, trans. Shlomo Eidelberg (Madison: University of Wisconsin Press, 1977), includes Hebrew chronicles of the First and Second Crusades.

For a comprehensive collection of primary source information about the military order of the Templars, see *The Templars*, translated by Malcolm Barber and Keith Bate (Manchester: Manchester University Press, 2002). Another recent translation of the rule is *The Rule of the Templars*, translated by J. Upton-Ward (Woodbridge: Boydell, 1992).

The World of El Cid: Chronicles

of the Spanish Reconquest, translated and annotated by Simon Barton and Richard Fletcher (Manchester: Manchester University Press, 2000), consists of the main narrative sources of eleventh- and twelfth-century Spain.

Secondary sources

Pilgrimage to Rome in the Middle Ages, by Debra J. Birch (Woodbridge, UK: Boydell Press, 1998), is a fine analysis of pilgrimage to Rome. Marilyn Stokstad's *Santiago de Compostela in the Age of the Great Pilgrimages* (Norman, OK: University of Oklahoma Press, 1978) provides a fascinating and colorful account of pilgrimage to Santiago. *Pilgrimage: An Image of Medieval Religion* (London: Faber & Faber, 1975; paperback ed. 2002), by Jonathan Sumption, is an intriguing study of pilgrimage, although the documentation style is difficult to follow.

The historiography of the crusades is voluminous. Among the most famous works are Stephen Runciman's *A History of the Crusades*, 3 vols. (New York: Harper and Row, 1964–67) and K.M. Setton, ed., *A History of the Crusades*, 2nd ed., 6 vols. (Madison WI: University of Wisconsin Press, 1969–1989). Four shorter studies are: Thomas F. Madden's *A Concise History of the Crusades* (Savage, MD: Rowman & Littlefield, 1999); *The Crusades: A Short History* (London: Athlone, 1987), by Jonathan Riley-Smith; and *The Crusades: 1095–1197*, by Jonathan Phillips (Harlow, UK: Longman, 2002).

Another helpful introduction to issues surrounding the historiographical discussion is the brief volume by Jonathan Riley-Smith, *What Were the Crusades?* (3rd. ed., London: MacMillan, 2002), and Riley-Smith's *The First Crusade and the Idea of Crusading* (London: The Athlone Press, 1993) provides a thorough and thoughtful presentation of the issues surrounding the First Crusade.

The Crusades: Islamic Perspectives, by Carole Hillenbrand (Edinburgh: Edinburgh University Press, 1999), is an outstanding work which presents views of the impact of the crusades on the Muslim world. Another recent work is Geoffrey Hindley's *The Crusades: A History of Armed Pilgrimage and Holy War* (London: Constable, 2003), which places the crusades in a broader perspective."

Two volumes by Jaroslav Folda, *Crusader Art in the Twelfth Century* (Oxford: Oxford University Press, 1982) and *The Art of the Crusaders in the Holy Land, 1098–1187* (Cambridge: Cambridge University Press, 1995), provide an interesting study of art in the Crusader kingdoms. *The New Knighthood: A History of the Order of the Temple*, by Malcolm Barber (Cambridge: Cambridge University Press, 1994), is an fine examination of the crusading order from its origins to its extermination by Philip IV. *European Jewry and the First Crusade*, by Robert Chazan (Berkeley: University of California Press, 1987), offers an excellent analysis of the violence perpetrated against Jews, and includes translations of two Hebrew

chronicles that reflect the experience.

The Jews of Spain: A History of the Sephardic Experience, by Jane S. Gerber (New York: Free Press, 1992), gives a comprehensive survey of the Jews in Spain, including a chapter on Jewish adaptation to the Christian Reconquista. Kenneth R. Stow's *Alienated Minority: The Jews of Medieval Latin Europe* (Cambridge, MA: Harvard University Press, 1992) provides a fine analysis of the Jewish experience during the European Middle Ages. Two excellent accounts of the Reconquista are *The Reconquest of Spain*, by D.W. Lomax (London: Longman, 1978), and Bernard F. Reilly's *The Contest of Christian and Muslim Spain: 1031–1157* (Oxford: Blackwell, 1992).

Medieval Monasticism: Forms of Religious Life in Western Europe in the Middle Ages (3rd ed., London: Longman & Co., 2001), by C.H. Lawrence, describes in detail the development of monasticism and the major monastic orders. Two classic works by Jean Leclerq concerning the Cistercian movement are *Bernard of Clairvaux and the Cistercian Spirit* (Kalamazoo, MI: Cistercian Publications, 1976) and *The Love of Learning and the Desire for God*, translated by Catharine Misrahi (2nd ed., London: S.P.C.K., 1976). An excellent survey of the development of the Cistercian order which proposes a new chronology is Constance Berman's *The Cistercian Evolution: The Invention of a Religious Order in Twelfth-Century Europe* (Philadelphia: University of Pennsylvania Press, 2000).

8 ROMANESQUE CULTURE

EUROPEAN CULTURE IN THE ELEVENTH AND TWELFTH CENTURIES was deeply influenced by the development of the monastic movements discussed in the previous chapter. Monasteries were built in the grand style of Cluny or the unornamented fashion of Cîteaux, and monks were active in the production of manuscripts, which they copied and illuminated in their *scriptoria*; indeed, some scholars have viewed this era as the high point of monastic culture. Artists in the growing urban centers were also remarkably productive, and the activities of pilgrimage and crusade brought vital cross-cultural influences to their artistic and architectural creations.

The ambitious building endeavors of monastic establishments and the cathedral chapters of burgeoning towns resulted in a vast blanket of churches which spread across Europe. According to the French monk Raoul Glaber, who lived during the last part of the tenth century and the first part of the eleventh:

> On the threshold of the aforesaid thousandth year, some two or three years after it, it befell almost throughout the world, but especially in Italy and Gaul, that the fabrics of churches were rebuilt, although many of these were still seemly and needed no such care; but every nation of Christendom rivaled with the other, which should worship in the seemliest buildings. So it was as though the very world had shaken herself and cast off her old age, and were clothing herself everywhere in a white garment of churches. Then indeed the faithful rebuilt and bettered almost all the cathedral churches, and other monasteries dedicated to divers saints, and smaller parish churches.

The architectural style of the churches of this period has long been identified by the term "Romanesque." Some recent scholars have found it appropriate to eliminate this term, along with "Gothic," when discussing the art and culture of the Middle Ages, because there was so much overlap between the two styles. Furthermore, since the terms "Romanesque" and "Gothic" were initially negative descriptions of art in the Middle Ages, and did not come into use until long after the medieval era, some art historians see them as potentially misleading. Nonetheless, in an introduction to the study of this topic, it is useful to divide such a lengthy period of time into discrete parts. Therefore, for purposes of the following discussion, the term "Romanesque" will be used to define the culture of the period that includes the last quarter of the eleventh century and most of the twelfth. It will become evident that the beginning of the Gothic style also occurred during this era, about 1145, with the rebuilding of the Abbey of St.-Denis under the direction of Abbot Suger. However, Gothic style, which will be discussed in Chapter 13, is a term most often used to characterize artistic and architectural expression beginning in the late twelfth century and lasting in some areas until the fifteenth.

Romanesque Style

"Romanesque," or "Roman-like," was a term first employed by nineteenth-century scholars, who saw the development of architecture in the eleventh century as similar to the emergence of the vernacular Romance languages from Latin. They used it to define and categorize the visual arts of the period, as well as the literature of the late eleventh and twelfth centuries. Originally meant to be pejorative, the term identified the Roman origins of the style, as demonstrated by the use of barrel vaults and rounded arches in church architecture. This stylistic adaptation was, in part, a natural aesthetic response of medieval architects to the forms of massive Roman ruins, such as the Pont du Gard, which they encountered in southern France.

Scholars have also seen the development of Romanesque art and architecture as showing a desire on the part of Carolingian rulers to imitate the styles and monuments of the glorious Roman past, which they wished to claim as reflections of their own power. As we have seen, there were obvious instances of deliberate emulation, such as the interior of Charlemagne's chapel at Aachen (see figs. 30 and 31) as well as less evident borrowings.

More recent scholarship, which has emphasized the cross-cultural nature of artistic contact, sees the art of ancient Rome as jut one among the many influences on so-called Romanesque art. Another important source, for example, was the Germanic artistic tradition of the sixth to ninth centuries, as exemplified by the Lindisfarne Gospels and the treasure from Sutton Hoo (see Chapter 4). The patterns of this earlier era were continued by artists of the eleventh and twelfth centuries, who filled the background spaces of illustrations and carvings with interwoven patterns such as foliage tendrils and linked chains. This tradition also fostered the intense fascination with bizarre monsters and animal forms that characterizes much Romanesque art.

Other significant influences came from two cultures outside the boundaries of western Europe: Byzantium and Islam. As discussed earlier, a widespread diffusion of artistic motifs had taken place as a result of the crusades and diplomatic contacts, as well as travel and pilgrimage. The subsequent cross-fertilization was of great importance in the development of medieval art. The artists of the Byzantine Empire also continued to provide Hellenistic models for western artists of the Romanesque era, and provided a fertile source for formal, technical, and iconographic ideas that spread rapidly as a consequence of the expansion of Christendom.

The architectural forms borrowed from the Islamic world proved to be of lasting significance. Of particular importance was the adoption of the pointed arch, which was being used extensively throughout northern Europe by the early years of the twelfth century. Earlier scholars believed that the style was transmitted through the Italian coastal city and republic of Amalfi. It has recently been suggested, however, that this architectural feature, which also became a prominent attribute of Gothic architecture, was borrowed by the Normans when they conquered the island of Sicily in the 1070s (see Chapter 9). The Muslims living there had used pointed arches, as well as barrel vaults, as early as the eighth and ninth centuries. Norman architects appear to have quickly adopted the pointed arch for use in their churches in England and France.

The synthesis of Roman, Byzantine, and Islamic influence, and the widespread development of the resulting artistic trends, meant that Romanesque was essentially an "international" style. However, regional differences may clearly be discerned, as we shall see.

Architecture

Although architects of the Romanesque period continued to use the basic model of the Roman basilica (see Chapter 1), the churches and cathedrals of the eleventh and twelfth centuries were larger and more richly ornamented than those of the preceding era. As noted earlier, the extended transept and large apse resulted in a shape that resembled a cross, and was known as **cruciform**. Generally speaking, these buildings were more "Roman-looking" than their predecessors in the sense that they featured heavy supports and rounded arches as aesthetic as well as structural components. The effect was one of somber and dignified solidity, characterized by bulk and thickness.

The naves of these churches were covered by stone vaults rather than wooden roofs. This was a practical solution to the problem of highly flammable timber roofing materials, as well as a way of overcoming the inherent limitations of size and style placed on medieval architects and builders by the use of wood. Furthermore, the incorporation of stone vaults greatly enhanced the acoustic properties of the medieval churches and cathedrals, creating a superb sonorous venue for the performance of Gregorian chant and a magnificent space for the celebration of the liturgy. Indeed, the development of the stone vault was the most important technological innovation of eleventh- and twelfth-century architects. (**Fig. 63** illustrates the style of Romanesque vaulting.)

Initially, when architects looked to Roman building techniques in order to solve the problem of vaulting the nave, they adopted the **barrel vault**, which replicated the shape of a half-cylinder. The barrel vault was essentially a long tunnel of stone, which was often strengthened by

63 During the eleventh and twelfth centuries, architects developed a system of vaulting that made possible the large windows of the later Gothic style (see chapter 13). As shown in diagram (a), the rounded Romanesque arch, derived from Roman building technique, distributed weight laterally and was used to create a dome-shaped vault, as shown in diagram (c). The later development of the Gothic pointed arch, shown in diagram (b), which thrust the weight more directly towards the ground, made possible the ribbed vault of diagram (d), with its lighter and more flexible structure.

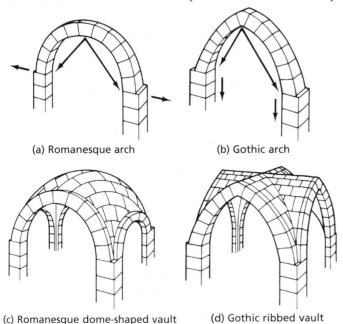

(a) Romanesque arch (b) Gothic arch

(c) Romanesque dome-shaped vault (d) Gothic ribbed vault

transverse arches placed at intervals along the nave. A more advanced and sophisticated solution was the use of the **groin vault**, sometimes called a cross vault, which was formed by two barrel vaults intersecting at right angles. This structure provided more support, as architects aimed to create buildings that soared heavenward. This goal was further advanced by the development of the ribbed vault. This vault was crossed by diagonal load-bearing arches, or ribs; it later became a basic component of Gothic architecture.

Whatever the style of vaulting, the stone roofs of Romanesque buildings were enormously heavy. Because architects had not yet developed the flying buttress, the supporting walls were necessarily massive and thick, and the windows were relatively small, resulting in interiors that were dark and mysterious. These features are found in two of the most famous Romanesque churches, both of them located on the pilgrimage routes of southern France: St.-Sernin at Toulouse and Ste.-Madeleine at Vézelay.

St.-Sernin and Ste.-Madeleine

St.-Sernin in Toulouse, begun about 1080, is a "pilgrimage" church, one of the many churches built to accommodate the crowds of travelers along the pilgrimage routes, in this case to the shrine of Santiago de Compostela in northwestern Spain. As mentioned in Chapter 7, pilgrimage constituted an important source of revenue for medieval towns and monastic establishments, both through direct offerings by the pilgrims and the various charges that could be levied on visitors. Impressive churches were therefore often situated on hilltops so that they would be visible from miles away, acting as beacons to the pilgrims. Parishes would also vie with one another for the ownership of important relics, such as teeth, bones, or clothing of the apostles and martyrs, which would attract travelers and give evidence of unusual divine favor.

St.-Sernin, which held, among other sacred objects, the head of St. Bartholomew and a stone from the Holy Sepulcher, was typical in its possession of saints' relics. These precious vestiges of sanctity were elaborately displayed in accessible chapels adjoining the transept and apse, where they could be viewed and venerated by the pilgrims.

In order to accommodate the large number of worshipers who visited St.-Sernin, the nave and transept were larger than those of the churches of the preceding centuries, and the apse was surrounded by a capacious **ambulatory** so that the crowds of pilgrims could easily pass through to view the relics contained in the **apsidal chapels (fig. 63)**.

As may be seen in the ground plan, there were two aisles on either side of the nave, and the inner aisle continued around the arms of the transept and

64 The church of St.-Sernin, in Toulouse, France (constructed *c.* 1080–1120) is a fine example of the so-called "pilgrimage" churches that were built along the most important routes traveled by pilgrims. The ground plan incorporated a nave and transept larger and more impressive than those of earlier churches, and included an ambulatory around the apse that enabled the crowds of pilgrims to venerate the precious relics on display in the apsidal chapels.

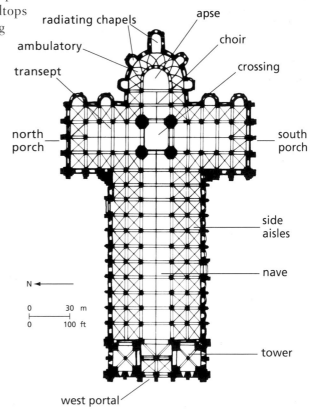

radiating chapels
apse
ambulatory
choir
transept
crossing
north porch
south porch
side aisles
nave
N
0   30 m
0   100 ft
tower
west portal

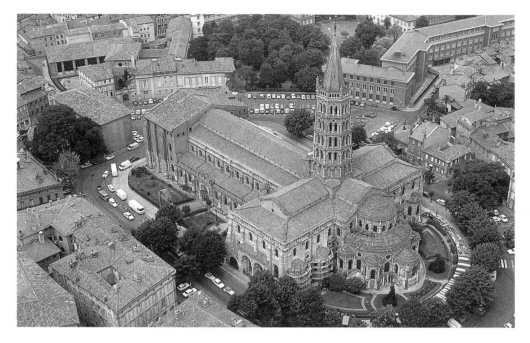

65 This exterior view of St.-Sernin shows clearly the typical cruciform shape of Romanesque churches, as well as the apsidal chapels radiating from the apse. The style is characterized by rounded arches, small windows, and thick walls.

66 A cross-section of the elevation of St.-Sernin shows that the aisles are covered with groin vaults, and that the bays are framed by two piers which support an arch. The nave is covered by a barrel vault, creating a harmonious aesthetic unity. The elevation at St.-Sernin has only two parts, rather than the more usual three, reflecting the concern of the builders that the vault be stable.

the apse. These features created a complete circuit beginning with the two towers of the west facade, which some scholars have defined as a "processional path" for the pilgrims. The ambulatory itself was adorned with apsidal chapels that radiated from the apse and continued along the eastern side of the transept. A pilgrim entering the church would move along the aisles and then into the ambulatory, stopping in the chapels along the transepts and apse to venerate the saints' relics. This design made it possible for crowds of travelers to view the sacred remains contained in the chapels without interfering with the services taking place at the high altar.

The interior geometry shown in the ground plan is clearly reflected in the exterior view of the cathedral (**fig. 65**), where it is possible to recognize the cruciform shape created by the nave and transept, as well as the chapels that crown the apse and transept. At St.-Sernin, as in other pilgrimage churches, the ambulatory, apse, and adjoining chapels form a unit known as the **pilgrimage choir**—a term that emphasizes the ubiquitous presence and activity of the pilgrims.

Since St.-Sernin is typical of the churches built in Romanesque style, it is important to discuss its technical features in some detail. The aisles of St.-Sernin are covered with groin vaults, made up of square bays, or vaulted compartments, which serve as the basic unit, or module, for the other dimensions. The bays, like those in most Romanesque or Gothic churches, are framed by two piers which support an arch. (**Fig. 66** shows a section of the nave elevation of

St.-Sernin.) As may be seen in the ground plan, the nave and the transept bays are composed of two units each, while the crossing and facade have four units. The piers that define the bays are ornamented with **colonnettes**—half-columns which are attached to the piers and then continue across the vault as transverse arches.

The nave exhibits the tall proportions typical of Romanesque architecture. A harmonious and coherent order is created by the barrel vault covering the nave, the groin-vaulted aisles, the arches, colonettes, and other decorative features (**fig. 67**). The succession of regular bays created by the division of the vault by piers, colonettes, and transverse arches emphasizes the processional nature of the interior, and the repetition of the rounded arches at the gallery level unifies the design.

There is no clerestory at St.-Sernin, resulting in a darkened upper vault. Windows at this time were restricted in size and confined to the outer walls of galleries and aisles since architects had not yet developed techniques that would allow large windows to be supported as a feature of the churches.

Another important pilgrimage church was built around the same time at Vézelay, in central France, and dedicated to Ste.-Madeleine (Mary Magdalene). It became a promi-

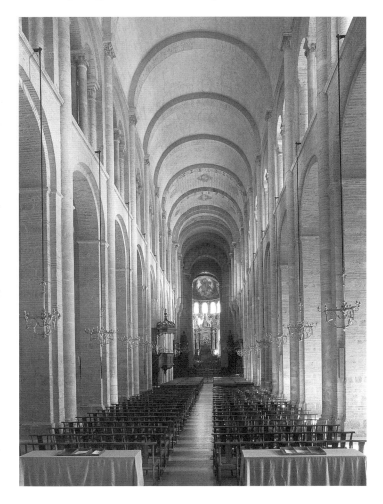

67 The balanced aesthetic order that characterized medieval ecclesiastical buildings is typified by the awe-inspiring nave of St.-Sernin which is over 377 feet long (115 m). Constructed of pink granite, the design is unified throughout by rounded arches, which may be seen on both the nave and gallery levels, as well as in the barrel vault.

nent site for pilgrimage after 1058, when Pope Stephen IX confirmed the parish's possession of authentic relics of St. Mary Magdalene. Her cult became tremendously popular at Vézelay, even overshadowing devotion to the Blessed Virgin. The original church proved to be too small to accommodate the crowds who flocked to the shrine, and a new building was begun in 1096 by Abbot Artaud, who may have been inspired by the building program at Cluny (see Chapter 7).

In 1120, there was a disastrous fire at the church which killed a number of pilgrims and destroyed the nave, but the body of Mary Magdalene resting in her shrine (as well as other precious holdings) was miraculously spared. The circumstances were described in some detail by Hugh of Poitiers, who wrote his *Vézelay Chronicle* in the mid-twelfth century:

> In the vault above the tomb of God's blessed lover Mary Magdalene such a blaze accidentally broke out that even the supports above it, which the French call beams, were burnt. But the wooden image of Mary, blessed mother of God, which stood on the floor of the vault, was not harmed by the fire at all,

although it was a little blackened . . . it was clear as crystal that the image itself would not have been affected by smoke in the slightest, except by divine dispensation for the purpose of revealing, when it was repaired, the inestimable treasure hidden within it. For when this image was sent to the restorer, he declared that it had, so it seemed to him, a cunningly hidden little door between its shoulders. Prior Gilo ordered the image to be carried into the sacristy, [where] he took a knife and scratched off the paint himself; but they could not discover any sign of a joint in the uncovered wood. Then he took a little iron hammer and tried to discover by ear what none could discern with his eyes, and hearing a sort of hollow sound, the bold man, armed with joyful hope, piously broke open the little door with his own hands. He found in it hairs of the chaste Virgin . . . and part of the tunic of the same Mary, mother of God, and a bone of the blesséd John the Baptist. He also found bones of the blesséd apostles Peter, Paul, and Andrew in one bundle, and one joint of the thumb of the blesséd James the Lord's brother, and two bundles of bones of the blesséd apostle Bartholomew, and most of an arm of one of the Innocents, relics of St. Clement, and a portion of the hair of the queen St. Radegund; a piece of the vestments of the three boys Shadrack, Meshak, and Abednego, and a section from the purple robe in which our Lord Jesus Christ was clothed during his passion . . . After they had carefully inspected all these things they returned them to the place where they had been before, and placed the statue with these saints' relics over the high altar.

68 The pilgrimage church of Ste.-Madeleine at Vézelay, France (constructed c. 1104–1132), was a popular goal of pilgrims, who traveled there to view the relics of St. Mary Magdelene. The nave of the church is unusually dramatic, with arches composed of alternating reddish-brown and white *voussoirs* (wedges), reminiscent of Muslim, or perhaps Carolingian, style.

Soon after the fire, the church was rebuilt in stone, and the dedication of the new building was celebrated about 1140. The architects of Ste.-Madeleine incorporated widely spaced compound piers into the design. This allowed them to eliminate the **triforium** gallery, and to insert large clerestory windows, which provided illumination within the building. Because of the widely spaced supports and the large window openings, the groin vault was slightly flattened and reinforced with iron rods, which provided a strong structural framework. The most visually compelling aspects of the nave at Vézelay, however, are the transverse arches, which are composed of alternating reddish-brown and white *voussoirs*, or wedges (**fig. 68**). The vibrant aesthetic effect is reminiscent of Islamic architectural detail (see the discussion of the Great Mosque of Córdoba in Chapter 3), and is indicative of the Muslim influence on Romanesque architecture. Some scholars have remarked that the style also recalls Carolingian polychrome (multicolored) masonry, such as that in the Palatine Chapel at Aachen.

In addition to possessing great architectural importance, the church at Vézelay was the site of dramatic historical events during the twelfth century. It was from Véze-lay that the Second Crusade was launched by Bernard of Clairvaux in 1146; Thomas Becket raged against his enemies in a famous sermon delivered there; and kings Richard the Lionheart and Philip Augustus met there before they departed on the Third Crusade in 1190 (see Chapter 9).

The pilgrimage churches of southern France are excellent examples of Romanesque architecture, but the style was not confined to that region alone. Important Romanesque structures built during the eleventh and twelfth centuries may also be found in England and the Rhineland.

Durham Cathedral

As discussed in Chapter 6, the widespread building of castles was one of the first endeavors undertaken by the Normans after their invasion of England in 1066. Even before the conquest, however, architects and masons had traveled to England from the Continent, and Norman building techniques were well established. As the Normans imposed their rule and their taste on the country, the nobles and church prelates undertook the building and rebuilding of castles and churches, which, in addition to their practical value, functioned as symbols of the power, prestige, and control of the new monarchy.

One of the most impressive and important of the early Anglo-Norman structures was the cathedral at Durham, which was built on a cliff above the River Wear (**fig. 69**). This imposing site possessed effective natural defenses which the cathedral shared

69 The cathedral at Durham, built on a cliff above the River Weir, is a fine example of Anglo-Norman architecture. Heavily fortified with towers and crenellations, the cathedral (begun in 1093) shared this imposing site with a castle. Buildings such as this provided a majestic visual emblem of the authority and control of the new Norman rulers.

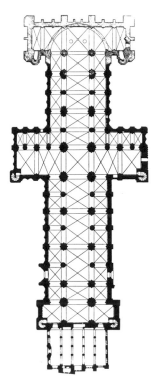

70 The ground plan of Durham Cathedral illustrates side aisles which consist of virtually square compartments, while the nave is composed of oblong bays. Intersecting ribs support the groin vaults—an important innovation that influenced the development of Gothic architectural style.

71 Visible in this photograph are the massive and unusual columns in the nave of Durham Cathedral. They are incised with decorative chevrons, spiral fluting, and zigzag designs—motifs that are reflective of both Viking and Anglo-Saxon techniques. The design is unified by arches connecting the columns, engraved with rolled moldings and chevron ornament.

with a castle, since Durham was the military as well as ecclesiastical headquarters for the north of England. It was not only a center of religious activity; it also served as a visual reminder of the authority of the new Norman rulers. Begun in 1093 by the Norman bishop William de Carlief, who was eager to replace the existing Saxon church, the construction of the building took place over forty years.

As one would expect, Durham possessed important relics—the body of St. Cuthbert, which the monks had discovered in 1104 when they opened the coffin to find the saint's remains incorrupt and exuding a fragrant aroma. According to Bede's *History of the English Church and People*, the body proved to be "intact and whole, as if it were still alive, and the joints of the limbs flexible, and much more like a sleeping than a dead man." The monks placed it in the east end of the partially finished cathedral, where it rests today.

The ground plan of Durham Cathedral illustrates aisles consisting of almost square groin-vaulted compartments (**fig. 70**). The nave is one-third wider than St.-Sernin at Toulouse, and has a greater overall length (400 feet/122 m). The bays of the nave, separated by strong transverse arches, are decidedly oblong, and their groin vaults are supported by intersecting ribs which form a double-X design. This vaulting system was the most important innovation in the building; rib vaults such as those at Durham were an important step in the development of Gothic architecture. As described earlier, rib vaults are, in essence, groin vaults with arches that intersect in the middle; these are affixed along the diagonal lines from one corner to the other. In addition to these ribs, there are slightly pointed transverse arches which frame the double-cross vaults. The massive piers at Durham, as well as exterior wall buttresses, support and stabilize the vault. Further, hidden buttresses in the galleries point to the future development of flying buttresses (see Chapter 13). As at Vézelay, the most striking visual feature in the nave is the decorative detail; the columns are ornamented with incised patterns of zigzag and chevron motifs, reminiscent of Viking and Anglo-Saxon artistic style (**fig. 71**).

The Romanesque style that characterized French churches and Norman structures such as Durham Cathedral also spread eastward into the areas of central Germany, where it became an expression of imperial power as well as religiosity. Perhaps the finest example is Speyer Cathedral.

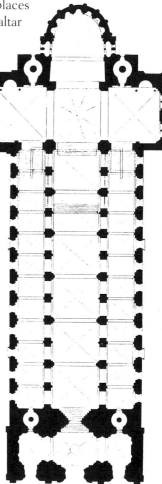

72 The ground plan of Speyer Cathedral (begun in 1030) shows the commonly used geometrical methods of medieval architects. The nave consists of square bays, while the side aisles are half as wide; hence, two bays of the side aisles equal one bay of the nave.

Speyer Cathedral

The cathedral at Speyer, in western Germany, was built on the site of earlier places of worship. Excavations of Roman fortifications have produced two objects—an altar marked with the monogram of Christ, and an oil lamp bearing the Greek letters *XP* (Chi-Rho—the first two letters of Christ's name)—which indicate that Christian worship took place there as early as the fourth or fifth century. The earliest record of a bishop of Speyer dates from 342, and there is a continuous list of bishops from the sixth century forward.

Documents exist indicating that the Merovingian king Childeric II released the church from obligations to pay taxes in 665, an act which indicates his patronage and close association with the bishopric of Speyer. There were two patron saints for this early church—the Virgin Mary and Pope Stephen I (r. 254–257). Between 782 and 854 a new church was built, probably under the leadership of Bishop Gerhard of Speyer.

In 1024, Conrad II (r. 1024–1039) was elected as German king (see Chapter 6), an event that proved to be of great importance for the diocese of Speyer and its cathedral (**fig. 72**). The architectural style was a typical adaptation of French Gothic. Conrad chose the diocese and its cathedral as the dynastic and royal burial place of the Salians, and patronized the building of a new cathedral. In 1025, he laid the foundation stone for the new structure, and throughout his reign he continued to patronize the diocese with generous donations.

At the time the cathedral was built, the main street was designed as a *Via Triumphalis* (triumphal way) which led from the city's west gate to the west porch of the cathedral. This path was used by the emperors and the bishops for ceremonial entries into the city, which became a favorite residence of the royal family.

Conrad's successor, Henry III, continued the building of the cathedral after his father's death in 1039, and donated a valuable Gospel book, the *Codex Aureus*, to the diocese. During Henry's reign (r. 1039–1056), the cathedral

received one of its most prized possessions—the head of Pope Stephen I—which was brought from Italy in 1047.

The consecration of the cathedral in 1061 was attended by Henry's successor, Henry IV (king of Germany 1056–1106; elected Holy Roman Emperor in 1084). A mere twenty years later, Henry began a massive rebuilding of the cathedral, for political as well as artistic reasons. Henry was at that time involved in the struggle with the papacy known as the "Investiture Controversy" (see Chapter 6) and the diocese of Speyer was unwavering in its loyalty to the emperor. As the largest building of the era, the cathedral was a powerful symbol of the might of Henry IV—one that the emperor wished to emphasize. With a nave measuring 435 feet (133 m), Speyer Cathedral is one of the largest churches in Europe. The height of the groin vaults is 107 feet (33 m) from the floor of the nave, and, as the art historian Marilyn Stokstad has remarked, its sheer size and majestic qualities made Speyer Cathedral a "symbol of imperial challenge to the rest of the Christian world" (**fig. 73**).

73 The Romanesque architectural trend spread rapidly throughout the European continent: the cathedral at Speyer, Germany, begun in 1030, was remodeled in the new style in 1080 and 1172–1178. The completed building, patronized by the German emperors, extended to the vast length of 435 feet (133 m), making it one of the largest churches in Europe.

Since Henry IV was under a sentence of excommunication when he died in 1106, he could not be buried in the cathedral with his ancestors. He was therefore interred in an adjoining chapel, known as the Afra Chapter, which had not been consecrated at the time. In 1111, his son Henry V (1106–1125) was able to have the excommunication lifted, and his father was reburied in the cathedral. To celebrate the event, Henry V granted certain privileges to the citizens of Speyer, releasing them from the death taxes then in effect, and allowing them to mint their own coinage, levy their own taxes, and hold judicial proceedings. To make certain that these decrees could not be rescinded, they were recorded in gilt letters above the main entrance to the cathedral. This was a step towards the later freedom from obligations to the emperor held by the city of Speyer, although the bishop continued to be lord of the city. In addition to the political interest of the cathedral generated by imperial associations, the building itself provides a fine example of Romanesque style as it was disseminated from its French interpretation. The architects employed a system of compound piers and wall arcades which created a contrast of light and shade, as at Toulouse and Vézelay. Furthermore, as an imperial cathedral, it established the style for German ecclesiastical architecture during the Romanesque era.

The Romanesque churches in France, and elsewhere throughout Europe, were decorated with sculptures that served several purposes. They were highly ornamental, of course, but more significantly, they told the story of Christianity to a largely illiterate population. Common themes, such as the Last Judgment or scenes from the Old and New Testaments and the lives of the saints, appeared as dramatic creations in stone, designed to inspire fear as well as devotion in the viewers. These sculptures demonstrate how the Christian religion gave to much of the art of the Middle Ages its intrinsic purpose and its specific imagery.

Sculpture

The artists and sculptors of the Romanesque period were encouraged to view their talents, skills, and abilities as gifts from God. For example, in the first quarter of the twelfth century, a treatise titled *De diversis artibus* (*On the Diverse Arts*) by the German artist and philosopher Roger of Helmarshausen, writing under the pseudonym Theophilus, offered the following advice to his peers:

> Through the spirit of wisdom, you know that all created things proceed from God, and without Him nothing is.
> Through the spirit of understanding, you have received the capacity for skill—the order, variety, and measure with which to pursue your varied work.
> Through the spirit of counsel, you do not bury your talent given you by God, but, by openly working and teaching in all humility, you display it faithfully to those wishing to understand.
> Through the spirit of fortitude, you drive away all the torpor of sloth, and whatever you essay with energy you bring with full vigor to completion.
> Through the spirit of knowledge accorded you, you are, in the abundance of your heart, the master of your skill and, with the confidence of a full mind, employ that abundance for the public good.
> Through the spirit of godliness, you regulate with pious care the nature, the purpose, the time, measure, and method of the work and the amount of the reward lest the vice of avarice or cupidity steal in.
> Through the spirit of fear of the Lord, you remember that you can do nothing of yourself; you reflect that you have or intend nothing unless accorded by God, but by believing, by acknowledging and rendering thanks, you ascribe to the divine compassion whatever you know, or are, or are able to be.

Thus, according to Theophilus, grateful artists would labor selflessly, recognizing that they were, in essence, vehicles of God's creative activity.

Nonetheless, many medieval artists were named and identified in documents, although specific works were generally not attributed to them. Some artists did sign their works, but their signatures are generally unobtrusively placed, often at the base of a column, or on a capital. In the cathedral of St.-Lazare at Autun in central France there is a signature that has long been a particularly famous example. It reads *Gislebertus hoc fecit*— "Gislebertus made this"—and was inscribed below the feet of Christ on the

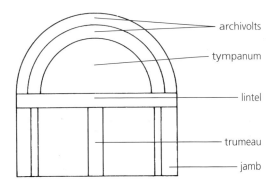

74 A cathedral or church portal usually consisted of the components shown in this drawing: the jambs flank the doors on either side, the trumeau separates the doors, and the lintel is the horizontal part of the doorframe, above which is the semi-circular tympanum surrounded by archivolts (ornamental moldings).

archivolts

tympanum

lintel

trumeau

jamb

tympanum. Scholars have theorized that the prominent placing of the inscription was, perhaps, an act of homage to God, but they have also suggested that it may have been inspired by the pride of Gislebertus in his own work.

Recent scholarship has produced another possibility: that Gislebertus was not a sculptor, but rather a nobleman who patronized the cathedral, and who wished to have his name placed in a prominent position on the building. The tympanum thus recorded a gift to the church, and attested to the aristocratic involvement in the activities of the community. In this interpretation, the sculptor remains anonymous. Nonetheless, whoever created the magnificent works at Autun—whether Gislebertus or an unknown artist—they remain among the finest examples of the art of the Romanesque period. Hence, we will examine several of them in detail.

The sculptures at Autun, which were created between approximately 1125 and 1135, show many typical aspects of the Romanesque sculptural style, such as the use of distortion, angular poses, and variations in scale among the diverse figures. Imaginative and original details such as these would have been the individual contribution of the sculptor to the artistic design, whose general form had been determined by the bishop and canons in charge of the building program.

A visitor entering the central doorway of a cathedral (**fig. 74**) first encountered the sculptures in the tympanum, which portray the Last Judgment in vivid and frightening detail (**figs. 75** and **76**). Christ occupies the center of the design; he is seated on a throne

75 The sculptural program in the tympanum above the west door at Autun Cathedral, France, portrays the Last Judgment in gruesome detail. Christ is enthroned in the center, surrounded by a *mandorla*. The figures on the left side are ascending to eternal bliss in heaven, while those on the right are being dragged to the torments of hell. This theme was often used over the portals of medieval cathedrals to remind worshipers of their ultimate destiny.

with outstretched arms, and surrounded by a *mandorla*, the sign of glory, which is supported by four angels. Inscribed on the *mandorla* are the words: "I alone dispose of all things and crown the just/Those who follow crime I judge and punish." The figures on the left side of the tympanum, under the first phrase, are shown as they float towards heaven, while those on the right undergo the agonies of the damned. At either side are angels blowing trumpets that proclaim the Day of Judgment.

The imagery is continued in the lintel. The elect are shown on the left side with apostles, who accompany them in their resurrection; on the right are the damned, all nude, with several figures covering their faces in terror. A miser, clearly screaming, has a bag of money hanging around his neck and is encircled by a snake. The breasts of an adulterous woman are being bitten by two snakes, while enormous, claw-like hands strangle the figure next to her. Directly above in the tympanum, a confrontation between the Archangel Michael and a devil is shown. The devil has a monstrous head, tail, and claws attached to a skinny body which is half-human, half-reptile. An even larger and more dreadful devil stands behind, carrying a toad, often a symbol of evil in medieval art. It is evident that images such as these were designed to strike fear into the hearts of medieval worshipers, who fervently believed in the impending reality of divine judgment (fig. 76).

To quote Theophilus once again:

> If, perchance, the faithful soul
> . . . beholds how great are the joys
> of heaven and how great the
> torments in the infernal flames,
> it is animated by the hope of its
> good deeds and is shaken with
> fear by reflection on its sins.

The same attitude is shown by the visual message at Autun, which echoes the prevailing pastoral admonition to obey the commandments of God or suffer the inevitable consequences of damnation.

The arches that surmount the tympanum suggest the universality and timelessness of God. They are carved with illustrations of the calendar, indicating the progress of the sun through the twelve signs of the zodiac. The signs are accompanied by the related occupations of each of the

76 An angel blows a trumpet, signifying Judgment Day, in this detailed view of the fate of the souls facing eternal damnation from the tympanum at Autun. Human figures writhe in agony as they are clutched by snakes and devils with spindly bodies and horrifying heads.

twelve months. This juxtaposition of religious and secular, even pagan, imagery may seem incongruous to twenty-first-century viewers, but people in the Middle Ages were far more willing to accept an amalgamation of cosmological traditions, seeing such expression as a manifestation of the various facets of God's activity in the world.

The skill and imagination of the sculptor at Autun are further demonstrated in his portrayal of Eve, found in the north doorway (**fig. 77**). This is one of the most beautiful and sensitive sculptures of the entire Romanesque era. Eve lies on the ground, resting on her elbow, about to pick an apple from a heavily laden branch of the Tree of Knowledge, which is being offered to her by Satan. She does not look at the fruit, but holds her hand close to her mouth in a gesture that may indicate that she is whispering to Adam. Although she is modestly covered with a vine, the sculptor was not hesitant to carve her breasts in a sensuous, even erotic, way. In an era when large-scale nudes were rare, this seductive work is a tribute to the artist's genius and individuality.

Another of the brilliant artists of the Romanesque era worked in the early twelfth century at Souillac, in southern-central France. There, the subject of the tympanum above the main door of the church was the pledge made to Satan by Theophilus the apostate (one who has rejected his religion). Below, on the trumeau, or central supporting column of the portal, a tangle of monsters engage in a ferocious struggle (**fig. 78**). Lions and **griffins** appear in pairs, with their opposing bodies creating an almost heraldic design. The turned heads of the griffins strain to gnaw at the bodies of birds and animals, which appear to slither and plunge towards the bottom of the column. At the top, a naked man is being attacked by two monsters—a griffin, which bites his torso, and a hairy wolf or lion, which grasps his head between vicious jaws. This sculpture visually summarizes many of the artistic trends and preoccupations of the previous several centuries, inherited by the Romanesque world from its Germanic, pre-Carolingian predecessors. The delight in fantastic images, the fascination with interwoven design, and the tension of violent struggling forms that characterized the arts of tribal tradition are found here in a splendid construction.

Bernard of Clairvaux, whose opinions concerning Cluniac artistic and liturgical practice were discussed in Chapter 7, viewed such sculptures with dismay, fearing that monks and other worshipers would be distracted by the vivid forms from contemplating the word of God. In his famous *Apologia ad Willelmum*, written shortly before the trumeau at Souillac was created, he warned:

> In the cloisters, under the eyes of the brethren engaged in reading, what business has there that ridiculous monstrosity, that amazing misshapen shapeliness and shapely misshapenness? Those unclean monkeys? Those fierce lions? Those monstrous centaurs? Those semi-human beings? Those spotted tigers? Those fighting warriors? Those huntsmen blowing their horns? Here you behold several bodies beneath one head; there again several heads upon one body. Here you see a quadruped with the tail of a serpent; there a fish with the head of a quadruped. There an animal suggests a horse in front and half a goat behind; here a horned beast exhibits the rear part of a horse. In fine, on all sides there appears so rich and so amazing a variety of forms that it is more delightful to read the marble than the manuscripts, and to spend the whole day in admiring these things, piece by piece, rather than in meditation on the Law of God.

Bernard was equally disturbed by the use of sumptuous liturgical vessels in religious ceremonies, as mentioned earlier. He viewed ornate chalices and candlesticks made of jewels and precious metals as potential distractions for worshipers. His feelings were not universally shared by his contemporaries, however, many of whom believed that the spirit was led closer to God by the contemplation of beauty.

Ecclesiastical Art

Many medieval people recognized that the wealth and power of the Church were symbolized by the sacred objects made of gold or silver, precious stones, and enamels that were used in liturgical services. Indeed, goldsmiths and other metalworkers were encouraged in the continued production of precious liturgical objects, which were necessary for the celebration of the Mass and office. The artist and philosopher Theophilus (Roger of Helmarshausen), for example, wrote:

> Come now, therefore, my wise friend—in this life happy in the sight of God and man and happier in the life to come—by whose labor and zeal so many sacrifices are offered to God, be inspired henceforth to greater deeds of skill, and with the utmost exertion of your mind prepare to execute what is still lacking in the vessels of the House of God, without which the divine mysteries and service of the Offices cannot continue. These are they: chalices, candlesticks, censers, cruets, shrines, reliquaries for holy relics, crosses, covers for Gospel books and the rest of the things which usage necessarily demands for the ecclesiastical rites.

78 The trumeau of the church at Souillac, in central France, incorporates knots of swirling monsters, engaged in fierce combat. The intricate design recalls the interwoven forms of Germanic tribal art, as well as the earlier fascination with animal figures evident in works such as the buckle from Sutton Hoo (see fig. 14).

A fine example of a gold candlestick that embodies the influence of Anglo-Saxon metalworking technique is shown in **fig. 78**. Known as "the Gloucester Candlestick," it was presented to the church of St. Peter at Gloucester, in the west of England, around the year 1110 by the prior, Peter. It was cast, rather than being engraved or embossed, and the elaborate technique of pierced hollow casting made possible the glittering effect of the three-dimensional twisting and writhing figures reminiscent of Germanic tribal imagery.

Pilgrims and other worshipers who entered medieval churches were often given the opportunity to gaze on, and sometimes to touch, the sacred vases, crosses, and **reliquaries**, which contained the precious relics of the saints. These reliquaries were often designed to replicate the part of the body held inside, such as an arm or a skull. Among the most popular reliquaries were the **champlevé** enamel containers known as *chasses*, made in the French town of Limoges. These reliquary *chasses* usually replicated the shape of early Christian **sarcophagi**, recalling the early martyrs of the Church, and establishing a link between the relics of the saints contained inside and their holy predecessors. Many fine examples of these reliquaries exist, including fifty-two that commemorate the martyrdom of St. Thomas Becket (see the discussion in Chapter 9). These, which form the largest group of Limoges *chasses* dedicated to an individual saint, were widely disseminated. They can be traced throughout Europe—as far north as Sweden and as far south as Sicily. The Becket reliquaries were produced between 1180 and 1220, during the astonishing growth of the cult of the murdered archbishop. The example shown in **fig. 80** is typical of the style of these objects.

79 The imagery on the magnificent gold "Gloucester Candlestick" represents the battle of human beings against the temptations of Satan, and their efforts to reach the divine illumination of Christ. The human figures are striving upward through the tangled mass of intertwined monsters and foliage, attempting to reach the symbols of the Evangelists halfway up (at the knot), and from there, striving towards the light at the top.

80 During the twelfth century, there were many reliquaries created at Limoges, France, using the enamel technique known as champlevé, in which the area to be covered with glass is cut away from the metal plate, rather than being partitioned with narrow strips, as in cloisonné work. This marvelous casket is one of many created in honor of St. Thomas Becket.

Becket is shown at the altar, being attacked by his assailants (there were actually four knights, rather than the three shown on the *chasse*). To his left are two clergymen, observing the action, but unable to defend him. The lid of these reliquaries generally has a scene showing either the saint's burial or the ascent of his soul into heaven; this example shows both episodes side by side.

The narrative artistic style of the reliquary exemplifies many figural characteristics of the Romanesque period, such as the stylized bodies in dance-like attitudes indicative of motion towards the archbishop, the arcs suggesting modeling of the legs and circles marking the knees, and the deep folds in the garments.

The iconography of the Becket martyrdom was also used in the needlework found on vestments, altar frontals, and **miters**, such as the example in **fig. 81** where the hand of God appears between two crescents above the scene of the murder. Narrative features such as those embroidered on vestments or incised into metal reliquaries were designed to bring the legend of the martyred archbishop to the attention of worshipers. They were emblematic of a world in which people were constantly reminded of the legends of the saints and biblical characters. These qualities were also characteristic of manuscript illuminations from approximately the same time.

81 The martyrdom of Becket was a popular image for stained glass, manuscript illumination, and ecclesiastical vestments during the centuries following his murder. An embroidered miter, worn by a bishop, shows the killing in gruesome detail, with the saint's brains oozing out from the wound inflicted by one of the knights. The hand of God reaches down towards the martyr from the point of the cap.

Manuscript Illumination

Illuminations of texts were used in medieval manuscripts to explicate and depict both biblical and hagiographical writings. These books were in increasingly high demand as a result of the foundation of numerous monastic communities during the twelfth century. An important development during the Romanesque era was the production of manuscripts by laypeople employed in monastic houses. Although historians once believed that lay production did not begin until the thirteenth century, scholars have recently shown that lay book illuminators and copyists were working in several English monasteries during the earlier period. The paid scribes copied works by the Church Fathers while the monks were engaged in producing books for liturgical services.

The illuminators employed a variety of styles and techniques, ranging from simple monochrome line drawings to fully painted works that involved the use of gold and textured effects. There were many procedures, with designs being executed in various combinations of painting and drawing.

A typical example of a hagiographical illumination, again taken from the artistic works depicting the martyrdom of Becket, appears in a late twelfth-century manuscript now

82 Like the reliquaries and the embroidered liturgical vestments, most of the manuscript illuminations depicting the events of Becket's life focus on the moment of his martyrdom. One exception is this example, which is probably the earliest image of the circumstances surrounding the murder. In a colorful series of pictures—a "continuous narrative"—the last hours of the saint are illustrated. In the upper frame, the archbishop is told by one of his clerks that the knights are waiting to converse with him; below on the left the murder is portrayed; and on the right the shrine of the saint is visited by the penitent knights.

in the British Museum (**fig. 82**). The illustration, which is probably the earliest image of the murder in the cathedral, relates the circumstances of Becket's final hours. In the upper lefthand corner, he is dining with two of the monks from his group of close companions. He is told by another of his clerks that four knights have arrived at his residence in Canterbury, and wish to speak with him. The space of the narrative is clearly delineated by the architectural feature of a peaked doorway, from which the messenger emerges to summon Becket. The lower part of the image depicts the martyrdom on the left, again separated from the companion image by an arch, through which the altar may be glimpsed. On the right, the artist moves us forward in time, as we see the knights doing penance at Becket's shrine. This final image is not historically accurate, according to the accounts of Becket's biographers, but was no doubt included to emphasize to the reader the importance of making recompense for one's sins.

The legends of saints such as Thomas Becket, who was canonized only three years after his murder, were one popular source of subject matter for narrative forms. Equally compelling were tales of heroes who struggled on the battlefield for God and monarch, such as the famous *Song of Roland*.

Literature: *The Song of Roland*

One of the most celebrated literary works of the entire Middle Ages is an anonymous epic poem, or *chanson de geste* ("song of heroic deeds"), known as *The Song of Roland*. The plot of the poem concerns a historical event that took place during the reign of Charlemagne, some 200 years before the poem emerged in its written form (though scholars assume that it existed as part of the oral tradition before that time). In 778, the emperor Charlemagne marched into Spain to fight off the advancing Muslim forces (see Chapter 4). As he did so, he separated his army into two parts; he led one part across the western Pyrenees towards Pamplona, and sent the other to Gerona. Both cities fell to his troops, and the two armies then proceeded to besiege Zaragoza. Charlemagne was soon faced with an uprising in his kingdom, however, and was forced to abandon the Spanish campaign. On his return north, as he crossed the Pyrenees at Roncevaux, the rear guard of his army was ambushed by Basque soldiers, who lay in wait along the high wooded areas on either side of the pass. After slaughtering Charlemagne's men and pillaging their baggage train, the Basque force disappeared into the woods.

This incident was mentioned as early as 830 by the chronicler Eginhardt (also known as Einhard), who recounts in the *Vita Carolinga* ("Life of Charlemagne"), "In the action were killed Eggihard the king's seneschal [steward], Anselm count of the palace, and Roland duke of the Marches of Brittany, together with a great many more." During the following two centuries, this brief mention of Roland developed into a legend of heroic proportion. Roland became the nephew of the emperor, "the right hand of his body," the greatest warrior of his age. He was accompanied in his adventures by his close companion Oliver and twelve peers, chosen as the bravest and most chivalrous of French knights.

The plot of the tale revolved around treachery committed by Roland's own stepfather, Count Ganelon, who engineered a consipiracy with the Muslim king Marsilion. The primary purpose of their intrigue, which derived from Ganelon's intense jealousy of his stepson, was the slaying of Roland and the peers. They were ultimately successful in killing the hero and his companions, but they faced deadly consequences when Charlemagne learned of their perfidy. Thus, with the addition of heroic characters who represent the eternal struggle between evil and good, a relatively insignificant historical event became the setting for a masterful work of epic literature.

The Song of Roland probably reached its completed state in the late eleventh century. The reasons for its popularity at that time are not difficult to discern. As discussed in Chapter 7, the Christian movement known as the Reconquista had resulted in battles against the Muslims such as those described in the poem, and religious fervor regarding expulsion of the infidel from Europe was widespread. Furthermore, heroic legends and tales such as *The Song of Roland* were growing in popularity along the pilgrimage paths and trading routes of Europe. These often featured local heroes, and were frequently associated with the great monastic establishments and important towns along each road. The route through the pass at Roncevaux, the site of Roland's death, led to the popular shrine of St. James at Compostela, and it was appropriate that travelers be regaled with local legends as they trudged along the path.

The poem features an ideological component as well as an exciting and entertaining story, since the work embodies many of the qualities of idealized feudal relationships. Roland's devotion to his God and to his leader, the emperor Charlemagne, is intrinsic to the ethical dimension of the tale; loyalty is extolled as the greatest virtue, while betrayal constitutes the worst sin. The story encapsulates the perfect feudal hierarchy—God, king, and vassal—which some scholars have viewed as a glorification of the royal authority of the Capetian monarchy, that had established itself in France by the time the *Song* first appeared in written form. At one point in the poem, when the French knights are sent into battle, Roland urges his men to confirm dedication to king and "sweet France" (stanza 88):

> Here we must stand to serve on the King's side.
> Men for their lords great hardship must abide,
> Fierce heat and cold endure in every clime,
> Lose for his sake, if need be, skin and hide.

And again:

> When the King gave us the French to serve this need
> These twenty thousand he chose to do the deed;
> And well he knew not one would flinch or flee.
> Men must endure much hardship for their liege,
> And bear for him great cold and burning heat,
> Suffer sharp wounds and let their bodies bleed.

Equally important is the hero's loyalty to his fellow soldiers. One of many examples of this recounts a circumstance in which Roland is fighting side by side with Archbishop Turpin, who, like other members of the clergy, was not banned from armed combat at this time. Roland calls to him:

For love of you here will I make my stand,
And side by side we'll take both good and bad.
I'll not desert you for any mortal man.

Roland's deep affection for his companions is given voice as he watches the death of Oliver, his close friend (stanza 151):

With tender words he bids him thus goodbye:
"Sir, my companion, woe worth your valiant might!
Long years and days have we lived side by side,
Ne'er didst thou wrong me nor suffer wrong of mine.
Now thou art dead I grieve to be alive."

The poem also portrays Roland's psychological response to the surrounding carnage (164):

The County Roland, seeing his peers lie dead,
Begins to weep for ruth and tenderness;
Out of his cheeks the color all has fled,
He cannot stand, he is so deep distressed,
He swoons to earth, he cannot help himself.

The tragic component of the tale is Roland's refusal to summon aid when his soldiers are besieged in the pass. With heroic determination, he believes that he will be judged as less than brave if he sounds the call for help, and he delays blowing his **oliphant** until it is too late for rescue. The description of Roland's own death echoes accounts of saintly martyrdom and embodies dedication to the ultimate liege lord, as he extends his "right-hand glove" to God (175). This linking of vassalage and the Christian religion is intrinsic to the meaning of the epic, as Roland is presented as the ideal Christian knight.

Now Roland feels his time is at an end;
On the steep hill-side, toward Spain he's turned his head,
And with one hand he beats upon his breast;
Saith: "*Mea culpa*; Thy mercy, Lord, I beg
For all the sins, both the great and the less,
That e'er I did since first I drew my breath
Unto this day when I'm struck down by death."
His right-hand glove he unto God extends;
Angels from Heaven now to his side descend.

In addition to the incorporation of feudal values based on traditions of vassalage, the poem reflects a preoccupation with holy war. This was perhaps a result of the rhetoric urging knights to undertake the First Crusade at the end of the eleventh century, which ignited religious fervor against the Muslims. Roland epitomizes the Christian knight, burning with religious zeal, who attacks the "accursed tribesmen—as black as ink from head to foot"; his mission calls to mind St. James, the "Moor-Slayer."

The primary objective of Charlemagne in *The Song of Roland* is the defeat and Christianization of the "pagans," who are viewed as "a people who have no love of God." They are, however, admired as worthy opponents. In describing one emir, or Muslim ruler, the words of the poet tell us that:

> From Balaguet there cometh an emir;
> His form is noble, his eyes are bold and clear,
> When on his horse he's mounted in career
> He bears him bravely armed in his battle-gear,
> And for courage he's famous far and near;
> Were he but Christian, right knightly he'd appear.

As one might expect, the Muslims are defeated in the poem, since "Wrong is with the heathen . . . and right is with the Christians." Zaragoza falls to the forces of Charlemagne, and Ganelon is punished for his treachery by being drawn and quartered. At the end of the poem, Christianization of the infidel is symbolized by the baptism of Bramimond, the Muslim queen of Spain. She has been renamed Juliana, and "Christian is she, informed in the True Way."

The Song of Roland represents a link in the epic tradition between *Beowulf* and the works of the thirteenth and fourteenth centuries, such as *Sir Gawain and the Green Knight*. It held great appeal for people in the Middle Ages because it presented stirring conflicts involving heroes who embodied the virtues of true Christian knighthood, based within the familiar system of vassalage. The poet describes the battle scenes in vivid detail, with swords bloody to the hilt, broken lances, riderless horses, torn **hauberks**, and piles of dead soldiers heaped on the ground. This style of vibrant narrative was also characteristic of the Bayeux Tapestry, which we first encountered in Chapter 6, although the religious focus of that narrative was less intense.

The Bayeux Tapestry

The Bayeux Tapestry (which is in fact, not a tapestry but an extensive embroidered panel of wool on linen) is about 232 feet(71 m) in length and a mere 20 inches (50 cm) high, and describes the events leading to the conflict between Harold of Wessex and William the Conqueror at the Battle of Hastings in 1066. It represents a tradition of narrative needlework of which very few examples survive. One similar panel, no longer extant, commemorated the Battle of Maldon, which took place in England during the Danish wars. It depicts the invaders being resisted by Byrhtnoth, the Ealdorman (Chief Military Officer) of Essex, who has challenged them to battle in 991—a conflict that is described in the poem *The Battle of Maldon*. The embroidery was commissioned by Byrhtnoth's widow, who presented it to Ely Minster (cathedral) along with gifts of manors and a golden necklace. The embroidered hanging was decorated with the deeds of her husband as a memorial of his virtues.

Scholars assume that this kind of secular narrative art had been practiced in England for a long time, and that the Bayeux Tapestry embodies a refinement of this tradition. The current consensus is that the tapestry was commissioned by Bishop Odo, the half-brother

of William the Conqueror, probably before 1082. It appears to have been designed by one person, whom scholars assume to have been male, and who was likely to have been an Englishman living in Canterbury. The tapestry was also likely to have been embroidered in different workshops, probably by Anglo-Saxon women, either lay or clerical. Historical texts reveal that women of all classes in Anglo-Saxon society practiced the skill of embroidery, and that their work was highly praised by those who saw it, especially European travelers. For example, William of Poitiers, a Norman who was not usually complimentary in his remarks concerning the "barbaric" people of England, praised the women as being "very skilled with the needle and in weaving with gold."

The tapestry portrays the history of the Battle of Hastings in a series of separate scenes that are arranged in chronological order, although the images sometimes shift backward and forward within a brief space of time. It is, in a sense, a narrative presentation akin to *The Song of Roland*. The designer of the tapestry borrowed rhetorical images from the genre of the *chanson de geste*, and presumably its audience was familiar with the stylistic conventions. Both works incorporate a cycle of scenes that deal with the relationships of feudal society, primarily the associations between kings and nobles, such as alliances and oaths of vassalage. Both works also feature images of fierce battles and intense hand-to-hand combat, and recount the death throes of heroic leaders (**fig. 83**). The tapestry, however, is less able to probe the psychological states and emotional reactions of the protagonists, and its important characters do not have the symbolic stature of Charlemagne. It does, nonetheless, present an elaborate kind of visual propaganda, addressed to a narrowly elite segment of eleventh-century society, whose members had an intense interest in the outcome of the events described.

As we have seen, the years between 950 and 1100 were vital to the development of western art, architecture, and literature. No less important, however, were the contemporaneous accomplishments in the field of music.

83 This dramatic panel from the Bayeux Tapestry shows the climax of the Battle of Hastings. The caption, *"Harold Rex Interfectus Est"* tells us that "King Harold was killed," and other soldiers are falling under the Norman onslaught. In the border below, the weapons and armor of the dead are being stripped off and taken by the victors.

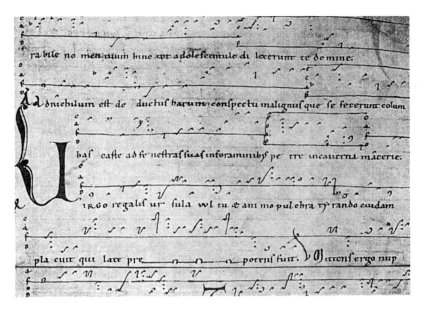

ra bile no men namm hinc cor adolescemulo di lererum te domine.

Donichilum est de ductus barum conspectu malignus que se fererum colam

bas caste ad fr nestras suas inforaminibus pe irv incauerni macerie.

IRCo regalis ur sula wl tu et am mo pulchra ry rando cuidam

pla euit qui late pre— — — — poterus fuit. Crensi ergo nup

84 The first music theorist to describe staff notation was Guido of Arezzo. Initially, the staff consisted of two lines, with a red line indicating the pitch F and a yellow (or green) one signifying C. Eventually, the staff was expanded to four lines—a pattern used throughout the Middle Ages. Although modern musical notation employs a five-line staff, liturgical chant continues to be written on the older four-line structure. The letters in the left margin eventually developed into clefs.

Music

During the late tenth and eleventh centuries the invention of musical notation made it possible to write music down in a form that enabled melodies to be passed from composer to singer, and from one historical era to another. In addition, music began to be structured according to definite rules and principles of order. The resulting theories concerning modes and rhythm were defined in musical treatises (see below).

By the eleventh century, the chant used in liturgical services had been standardized to a degree, and indications for pitches were provided above the syllables of the chant text (see the discussion in Chapter 4). These symbols did not indicate an exact pitch, however, and served basically as a reminder of melodies already known to the singer. A great deal of emphasis continued to be placed on memorization, and various diagrams and charts were used to aid the singers in learning the various chants to be sung in the liturgy. These were similar in nature to the mnemonic devices that were frequently used to assist in the memorization of biblical and theological passages during the eleventh and twelfth centuries.

One of the most innovative teachers and musicians of the era was Guido of Arezzo (*c.* 1000–1050), a Benedictine monk who was the first theorist to discuss staff notation. Guido described a rudimentary two-line staff, with a red line indicating the pitch F and a yellow one for C. His staff was eventually expanded to four lines and the indications for F and C were provided by clefs, thereby establishing a notation that has remained in use for chant until the present day (**fig. 84**). This system indicated pitch with accuracy, but it did not show rhythm. The development of symbols that specified rhythmic clarity remained a challenge to be solved by thirteenth-century composers.

Guido also codified a system of six **solmization** syllables (ut [do], re, mi, fa, sol, la), and developed a pedagogical aid often identified as the "Guidonian hand" (**fig. 85**). His method of solmization has remained in use, with few modifications—including the addition of a seventh syllable, ti—up to the present time. Guido's system resulted in the ability to "produce an accomplished singer in the space of one year, or at the most in two," whereas before the invention of his pedagogical technique, ten years of study had resulted in "only an imperfect knowledge of singing."

Guido described his system in a letter to a colleague:

> Moved by a divinely inspired charity, I have brought to you, and to as many others as
> I have been able, a grace divinely bestowed on me, the most unworthy of men;
> namely, that those who come after us, when they learn with the greatest ease the

ecclesiastical melodies which I and all my predecessors learned only with the greatest difficulty, they will desire for me and for you and my other helpers eternal salvation, and by the mercy of God our sins will be remitted, or at least from the gratitude of so many will come some prayer for our souls.

Like the artists of the era, Guido attributed his achievements to God, "for our actions are good only when we ascribe to the Creator all that we are able to accomplish." But his attitude was not totally altruistic; he was convinced that his work would bring about the remittance of sins and eternal salvation.

Guido of Arezzo and other music theorists and teachers worked to train musicians who would participate in the liturgical services of the Church, and developed the skills that allowed them to notate music for this purpose. Hence, it is not surprising that our knowledge of secular music is virtually nonexistent prior to the eleventh century. Scholars assume that people sang and played various instruments, but we have no way of knowing how this music sounded or how it was received by the people who listened to it. We do know from the negative comments of churchmen that there were itinerant musicians known as *jongleurs*—vagabonds who traveled from castle to castle, dancing, singing, playing instruments, performing magic tricks, and exhibiting trained bears. As may be imagined, they were viewed, at best, as a dangerous influence, and were accused by the clergy of corrupting the morals of decent people with their fashions of dress and hairstyle. According to the *History* of the Benedictine monk Raoul Glaber:

85 Another of Guido's innovations was the pedagogical aid known as the "Guidonian Hand," a system he borrowed from the makers of almanacs, who developed it to keep track of the calendar. As illustrated in this table from a thirteenth-century musical treatise, the solmization syllables (ut [do], re, mi, fa, sol, and la) were assigned to the joints of the fingers, and the teacher could indicate a melody to the student by pointing to the proper knuckle.

> In about the year 1000 of the incarnate Word, when King Robert married Queen Constance of the region of Aquitaine, thanks to the queen, men of all the vainest frivolity began to stream from the Auvergne and Aquitaine into France and Burgundy. Perverted in their customs and dress, their armor and horse trappings badly put together, they shaved their hair from halfway down their heads, went beardless like *jongleurs*, wore the most disgusting yellow boots and leggings, and were entirely devoid of any law of faith or peace. And so alas the whole of the French people, until recently the most decent of all, together with the Burgundians, seized avidly on their abominable example, till at length everyone came to conform to their wickedness and infamy.

Judging from iconography, rather than musical evidence, we assume that instruments often accompanied the voice in the performances of secular musicians. Various instruments were used, including the harp, which was the oldest medieval instrument; it had been imported to Europe from Ireland or Britain some time before the ninth century.

The most important bowed instrument was the **vielle** or **fiedel**, which was the forerunner of Renaissance instruments such as the viol. The medieval *vielle* had five strings, and iconographic images indicate that it was made in a variety of shapes. Another bowed string instrument was the **rebec**, which was gourd-shaped and had three strings. The **organistrum** also employed strings, although these were sounded by a crank-driven wheel, rather than a bow. The **lute** and the **psaltery**, a kind of zither, also appear frequently in manuscript illuminations and sculptural groupings. Wind instruments included flutes (both transverse and vertical), **shawms**, trumpets, and bagpipes. Drums began to be used in the twelfth century. Most of these instruments found their way into Europe from Asia, either through contacts with Byzantine musicians or the Muslims in north Africa and Spain. **Fig. 86**, taken from a collection of images of *Minnesänger*, the German equivalent of troubadors, shows typical instruments of the time.

The early development of polyphony

Another important musical development that took place prior to the eleventh century was the embryonic use of polyphony, or the sounding of more than one pitch at a time. The earliest form of polyphony is known as *organum*. It was first described in treatises by two nearly contemporary theorists, Regino of Prüm (d. 915) and Hucbald (*c.* 840–930). Hucbald clearly explains the simultaneous sounding of different pitches:

> Consonance is the judicious and harmonious mixture of two tones, which exists only if two tones, produced from different sources, meet in one joint sound, as happens when a boy's voice and a man's voice sing the same thing, or in that which they commonly call *organum*.

Organum was described in more detail, with musical examples, in two important treatises of the late ninth century: the *Musica enchiriadis* (Music Manual) and the *Scholia enchiriadis* (Commentary on the Manual). The *Scholia enchiriadis* defined different types of *organum*, all of which were derived from one basic principle: the simultaneous duplication of a chant melody by another voice sounding in parallel motion at the interval of an octave, fifth, or fourth. The voice sounding the chant melody was known as the *vox principalis*, or principal voice. Simple *organum* resulted when the principal voice was doubled by one other voice, known as the *vox organalis*. If one or both voices were doubled at the octave, the result was known as composite *organum*. When the interval between the voices was strictly maintained, the result was often known as strict or parallel *organum*. If the strict adherence to parallel motion was temporarily abandoned by the voices in a phrase beginning at the unison and moving to the interval of a fourth or fifth, the result was often referred to as free *organum* or modified parallel *organum*. **Fig. 87** shows a manuscript source and **fig. 88** provides a modern transcription of parallel *organum* at the octave and fifth; **fig. 89**, transcribed from the *Musica enchiriadis*, illustrates modified parallel *organum*.

86 King Wenzel is enthroned in the center of this image, with his various knights, courtiers, and entertainers around him. The hierarchy is shown by the relative size of the figures, with the knight and the courtier next in size to the monarch. The musicians, who carry a *shawm* and a *vielle*, are the smallest and, hence, the least important.

87 The earliest form of polyphony is known as *organum*. Originally, as may be seen on the left in this example from the ninth-century *Musica enchiriadis* (Music Manual), the intervallic distance between the lower voice, which sang the chant melody, and the upper voice, was strictly maintained—a technique resulting in "strict" or parallel *organum*. If either one or both voices was duplicated at the interval of an octave, as indicated on the right, the result was known as composite *organum*.

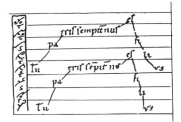

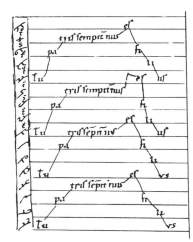

a) At the fifth below

Nos   qui vi - vi-mus, be - ni - di - ci-mus Do-mi-no,   ex hoc nunc et us-que in sae-cu - lum.

b) At the octave, above and below

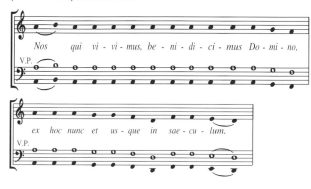

88 Parallel *organum* and composite *organum* have been transcribed into modern notation in this example ("We who are living will bless the Lord from this time forth and forever", Psalm 113:27). The initials V. P. indicate the *vox principalis* (the chant melody), and V. O. stands for *vox organalis* (the voice singing the melody which forms the *organum*). When the chant melody is duplicated at the octave, the *vox organalis* is not identified with V. O.

c) Three forms of composite *organum* at the fifth

89 The musical style known as modified parallel *organum* is shown in this modern transcription. The *vox principalis* intones the chant melody, while the *vox organalis* sings below. As may be seen in this example, the voices begin and end together (in unison), singing the same pitch.

During the following century composers experimented with various possibilities of range and the crossing of voices, a development to be discussed in Chapter 13.

Although the sound of this eleventh- and twelfth-century *organum* may initially seem strangely bare to the modern ear, it is ideally suited to the architectural style of the Romanesque cathedral. A vibrant, sonorous effect is created when this polyphonic chant style reverberates within the stone vaults of a lofty cathedral nave, inspiring awe in the minds of modern listeners just as it did in the hearts of the people of the eleventh and twelfth centuries.

Summary

The eleventh and twelfth centuries, often defined as the Romanesque era, represent the high point of the great age of pilgrimage and monastic culture. In architecture, the magnificent churches and cathedrals that appeared along pilgrimage routes and in developing cities derived their inspiration from Roman monuments, and incorporated Islamic technical innovations, most notably the pointed arch. They were decorated with elaborate sculptures that were didactic in their intent, proclaiming Christian scriptural narratives and doctrine to the illiterate worshipers who entered the portals. The legends of the Bible and the lives of the saints were vividly portrayed with bold iconographic forms influenced by the pre-Carolingian Germanic world. Similar images may also be seen in manuscript illuminations and on the ecclesiastical treasures created for use in the liturgy.

The development of literature in the Romanesque period was also influenced by the Germanic and Christian narrative traditions. One example is the famous *Song of Roland*, an epic poem based on a historical event from the reign of Charlemagne.

During this era, music theorists and composers developed a system for writing music in a clearly notated form, thereby enabling the transmission of specifically defined melodies—and eventually harmonies—from musician to musician and century to century. In addition, the beginning of polyphony laid the foundation for the sophisticated genres that characterized the music of the thirteenth century. Thus, Romanesque culture in all its forms provided the groundwork for the flowering of art, architecture, music, and literature of the Gothic period.

Suggestions for Further Reading

Primary sources

The Vézelay Chronicle, by Hugh of Poitiers, translated by John Scott and John O. Ward (Binghamton, NY: Center for Medieval and Renaissance Studies, 1992), gives an excellent translation of fascinating source material, along with fine articles about the abbey.

The last two chapters of *Early Medieval Art: 300–1150* (*Sources and Documents*), by Caecilia Davis-Weyer (Englewood Cliffs, NJ: Prentice-Hall, Inc., 1971), contain sources pertaining to early and late Romanesque art and architecture.

Music in the Western World: A History in Documents, selected and annotated by Piero Weiss and Richard Taruskin (New York: Macmillan, Inc., 1984), presents documents from the era discussed in this chapter.

The Song of Roland is available in many translations, including one by D.D.R. Owen (Woodbridge, UK: Boydell Press, 1990) and another by

Dorothy L. Sayers (Harmondsworth, UK: Penguin Books, 1957).

Secondary sources

Chapters 9, 10, 11, and 12 of *Medieval Architecture in Western Europe from A.D. 300 to 1500*, by Robert G. Calkins (Oxford: Oxford University Press, 1998), provide a thorough description of Romanesque architecture. *Early Medieval* by George Henderson (Harmondsworth, England: Penguin Books Ltd, 1972), traces the development of Romanesque art and demonstrates the ways in which it shares qualities and values with literature of the era. *Romanesque Art*, by Andreas Petzold (New York: Harry N. Abrams, 1995), is a beautifully illustrated analysis of the origins and development of the Romanesque style within a broad social and intellectual context. *Medieval Art*, by Veronica Sekules (Oxford: Oxford University Press, 2001), organizes the history of medieval art thematically, rather than chronologically, and places artistic expression within the context of social history. Chapters 7 and 8 of *Medieval Art*, by Marilyn Stokstad

(New York: Harper & Row, reprint ed., 1988), provide a lucid introduction to the art of the Romanesque period in various areas of Europe.

An engrossing account of artworks portraying the cults of saints is given in *The Medieval Cult of Saints: Formations and Transformations*, by Barbara Abou-El-Haj (Cambridge: Cambridge University Press, 1994). Linda Seidel's work *Legends in Limestone: Lazarus, Gislebertus, and the Cathedral of Autun* (Chicago: University of Chicago Press, 1999) presents a fascinating new theory concerning the identity of Gislebertus, as discussed in this chapter.

Decorative objects created for ecclesiastical use are thoroughly described in *Ars Sacra: 800–1200* by Peter Lasko. The 2nd edition (New Haven: Yale University Press, 1994) features splendid illustrations.

Romanesque Manuscripts: The Twelfth Century, by Walter Cahn (2 vols., London: Harvey Miller Publishers, 1996), is a comprehensive study of manuscript illumination in France during the

Romanesque period. *Medieval Illuminators and their Methods of Work*, by Jonathan J.G. Alexander (New Haven: Yale University Press, 1992), gives a fascinating account of the techniques of medieval artists and the process of manuscript illumination.

Two works that explore the social, political, and artistic meaning of the Bayeux Tapestry are *The Rhetoric of Power in the Bayeux Tapestry*, by Suzanne Lewis (Cambridge: Cambridge University Press, 1999), and *The Mystery of the Bayeux Tapestry*, by David J. Bernstein (London: Weidenfeld and Nicolson, 1986).

Medieval Music, by Richard Hoppin (New York: W.W. Norton & Co., 1978), provides a detailed analysis of music in the Middle Ages and explores its function in society. Less comprehensive but still valuable surveys are given by John Caldwell in *Medieval Music* (Bloomington, Indiana: Indiana University Press, 1978), and David Fenwick Wilson, *Music of the Middle Ages* (New York: Schirmer Books, 1990).

9 POLITICS AND THE CHURCH IN THE TWELFTH CENTURY

DURING THE TWELFTH CENTURY, many of the political regimes established during earlier periods continued to be strengthened and developed. The monarchies of England and Germany passed to new dynasties, both of which became powerful forces in European politics. The Capetians continued to rule France, and, although their land holdings were not as great as those of their vassals, shrewd and effective Capetian monarchs were able to consolidate their power.

The leaders of northwestern Europe continued their attempt to extend their hegemony towards the Mediterranean, through new crusading movements as well as invasion. Christian monarchs from England, France, and the Holy Roman Empire led forces that sought to expand control in the Holy Land, and the leaders of Christian Spain continued the Reconquista, striving to regain more of the peninsula from the Muslims. The Normans also moved to assert their authority in southern Italy and Sicily by establishing a ruling dynasty there, taking advantage of a political struggle between the Lombards and the representatives of the Byzantine ruler to assert their own authority. The expansion to the areas bordering the Mediterranean brought the people of the north into significant contact with Byzantine and Muslim societies, resulting in a rich cross-fertilization of cultural and intellectual life.

England

William Rufus and Henry I

When William the Conqueror died in 1087, his power and property were divided among his three sons (see table, facing page.) Normandy was left to his oldest son, Robert, and England to his second son, William Rufus ("the Red"). Henry, the youngest son, received a bequest equivalent in modern terms to several million dollars, and used part

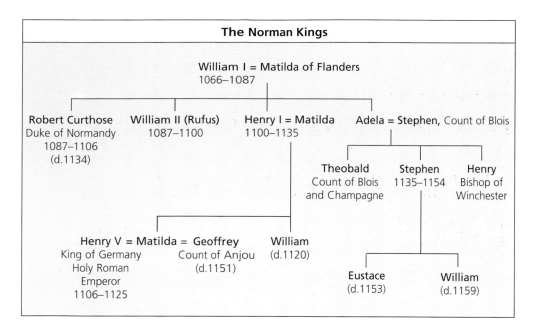

The Norman Kings

```
                      William I = Matilda of Flanders
                           1066–1087

Robert Curthose    William II (Rufus)    Henry I = Matilda    Adela = Stephen, Count of Blois
Duke of Normandy      1087–1100          1100–1135
   1087–1106                                              Theobald      Stephen      Henry
   (d.1134)                                             Count of Blois  1135–1154  Bishop of
                                                       and Champagne              Winchester

   Henry V = Matilda = Geoffrey    William
King of Germany   Count of Anjou   (d.1120)                Eustace       William
  Holy Roman        (d.1151)                               (d.1153)      (d.1159)
   Emperor
  1106–1125
```

of the money to buy a portion of Normandy from his brother Robert. He then proceeded to sow seeds of discord between his siblings.

As king of England, William Rufus proved to be "excessively devoted to money and to cruelty." Although the *Anglo-Saxon Chronicle* may have exaggerated when it claimed that he was "strong and fierce to his country and his men and to all his neighbors, and very terrible . . . hateful to nearly all his people, and odious to God," most contemporary authors tend to share this opinion. Certainly there was no great mourning when, in 1100, William was mysteriously killed by an arrow while hunting—an "accident" that had been prefigured by "blood bubbling out of the earth." His brother Henry, who was present when the shooting occurred, quickly seized the opportunity to assert his claim to the throne. Within three days he had appropriated the treasury, secured the loyalty of the royal council, and been crowned in Westminster Abbey (August 5, 1100) by the bishop of London. Henry's claim to the throne was actually weaker than that of Robert, his older brother, but Robert was on crusade, and could not assert his rights.

Henry issued a "Coronation Charter," in which he promised to observe customary feudal practices, especially those regarding vacancies in Church offices and the inheritances of his vassals. His proclamation sought to reverse the corrupt practices of his brother William Rufus, who had greedily taken advantage of any opportunity to appropriate funds attached to ecclesiastical benefices and secular fiefs.

In order to consolidate his power, Henry needed the support of the Anglo-Saxons and the Scots. He therefore shrewdly linked himself to the "true royal family of England" by marrying the great-granddaughter of Edmund Ironside (see p. 167), a Scottish princess named Matilda, also known as Maud. Henry soon needed to take advantage of this affiliation. When Robert invaded from Normandy, intending to wrest the English throne from his brother, Henry was able to amass an army made up of knights who owed him liege service as well as a number of native Englishmen. The brothers ultimately

90 Henry I evidently felt extremely apprehensive about the possible results of his extortionary taxation, because he was reported to have suffered from three nightmares in a single night, illustrated in this mid-twelfth-century *Chronicle of Florence and John of Worcester*. In the first image, the king fears that his power will not be adequate to control the angry peasants, who threaten him with their farming tools. He was also frightened by the actions or the upper social classes, who were equally infuriated by his monetary demands. In the second vision, knights accost him, swords in hand, and in the third, bishops attack him with the points of their staves.

settled their differences through negotiation, with Henry agreeing to pay Robert an annual subsidy. The truce was relatively short-lived, however, and in 1104–1105 Henry gathered his forces and invaded Normandy. The English were victorious at the Battle of Tinche-bray in 1106, and Henry imprisoned his brother, who remained comfortably incarcerated until his death twenty-eight years later.

Henry proved to be a powerful monarch who significantly strengthened royal admin-istration during his reign of thirty-five years. Known as the "Lion of Justice," he gener-ally ruled with equity. However, like some modern leaders, he was resented for his heavy taxation. For example, the *Anglo-Saxon Chronicle* reported that, in 1116, "this land and people were often severely oppressed by the taxes that the king collected both in and out of the boroughs," and that 1124 "was a very troublous year; the man who had any property was deprived of it by harsh taxes and harsh judgments at court; the man who had none died of hunger" (**fig. 90**). In contrast, the English monk and historian, William of Malmesbury (1090–1143), wrote that Henry was loved by the common people and feared by the magnates because of the "rectitude of his conduct." He also praised Henry for his self-control: the king was "plain in his diet . . . deplored lapses into drunkenness both in himself and others . . . and [was] wholly free from carnal desires, for . . . his intercourse with women was undertaken not for the satisfaction of his lusts but from his desire for children." Purely in his quest for an heir, he fathered two or three legitimate children and at least eight illegitimate sons and eleven illegitimate daughters.

Henry's oldest son, named William, was carefully trained and educated for suc-cession to the throne. When the boy was twelve, Henry arranged that "all the free men of England and of Normandy, of every rank and condition, to whatever lords they were subject, were obliged to submit themselves to him by oath and homage." According to William of Malmesbury, "it was confidently expected that in him the hopes of England . . . might again through this youth blossom and bring forth fruit. But God saw otherwise." In 1120, when William was seventeen, he and his brother and some close friends, all "flown with wine," drowned in a boating accident, known in history as the "White Ship Disaster." It was said at the time that "No ship ever brought so much misery to Eng-land." The boys' bodies could not be found, and "they became food for the monsters of the deep."

The accident destroyed Henry's carefully designed plans for the succession of his son, and since his second son had also perished in the shipwreck, he attempted to secure the throne for his daughter, Matilda. She had been married at age eleven to the Holy Roman Emperor Henry V, but his death had left her a childless widow. Her father secured pledges from his barons that they would support Matilda as the royal heir, and then arranged a marriage for her with Geoffrey of Anjou. In 1133, she gave birth to a son who would rule England as Henry II.

Unfortunately, when Henry I died in 1135, the barons refused to stand by their promises to accept the rule of a woman. Instead, they supported the claim of a power-ful landowner, Stephen of Blois, who was a grandson of William the Conqueror. Stephen secured the throne, claiming that courtiers at Henry's deathbed had heard the old king name him as successor.

Stephen proved to be a weak king. As the *Anglo-Saxon Chronicle* reported: "In this king's time there was nothing but disturbance and wickedness and robbery, for . . .

when the traitors understood that [Stephen] was a mild man, and gentle and good, and did not exact the full penalties of the law, they perpetrated every enormity." Furthermore, the barons who had done homage to Stephen did not keep their pledges:

They oppressed the wretched people of the country severely with castle-building. When the castles were built, they filled them with devils and wicked men. Then, both by night and day they took those people that they thought had any goods—men and women—and put them in prison and tortured them with indescribable torture to extort gold and silver—for no martyrs were ever so tortured as they were. They were hung by the thumbs or by the head, and corselets [pieces of heavy body armor] were hung on their feet. Knotted ropes were put round their heads and twisted till they penetrated to the brains. They put them in prisons where there were adders and snakes and toads, and killed them like that. Some they put in a "torture-chamber"—that is, in a chest that was short, narrow, and shallow, and they put sharp stones in it and pressed the man in it so that he had all his limbs broken.

18 – The Angevin Empire 1154

KEY

Angevin Empire in 1154

Capetian Domain

0   200 km
0   125 miles

N

According to the *Chronicle*, oppression such as this lasted the entire nineteen years of Stephen's reign. The chaotic situation was not improved when Matilda began to assert her claim to the throne in 1139. During the next decade, Stephen and Matilda were at war, which naturally resulted in disruption to trade and domestic tranquillity. A virtual state of anarchy persisted until Stephen promised, in 1153, to support Matilda's son, Henry of Anjou, as his successor. When Stephen died in 1154, Henry of Anjou was able to ascend the throne unopposed as King Henry II (r. 1154–1189), and the era of Angevin rule began.

The Angevin Empire

At the time Henry II succeeded to the throne, he had recently married Eleanor of Aquitaine, the divorced wife of Louis VII, king of France (see below). The lands over which Henry and Eleanor ruled—Anjou, Aquitaine, Normandy, and England—constituted the Angevin Empire, an expanse that included much of France, as well as England (**Map 18**).

Henry deliberately set about to return his realm to the policies of his grandfather, Henry I. He was able to achieve this partly as a result of his own forceful personality, and partly because England was ready for a strong monarch who could establish peace in a country torn by anarchy. He spent the first ten years of his reign using his privilege of office to consolidate his authority. Among other measures, he demanded that the barons swear allegiance to him as their liege lord, he disbanded mercenary troops, and he destroyed more than 1,200 illegal castles and fortifications which had been built without royal permission during the reign of Stephen. In re-establishing royal control, he concentrated on three areas: finance, military power, and the administration of justice. He strengthened the tax base through efficient collection of money due him, especially **scutage**, which vassals were supposed to pay to their lord in lieu of military service. He also reinstituted the fyrd, an army assembled from commoners, which had fallen out of use, and he placed his own men in local courts, sending royal justices to hear judicial cases.

One of the most important events of Henry's reign was his dispute with Thomas Becket, archbishop of Canterbury from 1162 to 1170 (see also Chapter 8). Before his appointment to the see of Canterbury, Becket had served Henry as chancellor of England, and been one of the king's closest friends and advisers. Once Henry appointed him archbishop, however, Becket took seriously his role as the leading Church prelate in England, and this sometimes placed him in direct opposition to the king.

One major source of friction between Henry and Becket was a disagreement over the trials of churchmen who had been accused of crimes. The king believed that clerics charged with criminal behavior should be tried in secular courts, and the archbishop insisted that the cases be heard in ecclesiastical courts. There were other contentious issues as well, in which the archbishop steadfastly continued to support the interests of the Church and to oppose the wishes of the king. When Becket would not agree to his demands, Henry began to harass him, accusing him of financial wrongdoing while serving as chancellor. The royal threats became progressively more serious, and in 1164 the archbishop fled into exile in France, where he spent the next six years.

In 1170, believing that his differences with the king had been resolved by the intervention of Pope Alexander III, Becket returned to England. Shortly afterwards, however, problems again arose, and it was clear that amicable relations were impossible. During Christmas week, 1170, Henry, away in France, uttered the fatal words that impelled four of his knights to return to England to seek out the archbishop: "What miserable drones and traitors have I nourished and promoted in my household, who let their lord be treated with such shameful contempt by a low-born clerk!" Whether it was the intent of Henry's men to murder Becket, or simply to arrest and imprison him, as they claimed, will probably never be clear. What is known is that they rode to Canterbury, where they approached the archbishop, demanding that he conform to the wishes of the king. When he refused, and left the meeting to attend the evening service in the cathedral, the knights followed him. One of the most dramatic of many accounts of the murder may be found in the office written for the feast day of the martyred archbishop:

As they were leaving, the archbishop went into the church, so that he might perform the evening praises [Vespers] to Christ. The accomplices of Satan followed him, wearing armor and with swords drawn, with a band of armed men behind them. Although the entrance to the church was blocked by the monks, the priest of God, soon to be the sacrificial victim of Christ, came running up and opened the door for his enemies, saying "The church ought not to be bolted shut like an armed camp." Rushing in, some said, "Where is the traitor?" Others questioned, in a furious voice, "Where is the archbishop?" The fearless confessor of Christ went out to meet them face to face. While they were threatening him with death, he said, "I willingly will accept death for the Church of God, but I warn you in God's name not to injure any of my companions." Indeed, imitating Christ in his suffering, he said, "If you seek me, allow these men to go." Rushing in toward the pious pastor, the rapacious wolves, unworthy sons against their own father, most cruel executioners against the sacrificial victim of Christ, cut off the consecrated crown of his head with deadly swords, and hurling down the anointed of the Lord onto the ground, cruelly sprinkled his brains along with his blood on the floor (horrible also to relate).

Thus the chaff overwhelms the grain of the fields, thus the custodian of the vineyard among the vines, the general in the camp, the shepherd in the sheepfold, the husbandman in the threshing floor, was murdered; thus the just man, slain by the unjust, exchanged his house of clay for the palace of heaven.

Becket was canonized by Pope Alexander III within three years of his murder, and his cult spread throughout Europe with astonishing rapidity. As discussed in Chapter 7, his shrine in Canterbury Cathedral became an important pilgrimage site, and drew throngs of people during the following centuries. Henry claimed that he had no intention of causing the archbishop's murder, but in 1174 he traveled to Becket's tomb to do penance for his part in the tragedy.

Henry ruled until his death in 1189. The last decades of his reign were fraught with problems initiated by his wife, Eleanor, from whom he had become estranged, and his sons, who were encouraged by the French king, Philip II "Augustus" (r. 1180–1223) to rebel against their father.

Henry had attempted to secure the succession to the throne smoothly, directing that his oldest son, Henry, be crowned in 1170. Unfortunately, the "Young King," as he was known, died in 1183, so that once again, a king's careful planning did not result in a smooth transition. However, Henry did have three remaining sons—Richard, Geoffrey, and John—two of whom would eventually wear the crown of England (see table, facing page). Shortly before Henry's death, Richard and John, in coalition with Philip Augustus of France, forced the old king to submit to their desired policies. His painful reaction was reflected in his final words, which, according to legend, were: "Shame, shame on a conquered king." His emotional response seems to have miraculously continued after death. As recounted by an anonymous contemporary chronicler in *The Deeds of King Henry II*:

The day after his death, when he was borne to burial, he lay in state robed in royal splendor, wearing a gold crown on his head, gauntlets on his hands and a gold ring on his finger, holding the scepter in his hand, with gold-braided shoes and spurs on his feet, girded with his sword, and his face uncovered. When this had been reported to Earl Richard, his son, he came post-haste to meet the cortège. At his

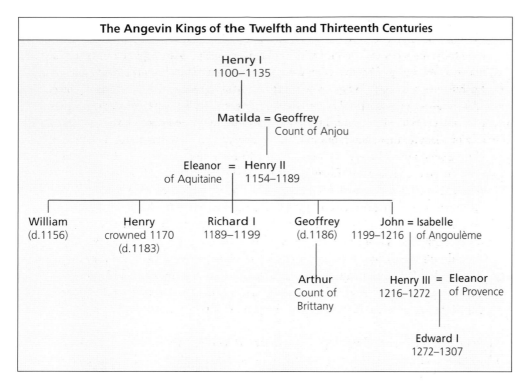

The Angevin Kings of the Twelfth and Thirteenth Centuries

Henry I
1100–1135

Matilda = **Geoffrey**
Count of Anjou

Eleanor = **Henry II**
of Aquitaine | 1154–1189

William (d.1156)   **Henry** crowned 1170 (d.1183)   **Richard I** 1189–1199   **Geoffrey** (d.1186)   **John** = **Isabelle** 1199–1216 | of Angoulème

Arthur Count of Brittany   **Henry III** = **Eleanor** 1216–1272 | of Provence

Edward I 1272–1307

coming blood began to flow forthwith from the dead king's nostrils as if his spirit was moved with indignation. Whereupon the said earl weeping and lamenting followed his father's corpse in procession as far as Fontevrault, where it was given burial.

And Benedictine monk and chronicler, Roger of Wendover reported that Richard, known as Richard the Lionheart (r. 1189–1199), was crowned shortly thereafter, promising that

> . . . he would observe peace, honor, and reverence, all his life, towards God, the holy Church and its ordinances: he swore also that he would exercise true justice toward the people committed to his charge, and abrogating all bad laws and unjust customs, if any such might be found in his dominions, would steadily observe those which were good.

Richard was first and foremost a warrior. According to the twelfth-century *Itinerarium Regis Ricardi*, "he surpassed all others both in his good character and in his great strength. Memorable in war and in his rule, his mighty deeds overshadow every manifestation of glory, however distinguished." Soon after his coronation, Richard eagerly "took up the cross" to set out on the Third Crusade. He was joined by two other western European monarchs, Frederick Barbarossa and Philip Augustus (see below).

While Richard was away, England was governed by a council led by his mother, Eleanor, and the archbishop of Canterbury Hubert Walter. During Richard's absence, his brother John attempted to wrest control of the government from the council, but he was destined to wait for his turn as king.

As Richard was traveling back to England after the crusade, he was captured by his enemy, the duke of Austria, who then, for a sum of money, delivered him into the custody of Emperor Henry VI of Germany. According to legend, while the king was imprisoned, he passed the long days in composing poetry and music, having been trained in the troubadour tradition fostered by his mother, Eleanor (see Chapter 10). Indeed, his whereabouts were supposedly discovered when one of his knights, searching for him, heard the king whistle a familiar troubadour melody. The following *Lament* gives an impression of Richard's psychological state while imprisoned in the German castle:

Ah, certes will no prisoner tell his tale
    Fitly, unless as one whom woes befall,
Still, as a solace, songs may much avail:
    Friends I have many, yet the gifts are small—
Shame! that because to ransom me they fail,
    I've pined two years in thrall [bondage].
But all my liegemen in fair Normandy,
    in England, Poitou, Gascony, know well
That not my meanest follower would I
    Leave for gold's sake in prison-house to dwell;
Reproach I neither kinsman nor ally—
    Yet I am still in thrall.

Alas! I may as certain truth rehearse,
    Nor kin nor friends have captives and the dead:
'Tis bad for men, but for my people worse,
    If to desert me they through gold are led;
After my death, 'twill be to them a curse
    If they leave me in thrall.

No marvel, then, if I am sad at heart
    Each day my lord disturbs my country more;
Has he forgot that he too had a part
    In the deep oath which before God we swore?
But yet in truth I know, I shall not smart
    Much longer here in thrall.

A huge ransom was demanded for Richard's safe return—£100,000—and the English managed to raise the sum by means of extraordinarily high taxation. Upon delivery of the ransom, Richard was released. He returned to rule England, but his time on the throne was short-lived (in fact, he spent only six months of his ten-year reign actually in his kingdom). In 1199, he was killed by a poisoned arrow while besieging the castle of an unruly vassal in southern France, and his brother John assumed the throne.

France

Louis VI ("the Fat") became king of France in 1108, ruling over a royal domain that was quite small in relation to the holdings of his vassals (see Map 12). Furthermore, his actual power was limited by the strength of the French magnates. He set about attempting to assert his authority, guided in his actions by Suger, the abbot of St.-Denis, who was an intelligent statesman, as well as an influential artistic patron (see Chapter 10). The king, with the advice of Suger, built an extensive staff of competent administrators, which eventually developed into an efficient royal bureaucracy. Suger's biography of the king, *The Life of Louis VI*, praised, with relative accuracy, the abilities and achievements of the king, who "proved himself an illustrious and courageous defender of his father's realm. He provided for the needs of the Church, and strove to secure peace for those who pray, for those who work, and for the poor. And no one had done this for a long time." Louis was determined to limit the power of his unruly vassals, and, as Suger described in his biography: "He stormed the strongest tower as if it were the hut of a peasant, and put to confusion the wicked men and piously destroyed the impious." When the barons saw that the king was quite able to tear down castles and deprive his vassals of their fiefs, they became more willing to submit to royal authority.

Shortly before the end of his reign (1137), Louis was presented with the opportunity to extend his territory significantly when the powerful Duke William of Aquitaine died, leaving only a young daughter, Eleanor, to inherit his holdings. According to feudal custom, it was the right of the vassal's liege lord to determine the marriage of a minor female, and Louis arranged Eleanor's marriage to his son, the future Louis VII (r. 1137–1180), thereby significantly expanding the holdings of the French crown. The addition of Aquitaine to the royal domain was not without problems, however; the vassals of the duke of Aquitaine were among the most difficult in the kingdom, and the king had very little real control over them.

Eleanor and Louis were married for fifteen years—but their natural incompatibility surfaced soon after the wedding ceremony. Louis, who became king within a year after their marriage, was a serious, pious, sober man, while Eleanor was devoted to the ideals of courtly troubadour society as practiced in southern France. She was perceived by the royal court to be shallow and frivolous, and unfit to reign as queen. The differences in temperament between Louis and Eleanor were exacerbated while they were on the Second Crusade, when Eleanor was accused of "flirtatious" behavior with her uncle Raymond, prince of Antioch. Furthermore, Eleanor had not borne a son; she and Louis had only two daughters. The couple agreed to separate, and a council of French bishops declared the marriage annulled on the grounds of **consanguinity**—Eleanor and Louis were too closely related. Within a short time, Eleanor had married Henry, duke of Normandy and count of Anjou, soon to be King Henry II of England. Louis later married Adèle of Blois, with whom he had a son, Philip, who was known as Philip Augustus when he became king. (The table on p. 270 contains a genealogical chart of the Capetian royal house.)

Louis had a positive relationship with the Church. He made frequent forays outside his domain to protect ecclesiastical establishments, and he received, in turn, several important ecclesiastical holdings as fiefs. In addition to supporting the Church, Louis

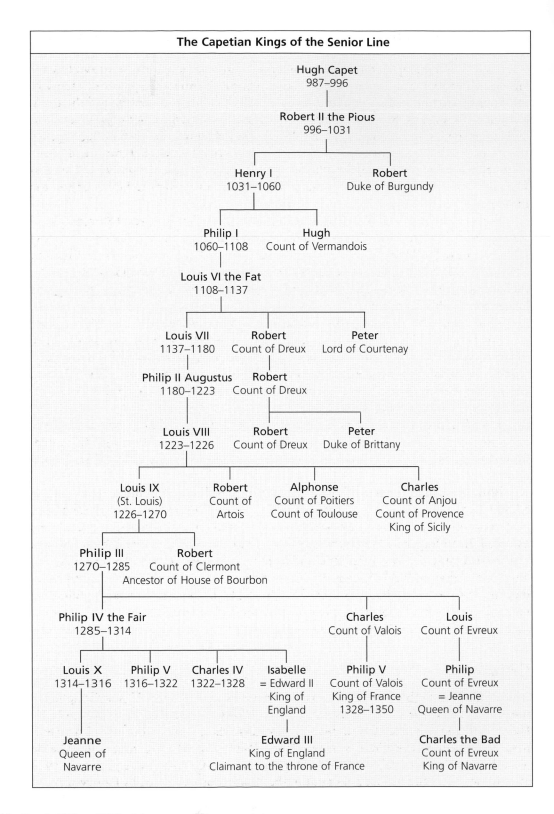

The Capetian Kings of the Senior Line

Hugh Capet
987–996

Robert II the Pious
996–1031

Henry I
1031–1060 — **Robert** Duke of Burgundy

Philip I
1060–1108 — **Hugh** Count of Vermandois

Louis VI the Fat
1108–1137

Louis VII
1137–1180 — **Robert** Count of Dreux — **Peter** Lord of Courtenay

Philip II Augustus
1180–1223 — **Robert** Count of Dreux

Louis VIII
1223–1226 — **Robert** Count of Dreux — **Peter** Duke of Brittany

Louis IX (St. Louis) 1226–1270 — **Robert** Count of Artois — **Alphonse** Count of Poitiers Count of Toulouse — **Charles** Count of Anjou Count of Provence King of Sicily

Philip III
1270–1285 — **Robert** Count of Clermont Ancestor of House of Bourbon

Philip IV the Fair
1285–1314 — **Charles** Count of Valois — **Louis** Count of Evreux

Louis X 1314–1316 — **Philip V** 1316–1322 — **Charles IV** 1322–1328 — **Isabelle** = Edward II King of England — **Philip V** Count of Valois King of France 1328–1350 — **Philip** Count of Evreux = Jeanne Queen of Navarre

Jeanne Queen of Navarre

Edward III King of England Claimant to the throne of France

Charles the Bad Count of Evreux King of Navarre

fostered the development of the city of Paris as a royal capital, a policy later continued by his son Philip.

Louis VII managed to maintain the growth in royal authority achieved by his father, and he took whatever action he could to curb the expanding power of Henry II. He supported Thomas Becket in his struggle with the king, and encouraged the revolt of Henry's sons against him. His own authority, however, was eroded by the powerful Blois family. His son Philip (r. 1180–1223) saw the necessity of buttressing royal strength against the house of Blois, and in order to assert his authority, he married the niece of the count of Flanders and formed an alliance with Henry II. These actions were successful, and Philip was king in all but name for at least a year before he inherited the throne in 1180.

Philip, known as Philip Augustus, realized that the greatest threat to French royal stability was the power of the Angevin monarchs, and in spite of his agreement with Henry II, he encouraged Henry's sons to revolt against their father. When Henry died in 1189, Philip was in an alliance with both Richard the Lionheart and John. As soon as Richard assumed the throne, however, Philip regarded him as a potential menace, and no longer courted his friendship.

Philip and Richard both participated in the Third Crusade, departing from Vézelay early in 1190. They quarreled constantly, and in July 1191 Philip decided to leave the campaign and return home. He claimed to be ill, but it is more likely that he had a political motive, seeing an opportunity to appropriate some of Richard's land. When Richard was imprisoned in Germany, Philip agreed to support John in seizing the throne, but the plot was not successful.

After Richard's death, John did finally assume the throne. Philip saw him as a less dangerous rival, however, and was successful in wresting much of the Angevin Empire from Plantagenet control—an achievement that quadrupled the revenue of the French crown.

Philip was also successful in strengthening royal power in other ways. In the administrative system, the royal court proved to be an effective instrument for asserting the rights of the king over the dukes and counts. Furthermore, building on the nucleus established by Suger and his father, Philip expanded the bureaucracy by creating a new class of officials drawn from the middle ranks of society. These were bound to the king, rather than to local officials, and since they owed their positions to royal favor, they were devoted to the interests of the king. By the time of his death in 1223, Philip had immeasurably strengthened French royal power, and had laid the foundations for the royal absolutism of the following centuries.

Germany

In 1125, following the death of the last of the Salian kings, Henry V (see Chapter 6), the princes of Germany elected Lothair, duke of Saxony, who reigned from 1125 to 1137. His actions as king fulfilled the desires of the electors, who chose him because of his weakness. When he died, the princes selected Conrad III (r. 1137–1152), of the Swabian house of Hohenstaufen (see table, p. 272.) During his reign Germany was plunged into a state of near anarchy, as Conrad's right to the throne was contested by Henry, duke of

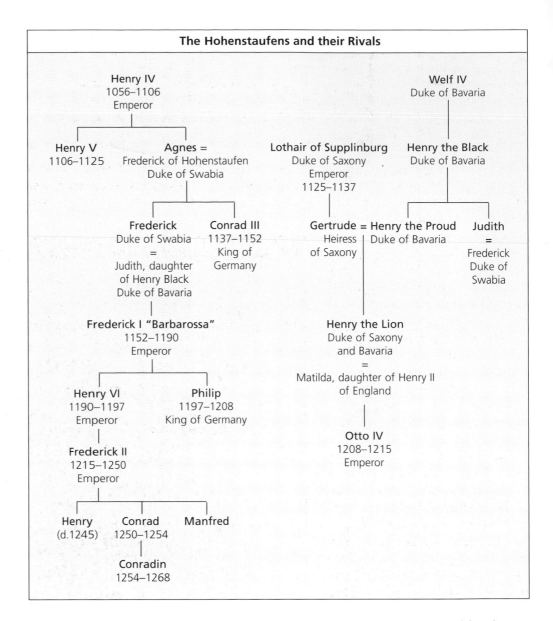

The Hohenstaufens and their Rivals

Henry IV
1056–1106
Emperor

Welf IV
Duke of Bavaria

Henry V
1106–1125

Agnes =
Frederick of Hohenstaufen
Duke of Swabia

Lothair of Supplinburg
Duke of Saxony
Emperor
1125–1137

Henry the Black
Duke of Bavaria

Frederick
Duke of Swabia
=
Judith, daughter
of Henry Black
Duke of Bavaria

Conrad III
1137–1152
King of
Germany

Gertrude = Henry the Proud
Heiress │ Duke of Bavaria
of Saxony

Judith
=
Frederick
Duke of
Swabia

Frederick I "Barbarossa"
1152–1190
Emperor

Henry the Lion
Duke of Saxony
and Bavaria
=
Matilda, daughter of Henry II
of England

Henry VI
1190–1197
Emperor

Philip
1197–1208
King of Germany

Otto IV
1208–1215
Emperor

Frederick II
1215–1250
Emperor

Henry
(d.1245)

Conrad
1250–1254

Manfred

Conradin
1254–1268

Bavaria. This Henry, head of the Hohenstaufens' rivals, the influential Welf family, was married to Gertrude, the daughter and heiress of Lothair; their son, Henry the Lion, inherited the duchies of both Saxony and Bavaria.

Frederick Barbarossa

The political climate changed, however, after Conrad's death in 1152, when the warring nobility decided to elect a strong king who could bring order and stability to the country. They chose a member of the Hohenstaufen dynasty and nephew of Conrad, Frederick I ("Barbarossa" or "Red Beard"), duke of Swabia, who reigned as German king and Holy Roman Emperor from 1152 to 1190. He was "desired by all, and with the approval of all," and he proved able to provide the necessary leadership. His mother was a member of the Welf family, and, according to the historian Otto of Freising:

> The princes, considering not only the energy and courage of the aforesaid young man, but also this fact, that as a member of both families, he might be able to bridge the gap between these two walls like a cornerstone, judged that he should be made the head of the kingdom.

Frederick required the German princes to swear homage to him, but he also allowed them to develop their own interests. He relied on the stronger magnates to curb the power of the lesser lords, who were forced into vassalage. In this way a more fully developed pattern of feudalism became a reality in Germany, although Frederick was careful to ensure that all feudal oaths acknowledged the king as overlord.

Thus, rather than attempting to reduce the power of the princes, Frederick was able to expand his authority into the kingdoms of Burgundy and Italy, with the ultimate goal of creating an empire that stretched from the North Sea to the Mediterranean. In 1156, he married Beatrice of Burgundy, thereby laying claim to her lands. He then turned to restoring imperial interests in Lombardy (**Map 19**). Since the reign of Henry IV, the nobility and merchant classes of the Lombard cities had become increasingly independent of imperial authority. They had freed themselves of the political control of the bishops, who were, in effect, representatives of the emperor, and had established self-governing communes. These communes were in competition with one another, however, and were thus unable to band together when Frederick resolved to reassert imperial control and marched into Italy. He then claimed that, as emperor, he should have a voice in choosing town officials, and that he was entitled to regular revenue from the communes.

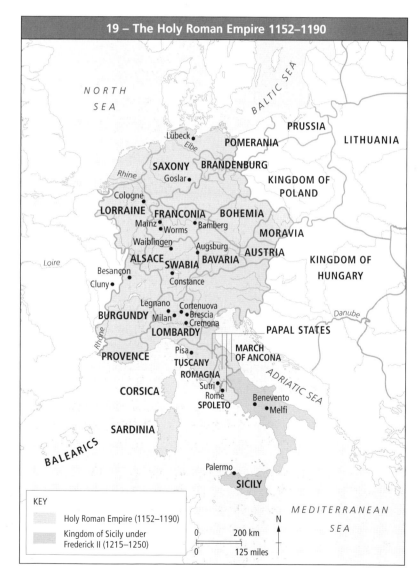

19 – The Holy Roman Empire 1152–1190

KEY

Holy Roman Empire (1152–1190)

Kingdom of Sicily under Frederick II (1215–1250)

0 — 200 km
0 — 125 miles

The papacy was immediately threatened by Frederick's action. The pope, Adrian IV (r. 1154–1159), was determined not to lose the gains in independence that had resulted from the Investiture Controversy (see Chapter 6). The two men met at Rome in 1155, but their encounter was troubled by questions of protocol. Would the king be willing, for example, to fulfill the usual custom of holding the pope's stirrup as he dismounted? Though the king finally complied with the established custom, it was indicative of problems to come; the pope did, however, crown him.

The pope was not unwilling to confirm the title of emperor as long as it held limited meaning, but he felt it necessary to assert his own authority. Accordingly, in 1157, he sent two legates to an imperial diet, or assembly, with a letter that referred to Frederick's possession of the empire as a *beneficium* (fief) held from the pope. Frederick responded with outrage in a "Manifesto," rejecting the claim and complaining that "from the head of the holy Church on which Christ impressed the character of his peace and love, causes of dissension, seeds of evil, the poison of a pestiferous disease seem to emanate." He feared that

> . . . the whole body of the Church will be tainted, the unity riven, a schism be
> brought about between the kingdom and the priesthood . . . [and] whoever shall say
> that we received the imperial crown as a benefice from the lord pope, contradicts
> the divine institutions and the teaching of Peter, and shall be guilty of a lie.

Adrian was forced to rescind his claim, asserting that his letter did not imply the meaning of *beneficium* as fief, but only as a "benefit."

When Adrian died in 1159, the cardinals elected Alexander III as pope. Frederick did not concur with the choice, and named his own alternative (rejected by Rome and labeled the "anti-pope"), creating a bitter feud with the papacy at the very time he was attempting to assert his authority in Italy.

In 1162, Milan was overrun by Frederick's army, and the emperor brought additional knights to rule northern Italy in his name. By 1167, the harsh measures employed by the imperial forces forced the communes to put aside their differences and form a defensive alliance with the support of the pope, known as the Lombard League. After several years of fighting, the Italian armies defeated imperial forces at the Battle of Legnano in 1176. Frederick was forced to make peace with the communes, and to recognize Alexander as pope. As stipulated in the treaty of Anagni:

> The emperor and the empress, and their son, King Henry, and all the princes
> promise to accept Pope Alexander III as the catholic and universal pope, and to
> show him such reverence as their predecessors were wont to show to his
> predecessors.

Frederick also agreed to return lands taken from the Church, and to restore to the pope the control of the civic government of Rome. Further, "The pope and the emperor will mutually aid one another in maintaining the honor and the rights of the empire and the Church."

Frederick's humiliating defeat was partly the result of the political situation in Germany. Many of the princes there had refused to send troops to support him. Most notable among these was Henry the Lion, the arrogant and ambitious duke of Saxony and Bavaria. Henry had requested that Frederick give him control over the area of Goslar, and when the emperor refused, he denied military aid for the imperial campaign in Italy.

Frederick returned to Germany, summoned Henry to court, and accused him of failing to fulfill his duties as a vassal of the emperor. He was charged with "oppressing the churches of God and the nobles of the empire by seizing their lands and violating their rights." Furthermore, Henry, "former duke of Bavaria and Westphalia . . . refused to obey our summons to present himself before us and has therefore incurred the ban." Henry was judged "contumacious," and by the unanimous sentence of the princes, was deprived of his fiefs. Thus, unable to rally effective support from his peers, he had no recourse but to accept the sentence, and was forced to go into exile at the court of his father-in-law, Henry II of England. Frederick, acting "under the advice of the princes," divided Henry's fiefs among them. This naturally earned him the support of the magnates, and he was able to emerge as the uncontested ruler of Germany.

Now that his position in his homeland was secure, Frederick returned to Italy, where he made conciliatory agreements with the communes of the Lombard League, guaranteeing that "the members of the league shall exercise freely and without interference from us all the rights which they have exercised of old." The cities were, however, obliged to pay taxes or tribute to the emperor, and the consuls of cities were required to "take the oath of allegiance to the emperor before they were invested with office." The emperor's vassals took the oath of fidelity to him, and received imperial investiture (see the discussion of investiture in Chapter 6). Furthermore, "all other persons between the ages of fifteen and seventy shall take the ordinary oath of fidelity to the emperor unless there be some good reason why this oath should be remitted." The cities of the League did retain a large measure of independence, however, since it was permitted for citizens to hold lands according to the customs of each city, and for the city government to erect fortifications. In addition, the League itself was permitted "to maintain its organization as it now is or to renew it as often as it desires."

Frederick next laid claim to some lands in central Italy, thus extending his base of power to that region. He divided the area into administrative districts and placed German officials in charge of collecting revenues. The emperor also arranged for his son to marry Constance, the aunt of William II of Sicily, who had a potential claim to that throne.

In 1190, while participating in the Third Crusade (see below), Frederick decided to swim in a river close to the castle of Selefke, on the road to Tarsus, in Asia Minor. According to one chronicler:

> It was very hot and he was a good swimmer. But the cold water overcame him and he sank. So the emperor, powerful by land and sea, met with an unfortunate death . . . If he had lived he would have been a terror to all the Orient, but by his death the army lost all its courage, and was overwhelmed with grief. His intestines and flesh were buried in Tarsus, but his bones were carried to Antioch and buried with royal ceremony.

Although Frederick failed in his attempt to create an empire extending from the northern tip of Europe to its southernmost point, he did establish a new sort of monarchy—one that was more feudal than those of his predecessors, and whose sources of power and revenue lay outside the German borders.

By the time of his death, the future political structure of Germany had not yet been determined, however. Although Frederick had demonstrated his power over the princes in his struggle with Henry the Lion, he had agreed that any fiefs that escheated to the crown would be regranted in a year and a day. This prevented his successors from amassing fiefs through the process of annexation—a means used by contemporaneous French kings to enhance their power. Furthermore, such widely separated sources of revenue as Tuscany and Frederick's own duchy of Swabia did not provide a stable foundation for a strong monarchy. However, if his successor had turned his attention to strengthening imperial control in Germany, subsequent history would probably have been very different.

Following Frederick's untimely death, the throne was inherited by his son, Henry VI (r. 1190–1197), who further shifted the imperial focus away from his homeland. Henry was assured of succession to the German throne, since he had already been crowned. However, he was soon tempted, as his father had been, by the throne of Sicily, where William II (r. 1166–1189) had died without an heir. The Mediterranean island soon became the center of imperial aspiration.

Rome and the Papal States

During the eleventh and twelfth centuries, the role of the papacy was transformed. Whereas the concerns of the papacy had previously been local, centered in the diocese of Rome, the bishop of Rome now became monarch of the entire western church, dedicated to reform and independence from secular control.

The early stages of this development took place during the papacy of Gregory VII, whose "Gregorian reform" and struggle with Emperor Henry IV were discussed in Chapter 6. The growing importance of the pope was evident when Urban II urged the First Crusade in 1087, and subsequent popes had become even more influential in European politics. The tradition of papal supremacy was appropriately summarized in the mid-twelfth century by Bernard of Clairvaux for the edification of Pope Eugenius III:

> According to your canons, some are called to a share of the responsibilities, but you are called to the fullness of power. The power of others is confined within definite limits, but your power extends even over those who have received power over others . . . [The pope] must rule not the people of this or that city or region or kingdom, . . . not one people but all people . . . the universal Church spread throughout the world, made up of all the churches.

In addition to directing the relationship between the Church and secular powers, the popes used their authority to reform and revitalize the structure of the Church, giving much power to the College of Cardinals and providing strict standards for clerical discipline. The popes also labored to inculcate Christian standards of behavior in the laity, sending **papal legates** throughout Christendom to link the directives of the papacy with the churches and courts of secular life. Hence, Roman pontiffs were deeply involved with the political issues of European society during the following centuries.

An important focus of interest for the papacy was the emergence of the Norman principalities in southern Italy and Sicily, since the new kingdoms were bound to the pope through feudal ties; the Norman princes swore fealty to the apostolic see, and the pope clearly delineated their responsibilities as vassals in a series of documents. Thus, as we shall see, the claims of the popes to feudal overlordship had practical results in their relations with their Norman neighbors.

The Norman Kingdoms of Southern Italy and Sicily

Sicily had been conquered by the Muslims in the first part of the ninth century, and their occupation of the island constituted a potent threat as a base of operations for their forays into southern Italy. The Muslims continued to capture cities, ransack the countryside, and threaten coastal settlements on the mainland, until they were finally driven from the island of Sicily by a coalition of papal soldiers and Byzantine naval forces. Their expulsion did not, however, bring peace to southern Italy, which remained in a state of political chaos. Some areas had long been ruled by Lombard chieftains, while others were controlled by Byzantine officers, and the competing factions were engaged in a succession of minor conflicts. Furthermore, the Muslims continued to harass travelers in the Mediterranean from their bases in northern Africa, making trade and pilgrimage to Rome hazardous ventures.

This turbulent situation provided an opportunity for northern European powers to interfere. In 982, the German emperor Otto II marched south from the city of Salerno under the pretext of "defending the Christian population." Although his expedition was a dismal failure, it proved to be the first in a series of incursions by warriors from the north.

In the eleventh century, according to legendary history, a group of Norman knights returning from a pilgrimage crossed into southern Italy. Observing the widespread political strife, they saw a potential outlet for their military abilities. Initially they functioned as mercenaries, fighting for monetary reward rather than out of loyalty to a leader. The Norman knights soon realized, however, that more permanent rewards could be gained by seeking to establish themselves as members of the ruling class. The first to do so was Rainulf, who in 1030 became count of Aversa.

The most famous of the Norman adventurers were three sons of a minor Norman nobleman named Tancred de Hauteville. They took part in a Byzantine expedition to conquer Sicily in 1038, and when the attack was unsuccessful, they turned against their employers and defeated them. By ruthless pillaging, the brothers were able to accumulate a fortune which provided the foundation for a famous dynasty. William de Hauteville became count of Apulia in 1042, although he did homage to an overlord, the Lombard Prince Gaimar of Salerno. His half-brother Robert, called Guiscard ("the Cunning"), established himself through marriage to Sichelgaita, the colorful and courageous Lombard princess mentioned in Chapter 5. Thus, in Italy, just as they were about to do in England, the Normans assimilated themselves into the aristocracy through a combination of military skill and diplomatic acumen. The Norman claim to southern Italian lands was confirmed in 1047 at an assembly held in Capua, attended by the emperor Henry III, and in 1059 Pope Leo IX officially recognized Robert as duke of Apulia and Calabria, and received homage from him for these fiefs.

Robert then turned his attention to conquering the remaining southern Italian land held by the Byzantine emperor, and sent his brother Roger to invade Sicily. Both expeditions were ultimately successful. Bari fell to Robert in 1071, bringing the last of the Byzantine areas of Italy under his control, and Palermo was conquered by the two brothers in 1072. The emirate of Taormina fell in 1079, and Roger completed the conquest of all of Muslim Sicily during the next twelve years (see Map 17).

In 1080, Roger swore fealty for his holdings to Pope Gregory VII, rather than Emperor Henry IV of Germany, as might have been expected. Scholars have seen this action as indicative of a quest on the part of the Norman rulers to establish international recognition. An alliance with the papacy was an important step along the path leading to the creation of a kingdom.

Roger I was able to build a strong centralized government by adapting the existing Sicilian administration to his needs. He ruled commoners and clergy through a bureaucracy that attempted to treat the Lombard, Byzantine, and Muslim citizens equally. Arabs and Jews were subject to a special tax, but the Norman charters, like Arab documents, demanded that "Latins, Greeks, Jews, and Saracens shall be judged each according to their own law," and by their own judges. This royal desire for justice and inclusive administration was demonstrated by the fact that government documents were issued in three languages: Latin, Greek, and Arabic.

Roger's court was characterized by formal ceremony and autocratic power, reflecting Byzantine tradition, and many of the administrative positions were of Byzantine or Islamic origin. Norman custom was recognizable in the appointment of officials such as **justiciars**, chamberlains, and constables, as well as the *curia*, an assembly of nobles who might be consulted for advice; however, the dignitaries clearly disseminated the directives of an all-powerful monarch. A traditional feudal hierarchy pertained in the organization of the barons and knights, and their responsibilities and obligations to the king were recorded in a "catalog of barons." Roger also employed a large and effective mercenary force, and he maintained a strong fleet.

The tolerance that characterized the government of Norman Sicily pervaded the island's cultural and religious life as well. For example, a Muslim writer who visited Palermo in 1184 remarked that the numerous Muslims who served as important government functionaries were given the freedom to practice their own faith. Thus, although the king fostered the spread of Latin Christianity through the endowment of new monasteries, both Greek and Latin, it is evident that other religious traditions were permitted.

When Roger I died, his third wife, Adelaide, became regent for Roger's heir, who was still a minor. Adelaide was of northern Italian origin, and her family associations resulted in a significant immigration of Lombards to Sicily. During her reign, Palermo was designated as the capital, probably because she observed that Sicily was less chaotic politically than southern Italy, and it provided a better source of revenue.

The date when Roger II assumed control of the throne is uncertain, though he certainly became count of Sicily before 1113, when his mother was foolish enough to marry King Baldwin of Jerusalem. According to eyewitnesses, her fleet presented a dazzling appearance as she departed for the Holy Land; her galley had a gold- and silver-plated prow, and the interior was carpeted with a cloth of woven gold. The marriage undoubtedly resulted in a significant loss of wealth to Sicily. Baldwin seems to have been interested only in Adelaide's dowry, which he needed to provide pay in arrears for his soldiers. In any case, he already had another wife, and when he had spent Adelaide's money, he easily convinced the pope to annul the marriage.

Some scholars have suggested that Roger may have encouraged his mother's misadventure in order to further his own cause. In any case, he soon proved himself to be a highly effective ruler, building his inherited country into a kingdom. When Robert Guiscard's grandson died in 1127, Roger took his holdings in southern Italy, and in 1130 his ambitions were realized when he was given the title "king of Sicily, the duchy of Apulia, and the principality of Capua," as vassal of the pope. The aristocracy ostensibly shed their Norman identity and their rulers were called "king of the Sicilians." Roger's kingdom extended north to the Papal States, where its frontier was marked roughly by the Tronto River on the Adriatic and the Garigliano River on the Tyrrhenian Sea.

The Norman kings of Sicily patronized scholars of Muslim and Byzantine origin, including the Arab geographer al-Edrisi, who dedicated his *Book of King Roger* to Roger II. Roger's son, William I of Sicily, who reigned from 1154 to 1166, also supported various intellectuals, including the Greek Eugenios, who was the translator of Ptolemy's *Optics* from Arabic into Latin, and Henry, known as "Aristippus," who translated Plato's *Meno* and *Phaedo* from Greek into Latin. There was an important school of Greek philosophy at Apulia, where famous scholars such as John of Salisbury came to study, and the medical school at Salerno was internationally recognized as the most important in Europe (see Chapter 13).

The court of Roger II was a particularly cosmopolitan synthesis of cultural influences from Byzantium, Islam, and the west. The combination is best exemplified by the Palatine Chapel, which was Roger's personal chapel in the palace at Palermo (**fig. 91**). The elaborate ceiling, made of painted wood, was constructed by Muslims, and Byzantine craftsmen were employed to create the mosaic program, which reflected the religious and political attitudes of western Europe. The saints portrayed in the mosaics were St. Martin and St. Dionysius, both of whom were associated with French tradition.

91 The Palatine Chapel in the royal palace of Roger II at Palermo, Sicily, was used as a public audience hall, as well as a private place of worship for the rulers. The most striking feature of the chapel is an intricate ceiling made of painted wood, which resembles a stalactite formation. Muslim artists created the ceiling, and Byzantine craftsmen were employed to produce the elaborate mosaics decorating the walls and arches of the room—a vivid demonstration of the cultural influences at work within the Sicilian court.

Roger's royal aspirations are made abundantly clear in a mosaic from the Church of the Martorana in Palermo (**fig. 92**). His ceremonial robes are depicted in a distinctly Byzantine style, and he is being crowned by Christ himself, rather than by the pope. This imagery reflects Byzantine iconographical tradition, as discussed in Chapter 2.

William II (r. 1166–1189), who married Joanna, the daughter of Henry II, also patronized ecclesiastical establishments and artists as well as scholars. The cathedral he founded at Monreale is famous for its mosaic program as well as its architectural features. In one of the mosaics, William is portrayed offering a model of the church to the Virgin Mary (**fig. 93**). Images such as this, in which the donor is shown presenting a representation of the building to Christ

92 Roger II's divine right to rule is emphasized in this beautiful mosaic, in the twelfth-century Church of the Martorana in Palermo, which shows Christ, rather than the pope, crowning the monarch. The use of typical Byzantine imagery and the medium of mosaic may symbolize Roger's desire to conquer the Byzantine Empire.

93 This mosaic from the cathedral at Monreale shows its founder, William II, dressed in elaborate robes, offering a model of the building to the Virgin Mary; he is blessed by the hand of God, which appears between the observing angels. William intended the cathedral to serve as the burial place for himself and subsequent Norman rulers.

or the Virgin Mary, were common features of twelfth-century architectural decoration. They are often found in stained-glass windows as well as mosaic ornament.

Among the portraits of saints in the mosaics at Monreale is the earliest-known image of the martyred archbishop of Canterbury, Thomas Becket. Scholars have speculated that William's wife, Joanna, a daughter of Henry II, may have wished to have Becket portrayed in the cathedral that she and her husband sponsored as a form of penance for her father's role in the archbishop's murder. Whatever the motivation for the portrait, the mosaic imagery in Sicilian churches and palaces built during the reigns of Roger II, William I, and William II had enormous influence in the development of the art of northwestern Europe, especially in Germany and England. One example of this strong effect may be seen in the illuminations in the Winchester Bible, created by seven different artists in England around 1160–1175. Today it is in the library of Winchester Cathedral.

William's marriage to Joanna in 1177 was an example of the careful establishment of alliances with European countries that the Norman rulers cultivated through marriage diplomacy. They also preferred to encourage friendly relations with neighboring Arab countries, and did not participate directly in the crusades, but chose to profit instead from the luxury trade emanating from Egypt and the ports of northern Africa.

The Norman dynasty in Sicily ultimately collapsed, as we saw earlier in this chapter, with the death of William II, who had no male heir. William thus arranged the marriage of his aunt Constance to Henry, the son of Emperor Frederick Barbarossa. This was not a popular action, and when William died and Henry VI arrived to claim his wife's inheritance, civil war erupted. Henry was eventually victorious, and was crowned king of Sicily in 1194. The rich Mediterranean jewel was now a possession of the Hohenstaufens, and it became a focus of the imperial designs of the thirteenth century.

Spain and Portugal

By the early twelfth century, as discussed in Chapter 7, Christian monarchs had extended their control over northern Spain. The Castilian kings had moved as far south as the Tagus River, and the Aragónese and the Catalans had advanced to the Ebro. By 1077, Alfonso VI of Castile (r. 1065–1109) had been successful in establishing Christian hegemony throughout the area.

The last years of Alfonso's reign were characterized by the struggle of the king to unite Castile with Aragón, and witnessed the economic triumph of ranching interests, as well as the advance of clerical power. During the same period, a number of contentious issues also arose between townspeople and peasants. These are well documented by an anonymous chronicler of the abbey of Sahagun, or San Fagondey, in León, north-central Spain:

> Accordingly, inasmuch as the said king [Alfonso VI] had ordered . . . that there should be a town there, townsmen [burguéses] of many and various kinds and trades came from all parts of the world—smiths, carpenters, tailors, furriers, and shoemakers. These men also included many from foreign provinces and kingdoms—Gascons, Bretons, Germans, English, Burgundians, Normans, Toulousains, Provençals, Lombards, and many other merchants of divers nations and strange

languages. And thus he populated and created a considerably sized town. Then the king decreed and ordered that none of those living in the town should have a field, vineyard, orchard, plot, or mill within the lands of the monastery unless the abbot should grant it on terms and conditions; but they could have houses in the town, provided that they each paid a yearly sum of money to the abbot as a rent and in recognition of his lordship. . . . Furthermore, he ordered that all should bake their bread in the monastery's oven, and this was such a vexing and troublesome matter for the townsmen and inhabitants that they entreated the abbot with many prayers to make it legal and permissible for them to bake their bread wherever they wished, provided that they each paid him a yearly sum of money. This was granted to them and written up in a signed document whereby every year all the townsmen and inhabitants would each pay two sums of money to the monastery: one sum at Christmas for the oven, and another at All Saints as rent and recognition of lordship. . . . and because the merchants and burguéses of Sahagun disposed of their merchandise peacefully and traded without fear, they came and brought goods from all parts, such as gold and silver and even all kinds of fashions of clothes. Thus the townsmen and inhabitants were very rich and well supplied with many delightful things.

When Alfonso VI died in 1109, he left only his widowed daughter, Urraca, to inherit the Castilian throne. According to custom, a woman alone could not govern, and she was soon married to the only reigning king in Spain, Alfonso I ("the Battler"), king of Aragón (r. 1104–1134). The marriage was a political and conjugal disaster from the beginning. The queen was stubborn and independent by nature, and Alfonso the Battler, besides being a misogynist, was a pious crusader who devoted himself to military campaigns against the Muslims. Furthermore, the transition to a new monarchy coincided with a period of revolt by the rural workers and the townspeople of Aragón. The peasants demanded that the customary services due to their landlords be lessened, and the residents of the towns resisted paying a supplementary Easter tax. Moreover, they sought royal, rather than monastic, control of the forests, vineyards, and mills. There was also dissension within the clergy, as the rural clerics protested against the economic privileges granted to the Cluniac monasteries. The revolt rapidly spread into the area of Castile and León.

The clergy and nobility in both kingdoms sought the support of Queen Urraca, while the peasants and the townspeople rallied around Alfonso. The problem of these competing alliances was ultimately solved when the nobles secured a papal annulment of the marriage, citing consanguinity (the king and queen were second cousins). Furthermore, in 1116 and 1117 the pope issued several bulls (edicts) that required landholders to return to the monasteries all the lands that they had confiscated within the last five years. Alfonso ultimately withdrew from the struggle and returned to his crusading activity, leaving Urraca's son by her first marriage to succeed him as Alfonso VII of Castile-León.

The social revolt resulted eventually in the victory of the aristocracy, and some of the townspeople who had led the revolt were forced to leave the country. Society continued to be composed of aristocrats and peasants, warriors, priests, and shepherds, while the development of urban social classes was less rapid than in other areas of Europe.

The Spanish kings found it expedient to form close alliances with the papacy, and to ready themselves for continued war "for the Faith," against the Muslims. This bellicose attitude led Alfonso, according to the Arab chronicler al-Maqqari, to "send messengers . . . summoning all the Christian nations to come and help him" to expand Christian power. In 1118, a council was held at Toulouse to discuss plans for an attack against the Muslims, and Pope Gelasius II (r. 1118–1119) granted remission of sins to all those who participated. The recognition of Spain as a valid area for crusade was further specified in a bull of Eugenius III (r. 1145–1153), issued in 1148.

There were several advantages in the declaration of an official crusade. It enhanced military morale, encouraged Hispano-Christian political unity, and provided financial support through the granting of special subsidies. Furthermore, the twelfth century witnessed the creation in Spain of military orders modeled on the Templars and the Hospitallers; these were the Order of Calatrava, founded in 1158, and the Order of Santiago, which was confirmed by the pope in 1175.

Early in the twelfth century, the kingdom of Portugal began to develop as a separate entity. Before this time, much of the northern area of modern Portugal had been a dependent constituency of the Spanish kingdom of León, but in the 1130s the count of this territory—Alfonso Henrigues—rebelled, attacking both the Muslims and his cousin and overlord, the king of Léon. As the result of a victory over the Muslims at Ourique in 1139, Alfonso began to call himself "King of Portugal," although he was forced to recognize his cousin as overlord. The title of king was officially confirmed by the pope in 1179, when Alfonso pledged vassalage to the papacy. A fortuitous occurrence in 1143 enabled Alfonso to expand his territory to the south, when crusaders from England, Flanders, and Germany captured Lisbon and gave the territory to the Portuguese king. Thus, by the middle of the twelfth century, Portugal, Castile, and Aragón were the most significant Christian kingdoms in the Spanish peninsula, which was now half Muslim and half Christian.

In the meantime, a new and more aggressive Muslim cult was developing in northern Africa, led by a zealous preacher, Mohammed Abda. Abda and his followers, known as Almohades, advocated a return to the precepts of the Qur'an—to the "true religion"—and his fanatically monotheistic tribe was able to defeat the Almoravides in northern Africa, thereby establishing their control of a region extending from Egypt to Morocco. By 1147, they had moved north and conquered southern Spain. The Almohades were able to bring prosperity to the areas under their hegemony, and gradually lost some of their fanaticism as they were assimilated into the existing society. Their years of rule in southern Spain (1147–1214) were characterized by cultural development, and continued the earlier widespread interest in Persian philosophy and art, Greek philosophy and medicine, mathematics, and literature. Two of the most famous scholars of the twelfth century were educated in this milieu: Ibn Rushd, known in the west as Averroës (1126–1198), and Maimonides (1135–1204), also known as Rabbi Moses ben Maimon.

Averroës achieved the deepest understanding of Aristotle of any philosopher prior to the thirteenth century. He studied all of the works of Aristotle, although only his commentaries on logic, natural philosophy, cosmology, psychology, and metaphysics have survived. The Almohad rulers were suspicious of writings that attempted to harmonize Islamic teaching and Greek philosophy, and some of the writings of Averroës were destroyed as a result of official inquiry by the Almohad authorities. Nevertheless, his writings concerning Aristotelian philosophy were particularly influential in the recovery of Aristotle's thought that characterized the intellectual life of western Europe in the thirteenth century (see Chapter 13). At that time, Averroës' commentaries were soon recognized as the most authoritative works on Aristotle, and when they were translated into Latin he became known among scholars as "the Commentator."

Maimonides was educated in Spain, but, finding the intellectual climate restrictive, he moved to Egypt during the reign of the Almohades. There he functioned as court physician to the local ruler, and served his fellow Jews as their chief rabbi. Maimonides, like Averroës, believed that the writings of Aristotle represented the high point of philosophical discourse, and his goal was to synthesize Aristotelian thought with the Jewish intellectual and religious tradition. His most famous work, the *Guide to the Perplexed*, is a rigorous assimilation of Jewish theology and Aristotelianism.

The rule of the Almohades came to an end in the thirteenth century. By 1212, the Christian soldiers from the northern kingdoms, responding to the papal call for a crusade, were once again marching on areas under Muslim control, and they achieved a significant victory at the Battle of Las Navas de Tolosa, south of Toledo. This broke the power of the Almohades, and the Christians returned to their usual practice of fighting among themselves until the Reconquista resumed in earnest in 1236 under Fernando III (see Chapter 11).

The Second and Third Crusades

In 1144, the Greek city of Edessa, recaptured from the Muslims in the First Crusade, was again conquered by the emir of Mosul. This prompted Pope Eugenius III, after his election the following year, to preach another crusade to the knights of western Europe:

> Now, because of our sins and the sins of the people in the east . . . the city
> of Edessa . . . has been taken by the enemies of the cross of Christ, and many
> Christian fortresses have been seized by them. The archbishop of Edessa and his
> clergy and many other Christians have been killed there. The relics of the saints
> have been trampled under foot by the infidels and scattered. You know as well as
> we how great a danger is threatening the Church and the whole Christian world.
> If you bravely defend those things which the courage of your fathers acquired, it will
> be the greatest proof of your nobility and worth. But if not, it will be shown that you
> have less bravery than your fathers. Therefore we exhort, ask, command, and for the
> remission of your sins, we order all of you, and especially the nobles and the more
> powerful, to arm yourselves manfully to defend the oriental Church, and to attack
> the infidels and to liberate the thousands of your brethren who are now their
> captives, that the dignity of the Christian name may be increased, and your
> reputation for courage, which is praised throughout the world, may remain unimpaired.

Eugenius was concerned that only seriously committed knights should go on the crusade, and he cautioned the knights to avoid clothing themselves in ways that might indicate frivolous intent:

Since those who fight for the Lord should not have their minds set on fine clothing, or personal decoration, or [hunting] dogs, or falcons, or other things which savor of worldliness, we urge you to take care that those who undertake so holy a journey shall not deck themselves out with gay clothing and furs, or with gold and silver weapons, but that they shall try to supply themselves with such arms, horses, and other things as will aid them to defeat the infidels.

Eugenius's plea was reinforced by Bernard of Clairvaux, who brought his considerable persuasive powers to bear in convincing the nobles to take the cross. Bernard's views of crusading knighthood and its spiritual rewards were described with his customary eloquence in his treatise "In Praise of the New Knighthood":

The knight of Christ, I say, is safe in slaying, safer if he is slain. He is accountable to himself when he is slain, to Christ when he slays. "For he beareth not the sword in vain: for his is the minister of God, a revenger to execute wrath upon him that doeth evil, to praise him that doeth good." For when he kills a malefactor, he does not commit homicide but, I might say, malicide, and is clearly reputed to be the vindicator of Christ, bringing punishment to evildoers, and praise in truth to good men. Moreover, when he is himself killed, it is known that he does not perish, but triumphs. The death he inflicts is Christ's gain; the death he dies, his own. The Christian is glorified in the death of a pagan, because hereby Christ is glorified; in the death of a Christian, the liberality of the King is shown, when the knight is led to his reward.

The force that departed on the Second Crusade was led by two of the monarchs of western Europe: Louis VII of France and Conrad III of Germany, Frederick Barbarossa's predecessor. Although we cannot determine the number of knights who accompanied them, their armies were probably not sizeable, since few important noblemen joined them in their adventure. Louis, as was mentioned earlier in this chapter, was accompanied by his wife, Eleanor, who brought with her a number of court ladies. They no doubt aroused a great deal of attention, since they costumed themselves as Amazons, riding bare-breasted until sunburn got the better of them.

Conrad's army made its way across land to Nicea, and from there began the march to Edessa. Within ten days his forces were attacked by Turks, and almost completely destroyed. Conrad and a small portion of his army managed to retreat to Nicea, where they planned to board a ship for the Holy Land. Louis, who arrived at Nicea in time to witness Conrad's return, decided to move on by way of land. His army was also subjected to Turkish attack, and he lost his provisions and many of his horses. He then marched his men to the coast, where most of them boarded ships for Antioch. Unfortunately, there were not enough ships for the entire army, and those who attempted a land crossing were soon annihilated by the Turks.

After arriving at Antioch, Louis decided to travel on to Jerusalem, where he met Conrad and the remainder of his army. The two kings joined forces to attack Damascus, and the siege was successful in its initial phases. Conrad and Louis soon quarreled, however, with the result that the former returned home. Louis could not proceed with the assault on his own, and gave up the fight. So ended the Second Crusade—a phase in the ongoing Holy War that brought nothing of benefit to the Christian forces. The survivors of the crusade complained bitterly that their failure to capture Damascus was the result of the defection by supporting troops recruited from the crusader kingdoms, who had been tempted away by Muslim gold.

Towards the end of the twelfth century, the European knights responded to yet another call to free the Holy Land. As recounted by the Christian writer, Otto of St. Blasien in his *Chronicle*:

> In the year 1187, Saladin, king of the Saracens, seeing the very base conduct of the Christians, and knowing that they were afflicted with discord, hatred, and avarice, thought the time was favorable and so planned to conquer all Syria with Palestine. He collected a very large army of Saracens from all the orient and made war on the Christians. Attacking them everywhere in Palestine with fire and sword, he took many fortresses and cities and killed or took prisoner all their Christian inhabitants, and put Saracen colonists in their place. The king of Jerusalem and the noble prince Reinaldus [of Chatillon, governor of Kerak], and other nobles collected a large army and went out to meet Saladin. The True Cross was carried at the head of the army.

The battle between the forces of Saladin (r. 1169–1193) and those of Reinaldus and the king of Jerusalem took place at Hattin on July 4, 1187. It proved to be an unmitigated disaster for the Christian forces. Their army was annihilated, and most of the leaders were taken prisoner; according to Otto, several were personally beheaded by Saladin. Even worse, the True Cross, most precious of all relics—on which Christ was believed to have died—was captured by the Muslims.

As may be anticipated, the Muslim chronicler, Baha al-Din Ibn Shaddad, provided a very different perspective in his *Rare and Excellent History of Saladin*, explaining the background for Saladin's actions:

> The forces of Islam surrounded the forces of unbelief and impiety on all sides, loosed volleys of arrows at them and engaged them hand to hand. One group fled and was pursued by our Muslim heroes. Not one of them survived. Another group took refuge on a hill called the Hill of Hattin, the latter being a village near which is the tomb of Shu'ayb (on him and on the rest of the prophets be blessings and peace). The Muslims pressed hard upon them on that hill and lit fires around them. Their thirst was killing and their situation became very difficult, so that they began to give themselves up as prisoners for fear of being slain. Their commanders were taken captive, but the rest were either killed or taken prisoner . . . The sultan [Saladin] had vowed to kill Prince Reynald [Reinaldus] if he got him in his power. This was because a caravan from Egypt had passed through his land at Shawbak during the state of truce. They halted there under safe conduct, but he treacherously killed them. The sultan heard of this and religion and his zeal encouraged him to swear that, if he seized his person, he would kill him. After God had bestowed the great victory on him, the sultan sat in the entrance lobby of his tent . . . and, having summoned Prince Reynald, confronted him as he had said. He said to him, "Here I

am having asked for victory through Muhammad, and God has given me victory over you." He offered him Islam but he refused. The sultan then drew his scimitar and struck him, severing his arm at his shoulder. Those present finished him off and God speedily sent his soul to Hell-fire.

After the battle at Hattin, Saladin moved immediately to conquer most of the Christian territory, including Jerusalem, accomplishing his objective within three months. According to Otto of St. Blasien, "Jerusalem was taken [on October 2, 1187], and the holy places were profaned and inhabited by pagans."

Although the call for a new crusade against the infidel was proclaimed within a short time, it took nearly two years for the knights of western Europe to prepare themselves to travel to the Holy Land. The first to respond was Frederick Barbarossa, who was able to gather a large and efficient army. He was joined by Richard I (Richard the Lionheart) of England and Philip Augustus of France, who had been convinced by papal representatives to cease quarreling with each other and join the Third Crusade. Since both monarchs would be away on crusade, neither one could take advantage of the absence of the other to make territorial incursions. When Saladin heard of the massive forces arrayed against him, he summoned additional troops to fend off the invading crusaders.

As mentioned earlier, Frederick drowned on the way to the Holy Land—an accident that the Muslims viewed as a miraculous sign of Allah's favor. Philip Augustus and Richard, by now under way, seemed to be in no hurry to reach the battle front. They stayed in Sicily for the winter, before moving on eventually to Acre, in what is now northwest Israel, which they conquered on July 12, 1191. The city would remain the capital of the crusader states for a century.

Soon afterwards, Philip returned to France on the pretext of ill health, and Richard made plans to push on towards Jerusalem. Before departing, however, he massacred the Muslim prisoners at Acre. According to Baha al-Din Ibn Shaddad in his history of Saladin:

When the king of England saw that the sultan hesitated to hand over the money, the prisoners, and the Cross, he dealt treacherously towards the Muslim prisoners. He had made terms with them and had received the surrender of the city on condition that they would be guaranteed their lives come what may, and that, if the sultan delivered what was agreed, he would free them together with their possessions, children, and womenfolk, but that, if the sultan refused to do so, he would reduce them to slavery and captivity. The accursed man deceived them and revealed what he had hidden in his heart. He carried out what, according to the subsequent reports of his co-religionists, he had intended to do after taking the money and the prisoners. He and all the Frankish forces, horse and foot, marched out at the time of the afternoon prayer on Tuesday 27 Rajab [August 20] and came to the wells beneath the Tell al-'Ayyadiyya. They brought their tents forward as far as that and then moved on into the middle of the plain between Tell Kaysan when the Franks moved their tents forward to Tell al-Ayyadiyya. The enemy then brought out the Muslim prisoners for whom God had decreed martyrdom, about 3,000 bound in ropes. Then as one man they charged them and with stabbings and blows with the sword they slew them in cold blood, while the Muslim advance guard watched, not knowing what to do because they were at some distance from them. The Muslims had already sent to the sultan and informed him of the enemy's move and their new position and he had sent reinforcements. When the enemy had finished, the Muslims attacked them and a great battle ensued, in which men were killed and wounded on both sides. It continued until nightfall.

In the morning the Muslims investigated what had happened, found the martyrs where they had fallen and were able to recognize some of them. Great sorrow and distress overwhelmed them for the enemy had spared only men of standing and position or someone strong and able-bodied to labor on their building works. Various reasons were given for this massacre. It was said they had killed them in revenge for their men who had been killed or that the king of England had decided to march to Ascalon to take control of it and did not think it wise to leave that number in his rear. God knows best.

Saladin's forces harassed the army as it moved south, "lying in wait at a distance out of sight like a lion in his den, and . . . intent on killing the friends of the cross like sheep led to the slaughter," but Richard was able to repulse Saladin at Arsuf. The two armies fought various skirmishes along the coast, since Richard was reluctant to risk moving inland to Jerusalem because his army might be cut off from its supply lines. When he finally did approach the Holy City, the Muslims were able to withstand his advance.

Fighting continued for more than a year, alternating with negotiations between Richard and Saladin. The two leaders finally agreed on a treaty that left Jerusalem under Muslim control, but which granted permission for Christians to visit the holy sites; the crusaders were also allowed to retain the coast from Tyre to Jaffa. Thus, the achievements of the Third Crusade were modest. Most of the Holy Land was still in Muslim hands. Saladin had successfully held off the invading forces led by the most important kings of western Europe. And while the crusader states continued to control Acre and the coastal area during the following half-century, this was due primarily to the dissension that occurred among Saladin's heirs after his death in March, 1193.

Summary

During the twelfth century, the kings of the northern European countries—England, France, and Germany—furthered their royal interests through the establishment of military power and bureaucratic control. In England and France, the Plantagenet dynasty founded by Henry II and Eleanor of Aquitaine ruled a vast area known as the Angevin Empire. Their holdings were thus far greater than those of the French kings, although the Capetians continued to solidify their rule during the reigns of Louis VI, Louis VII, and Philip Augustus. The throne of Germany passed to the Hohenstaufen dynasty, and Frederick I ("Barbarossa") expanded his imperial holdings into Burgundy and Italy.

One of the most fascinating developments of the twelfth century occurred in southern Italy and Sicily, where Norman adventurers were able to establish themselves as rulers. Roger I, Roger II, and William II presided over sophisticated courts cast in the Byzantine mold, where they patronized scholars and artists and fostered a brilliant intellectual environment.

In Spain, the Reconquista continued, as Christian forces from the north moved south to conquer Muslim territories, and to extend the control of Christian kingdoms. The Islamic culture in the south provided a fertile environment for scholarly activity, and important translators worked to produce Arabic versions of ancient Greek treatises. The twelfth century also witnessed the initial phases of Portuguese autonomy, as King Alfonso was able to develop an independent realm.

Louis VII and Conrad III of Germany participated in the Second Crusade, which proved to be an ineffective chapter in the struggle against the Muslims for control of the Holy Land. The Third Crusade, led by Frederick Barbarossa, Richard the Lionheart, and Philip Augustus, was equally ineffectual, as they were not able to inflict a decisive defeat on the forces of Saladin. A truce was ultimately negotiated that left the crusaders in control of Acre and some coastal areas; Jerusalem continued to be ruled by the Muslims, but visitation privileges were granted to Christian pilgrims.

The political developments of the twelfth century, coupled with the revival of towns and trade to be discussed in the next chapter, took place alongside a vibrant revival of intellectual life—an era often characterized as one of renaissance and renewal.

Suggestions for Further Reading

Primary sources

The translation of Baha al-Din Ibn Shaddad's *The Rare and Excellent History of Saladin*, by D.S. Richards (Aldershot, U.K.: Ashgate, 2001), presents a vivid account of the Muslim view of Saladin's reign. Peter W. Edbury's volume *The Conquest of Jerusalem and the Third Crusade: Sources in Translation* (Aldershot, U.K.: Scolar Press, 1996) provides a translation of the Old French continuation of the chronicle of William of Tyre, covering the years 1184–1197, and a valuable collection of sources, including an account of the Battle of Hattin and the adventures of Richard the Lionheart in the Holy Land.

An excellent collection of sources that give the Muslim perspective on the crusades may be found in *Arab Historians of the Crusades*, by Francesco Gabrieli (London: Routledge & Kegan Paul, 1969).

Documents concerning the reigns of English kings discussed in this chapter are collected in *English Historical Documents: 1042–1189*, vol. 2, edited by David C. Douglas and George W. Greenaway (2nd ed., London: Eyre Methuen, 1981). Abbot Suger's *The Deeds of Louis the Fat*, translated by Richard Cusimano and John Moorhead (Washington, D.C.: Catholic University of America Press, 1992), is an excellent contemporaneous biography of the twelfth-century French ruler.

Letters of the Queens of England: 1100–1547, edited by Anne Crawford (Phoenix Mill, UK: Alan Sutton, 1994), includes letters of the Angevin queens Eleanor of Aquitaine, Berengaria of Navarre, Isabella of Angoulême, and Eleanor of Provence.

Secondary sources

The Making of England to 1399, by C. Warren Hollister, Robert C. Stacey, and Robin Chapman Stacey (8th ed., Boston: Houghton Mifflin Co., 2001), provides a good introduction to the political and social history of England. *Thomas Becket*, by Frank Barlow (Berkeley: University of California Press, 1986), is the best biography of the martyred archbishop. W.L. Warren's biography *Henry II* (Berkeley: University of California Press, 1973) provides a comprehensive view of Henry and the Angevin Empire.

A classic account of the Capetian kings is Robert Fawtier's *The Capetian Kings of France:*

Monarchy and Nation, 987–1328, translated by Lionel Butler and R.J. Adam (New York: St. Martin's Press, 1960).

Two excellent books that analyze the development of the papacy during the eleventh and twelfth centuries are *The Papal Monarchy: The Western Church from 1050 to 1250*, by Colin Morris (Oxford: Clarendon Press, 1989), and I.S. Robinson's *The Papacy: 1073–1198* (Cambridge, England: Cambridge University Press, 1990). The latter contains a particularly interesting chapter analyzing the relationship between the papacy and the Norman kingdoms of southern Italy and Sicily.

Medieval Sicily: 800–1713, by Dennis Mack Smith (London: Penguin 1968), gives a clear and readable account of the history of the Mediterranean kingdom. Part 1 covers the era from 800 to 1200, while Part 2 discusses the years from 1200 to 1375.

Angus MacKay's *Spain in the Middle Ages: from Frontier to Empire, 1000–1500* (London: Macmillan 1977) provides a good introduction to medieval Spain which focuses on economic history. Another fine analysis of Spain may be found in *A History of Spain and Portugal*, vol. 1, by Stanley G. Payne (Madison: University of Wisconsin Press, 1973).

As mentioned earlier, *A History of the Crusades*, 3 vols., by Stephen Runciman, is a thorough analysis of the crusades. More recent works include the fine study by H.E. Mayer, translated by John Gillingham, *The Crusades* (2nd ed., Oxford: Oxford University Press, 1988). Helpful contextual and background information for the Second and Third Crusades is presented in *Defenders of the Holy Land: Relations between the Latin East and the West, 1119–1187*, by Jonathan Phillips (Oxford: Clarendon Press, 1996). *A History of the Crusades*, vol. 1, edited by Marshall W. Baldwin (Philadelphia: University of Pennsylvania Press, 1955), is a collection of still-valuable articles by important scholars covering the first hundred years of the crusading movement.

THE TWELFTH-CENTURY RENAISSANCE

10

THE TWELFTH CENTURY was first conceptualized as a period of "renaissance" in the nineteenth century. The idea of a "twelfth-century renaissance" did not become firmly fixed in the historiographical tradition, however, until the publication of *The Renaissance of the Twelfth Century*, by Charles Homer Haskins, in 1927. As with many other time-honored concepts, the idea has been questioned by recent scholars, who have suggested that the intellectual movement of the twelfth century pales into insignificance when compared to the Italian Renaissance of the fifteenth and sixteenth centuries, and does not deserve to share the definition.

Furthermore, the proliferation of subjects considered by historians of the twelfth century, which includes the revival of science, law, and the Latin classics, as well as the growth of vernacular literature and the beginnings of Gothic style, may not exhibit a sufficient number of unifying features to be grouped under one rubric. Additional objections have been raised about the wide dissemination, or occasional lack, of certain intellectual features that purport to serve as defining characteristics.

The following discussion will not attempt to resolve these disagreements, but will, rather, contribute to the debate through a series of examples. Taken together, these provide insight into the exciting achievements of people in an era defined by one scholar as "the long twelfth century," from 1100 to 1250.

The Development of Urban Life

The period between 1100 and 1250 was an era of continuous economic growth that was so widespread and intense that some scholars have identified it as an "economic revolution." Because the change took place over a long period of time, it is probably inaccurate to describe it as a "revolution," but the movement certainly produced dramatic results. As discussed in Chapter 5, the population began to increase dramatically during the eleventh century, as a result of better nutrition and more peaceful political circumstances, and the rate of growth did not diminish until the disaster that befell Europe in the fourteenth century—the Black Death (see Chapter 14). The increase in population was accompanied by the reclamation of land for additional cultivation as well as new colonization. Trade expanded dramatically throughout the Mediterranean region, and the North Sea developed its own loose commercial organization. These twin networks were connected by the fairs in the Champagne region of northern France, which offered the opportunity for merchants from the south to establish commercial relationships with those from the north. The increased use of cash and credit fueled the economy, resulting in the phenomenon of commercialization.

By the twelfth century, the urban growth that had taken root during the previous hundred years resulted in a number of sizeable cities. Long-distance trade was well established, and supported the flourishing economies in urban areas such as Venice, Genoa, Cologne, and London. William FitzStephen, a historian writing in the twelfth century, described in detail the glories of London, and although he ignored problems such as overcrowding and lack of sewage disposal in his description of England's capital, his remarks about the trading network reveal an atmosphere bustling with activity. According to FitzStephen:

> Among the noble and celebrated cities of the world, that of London, the capital of the kingdom of the English, is one which extends its glory farther than all the others and sends its wealth and merchandise more widely into distant lands . . . To this city from every nation under heaven merchants delight to bring their trade by sea. The Arabian sends gold; the Sabaean [from southern Arabia] spice and incense. The Scythian [from the present-day Crimea] brings arms, and from the rich, fat lands of Babylon comes oil of palms. The Nile sends precious stones; the men of Norway and Russia, furs and sables; nor is China absent with purple silk. The Gauls come with their wines.

FitzStephen's comments demonstrate the widespread nature of commercial contacts, and reflect a vital aspect of urban life in the medieval world, since foreign trade formed a significant source of revenue. It is important to remember, however, that most cities relied equally on the surrounding local economies. The urban dwellers depended on the agricultural surplus of the adjoining rural areas for sustenance and, in return, provided markets and goods for the agrarian population. The burgeoning cities also served as a magnet to free peasants and serfs who sought to improve their lives (a serf who escaped from the manor would be legally free if he or she remained away from the manor for a year and a day).

Within the cities, economic life was organized according to the "guild system." These **guilds** were associations formed by both craftsmen and merchants. Their function was to regulate the practice and determine the standards of quality of a given craft, such as clothmaking or shoemaking, or, in the case of the merchants, to establish firm guidelines for trading activity. The formation of protective associations included every occupation, extending to the professions, as well as crafts and commerce; in addition to clothworkers, for example, there were guilds of musicians and even of prostitutes.

A craft guild was composed of "masters"—experts in a given craft who owned their shops. These guild officials agreed on prices and conditions of labor, and carefully limited access to the practice of their craft. The masters took in apprentices, who generally spent six years living with the master's family, learning the rudiments of the trade and performing general tasks such as cleaning and running errands. When they had served the period of apprenticeship and had become sufficiently accomplished, they reached the next level—that of day laborer or journeyman (from the French *journée*, meaning day). The journeyman usually lived on his own, and received a small wage, which seems not to have been enough to support a family; in fact, some towns passed laws that prevented a man from marrying until he became a master. If the journeyman aspired to master status, he was required to produce a "masterpiece"—an example of his craft that would be judged by the masters of the guild. However, a finely wrought example did not necessarily guarantee him the opportunity to acquire his own shop; the economy of the city must be judged by the guild to be strong enough to support another establishment in a given craft. Hence, the guild system protected those in the highest positions and carefully limited competition.

Women worked along with their husbands in the various trades, and a widow often carried on the business after her husband's death. Sometimes women were recognized as guild members in their own right, as in the musicians' guild described below. Some trades were dominated by women, such as the clothmaking industry in Paris, where records indicate that the silkmaking guild was composed primarily of women.

The guilds also provided social services to their members, such as health care in guild-operated hospitals, pensions for widows and retired craftsmen, and support for the children of a deceased member.

The merchant guilds offered functions similar to the craft guilds. They enforced a rigid pricing system and restricted competition. In addition, they often controlled the rights of citizenship in a city.

The members of a guild generally lived in close proximity to each other, congregating in a particular area of the city. As FitzStephen remarked in his description of London, "Those engaged in business of various kinds, sellers of merchandise, hirers of labor, are distributed every morning into their several localities according to their trade." This custom was also true of Parisian guilds, as may be seen in information regarding the musicians of Paris, who lived in the parish of St.-Josse. Medieval tax records from 1292 clearly indicate that the inhabitants of this area were engaged in the musical profession. They identify the residents as trumpeters, *jongleurs*, and minstrels, and include women who were called *jongleresses* (sometimes *jongleuresses*: female minstrels) (**fig. 93**). Their surnames, which indicate cities and provinces outside the capital city, reveal that many musicians had come to Paris to seek their fortunes. Eventually

94 Various musical instruments are shown in this illumination taken from a fourteenth-century manuscript of *De arithmetica* by Boethius. King David is shown at the top, strumming a psaltery, and various minstrels (clockwise from the right) play a lute, clappers, trumpets, *nakers* (drums), bagpipes, *shawn*, tambourine, and rebec. The lady in the center, who symbolizes the art of Music, plays a portative (portable)

these musicians, following the example of members of other professions, decided to regulate the practice of their craft. In 1321, they drew up statutes for a minstrels' guild which were officially registered with the city government in 1341. The original signers numbered thirty-seven, and included both men and women.

The statutes, some of which were undoubtedly established to correct contemporary abuses, were addressed to the warden of the provost of Paris:

> Know that we, by common accord, the menestrels and menestrelles, *jongleurs* and *jongleresses* living in the city of Paris whose names are here signed, have ordained the points and articles contained and set forth below for the reformation of our craft and the common profit of the city of Paris. The persons named below have testified and affirmed by their oaths that they will be profitable and valuable to their avowed profession and to the community of the city, as indicated by the following points and articles:

> (1) No *trompeur* of the city of Paris may enter into a contract at a feast for anyone except himself and his companion, or for any other who wish to bring *taboureurs*, *vielleurs*, *organeurs*, and other *jongleurs* from other *jongleries* with them, taking anyone they wish, and receiving payment from them. They take inferior musicians and ignore the better players; even though they perform less well, the same salary is demanded. Because of this good people are deceived and the reputation and common profit of the profession are damaged.

> (2) *Trompeurs* or other minstrels who have been hired to play for a function must wait until it ends before they move on to another engagement.

> (3) Those who have agreed to play are not to send a substitute, except in case of illness, imprisonment, or other emergency.

> (4) *Menestreurs, menestrelles*, or *aprentiz* who advertise themselves or others at feasts or weddings in Paris will be fined.

> (5) An apprentice minstrel who goes to a tavern should not discuss the details of his profession by word, signal, or custom, or engage any performer to play other than himself, except for his children by marriage or his daughters whose husbands are away in foreign countries or separated from their wives. He must direct any inquiries to the guild headquarters with the words "Sir, the laws of my profession forbid me to engage anyone but myself, but if you seek minstrels or apprentices, go to the *rue aus jongleurs* [street of *jongleurs*], and there you will find good ones." Any infraction of the rule is to be punished by a fine imposed by the master of apprentices. If payment is not made, the apprentice will be banished from the profession for a year and a day, or less time if he subsequently pays the fine.

> (6) When a prospective customer appears in the *rue aus jongleurs* he is to be allowed to approach whatever performer he wishes to engage without interference from rivals.

> (7) Apprentices must observe the same rules as fully accredited members of the profession.

> (8) and (9) All minstrels, whether Parisian or from other areas of France, must swear

to obey the statutes. Any outside minstrel arriving in Paris, either master or apprentice, is required to swear to the provost of St.-Julien that he will obey the statutes or else be banished for a year and a day.

(10) Finally, two or three worthy representatives of the profession are to be chosen to enforce the statutes. These officials are to be elected each year by the guild members and confirmed by the provost of Paris in the name of the king. Their duties include imposing fines; each infringement of the rules is to be punished by a fine of ten *sous*, half of such income to go to the guild and half to the crown.

These statutes served to create a monopoly of guild profits, to guarantee the interests of the members of the guild, and to establish rules for the administration of the organization. These are objectives that were typical of medieval guilds in general. More specific to the practice of music as a liberal profession were the statutes that ensured the honor of the profession, such as the first, which prevented the hiring of inferior musicians who would dishonor the art by their ineptitude.

Several decades later, new statutes were drawn up for the guild, and were confirmed by the royal seal. New articles were incorporated which defined professional standards more clearly. Minstrels must now audition for admission to the guild, and, if they aspired to the "mastership," they must also pass an examination concerning the principal rules of music. Unqualified minstrels who played at important gatherings were fined, and an "unlicensed" musician was formally forbidden to associate with those of higher rank. This hierarchical system was characteristic of the medieval guild system in general, and indeed of all of medieval existence.

Another article fixed the duration of the apprenticeship at six years, a term prescribed by the statutes of most arts and crafts guilds. If any master shortened the time without the permission of the director of the guild, the penalty was exclusion from the practice of the profession for one year and one day. The apprenticeship period of six years served to develop high standards in performance, but the fledgling minstrel was playing without salary during this time, and this, coupled with the fee due upon receiving the mastership, served to limit the number of masters in order that the profits of the profession be shared with fewer people.

A typical contract demonstrated that a musical apprentice bound himself to a master for six years, swearing to serve him and to work to learn to play the instrument that the master deemed most appropriate. In return, the master provided the apprentice with the necessities of life—food, shelter, and clothing—and at the end of the term paid his apprentice four gold francs and bought him a suitable instrument.

The guild system, as demonstrated in the example of the musicians' guild, offered training in a trade or profession, coupled with the guarantee of a livelihood. As may be seen, women were full participants in this guild as in many others, and received, in addition, benefits as wives of guild members. The hierarchical system provided a way of organizing the economic and commercial life of the medieval cities. Other examples abound, including the guilds that participated in the building trades. Many were involved in the construction of a church or cathedral, such as the guilds of glassworkers and stonemasons. They contributed to, indeed created, the buildings that remain among the most enduring achievements of the twelfth century.

The Birth of Gothic Architecture

The artistic style known as Gothic emerged during the twenty years between 1130 and 1150 alongside the tradition identified earlier as Romanesque (see Chapter 8). The Gothic only gradually replaced Romanesque forms, with the great flowering of the new style occurring in the thirteenth century (see Chapter 13).

In defining the development and characteristic features of this new style, architectural historians generally point to two buildings in France from the twelfth century:

95 The diffusion of light through the brilliantly colored stained-glass windows in the choir and ambulatory of the Abbey Church of St.-Denis, France (1140–1144) was thought by Abbot Suger to be the manifestation of the divine light of God. The large panels of glass were made structurally possible by the use of the pointed arch and the rib vault. The style of the building, which is often cited as the birth of Gothic form, spread rapidly throughout Europe.

Abbot Suger's church at St.-Denis, just north of Paris, and Henri Sanglier's cathedral at Sens, southeast of Paris. These structures exhibit features that became hallmarks of Gothic form, such as the pointed arch, which had been a component of both Islamic and Anglo-Norman architecture, and the cross-ribbed vault, whose modifications led to the codification of Gothic style. Suger (1081–1151), in particular, has traditionally been credited with sponsoring the innovations that led to the new aesthetic, although recent historians have questioned the originality of his contributions. They have suggested that his fame resulted in large part from his own writings concerning the development and consecration of the building, and that his direct influence on the creation of the new style was less substantial than has generally been assumed.

In a sense, the choir in Suger's church at St.-Denis may be viewed as the most fully developed example of the Romanesque pilgrimage church—resplendent and spacious, but also intimate. More importantly, the pivotal nature of its significance is shown by the fact that the newly built choir, with its massive windows and pointed arches (**fig. 95**), was immediately accepted as the basis of a new architectural style. Additionally, it was a splendid building with special links to the monarchy, since it was the most important royal burial place, and the crown and coronation regalia of the French kings were kept near the relics of St.-Denis. Suger must have been well aware that the creation of a magnificent new structure would enhance the prestige of the Capetian dynasty, and he was careful to emphasize the sacred nature of kingship in the artistic decorations of the church, closely associating the monarchs of France with Old Testament kings.

Suger's original intention was to expand the basilica he mistakenly attributed to the patronage of the Merovingian king Dagobert—he believed that the eighth-century edifice actually dated from the seventh century (**fig. 96**). While expressing appreciation for the "inestimable splendor" of the earlier church, and recognizing the legend that Christ himself had consecrated the nave, he was concerned about its limited size. As he remarked in his work *De consecratione* ("On Consecration"), which concerned St.-Denis, the extant structure was increasingly unable to accommodate the crowds of visiting pilgrims:

> [Due to its smallness, and because of] the number of the faithful growing and frequently gathering to seek the intercession of the Saints—the aforesaid basilica had come to suffer grave inconveniences. Often on feast days, completely filled, it disgorged through all its doors the excess of the crowds as they moved in opposite directions, and the outward pressure of the foremost ones not only prevented those attempting to enter from entering but also expelled those who had already entered. At times you could see, a marvel to behold, that the crowded multitude offered so much resistance to those who strove to flock in to worship and kiss the holy relics, the Nail and Crown of the Lord, that no one among the countless thousands of people because of their very density could move a foot; that no one, because of their very congestion, could [do] anything but stand like a marble statue, stay benumbed or, as a last resort, scream. The distress of the women, however, was so great and so

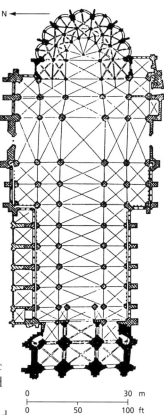

N ←

0   30 m
0   50   100 ft

96 The parts shaded black in this ground plan of St.-Denis were added by Abbot Suger. The splendid new choir and ambulatory provided an impressive path for visiting pilgrims, and served as an appropriate burial place for the Capetian monarchs.

intolerable that you could see with horror how they, squeezed in by the mass of strong men as in a wine press, exhibited bloodless faces as in imagined death; how they cried out horribly as though in labor; how several of them, miserably trodden underfoot [but then] lifted by the pious assistance of men above the heads of the crowd, marched forward as though upon a pavement; and how many others, gasping with their last breath, panted in the cloisters of the brethren to the despair of everyone . . . [realizing this] I zealously strove to have it corrected . . . [and when I was placed] at the head of the so important administration of this sacred church . . . [I] resolved to hasten, with all [my] soul . . . to the enlargement of the aforesaid place.

Although Suger's initial impulse may have been to enlarge the existing structure, his aesthetic ideals informed the choice of style, which incorporated features of the highly evolved Romanesque structures of Normandy and England. As discussed in Chapter 8, the builders of the eleventh-century Anglo-Norman churches had perfected the groin vault, which was the necessary antecedent to the ribbed vault, in which the groins were replaced by crossed pairs of thin arches or ribs (see fig. 63).

Suger's most important aesthetic contribution, however, consisted of transforming the outer walls of the choir into an almost continuous band of brilliantly colored stained-glass windows. As discussed earlier, the walls of Romanesque buildings, without the weight-bearing pointed arches and buttresses, could not sustain such expansive glazing. In describing the innovative structure, Suger remarked:

The dimensions of the old side aisles should be equalized with the dimensions of the new side aisles, except for the elegant and praiseworthy extension, in [the form of] a circular string of chapels, by virtue of which the whole [church] would shine with the wonderful and uninterrupted light of most luminous windows, pervading the interior beauty.

In order to accomplish the tasks, Suger employed master craftsmen:

Now, because [these windows] are very valuable on account of their wonderful execution and the profuse expenditure of painted glass and sapphire glass, we appointed an official master craftsman for their protection and repair, and also a skilled goldsmith for the gold and silver ornaments, who would receive their allowances and what was adjudged to them in addition, viz., coins from the altar and flour from the common storehouse of the brethren, and who would never neglect their duty to look after these [works of art].

Suger's aesthetic innovation was derived from a theological concept that envisioned the church as a miniature replica of the celestial Jerusalem—heaven on earth. This was a reflection of the prevailing world view, which understood the physical world (the microcosm) to be a reflection of the heavenly realm (the macrocosm). Several scholars have suggested that the possible source of this idea was the mystical writings of a sixth-century Christian Neoplatonist from Syria. He wrote under the name of

Dionysius the Areopagite, a biblical personality converted by St. Paul at Athens (Acts 17:34). Now referred to as Pseudo-Areopagite (or Pseudo-Dionysius), his works emphasized the properties of light in allowing the worshiper's spirit to ascend to God. A more practical view suggests that the splendid glazing of the windows served to impress the visiting pilgrims. Whatever the reason, which will no doubt remain undetermined, the fashion for expansive colored windows became a hallmark of the new Gothic buildings that appeared all over Europe in the following century.

In addition to the birth of the Gothic cathedral, the culture of the twelfth century provided the seeds for the development of another important institution—the great medieval university (see Chapter 12). Although scholars now agree that universities did not officially emerge until the thirteenth century, their origins may be found in the earlier educational institutions that resulted from a significant growth in learning opportunities, which began to extend beyond the boundaries of monastery and cathedral schools.

Education in the Twelfth Century

Both monastic and cathedral schools existed before 1100, though they were dedicated to different purposes. The monastic schools were devoted to the preservation of the Christian intellectual heritage, and trained their students, both male and female, to fulfill the needs of the monastery, preparing them to participate in liturgical functions and providing them with the tools for a life of prayer and meditation. Since the students were often oblates, given to the monastery as children, they were trained from an early age to be unquestioningly obedient, and to view themselves as part of a long tradition which they were pledged to preserve.

The monastic educational technique was based on the assimilation of received truth and the acceptance of inherited doctrine, rather than inquiry and the search for new solutions to problems. The importance of *auctoritas* (authority) was stressed, and it was assumed that intellectual work consisted of synthesizing the revered writings of predecessors such as the Church Fathers or the theologians of the Carolingian period. It was assumed that God would provide, through intuition and revelation, the solutions to difficult problems. Thus, devotion and spiritual communion with the Divine were prominent features of monastic training and the monastic existence in general.

Not much is known about the activities of cathedral schools before 1100. Their students, unlike those of the monastic schools, attended for specific periods of time, rather than being committed to a lifetime within the monastery; hence, the cathedral establishments did not foster traditional attitudes. They were attached to the secular world, and their curriculum provided boys with the skills necessary for a career in royal administration or bureaucracy. They offered a basic education in literacy and rhetoric, probably building on the old Roman *Trivium* and *Quadrivium* (see Chapter 2).

Some scholars have suggested that the cathedral schools encouraged the pupil to model himself on his master, copying his intellectual style and behavior in addition to absorbing the knowledge he provided. Because training began in early youth, instruction by rote was most common, with emphasis on the rules of grammar. However, one twelfth-century description of cathedral schools in London gives an image of a vibrant and challenging intellectual life:

In London the three principal churches (that is to say, the Episcopal Church of St. Paul, the Church of the Holy Trinity, and the Church of St. Martin) have famous schools by special privilege and by virtue of their ancient dignity. But through the favor of some magnate, or through the presence of teachers who are notable or famous in philosophy, there are also other schools. On feast-days the masters hold meetings for their pupils in the church whose festival it is. The scholars dispute, some with oratory and some with argument; some recite enthymemes [syllogisms in which one premise is suppressed]; others excel in using perfect syllogisms. Some dispute for ostentation like wrestlers with opponents; others argue in order to establish the truth in its perfection. Sophists who speak paradoxes are praised for their torrent of words, while others seek to overthrow their opponents by using fallacious arguments. Now and then orators use rhetoric for persuasion, being careful to omit nothing essential to their art. Boys of different schools strive against each other in verses, or contend about the principles of grammar and the rules governing past and future tenses.

In addition to cathedral and monastic schools, there was a third educational institution in the twelfth century. This was the noble household, in which tutors were employed to provide training for children, and it seems, judging from examples such as Marie de France and Heloise (to be discussed below), that here both boys and girls were given educational opportunities. An extension of this pattern may also be seen in the royal or episcopal court, where a quasi-school might be created to educate the royal family. This venue was especially important in the development of a specifically "courtly" education, which emphasized literacy and ultimately provided patronage to the authors of vernacular literature. As we shall see in the course of this chapter, prominent individuals emerged from all three educational settings. Their careers demonstrate the shift of focus from assimilation and repetition of the past to the fostering of an independent creative and intellectual life.

Courtly Literature

During the twelfth century, inspired perhaps by the crusades, a new genre of historical writing emerged that combined historical fact with stirring tales of adventure and heroism. One of the most popular authors of these chronicles was Geoffrey of Monmouth, who wrote in the first half of the twelfth century. When creating the exciting tales that make up his *History of the Kings of Britain*, Geoffrey drew on Celtic narrative traditions about the legendary King Arthur. His inaccurate but imaginative reconstruction of history glorified the Anglo-Norman kingdom in an attempt to provide the newly established Norman regime with venerable historical and mythical roots. In the process of creating a new political image, Geoffrey's account blackened the reputations of the Anglo-Saxon and Viking people of England, and also the French kingdom. Writing some twenty years before Henry II took the throne, his portrait of Arthur prepared the way, in a sense, for the ambitious designs of the Plantagenets, and introduced a new code of values for courtly behavior.

Geoffrey traced King Arthur's geneology back to the ancient Trojans, and linked his ancestors with Julius Caesar. He portrayed Arthur as a medieval Christian king in the mode of Charlemagne, although it is clear from the narrative that Arthur is fighting for personal glory rather than a higher power. In one part of the narrative, Geoffrey describes Arthur arming himself for battle with the Saxons. Just as in the *Song of Roland*, his weapons are personified as companions:

> Arthur . . . set upon his head a helm of gold graven with the image of a dragon. Upon his shoulders he bore the shield that was named Pridwen, wherein, upon the inner side, was painted the image of holy Mary, Mother of God, that many a time called her back unto his memory. Girt was he also with Caliburn, best of swords, that was forged within the Isle of Avallon; and the lance that graced his right hand was called by the name Ron, a tall, stout lance, fully able to do slaughter. Then, stationing his companies, he made a hardy assault upon the Saxons . . . Whomsoever he [Arthur] touched, calling upon God, he slew at a single blow, and he did not once slacken in his onslaught until he had slain four hundred and seventy men single-handed with his sword Caliburn.

According to Geoffrey, after Arthur had stopped the Saxon invasion, he proceeded to bring Ireland under his control, and then turned to subjugate the inhabitants of Iceland. Soon his fame reached "even unto the uttermost ends of the earth," and kings of distant realms were frightened, lest he invade their territories. When Arthur heard about his fierce reputation, "his heart was uplifted for that he was a terror unto them all, and he set his desire upon subduing the whole of Europe unto himself." Geoffrey praised Arthur's virtues, extolling his generous nature and pointing to his benevolence in the settlements of victory, as well as to his brilliant and festive court, which surpassed all other kingdoms in "plenty of riches, in luxury of adornment, and in the courteous wit of them that dwelt therein."

The Arthurian legend recounted by Geoffrey of Monmouth was carried forward in France during the twelfth century in the popular work of Chrétien de Troyes (1135–1183), a native of the Champagne region, whose *Lancelot* was written in vernacular French verse (**fig. 97**). This **romance**, like others of its genre, was probably read aloud in a courtly

97 In the romance, *Lancelot*, by Chrétien de Troyes, the hero must undergo various trials to attain the love of Queen Guinevere, the wife of his liege lord, King Arthur. This illumination from a fourteenth-century manuscript illustrates one of the tests: Lancelot is crossing a bridge that is "just like a sharp sword" in order to reach his lady in the tower. Courtly verse romances such as this were a popular aspect of medieval aristocratic culture.

setting, but its creation took place at approximately the same time as the development of a "textual" culture—one that depended on written texts rather than relying entirely on oral tradition. Verse romances such as *Lancelot* reflected the values and concerns of an emerging aristocratic society that was increasingly sophisticated and literate.

It has been suggested by recent scholars that the term "courtly love," which has long been used when describing this literature, has no precise meaning or content, and should therefore be discarded. Some interpretations view the positioning of the woman on a pedestal as a form of abasement, relegating her to a position of objectification. Scholars who share this view tend to see "courtliness" as a "mode of coercion" which, in effect, reflects a tradition of misogyny rather than an idealization of the beloved. Nonetheless, however the reader may interpret the works attached to the canon of "courtly literature," poems and stories such as those of Chrétien de Troyes form an important link in the western tradition of the love tale which has endured from the twelfth century to the present.

Chrétien's influence was widespread. Not only was he a prolific writer, but he also established a new genre—that of the romance, which was widely imitated by other authors who wrote for a courtly audience.

Chrétien's patron was Marie, Countess of Champagne—a daughter of Eleanor of Aquitaine and King Louis VII of France. Marie, Chrétien tells us in the introduction to *Lancelot*, gave him "the subject matter and the meaning" of his romance, and he remarks further that "since my lady of Champagne wishes me to begin a romance, I shall do so most willingly, like one who is entirely at her service in anything he can undertake in this world." Although the poet claims that he is not intent on flattering her, [someone] "might say, and I would agree, that she is the lady who surpasses all women who are alive." Scholars generally concur that Marie probably did suggest the source story—a typical medieval romance—and that Chrétien then wove the themes into an enduring masterpiece.

The medieval romance commonly presented as the central feature of the plot an adulterous love affair in which the heroine was married, often to the superior lord of her lover. This situation is exemplified in Chrétien's *Lancelot*, in which Guinevere, King Arthur's queen, is loved by one of Arthur's knights, Lancelot. Like his counterparts in other romances such as that of Tristan and Isolde, and in troubadour poetry, Chrétien's hero is willing to undergo extreme tests of courage and physical stamina to prove his love to his lady. In the following passage, Lancelot is able to summon the strength to bend iron bars in order to be with his love:

> When Lancelot saw the queen leaning upon the window ledge behind the thick iron bars, he greeted her softly. She returned his greeting promptly, since she had great desire for him, as did he for her. They did not waste their time speaking of base or tiresome matters. They drew near to one another and held each other's hand. They were troubled beyond measure at being unable to come together, and they cursed the iron bars. But Lancelot boasted that, if the queen wished it, he could come in to her—the iron bars would never keep him out. The queen responded, "Can't you see that these bars are too rigid to bend and too strong to break? You could never wrench or pull or bend them enough to loosen them."

"My lady," he said, "do not worry! I do not believe that iron could ever stop me—nothing but you yourself could keep me from coming in to you. If you grant me your permission, the way will soon be free; but if you are unwilling, then the obstacle is so great that I will never be able to pass." [The queen grants her assent].

Thereupon the queen turned away, and Lancelot prepared and readied himself to unbar the window. He grasped the iron bars, strained, and pulled until he had bent them all and was able to free them from their fittings. But the iron was so sharp that he cut the end of his little finger to the quick and severed the whole first joint of the next finger; yet his mind was so intent on other matters that he felt neither the wounds nor the blood flowing from them.

Although the window was quite high up, Lancelot passed quickly and easily through it . . . He came next to the bed of the queen; Lancelot bowed low and adored her, for he did not place such faith in any holy relic. The queen stretched out her arms toward him, embraced him, clasped him to her breast, and drew him into the bed beside her, looking at him as tenderly as she could, prompted by Love and her heart. She welcomed him for the sake of Love; but if her love for him was strong, he felt a hundred thousand times more for her. Love in other hearts was as nothing compared with the love he felt in his. Love took root in his heart, and was so entirely there that little was left for other hearts.

Now Lancelot had his every wish: the queen willingly sought his company and affection, as he held her in his arms, and she held him in hers. Her loveplay seemed so gentle and good to him, both her kisses and caresses, that in truth the two of them felt a joy and wonder, the equal of which has never been heard or known. But I shall let it remain a secret forever, since it should not be written of: the most delightful and choicest pleasure is that which is hinted, but never told.

Lancelot had great joy and pleasure all that night, but the day's coming sorrowed him deeply, since he had to leave his love's side. So deep was the pain of parting that rising was a true martyrdom, and he suffered a martyr's agony: his heart repeatedly turned back to the queen where she remained behind. Nor was he able to take it with him, for it so loved the queen that it had no desire to quit her. His body left, but his heart stayed . . . On parting, Lancelot bowed low before the bedchamber, as if he were before an altar. Then in great anguish he left.

Romantic tales, including the Arthurian stories, also formed the subject matter of another writer, Marie de France. Marie, along with Chrétien, was among the most popular authors of the twelfth and thirteenth centuries. Her exact identity remains hidden in mystery, but it is generally believed that she was a French noblewoman living in England, probably at the Norman court. It has even been suggested that she may have been a half-sister of King Henry II. Her works comprise the first extensive body of vernacular writings by a woman. They include short narrative poems known as *lais*, in addition to a collection of animal fables and a supernatural tale, St. *Patrick's Purgatory*.

Although the dating of Marie's works remains inexact, they were probably written between 1160 and 1215. She was undoubtedly addressing an aristocratic audience—one in which literacy was becoming more prevalent, especially among women. Her career may exemplify the expanded opportunities that existed for noblewomen in the twelfth century.

Although they were not admitted to the cathedral schools, training in languages and Classical literature was becoming increasingly available on a tutorial basis.

Marie's *lais* depict complicated human situations in which love offers joy. However, this joy never exists in its most powerful form without pain, and it cannot last forever. As in the works of Chrétien, the lovers are prevented by circumstance from being together. Generally the heroine is married, often to a king or to her lover's superior lord, and the lovers ultimately bow to the demands of society.

The shortest of the *lais* of Marie is *Chevrefoil* (*The Honeysuckle*), which recounts an episode in the traditional love story of Tristan and Isolde, which Marie probably derived from oral sources. In this poem she uses the symbol of the honeysuckle wound around a hazel tree to symbolize the love that binds the lovers together. Once again we have the tale of an adulterous romance, in this case between a queen (Isolde) and a knight (Tristan). In the segment of the poem that follows, Tristan waits at the side of a road for the queen to pass by:

> This was the meaning of the message
> That he had imparted and told to her:
> That he had been there a long time,
> Had waited and remained
> To keep watch and to find out
> How he could see her,
> For he could not live without her.
> It was exactly the same with the two of
> them
> As it was with the honeysuckle
> That has attached itself to the hazel tree:
>
> When it has so entwined itself and taken
> hold
> And completely surrounded the trunk,
> Together they can survive quite well;
> But if someone then tries to sever them,
> The hazel tree quickly dies,
> And the honeysuckle as well.
> "My beloved, it is the same with us:
> Neither you without me, nor I without
> you!"

The tradition of the courtly romance and the romantic lyric established by Chrétien and Marie spread through the aristocratic circles of the European courts, including that of Henry the Lion in northern Germany. Vernacular writing based on the French heroic tales known as *chansons de geste* also permeated the bourgeois levels of Germanic society, where the mythological tradition preserved in the stories known as the *Nibelungenlied* had great appeal. These enchanting tales of heroism and magic, undoubtedly based on an oral tradition that extended back to the pre-Christian Germanic era, were written down during the last two decades of the twelfth century. The courtly tradition was less well established in Italy and Spain, although the Spanish *Poem of El Cid* provides a verse biography of a heroic warrior.

Developing concurrently with the courtly tale was the short love lyric, which was initially composed and sung in France during the eleventh century. The composers of these poems were originally from the aristocracy, although many poets and musicians of subsequent generations were drawn from the middle class as well. These men and women, known respectively as **troubadours** and ***trobairitz***, usually composed both the lyrics and the music of their songs.

The man who is generally identified as the first troubadour was William IX, duke of Aquitaine (d. 1127). We assume that he, like similar poets, composed **monophonic** music to accompany his poetry, which was generally sung syllabically (one syllable per note), with texts in stanzas sung to the same melody. Eleven of his poems are extant, but they have, unfortunately, been preserved without music, except for one incomplete stanza.

The poems of the troubadours and *trobairitz* were written in the vernacular language of southern France, the *langue d'oc*. They dealt primarily with romantic love, set within the conventions of chivalry—a tradition that established honorable conduct for a knight and advanced the glorification of women and the love service of men. As in the works of Chrétien and Marie, love was treated as a malady; it was often a condition in which erotic desire could not be consummated.

The origins of troubadour poetry are obscure. It may be that Roman poetry continued to be recited in western Europe during the early Middle Ages, and provided a model for the creation of these songs. Some scholars have also suggested that Arabic love poetry was influential, lending verse structures, if not ideas, to the new art form, which may represent an early example of multiculturalism. Others seek its derivation in religious lyrics of the time.

Many of these poems dealt with the emotions aroused by love for an unattainable woman. Often she was married, as in the tales of Chrétien and Marie de France, sometimes to the liege lord of the poet–musician. The virtues of the lady are typically extolled in expansive language, as in this poem by Duke William:

I shall write a new song
before the wind or ice or rains come;
my lady tries me and tests me
as to how and in what way I love her;
yet never, for any quarrel she may bring
    me,
shall I loosen myself from her bond.
For rather I surrender and give myself to
    her,
so that in her charter she can inscribe
    me.
And do not hold me as a drunk
if I love my noble lady,
for without her I cannot live,
such great hunger do I have for her love.
For she is whiter than ivory,
wherefore I adore no other lady.
If soon I do not have help
so that my noble lady may love me,
I shall die, by St. Gregory's head,
if she does not kiss me in the bedroom
    or in the arbor.

What advantage will you have, gracious
    lady,
if your love keeps me far away?
It seems that you want to become a
    nun.
And know, because I love you so much,
that I fear that pain may wound me
if you do not right the wrong of which I
    complain to you.
What advantage will you have, if I join
    the cloister,
and you do not retain me as yours?
All the joy of the world is ours,
Lady, if we love each other.
There to my friend Daurostre
I say and command that he should sing
    and not howl.
For her I shiver and tremble
because I love her with such a noble
    love
that I do not believe there ever was born
her equal, in semblance, in the great
    line of Adam.

This poem expresses desire in rather subtle terms, whereas a stanza drawn from another of Duke William's verses is more explicit:

I still remember one morning
when we put an end to our quarrel,
and when she gave me such a great gift:
her love and her ring.
May God let me live
until I may have my hands under her cloak!

Troubadour poetry often expresses longing for a beloved lady who is far away ("the love from afar"). One example was written by Jaufré Rudel, a poet who worked shortly before the middle of the twelfth century, and apparently participated in the Second Crusade, from which he did not return. His poem reflects a willingness to go on a pilgrimage, or to be a prisoner of the Muslims, if only he could be near to his beloved:

When the days are long in May,
I am pleased by the sweet song of birds
    from afar;
and when I departed from there,
I remember a love from afar:
I go depressed and bowed down,
So that neither song nor hawthorn
    flower
pleases me any more than icy winter.
I do hold the Lord as true,
through whom I shall see the love from
    afar,
but for one good that befalls me from it,
two ills do I suffer, because she is so far
    away from me.
Ah! if only I were a pilgrim there,
so that my staff and my cloak
might be seen by her beautiful eyes!
It will truly be a joy for me when I ask
    her,
for the love of God, for shelter far away
and, if it pleases her, I shall dwell
close to her, even if I am from afar.
Then the pleasant conversation will
    begin,
when the lover from afar shall be so near
that with beautiful words he may enjoy
    sweet solace.

With sorrow and happiness I shall leave
    her,
if I do not see it, that love from afar.
But I do not know when I shall see her,
as our lands are far removed from one
    another
there are many passes and roads,
and because of this I cannot foretell
    anything
but may all this be as it pleases God!
Never again shall I enjoy love
if I do not enjoy this love from afar,
for I know no one fairer or nobler than
    she,
in any place, near or far;
so great and noble is her worth
that there, in the Saracens' realm,
I wish I could give myself up as a
    prisoner for her!
May God, who made everything that
    comes and goes
and created that love from afar,
grant me the power, for I have the
    courage,
to see that love from afar,
truly, and in such a dwelling
that the bedroom and the garden
may seem to me, always, a palace.
He tells the truth who calls me covetous

and desirous of the love from afar,
for no other joy pleases me as much
as the possession of the love from afar.
But what I want is kept from me,
for thus my godfather cursed me
that I should love but not be loved.
But what I want is kept from me.
May the godfather truly be cursed
who enchanted me so that I should not
  be loved.

The poetry of the *trobairitz*, or women troubadours, reflects a similar attitude toward love, although at times their words are even more explicit that those of the male poets. The most famous of the female poets was the Comtessa de Dia (*c.* 1150–1200), "a beautiful and good woman," who "was in love with Rambaud d'Orange and made about him many good and beautiful songs." The comtessa, married to the Provençal lord Guillaume de Poitiers, was not shy in describing her desires:

I have been in a cruel torment
because of a knight I have had;
and I want it to be known always
how I have loved him passionately;
now I see that I have been deceived
because I did not give him my love,
and therefore I have been suffering great
  anguish
in bed and when I am dressed.
I would truly love to hold
my knight, naked, in my arms one night,
and that he would consider himself in
  ecstasy
if only I would serve him as a pillow;
for I am more in love with him
than was Floris with Blanchefleur:
I give him my heart and my love,
my mind, my eyes and my life.
Dear friend, charming and good,
when shall I have you in my power?
If only I might lie with you one night
and give you a loving kiss!
Rest assured that I would have a great
  desire
to have you in place of my husband,
provided that you would have sworn
to do everything that I might want.

The poetry of the troubadours and *trobairitz* can be categorized into several genres. One important type is the *alba*, or dawn song, known in German as a *Wächterlied* (Watchman's Song), and in French as an *aubade*. Its theme is the parting of two lovers at dawn, after they have been awakened by the chirping of birds or the call of the watchman. Another popular genre was the *pastourelle*, frequently found in dialogue form, in which an innocent shepherdess is seduced by a knightly courtier. Dialogue is even more important in the *tenso*, a debate poem, and political topics are often explored satirically in the *sirvente*.

The troubadour tradition spread to northern France when Eleanor of Aquitaine married Louis VII in 1137, the year he was crowned. As the granddaughter of the first troubadour, Duke William IX, she was a lover of the poetic art, and the patron of many poets and composers. In northern France these poets were known as **trouvères**; they wrote poetry in the language of northern France, the *langue d'oil*. As a result of Eleanor's eventual divorce and remarriage to Henry of Anjou, duke of Normandy, who soon became king of England (see Chapter 9), the enthusiasm for courtly poetry spread to the British Isles. In Germany, composers in a similar tradition were called *Minnesänger* (Minnesingers); they sang of an abstract love (*Minne*), which often communicated a distinctly religious attitude (**fig. 98**). In Spain, the songs reminiscent of troubadour poems and melodies were known as *cantigas*.

The popularity of chivalric verse with accompanying music was widespread throughout Europe, and interest in the medium extended to the end of the thirteenth century, when the turmoil of the Albigensian Crusade in southern France (see Chapter 12) ended the great flowering of poetic composition. Assessing only the body of troubadour poetry, we find that approximately 2,600 poems have been preserved, with about 275 melodies. As mentioned above, these works were important in influencing the forms and content of the poems composed in areas beyond southern France, though the greatest output was confined to that region.

In addition to the widespread interest in secular song in the vernacular languages, there was also a prominent tradition of Latin monophonic poetry with musical accompaniment. The earliest collection of such works is commonly known as the "Cambridge Songs," after the manuscript that contains them, which is presently in the University of Cambridge Library. The texts of these songs demonstrate the wide variety of topics found in this genre. They include religious poems, laments, songs in praise of kings and bishops, folk stories, and erotic poems. They were probably performed by wandering scholars known as

98 A knight and his lady-love sit under a tree hung with a shield proclaiming *AMOR* (Love) in this image from an early fourteenth-century manuscript featuring sumptuous illuminations of *Minnesängers*. The lovers seems to be discussing the subject matter of a book, perhaps on the nature of love?

goliards (who were often clerics unable to secure a permanent position in the church). The name "*goliards*" is thought to have been derived from a synthesis of *gula* (Latin for gullet) and *Golias* (Goliath), an allusion to the goliards' reputation for gluttony. Many of the *goliard* songs, which extol the pleasures of eating, drinking, gambling, and amorous quest are supposed to have been written by the legendary Golias, the mythical head of a fictional "Order of *Goliards*." Although the subjects of such songs were not scholarly, the men who composed them were well educated and highly accomplished; they were justifiably proud of their poetic artistry.

The development of courtly secular poetry and tales in the vernacular languages was an important aspect of the twelfth-century renaissance. Equally significant, however, were the literary accomplishments of men and women living in the ecclesiastical and monastic environments, who were able to expand and eventually to transcend the narrow confines of their worlds. The next two sections examine the careers of three people who were particularly fine examples of the individualism of the era: Hildegard of Bingen, and Abelard and Heloise.

Hildegard of Bingen

Hildegard of Bingen (1098–1179) was one of the most extraordinary figures of the twelfth century. Her accomplishments bridged a wide range of disciplines, including theology, medicine, and music. In addition to her ecclesiastical and creative activities, she was a potent force in twelfth-century politics, giving advice in extensive correspondence with various popes and Church prelates, as well as political figures such as Frederick Barbarossa.

Hildegard was born into an aristocratic family at Bermersheim, near Mainz. She was given as an oblate to the Church at age eight because, according to her biographer, her parents believed that they should offer her, their tenth child, as a "tithe," just as they gave ten percent (a "tithe" or tenth) of their income to the Church. The young girl was placed in the care of a noblewoman, Jutta of Spanheim, an **anchoress** who was affiliated with the Benedictine monastery at Disibodenberg. By the time Hildegard was thirteen or fourteen, a number of girls had been placed in Jutta's custody, and the recluse's cell had become a small convent, under the supervision of the monastery.

Very little information exists about Hildegard's education or life before the age of thirty-eight. Judging by her later accomplishments, she must have received instruction from Jutta in the basic skills of literacy and music, as well as training in the Benedictine liturgical tradition. From early childhood she experienced visions, which she described in her later work, *Scivias* (*Know the Ways of the Lord*), and confided her experiences to Jutta and the monk Volmar, who became her trusted friend and assistant. Jutta died in 1136, and Hildegard was elected abbess of Disibodenberg by the unanimous vote of the nuns.

In 1141, according to the preface of *Scivias*, Hildegard experienced a vision which she regarded as a sign that she should seek a wider forum for her efforts:

> And it came to pass in the eleven hundred and forty-first year of the incarnation of Jesus Christ, Son of God, when I was forty-two years and seven months old, that the heavens were opened and a blinding light of exceptional brilliance flowed through my entire brain. And so it kindled my whole heart and breast like a flame, not burning but warming . . . and suddenly I understood the meaning of the expositions of the books, that is to say of the psalter; the Evangelists, and other catholic books of the Old and New Testaments.

Accompanying the vision, she heard a command: "O fragile one, ash of ash and corruption of corruption, say and write what you see and hear." Hildegard relates that, feeling unworthy, she "refused for a long time the call to write . . . until weighed down by the scourge of God, I fell onto a bed of sickness." Hildegard soon confided her difficulties to Volmar, and with his help, and the permission of the abbot of Disibodenberg, she began to write down the visions that ultimately formed the *Scivias*. "Rising from my sickness with renewed strength, I was just able to bring the work to a conclusion in the space of ten years." Hildegard believed that the purpose of her life was to act as the mouthpiece

99 Hildegard of Bingen experienced her visions in brilliant color and with elaborate detail. In the *Book of Divine Works*, Part 1, Vision 1, Hildegard receives a divine message, as her secretary, Volmar, writes down the details of the event, and a companion stands behind.

of the Lord, writing down and conveying his messages to her listeners and those who read her works. **Fig. 99** shows her receiving a vision, as Volmar records the experience.

Hildegard was given official papal sanction for her work in 1148, when a commission was sent to investigate her writings. The papal representatives were satisfied that the visions were authentic, and it was decreed that she should transcribe and make known whatever knowledge she received from the Holy Spirit.

In about 1150 Hildegard experienced a vision instructing her to move her congregation of nuns away from Disibodenberg to found a new convent at Rupertsberg, near Bingen, where the River Nahe joins the Rhine. The creation of a new establishment meant forsaking the wealth and relative comfort she had known at Disibodenberg, but it also provided her with more autonomy than she had known previously.

Although Hildegard was faced with many new administrative duties, she was able to continue her writing and composing. Most of her hymns and sequences were written during the early years at Rupertsberg, as were her works on science and medicine, notably the *Physica* (*Natural History*) and *Causae et curae* (*Causes and Cures*), which survive in fragmentary form. Her next major work, *Liber vitae meritorum* (*Book of Life's Merits*), was written between 1158 and 1163. She then began her most famous theological work, *Liber divinorum operum* (*Book of the Divine Works*), which she finally completed in 1174, five years before her death.

During these years Hildegard was also engaged in a series of preaching tours, speaking publicly in Trier, Cologne, Werden, and Liege, among other places. It was extremely unusual for a woman to be preaching publicly in the twelfth century, and it is indicative of Hildegard's fame that she was sought out for such activity. Furthermore, it was physically taxing; even though river transportation would have been available for some of these trips, much overland travel must have been required, and whether by foot or on horseback, it would have been extremely difficult. Her last major journey took place in 1170, when she was seventy-two years old. At that time she visited a number of monasteries, including Maulbronn, Hirsau, Kirchheim, Zwiefalten, and Hordt, involving travel of more than 250 miles (400 km).

In addition to her preaching tours, Hildegard engaged with the world outside her convent through an extensive correspondence with important ecclesiastical and political dignitaries. As shown in the following excerpt from a letter written *c.* 1170–1173 to Philip, archbishop of Cologne, she did not hesitate to reprimand her superiors, even popes and archbishops. Hildegard is chastising the archbishop in quite graphic terms for the sin of avarice (greed). She points out that he must make a choice between good and evil:

In a vision I saw, as it were, the sun shining with excessive heat upon mud filled with worms, and these creatures stretched themselves out in the joy of the heat, but, eventually not being able to bear the excessive heat, they hid themselves away, and the mud sent forth a noisome stench. I saw also that the sun shone in a garden, in which roses and lilies and all kinds of herbs grew, and the flowers grew abundantly by the heat of the sun, and the herbs sent forth innumerable roots and gave forth an exceedingly delightful odor, so that many people, suffused with this lovely fragrance, rejoiced in this garden as if it were paradise. And I heard a voice from above saying to you: "Make your decision, O man, whether you wish to remain in this garden of delights or to lie with the worms in that stinking excrement. You must determine whether you will be a lofty temple beautifully adorned with towers, in whose windows one can see the eyes of doves or whether you will be a wretched hovel thatched with straw, scarcely large enough to hold a peasant and his family. . ."

O father, I say to you in truth that I saw and heard all these words in a true vision, and I have written them to you in response to your command and petition. Therefore, do not be amazed at these things, but reflect on all your life from your childhood up to the present time. Also, change your name, that is, from wolf to lamb, because wolves gladly seize the sheep.

The imagery used in this letter is typical of Hildegard's style of expression, as may be seen throughout her prose works, as well as her poetry. Her language is always colorful, and she makes frequent use of biblical references and allusions. The mystical qualities of her visionary writings made her works famous in their own time, and she has become a rediscovered "cult figure" in our day.

Abelard and Heloise

Peter Abelard (1079–1142) was one of the most important philosophers and theologians of the twelfth century, and his writings exemplify the cultural and intellectual movement of the twelfth-century renaissance. He was born in Brittany, a son of Berengar, lord of Pallet, who planned that he would have a brilliant military career. However, the young man had different ideas about his future. As he wrote in his autobiography, he was "so enthralled by [his] passion for learning" that he "fled utterly from the court of Mars that [he] might win learning in the bosom of Minerva."

When he was about fifteen, Abelard began to study logic under the famous master Roscelin of Compiègne, and his determination to apply the rules of logic to every aspect of existence came to dominate his intellectual life. He was such a dedicated student that, as he remarked in his autobiographical work *Historia calamitatum* (*The Story of My Misfortunes*), he would travel to any town where he could find a teacher of logic and dialectic. He eventually arrived in Paris, where he studied under the director of the cathedral school of Notre-Dame, William of Champeaux.

Abelard proved to be an extremely precocious student, although he was described by contemporaries as being "so arrogant and self-opinionated that he would scarcely demean himself to listen to his masters." He made such rapid progress that he was soon able to defeat his teacher in a public debate. After gaining a certain amount of fame as a result, the twenty-five-year-old philosopher decided to establish his own school in nearby Melun. Abelard's autobiography reveals that "From this small inception of my school, my fame in the art of dialectics began to spread abroad, so that little by little the renown, not alone of those who had been my fellow students, but of our very teacher himself, grew dim and was likely to die out altogether." He soon moved his school to Corbeil, which was closer to Paris, "for there [he] knew there would be . . . more frequent chance for [his] assaults in our battle of disputation." By "disputation," or *disputatio*, Abelard meant a new method of teaching, which involved posing a problem and discussing it through question and answer before ultimately arriving at a resolution. He insisted that this technique should replace the standard method of *lectio*—a lecture by a teacher that was read aloud sentence by sentence and copied by the students—and he put it to use in his philosophical work, as well. Abelard's method became widely influential, ultimately leading to the great philosophical **summmae** ("summaries") of the Gothic era.

By 1108, Abelard was back in Paris, where his practice of challenging men of established reputation in ways that brought them public disgrace soon made him a notorious celebrity—one who attracted devoted followers as well as tenacious enemies. His public disputations became a popular feature of the vibrant intellectual life of the Parisian schools. He was invited to teach theology and dialectics at the school of Mont Ste.-Geneviève, which eventually developed into the University of Paris, and by 1113 he was teaching at the cathedral school of Notre-Dame. His popularity as a lecturer grew rapidly, resulting in fame, wealth, and honors, as well as "bitter envy."

At about this time, Abelard met a young woman named Heloise, 22 years his junior, who was the niece of Fulbert, a canon at Notre-Dame. As Abelard remarked, she was "of no mean beauty, [and] she stood out above all by reason of her abundant knowledge of letters." Abelard tells us that he "determined to unite [her] with myself in the bonds of love, and indeed the thing seemed to me very easy to be done," since "so distinguished was my name, and I possessed such advantages of youth and comeliness, that no matter what woman I might favor with my love, I dreaded rejection of none." Abelard then relates how, "utterly aflame with [his] passion for this maiden," he was able to convince Heloise's uncle to appoint him as tutor to the young woman, and to invite him to live in his house. He continues:

> By Fulbert's own earnest entreaties he fell in with my desires beyond anything
> I had dared to hope, opening the way for my love; for he entrusted her wholly to my
> guidance, begging me to give her instruction whensoever I might be free from the
> duties of my school, no matter whether by day or by night, and to punish her sternly
> if ever I should find her negligent of her tasks. In all this the man's simplicity was
> nothing short of astounding to me; I should not have been more smitten with
> wonder if he had entrusted a tender lamb to the care of a ravenous wolf.

The teacher and his pupil became intellectually close, as Abelard comments in his autobiography, and then, as he recounts:

> We were united first in the dwelling that sheltered our love, and then in the hearts
> that burned with it. Under the pretext of study we spent our hours in the happiness
> of love, and learning held out to us the secret opportunities that our passion craved.
> Our speech was more of love than of the books which lay open before us; our kisses

far outnumbered our reasoned words. Our hands sought less the book than each other's bosoms; love drew our eyes together far more than the lesson drew them to the pages of our text.

When Heloise "found that she was pregnant," Abelard arranged for her to be taken to his home in Brittany, where she gave birth to their son, Astrolabe. Abelard approached her uncle Fulbert, pointing out that "what had happened could not seem incredible to any one who had ever felt the power of love, or who remembered how, from the very beginning of the human race, women had cast down even the noblest men to utter ruin." He offered to marry Heloise, provided that the marriage remained secret, so that Abelard "might suffer no loss of reputation." Fulbert accepted the proposal, but Heloise objected, pointing out to Abelard that his work would suffer, since there could be no possible concord "between scholars and domestics, between authors and cradles, between books or tablets and distaffs, between the stylus or the pen and the spindle." Heloise marshaled Classical sources to support her arguments against marriage, but she and her lover were finally wed in secret. When the union became publicly known, and had become the subject of various poems and songs, Abelard sought to preserve his reputation by sending Heloise to the convent of Argenteuil. Fulbert saw this as a shirking of responsibility, and proceeded to inflict a dire revenge. He hired a gang of thugs, who broke into Abelard's room with the assistance of his servant, where, as Abelard recounts, "They took cruel vengeance on me of such appalling barbarity as to shock the whole world; they cut off the parts of my body whereby I had committed the wrong of which they complained."

The following morning "the whole city was assembled before my dwelling," uttering "lamentations and outcries." After this public disgrace, seeing "how justly God had punished me in that very part of my body whereby I had sinned," Abelard entered the monastery at St.-Denis to become a Benedictine monk. True to form, he thought it necessary to challenge the existing tradition by proving that the patron saint of the abbey was not identical with Dionysius the Areopagite, the biblical figure converted by St. Paul, who had become identified with St.-Denis in the ninth century. Asked to leave the monastery, he resumed teaching in Paris, but again created a controversy which ultimately resulted in the condemnation of his teaching on the Holy Trinity by a council held at Soissons in 1121.

In 1126, Abelard was elected abbot at the abbey of St. Gildas in his native Brittany. However, the demands of the resident monks made his life at the abbey difficult, and he eventually returned to Paris, where he resumed teaching.

Heloise became prioress of the convent of Argenteuil, where she had taken vows at the age of nineteen. She seems to have felt no vocation for the monastic life at this time, though she remained a nun for the rest of her life and became abbess of the Paraclete, a convent founded by Abelard, by 1132. Her feelings of longing and frustration were poured out in a letter to Abelard, which has been viewed by feminist scholars as a prime example of female capitulation to male authority and emotional domination:

You know, beloved, as the whole world knows, how much I have lost in you, how at one wretched stroke of fortune that supreme act of flagrant treachery robbed me of my very self in robbing me of you; and how my sorrow for my loss is nothing compared with what I feel for the manner in which I lost you. Surely the greater the cause for grief, the greater the need for the help of consolation. You alone have the power to make me sad, to bring me happiness or comfort; you alone have so great a debt to repay me, particularly now when I have carried out all your orders so implicitly that when I was powerless to oppose you in anything, I found strength at your command to destroy myself. I did more, strange to say—my love rose to such heights of madness that it robbed itself of what it most desired beyond hope of recovery, when immediately at your bidding I changed my clothing along with my mind, in order to prove you the sole possessor of my body and my will alike. God knows I never sought anything in you except yourself; I wanted simply you, nothing of yours. I looked for no marriage-bond, no marriage portion, and it was not my own pleasures and wishes I sought to gratify, as you well know, but yours. The name of wife may seem more sacred or more binding, but sweeter for me will always be the word mistress, or, if you will permit me, that of concubine or whore. I believed that the more I humbled myself on your account, the more gratitude I should win from you, and also the less damage I should do the brightness of your reputation . . . God is my witness that if Augustus, Emperor of the whole world, thought fit to honor me with marriage and conferred all the earth on me to possess for ever, it would be dearer and more honorable to me to be called not his Empress but your whore.

Heloise goes on to beg Abelard to send her a letter; otherwise she might be led to concur with the words of others, who suggest that "It was desire, not affection, which bound you to me, the flame of lust rather than love." He responded that he had not written because he had always had such confidence in her "own good sense" that he did not think it was necessary. These letters began a correspondence that was to last for years, and which included not only personal communications, but also directions by Abelard for the proper conduct of a monastic establishment for women.

Abelard continued to teach and write in Paris after 1136. His most famous work, *Sic et non* (*Yes and No*), was written during this period. This treatise consisted of a series of texts from scripture and the Church Fathers on 150 theological points, arranged in groups that appeared to be mutually contradictory. The purpose of this system was to encourage methodical doubt, for, as Abelard wrote in the prologue, "Careful and frequent questioning is the basic key to wisdom," and "By doubting we come to questioning, and by questioning we perceive the truth." He further challenged, in his *Introduction to Theology*: "Now . . . it remains for us, after having laid down the foundation of authority, to place upon it the buttresses of reasoning." Although Abelard presented the basic principles of textual criticism in *Sic et non*, he did not propose solutions to the contradictory expressions. Such conclusions were eventually worked out, and Abelard's procedure became an important part of the Scholastic Method, to be discussed in Chapter 13.

Inevitably, Abelard once again became the center of an intense controversy. His theological views and philosophical methodology drew the ire of St. Bernard of Clairvaux, who wrote to Pope Innocent II and to numerous bishops, criticizing Abelard's doctrine and approach. In a letter to the Pope, Bernard railed against Abelard:

We have escaped the lion [a reference to Peter Leonis, the anti-pope] only to fall victims to the dragon [Abelard] who is, perhaps, more dangerous lurking in his lair than the lion raging in the open. Although he is no longer lurking in his lair: would that his poisonous writings were still lurking in their shelves, and not being discussed at the crossroads! His books have wings: and they who hate the light because their lives are evil, have dashed into the light thinking it was darkness. Darkness is being brought into towns and castles in the place of light; and for honey poison or, I should say, poison in honey is being offered on all sides to everyone. His writings "have passed from country to country, and from one kingdom to another." A new gospel is being forged for peoples and for nations, a new faith is being propounded, and a new foundation is being laid besides that which has been laid. Virtues and vices are being discussed immorally, the sacraments of the Church falsely, the mystery of the Holy Trinity neither simply nor soberly. Everything is put perversely, everything quite differently, and beyond what we have been accustomed to hear.

Abelard was determined to answer these charges in person, and Bernard agreed to meet him. Accordingly, a council was arranged at Sens, attended by the king and most of the bishops of France, including the papal legates. To the amazement of everyone, when St. Bernard called on Abelard to justify the points in question, he refused to answer, and referred the whole issue to the pope. A list of contentious issues was drawn up and sent to Rome, and Abelard began his journey to appear in person before the papal court. But he was met en route, at Cluny, with the news that his books had been publicly burned in Rome and he had been officially condemned on July 16, 1140. Deeply disheartened, he remained at Cluny, where he died two years later, having finally made peace with his intellectual enemy St. Bernard.

Summary

The twelfth century was a time of renaissance and renewal in western Europe, as economic development and political stability fostered the growth of urban areas. The inhabitants of the burgeoning cities organized their social and economic lives in a system of associations known as guilds, which controlled the training, skill levels, products, and incomes of the guild members, in addition to providing social benefits.

In the cities, the cathedral schools provided increased educational opportunities in which the development of literacy was encouraged. Education was also more widely available in courts and noble households, where tutors were hired to train noble children, both boys and girls, in basic writing and the skills of arithmetic. A more literate "courtly" environment encouraged the production of literature in the vernacular, which featured plots reflecting the concerns and tastes of a more sophisticated aristocracy.

During this era individualism became more pronounced, with people such as Abbot Suger, Abelard, and Hildegard of Bingen breaking free from the constraints of tradition to establish new directions in architecture, music, theology, and philosophy. The cultural and religious contributions of these individuals and others like them provided the foundations for the Gothic cathedral, the philosophical *summa*, the medieval university, and the great literature of the thirteenth and fourteenth centuries.

Suggestions for Further Reading

Primary sources

Abbot Suger: On the Abbey Church of St.-Denis and its Art Treasures, edited and translated by Erwin Panofsky (2nd ed. by Gerda Panofsky-Soergel, Princeton: Princeton University Press, 1979), recounts the views of Suger, which resulted in the beginning of Gothic style at St.-Denis.

The Romance of Arthur: An Anthology of Medieval Texts in Translation, edited by James J. Wilhelm (New York and London: Garland Press, 1994), offers selections from the writings of Geoffrey of Monmouth and Chrétien de Troyes, among others. The poetry of Marie de France may be found in *The Lais of Marie de France*, translated by Robert Hanning and Joan Ferrante (New York: Dutton, 1978).

There are many excellent anthologies of troubadour poetry. One of the more recent volumes is *Troubadour Lyrics: A Bilingual Anthology*, by Frede Jensen (New York: Peter Land, 1998), which offers good modern translations. The works of *trobairitz* may be found in *Unsung Women: The Anonymous Female Voice in Troubadour Poetry*, by Carol Jane Nappholz (New York: Peter Lang, 1994), and *Songs of the Women Troubadours*, edited and translated by Matilda Tomaryn Bruckner, Laurie Shepard, and Sarah White (New York: Garland Press, 1995).

Hildegard of Bingen: Selected Writings, translated and edited by Mark Atherton (London: Penguin Books, 2001), is a good introductory anthology. Selected letters of Abelard and Heloise, as well as Abelard's autobiography, *Historia calamitatum* (*The Story of My Misfortunes*), are contained in *The Letters of Abelard and Heloise*, translated by Betty Radice (Middlesex, UK: Penguin Books, 1974).

Secondary sources

The classic work concerning twelfth-century intellectual life is *The Renaissance of the Twelfth Century*, by Charles Homer Haskins (Cambridge, MA: Harvard University Press, 1927). This book remains the essential introduction to study of the period. A valuable contribution is *The Twelfth-Century Renaissance*, by R. N. Swanson (Manchester and New York: Manchester University Press, 1999), which incorporates much recent scholarship in an excellent overview of the topic. *Renaissance and Renewal in the Twelfth Century*, edited by Robert L. Benson and Giles Constable (Cambridge, MA: Harvard University Press, 1982, reprint ed. Toronto: University of Toronto Press, 1991), is a fine collection of articles by leading scholars dealing with the social and intellectual history of the twelfth century.

The Rise of the Gothic, by William Anderson (London: Hutchinson, 1985), places the emergence of Gothic style within the context of twelfth-century politics and society. *The Gothic Cathedral: The Architecture of the Great Church (1130–1530)*, by Christopher Wilson (London: Thames and Hudson, 1990), gives a clear discussion of the development of Gothic style. Chapter 1 deals with Suger and St.-Denis. For a detailed analysis of the sculptural program at St.-Denis, see *Early Gothic St.-Denis: Restorations and Survivals*, by Pamela Z. Blum (Berkeley: University of California Press, 1992).

Lindy Grant's biography of Suger, titled *Abbot Suger of St.-Denis: Church and State in Early Twelfth-Century France* (London: Longman, 1998), presents a revised view of his role as royal adviser and ecclesiastical patron, placing his life within the context of twelfth-century society. *Artistic Change at St.-Denis: Abbot Suger's Program and the Early Twelfth-Century Controversy over Art*, by Conrad Rudolph (Princeton: Princeton University Press, 1990), argues that Suger's iconographical and architectural programs were an outgrowth of his response to the opposing twelfth-century monastic views of appropriate artistic expression, and were influenced only marginally by Pseudo-Dionysian light theology. Charles M. Radding and William W. Clark have produced a fascinating study of the relationship between architecture and scholarship in *Medieval Architecture, Medieval Learning: Builders and Masters in the Age of Romanesque and Gothic* (New Haven: Yale University Press, 1992).

Artists of the Middle Ages by Leslie Ross (Westport, CT: Greenwood Press, 2003) is an excellent study of medieval artistic activity.

Chrétien de Troyes, the Man and his Work, by Jean Frappier and translated by Raymond J. Cormier, (Athens, OH: Ohio University Press, 1982), provides a general introduction to Chrétien.

Erotic Dawn-Songs of the Middle Ages: Voicing the Lyric Lady, by Gale Sigal (Gainsville, FL: University Press of Florida, 1996), is an interesting study of the *alba*. *The World of the Troubadours: Medieval Occitan Society*, by Linda M. Paterson (Cambridge: Cambridge University Press, 1993), provides a fine analysis of the social milieu of the troubadours.

Hildegard of Bingen: A Visionary Life, by Sabina Flanagan (2nd ed., London: Routledge, 1998), is a readable and comprehensive introduction to the saint's life and works. Barbara Newman's *Sister of Wisdom: St. Hildegard's Theology of the Feminine* (Berkeley: University of California Press, 1989) presents Hildegard's thought in relation to traditional twelfth-century religious belief.

A biography of Abelard, together with an analysis of the legend of Abelard and Heloise through the subsequent centuries, may be found in *Abelard and Heloise*, by D.W. Robertson, Jr. (New York: Dial Press, 1972). An interesting interpretation of various facets of the legend surrounding the two lovers is presented in *Heloise and Abelard*, by the famous scholar Etienne Gilson (London: Hollis & Carter, 1953). A more recent biography of Abelard that emphasizes his contributions to intellectual history is *Abelard: A Medieval Life* by M.T. Clanchy (Oxford: Blackwell, 1997).

BEFORE 1200

Politics	Culture	Religion
ENGLAND/FRANCE *c.*1165–1218 life of Simon de Montfort 1199–1216 r. of John 1180–1223 r. Philip Augustus	1126–1198 life of Ibn Rushd, known as Averroës 1130 Irnernius (commentary on *Corpus juris civilis*) 1140 Gratian (*Decretum*) by 1140 University at Bologna *c.*1159–*c.*1201 life of Leonin *c.*1170–*c.*1236 life of Perotin	*c.*1140–1217 life of Peter Waldo 1170–1221 life of St. Dominic 1182–1226 life of St. Francis of A
SPAIN 1188–1230 r. of Alfonso IX **OTHERS** 1167–1227 life of Genghis Khan 1195–1203 r. of Alexius III	1184 Trinity Chapel (Canterbury Cathedral) begun 1194 Chartres Cathedral begun *c.*1195–*c.*1272 life of John of Garland (Johannes de Garlandia)	1198–1216 r. of Pope Innocent III

AFTER 1200

Politics	Culture	Religion
ENGLAND/FRANCE 1215 Magna Carta granted 1216–1272 r. of Henry III 1226–1270 r. of Louis IX 1272–1307 r. of Edward I 1285–1314 r. of Philip IV 1337–1453 Hundred Years War *c.*1347 Black Death 1358, 1381 Peasant revolts	1200 Charter granted to University at Paris 1200 Notre-Dame Cathedral, Paris completed by 1209 Chancellor established at University of Oxford 1220 Amiens Cathedral begun	1202–1204 Fourth Crusade 1207 Stephen Langton beco Archbishop of Canter 1221–1274 life of St. Bonaventure *Soul's Journey into Go* 1225–1274 life of St. Thomas Aqu (*Summa Theologica*) 1227–1241 r. of Pope Gregory IX
HOLY ROMAN EMPIRE 1215–1250 r. of Frederick II **SPAIN** 1217–1252 r. of Ferdinand III 1252–1284 r. of Alfonso X "the Wise" **OTHERS** 1203–1204 r. of Alexius IV	by 1233 University at Cambridge firmly established *c.*1250–1300 life of Guillaume d'Amiens *c.*1260 *Roman de la Rose* 1265–1321 life of Dante Alighieri (*The Divine Comedy*) *c.*1295–*c.*1351 life of Jean de Muris 1300–*c.*1377 life of Guillaume de Machaut 1304–1374 life of Francisco Petrarch (*Sonnets*) 1313–1375 life of Giovanni Boccaccio (*Decameron*) *c.*1322 Philippe de Vitry (*Ars nova*) *c.*1330 Jacques de Liège (*Speculum Musicae*) 1342–1400 life of Geoffrey Chaucer (*Canterbury Tales*) 1347–1385 Prague Cathedral built *c.*1347–1380 life of St. Catherine of Sienna 1351–1412 Gloucester Cathedral built *c.*1358 Jean Froissart (*Chronicles*) *c.*1364–1430 life of Christine de Pizan *c.*1373–1440 life of Margery Kempe	1294–1303 r. of Pope Boniface VI 1378–1417 Great Schism

PART III

THE HIGH MIDDLE AGES

c. 1200–*c.* 1400

11 POLITICS IN THE THIRTEENTH CENTURY

T HE THIRTEENTH CENTURY IN EUROPE was a time of vigorous expansion, geographically, economically, and intellectually. Burgeoning trade encouraged the development of extensive mercantile networks, which brought fruitful interaction between the citizens of Europe and those of the Mediterranean and North seas. Urban life continued to flourish, as economic growth made cities attractive to an ever-growing portion of the population.

The positive attitudes engendered by successful economic development encouraged geographic growth, as western European monarchs began to see the Mediterranean area and the Baltic countries as opportunities for a fruitful extension of their hegemony. Their attempts took various forms. Several kings undertook new crusades to the Holy Land, German princes expanded to the area of the Baltic Sea, Spanish monarchs continued the Reconquista, and the Holy Roman Emperor Frederick II attempted to establish a kingdom that would extend from the North Sea to Sicily.

At the same time, the rulers of western European countries such as England and France strengthened their control over their own subjects through the development of legal codes and strong bureaucracies, establishing patterns that were replicated in Spain and Hungary. They often granted privileges to the urban middle class in order to gain support for the crown in their struggles with the nobles of the realm.

The Byzantine Empire continued to wither militarily, but its cultural and intellectual growth did not experience decline until the disastrous events of the Fourth Crusade and the emergence of the Mongol Empire. By the end of the thirteenth century, Europe, both east and west, had assumed a much larger and more diverse configuration.

England

King John and Magna Carta

When Richard the Lionheart was struck down by a poisoned arrow while besieging the castle of an unruly vassal in 1199, the throne of England passed to his younger brother John (r. 1199–1216). Historians have generally judged John harshly, pointing to his tyrannical attitudes, his fiery temper, and his unscrupulous conduct, especially his unfortunate habit of seducing the wives and daughters of his vassals. Recent scholarship, however, has viewed him somewhat more positively, remarking that he was an excellent administrator and that he was quick to see the advantage of allying himself with the newly emerging merchant class in the cities—an opportunity that his father and brother had failed to perceive.

At the time of Richard's death, John was not the only claimant to the throne. He had a rival in the person of Arthur, the son of an older brother who had died. However, Hubert Walter, archbishop of Canterbury, declared in favor of John, who duly ascended the throne.

When Archbishop Walter died early in his reign, John became involved in a dispute with Pope Innocent III (r. 1198–1216) concerning the appointment of a new prelate. The monks at Canterbury elected one of their own members, a man unacceptable to the king. John then forced a new election, which resulted in the choice of his own preferred candidate. The pope, however, insisting on proper procedure, mandated another election, this time by monks who were then in Rome. The result was the choice of the pope's candidate, Stephen Langton, a professor of theology at the University of Paris. Langton was consecrated as archbishop in 1207, but John refused to allow him to come to England, threatening to kill him or to burn down Canterbury Cathedral. In 1208, Innocent retaliated by laying an interdict on the entire country, which meant that liturgical services were suspended, including marriages, baptisms, and burials. This caused great consternation, since the people of England were denied the basic rituals of their religion. John responded by seizing Church property—a policy initially tolerated by the populace. But when the king began to impose illegal taxation and to enforce ancient forestry laws which barred the people from gathering wood, his popular support evaporated. To make matters worse, John let two recalcitrant nobles and two bishops die in prison, further alienating him from the people. The situation was ultimately resolved in 1213, when Pope Innocent threatened to depose John; it is probable that he also offered papal support for a French invasion of England, although this cannot be proved. The king capitulated, accepting Stephen Langton as archbishop of Canterbury, and submitting England to the pope as a fief, thereby guaranteeing a large annual payment to Rome.

John's activities outside the confines of England were equally problematic. Early in his reign he faced hostility from the clever and ambitious French king Philip Augustus, who was John's overlord for his possessions in France. Through a series of incursions into the Angevin lands between 1202 and 1204, which resulted from squabbles over feudal procedure, Philip was able to wrest control of both Normandy and Anjou from the English crown; ultimately English ties were maintained in Aquitaine alone.

After a decade of attempts to coordinate forces of opposition against Philip Augustus, John joined the north German prince Otto of Brunswick in a two-pronged attack on France in 1214, hoping to regain some of his lost possessions. John assaulted Anjou, and Otto's forces attacked Paris from the north. The invasion was unsuccessful, and the coalition army was disastrously crushed at the Battle of Bouvines, effectively ending any hope that the English would regain their French possessions. This humiliating defeat engendered tremendous opposition in the kingdom, and seriously affected the amount of support enjoyed by John. Indeed, his subjects began to refer to him as "John Lackland," or "John Softsword."

The result of this growing resistance to the king is well known. In 1215, following an uprising in which his barons occupied London, John met the magnates, together with the archbishop of Canterbury, in a field at Runnymede, near to present-day Windsor, where they presented him with a list of demands. Although this document was long viewed as the first step towards representative government, in reality it was primarily a conservative charter which attempted to define the rights of the nobility in relation to the crown; the barons' demands were intended to ensure protection from the unreasonable exactions of the king. The initial list, dated June 15, 1215, was codified and issued soon thereafter by the **Chancery**—the office responsible for issuing royal documents.

The provisions of Magna Carta ("the Great Charter"), as the document is known because of its great length, concerned the rights of the Church, feudal relations between the king and his vassals, and the procedures and practices of royal government. Several provisions, absent from the version of Magna Carta reissued in 1216 by the council acting as regents for John's young son, Henry III, satisfied the initial demands of John's magnates by giving some authority to the barons and clergymen. The first clause grants that "the English church shall be free, and shall have its rights undiminished and its liberties unimpaired," while another establishes a council of twenty-five barons to oversee the government:

> For God and the betterment of our kingdom and for the better allaying of the discord that has arisen between us and our barons we have granted all these things aforesaid, wishing them to enjoy the use of them unimpaired and unshaken for ever, we give and grant them the under-written security, namely, that the barons shall choose any twenty-five barons of the kingdom they wish, who must with all their might observe, hold, and cause to be observed, the peace and liberties which we have granted and confirmed to them by this present charter of ours, so that if we, or our justiciar, or our bailiffs or any one of our servants offend in any way against anyone or transgress any of the articles of the peace or the security and the offence be notified to four of the aforesaid twenty-five barons, those four barons shall come to us, or to our justiciar if we are out of the kingdom, and, laying the transgression before us, shall petition us to have that transgression corrected without delay. And if we do not correct the transgression, or if we are out of the kingdom, if our justiciar does not correct it, within forty days, reckoning from the time it was brought to our notice or to that of our justiciar if we were out of the kingdom, the aforesaid four barons shall refer that case to the rest of the twenty-five barons and those twenty-five barons together with the community of the whole land shall distrain and distress us in every way they can, namely, by seizing castles, lands, possessions, and in such other ways as they can, saving our person and the persons of our queen and our children, until, in their opinion, amends have been made; and when amends have been made they shall obey us as they did before.

Another provision provides direction as to how the council of twenty-five barons would operate:

> All fines made with us unjustly and against the law of the land, and all amercements

[fines] imposed unjustly and against the law of the land, shall be entirely remitted, or else let them be settled by the judgment of the twenty-five barons who are mentioned below in the clause for securing the peace, or by the judgment of the majority of the same, along with the aforesaid Stephen, archbishop of Canterbury, if he can be present, and such others as he may wish to associate with himself for this purpose, and if he cannot be present the business shall nevertheless proceed without him, provided that if any one or more of the aforesaid twenty-five barons are in a like suit, they shall be removed from the judgment of the case in question, and others chosen, sworn and put in their place by the rest of the same twenty-five for this case only.

The clauses that pertain to feudal practices guaranteed, among other issues, the rights of inheritance and wardship that had been frequently abused by John. These provisions restored traditional procedures that had been observed before his reign. In addition to specifying the payments for relief, for example, the document provides some protection for widows:

A widow shall have her marriage portion and inheritance forthwith and without difficulty after the death of her husband; nor shall she pay anything to have her dower or her marriage portion or the inheritance which she and her husband held on the day of her husband's death; and she may remain in her husband's house for forty days after his death, within which time her dower shall be assigned to her.

And,

No widow shall be forced to marry so long as she wishes to live without a husband, provided that she gives security not to marry without our consent if she holds of us, or without the consent of her lord of whom she holds, if she holds of another.

These provisions, as well as those governing trade and the activities of merchants, appeared in both versions of the charter. Economic stipulations guaranteed, for example, that:

All merchants, unless they have been publicly prohibited beforehand, shall be able to go out of and come into England safely and securely and stay and travel throughout England, as well by land as by water, for buying and selling by the ancient and right customs free from all evil tolls, except in time of war and if they are of the land that is at war with us.

The charter also established measures for various commodities:

Let there be one measure for wine throughout our kingdom, and one measure for ale, and one measure for corn, namely "the London quarter"; and one for cloths whether dyed, **russet** or *halberget*, namely two **ells** within the **selvedges**. Let it be the same with weights and with measures.

As may be seen from the foregoing examples, Magna Carta was essentially a conservative document designed by the nobility and the clergy for the purpose of regulating life in England. It is a practical document, rather than a great statement for personal freedom, although the seeds of parliamentary government and limited monarchy may be discerned in some of its provisions.

John evidently had no intention of keeping the charter, and he appealed to Pope Innocent, by now a close ally, to declare it null and void. As a result, in a statement issued in August of 1215, the pope proclaimed that:

> . . . we utterly reject and condemn this settlement, and under threat of excommunication we order that the king should not dare to observe it and that the barons and their associates should not require it to be observed: the charter, with all undertakings and guarantees, whether confirming it or resulting from it, we declare to be null, and void of all validity for ever. Wherefore, let no man deem it lawful to infringe this document of our annulment and prohibition, or presume to oppose it. If anyone should presume to do so, let him know that he will incur the anger of Almighty God and of saints Peter and Paul his apostles.

Not only did the pope reject the charter, but the council of twenty-five barons alienated many people through its tactless behavior. The barons' actions ultimately led to a revolt and a period of vicious fighting, which drew to a close without clear resolution. In the fall of 1216, John died, leaving as his successor his nine-year-old son, who would eventually come to the throne as Henry III.

Henry III

The period of rule by a council of regents while Henry was still a child returned England to order and unity. The leader of the council, William Marshall, earl of Pembroke, was able to gain back the loyalty of many barons, leading to a more stable political environment.

Henry finally ascended the throne in 1232. He was well-educated and pious, but his weak nature led to a propensity for falling under the influence of strong personalities. His court was dominated by foreign nobles who became his most influential advisers, and naturally this situation created an atmosphere of suspicion and distrust among the English barons. In addition, Henry became involved in grandiose foreign ventures, such as an attempt to take back the French lands lost during the reign of John. In order to undertake projects such as this, he was forced to levy exorbitant taxes, and he often convened the council of twenty-five barons for the purpose of approving taxation, rather than to ask its advice.

Henry gradually lost the support of the council, and in 1242 it refused to grant him money for his wars, expressing a lack of approval for his administration of royal government, and insisting that it should be consulted before the king embarked on any more foreign adventures.

However, in 1258 the pope, seeking an alliance with a strong foreign power, approached Henry, offering the crown of Sicily to Henry's younger son, Edmund Crouchback. In order to establish English control, it was necessary to send an expeditionary force. The adventure proved to be a disastrous failure, and the barons lost patience with royal schemes such as this, which had placed the country deeply in debt. They issued a document known as the "Provisions of Oxford," which declared that a council of fifteen members, chiefly barons, would share with the king the responsibility of governing the realm. They were given the responsibility of overseeing the office of the **Exchequer** and the power to appoint the chancellor and other important officials of the state. Furthermore, the "Provisions" declared that the great council of all the magnates, now known as "Parliament," would meet three times a year.

The "Provisions of Oxford," meekly accepted by a weak king, proved to be a failure because of factionalism among the barons, but the document indicates the predilection of the powerful magnates towards royal administration. They had no intention of abolishing the monarchy, but simply wished to establish a measure of control over the arbitrary actions of the king.

When the measures stipulated in the "Provisions" failed, Henry III returned to governing alone, and his corrupt and inept administration once again caused baronial rebellion. A group of opposing magnates, under the leadership of Simon de Montfort, earl of Leicester, defeated the forces of the king at the Battle of Lewes in 1264, and the king himself was taken prisoner.

De Montfort, together with two baronial colleagues and a committee of magnates, ruled England for fifteen months in the name of the king. Parliaments were called frequently during this time, and included, in addition to great magnates, royal officials, and the clergy, representatives from all classes of society. In a system probably designed to broaden de Montfort's own base of support, two knights were sent from every shire, and two burghers from every town. This became the pattern for parliamentary representation in subsequent decades. However, de Montfort lacked the full support of the barons, relying instead on the lesser landholders and the residents of the towns. As was often the case with aristocratic rebellions, many magnates remained loyal to the crown, and supported Henry's son, Lord Edward. Under his leadership, the forces of de Montfort were defeated at Evesham in 1265, and England returned to monarchical governance.

Edward was able to gain the allegiance of a majority of the barons, and left on crusade, leaving Henry III to govern until his death in 1272.

Edward I and the development of English law

Edward was crowned upon his return from the Holy Land in 1272, and ruled England until 1307. He proved to be an able monarch, initiating a significant amount of new legislation; indeed, he is sometimes known as the "English Justinian."

One of Edward's most important innovations was the reorganization of the royal administration. The major offices during his reign included the Exchequer, responsible for the collection of taxes and the overseeing of the accounts of sheriffs and other local officials, and the Chancery—responsible for issuing royal documents. The proclamations of the king were verified by attaching the great seal—a round wax seal showing the seated ruler on one side and an equestrian portait on the other. Whereas the offices of the Chancery and the Exchequer had been joined during the reign of Henry II, they became distinct specialized branches under Edward. In addition, there were Parliament, the "large council," and a smaller council of royal advisers. Edward also had a "household," which

traveled with the king. Its staff comprised treasury officials, writing clerks, and the keeper of the Privy ("Private") Seal, which provided the king and his Chancery with the means of issuing documents with the necessary emblem of sovereign authentication of the great seal while away from the royal court.

Edward faced the same problem as his predecessors with regard to raising money for wars, and he needed to levy frequent additional land taxes. In order to provide sanction for these taxes, in 1295 he convened a "Model Parliament," consisting of barons, Church prelates, lower clergy, knights, and burgesses (**fig. 100**). Summoned by the king, it furnished a pattern for subsequent parliaments. There were two representatives from each of 110 boroughs, two knights from each of the boroughs, ninety bishops and abbots, forty-one barons, and various representatives from the lower clergy. There was no division into two houses—a feature that eventually came to characterize Parliament. At this time, the function of Parliament was to assist the king in governing the realm, and

100 Edward I is shown in this illumination wearing full royal regalia, as he presides over a session of Parliament. The artist has faithfully represented the governmental hierarchy. The Prince of Wales is on Edward's left and slightly below, and Alexander, king of Scotland, is seated to his right. The archbishops of York and Canterbury sit at the ends of the platform. Members of the clergy appear down the left side of the illustration, with barons on the right; between them royal judges are seated on bags of wool.

to approve the taxation. Although Parliament gave counsel and heard complaints against royal officials, it remained essentially an extension of the king's will.

The most important of the documents issued during Edward's reign were designed to enhance the king's power by ensuring that the holding of land was regulated by the king. The Statute of Mortmain (1279), for example, prevented religious bodies from acquiring new lands, and the Second Statute of Westminster (1285) established **primogeniture**, decreeing that the land in the kingdom should pass from father to oldest son. In 1290, the Third Statute of Westminster, known as *Quia Emptores*, prevented further subinfeudation in England.

In addition to strengthening royal governance through legal measures, Edward was also determined to expand his realm. He ended a lengthy struggle with Wales by conquering the area in 1282–1283, and in 1284 the Statute of Wales was issued, incorporating Wales into England (see Map 18). Edward constructed castles in the newly conquered territory, such as Conwy Castle (**fig. 101**) in North Wales, and invested his son as Prince of Wales. His attempts to bring Scotland under English dominance were less successful, however, and his war with Philip IV of France was equally

101 Conwy Castle, in the county of Gwynedd, Wales (constructed c. 1283–1292) is typical of the fortifications constructed by Edward I to secure the newly incorporated area. The fortress was strategically placed to provide vantage points for watching over vast expanses of land in order to see approaching enemies. Furthermore, in addition to their practical function as battlements, features such as the massive circular towers, with their jagged crenellations, also provided a visual symbol of English power and authority.

inconclusive, although he was able to maintain English control over the Gascony region in southwestern Aquitaine.

When Edward died in 1307, England was firmly under royal control. Although he had exhausted the treasury with his wars, and had failed to fulfill his grandiose attempts to regain the Angevin Empire and to bring Scotland into the realm, Edward's legal measures had established a firm foundation for future royal governance.

France

The later reign of Philip Augustus

Philip Augustus proved to be one of the most effective of the Capetian kings, especially in terms of his relationships with the Angevin kings of England. During the reign of Henry II, he sowed seeds of discord between the king and his sons, encouraging Richard and John to rebel against their father; in addition, he encouraged Henry's French vassals to revolt. He accompanied Richard on the Third Crusade, but returned to France before the climactic encounters with Saladin, and he endorsed the captivity of the English monarch in Germany. After Richard's death he withdrew from his previous alliance with John, whom he now viewed as an opponent, rather than an ally (see Chapter 9). As discussed earlier, John's attempts to recover his land in France were unsuccessful, and Philip was able to expand the French royal domain significantly. Most of the new land was taken from England, but Philip was also industrious in the appropriation of vacant fiefs and those of disloyal vassals. Thus, at the end of his reign, in 1223, the realm was approximately four times as large as it had been in 1180 (**Map 20**).

Philip established his authority in these newly acquired areas by appointing *prevots*—non-feudal civil servants who were in charge of the administration of royal estates. He also created the offices of ***bailli*** and **seneschal**, royal officials drawn from the

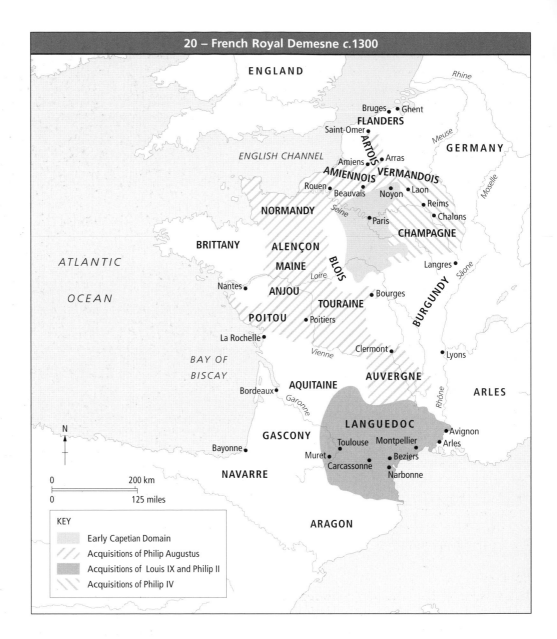

20 – French Royal Demesne c.1300

ENGLAND

Rhine

Bruges • Ghent
FLANDERS
Saint-Omer •
ARTOIS

GERMANY

Meuse

ENGLISH CHANNEL
Amiens • • Arras
AMIENNOIS **VERMANDOIS**
Rouen • • Beauvais Noyon • Laon •
NORMANDY • Reims
Seine • Paris • Chalons
CHAMPAGNE

Moselle

ATLANTIC

BRITTANY **ALENÇON**
MAINE **BLOIS**
Langres •
Loire
Saône
OCEAN
Nantes • **ANJOU**
POITOU **TOURAINE** • Bourges
• Poitiers
BURGUNDY
La Rochelle •

BAY OF
BISCAY
Vienne
Clermont •
• Lyons

AUVERGNE

ARLES

Bordeaux • **AQUITAINE**
Garonne
Rhône

N
LANGUEDOC • Avignon
GASCONY Toulouse • Montpellier • Arles •
Muret • • Beziers
Bayonne • Carcassonne • Narbonne •

0   200 km

0   125 miles

NAVARRE

ARAGON

KEY
Early Capetian Domain
Acquisitions of Philip Augustus
Acquisitions of Louis IX and Philip II
Acquisitions of Philip IV

lower nobility and the middle class, who were paid for their services. As a result of the development of education and the spread of literacy among the urban classes, there were many able candidates for these positions. The responsibilities of these new bureaucrats were administrative, and included financial and judicial duties. By employing civil servants who were dependent on, and hence devotedly loyal to, the king, the monarchy gained in popularity and strengthened its position in relation to the nobility.

In order to provide a further counterbalance to the power of the nobles, Philip gave charters to cities, which included special privileges for merchants, and he encouraged the growth of Paris as the capital. He actively fostered building projects in the

city, widening streets and constructing a magnificent palace near the cathedral of Notre-
Dame, whose facade was completed during his reign. In addition, he began the
construction of a fort, known as the Louvre,
on the right bank of the Seine so as to protect the city at its most vulnerable point. He
also issued a charter to the University of Paris
in 1200, thereby establishing an institution
that would become a preeminent center of
learning (see Chapter 13).

Philip's successor, Louis VIII, reigned
for the brief period of three years (r.
1223–1226), before he died in a military campaign against the Albigensians in southern
France (see Chapter 12). His heir was a twelve-
year-old son, also named Louis, who became
Louis IX (1226–1270). While the new king
was still a minor (1226–1234) and again later,
while he was on crusade (1248–1252), France
was governed by his mother, Blanche of Castile,
who proved to be a capable and effective
regent. Indeed, some scholars have asserted
that she was one of the most impressive rulers
of the entire Middle Ages (**fig. 102**). As was
common during a period of regency, the vassals of the crown attempted to weaken the
power of the regent through coalition and
rebellion, but Blanche personally led armies

102 This page from
the *Bible abregée*
(c. 1250) clearly shows
the influential position
enjoyed by Blanche of
Castile as mother of the
young king, Louis IX.
Blanche, top left,
appears to be giving
advice to the young
monarch, top right. In
the frames below, a
monk gives instructions
to the scribe, who is
preparing the vellum for
text and illumination.

into the field to quell these potential revolts. She was also a forceful negotiator, and when
Louis came of age in 1234, she was able to deliver a strong, unified kingdom into his hands.

Louis IX

Louis IX, or St. Louis, is commonly regarded as the greatest king of medieval France.
He was serious and conscientious, believing that God had placed him on the throne to
rule in a Christian manner. As a result, he was pious, generous, and hardworking, and was
intent on providing justice for his subjects; in addition to these virtues, he was valiant
in battle. As his biographer Joinville relates:

> St. Louis loved God with his whole heart and it was on him that he modeled his
> actions. This could be seen in that, as God died for the love of his people, so did the
> king more than once put his own body in danger of death for the love he bore his
> people; and this although, had he wished it, he might well have been excused.

The king's religious faith was strengthened by his daily schedule, which was arranged so as to allow him to attend not only a requiem Mass and the Mass of the day, but also the hours of the Divine Office. Joinville reports that he also said the Office of the Dead privately in his room before hearing Vespers and Compline.

Louis was also extremely temperate in eating and drinking, mixing his wine with water and cautioning his companions to "water their wine," lest when they were old men they should be drunk every evening: "It was a mighty ugly thing for a good man to get drunk." He was also noted for his generosity. As well as being "very compassionate to the poor and suffering," Louis, according to Joinville,

> daily gave countless generous alms, to poor religious, to poor hospitals, to poor sick people, to other poor convents, to poor gentlemen and gentlewomen and girls, to fallen women, to poor widows and women in childbed, and to poor minstrels who from old age or sickness were unable to work or follow their trade.

Although he was in many ways an exemplary king, Louis did, unfortunately, share some of the less tolerant attitudes of his contemporaries regarding Jews and heretics, perhaps as a result of his deep devotion to Christianity. He supposedly "could not bear" the sight of a Jew, and was concerned lest their "poison" infect his kingdom. He was also convinced that Hebrew biblical commentaries were pernicious, and in 1242 he watched as two dozen cartloads of the Talmud, condemned as an anti-Christian polemic, were burned in Paris.

Louis did not change the administrative structure he inherited to any degree, nor did he contribute in any way to the development of representative government—indeed, his nobles acted primarily as mere advisers. He did, however, establish a group of royal officials, known as **enquêteurs**, whose function was similar to the old *missi dominici* of the Carolingian period (see Chapter 4). These emissaries traveled throughout the kingdom, listening to grievances and holding local courts. They ultimately returned to Louis with notice of these complaints, and he then took suitable action.

The king's belief that every citizen was entitled to justice led to the evolution of the French court system. The extraordinary number of cases presented to the court of the king meant that the hearings could no longer take place at a traveling court, as had been the custom. Therefore, Louis established a permanent royal court at Paris, called *Parlement*, which met regularly, regardless of the absence of the king and powerful nobles. It is important to note that, despite the similarity in names, Parliament in England was a legislative assembly, whereas the French *Parlement* was a judicial body. Professional jurists generally decided the issues in *Parlement*, although in cases where an important nobleman was involved, a jury of his peers was called.

During the reign of St. Louis, France was at peace, although the king did go on two crusades (the Seventh and Eighth), one lasting from 1248 to 1250, and the other in 1270. Both were discouraging failures. During the first of these, the French armies attacked Egypt and easily took the port city of Damietta. As they attempted to move inland, they became confused by the twisting branches of the Nile, and were easily defeated by the Egyptians; Louis himself was captured, along with many of his nobles. The king was later ransomed and released, and was able to travel on to the Holy Land, where he spent the next four years helping to fortify the remaining Christian strongholds. He was convinced that his failure in Egypt was a result of his own sinful behavior, and he became even more dedicated to self-purification.

Louis brought many sacred objects back to France from the Holy Land, including some supposed relics of the Crucifixion: the Crown of Thorns, a piece of the lance that pierced Christ's side, the sponge, and a fragment of the True Cross, which he had purchased from his cousin Baldwin of Flanders, who was then ruling as the Byzantine emperor (see below). In order to provide a proper setting for these precious items, he built a chapel at Paris, known as the Ste.-Chapelle. Glittering with immense stained-glass windows and gilded sculptures of apostles and angels, the jewel-like building represents the apogee of the Gothic style (**fig. 103**). The upper chapel, shown in the illustration, adjoined the king's apartments, and was reserved for royal worship; a lower chapel, dedicated to the Virgin, was used as a parish church for members of the royal household. It was the king's intention to create a new "holy land" at Paris; in addition, the sumptuous quality of the interior of the chapel glorified not only the Christian God, but also the Capetian dynasty.

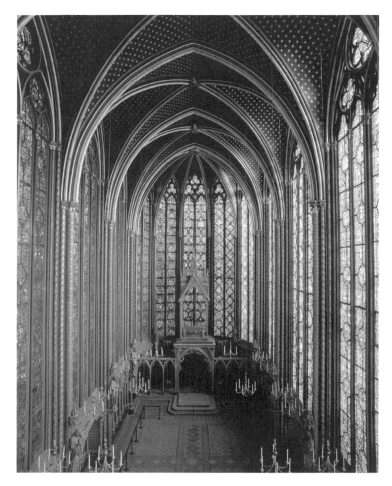

103 The small palace chapel at Paris known as Ste.-Chapelle was built (1246–1248) by Louis IX to provide a suitable place for displaying the precious relics he acquired while on a crusade to the Holy Land, including Christ's Crown of Thorns and a fragment of the True Cross. The building is one of the most glorious examples of Gothic style, featuring huge stained-glass windows. Because of the gilded sculptures and the glistening light that streams into the upper chapel, it has been called a medieval "jewelbox."

In 1270, Louis undertook another crusade (the Eighth), this time to Tunis. As he was traveling, he contracted dysentery and died almost immediately. His army disbanded and returned to France. In 1297, after a papal committee had made careful "inquisition into the life, the works, and miracles of this saintly king," Louis was canonized by Pope Boniface VIII.

St. Louis was succeeded by his son Philip III, who ruled from 1270 to 1285. Philip, who retained the policies and wise councillors of his father, added to the royal domain through marriage, and succeeded in preserving the peace. However, he was not an active king, and, in any case, it would have been impossible to live up to the reputation of his father.

Philip IV

Philip III was followed on the throne by Philip IV ("the Fair") (r. 1285–1314), one of the most important rulers of medieval France. He continued his father's and grandfather's policies of centralizing government and curbing abuses by the nobility. Like his earlier predecessor, Philip Augustus, however, Philip IV also became involved in expensive wars. His primary objectives were to drive the English from their remaining possessions in Aquitaine, and to extend the boundaries of France to include the rich area of Flanders. He also waged campaigns along the border areas of the German empire.

Facing the same problems of military expense as his English counterpart, Edward I, Philip was forced to seek sources of taxation beyond the ordinary. It occurred to his advisers that a large portion of the land of France (approximately one-fourth) was held by the Church, and was therefore exempt from taxes. Philip, claiming that the circumstances of war were "unusual," decided that he should be allowed to levy a tax on Church lands. His attempt to tap this source of revenue led him into a major confrontation with the pope, Boniface VIII.

Thundering forth from Rome, Boniface declared in a papal bull known as *Clericis Laicos* (1296) that only the pope held the authority to tax the clergy, and he expressly forbade the bishops and clergy to pay taxes, or provide aids or loans, "without the permission of the pope." If they did make payments "by whatever name or pretext," they would "incur the sentence of excommunication." He further threatened to excommunicate kings who attempted to assess payments without papal permission: "If the ones shall pay, or the others receive anything, they shall by that very act fall under the sentence of excommunication."

Philip reacted by arresting a bishop in southern France on charges of treason. This action precipitated another papal bull, *Unam Sanctam* (1302), which declared that the papacy held authority over secular rulers:

> We are taught by the words of the Gospel that in this Church and in her power there are two swords, a spiritual one and a temporal one. For when the apostles said "Here are two swords" (Luke 22:38), meaning in the Church since it was the apostles who spoke, the Lord did not reply that it was too many but enough. Certainly anyone who denies that the temporal sword is in the power of Peter has not paid heed to the words of the Lord when he said, "Put up thy sword into its sheath" (Matthew 26:52). Both then are in the power of the Church, the material sword and the spiritual. But the one is exercised for the Church, the other by the Church, the one by the hand of the priest, the other by the hand of kings and soldiers, though at the will and sufferance of the priest. One sword ought to be under the other and the temporal authority subject to the spiritual power . . . Therefore, if the earthly power errs, it shall be judged by the spiritual power, if a lesser spiritual power errs it shall be judged by its superior, but if the supreme spiritual power errs it can be judged only by God, not by man, as the apostle witnesses, "The spiritual man judgeth all things and he himself is judged of no man" (1 Corinthians 2:15) . . . Therefore, we declare, state, define, and pronounce that it is altogether necessary to salvation for every human creature to be subject to the Roman pontiff.

Philip reacted by ordering his agents to travel to the pope's residence at Agnani, south of Rome, to capture the pontiff and bring him to France to face a trial on charges of heresy. The king's men probably subjected the pope to physical abuse, and although the townspeople of Agnani expelled Philip's men from the pope's palace, the pontiff (who was eighty-two) died a month later. Philip and his henchmen were pardoned by the newly elected pope, Benedict XI, who reigned only a year; the next pope, significantly, was French, and the papacy stood at the threshold of the Avignon papacy, the so-called "Babylonian Captivity," during which the popes were in residence in southern France for much of the fourteenth century (see Chapter 14).

In order to amass support in his struggle against Pope Boniface VIII, Philip had summoned a legislative body known as the *Etats-Généraux* (Estates General), which comprised delegates from the nobility, the French clergy, and representatives of towns. One of the first actions of this assembly was to declare the pope a heretic and a criminal who was subject to the French king. The fact that the clergy supported the king against the pope is indicative of an embryonic nationalism that was beginning to be evident in the monarchies of western Europe. The king also enjoyed the loyal support of the citizens of the towns, who joined the clergy in urging governmental reform.

One of the most infamous events during the reign of Philip was his disbanding of the Templars. This order of crusading knights was in control of the royal finances (see Chapter 7). It was their responsibility to audit annually the accounts of the royal tax collectors. By 1300, the Templars were unable to deal efficiently with the complicated administration of the rapidly growing economy, and Philip, realizing the potential wealth that would result from seizing the holdings of the order, charged them with corruption and embezzlement. The methods he used were ruthless and cruel, including stealth, torture, extraction of confessions from the leaders, and burning of those who later retracted their statements. Pope Clement V (r. 1305–1314) tried in vain to establish an inquiry into the Templars' activities, and those of Philip. Eventually, under threat from the French king, in 1312, the pope disbanded the order. By that time Philip had taken their real estate and capital holdings in France, and other European kings had followed suit.

Germany, Italy, and Sicily

After the death of the Holy Roman Emperor Henry VI in 1197, his heir, the infant Frederick II (r. 1215–1250), was placed under the guardianship of Pope Innocent III. Frederick lived in Sicily during his childhood, and thought of this area, rather than Germany, as his home.

Frederick was given a brilliant education, and his intellectual accomplishments earned him the nickname *Stupor mundi* ("Wonder of the World"). According to the *Cronica* (*Chronicle*) written by a thirteenth-century Italian Franciscan friar and historian named Salimbene di Adam, Frederick "knew to read, write, and sing, to make songs and music . . . [and] to speak with many and varied tongues." As an adult he was a great patron of the arts, and assembled a number of scholars, including Muslims, who worked in a center for translation at Palermo. He also established the University of Naples, one of the earliest university foundations by a secular ruler.

Because of his Sicilian upbringing, Frederick was deeply influenced by Muslim culture. He kept a splendid court, dressed in sumptuous garments of the Islamic style, and was rumored to possess a harem of beautiful Muslim women. Furthermore, he was not in the least opposed to establishing friendly alliances with Muslim princes. His actions were regarded by the papacy as suspicious, and the popes who reigned during his tenure as emperor saw him as less than the ideal Christian ruler.

Frederick was fascinated by scientific investigation, and some of his experiments were judged by his contemporaries to indicate a cruel nature. According to the *Chronicle* of Salimbene:

> Frederick cut off a notary's thumb who had spelt his name Fredericus instead of Fridericus . . . he enclosed a living man in a cask that he might die there, wishing thereby to show that the soul perished utterly . . . [and] he fed two men most excellently at dinner, one of whom he sent forthwith to sleep, and the other to hunt; and that same evening he caused them to be disembowelled in his presence, wishing to know which had digested the better: and it was judged by the physicians in favor of him who had slept.

Shortly after assuming the throne in 1212, Frederick toured his northern possessions, but then returned to live in Italy, preferring this area as a base of power (see Map 21). He left the northern part of his realm in the hands of the princes, granting them full rights over their lands; he guaranteed, among other things, that:

> Each prince shall possess and exercise in peace according to the customs of the land, the liberties, jurisdiction, and authority over counties and hundreds which are in his own possession or are held as fiefs from him.

The rights granted to the nobles included economic matters as well as issues of jurisdiction, and put the princes in authority over the burgeoning urban areas in Germany. By extending princely control over the towns in this way, Frederick abandoned a great source of potential strength and support for the monarchy. This policy did nothing to enhance his own power in Germany, but it did serve to pacify the princes. The result, however, was that, once Frederick had given them what they wanted, they paid little attention to his further imperial designs, and refused to lend support to his campaigns in Italy.

The popes, especially Gregory IX (r. 1227–1241), were suspicious of Frederick's activities. Gregory issued a sentence of excommunication, claiming that Frederick had failed to go on a crusade, as he had promised. The emperor promptly addressed the issue by setting out for the Holy Land in 1228, without resolving his differences with the Church.

Frederick's experience in the ongoing Holy War was quite different from the earlier crusades. He traveled to Palestine, where he entered Jerusalem. He then negotiated with the sultan of Egypt, who was in control of Jerusalem, and finally convinced him to cede Jerusalem, Bethlehem, and Nazareth, among other towns, together with a broad access route. Freedom of worship would be granted to both Christian and Muslim worshipers. It should be noted that Frederick had actually accomplished what all the other crusaders had set out to achieve, largely through the force of his personality, rather than arms. The crusade was brought to an abrupt close when Frederick learned that papal armies had invaded his Italian lands, and he hurried home to meet the assault.

Frederick easily defeated the papal armies, and then moved to strengthen and centralize his administration in Italy. In a document known as the *Constitution of Melfi* published in 1231, the emperor's authority was emphasized, the privileges of both nobles and townspeople were diminished, and the adjudication of major legal cases, both civil and criminal, was assigned to royal courts. The same year, Frederick issued the *Constitution in Favor of the Princes*, which stipulated the various powers the magnates could employ in their territories to establish and maintain order.

The ultimate result of Frederick's policy towards Germany was the institutionalization of fragmented power by allowing each prince to build his own realm without interference from the emperor. In the future, the princes of Germany had no intention of allowing royal supremacy to reassert itself. The crown was granted according to the elective principle, and the princes were careful to choose a weak individual who offered no threat to their authority. Hence, rather than developing into a strong monarchical state like France and England, Germany remained a tenuous alliance of princes under the loose control of an elected emperor. Although when Frederick died in 1250, he was followed on the throne by his weak and ineffectual son Conrad (r. 1250–1254), most scholars think that the Hohenstaufen Empire actually died with him.

The period after Conrad's death was one of conflict and confusion. No one candidate was able to amass enough support to be elected as emperor, and the princes kept the German throne empty while they proceeded to build numerous castles to assert their control over their local areas. The lands of the Hohenstaufens were seized and divided among the magnates. Ultimately, in 1273, the princes, who had organized themselves into a body known as the *Diet*, elected Rudolf of Habsburg, who ruled until 1291. Recognizing that he could not assert his authority over the nobles, he used his energy and resources to extend his domain into eastern Europe—a policy that was acceptable to the princes, since it did not affect their interests.

The governance of the Sicilian kingdom, comprising Sicily and Naples, was also problematic. Although it had been weakened by Frederick's expensive military operations, it remained an important Mediterranean power. As we saw earlier in this chapter, the island was coveted by Henry III of England, but since it was historically a papal fief, the papacy wished to enhance its own position. By awarding the kingdom of Naples and Sicily to Charles of Anjou, the younger brother of King Louis IX of France, the pope intended that French power would drive out the claimant to the throne, Manfred, an illegitimate son of Frederick II. Noted for his ambition and cruelty, Charles killed his rival and was able to occupy the throne in 1266.

Charles was extremely unpopular with the Sicilians, who viewed his French soldiers as an army of occupation. In 1282 the citizens of Palermo began a riot when a French soldier accosted a young married woman on her way to an evening church service, and the uprising eventually spread to the rest of the island. The French were forced to retreat to Naples, and a war ensued, which lasted some twenty years. This conflict was known as the "War of the Sicilian Vespers," since the riot had begun while the bells were tolling to announce the evening service. By 1302 the island had established its independence from the Italian mainland, but the citizens were never able to recover fully from the effects of war, and Sicily sank into poverty.

Spain

In the course of the thirteenth century, Castile and Aragón emerged as the most important Spanish kingdoms. In 1230, Castile was reunited with León after a separation that had lasted seventy-three years, during which the kingdom of León was ruled by its own kings Ferdinand II (r. 1157–1188) and Alfonso IX (r. 1188–1230). The new leader of the combined kingdom after 1230 was Ferdinand III ("San Fernando;" king of Castile since 1217), who undertook further vigorous expansion into Muslim Spain. In 1236, the southern city of Córdoba was captured, followed in 1238 by Valencia and in 1248 by Seville. Thus, by the middle of the thirteenth century, the Muslims were confined to the area around Granada, where they remained until 1492.

Ferdinand III

Ferdinand's accomplishments are reflected in the words that the dying king (d. 1252) supposedly said to his son, Alfonso X:

> You are richer in lands and good vassals than any other king in Christendom . . .
> I leave you the whole realm from the sea hither, which the Moors won from Rodrigo,
> king of Spain. All of it is in your dominion, part of it conquered, the other part
> tributary. If you know how to preserve in this state what I leave you, you will be as
> good a king as I was, and if you win more for yourself, you will be better than I was,
> but if you diminish it, you will not be as good as I was.

Spanish writers of the time were exultant when they reflected on their victories. Their sense of pride is encapsulated in the words of Vincentius Hispanus, a professor of canon law: "The Spaniards alone gained an empire by their valor."

Muslim writers and poets, by contrast, expressed a sense of loss and despair, and many chose to emigrate from their native country. A thirteenth-century poem by al-Rundi typifies their emotional response:

> As a lover does when torn from his beloved;
> They weep over the remains of dwellings devoid of Muslims,
> Despoiled of Islam, now peopled by Infidels!
> Those mosques have now been changed into churches,
> Where the bells are ringing and crosses are standing;
> This misfortune has supposed all that has preceded,
> And as long as Time lasts, it can never be forgotten!
> What an opprobrium, when once powerful people
> Have been humbled to dust by tyrants and injustice!
> Yesterday they were kings in their own palaces,
> Today they are slaves in the land of the Infidels!

There was no direct attempt by the Christians to expel, assimilate, or convert the Muslims living in the newly conquered territories. However, many of the Muslims preferred to join their co-religionists in Granada. Those who remained in Christian Spain, called **mudéjares** in Spanish, became a major problem for the kings who followed Ferdinand III.

Alfonso the Wise

Alfonso X (1252–1284), Ferdinand's successor as king of León and Castile, is known as *El Sabio*, "the Wise" or "the Learned." He was well educated and accomplished in the arts of war, and when he ascended the throne he seemed ideally suited to carry on his father's policies of expansion. But the most important feature of his reign was the cultural achievement of the writers, scholars, and musicians he patronized.

Alfonso was a scholar whose impact on the cultural life of thirteenth-century Spain was profound. He believed that his people should be educated, and he insisted that scholarship and literary efforts be presented in the vernacular, so as to attract the widest possible audience. His program of patronage included the completion of a vernacular encyclopedia, called the *Setenario*, begun during the reign of his father, which described the Seven Liberal Arts and basic Christian beliefs and practices. Alfonso was also interested in science, and many of the translations he commissioned were Arabic scientific treatises.

One of the king's finest accomplishments was a collection of songs, the *Cantigas de Santa María*, which was compiled at his court and contained several compositions by Alfonso himself (**fig. 104**). For the most part, the songs deal with miracles performed by the Virgin Mary, which are systematically arranged. The songs are typical expressions of the cult of the Virgin Mary, which was a prominent feature of thirteenth-century culture throughout Europe.

The political achievements of Alfonso "the Wise" are generally deemed less significant than his cultural and intellectual accomplishments. He was certainly unsuccessful in one of his main political ambitions. Through his mother, who was a granddaughter of Frederick Barbarossa, Alfonso had a claim to the throne of the Holy Roman Empire. Although his rights were substantial, and he spent an exorbitant amount of money in an attempt to secure the position, the pope refused to recognize him, effectively ending his imperial venture.

Partly because he became enchanted with this quest for the crown of the Holy Roman Empire, Alfonso was distracted from solving problems within his own realm. This is not to say that he had no ambitions in this area, but his enormous expenditure of resources, together with his tendency towards absolutism and his indecision concerning his successor on the throne, brought his reign to a less than stellar end.

104 King Alfonso X, "the Wise," was a scholar and important patron of the arts. One of the finest examples of the work of artists and muscians at his court was the collection of songs, *Cantigas de Santa María*, which contained some of the king's own compositions. This illustration from the *Cantigas* depicts Alfonso surrounded by singers and instrumentalists, who play lutes and rebecs.

Alfonso continued the policies of royal centralization that had characterized his predecessors, strengthening his control through a code of municipal law, the *Fuero Real*, which he imposed upon many towns, and the *Espéculo de las leyes*, which was intended to become a uniform law throughout his realm. The vision of royal power embodied in these codes was at variance with the traditional views of balance between a king and his subjects. The nobles accused Alfonso of depriving them of their rights, and the townspeople were alarmed at the prospect of losing their traditional privileges; they were also resentful of the king's demands for extraordinary taxation.

Like those of King John in England and King Philip in France, Alfonso's subjects complained that his quest for empire "brought great poverty to the kingdoms of León and Castile." The magnates began to plot with Alfonso's enemies, and they ultimately confronted the king at Burgos, demanding that he make concessions regarding onerous taxes. The king acceded to their demands, confirming the traditional customs of the nobility and also the leaders of the towns. In return, the towns granted him a tax levy every year to aid in his plans for expansion, which ultimately proved fruitless.

Alfonso's reign and character were effectively summarized by a contemporary Catalan historian, Bernat Desclot:

> He was the most generous man who ever lived, for there was no man, or knight, or minstrel who came to ask anything from him who went away empty-handed. On this account his realm was much less wealthy and the people could not endure the burdens he caused them or the many evil laws he imposed . . . For this reason the barons of Castile and León and of the whole realm deprived him of his sovereignty.

The end of Alfonso's reign was sullied by a quarrel between the king and his son Sancho regarding the succession to the throne. Alfonso's eldest son, Ferdinand, had been killed in battle, and his second son, Sancho, proclaimed himself heir, disregarding the claims of Ferdinand's sons. Alfonso was not in favor of Sancho's succession, but eventually, deserted by family members as well as noble supporters, he attempted a reconciliation with him. He did not, however, change his will, which disinherited Sancho. Nonetheless, when the king died, Sancho seized the entire inheritance, and reigned as Sancho IV (r. 1284–1295).

Muslims and Jews in thirteenth-century Spain

The kings of the thirteenth-century Spanish peninsula ruled over a population that was religiously diverse. The changes that had resulted from the Christian reconquest were substantial. Large numbers of Muslims and Jews were assimilated into the Christian kingdoms, but others left their ancestral homes to migrate to Muslim-held Granada or even North Africa. Substantial areas were thus left open to Christian colonists from the north, especially in the southern regions of Andalucía, the Alentejo, and the Algarve. Here the new settlers tended to congregate in the urban areas, while the Muslims generally remained in the countryside. Christian colonization was widespread, and continued unabated until the coming of the Black Death in 1348 (see Chapter 14).

The ethnic composition of Spain remained essentially unchanged, with the exception of port cities such as Seville, where foreign merchants, primarily the Genoese, settled. The most significant change experienced by the Christian kingdoms was that large numbers of Muslims and Jews were contained within the newly established borders. It seems that Granada, by contrast, had relatively few Jews and Christians among its people.

The *mudéjares* were legally protected but generally had limited freedom. Many were slaves who worked at agricultural or domestic tasks for nobles, bishops, monasteries, and other members of the upper class. Most Muslims lived in rural areas, but there were Muslim communities in the cities where they lived in circumscribed districts. As long as they paid a tribute to the king, they were allowed to govern themselves according to their own laws. They also enjoyed religious liberty, although the most important mosques were often taken by the Christians and converted to Christian use. The *muezzin* was forbidden by Pope Clement V as a means of summoning the congregation to worship, and Muslims were not allowed to invoke Muhammad's name in public, or to make pilgrimages to the tombs of holy men. Christians were urged to attempt conversion of their Muslim neighbors "by good words or suitable preaching," but were cautioned not to use force, "for the Lord is not pleased by the service that men give him through fear." If a Christian converted to Islam, he would lose his inheritance, and if he were found in Christian lands, he would "die for his error." As these provisions may suggest, there were frequent conversions and reconversions in the frontier areas of the Christian kingdoms.

Other restrictions placed on the Muslims included a requirement to wear their hair cut short without a forelock, although they had long beards, as stipulated by their own tradition. They were forbidden to wear bright colors, such as red, vermilion, or green, and their shoes could not be white or gilded. They were not allowed to live in Christian houses, or to hire Christian workers, or to employ Christian women to nurse their children. If a Muslim was caught in a sexual relationship with a Christian virgin, he was to be stoned, and she lost half of her possessions for the first offense, and the rest if she continued the liaison. If the woman was married, her husband could punish her in any way he wished, including burning her.

The Jews in Christian Spain faced similar restrictions. They were required to wear distinctive clothing, usually with a yellow badge or a six-pointed star on the front and back. They were forbidden by law to own Christian slaves, or to have intercourse with Christians, or to harass a Jew who had converted to Christianity. The Jews did possess a measure of religious liberty, however, and enjoyed freedom of worship, although they were not allowed to build new synagogues or to enlarge existing ones without permission from the king.

Like the Muslims, Jews in Spain settled mostly in cities, where they lived in isolated communities, called **juderías**, and governed themselves under the direction of a council of elders. They were subject to most of the same taxes as the Christians, but paid, in addition, a monthly fee of thirty **dineros** in memory of the thirty pieces of silver received by Judas for betraying Jesus.

The Muslim and Jewish populations both made significant contributions to cultural and economic developments in the Spanish kingdoms, and eventually served as a conduit for the transmission of ancient learning to northern Europe, thereby providing an important link between the Christian and Muslim worlds.

The Northern Crusades

Until recently, the crusading movement in northern Europe has received much less scholarly attention than the crusades to the Holy Land or the Spanish Reconquista against the Muslims. It has not been emphasized that when Bernard of Clairvaux began to encourage German knights to go on crusade in the middle of the twelfth century, he discovered that many Germans were also eager to take action against non-Christians in the north. Bernard gained papal recognition for these crusades, which were begun by the king of Denmark and the duke of Saxony. These two leaders were able to establish control over much of the area east of the Oder River, taking some territory directly and awarding it to their followers as booty. Other land continued to be held by Slavic princes, who surrendered and became vassals of the Christian rulers.

In 1198, the newly elected Pope Innocent III preached the first of several crusades, this one against the Livs, a tribe living on what is now the coast of Latvia. A crusading order was established to lead the armies; it was known as the Order of Sword Brothers, and was later absorbed by another order, the Teutonic Knights, created in the aftermath of the Third Crusade. Innocent created a bishopric, "the see of Riga," which was strategically placed at the mouth of the Dvina River. The armies forced the native population to surrender and accept their religion, often by promising military aid against their enemies, or, if that failed, by brute force. By the beginning of the fourteenth century, the crusaders had overtaken Livonia, Prussia, Estonia, and Finland; Lithuania alone was able to remain independent.

These northern crusades had a great impact on the future of the Baltic territories. The region was colonized by German lords and peasants, who brought with them their customs and traditions, creating a link between their new homeland and their relatives to the south and west. As churches and monasteries were established, cities gradually began to develop in the region. Eventually guilds and universities, as well as castles and manors, spread throughout the Baltic area.

The Borderlands of Western Europe

In the areas bordering western Europe, Christianization continued to proceed rapidly. As discussed in Chapter 6, during the tenth and eleventh centuries bishoprics were established by German missionaries in Hungary, Poland, and Bohemia, with the new foundations being subject to the inspection and control of German ecclesiastical authorities. In Scandinavia, the earliest sees were founded in Denmark, and by the eleventh century a territorial network of nine (later eight) bishoprics was in existence. In the twelfth century the Danish church was granted its own archbishopric, at Lund in Scania (now in Sweden). The other Scandinavian countries—Sweden, Norway, and Iceland—had a more sporadic Christian development, but by the twelfth century there were a number of bishoprics, extending from Iceland to Uppsala.

These areas were also bound together by trade. In the twelfth century Henry the Lion had taken possession of the strategically important town of Lübeck, and had welcomed the merchants:

At his bidding the merchants at once returned with joy and . . . started to rebuild the churches and the walls of the city. The duke sent messengers to the cities and kingdoms of the north—Denmark, Sweden, Norway, Russia—offering them peace so that they should have free access to his city of Lübeck. He also ordained there a mint and tolls and most honorable civic rights. From that time on, the business of the city prospered and the number of its inhabitants multiplied.

From this time Lübeck became the center of a burgeoning trading network, and by the end of the thirteenth century trade among the Baltic countries, Scandinavia, and Russia was firmly established.

Hungary was also populated by many German immigrants during the central Middle Ages. In the eleventh century the Hungarian kings, who had established their authority in the area along the Danube River, moved northeast towards the Carpathian Mountains, asserting their hegemony over the Slavic and German residents of the area. It is interesting to note that the feudal nobility, of mixed ethnicity but primarily Hungarian, forced the thirteenth-century king, Andras II (r. 1205–1235), to issue a document similar to Magna Carta, known as the Golden Bull, which granted privileges such as exemption from taxation.

In the eleventh century the Hungarian kings extended their control southward to Croatia, which enabled them to vie with the Venetian Republic for the lucrative Adriatic trade. As will be discussed in the next section, the Hungarian takeover of the city of Zara became a contributing factor in events of the disastrous Fourth Crusade.

The Byzantine Empire and the Fourth Crusade

During the century following the First Crusade, the Byzantine Empire continued to experience the military and political decline that had been endemic during the previous hundred years. Although the rulers of the Comneni dynasty who followed Alexius Comnenus (r. 1081–1118) were generally shrewd and politically skillful, they were blamed for initiating the crusades, and were criticized for their inability to bring them to a close.

As long as the crusaders took the land route through Constantinople, the emperors were able to negotiate agreements with them that would provide for the return of conquered lands to the empire in exchange for military assistance and supplies. The crusaders did not intend to live up to these arrangements, however, and the Byzantine rulers were equally untrustworthy. As the twelfth century progressed, the distrust between the western European and Byzantine powers escalated. This factor, in addition to the constant rivalry over shipping routes, contributed to the rift between east and west that had originally centered on religious differences. Indeed, the religious controversies themselves actually began to dissipate, as people realized that mass conversion would not occur. The lessening of tension seems to have led to an atmosphere of increased tolerance among Christians of both Roman and Orthodox traditions, Muslims, and Jews.

The political and military decline of the twelfth and thirteenth centuries was not mirrored in the economic and cultural situation of the empire, which remained healthy. Although the imperial holdings comprised probably only two-thirds of the area controlled in the tenth century, most of the land lost during the twelfth was situated on the sparsely populated and agriculturally poor Anatolian plateau. The most fertile and populous territory remained part of the empire, and trade, as well as agriculture, continued to prosper and thrive. Indeed, in 1204, when crusaders entered Constantinople, which at that time had a population of approximately 400,000 (see below), they were astonished to find the largest and wealthiest city they had ever seen.

During the twelfth century the Byzantine merchants and large landowners continued to become more prosperous, and the peasants who held small agricultural tracts made up a minority of the population for the first time in the history of the empire. This development was a result of increasing demographic growth which was confined to an area where geographic expansion had ceased. The scarcity of land caused it to become more expensive, whereas labor was more plentiful, and hence less valuable. The existing land was consolidated in the hands of those with the most money, including nobles, government officials who had become wealthy, and monastic establishments.

The growing power and influence of the wealthy aristocrats were a threat to the emperors, and by 1200 several local magnates had, in fact, taken control of territories in central Thrace and Greece. Sensing potential danger, the emperors, rather than continuing the previous policy of drawing military officers from the ranks of the aristocracy, began to hire mercenaries to staff the officer class; these men held no loyalty to the crown. Furthermore, the appropriations for the military decreased during this period, and the naval fleet was drastically weakened, leaving the empire in an increasingly vulnerable position.

Byzantium was coveted as a rich prize by several foreign powers, in addition to western Europeans such as the Normans, who had attempted to invade in the eleventh century. Forces of Arabs, Turks, Syrians, Armenians, and Kurds had assaulted parts of the empire during the eleventh and twelfth centuries, and had managed to take large areas in Palestine and Asia Minor. In addition, portions of the Balkan lands were overrun by groups of Bulgars, Pechenegs, and Cumans. The ineffectual emperors were seemingly unable to prevent these incursions and losses of territory, and in 1200 there was a revolt in Constantinople itself. This proved to be an opportune time for action from the west, for the recently elected Pope Innocent III had called for a new holy war in hopes of redeeming the losses and humiliations of the Second and Third Crusades.

Those setting out on this Fourth Crusade made their preparations, deciding to take the sea route rather than traveling over land, since they believed that the Byzantines could not be trusted. They struck a bargain with the Venetians, who contracted to take them to Egypt, their determined destination, and to provide horses and supplies upon their arrival. When the time came for the crusaders to pay, however, they were unable to collect the agreed amount, some 85,000 marks. In lieu of a cash payment, the Venetians convinced the crusaders to join them in attacking the city of Zara, a former Venetian possession then under Hungarian control. The assault was successful, and Zara was returned to Venetian jurisdiction. However, this premeditated attack on a Christian city enraged Pope Innocent, who excommunicated the entire crusading army.

The crusaders spent the winter of 1202–1203 in Zara, where they were contacted by Alexius (eventually Emperor Alexius IV, in r. 1203–1204), a Byzantine prince who had been deposed by a national revolt in 1201. Alexius asked them to aid him in regaining his throne, which had been usurped by another Alexius, known as Alexius III. He promised to provide them with money, supplies, and soldiers so that they could continue on to the Holy Land once he had regained power, and they accepted his offer. Soon the crusaders were at the walls of Constantinople.

After a period of convoluted political maneuvering, it became evident that Alexius was not able to fulfill his side of the bargain, and the crusaders, together with Venetian forces, attacked the city. When they had breached the walls, they set large areas of the city on fire, and most of the population fled, together with the emperor, Alexius III. As described by Geoffrey de Villehardouin (d. 1213), a French crusader who was a witness to the disaster:

> Then followed a scene of massacre and pillage: on every hand the Greeks were cut down, their horses, palfreys, mules, and other possessions snatched as booty. So great was the number of killed and wounded that no man could count them. A great part of the Greek nobles had fled towards the gate of Blachernae; but by this time it was past six o'clock, and our men had grown weary of fighting and slaughtering.

The besieging forces triumphantly entered the city, and the crusaders placed one of their own number, Baldwin of Flanders, on the Byzantine throne.

One of the participants in the looting of Constantinople was Martin, abbot of the Cistercian monastery of Pairis, in the Alsace region. Upon returning to his monastery, he directed one of the monks, named Gunther, to write an account of the crusade. Gunther's work, the *Hystoria Constantinopolitana* (*A Constantinopolitan History*), combined prose and poetry in an elaborate justification of the actions of the crusaders, which Gunther saw as being the "decision of Divine Goodness . . . so arranged, through this pattern of events, that this people, proud because of its wealth, should be humbled by their very pride and recalled to the peace and concord of the Holy Catholic Church." Gunther wrote that it was appropriate for pilgrims to grow rich on the spoils of the Byzantine Empire, and that the western church, "illuminated by the inviolable relics of which these people had shown themselves unworthy, should rejoice forever." The crusaders had been galvanized by his poetry:

> Break in! Now, honored soldier of Christ, Break in!
> Break into the city which Christ has given to the conqueror.
> Imagine for yourself Christ, seated on a gentle ass,
> The King of Peace, radiant in countenance, leading the way.
> You fight Christ's battles. You execute Christ's vengeance,
> By Christ's judgment. His will precedes your onslaught.
> Break in! Rout menaces; crush cowards; press on more bravely;
> Shout in thundering voice; brandish iron, but spare the blood.
> Instill terror, yet remember they are brothers
> Whom you overwhelm, who by their guilt have merited it for some time.
> Christ wished to enrich you with the wrongdoers' spoils,
> Lest some other conquering people despoil them.
> Behold, homes lie open, filled with enemy riches,

And an ancient horde will have new masters.
Yet you, meanwhile, curbing heart and hand,
Postpone and disdain the pillage of goods until the right moment!
Throw yourself on the timorous; press firmly upon the conquered;
Do not allow the fatigued to recover and regain strength.
Immediately upon the enemy's expulsion from the entire city,
There will be time for looting; it will be proper to despoil the conquered.

The sack of Constantinople was an unparalleled disaster. The city was full of ancient Greek art treasures, as well as exquisite artifacts of Byzantine manufacture. The Venetians understood the value of these objects, and took them to use as ornaments for their own buildings and public squares. The Franks had no such appreciation, however, and were wanton in their destruction of artworks and sacred monuments. In Hagia Sophia itself, they were seen tearing down the embroidered silk wall hangings, destroying silver liturgical vessels, and trampling icons and liturgical books underfoot.

Eventually the crusading army ceased its destructive rampage, and as its members moved through the Byzantine palaces, they began to amass the remaining spoils of conquest, which were vast. According to Villehardouin, they took "gold and silver, table-services and precious stones, satin and silk, mantles of squirrel fur, ermine, and miniver [unspotted ermine or any white fur], and every choicest thing to be found on this earth . . . [indeed], so much booty had never been gained in any city since the creation of the world."

Following the Fourth Crusade, the areas left unconquered by the European armies was less than half of the territory held by the Byzantine Empire in the mid-eleventh

century. These were consolidated into three "states": the Principality of Epirus (present-day northern Greece and Albania); the Empire of Nicea, including the cities of Nicea (today Iznik, Turkey) and Heraclea Pontica (Eregli); and the Empire of Trebizond, which included a narrow band of land on the southeast coast of the Black Sea.

In 1264, a new dynasty, the Palaeologi, was able to regain Constantinople from the Europeans. Eventually they recovered most of the territory that had constituted the empire in 1204, but in terms of military strength, economic production, and cultural and intellectual influence, the Byzantine Empire never recovered fully from the Fourth Crusade (**Map 21**). The fact that it managed to survive at all was largely as a result of diplomatic efforts and strong fortifications. But the empire's potential enemies were also distracted by having to attend to serious new threats that had emerged during the thirteenth century, coming primarily from a new power in the east: the Mongols.

The Rise of the Mongols

The Mongol Empire that emerged in the thirteenth century (sometimes called the Tatar or Tartar Empire) was the creation of one man, a ferocious warrior known as Genghis (or Jenghis) Khan (1167–1227). Genghis was able to organize groups of formerly nomadic tribesmen living in Central Asia into a powerful and cohesive Mongol force that swept through China, breaking through the Great Wall, and forcing the population to submit in a campaign that has been described as the conquest of 100 million people by 100,000 soldiers. The Mongols then turned west towards Russia and Europe (**Map 22**), conquering everything in their path by virtue of military superiority coupled with terror tactics verging on the sadistic.

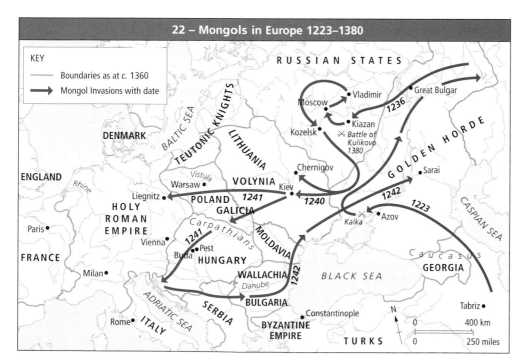

The Mongols' assault on Kiev was typical of their methods. As described in 1245 by a papal legate and famous traveler, Archbishop Plano Carpini:

> they went against Russia and enacted a great massacre in the Russian land, they destroyed towns and fortresses and killed people, they besieged Kiev, which had been the capital of Russia, and after a long siege they took it and killed the inhabitants of the city; for this reason, when we passed through that land, we found lying in the field countless heads and bones of dead people; for this city had been extremely large and very populous, whereas now it has been reduced to nothing: barely two hundred houses stand there, and those people are held in the harshest slavery.

Genghis demanded two things of the peoples he conquered: the payment of a tribute and the military service of all adult males. When he encountered resistance, it was not unheard of for him to order the slaughter of every living creature in a city, both human and animal. Furthermore, the Mongols had no hesitation in defiling the religious monuments of the people they attacked, as may be seen in this account by a Russian historian:

> The churches of God they devastated, and in the holy altars they shed much blood. And no one in the town remained alive: all died equally and drank the single cup of death. There was no one here to moan, or cry—neither father and mother over children, nor children over father and mother, neither brother over brother, nor relatives over relatives—but all lay together dead. And all this occurred to us for our sins.

The Mongols moved west as far as Poland and Hungary, but the most lasting effect of their assaults was in Russia, where they established their headquarters in the lower Volga area. From this center they created an empire known as the Golden Horde, named for the golden color of the leader's tent. They remained there for a century and a half, dominating the surrounding principalities and controlling trade routes from their strategic position.

Following their conquest, the Mongols left the laws, customs, and traditions of the Russians in place, although they collected taxes and recruited soldiers based on a population census. As long as the Russian princes paid homage and tribute to the Khan—the Mongol ruler—the conquerors allowed them to govern their own people. In this way, although they did not interfere significantly with Russian life, the Mongols retained effective control from 1240 to 1380.

The effects of Mongol domination have long been a source of historical debate, in which scholars of the last generation, especially those trained in Russia, have asserted that the Mongol presence resulted in a cultural regression that held back the development of Russia for 150 to 200 years. Recent historians, however, have seen the contributions of the Mongols in a more positive light, giving them credit for establishing a link that made commerce between Europe and Asia a possibility. As a result of Mongol control, merchants, traders, missionaries, and diplomats began to travel to China, and adventure stories such as those of Marco Polo fueled the desire of others to visit the exotic locales in search of the fabled treasures of the east.

Summary

The thirteenth century was, in some ways, a continuation of the vibrant experience of the twelfth-century renaissance. Galvanized by economic prosperity, the people of western Europe were searching for greater security and for ways to expand their world. To consolidate their power, the monarchs of Europe centralized their authority through the development of law codes and extensive bureaucracies, often granting privileges to urban citizens as a way of buttressing their power against the restive nobility.

To pursue their dreams of expansion, European monarchs used a variety of means, including mercantile opportunism and military aggression. In France, the kings were able to retake most of the land that had belonged to the Angevin Empire, thereby significantly expanding the royal domain. Frederick II, the German emperor, looked to the Mediterranean, hoping to establish a kingdom reaching from the North Sea to Sicily, and the Spanish kings continued their advance into Muslim territory, eventually conquering all of the Spanish peninsula with the exception of Granada. There were several crusades to the Holy Land, but there were also holy wars against the heathens of the Baltic region, resulting in significant colonization by Germanic Christians, and an eventual "westernization" of the area.

The Byzantine Empire suffered the sack of Constantinople in 1204, when the western European armies participating in the Fourth Crusade allied themselves with the Venetians. The once glorious empire had not yet fully recovered when it faced a new threat from Asia—the specter of Mongol power under the leadership of Genghis Khan.

By the end of the century Europe had experienced a significant shift of focus. No longer isolated and directed inward, Europeans now experienced a more international and cosmopolitan environment. The result of their self-confident aggression had been the creation of new opportunities and a new world view.

Suggestions for Further Reading

Primary sources

Materials regarding the reign of the English kings from John to Henry III are contained in *English Historical Documents*, vol. 3 edited by H. Rothwell (London: Eyre & Spottiswoode, 1953–1969). Joinville's *Life of St. Louis* and Villehardouin's *The Conquest of Constantinople*, translated by M.R.B. Shaw, are published together as *Chronicles of the Crusades* (New York: Penguin Books, 1963). These give fascinating accounts of the Fourth Crusade and the life of Louis IX.

A facsimile edition of *La música de las Cantigas de Santa María*, 3 vols. (Barcelona, 1943–64), by Higini Anglès, contains images of the illuminations as well as a transcription of the music. The detailed commentary is in Spanish and German.

The History and the Life of Chinggis Khan: The Secret History of the Mongols, translated by Urgunge Onon (Leiden: E.J. Brill, 1997), is an important source for Mongol history.

Secondary sources

A stimulating general discussion of the expansion of Europe may be found in *The Making of Europe:*

Conquest, Colonization and Cultural Change (950–1350) by Robert Bartlett (Princeton: Princeton University Press, 1993).

W.L. Warren's King John (2nd ed., New Haven: Yale University Press, 1997) is an excellent biography of the controversial monarch. See also the study by Ralph V. Turner, King John (London: Longman, 1994). Recent views of John's reign may be found in the stimulating articles contained in King John: New Interpretations, edited by S.D. Church (Woodbridge: Boydell Press, 1999).

John W. Baldwin's The Government of Philip Augustus: Foundations of French Royal Power in the Middle Ages (Berkeley: University of California Press, 1986) is a fine study of the French monarchy in the late twelfth and early thirteenth centuries. Two fascinating biographies of monarchs discussed in this chapter are St. Louis: Crusader King of France, by Jean Richard (Cambridge: Cambridge University Press, 1992), and David Abulafia's Frederick II: A Medieval Emperor (London: Allen Lane, Penguin Press, 1988).

A History of Medieval Spain, by eminent historian Joseph F.

O'Callaghan (Ithaca: Cornell University Press, 1975), is a detailed and comprehensive study of Spain in the Middle Ages. Alfonso X, the Cortes, and Government in Medieval Spain is a collection of papers by Joseph F. O'Callaghan (Aldershot: Ashgate, 1998), most of which deal primarily with legal and economic issues. See also the same author's biography The Learned King: The Reign of Alfonso of Castile (Philadelphia: University of Pennsylvania Press, 1993). Peter Linehan's History and the Historians of Medieval Spain (Oxford: Clarendon Press, 1993) is an encyclopedic analysis of the historiography, as well as the history, of medieval Spain. The Lara Family (Cambridge, MA: Harvard University Press, 2001) provides a fascinating glimpse of the relationship of the Spanish monarchy to an important noble family. The Legacy of Muslim Spain, edited by Salma Khadra Jayyusi (Leiden: E. J. Brill, 1992), is an excellent collection of articles dealing with Spanish history, as well as cultural and intellectual developments.

Two works by Warren Treadgold—A History of the

Byzantine State and Society (Stanford, CA: Stanford University Press, 1997) and A Concise History of Byzantium (New York: Palgrave, 2001)—provide fine analyses of twelfth-century Byzantium and the Fourth Crusade. The third volume of Steven Runciman's A History of the Crusades (also cited in Chapter 7 above) gives a stirring account of the Fourth Crusade, as well as an excellent discussion of the crusades of Louis IX. An excellent survey of Russian history is Nicholas V. Riasonovsky's A History of Russia, 6th ed. (New York: Oxford University Press, 2000).

An interesting collection of articles concerning Byzantium, Russia, and the Balkans is contained in Dimitri Obolensky's The Byzantine Inheritance of Eastern Europe (London: Variorum Reprints, 1982).

Barbara Hill's Imperial Women in Byzantium: 1025–1204 (London: Longman, 1999) offers a fascinating analysis of the role of the empresses in Byzantine society.

David Morgan's The Mongols (Oxford: Oxford University Press, 1986) is the most accessible introduction to the history of the Mongols.

NEW CURRENTS IN RELIGION

12

T HE THIRTEENTH CENTURY was a time of intense and rapid change in almost every aspect of human activity. Partly as a result of the growth of urban society, new varieties of religious and spiritual expression emerged as a response to social need, rather than as a desire to reform existing religious establishments.

As the population of the cities and towns increased in the twelfth century, social and economic transformations took place that created a vastly different style of life from the primarily rural existence of previous eras. As discussed earlier, cities were essentially places of commerce, which had developed rapidly between 1100 and 1200 as people became more concerned with a quest for profit. However, this drive for money, together with government taxation and the vagaries of economic fluctuation, often resulted in exploitation of the poorest members of the community. This situation spawned a number of problems for which society and the Church were unprepared. Social and economic forces were fostering rapid change, and the Church became progressively unable to deal with the realities of urban life and to respond to new social needs.

The parish churches of the Middle Ages were rural establishments, unable to fulfill the needs of a transient urban population; in the cities, the time-honored pattern simply did not work. First of all, the number of urban churches was inadequate to deal with the concentration of people in the city. Second, when poverty emerged as a major problem—with a vast monetary gap between ordinary people and wealthy merchants as well as the potentates of the Church—the ecclesiastical authorities tended to ignore the problem rather than addressing the situation.

Inevitably, by the late twelfth century new religious groups were beginning to arise that responded to the needs of this growing and disenfranchised population. The earliest of these movements were regarded as heresies because their teachings differed from orthodox Christian doctrine. Furthermore, many of these movements were anticlerical in nature, as people began to question the validity and necessity of the clergy. Certainly, similar heresies must have existed in medieval Europe before the twelfth century, but we have very limited information about them. One of the earliest of the documented expressions of social and spiritual discontent was initiated by a prosperous merchant of the French city of Lyons, Peter Waldo (or Waldes), whose followers were known as the Waldensians.

New Approaches to the Apostolic Life

The Waldensians

An anonymous chronicle written about 1218 reports that in 1173, Peter Waldo (c. 1140–1217), a man who had "made himself much money by wicked usury," heard a troubadour recount the legend of St. Alexis, the son of a wealthy Roman who gave away his possessions and existed as a wandering beggar seeking alms. Waldo immediately decided to follow the model of Alexis, divesting himself of his wealth and possessions, and seeking to return to the precepts of the **apostolic life**—a pattern of living that sought to emulate the early disciples of Christ.

Waldo asked his wife to choose between his real estate holdings and his personal property, and although she was unhappy at being forced to make a choice, she kept the real estate. Waldo gave part of the remaining money to his daughters, placing them in a convent. He repaid all of the assets he had gained from usury, and distributed the rest of his possessions, which were considerable, among the poor.

Having given away everything, Waldo was forced to beg for his daily sustenance. According to an anonymous thirteenth-century chronicle, when his wife learned that he had assumed a **mendicant** lifestyle, she went to the archbishop, complaining that her husband begged his bread from someone other than her. Waldo was summoned at the archbishop's request, and his wife, "clinging to her husband's garments, cried, 'Is it not better, O my husband, that I, rather than strangers, should atone for my sins through alms to you?' And from that time forth, by command of the archbishop, he was not permitted in that city to take food with others than his wife."

Waldo was deeply concerned by the growing division between the views and actions of the wealthy urban commercial classes and the traditional Christian doctrine of concern for the poor, which had been emphasized by St. Bernard of Clairvaux, among others. In this, he was a forerunner of St. Francis of Assisi (see below).

Waldo did not join a monastic order, as might have been expected, because he held a deep belief that laymen (and laywomen) should preach the Christian gospel. According to charges brought against him in 1254 by the Dominican inquisitor Reinerius Saccho in *On the Sects of Modern Heretics*, Waldo taught that salvation was to be attained through personal initiative, and that "Every good layman is a priest . . . we are not to obey prelates, but only God." In order to make Christ's message available, he persuaded two priests to translate parts of the New Testament into French, so that people could read the scripture for themselves.

In 1177, Waldo gathered about him a group of like-minded believers who eventually became known as the "Poor of Lyons." They developed their own devotional traditions, often gathering in communal worship to read the Bible, sing hymns, and recite psalms. They also followed Waldo's own example by giving their possessions to the poor, and became "devotees of voluntary poverty." As described in 1179 by Walter Map, the chronicler of Henry II of England: "They go about two by two, barefoot, clad in woolen garments, owning nothing, holding all things common like the apostles, naked, following a naked Christ." The Waldensians began to preach "against their own sins and those of others," and their activities eventually constituted an evangelistic enterprise: "the teaching of all nations."

Initially there was no argument between Waldo and the Church concerning doctrine. In 1179, Pope Alexander III (r. 1159–1181) considered the case, and determined that Waldo was not really a pernicious influence and could continue to pursue his life of poverty. He stipulated, however, that Waldo could continue to preach only if he obtained a license from the bishop. Waldo applied for the required document, but his petition was rejected. Nevertheless, since he believed that preaching was an essential doctrine of the New Testament, he continued to speak publicly, and vigorously expanded the geographical area of his mission.

The Waldensians were viewed by the Church prelates as illiterate and unsophisticated believers who "saw themselves as experienced persons, although they were nothing more than dabblers." Their teachings were offensive to the ecclesiastical authorities, who railed against them: "Shall the Word be given to the ignorant, whom we know to be incapable of receiving it, much less of giving in their turn what they have received? Away with this, erase it!" In 1181, the preaching of the Waldensians was officially condemned as heretical by the pope.

Although Waldo's message was originally one of consolation, it became increasingly and virulently anti-sacramental and anti-clerical as the Waldensians met severe resistance from the Church. Charges brought against the group by Saccho emphasized this aspect of Waldo's teaching:

> [the Waldensians] say that the Romish Church, is not the Church of Jesus Christ, but a church of malignants . . . And they say, that they are the church of Christ, because they observe both in word, and deed, the doctrine of Christ, of the Gospel, and of the Apostles.

The Waldensians believed that nothing except the teachings of Christ was necessary for salvation, and hence that the Church and the sacraments were totally unnecessary. As their ideas developed, they began to assault the very foundations of Church doctrine, eventually espousing doctrines that were unquestionably heretical. As a result they were driven from Lyons, and migrated to Italy, northern Spain, and the Moselle valley in Germany, where they continued their preaching mission.

The Beguines

Another lay religious movement was begun some time in the twelfth century by women in the Low Countries (now modern Belgium, Luxembourg, and the Netherlands), known as **Beguines** (the few male participants were known as **Beghards**). Like the Waldensians, these women sought to imitate the apostolic life by renouncing wealth, earning their living by manual labor, and participating in charitable activities. According to one of their staunchest advocates, the preacher Jacques de Vitry, "many [of them], scorning the riches of their parents and rejecting the contemptible and wealthy husbands offered them, live in profound poverty . . . content with vile clothes and modest food." By the thirteenth century, there were established communities in France and Germany in addition to the Low Countries. The city of Cologne, for example, had about sixty clusters of Beguines.

Most of these women, who were either unable or unwilling to become part of an established nunnery, lived together as a communal sisterhood in homes known as **Beguinages**, although some lived on their own or remained at home with their families. A large Beguinage in Ghent is described thus in a Flemish **chartulary** titled *Cartulaire du Beguinage de Sainte-Elizabeth à Gand*:

> the Beguinage of Sainte-Elizabeth . . . is encircled by ditches and walls. In the middle of it is a church, and next to the church a cemetery and a hospital, which the aforesaid ladies endowed for the weak and infirm of that same Beguinage. Many houses were also built there for the habitation of the said women, each of whom has her own garden, separated from the next by ditches or hedges; and two chaplains were established in this place by the same ladies.

The Beguines supported themselves at a meager level by weaving and spinning, and by "washing the wool and cleaning the pieces of cloth sent to them from the town." Some Beguines wrote, preached, and taught, but this occasionally led to condemnation by the ecclesiastical authorities. They did not take formal ecclesiastical vows, but did pledge themselves to poverty and chastity. Their communities developed no hierarchical structure or general administration, although each Beguinage had a "mistress of work, whose duty is to supervise the work and the workers, so that all things are faithfully carried through according to God's will," and a principal mistress, whose duty was the "correction of those who transgress against the praiseworthy rules of the said place."

The Beguines were extremely ascetic in their habits. According to the chartulary,

> Many of them are satisfied for the whole day with the coarse bread and pottage which they have in common in each convent, and with a drink of cold water they lessen their thirst rather than increase their appetite. And many among them are accustomed to fast frequently on bread and water, and many of them do not wear linen on their bodies, and they use straw pallets instead of beds . . . [they wear] a habit which is gray in color, humble, and of a coarse shape, and none may have anything which is unusual or suspect in its shape, sewing, or belting, or in the way of nightcaps, hoods, gloves, mitts, straps, purses, and knives.

The restrictions and sacrifices of such a life appealed to women of means; for the poor, the spiritual attraction of poverty held little value. The attempt on the part of the Beguines, and of the Waldensians, to recreate the apostolic life was also embraced by the urban classes, who sought to experience a spiritual purity that they saw as unavailable to them in the organized Church.

The Brethren of the Common Life

Another movement similar to Waldensians—the *Devotio moderna* ("Modern Devotion"), whose members were eventually known as the "Brethren of the Common Life"—was begun in Holland in the late fourteenth century by Gerhard Groote. The primary focus of the founder was the freedom for each individual to discover for himself a way of life compatible with his religious needs. Groote described his motivation in a letter to the rector at Hildesheim (now in northwest Germany):

> We are not members of an Order, but religious men trying to live in the world. . . .
> Our way of life springs and has always sprung from an inner kernel of devotion. Let
> us therefore not bring upon ourselves at once the destruction of our good name, our
> peace, our quiet, our concord, our charity. Our voluntary life as brethren is very
> different from the irrevocable necessity of those who live under the Rule and
> statutes of a religious Order.

Groote had a strong aversion to mendicant existence, and emphasized the virtue of manual work as an essential component of the religious life. As he wrote, "Labor is wonderfully necessary to mankind in restoring the mind to purity." Thus, he envisioned that his followers would work for their living. This proved to be more difficult than it seemed, given the overpopulated conditions of the towns of the later Middle Ages and the control of the craft industries by the guilds.

Groote's solution was to enter the business of book production. Here he found a whole range of skills that the brothers could practice. They organized themselves into groups which copied and produced books, adopting their own style of writing and their own characteristic bindings. The Brethren of the Common Life were also among the first to enter the new industry of printing. In addition to producing books for themselves, they supplied collegiate, parochial, and cathedral churches with accurate texts of both devotional and liturgical works. Their activities enabled them successfully to combine a religious way of life with the merit of earning a living through manual labor, while meeting their own religious and devotional needs.

The followers of Peter Waldo, the Beguines, and the Brethren of the Common Life were not the only lay religious sects to become widespread in the twelfth, thirteenth, and fourteenth centuries. Another group, which professed a more dangerous heresy, arose in southern France. Connected with the town of Albi, they became known as the Albigensians or "Cathars" (meaning "the Pure," from the Greek *katharos* [pure]).

The Cathars

The Cathar, or Albigensian, heresy also developed in cities, primarily among skilled craftsmen. Thought by some historians to have originated in a widespread heresy that had appeared in the Byzantine Empire in the tenth century, the doctrine of the Cathars taught dualism. They believed that there were two divine sources of being and elements in the universe, which they defined as Good and Evil. The God of Good, or the "benevolent God," was the source of light, spirit, and Christ, and the God of Evil, the "malevolent God," was the originator of darkness, flesh, and the Antichrist. Indeed, all physical matter was a product of the Devil, since it was antithetical to immaterial spirit. The Cathars thought that the established Church was on the side of Evil, and hence constituted a false church. They found much evidence around them to substantiate their belief that the "Church of Rome was a den of thieves, and that it was the harlot of which we read in the Apocalypse."

The Cathars taught there were two categories of adherents: the "believers" or *credentes*, and a higher level, the "elect," known as **perfecti**, whom all should strive to emulate. These individuals embraced a life of sexual abstinence and a largely vegetarian diet in order to suppress the desires of the flesh and elevate the spirit towards true Goodness. A predictably hostile view of the Cathars was expressed by Peter, a monk from northern France, writing in the thirteenth century:

> Certain of the heretics were called the Perfect or Good Men; the others were called the believers of the heretics. Those who were called Perfect, wore a black cloak; they falsely claimed that they kept themselves chaste; they abhorred the eating of meat, eggs, and cheese . . . [others] were called believers of the heretics, who lived after the manner of the world, and who, though they did not attain so far as to imitate the life of the Perfect, nevertheless hoped to be saved in their faith; and though they differed as to their mode of life, they were one with them in belief and unbelief. Those who were called believers of the heretics were given to usury, rapine [pillage or plunder], homicide, lust, perjury, and every vice; and they, in fact, sinned with more security, and less restraint, because they believed that without restitution, without confession and penance, they should be saved, if only, when on the point of death, they could say the Lord's Prayer, and received imposition of hands from their teachers.

Women took an active part in the Cathar movement, perhaps because the lack of hierarchy made it possible for them to assume more prominent religious roles than were available to them in the traditional Church. Cathar doctrine did not prevent women from becoming *perfecti*, or from preaching or administering the last rites. Although many women did achieve "perfect" status, evidence indicates that relatively few of them functioned as deliverers of the **consolamentum** or "consolation." This spiritual baptism was bestowed through the laying-on of hands by one of the established *perfecti*. It seems likely that the leadership of women was probably limited to emergency situations.

It seems probable that many members of the merchant class joined the movement, since this group generally controlled the government of towns. Because the Cathars did not preach against usury, they provided a viable and attractive alternative to the view of the traditional Church, as well as to that of the Waldensians.

By the end of the 1170s, Catharist doctrine was being preached openly, and by 1204 the Albigensian heresy had spread throughout southern France. The Church, understandably, perceived it as a threat. According to the monk Peter:

> Just as one bunch of grapes takes on its sickly color from the aspect of its neighbor, and in the fields the scab of one sheep or the mange of one pig destroys an entire herd, so, influenced by the proximity of Toulouse, neighboring towns and villages in which heresiarchs had put down their roots were wonderfully and woefully infected by this spreading disease as the sprouts of its infidelity multiplied.

Pope Innocent III sent his legates to quell the Cathar activity, but the heretics had the good will of the powerful lords in the region, who "warmly cherished and protected

105 Restored to its former glory in the nineteenth century, the walled city of Carcassonne provides a fine example of a medieval urban settlement. In this photograph, the area in the foreground is plowed in strips, as it would have been in the Middle Ages. In the event of siege, the residents of the "suburbs" could abandon their fields and take refuge behind the walls of the city. Unhappily, this tactic did not protect them when Carcassonne was attacked during the Albigensian Crusade in the early thirteenth century.

them against God and the Church." The pope asked the king of France, Philip Augustus, to intervene, but he refused. By 1209, however, the situation had escalated, and Philip agreed that his vassals could take part in a crusade against the heretics. An army from northern France attacked the town of Béziers, where the soldiers slaughtered 7,000 people hidden in a church. When one crusader asked how he could tell the heretics from the true Christians, the papal legate responded, "Kill all! Kill all, for God will know his own."

The army then turned to the walled city of Carcassonne (**fig. 105**), "till now glorying in its wickedness, abounding in riches, and well fortified." According to the chronicler Roger of Wendover, a relatively objective English cleric of St. Albans Abbey:

> [The crusaders] crossed the entrenchments and scaled the walls amid showers of missiles from the crossbows, and the blows of the lances and swords of its wicked defenders. After this they set up their engines of war, and on the eighth day the greater suburb was taken after a great many of the enemy, who had incautiously exposed themselves, were slain, and the suburbs of the city, which seemed larger than the body of the town, were altogether destroyed. The enemy being thus confined in the narrow streets of the city, and suffering as well from their numbers as from want of provisions more than is credible, offered themselves and all their property, together with the city to the crusaders, on condition of their lives being preserved out of mercy.

The crusade continued under the leadership of Simon de Montfort, who was named ruler of Carcassonne. Various conquests in the area were achieved by the crusaders, accompanied by the enthusiastic slaughter of heretics. In 1218, de Montfort was killed in Toulouse, and his son was forced to surrender the fief to the French king. Thus, the ultimate achievement of the Albigensian crusade was a significant expansion of royal authority into southern France. The power of the nobles who had protected the heretics was destroyed, and the Albigensians, as well as the Waldensians who were still alive, were left to the mercy of the Church. Facing numerous heresies, the clerical establishment required an effective ecclesiastical organization to deal with the problem. They found their answer in the process of Inquisition.

The Inquisition

By the thirteenth century, various heresies had spread throughout Europe. A German chronicle of the time shows that the teachings of the Waldensians, the Cathars, and other sects had been adopted in various forms:

> Many [of the heretics] were versed in the Holy Scriptures, which they had in German translation. Some, indeed, performed a second baptism; some did not believe in the sacrament of the Lord's body; some held that the body of the Lord could not be consecrated by evil priests; some said that the body of the Lord could be consecrated with salver and chalice in any place whatsoever, equally well by a man or a woman, whether ordained or not; some judged confirmation and extreme unction to be superfluous; some scorned the supreme pontiff, the clergy, and the monastic life; some denied the value of prayers of the Church for the souls of the dead; some took their own mothers in marriage, making amends for the consanguinity that existed by the payment of eighteen pence; some kissed a pallid man or even a cat, and performed still worse acts; some, believing all days to be the same, refused to keep holidays or fasts, and thus worked on feast days and ate meat on Good Friday. Let this suffice as a catalogue of their errors, not that we have listed them all but only noted the most outstanding.

During the twelfth century, heresy had generally been regarded as treason against society, and this view was formally endorsed by Pope Innocent III at the Fourth Lateran Council in 1215. The decree of the council declared that:

> We excommunicate and anathematize every heresy that raises against the holy, orthodox and Catholic faith . . . condemning all heretics under whatever names they may be known, for while they have different faces, they are nevertheless bound to each other by their tails, since in all of them vanity is a common element.

Innocent originally hoped that heretics could be brought back to the Christian fold through preaching and teaching, but his legates proved to be ineffectual, and he ultimately turned to interrogation by papal inquisitors.

Cases of suspected heretics could be brought to court by a Church official, usually an archdeacon, or by a private individual. However, the system did not work well where heretics were numerous. Archdeacons were often too busy, and individuals either sympathized with the heretics, or feared acts of revenge. Furthermore, the usual secular procedures—ordeals and lynchings—were not effective in preventing the spread of heresy.

The procedure of the Inquisition was technically an "official inquiry," undertaken to gather information about possible heretical activity, and to punish the offenders when identified. As described in a manual for inquisitors at Carcassonne, the official was to choose a place for the Inquisition that was "well suited to the purpose" of a secret inquiry.

The inquisitor would first summon the clergy and the people together and deliver a sermon which included the papal letters concerning the form and process of the investigation. He would then issue a general summons to all the inhabitants—"men from the age of fourteen, women from the age of twelve if perchance they shall have been guilty of an offense"—to appear before him to "answer for acts which they may have committed against the faith and to abjure heresy." An indulgence from imprisonment was granted if the people came voluntarily, as penitents. In describing the form of the required oath, the manual states:

> We require each and every person who presents himself for confession to abjure all heresy and to take oath that he will tell the full and exact truth about himself and about others, living and dead, in the matter of the fact or crime of heresy or Waldensianism; that he will neither harbor nor defend heretics of any sect whatever nor befriend them nor believe in them, but rather that he will in good faith pursue and seize them and their agents or, at least, will disclose them to the Church or to princes and their baillies, who are eager and able to seize them; and that he will not obstruct the Inquisition, but rather will set himself against those who impede it.

The person under investigation was questioned about his or her associations with the heretics or Waldensians, whether he traveled with them from place to place, whether he ate and drank with them, whether he had acted as a financial agent, whether he had participated in their religious services—in brief, "whether he was otherwise on familiar terms with or associated with heretics or Waldensians in any way."

Those heretics who wished to return to "ecclesiastical unity" were required to abjure heresy, by taking an oath to observe the faith and to pursue heretics, and actively participating in inquisitions. They also must serve penances, which sometimes included imprisonment. The possessions of the heretics, both the condemned and the imprisoned, were confiscated. The heretics who, of their own will, "return humbly to the bosom of Holy Church" were required to wear "two crosses, one on the breast and one on the shoulders, yellow in color, two palms in height, two in breadth, each arm three fingers in width. The clothing on which he wears the crosses shall never be yellow in color." In some places the penitent was compelled to shave his head as a distinguishing characteristic. He was required to attend Mass and vespers and general sermons in the village, and was often directed to undertake a pilgrimage.

Heretics who refused to renounce their faith, or who had recanted but then lapsed back into heresy, were released to the secular authorities. They were then generally sentenced to be burned at the stake. Further, anyone who befriended or aided a heretic was subject to excommunication, and if the Inquisitor learned of individuals who had died as heretics, it was decreed that "his bones be exhumed from the cemetery . . . and burned in detestation of so heinous an offense."

The Mendicant Orders

The same impulses towards recreating the apostolic life that spawned the heresies of the twelfth and thirteenth centuries also led to the development of two new religious orders—the Franciscans and the Dominicans. These monks, or **friars**, as they were known, were mendicants—that is, they owned no property and provided for their daily needs by working or accepting alms. They were instrumental in strengthening the Church; indeed, they constituted a force available to the pope in his attempt to combat heresy and to win heretics back to the traditional religious establishment. A few Dominicans functioned as inquisitors, but the great majority of friars in both orders worked to increase Christian zeal through preaching and teaching, and by personal example. They demonstrated that an evangelical life was possible within the confines of the established Church.

The revolutionary message of the new orders concerned the living of a devout life by the Christian laity. They held out the possibility that a person could attain salvation while living a life fully in the world, rather than withdrawing to ascetic isolation in the cloister. In essence, they offered a new theology of the secular life—one that held great appeal to the people of the late medieval world.

The first of these new orders, the Franciscans, was founded by the son of a wealthy merchant from Assisi.

The Franciscans

The circumstances of the origins of the Franciscan order are quite similar to those of the Waldensians. Francis Bernardone (1182–1226) was a young man who enjoyed pursuits such as singing courtly love songs and participating in the small-scale warfare that was endemic between his home town of Assisi and the neighboring towns. During one of these campaigns, he was taken captive and placed in prison. During his incarceration he became ill, and evidently began to seek religious consolation. Soon after his release, he was praying in the Church of St. Damian, when he heard a voice that seemed to emanate from the crucifix above the altar, saying, "Francis, go build my church." The young man understood the direction quite literally, and proceeded to take some merchandise from his father's shop. He sold the items and then gave the money to a local priest so that he could repair his church. Francis's father was enraged by this action, and imprisoned his son. Francis managed to escape, however, and sought the protection of the local bishop. Soon afterwards he repudiated his father in a dramatic scene. Stripping off his clothes, he proclaimed: "Hitherto I have called Pietro Bernardone father . . . Now I return to him his money and also the clothes I wore which are his. From now on I will say 'Our Father who art in heaven' and not 'father Pietro Bernardone'."

After breaking with his father, Francis spent his time repairing churches. He felt that he was called to serve God, but he did not understand exactly what role was intended for him. When attending a service one day, he heard the priest read from the gospel of St. Matthew: "As you go, preach the message, 'The kingdom of Heaven is at hand . . . Freely you have received, freely give.' Do not keep gold or silver or money in your girdles, nor wallet for your journey, nor two tunics, nor sandals, nor staffs." Francis perceived immediately what he should do, and began preaching about the rewards and virtues of the apostolic life.

Each day Francis worked to earn enough food for subsistence, and if work was unavailable, he accepted alms. He had an unusually appealing and charismatic personality, and was immediately sympathetic to the needs of others. He provided inspiration to those around him, and earned the immediate affection of those he met. Soon he had attracted a group of followers, for whom he drew up a rule. As Francis described this document in the testament he wrote at the end of his life:

> And when the Lord gave me some brothers, no one showed me what I ought to do, but the Most High Himself revealed to me that I should live according to the form of the holy Gospel. And I caused it to be written in few words and simply, and the Lord Pope confirmed it for me. And those who came to take this life upon themselves gave all that they had to the poor and they were content with one robe, patched within and without, and those who wished had a cord and trousers, and we wished for no more.

As this brief excerpt shows, Francis insisted on poverty—his followers were to have no personal possessions, and were forbidden to have money. The essential difference between the Rule of Francis and those of the established religious orders, such as the Cluniacs and Cistercians, was that the Franciscans were to subsist through manual labor and by begging. Furthermore, Francis's followers should not live in a cloistered environment, withdrawn from the world, but should reside among the people, actively preaching and ministering to the needs of the poor. As Francis stated in his testament, "Let the brothers take care not to receive on any account churches, poor dwelling-places, and all other things that are constructed for them, unless they are as is becoming the holy poverty which we have promised in the Rule, always dwelling there as strangers and pilgrims."

The teachings of Francis held special appeal for literate members of the urban laity who sought to model themselves on the earthly experience of Jesus as described in the gospels—to pursue the imitation of Christ. These articulate and thoughtful people were critical of what they saw as the moral laxity of the clergy and impatient with the practices of monastic spirituality. They were eager and willing to listen to the ideas of the Franciscan brethren, and many joined the order.

An especially appealing aspect of the Franciscan experience was the founder's affection for the beauty of nature and the world around him. His "Canticle to the Sun," in praise of nature, is one of the finest masterpieces of Italian poetry, and his beneficent attitudes towards animals and birds became a favorite subject of painters, especially Giotto. Furthermore, his miraculous ability to control wild animals became legendary. While this may seem extraneous to his career, an important part of Francis's doctrine was the glorification of the created universe, in contrast to the extreme asceticism of the Cathars. This view was presented in verses such as the following from his "Canticle":

> Praised be my Lord for our sister, mother earth,
> The which sustains and keeps us
> And brings forth diverse fruits with grass and
> flowers bright.

By extolling the beauty of the world, Francis was appealing to people at a deep emotional level, as well as responding to the claims of the heretics.

In 1210, Francis went to Rome to ask the pope for approval of his Rule, which, in its original form, was little more than a collection of Gospel references that extolled the virtues of poverty and the commitment to evangelical preaching. Francis was, at this time, in much the same position as Peter Waldo had been a generation earlier. The crucial difference, and the factor that enabled the Franciscans to develop into a great religious order, was that Francis did not eschew the priesthood and the sacraments, as many heretics did. In fact, he was devoted to these aspects of the Church, as shown in his *Testament*, where he wrote, "I wish to fear, love, and honor all priests as my lords," and further that, "We ought to honor and venerate all theologians, who minister to us the divine word, as those who minister to us the spirit of life." Pope Innocent was initially reluctant to grant Francis's request for the approval of his Rule, but when an adviser pointed out that it would be imprudent, at best, to deny the way of life advocated by Christ, the pope gave his consent. Francis and his followers were free to follow their Rule and to preach.

The ranks of the Franciscans (later known as the "Friars Minor") increased rapidly. They first extended the boundaries of their itinerant preaching throughout Italy, and in 1217 missionaries were sent to Tunis and Spain. In 1219, larger groups went to France, Germany, and Hungary. At first it was difficult for them to be accepted; people thought that they were heretics because of their lifestyle. Gradually, however, they were integrated into the European communities.

As the order grew, it became impractical to govern and coordinate their efforts without some form of systematic organization. Although Francis had originally conceived of a movement without any governance, this proved to be unworkable. In 1223, he therefore wrote a second version of his Rule, which became the permanent constitution of the Franciscans. This document reaffirmed the commitment to poverty, while at the same time establishing a permanent hierarchy of administration.

A series of changes followed the death of Francis in 1226. In 1230, the pope decreed that Franciscans could hold property and accept gifts to the order, and a bull of 1245 made the pope the legal owner of all buildings belonging to the order. The Franciscans also changed their initially hostile attitudes towards education, and from the 1220s onward, members of the order regularly attended universities. However, while these measures were accepted by the majority of the Franciscans, some of the friars were opposed to the abandonment of the strict observance of the rule of poverty mandated by Francis. These "Spiritual Franciscans" remained vocal, and were among the most virulent critics of the papacy during the fourteenth century.

The charisma and virtue of Francis attracted women as well as men, most prominently a young girl from an aristocratic family, now known as Clare of Assisi (1194–1253). Clare vowed to follow Francis in his practice of poverty and the apostolic life. As she wrote in her *Testament*:

> The Son of God became for us the Way and that Way our Blessed Father Francis, his true lover and imitator, has shown and taught us by word and example . . . For the Lord has placed us as an example and mirror not only for other men, but also for our Sisters whom God has called to our way of life, that they in turn should be a mirror and an example to those living in the world.

Clare gathered a group of like-minded women, and initially they worked alongside the Franciscans in ministering to the sick and destitute. Francis designated the restored church and house of St. Damian for the use of Clare and her companions, but he did not endorse the idea of full participation in the activities of the order. This reluctance may have been the result of social and ecclesiastical disapproval. Although the practice of poverty was not regarded as the exclusive province of males, it was unthinkable for women to wander about the countryside, preaching and begging for alms.

In 1219, Cardinal Hugolino, patron and cardinal protector of the Franciscans, provided a rule for the women that stipulated strict enclosure and adherence to the Rule of St. Benedict. Personal poverty was mandated, but the provisions of the Rule allowed the women to hold property in common. This was contrary to the wishes and beliefs of Clare, who had promised Francis that she would live in "holy poverty," according to the precepts of the holy gospel. She eventually composed her own Rule, the first religious rule drawn up by a woman. In emphasizing the commitment to poverty, she borrowed the phrase from the second rule of Francis: "The sisters are to appropriate nothing for themselves, neither house nor place, nor anything." They were to hold no property, individually or through an intermediary. This rule was eventually confirmed by Pope Innocent IV, two days before Clare's death. However, the provision against the holding of property applied only to her own convent. Other houses of the order, which became known as the "Poor Clares," remained enclosed monastic establishments of the traditional kind. The order attracted many recruits, but it was never as popular as uncloistered groups of women, such as the Beguines.

Another new religious order, also dedicated to the apostolic life, originated at approximately the same time as the Franciscans. This was the "Order of Preachers," also known as the Dominicans.

The Dominicans

The new order, founded by a Spanish priest named Dominic de Guzmán (1170–1221), differed in several ways from the early Franciscans. It was, from the beginning, an order that emphasized learning and education. In this it closely resembled the traditional monastic establishments, although its highest dedication was to the activities of the pastoral mission.

The origins of the order may be found in the ecclesiastical attempts to control the Cathar heresy. Dominic first encountered the Cathars in southern France, when he accompanied his bishop, Diego of Osma, on a diplomatic mission. At this time, the pope had assigned the responsibility of working to remove the heresy to the Cistercians, and it was evident that they had not made much progress in ridding the area of heretics. Dominic and Diego met with two Cistercian legates and offered to lend their help, pointing out that the Cistercians were perhaps not very effective because of their traditional clerical style; the Spaniards suggested that a better approach would be to emulate the practitioners of the apostolic life. As authentic preachers of the gospel, they could compete with the *perfecti*, the spiritual elite of the Cathar movement (see above). Dominic and Diego persuaded the Cistercians to join them in this new enterprise, and sent their large retinue of servants and clerks home with their horses. They then began an itinerant preaching tour on foot, walking from town to town to engage the Cathar leaders in public debate.

Some scholars have suggested that Dominic borrowed his ideas concerning absolute poverty from the Franciscans. This is probably not the case, however, since Dominic and Diego adopted the apostolic life before they could have known of Francis and his movement. For the founders of the Dominican order, it was, most probably, an independent application of the idea of the apostolic life current in the twelfth century.

Dominic continued his mission during the years of upheaval caused by the Albigensian Crusade. He had established a base of operations at Toulouse which became the headquarters of his preaching activities, and he attracted a number of recruits whom he trained as a community of assistants. In 1215, he went to Rome to ask for papal authorization of a new order. The Fourth Lateran Council, which was then in session, did not embrace his idea; evidently its members thought that there were too many new religious groups, and would not authorize a new monastic order. The prelates decreed that a new community should simply adopt an existing rule. Not surprisingly, Dominic chose the Rule of St. Augustine, since his religious affiliation was already with that order which adhered to a pattern for discipline and spiritual life created in the fifth century by St. Augustine of Hippo for his own cathedral clergy. Sometimes called the "Austin Canons," the Augustinian monks were committed to fulfilling ecclesiastical duties within society. They served in churches and cathedrals, and dedicated themselves to addressing social needs in the towns where they were located.

In 1216, Pope Honorius III (r. 1216–1227) granted papal confirmation, recognizing the existence of Dominic's order and confirming its possessions in Toulouse. The pope did not, however, ratify a new rule, and the Order of Preachers was officially a branch of the Augustinian canons regular.

In 1217, Dominic gave directions to his associates to leave Toulouse and to travel throughout Europe. Some were sent to Paris, some to Spain, and others to Bologna. The missions to Paris and Bologna seem to have been undertaken for the express purpose of infiltrating the finest intellectual centers in Europe—the universities that had emerged and developed in recent decades (see Chapter 13). Ultimately, the best recruits in the order were drawn from famous intellectual institutions such as these. Thus, the Preachers, or Dominicans, began a mission that comprised all of Europe, confirmed in 1218 by a papal bull requiring the support of prelates throughout Christendom.

Dominic was considerably more talented than Francis in matters of administration and organization. The first set of statutes governing internal matters was enacted at a "General Chapter," or annual assembly, of the order in 1228, and was essentially the work of Dominic himself. The new constitution was modeled on monastic tradition, and stipulated a daily choral recitation of the divine office, though this could be accomplished "briefly and succinctly." Manual labor was discarded in order to allow for study and preaching.

The testimony of one member of the order, Brother Ventura, at the canonization hearings for Dominic that took place in 1234 vividly reveals how the Rule was maintained by Dominic during his travels:

[Dominic] also said that on a journey or wherever he was, he wanted to be always preaching or talking or arguing about God, either in person or through his companions. He was also persistent in prayer, and said Mass every day if he could find a church, though he never did so without weeping. When he arrived at a hostel, if there was a church there he would go there first. When he was staying somewhere other than one of the convents, when he heard others saying Matins he would get up at once and recite Matins devoutly with his companions. After Compline, when he was on a journey, wherever he was, he observed silence with his companions and with everybody else, and did not want it to be broken until the hour of Terce the next day. When he was traveling, he would lie down at night on some straw, fully clothed, barely even taking his shoes off. (**fig. 106**)

Although the program included many features of traditional monastic practice, there was one revolutionary aspect of Dominic's Rule, which pertained to the constitution of the order. At every level of the hierarchy the officials were elected, and were made responsible to their subordinates for the conduct of their offices. The basic unit was the priory or convent, and its head (the prior) was elected by the members of the establishment. A companion was also elected to accompany the prior on his journeys to the meetings of the provincial chapter. The order was divided according to provinces, and the provincial prior was elected by a committee composed of the heads of the houses and two representatives chosen by each priory. The provincial chapter was usually quite large, so the conduct of business was delegated to a steering committee, which could, among other things, hear complaints against the provincial prior, and remove him from office, if necessary. The most important unit was the General Chapter, which met annually. It was composed of an elected master general, who presided, and one representative elected by the chapter of each province. The representative form of the government of the Order of Preachers succeeded in institutionalizing obedience to a superior, thus abolishing the dependence on an established hierarchy; the Dominicans were instead able to determine their own leadership. Their structure provided a model that influenced many other religious organizations, including the Franciscans.

In the course of time, the two mendicant orders began to resemble each other in important ways. The Dominicans had, from the outset, adopted Francis's doctrine of poverty, and, like the Friars Minor, they had a significant impact on lay society. The Franciscans, who originally expressed pride in their lack of education and intellectual rigor, eventually entered the university environment, emulating the Dominicans in intellectual achievement. Furthermore, both Franciscans and Dominicans were exempt from the jurisdiction of bishops, and reported directly to the pope.

Like Francis, Dominic attracted female followers from the beginning. He seems to have believed in strict enclosure for his women converts, and he provided for them a fully developed monastic constitution. A prominent issue was the relationship between

106 Two of the modes of prayer advocated by St. Dominic are shown in these illuminations from *De modo orandi* (*Concerning the Way of Praying*), an anonymous manuscript housed in the Vatican Library. The saint, who was noted for being "persistent in prayer," is shown in a prostrate position before a crucifix, and then standing, with his arms extended towards the image of Christ.

the friars and their sister organization. In 1228, the General Chapter ordered the Dominicans to discontinue their ministry to the women's houses because it was seen as a distraction from the order's apostolic duty. However, Dominic's original houses were exempted from the ruling, and after several decades of effort, the sisters won full recognition as an associate order of the Dominicans. The Poor Clares faced the same opposition, since the Franciscans viewed their primary purpose as one of preaching and ministering to the urban laity. Attending to the religious needs of several houses of nuns was a time-consuming task which curtailed their most important duty. It is ironic that the two mendicant orders that abandoned the tradition of isolation and segregation from society, gave birth to two female orders that were forced to maintain strict enclosure.

The Franciscans and Dominicans were devoted to the mission of evangelizing the urban population of Europe, and their success was dependent on the resources of the burgeoning towns and cities. Only an urban environment could support organizations that relied upon begging. The rural population was too close to the subsistence level to be able to provide sustenance for a mendicant group in their midst, no matter how pious and well-intentioned they were. Only the residents of towns possessed the surplus needed to subsidize the friars.

The spiritual needs of the urban population had been relatively neglected, often being served by priests who lacked education as well as motivation. The success of the new orders depended, to a large degree, on their ability to capture the minds and hearts of their audiences through their preaching. The friars worked to speak directly to the needs of the people, often tailoring their sermons to a given audience, such as merchants, apprentices, or married people. In order to help their preachers, they developed literary aids such as the theoretical treatises *The Instruction of Preachers*, by the Dominican master-general Humbert de Romans, or *The Art of Preaching*, by Thomas Waleys, in addition to collections of model sermons. There were also compilations of excerpts and tales from the lives of the saints, which enabled the preachers to reach directly to the emotions of their listeners.

The work of the friars was only one aspect of a general shift of focus that was taking place within Christianity as a whole. Alongside it came a new emphasis on the human nature of Christ, as well as a heightened devotion accorded to the Virgin Mary.

New Forms of Spirituality

The humanization of Christ and the cult of the Virgin

During the twelfth and thirteenth centuries there was a dramatic change in the way people viewed the nature of Christ. Earlier in the Middle Ages, Christ had been portrayed as a triumphant ruler and a stern judge. By contrast, although Romanesque cathedrals still presented Christ as the ruler of Heaven, most representations now showed him as kindlier and more sympathetic. In the twelfth and thirteenth centuries, his human nature was emphasized in the artworks and sermons, which referred to his care for his followers, his preaching a message of love and forgiveness, and, above all, his bodily suffering on the cross. These changes reflect a new attitude towards Jesus and a new devotion to the "Man of Sorrows," which emphasized the human and physical aspects of his personality and experience (**fig. 107**).

This new attitude spawned innovative devotional rituals, such as the Stations of the Cross. In this Lenten service, worshipers processed past a series of paintings and sculptures that represented the human suffering endured by Christ at his crucifixion. Further, the Mass itself was altered during this era. Before this time, most laypeople did not partake of the bread and wine that represented the body and blood of Christ; they merely witnessed the elevation of these elements by the priests officiating at the communion ceremony, who were the only ones to consume them. Beginning in the thirteenth century the laity began to be offered the sacraments, representing a change in practice that intensified the message of Christ's love for humanity. These alterations signaled a new attitude on the part of the Church—one that was responsive to the changing needs of a society more attuned to emotional religious enthusiasm.

Some scholars have attributed this turn towards a more approachable Christ as an indication of the influence of St. Francis. Many people considered Francis to be a reflection of the gentle, loving, pious nature of Christ himself, and this impression was heightened by the circulation of the legend that Francis had received the stigmata— the wounds inflicted on Christ on the cross. For many people, this contemporary figure seemed almost to represent a rebirth of the Savior, who had returned to remind people of his love and their potential for salvation.

A similar humanization and approachability may be witnessed in the new devotional attitudes towards the Virgin Mary. Although in the eastern church she had been worshiped as the mother of Christ and the Queen of Heaven since the early Middle Ages, the western church did not accord any special devotion to her before the late eleventh century. At that time, for reasons that remain unclear, she began to be a focus of personal devotion which centered on her direct role in aiding the worshiper to attain salvation. Furthermore, the Virgin represented a model of motherhood, and was a paradigm of chastity, virtue, and humility. As such, she exemplified the female values of obedience and piety, qualities greatly valued by the Church and by society in general.

The cult that developed around Mary grew rapidly, escalating dynamically in the twelfth and thirteenth centuries. During this period thousands of churches and cathedrals were dedicated to her, and her cult was a major stimulus to the building of Gothic structures. Indeed, other than the crucifix, her image became the most popular focus for devotion. Countless artworks in various media portrayed the story of her life, and sermons emphasized her function as mediator and intercessor. Miraculous stories about her continuing activity in the world flourished; mystics claimed to have spoken to her directly in visions, and musicians and poets composed songs in her honor. It is evident that much of the verbal tradition of courtly love (see Chapter 10) was incorporated

107 By the twelfth century, the human aspect of Christ was valued more highly than his role as Ruler of Heaven. Artworks emphasized his agony on the cross, and sermons stressed his message of love and forgiveness. This "Man of Sorrows," which is half of a fourteenth-century diptych, represents the dead Christ with eyes closed and arms crossed. The other panel portrays the Virgin and Child.

into this cult of the Virgin. *Salve Regina*, an antiphon (a chant—in this case a votive anthem) by an anonymous French or German monastic poet and musician, beautifully encapsulates this new reverence:

> Hail, queen, mother of mercy:
> our life, sweetness and hope, hail.
> To thee we cry, as exiles, children of Eve.
> To thee we sigh, goaning and weeping
> in this vale of tears.
> Come, then, our counsellor,
> turn those merciful eyes upon us.
> And show Jesus, the blessed fruit of thy
> womb, to us after this exile.
> O gentle: O pious: O sweet virgin Mary.

108 The theme of pity (*pietà* in Italian), became a prominent feature of devotional art in the thirteenth century and beyond. Frequently shown standing by the cross or holding the body of her crucified son in her lap, Mary was portrayed as a suffering mother, rather than as Queen of Heaven. In this painted limestone sculpture from the Seeon Monastery near Salzburg, Mary's sorrowful gaze is directed at the large and ungainly body of her dead son.

Some scholars have pointed once again to the Franciscan emphasis on the emotional aspects of religion as providing this impetus towards this new devotion to the Virgin, with its vision of Mary as an earthly mother rather than Queen of Heaven. The Virgin was often portrayed by painters and sculptors either standing by the Cross, witnessing the death of her son, or holding his body in her lap. This theme of pity (*pietà* in Italian), appeared in sculptures and paintings (**fig. 108**), and was the subject of hymns such as the Franciscan *Stabat Mater Dolorosa*:

> Next the cross with tears unceasing,
> Worn by the sorrow aye increasing,
> Stood the mother 'neath her Son.

One of the most impressive compilations of Marian devotional material is the magnificent *Cantigas de Santa María* commissioned by Alfonso X ("the Wise") of Castile (see Chapter 11). This beautifully illustrated manuscript contained miracle tales about the Virgin in addition to devotional songs and hymns.

The cult of the Virgin spread throughout Europe during the High Middle Ages, providing an outlet for lay piety and emotional expression. An even more intense aspect of religiosity was expressed in the growth of a movement often identified as mysticism.

Mysticism

Mysticism, defined as the experience of direct, immediate contact with God, was not a new phenomenon in the thirteenth century. Signs from God had been an accepted mode of religious experience since before the Middle Ages. Several examples have been discussed in this book: Constantine's conversion at the Battle of the Milvian

Bridge, the divine revelation to St. Augustine to "take up [the Bible] and read," and the visions of Hildegard of Bingen, among others. What appears to have been different in the centuries following Hildegard's era was the extraordinary number of people from all walks of life who claimed to have had mystical experiences, usually accompanied by hypnotic trances, fainting, passionate cries, and even physical transformations.

Although there are accounts of male mystics, females far outnumber them in the records. It has been assumed that there were simply more women than men who had these experiences, but the vast difference may simply be indicative of the fact that more elaborate testimonies were required of females, since they aroused more suspicion on the part of the ecclesiastical authorities. Nonetheless, the most dramatic and evocative accounts come from the writings of women.

Female visionaries in the thirteenth and fourteenth centuries were generally found in the Low Countries, parts of Germany, and the towns of central and northern Italy, although many important mystics were located elsewhere, such as Birgitta of Sweden, the Frenchwoman Margaret of Oingt, and Margery Kempe from King's Lynn in Norfolk, England. The northern visionaries were often nuns, and the southern ones tended to be lay affiliates of the religious orders (**tertiaries**), although this is no more than a broad generalization. One important center was the convent of Helfta in Saxony, where

109 Devotional imagery was often used to stimulate mystical visions. For example, in this illumination from the *Passional of Abbess Kunigunde*, a nun prays before an image of the risen Christ. Although he is no longer bound to the cross, the wounds he suffered in his crucifixion are conspicuously displayed as reminders of his humanity and his agony.

devotion to the pierced heart of Jesus became the focus of the cult of the Sacred Heart. Furthermore, many German Dominican nuns expressed a high frequency of mystical experience. The best-known of the Italian mystics were affiliates of the mendicant orders, such as Margaret of Cortona, Angela of Foligno, and Catherine of Siena, but there were visionary nuns, as well. Their experiences were rooted in emotion and affective piety, and they were devoted, above all, to the Passion and death of Christ, to the Eucharist, and to the Virgin Mary. Often a devotional image was used as the impetus to visionary experience. **Fig. 109**, from a book of readings called the *Passional of Abbess Kunigunde* of Prague, shows a nun praying before an image of Christ, now freed from the Cross, but with his wounds prominently in evidence.

One of the most famous of the female mystics was Margery Kempe (*c.* 1373–1440), an Englishwoman whose autobiography describes her religious development. The work recounts her life in England, as well as pilgrimages to Jerusalem and Rome. Most fascinating are her conversations with the Virgin Mary, Jesus, and finally, with God. These are often accompanied by physical manifestations of the mystical experience, such as those described by Margery (who always wrote in the third person) on a visit to a church at Norwich:

> When she came in the churchyard of St. Stephen's, she cried, she roared, she wept, she fell down to the ground, so fervently the fire of love burnt in her heart. Afterwards she rose up again and went forth weeping into the church to the high altar, and there she fell down with violent sobbings, weepings, and loud cries beside the grave of the good vicar, all ravished with ghostly comfort in the goodness of our Lord who wrought so great grace for his servant who had been her confessor . . . and [later] she went to the church [to hear a service], where she saw a fair image of our Lady called a pity [a *pietà*]. And through the beholding of that pity, her mind was all wholly occupied in the Passion of our Lord Jesus Christ and in the compassion of our Lady, St. Mary, by which she was compelled to cry full loudly and weep full sorely, as though she should have died.

It is evident from the foregoing that Margery was deeply affected by the image of the *pietà*, and that she fully expressed her response through weepings and wailings. This was a typical reaction, also described by Angela of Foligno (1248–1309) and another female English mystic, Julian of Norwich (*c.* 1342–*c.* 1416), among many other visionaries. For example, the thirteenth-century preacher Jacques de Vitry, in recounting the life of Marie d'Oignies (1167–1213), a mystic from the town of Liège (now in Belgium) recalls how she was visited by Christ:

> One day, already chosen by you, she was visited by you and she considered the benefits which you had generously shown forth in the flesh to humanity. She found such grace of compunction therein that a great abundance of tears was pressed out by the wine press of your Cross in the passion and her tears flowed so copiously on the floor that the ground in the church became muddy with her footprints. Wherefore for a long time after this visitation she could neither gaze at an image of the Cross, nor speak, nor hear other people speaking about the passion of Christ, without falling into ecstasy through a defect of the heart.

Generally speaking, the women who experienced such visions were either nuns or believers who considered it to be of great importance to serve their communities. They were convinced that they were mediators and intercessors who could provide a connection between Christ and the people around them, and saw the recording of their visions as an important component of their mission.

Another tradition, which arose primarily among educated clerics, is often called "mystical theology," and refers to a mysticism based on a "scientific" analysis of the mystical experience, or the active pursuit of visionary experience through study. The movement had its roots primarily among the Dominican friars of Germany, and was perhaps stimulated by the contact of the Dominicans with the Beguines of northern Europe.

The most famous of mystical theologians was Meister Eckhart (*c.* 1260–1327), a German Dominican who had studied at the universities of Paris and Cologne. Eckhart became convinced of the impossibility of knowing God, and argued that it was only through "unknowing," a kind of self-annihilation, that the human soul could come to experience direct apprehension of the divine: "Divesting thyself of thyself and of everything external thereto does give it thee." Eckhart's sermons, from which this phrase is taken, were very popular, but the ecclesiastical authorities saw some of his views as pantheistic, and he was tried for heresy. Eckhart claimed that his teaching, were not in conflict with orthodox ecclesiastical teaching, but he died before the trial was over. A posthumous verdict excommunicated him, and all of his writings were ordered to be destroyed. Fortunately, some of his followers, known as the Friends of God, were able to rescue some of his sermons and other writings.

The mystical path was also quite appealing to the Franciscans, given their emphasis on faith and emotion as opposed to reason. The most famous Franciscan mystic was St. Bonaventure (c. 1217–1274), who was governor general of the order in the late thirteenth century (see Chapter 13). Bonaventure believed that one's dedication to faith and love was more important than rational speculation in achieving union with God:

> If you ask how [divine things] may be known, my answer is: turn to grace instead of doctrine, desire instead of knowledge, the groaning of prayer instead of the labor of study—in a word, to God instead of man.

Even the great Dominican philosopher and theologian Thomas Aquinas (1225–1274) came to a mystical realization of God. After years of study and rational thought, his glorious vision of the Divine convinced him that faith, rather than reason, was the way to the Godhead (see Chapter 13).

Most of the mystics advocated working within the established framework of orthodox ecclesiastical doctrine, and did not see themselves as rebelling against the existing Church. Their intense passion and devotion were indicative, however, of the changing attitudes towards religious experience common in the later Middle Ages, which emphasized personal and emotional involvement. Some mystics, however, and many heretics were suspected, and accused, of using practices and methods generally regarded as "magic" in their religious devotions. Understandably, the Church was alarmed by these reports of witchcraft, satanic worship, and magical activities, and moved to eradicate them.

Magic and Witchcraft

The evolution of magic in the medieval world had a long and complicated history, which resulted from a combination of magical lore inherited from the Classical Roman world, influences from Germanic tribal customs, and Celtic folklore. Some scholars have also suggested that the survival of early Christian "underground" cults was a contributing factor. A variety of "magical" practices had long been undertaken to heal disease, for example, or to increase the yield of a harvest, and these were deemed acceptable by the Church and learned authorities, although the distinction between "white magic" and "black magic" was blurred and uncertain.

By the twelfth century, however, the Church had defined key differences between the various systems of belief and the practice of magic, and ecclesiastical authorities were determined to rid society of the magicians, sorcerers, and witches who were thought to consort with demons. The occult practices of magic and witchcraft began to be closely associated with heresy, and images of the magician and the heretic were greeted with the same sort of revulsion. Eventually, inquisitional inquiries were extended to include interrogations of men and women accused of magical practices. It has been suggested that this was due, in part, to the changing perceptions of the Devil, who became an increasingly powerful and fear-producing figure in the popular imagination—due in large part to the teachings of the Church itself. This preoccupation with the Devil, and the accompanying fear of witches, has been linked by some historians to the growing emotionalism in the relationship between God and humans. The Devil was the arch-enemy against whom people must summon the protective aid of God through the ministry of the Church.

Before the twelfth century, the Devil and his associates were part of the tales of folklore, which depict them as responsible for actions ranging from the truly diabolical to the merely impish and mischievous. Indeed, even in the late Middle Ages, practices that might later be regarded as "satanic" remained as part of "folk Christianity" in the activities of "wysards" (wizards) and "cunning folk." However, in the systematic philosophical writings of thinkers such as St. Thomas Aquinas, Satan acquired a hierarchically organized body of assistants who were able to take on bodies and to communicate their wishes and demands to human beings. They could tempt men and women into their service, and often confirmed this allegiance through written contracts and distinguishing marks, which they placed on the bodies of their adherents. They could have sexual relations with humans, and were able to give people the power to fly and to transform themselves into animals. They frequently called their human servants to nocturnal assemblies known as "sabbats," at which they were required to renounce their Christian faith, desecrate the holy sacrament, and pay homage to the Devil. These gatherings were supposedly held in isolated places, often in fields or the secluded areas of mountain ranges.

One such gathering was described in a decretal letter from Pope Gregory IX (r. 1227–1241) to several northern German prelates:

> The following rites of this pestilence are carried out: when any novice is to be received among them and enters the sect of the damned for the first time, the shape of a certain frog appears to him, which some are accustomed to call a toad. Some kiss this creature on the hindquarters and some on the mouth; they receive the tongue and saliva of the beast inside their mouths. Sometimes it appears unduly large, and sometimes equivalent to a goose or a duck, and sometimes it even assumes the size of an oven. At length, when the novice has come forward, he is met by a man of marvelous pallor, who has very black eyes and is so emaciated and thin that, since his flesh has been wasted, seems to have remaining only skin drawn over the bone. The novice kisses him and feels cold, like ice, and after the kiss the memory of the catholic faith totally disappears from his heart. Afterwards they sit down to a meal and when they have arisen from it, from a certain statue, which is usual in a sect of this kind, a black cat about the size of an average dog, descends backwards, with its tail erect. First the novice, next the master, then each one of the order who are worthy and perfect, kiss the cat on its hindquarters; the imperfect, who do not estimate themselves worthy, receive grace from the master. Then each

returns to his place and, speaking certain responses, they incline their heads towards the cat. "Forgive us," says the master, and the one next to him repeats this, a third responding and saying, "We know master;" a fourth says, "and we must obey."

Thus prepared, the vassals of Satan were able, through charms and conjurings, to "ruin and cause to perish the offspring of women, the foals of animals, the products of the earth, and grapes of vines, and the fruit of trees, as well as men and women, cattle and flocks and herds of animals of every kind." Their powers were often invoked in matters pertaining to love and lust, and they could "cause immense hailstorms and poison winds with lightning, cause sterility in humans and animals, injure their neighbors in body and property, drive horses mad when their wealthy riders mounted them, and travel through air wherever they wished to go."

The now familiar image of women flying about on broomsticks (**fig. 110**) is indicative of the frequent accusations against female witches, although men were similarly charged. A fifteenth-century account taken from a sermon concerning the behavior of a witch tells how a woman had killed thirty children "by sucking their blood," and reports that she had killed "her own little son, and had made a powder out of him, which she gave people to eat in these practices of hers." This seems to have been a typical story, often featuring women who were old and poor, or who were outsiders in the village and hence suspected by their neighbors. They frequently exhibited unpleasant traits, such as insolence or aggressive behavior, and they spoke freely about their own sexual activities, as well as those of others; they usually had a bad reputation. These general characteristics probably account for the preponderance of women who were accused, convicted, and executed. The ratio of women to men in France, for example, was about four to one.

Fear of witches did not remain a medieval phenomenon. Indeed, the drive to exterminate witchcraft continued to develop in the following centuries, reaching its apogee in the well-known witch hunts of the sixteenth and seventeenth centuries throughout Europe and in the American colonies.

110 This drawing—probably the earliest image of women flying on broomsticks—appeared as a marginal illustration in a fifteenth-century manuscript of the poem *Le Champion des dames*, by Martin Le Franc.

Summary

The rapid changes taking place in European society in the twelfth and thirteenth centuries caused dramatic and radical alterations in the religious ideologies of the period and resulted in the development of new monastic orders and lay religious sects. These currents were first evident in the teachings of Peter Waldo, the founder of the Poor Men of Lyons, who advocated a return to the apostolic life, characterized by poverty and the preaching of the Gospel. Eventually the followers of Waldo began to advocate anticlericalism, and they were persecuted by the ecclesiastical authorities. Another group, the Cathars, or Albigensians, were viewed as even more heretical and were vigorously exterminated in the Albigensian Crusade. Other movements to emerge included the Beguines and the Brethren of the Common Life, who were also devoted to poverty and supported themselves through manual labor.

Two important new religious groups eventually received papal approval: the Franciscans and the Dominicans. These mendicants, or friars, as they became known, were dedicated to ministering to the urban poor, and espoused poverty, as the Waldensians and Cathars had done. These new monastic orders were directly responsible to the pope, and became important in the papal drive against heresy, magical practices, and witchcraft.

A further change in religious belief came in the form of a heightened emotional relationship between humans and God, Christ, and the Virgin Mary. A humanizing vision of Jesus, coupled with the development of the Cult of the Virgin, led to a more personal response in religious devotion. This tended to intensify the religious experience, and contributed to the growing number of people who claimed to have a mystical contact with God. Mysticism also became a prominent component of "mystical theology," which sought to encourage faith and mystical experience through intense study.

By the end of the thirteenth century, the highly organized ecclesiastical structure of the medieval Church had changed in order to accommodate these new religious currents. Although cloistered monasticism continued to exist, and indeed, exists in the present day, powerful new monastic orders and groups of lay people emerged with the purpose of meeting not only their own religious needs, but also those of the urban, laboring poor.

Suggestions for Further Reading

Primary sources
Heresies of the High Middle Ages, translated and annotated by Walter L. Wakefield and Austin P. Evans (New York: Columbia University Press, 1969), provides an extensive collection of documents concerning heretical movements from the eleventh through the fourteenth centuries. Another excellent collection of sources is *Heresy and Authority in Medieval Europe: Documents in Translation*, by Edward Peters (Philadelphia: University of Pennsylvania Press, 1980).

Chapters 5 and 6 of Emilie Amt's *Women's Lives in Medieval Europe* (New York: Routledge, 1993) include sources concerning the Beguines, as well as female Waldensians and Cathars.

St. Francis of Assisi: Writings and Early Biographies: English Omnibus of Sources for the Life of St. Francis, edited by Marion A. Habig, 4th ed. (Chicago: Franciscan Herald Press, 1983), is a fine collection of sources with helpful introductions. *Early Dominicans: Selected Writings*, edited by Simon Tugwell (New York: Paulist Press, 1982), is a good selection of sources, with an introduction.

A fine edition of *The Book of Margery Kempe*, edited by Lynne Staley (New York: W.W. Norton, 2001), includes a selection of medieval sources to provide context, and excellent critical articles.

The subject of witchcraft is admirably documented in *Witchcraft in Europe: 400–1700, A Documentary History*, edited by Alan Charles Kors and Edward Peters, 2nd ed. (Philadelphia: University of Pennsylvania Press, 2001).

Secondary sources
Religion and Devotion in Europe, c. 1215–c. 1515, by R.N. Swanson (Cambridge: Cambridge University Press, 1995), provides a survey of religion and devotion in the late

Middle Ages, discussing basic questions about medieval religious experience and presenting several issues of recent historiographical debate. Southern's classic work, *Western Society and the Church* (Hammonds-worth: Penguin Books, reprint ed. 1982), includes an interesting discussion of the friars, Beguines, and Brethren of the Common Life in the last two chapters.

An excellent collection of articles about the Waldensians is Peter Biller's *The Waldenses, 1170–1530* (Aldershot: Ashgate, 2001). The volume contains historiographical information as well as studies of preaching by the Waldensian Sisters and texts of the Inquisitors, among other topics. Biller's research concentrates on the Waldensian movement in Germany.

The Cathars and the Albigensian Crusade, by Michael Costen (Manchester: Manchester University Press, 1997), gives a detailed but exciting description of the activities of the Cathars in southern France, and discusses the response of secular powers, as well as the Church. A classic account of the Cathar inquisition is *Montaillou: The Promised Land of Error*, by Emmanuel Le Roy Ladurie, translated by Barbara Brey (New York: Scolar Press, 1978). *The Cathars*, by Malcolm Lambert (Oxford: Blackwell Publishers, 1998), gives a fascinating view of the origins and development of the Cathar movement in various areas of Europe, including an innovative chapter on the Catharist church in Bosnia.

Another excellent work by Malcolm Lambert is *Franciscan Poverty: The Doctrine of Absolute Poverty of Christ and the Apostles in the Franciscan Order* (St. Bonaventure, NY: Franciscan Institute, 1998), which provides a stimulating introduction to the doctrine of the Franciscan Order.

Texts and the Repression of Medieval Heresy, edited by Caterina Bruschi and Peter Biller (Woodbridge: Boydell Press, 2003), offers articles that discuss the attempts to repress heresy as reflected in various writings, including inquisitorial sources. Malcolm Lambert's *Medieval Heresies: Popular Movements from the Gregorian Reform to the Reformation* (2nd ed., Oxford: Blackwell, 1992) is a fine survey of the activities of Cathars and the Waldensians. The volume also includes a study of heretical movements in the fifteenth and early sixteenth centuries. *Repression of Heresy in Medieval Germany*, by Richard Kieckhefer (Philadelphia: University of Pennsylvania Press, 1979) is a specialized study of the activities of inquisitors in Germany.

Patricia Ranft's *Women and the Religious Life in Premodern Europe* (New York: St Martin's Press, 1998) provides a brief introduction to women's religious life, including discussions of Beguines, Cathars and Waldensians. *Women in Medieval Europe: 1200–1500*, by Jennifer Ward (London: Longman, 2002), discusses the religious experiences of nuns and laywomen. The last six chapters provide information about Beguines and mystics.

Richard Kieckhefer's *Magic in the Middle Ages* (Cambridge: Cambridge University Press, 1989, 2000) is a survey of the development of the practice of magic in the medieval world, including a discussion of Arabic learning and the occult sciences. *The Magician, the Witch, and the Law*, by Edward Peters (Philadelphia: University of Pennsylvania Press, 1978), is a fascinating study of magic and witchcraft in medieval Europe. Two books by Jeffrey Burton Russell, *Lucifer: The Devil in the Middle Ages* (Ithaca: Cornell University Press, 1984) and *Witchcraft in the Middle Ages* (1972), are excellent accounts of the practices of medieval witchcraft and devil worship. Another excellent analysis of witchcraft is Carlo Ginzburg's *Ecstasies: Deciphering the Witches' Sabbath*, translated by Raymond Rosenthal (New York and London: Penguin Books, 1991).

13 THE CULTURE OF THE HIGH MIDDLE AGES

THE THIRTEENTH CENTURY is generally regarded as the high point of medieval culture. It was an era characterized by the flowering of intellectual life and artistic expression. As commerce and trade developed, the growing urban centers provided the dynamic energy, both intellectual and economic, that produced institutions of higher learning. Patronage for cultural institutions became widespread, and led to new forms in art and architecture, literature, philosophy, and music. These were linked, according to some scholars, by a common thread of rational order.

The most notable manifestation of this new intellectual flowering was perhaps the founding of the first universities in Italy, France, and England. But this vibrant intellectual culture was also reflected in the work of the great philosophers of the time, who sought to relate the philosophies of the Classical period to their own world. In the visual arts, the Gothic cathedral rose heavenward in cities throughout Europe, while sculptors and illuminators also embraced the new and delicate Gothic style. In music, composers developed a rhythmic system that enabled them to create complex polyphonic musical works, and literature in the vernacular achieved growing popularity.

These artistic achievements were intimately connected with an important new institution that would profoundly affect the educational development of western civilization—the university.

The Medieval University

The university as we know it was essentially the creation of medieval Europe. Earlier educational centers such as the philosophical schools of ancient Athens (fourth century BC), the law school of Beirut (third to sixth century AD), and the imperial university of Constantinople (founded in 425) had some features that anticipated medieval universities, such as rudimentary administrative organization and a regular course of study. However, they possessed neither the corporate associations of masters and students governed by statutes and administrative machinery, nor the fixed degree procedures and curricula that characterized the medieval university. Although the intellectual roots of the university may be traced to Greco-Roman, Byzantine, and Arabic schools of thought, the creation of the institution itself seems to have been a response to the growing need for professional education in a society that was becoming more and more urban and bureaucratic.

The first evidence of university structure—a "proto-university," according to the historian Alan Cobban—can be traced to the southern Italian town of Salerno. By the twelfth century, the faculty of medicine at Salerno had achieved great fame, and the school of liberal arts, though a less celebrated component, was an important site for the reception and dissemination of Greek, Jewish, and Arabic science and philosophy. Although the institution was legally recognized as a center of medical study by the emperor Frederick II in 1231, it failed to acquire the kind of cohesive bureaucratic organization that would have guaranteed its development as a comprehensive institution. It remained essentially devoted to the specialized study of medicine, and did not develop the full course of study that characterized medieval universities such as Bologna, Paris, Oxford, and Cambridge.

Bologna

The first institution to transcend specialization was the university that emerged at Bologna, Italy, originally founded to train laymen in Roman law. This focus was a direct result of the expanded career opportunities that resulted from the burgeoning municipal life in the northern Italian cities. Furthermore, Bologna was well situated on an important crossroads in northern Italy, where pilgrims stopped on their journeys, and merchants from north of the Alps met Italian traders carrying goods from the Byzantine Empire. Thus, the city had long been characterized by a cosmopolitan atmosphere.

An even more important factor than location was the presence at Bologna of a charismatic teacher, Irnerius, who taught there between 1116 and 1140. Using a method somewhat akin to the dialectic of Peter Abelard (see Chapter 10), Irnerius wrote a commentary on the *Corpus juris civilis* of Justinian. His work provided a survey of Classical legal thought that could be easily communicated to students. Thus, the basic Roman legal texts were now available in a form that could be used as a foundation for specialized study. Irnerius's teaching established the fame of Bologna as a legal center, and students from distant areas of Europe flocked to the city.

Canon, or Church, law became an equally prominent aspect of the curriculum in 1140, when the monk Gratian, who taught at the Bolognese monastic school of San Felice, completed his *Concordia discordantium canonum* (*A Concordance of Differing Canons* often called the *Decretum Gratiani*). This work provided a convenient compendium of canon law, appropriate for the educational process.

From these twin legal curricula emerged Europe's first university. Its government, closely modeled on that of the emerging commune of Bologna, arose from the initiatives of Bolognese law students to form a protective organization. In order to understand this development, it is important to remember that Bologna was filled with students from diverse regions of Europe who were legal aliens. Without protection from local landlords, merchants, and authorities, the educational enterprise was at risk. It was natural that the students should decide to form protective associations or ***universitates***. These were ultimately subdivided into national groupings, known as "nations," which were presided over by elected student rectors. By the mid-thirteenth century the nations had formed into two major groups, the *Ultramontani*, which included students from north of the Alps, and the *Citramontani*, those from Italy.

The students created a governance structure for the university in which they held sovereign power. The daily administrative tasks were carried out by small executive committees comprising the student rectors and their supporting officials, all of whom were chosen by the nations. The teachers were elected annually by the students, and were dependent upon student fees for their income. Furthermore, they took an oath upon election, in which they swore to obey the jurisdiction of the student rector with regard to everything that affected the life of the university. The regulations exercised by the students were extremely rigorous, and, according to one scholar, amounted to a "quasi-totalitarian regime." The statutes of the university indicate that the students held powerful control over the teacher's professional life. He was fined if he began to lecture a minute late or if he continued beyond the predetermined time, in which case the students were required to leave the lecture hall immediately. At the beginning of each term, the students and the teacher reached an agreement about the material to be covered, as well as the schedule according to which it would be studied. If the teacher failed to meet the schedule, he would be subjected to a heavy fine. He would also be penalized financially if he did not give equal emphasis to all parts of the syllabus, or if he did not adequately explain a difficult topic. If he did not cover all items of a projected syllabus, he was required to repay all or part of his students' fees.

In order to guarantee the lecturer's close attention to these details, he was required to deposit a sum of money with a city banker on behalf of the students. Any infringement of the rules was subject to a student review board, presided over by the rector, which was empowered to deduct fines from this account. If the money ran out, owing to heavy fines, the lecturer was required to deposit an additional amount. If he refused to comply, he could not collect his salary, and his source of income was cut off. In addition, a system of secret denunciations was in place. The rectors were obligated to act on a charge if only two students had denounced a teacher; and students were urged, as part of their academic responsibility, to report on teachers who infringed the statutes in any way.

Lecturers were obviously willing to accept these terms, although not without some reservations, one would assume. Since, however, the circumstances of a salaried lectureship represented an improvement over collecting fees from the students individually, the teachers acquiesced in the system. Furthermore, many seem to have derived incomes from activities other than teaching, such as working as ambassadors for the commune. Eventually, the students lost their control over the nomination and activities of the teaching staff. By 1350, almost all lecturers were appointed and paid by the commune.

Although women were not able to matriculate at medieval universities, there is evidence that at least two women did receive doctorates in law and taught at Bologna. Both were daughters of law professors who were educated at home. They presented themselves as doctoral candidates, passed the examinations and defended their theses brilliantly, were awarded their degrees, and became part of the faculty.

Paris

The evolution of the University of Paris followed a quite different path from that of Bologna. In Paris the students had little effective control and the professors struggled for autonomy against ecclesiastical domination. The constraints on their free development came from the chancellor and chapter of the cathedral of Notre-Dame, whose schools were the foundation of the embryonic university. Originally, the students who attended these institutions on the Ile de la Cité (a small island in the Seine where the cathedral of Notre-Dame stands) stayed in the homes of the **canons** of the cathedral, who were the earliest teachers. The schools were under the jurisdiction of the chancellor of the cathedral, who derived his authority from the bishop of Paris. As the schools became famous, they attracted many students from outside Paris, and there was a severe housing shortage. The chancellor limited the admission to the schools, and many students moved across the river to the left bank of the Seine—an area that became known as the "Latin Quarter," since Latin was the language of education, as well as of the Church.

The schools of Notre-Dame did not diminish in importance, but in the twelfth century more schools were established near the bridges of the Seine, and in the environs of the collegiate Church of Ste.-Geneviève and the Abbey of St. Victor. The university that developed around the cathedral in the thirteenth century built on this burgeoning educational activity, as well as on the intellectual achievements of scholars who made Paris the preeminent university of northern Europe. One of these, Hugh of St. Victor (1096–1141), the head of the School of St. Victor, concentrated on biblical exegesis and mystical theology, and made a distinctive contribution to theological scholarship, as did other "Victorines," making Paris the center for theological discourse. Perhaps more important was Peter Abelard, whose career was discussed earlier (see Chapter 10); he was typical of the brilliant and charismatic masters who attracted an international student population. The most important component, however, was the stability of the cathedral of Notre-Dame, which provided the institutional framework around which the university could be formed.

Paris itself provided an ideal location for an academic community. It was a vital and growing area which could furnish accommodation for a large number of masters and students. In addition, the French kings recognized the advantages of fostering an academic population. Since they wished to promote the economic, social, and political development of the city, they had a positive attitude towards the university. This was a strong contributing factor in its successful emergence and survival.

By 1200, when Philip Augustus issued a charter for the university, an association of masters was no doubt already in place, and by 1215 they had acquired the right to elect officers and to establish statutes of governance. In that year the papal legate Robert de Curzon affirmed the right of the masters to create statutes, and also authorized them to fix rents for lodgings, to determine proper clothing for teachers, and to regulate lectures and disputations. The statutes proclaimed, for example:

> No one shall lecture in the arts at Paris before he is twenty-one years of age, and he shall have heard lectures for at least six years before he begins to lecture . . . he shall not be stained by any infamy . . . none of the masters lecturing in arts shall have a **cope** except one round, black, and reaching to the ankles, at least while it is new. Use of the **pallium** is permitted. No one shall wear with the round cope shoes that are ornamented or with elongated pointed toes.

Furthermore:

> Each master shall have jurisdiction over his scholar. No one shall occupy a
> classroom or house without asking the consent of the tenant, provided one has
> a chance to ask it. No one shall receive the licentiate from the chancellor or another
> for money given or promise made or other condition agreed upon. Also, the masters
> and scholars can make both between themselves and with other persons obligations
> and constitutions supported by faith or penalty or oath in these cases: namely,
> the murder or mutilation of a scholar or atrocious injury done a scholar, if justice
> should not be forthcoming, arranging the prices of lodgings, costume, burial,
> lectures, and disputations, so, however, that the university be not thereby
> dissolved or destroyed.

Statutes such as this provided a clear determination of the right of the masters to function as a guild—a *universitas magistrorum et scolarium* (a body of masters and students). Furthermore, although technically the right to grant licenses to teach remained with the chancellor, he was required by the pope to award the license to all candidates recommended by the masters in the various faculties.

As at Bologna, the students at Paris were grouped according to national origin, and informal associations of scholars from the same geographical areas were evident by the late twelfth or early thirteenth centuries. By 1249, there is definite evidence of a four-fold national division in the faculty of arts: French, Picard, Norman, and English–German. In the graduate faculties of theology, law, or medicine, there were no national groupings, but masters of arts who were studying for advanced degrees were classified in the nations until they acquired masterships or doctorates in a graduate discipline. Each of the four nations had a high degree of autonomy, with its own elected officers and proctor, statutes and archives, finances, seal, schools, assembly point, and feast days. The loyalty of students tended to be focused on the nation, rather than on the faculty of arts or the university as a whole, and this often led to feuding and even outright fighting among the nations. Sometimes the conflict became so severe that it required the intervention of a papal legate or, in extreme cases, the French king.

The university provided housing for poor students, such as the residence of St. Thomas of the Louvre. However, by 1228, this residence was experiencing difficulties. As indicated in a chartulary from that year, the representative of the bishop of Paris found, among other things, that

> certain scholars, who for a long time past had lived on the goods of that house, had
> reached a point of such insolence that unless they are received at night they break in
> and violently enter the house of the brothers. Others, as it were, sure of food, eat
> more than is expedient for those studying a long time; making little progress and
> unwilling to study, a burden to the studious, they in various ways molest the quiet
> and study of others.

The solution of the inspector was to limit to one year the amount of time a student could be housed at St. Thomas of the Louvre, unless special permission were given.

In the Middle Ages, as in the twenty-first century, housing was not the only significant expense for a university student. The purchase of books, which were copied by hand since printing had not yet been invented, also placed a hardship on those of lesser means, who were often exploited by booksellers eager to make a profit. The University of Paris attempted to place controls on the vendors in order to protect students, as may be seen in the following excerpt from a thirteenth-century chartulary:

> Also, since some of the aforesaid booksellers, given to insatiable cupidity, are in a way ungrateful and burdensome to the university itself, when they put obstacles in the way of procuring books whose use is essential to the students and by buying too cheaply and selling too dearly and thinking up other frauds make the same books too costly, although as those who hold an office of trust they ought to act openly and in good faith in this matter, which they would better observe if they would not simultaneously act as buyer and seller, we have decreed that the same booksellers swear, as has been stated above, that within a month from the day on which they receive books to sell they will neither make nor pretend any contract concerning those books to keep them for themselves, not will they suppress or conceal them in order later to buy or retain them, but in good faith, immediately they have received the books or other things, they will offer them for sale at an opportune place and time.

Some students, fortunate enough to be supported by their parents, misused their funds. As observed by Alvarus Pelagius, a representative of the pope, when writing in the early fourteenth century about conditions at the university:

> The expense money which they have from their parents or churches they spend in taverns, conviviality, games, and other superfluities, and so they return home empty, without knowledge, conscience, or money. . . . They contract debts and sometimes withdraw from the university without paying them, on which account they are excommunicated and do not care, but they may not be absolved.

The university curriculum was based on the Seven Liberal Arts—the *Trivium* (grammar, rhetoric, and logic), and the *Quadrivium* (arithmetic, geometry, music, and astronomy), inherited from the Roman educational system (see Chapter 2). Mastery of these subjects, especially logic and dialectical argument, was considered to be essential before moving on to the more advanced courses in theology and law. It seems that students often tended to pass through the arts curriculum as quickly as possible, seeking to enter one of the more lucrative fields. As the noted scholar John of Salisbury lamented as early as the twelfth century: "If you are a real scholar you are thrust out in the cold. Unless you are a money-maker, I say, you will be considered a fool, a pauper. The lucrative arts, such as law and medicine, are now in vogue, and only those things are pursued that have a cash value." These inclinations ran counter to the educational ideal, but were driven by the needs of society. The growth of European cities dictated the establishment of a course of study that concentrated on socially useful employment, rather than humanistic literary study.

Oxford and Cambridge

One might expect that universities following the Parisian pattern would have emerged in England, but this did not occur. There were many educational centers in the twelfth century from which a university might have evolved, such as Lincoln, Hereford, or York, but none of these developed into a full-blown **studium generale**.

Historians were long inclined to agree with the thesis of Hastings Rashdall, an eminent early twentieth-century scholar of medieval universities, that Oxford was founded by a group of students who returned to England from Paris around the year 1167, when Henry II decreed that they could not attend the University of Paris because of the potential influence of supporters of Thomas Becket. Current scholars think, rather, that the university at Oxford developed gradually, and they point to evidence that schools there were able to attract scholars of international reputation by the early twelfth century. Furthermore, if a migration from Paris did occur, it should be viewed as simply one component in a continuous development that extended throughout the twelfth century. By 1300, Oxford was commonly regarded as a university, with specialized curricula in arts, law, and theology.

The office of chancellor of the university was in evidence by 1209, and was originally linked to the bishop of Lincoln. Soon, however, the chancellor came to be elected by the masters, who submitted their choice to the bishop for his confirmation. Predictably, this led to a prolonged struggle between the various chancellors of the university and the bishops of Lincoln. The conflict was ultimately resolved in 1367, when Pope Urban V (r. 1362–1370) rescinded the right of episcopal confirmation. Subsequent English chancellors had far greater power than either the chancellor at Paris or the rector at Bologna.

Just as Bologna was famous for law, and Paris for theology, so Oxford established a reputation for excellence in mathematics and natural sciences. English scholars had been engaged in scientific experimentation since the early twelfth century. Their studies consisted primarily of using mathematical principles to improve their understanding of natural phenomena, and their efforts were spurred on by the rediscovery around 1150 of the works of Aristotle (see below). Since the English scientists were not subject to the same curricular restrictions at Paris where the study of Aristotle was prohibited, the emerging university at Oxford provided them with a supportive environment; hence, the scientific emphasis became a feature of the curriculum at the English university. Furthermore, the institution enjoyed the support of the monarchy and the papacy during the thirteenth through sixteenth centuries, and this led to the consistent advancement of the academic community (**fig. 111**).

Cambridge University was long regarded as lagging far behind Oxford in its evolution, and, in fact, it owed its foundation to an exodus of scholars from Oxford when classes were suspended there in 1209. By 1233, "the chancellor and university of scholars at Cambridge" were addressed by Pope Gregory IX, indicating that the university had formed a corporate entity that functioned under the

111 New College, Oxford, was founded in 1379, and the impressive quadrangle shown in this drawing from c. 1461–1465 remains almost unchanged today. On the right, steps lead up to the dining hall, and the passage just left of center goes through to the chapel and cloisters. The college library was located on the upper floor of the building on the right. The fellows and scholars of the college are shown in the foreground grouped around the warden, Thomas Chaundler, who served from 1455 to 1475.

direction of a chancellor. By the fifteenth century, the institution had achieved a reputation as a university of the highest quality.

The foundation of universities throughout France and Italy began early in the thirteenth century, and extended to the fifteenth. During this period similar institutions began to emerge in Spain. The universities in Germany, Bohemia, Poland, Hungary, Denmark, and Sweden developed somewhat later. For example, the earliest foundations in central Europe include the University of Prague, founded by Charles IV in 1347–1348, and universities at Vienna in 1365, Cologne in 1388, Krakow in 1367, Buda (in modern Hungary) in 1389, and Uppsala in 1477. By this time, the initial restrictions on the study of ancient Greek philosophy had been rescinded, and scholars at all of these institutions were able to incorporate the "New Learning" into their studies.

The Rediscovery of Aristotle and the Scholastic Method

In the early part of the thirteenth century, as discussed above, the curriculum at the University of Paris consisted of an arts course emphasizing logic and dialectical argument. The school of theology at Paris was conservative and intent on maintaining a traditional approach, and not at all interested in the intricate dialectical paths of philosophy. Parisian theologians tended to view this intellectual approach as antithetical to the proper study of their discipline. These attitudes led them to attempt preventing the study of the Aristotelian treatises that had begun to infiltrate the intellectual world of the university (**fig. 112**).

By 1200, a great portion of the work of Aristotle was available to western European scholars. The writings of "the philosopher" had largely been recovered, a result of the outward expansion of northern Europeans into southern Italy, the east, and especially Spain. Their incursions in these areas brought them into contact with unfamiliar centers of intellectual life which contained treasures hitherto unknown to medieval European scholars. The energetic attitudes that made political expansion possible were reflected in the intellectual orientation of the European scholars, who were eager to put to use the new sources of knowledge and thought.

As the Europeans moved into Antioch following the First Crusade, they encountered scholars who had translated many unknown works of the ancient world, and at Constantinople they discovered translators at work on Aristotelian logic, as well as the writings of early Christian churchmen such as St. John Chrysostom and St. Basil.

112 A university lecture by Henry of Germany is shown in this fourteenth-century manuscript illumination from a German version of Aristotle's *Ethics*. The scholars in the first two rows are, for the most part, paying close attention to the lecture, which they follow in their texts. In the back rows, much like present-day students, one man succumbs to sleep, while others are engaged in personal conversations.

A third area of interchange was Sicily, where, under the Norman monarchs, scholars of Latin, Greek, Arabic, and Hebrew were translating the works of Plato and Aristotle. An even more important center was Spain, where the writings of Aristotle had long been an object of intense study. As discussed in Chapter 9, the translations of Greek philosophical works by the Muslim scholar Averroës and the Jewish translator and theologian Maimonides had preserved ancient thought during the previous centuries. As the Reconquista progressed, there was eager patronage of scholars and translators by monarchs and bishops, as well as an atmosphere conducive to productive intellectual interchange.

The translations from these centers had a profound effect on the development of philosophy, and ultimately theology, as they filtered into the academic and intellectual centers of northwestern Europe. Scholars first turned to Aristotle's works on logic, which were concerned with the modes of propositions, the **syllogism**, and various methods of argument. As mentioned earlier, Abelard had established the basic principles of structuring textual criticism in *Sic et non*, but he had refrained from proposing conclusions (see Chapter 10). It was inevitable, however, that such solutions would eventually be worked out, and this procedure became an important hallmark of the "Scholastic Method." The technique of reconciling seemingly contradictory propositions was perfected into a fine art by the assimilation of Aristotelian logic. This method determined the content and form of academic instruction, the ritual of public disputations, and, most significantly, the process of argumentation in the Scholastic writings themselves.

The great treatises were organized according to a logical system so that the reader was led, step by step, from one proposition to another. The whole was divided into parts, which were, in turn, divided and subdivided into smaller parts. The result of this continuing subdivision was that almost every concept was split into two or more meanings. Every topic was formulated as a question, and the discussions began with the positioning of one set of authorities against the other. The argument proceeded to the solution, and was followed by an individual critique of the arguments that had been rejected.

The development of the Scholastic Method was retarded, to a degree, by the strong resistance to the study of the works of Aristotle on the part of ecclesiastical officials. Their opposition was clearly demonstrated in a decree passed at the provincial synod of Sens, in northern France, which stipulated: "Neither the writings of Aristotle on natural philosophy nor their commentaries are to be read at Paris in public or private, and this we forbid under penalty of excommunication." The statement that these works were not to be "read" meant that they were not to be used as texts for teaching. Scholars could, and did, read the works in private, and they were in use at other universities. Indeed, the newly founded university at Toulouse proclaimed in a brochure of 1229 that the masters there were free to use Aristotle.

The ban at Paris was reinforced in 1215, when the statutes of the papal legate Robert de Curzon decreed that the masters of arts "must not lecture on the books of Aristotle on metaphysics and natural philosophy, or on summaries of them." As we have seen, the prohibition was never instituted in Oxford and, by mid-century, the Parisian scholars probably felt the urge to "catch up" with the English university. In 1252, Aristotle's *De anima* (*On the Soul*) was included in the syllabus as an examination subject in the English nation at Paris, and in 1253 all the works of Aristotle were available for use by the entire faculty.

The theologians, meanwhile, had become less conservative. By the middle of the thirteenth century, theological scholars commonly produced during their careers a comprehensive manual, called a *summa*, which synthesized the entire tradition of theology by using philosophy and the dialectical method to explain their conclusions. The nucleus of their thought was, as might be expected, the tradition of scripture and the Church, generally as interpreted by St. Augustine of Hippo. In their commentaries, however, they drew on an ever-growing fund of ideas, derived from Neoplatonic and Muslim philosophy, as well as the newly discovered Aristotelian material.

The advent of the Franciscans and Dominicans at Paris lent a new refinement to this methodological development. Both orders sent their most brilliant members to occupy academic chairs at Paris, which were ultimately filled by eminent men. Two of the most famous were Bonaventure (a Franciscan), and Thomas Aquinas (a Dominican). They were among the scholars whose works exemplify the Scholastic Method.

Scholastic Philosophy

Bonaventure

St. Bonaventure (Giovanni di Fidanza) was born in Tuscany in *c.* 1221. He studied at the University of Paris from 1236 to 1242, and became a friar in 1243. The following year he began his theological studies, which continued until 1248, and in 1253 he advanced to the rank of master. In 1257, he was elected minister general of the Franciscan order. Pope Gregory IX named him cardinal bishop of Albano in 1273, and he died at the Council of Lyons in 1274. Bonaventure's many official positions meant that he was a public figure for much of his life. He was renowned for his "angelic purity" and his friendly disposition, as well as his outstanding intellectual powers. His ability to use the Scholastic Method in his theological works is surpassed only by his contemporary, Thomas Aquinas (see below).

Bonaventure's works are carefully organized. They are structured in a logical manner, with subdivisions clearly marked, but they also possess thematic unity. A devout follower of the precepts of St. Francis and St. Augustine, Bonaventure was primarily concerned in his writings with two problems: the ability of human beings to penetrate intellectually the mystery of God, and the progress of the individual human soul towards union with God. Like St. Francis, he viewed the world as a reflection of God, and thought that the meaning of human life consisted of progress towards the ecstatic vision. Though highly intellectual and rational, Bonaventure believed that true knowledge of the Godhead came as the result of a mystical vision. As he wrote in Chapter 7 of *The Soul's Journey into God*:

> In this passing over,
> if it is to be perfect,
> all intellectual activities must be left behind
> and the height of our affection must be totally transferred and transformed into God.
> This, however, is mystical and most secret,
> which no one knows except him who receives it,
> no one receives

except him who desires it,
and no one desires except him
who is inflamed in his very marrow by the fire of the Holy Spirit whom Christ sent
into the world.

Thomas Aquinas

The works of Aquinas, by contrast, lack a mystical cast. Aquinas's writings are much less emotional, remaining rational and impersonal in style, and his vocabulary is spare and precise, rather than florid and figurative. To many scholars, he is the authentic voice of reason, and the greatest interpreter of traditional Christian thought.

Aquinas, like Bonaventure, was born in Italy, in either 1225 or 1226. In 1230, he was offered by his parents to the monastery at Monte Cassino as a child oblate. In 1239, the monks at Monte Cassino were expelled by Frederick II, and Thomas became a student at the University of Naples. He joined the Dominican order in 1244, and in the next year traveled to Paris and Cologne. From 1248 he was a pupil of Albert the Great, who was the first scholar to master the works of Aristotle, and he taught at Paris as a bachelor of arts in 1252–1256. Between 1259 and 1268 Aquinas was in Italy, teaching and writing at Agnani, Orvieto, Viterbo, and Rome. He returned to Paris in 1269, and remained there until 1272, when he went to Naples to organize the course of studies at that university. Aquinas, too, died in 1274, on his way to the Council of Lyons. Not much is known of his personal life, though anecdotes report that he was extremely obese and quite silent— a "dumb ox" who remained preoccupied with philosophical speculations even when in the presence of King Louis IX.

Like the other great scholastics, Aquinas was a voluminous writer. He surpassed the others, however, in lucidity, in sense of proportion, and in his ability to construct a vast system of thought based on a few simple principles. Although his style is less expressive than that of Bonaventure, he joined his contemporary in searching for the ultimate approach to God. As he wrote in his *Commentary on the Sentences*:

> Wisdom by its very name implies an eminent abundance of knowledge, which
> enables a man to judge of all things, for everyone can judge well what he fully
> knows. Some have this abundance of knowledge as the result of learning and study,
> added to a native quickness of intelligence; and this is the wisdom which Aristotle
> counts among the intellectual virtues. But others have wisdom as a result of the
> kinship which they have with the things of God; it is of such that the Apostle says:
> "The spiritual man judges all things." The Gift of Wisdom gives a man this eminent
> knowledge as a result of his union with God, and this union can only be by love, for
> "he who cleaveth to God is of one spirit with Him." And therefore the Gift of
> Wisdom leads to a godlike and explicit gaze at revealed truth, which mere faith holds
> in a human manner as it were disguised.

Aquinas's greatest work—the *Summa theologica*—exemplifies the hierarchical structure and breadth of subject matter that characterized Scholastic philosophy. In the *Summa*, Aquinas posits 631 questions, on topics ranging from the nature of God and the angels, to the actions of human beings. He organizes points to support both positive and negative answers to such questions as: whether a human act is right or sinful in so far as it is good or evil; whether human virtue is a habit; or whether virtue is in us by nature.

The following example (Question 73, Article 2) demonstrates the methodology Aquinas used in structuring the *Summa*. It also shows clearly his technique of synthesizing biblical references and sources from the ancient world, including the writings of the Roman philosopher Cicero, the Stoics, and Aristotle's *Ethics*.

Whether All Sins Are Equal?

We proceed thus to the Second Article:

Objection 1. It would seem that all sins are equal. For sin is to do what is unlawful. Now to do what is unlawful is reproved in one and the same way in all things. Therefore sin is reproved in one and the same way. Therefore one sin is not graver than another.

Objection 2. Further, every sin is a transgression of the rule of reason, which is to human acts what a linear rule is in corporeal things. Therefore to sin is the same as to pass over a line. But passing over a line occurs equally and in the same way, even if one go a long way from it or stay near it, since privations do not admit of more or less. Therefore all sins are equal, since privations do not admit of more or less. Therefore all sins are equal.

Objection 3. Further, sins are opposed to virtues. But all virtues are equal, as Cicero states. Therefore all sins are equal.

On the contrary, Our Lord said to Pilate (John XIX: 11): He that hath delivered me to thee, hath the greater sin, and yet it is evident that Pilate was guilty of some sin. Therefore one sin is greater than another.

I answer that, The opinion of the Stoics, which Cicero adopts in the book on *Paradoxes*, was that all sins are equal; and from this opinion arose the error of certain heretics, who not only hold all sins to be equal, but also maintain that all the pains of hell are equal. So far as can be gathered from the words of Cicero, the Stoics arrived at their conclusion by looking at sin on the side of the privation only, in so far, namely, as it is a departure from reason. Hence, considering without reservation that no privation admits of more or less, they held that all sins are equal. Yet if we consider the matter carefully, we shall see that there are two kinds of privation. For there is a simple and pure privation, which consists, so to speak, in being corrupted. Thus, death is a privation of life, and darkness is a privation of light. Such privations do not admit of more or less, because nothing remains of the opposite habit; and hence a man is not less dead on the first day after his death, or on the third or fourth days, than after a year, when his corpse is already dissolved; and, in like manner, a house is no darker if the light be covered with several shades, than if it were covered by a single shade shutting out all the light. There is, however, another privation which is not absolute, but retains something of the opposite habit. It consists in becoming corrupted rather than in being corrupted: e.g., sickness, which is a privation of the due commensuration of the humors, yet so that something remains of that commensuration, or else the animal would cease to live. The same applies to deformity and the like. Such privations admit of more or less on the part of what remains of the contrary habit. For it matters much in sickness or deformity whether one departs more or less from the due commensuration of the humors or the members. The same applies to vices and sins, because in them the privation of the due commensuration of reason is such as not to destroy the order of reason altogether; or else evil, if total, destroys itself, as is stated in *Ethics IV*. For the substance of the act or the affection of the agent could not remain, unless something remained of the order of reason. Therefore it matters much to the gravity of a sin whether one departs more or less from the rectitude of reason; and accordingly we must say that sins are not all equal.

Reply Objection 1. To commit sins is unlawful because of some lack of order in them; and therefore those which contain a greater lack of order are more unlawful, and consequently graver sins.

Reply Objection 2. This argument looks upon sin as though it were a pure privation.

Reply Objection 3. Virtues are proportionately equal in one and the same subject. However, one virtue surpasses another in excellence according to its species; and, again, one man is more virtuous than another in the same species of virtue, as was stated above. Moreover, even if the virtues were equal, it would not follow that vices are equal, since virtues are connected, and vices or sins are not.

In this small example taken from the *Summa Theologica*, it is possible to see the rational techniques used by Scholastic philosophers such as Aquinas to bring order and clarity of structure to the vast treasury of thought that had accumulated in the previous 1,500 years. The balanced, rational design of the works of these great Scholastic philosophers has frequently been compared to that of the Gothic cathedral, which also exemplifies logical arrangement, division into discrete parts, and an aesthetic goal of encapsulating the presence of the divine.

The Gothic Cathedral

Great cathedrals such as those at Chartres, Paris (Notre-Dame), Cologne, and Prague were designed and built to provide a meaningful focus, both religious and aesthetic, for public worship. They drew people from the cities, as well as the surrounding areas, who came to attend liturgical services, to celebrate holy feast days, and to venerate the saintly relics contained in splendid shrines. The buildings themselves functioned as sites of holiness, and the many sculptures, carvings, and stained-glass windows proclaimed the Christian message. Cities vied with one another in the creation of these impressive monuments, building magnificent structures that soared towards heaven. The religious enthusiasm that led to the proliferation of these glorious churches is well documented; the records of Guillaume de Seignelay, bishop of Auxerre between 1207 and 1220, tell us:

> the construction of new churches everywhere heightened people's zeal. And so the bishop, seeing his own church at Auxerre, which was of ancient and crude construction, suffering from neglect and old age, while others all around were lifting their heads in marvelous beauty, determined to provide it with [a] new building so that it might not be inferior to these others in form and treatment.

The participation of the townspeople in the construction of cathedrals has long been debated. During the "Gothic revival" that took place in the nineteenth century, it was often mentioned that the people of Chartres had actually harnessed themselves to carts full of stone which they dragged to the cathedral site. Although recent scholars believe that these accounts were probably exaggerated, there is evidence indicating that the citizens, including women and children, were active participants in some areas, at least in helping to make the buildings ready for services. The records of Geoffrey of Loudun, bishop of Le Mans between 1234 and 1255, describe how the townspeople worked to clear the cathedral of construction rubble so that the relics of St. Julian could be brought and installed as scheduled:

On the morning after the Easter service, in the church of the Most Blessed Confessor, a great multitude was at hand, of every condition, sex and age of the whole city of Mans. To free the church of building debris they carried out the rubbish, vying with one another in their eagerness. Matrons were there with other women who, contrary to the way of women, not sparing their good clothes, carried the gravel outside the church in various garments, in clothes bright with green stripes or some other color. Many who carried the sweepings out from the church in their dresses rejoiced that the dresses themselves were stained with the dirty dust. Others, filling the tiny garments of babies with the rubbish from the church, carried it outside the church. Small wonder. It was fitting that the praise of infants attend the divine work. In order that infants and little children might seem to have contributed their labor to so great a service, three-year-olds and little children in whom one could already discern signs of holy faith and who until then could scarcely walk carried the dirt outside the church in their own little garments. Those who were older and stronger carried great pieces of wood and stone outside the church more quickly and easily than could be believed. The younger ones attended to light loads, according to their strength, while the older ones, according to theirs, toiled to carry heavy ones. In a short time they did voluntarily what many hired men had not accomplished over long periods of time. And this they did on their holiday, without interruption and without having been asked to do so. What more need be said? Such was the zeal of people's faith, such the ardor of their devotion, that onlookers marveled.

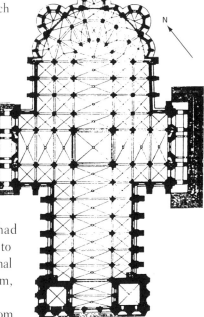

113 The ground plan of Chartres Cathedral (constructed 1194–1220) shows the basic features of most Gothic cathedrals: a central nave with side aisles and a transept; the choir terminating in an apse, around which an ambulatory provides a passageway enabling worshipers to view the relics in apsidal chapels.

By the thirteenth century, when the records of the cathedrals of Auxerre and Le Mans were being written, architects and builders had fully adapted the Romanesque forms and the innovations of Abbot Suger to their new designs (see Chapters 8 and 10). Although there was some regional variation, the Gothic cathedrals were essentially similar in basic form, with several features being common to all.

As may be observed in **fig. 113**, the ground plan, which developed from the early Christian basilica form, consists of a central nave with side aisles and a transept. The eastern portion of the nave forms the choir, which almost

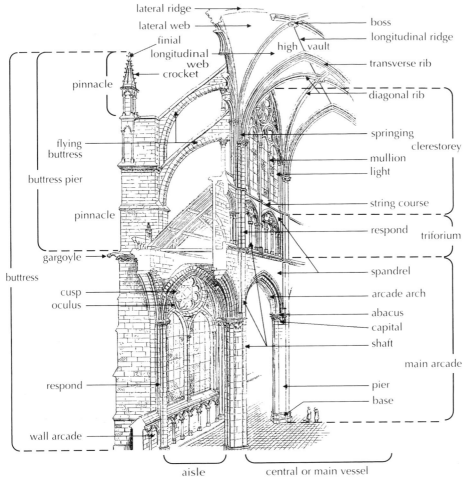

lateral ridge
lateral web
finial
longitudinal web
crocket
pinnacle
flying buttress
buttress pier
pinnacle
gargoyle
buttress
cusp
oculus
respond
wall arcade
boss
longitudinal ridge
high vault
transverse rib
diagonal rib
springing
clerestorey
mullion
light
string course
respond
triforium
spandrel
arcade arch
abacus
capital
shaft
main arcade
pier
base
aisle
central or main vessel

114 This cross-section elevation diagram of Amiens Cathedral (constructed 1220–1236) identifies the basic features of most Gothic cathedrals.

invariably terminates in a polygonal apse, or sanctuary, around which the aisles continue (the ambulatory). A series of small chapels opens out from these aisles, with the central one usually being more developed than the rest. The transept arms generally have rectangular ends, and the west end of the nave is almost always rectangular.

The nave is divided from the aisles by a row of piers which support the super-structure, consisting of the triforium and the clerestory. On the outer sides of the aisles are half-piers, against which are set the great exterior buttresses. The spaces between them are enclosed by low, thin walls with openings above them that extend from pier to pier and up to the arch of the aisle vaulting (**fig. 114**).

The vaults are constructed on a complete set of ribs—transverse, diagonal (groin), and longitudinal. These ribs form pointed arches, known as ogives (see fig. 63). The ribs are sustained by slender shafts, compactly grouped, and bonded at their bases and capitals to the great piers which rise from the pavement through the successive stories of the building to the nave cornice.

In addition to the shafts that support the main ribs of the vault, there are shorter ones carrying the archvaults (the arches of the main arcades), the ribs of the aisle vaulting, and the arches of the triforium. A rectangular buttress, which rises through the triforium and becomes an external feature in the clerestory, is added to the pier. Each pier is thus a compound member which consists of a great central column that incorporates smaller shafts, and a buttress. These piers support the vaults, their thrusts being so completely counterbalanced by the external buttress system that they need only be massive enough to bear the weight of the vaults.

The clerestory buttresses are reinforced by **flying buttresses**—segments of arches that rise from the outer abutments and extend over the aisle roofs. In this way, the ribs, strongly supported by the pier buttresses, and then by the flying buttresses, provided the architects of the Middle Ages with a solution to the problem of vaulting the basilica form. The "broken" arch, with ribs meeting in a point, made it possible to achieve an even height for the crown of the vault when the sides of the ground plan were not equilateral. The vault could now be adapted to a ground plan of any shape. In addition, the use of the pointed arch permitted a thinning of the piers and walls.

The ribbed vault has a decorative value as well as a structural one. It heightens the effect of the upward surge produced by the high, narrow naves where the vertical lines predominate, prolonging under the vaults the ascending direction of the long delicate shafts which, attached to the piers and walls, mount towards heaven (**fig. 115**). The aesthetic and devotional effect of the Gothic style fills the viewer with awe today just as it must have done in the Middle Ages.

Understandably, Gothic cathedrals have been a source of fascination for generations of scholars, extending back several centuries. Many interpretations have been suggested, including structural, symbolic, social, and intellectual speculations. Nineteenth-century Romantic critics viewed the cathedral as a soaring space which brought worshipers closer to an experience of the Divine. German nationalists saw the cathedral as being inspired by the tall trees of the forests of northern Germany. French scholars of the nineteenth century, such as Viollet-le-Duc, were more interested in the engineering feats of Gothic builders than in symbolic explanations. More recent scholars have viewed the cathedral as the Bible in stone for an illiterate populace. Others have suggested that the buildings represent a demonstration of the philosophical principles of Scholasticism—a *Summa theologica* in stone and glass—or a representation of the aesthetic and mystical precepts of St. Augustine. Regardless of their particular orientation, all seem to agree that an essential component of the High Gothic style is "light as form and symbol." As art historian Louis Grodecki wrote, "The notion of 'light-space' [represents] the medieval Church as the material realization of spiritual ideas, religious or philosophical."

Contemporary scholars have been interested as well in exploring archival sources relating to the builders themselves, and have sought to analyze the records of cathedral chapters to ascertain the methods and techniques used by medieval architects, sources of patronage, and participation by guilds of workers in stone and stained glass. One important medieval source for this kind of information comes from the historian Gervase of Canterbury, who wrote about the reconstruction of Canterbury Cathedral after a fire in 1174. In *Of the Burning and Repair of the Church of Canterbury*, Gervase describes the horror of the fire and the destruction of the cathedral. "The house of God, hitherto delightful as a paradise of pleasures, was now made a despicable heap of ashes, reduced to a dreary wilderness, and laid open to all the injuries of the weather." He then recounts the search for a competent architect who could provide advice concerning the possible

115 Amiens Cathedral is the largest Gothic cathedral in northern Europe. It has an interior height of 142 feet (43 m) and a surface area of over 26,000 square feet (2,415 square m). The soaring lines of the elevation and the vaulting lead the eyes of the viewer upwards, towards heaven. Today the cathedral is bare in comparison to its appearance in the Middle Ages, when it would have been filled with sculptures, banners, and tapestries.

116 A candle burning in the center of Trinity Chapel in Canterbury Cathedral marks the place where the shrine of St. Thomas Becket stood from the thirteenth century to the Reformation, when Henry VIII had the imposing structure destroyed. The chapel is surrounded with stained-glass windows which recount the life and miracles of the Canterbury martyr.

repair and rebuilding. Both French and English builders were summoned, but they could not agree as to the proper procedure. Among them was William of Sens, "a man active and ready, and as a workman most skillful both in wood and stone. [The monks] retained him, on account of his lively genius and good reputation, and dismissed the others."

Gervase's account of William's activities gives a fascinating view of the responsibilities of a medieval supervisor of works. William procured stone "from beyond the sea"; he "constructed ingenious machines for loading and unloading ships, and for drawing cement and stones. He delivered molds for shaping the stones to the sculptors who were assembled, and diligently prepared other things of the same kind." Work progressed rapidly during the first four years, but in 1178, William was injured in an accident. After he had prepared the machines for "vaulting the great vault, suddenly the beams broke under his feet, and he fell to the ground, stones and timbers accompanying his fall, from the height of the capitals of the upper vault, that is to say, of fifty feet [15 m]. Thus sorely bruised by the blows from the beams and stones he was rendered helpless alike to himself and for the work." William was confined to his bed, and he placed in charge of the construction "a certain ingenious and industrious monk, who was the overseer of the masons." The master continued to direct the work from his bed for some time, but finally decided to return to his home in France.

The man who took his place as director of the works was "William by name, English by nation, small in body, but in workmanship of many kinds acute and honest." The English William finished the transept and completed the vaulting, and laid the foundation for the enlargement of the east end, where a chapel for St. Thomas Becket was to be erected. Gervase goes on to describe in detail the placement of walls, piers, and columns, but admits that "if one wishes to understand all this, it will be revealed more clearly by the sight of the church than by words" (**fig. 116**).

As may be seen from the foregoing description, the duties of an architect were many and varied. According to medieval records, architects were known as "masons" until the end of the thirteenth century, and often in the next century, and there seems to have been no distinction in rank. An architect was probably trained as a mason, beginning with an apprenticeship as a stonecutter. His eventual rise to prominence no doubt depended on his general abilities and artistic gifts. The only personal record of an architect's activities and concerns in the thirteenth century is the lodge book of the French mason and architect Villard de Honnecourt. This work contains important information about the building techniques as well as the activities of the medieval architect.

The Gothic builders relied on geometry as the basis of their design. Because structural mechanics did not exist as a science before 1600, the dimensions of structural members were described by formulas that were expressed as relations between the sides of the square, the equilateral triangle, the double square, the pentagon, or their multiples. Indeed, the Gothic architect developed all magnitudes of his ground plan and elevation from a single dimension by using geometrical figures. The architect did not instruct the mason to build a pinnacle a certain number of feet in height. He said instead, "Make the height so many multiples of the length of the basic square." The knowledge of this method for determining architectural proportion was kept a professional secret until the fifteenth century, but there is important evidence in Villard de Honnecourt's *Sketchbook* that this was the technique in use in the thirteenth century. **Fig. 117** contains designs showing squares which deserve special attention. Under the one in the center is written: "How to lay out a cloister with its galleries and courtyard." The exterior square is twice the size of the inner one and is obtained by tracing the diagonal as one of its sides. The new square is twice as large as its predecessor. As ultimately revealed some two centuries later by Mathias Roriczer, the architect of Regensburg Cathedral, this technique was used by medieval architects to determine the dimensions of every detail (**fig. 118**). Thus, the art of taking an elevation from a plan by geometrical methods was the constructive basis of the entire edifice.

Architects and masons were joined in cathedral construction by sculptors and glassworkers. These artists were given the task of creating the figures and images that carried the stories of the Bible and the lives of saints to a largely illiterate community. As the French churchman and professor of canon law Guillaume Durand (1230–1296) remarked in his treatise *Rationale divinorum officiorum*:

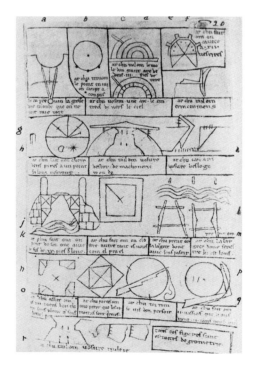

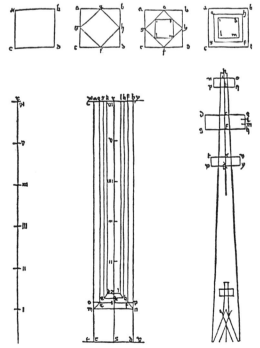

FAR LEFT **117** The sketchbook of the architect Villard de Honnecourt contains information about the geometric methods used by builders in constructing Gothic buildings. The square that appears in the center of this drawing demonstrates that measurements for a square twice as large as the original were obtained by tracing the diagonal as one of its sides.

LEFT **118** Drawings by Mathias Roriczer, the architect of the cathedral in the German city of Regensburg, confirm the assumption that geometrical techniques were used during the Middle Ages to determine the elevations of all aspects of a ground plan.

The glass windows in a church are Holy Scriptures, which expel the wind and the rain, that is all things hurtful, but transmit the light of the True Sun, that is, God, into the hearts of the Faithful. These are wider within than without, because the mystical sense is the more ample, and precedeth the literal meaning. Also, by the windows the senses of the body are signified: which ought to be shut to the vanities of this world, and open to receive with all freedom spiritual gifts.

The creation of stained-glass windows was a complicated process, involving the production of the glass itself, followed by painting and leading, and ultimately the setting of the panels. The low windows, often in **lancet** form, were easily seen by worshipers, and generally had complicated narratives drawn from the Bible and the lives of saints; here, many small scenes were arranged in geometric panels. The elevated clerestory windows contained large figures of Christ, the Virgin Mary, saints, and apostles. Their increased size made it possible for viewers to see them easily. High Gothic cathedrals also featured rose windows, which frequently appeared above the doors at the western entrance and the transepts. As mentioned earlier, the lives of Christ and the Virgin Mary provided a fertile source for creating devotional images that both instructed and inspired those who observed them.

One of the most famous examples in stained glass is the rose window in the north transept of Chartres Cathedral (**fig. 119**). Here the Virgin and Child are surrounded by four doves, representing the Gospels, and eight angels. In the circle of lozenges there are images of Old Testament kings and prophets—the forerunners of Christ. The golden lilies of France are prominently displayed, along with the heraldic castles of Castile. This last feature may be a reference to the patronage of Blanche of Castile (the mother of Louis IX of France), who may have commissioned the windows. Around the rim of the rose are checkered medallions with prophets in the center, and in the center of the lancets underneath, over the royal crest, stands St. Anne holding the infant Virgin Mary. Anne was given this place of honor because the cathedral possessed a precious relic—her head—which had been presented to the chapter by the Count of Blois when he returned from the Fourth Crusade in 1204. The lancets on Anne's right and left contain Old Testament prefigurations of Christ: Melchizedek, David, Solomon, and Aaron.

When entering a cathedral suffused by color and light, the medieval viewer, like the modern one, was immediately struck by glittering images such as these. The aesthetic appeal led directly to spiritual apprehension when the image represented a central doctrine of the Christian religion. As the artist Roger of Helmarshausen (writing under the pseudonym Theophilus) asserted early in the twelfth century:

> If [the human eye] gazes at the abundance of light from the windows, it marvels at the inestimable beauty of the glass and the variety of this most precious workmanship. But if a faithful soul should see the representation of the Lord's Crucifixion expressed in strokes of an artist, it is itself pierced.

The lives of saints were also prominently depicted, especially the legends of the patron saints of specific churches and cathedrals. One fine example is the series of windows in the Trinity Chapel at Canterbury, which records the miracles of St. Thomas Becket. There are images of the saint healing people stricken with many varieties of illness, including leprosy, fever, paralysis, and plague, and there are also windows that depict his raising of people from the dead, and his rescuing of individuals from natural disasters. Often there are several images that provide a continuous narrative. For example, the miracle of curing the plague in the household of a knight, Jordan Fitz-Eisulf, is recounted in nine sections (**fig. 120**). Images such as these brought hope to the thousands of pilgrims who visited Becket's shrine seeking relief from physical and spiritual ills.

At Chartres Cathedral, where some of the finest medieval glass survives, in addition to biblical windows and those recounting the lives of saints, there are windows known as the "trade windows," which present images of various groups of workers. In one window, masons are depicted cutting stones and building walls; in an accompanying image, workers are carving sculptures. Scholars have generally believed that these windows were created with money donated by the guilds in order to affirm their influence. It has recently been pointed out, however, that they are actually testaments to the control of the clergy, and that these stained-glass images are the "physical demonstration of the enormous authority of the church" over the common laborers.

Stained glass was initially used in the cathedrals of France and England, but it eventually became a prominent feature of Gothic churches throughout Europe, carrying forward Abbot Suger's vision of filling the churches and cathedrals with brilliant light, and

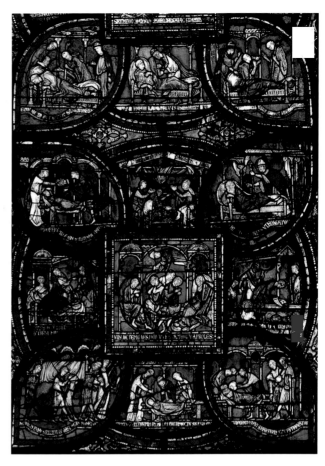

120 Trinity Chapel at Canterbury Cathedral contains many examples of continuous narrative, in which parts of the same tale appear in sequence. In the window pictured here, St. Thomas Becket is shown in the upper right corner, visiting the son of Jordan Fitz-Eisulf who has been stricken by plague. Subjects for the windows in Trinity Chapel were drawn from the book of Becket's miracles compiled by Benedict of Peterborough.

thereby capturing the essence of God within the sacred structure. As Suger had said in the twelfth century: "The great church windows are the Divine writings that let the light of the true sun, which is God, into the church, which means, into the hearts of the faithful, so that it can enlighten them all."

Equally important aesthetically were the sculptures that covered the exterior of Gothic cathedrals and enhanced the interior. The most famous of the sculptural cycles are those of Chartres, Amiens, and Reims. The iconographical programs of these cathedrals encompass Christian teaching and medieval learning to the degree that one famous scholar has called them encyclopedias in stone.

Gothic cathedrals continued the Romanesque tradition of placing an image of the Last Judgment in a prominent position, generally over the central door (see Chapter 8). The tympanum over the western portal at Chartres provides a typical example—one that illustrates the advance in sculptural style that had taken place by the thirteenth century. Here, rather than being in low relief, like the figure of Christ in the tympanum at Autun (see fig. 75), the central figure is almost three-dimensional, as are the symbols of the Evangelists surrounding him (**fig. 121**). The sculptures on the door jambs are also more realistic and less stiff, with undulating cascading draperies suggesting human anatomy beneath.

At Amiens, sculptors created figures that characterized the High Gothic style. An excellent example, which also typifies the humanized Christ, is *Le Beau Dieu*, placed on the trumeau of the central west portal. Here, broad folds of drapery follow a pattern that became almost a formula for Gothic sculptures. Vertical folds on one side of the figure provide a contrast with diagonal lines on the other, drawing the viewer's eye upwards to the gentle face and extended hand of the blessing Christ (**fig. 122**). This idealized style provided the basic pattern for sculptors from other areas of France, and eventually spread to Spain, Germany, Italy, and the Slavic countries.

The pier of the south portal at Amiens features a lovely Madonna and Child, known as the *Vierge Dorée* (Golden Virgin) because some of the original gilding remains on the sculpture (**fig. 123**). This sculpture of the Virgin is typical of the sensitive style of portrayal that developed out of the Cult of the Virgin and the emphasis on her value as an intermediary between humans and God. Her expression is similar to that of a loving earthly mother, but the elaborate crown on her head reminds the worshiper that she is the Queen of Heaven. This image of the Virgin was replicated in small scale in countless small sculptural works of the High Gothic period which were produced in gold, silver, and ivory, as well as in manuscript illuminations.

LEFT **123** The so-called *Vierge Dorée* (Golden Virgin) at Amiens is typical of artworks that emphasized the Virgin's role as an intermediary between God and human beings. Mary is shown here as a young mother admiring her baby, rather than as a stiff, severe, royal figure. The artist has created a natural effect with sweeping draperies which emphasize the S-curve of her body—a stance that was reproduced in countless medieval artworks, both large and small.

BELOW **124** The Cult of the Virgin inspired many exquisite works of art designed for private devotion. This lovely example, *The Virgin and Child of Sainte-Chapelle*, was carved in ivory and ornamented in gold. Although the Virgin originally wore a crown, her role as Queen of Heaven was not the most conspicuous aspect of this statuette. Instead, the relationship between mother and child was emphasized by the artist, drawing attention to Mary's human qualities.

Art Beyond the Cathedral

The Cult of the Virgin and the humanization of Christ that developed during the thirteenth century (see Chapter 12) also led to the creation of portable religious artworks which were used in private devotional settings. The finest examples were made for members of the nobility, who commissioned works for the devotional niches and chapels that were essential areas in their castles. Other elegant religious objects were created for use in convents and monasteries, where they became a focus for sacred veneration.

One of the most beautiful examples of small religious sculpture is *The Virgin and Child of Sainte-Chapelle* (**fig. 124**), which was registered in the oldest inventory of the royal chapel in Paris, compiled *c*. 1279–1285. Carved of ivory and delicately decorated in gold, the figure of the Virgin originally wore a gold crown studded with pearls and emeralds. Her breast was adorned with a gold flower centered with a large emerald, and she had an emerald finger ring which was "already lost in 1480." The two figures project a feeling of warmth and humanity; the Christ Child is responding to the fruit offered by his mother, and she smiles sweetly. There is no hint of future sorrow; the Virgin seems to represent an optimistic mother as well as the Queen of Heaven. This is perhaps the finest example of many small ivory sculptures designed for private devotional purposes, offering what one scholar has defined as a "rare combination of grandeur and intimacy."

Devotion to the Virgin assumed a heightened role as the Gothic era progressed. One example of manuscript illumination that demonstrates this tendency is found in the *Psalter and Hours of Yolande, Vicomtesse of Soissons* (perhaps created at Amiens, *c*. 1280). This work incorporates Gothic imagery, together with the heraldic arms of the patroness, as a frame for an image of Yolande praying to the Virgin and Child (**fig. 125**). There are

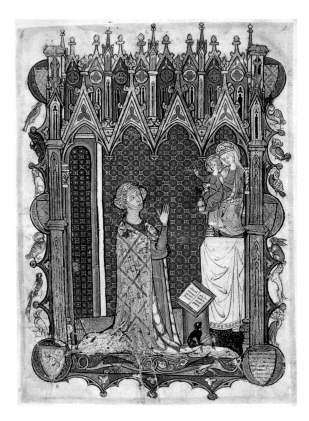

pointed arches, gables, pillars, buttresses, tendrils, and towers—all reminiscent of the architectural vocabulary of contemporaneous cathedrals. Also present are the playful birds and animals often in evidence in the borders of Gothic manuscripts.

The Gothic vocabulary was also used by goldsmiths and silversmiths in the creation of reliquaries—for example in one celebrated piece from the Aachen Cathedral Treasury (**fig. 126**). This work exemplifies the common practice of setting sculptural figures within an architectural framework. During the High Gothic era, it was perfectly natural for artists to borrow from the imagery employed in cathedrals. As the art historian Michael Camille has remarked, the "envelope [created by] the arch not only sustains and protects the figure, it elevates it, no matter how lifelike it has become, within an eternal, ecclesiastical order."

The thread of complex organization linking the philosophical treatises and the cathedrals of the thirteenth century may also be seen in the music of the era, as composers developed intricate systems that allowed them to create vertical harmonies of great beauty. Their works filled the lofty naves of European churches with splendid sonority.

Music

Paris, home of one of the greatest universities in medieval Europe, was also the primary center for the development of Gothic architecture, and it is not surprising that the city's composers assumed a leading role in the evolution of new musical styles.

Many thirteenth-century musical treatises were associated with the University of Paris, and the composers at Notre-Dame, known collectively at the "School of Notre-Dame," were pioneers in the development of **polyphonic** musical forms.

When Maurice de Sully became bishop of Paris in 1160, he initiated the construction of a new building to replace the Romanesque cathedral of Notre-Dame. The cornerstone was set in place in 1163, and the apse and choir were completed by 1182; the nave and transept were finished around 1200. During this forty-year period of construction, two generations of composers worked to produce a significant collection of sacred polyphony, which scholars now attribute to the School of Notre-Dame. Although most of these musicians remain anonymous, we do have the names of two important composers who made major contributions to the repertory—Leonin (*c.* 1159–*c.* 1201) and Perotin (*c.* 1170–*c.* 1236). This information comes from a document that appears to be a set of notes compiled by an English student at the University of Paris, known in music history as "Anonymous IV," since his is the fourth in a series of anonymous treatises published in the nineteenth century. Writing in the second half of the thirteenth century, he observed:

> Master Leoninus was generally known as the best composer of *organum*, who made the great book (*Magnus Liber*) of *organa* for Mass and Office for the enhancement of the Divine Service. This book was in use until the time of the great Perotinus, who shortened it and substituted a great many better ***clausulae***, because he was the best composer of **discant** [descant] and better than Leoninus . . . The book, or rather books, of Master Perotinus have remained in use in the choir of the Church of Our Blessed Virgin in Paris [i.e. Notre-Dame] until the present day.

The statements of Anonymous IV have been confirmed by other sources, including several manuscripts from France, Scotland, and Spain. These sources contain *organum* for two, three, and four voices, as described by Anonymous IV in another passage. We cannot assume that Leonin and Perotin composed all of the music contained in these compilations of Notre-Dame *organum*, but it is evident that the style developed at Notre-Dame by these men and their associates was extraordinarily influential in the evolution of polyphonic music. Just as the architectural features of the Gothic style in evidence at Paris appeared in cathedrals throughout Europe, so the musical characteristics that originated there later emerged in liturgical music composed in cities as diverse as Toledo, Spain, and St. Andrews, Scotland.

Leonin has been credited with establishing the style of Parisian *organum*, which was based on the distinction between two ways of setting the text: the syllabic or "group" style (one to four notes for each syllable), and the melismatic style (many notes for each syllable). The sections set in syllabic style, known as *clausulae*, provide the first evidence for the development of composition in strict rhythm. It was Leonin's unique contribution to replace the even, unmeasured flow of earlier polyphony with recurrent patterns of long and short notes. These different patterns are known as rhythmic modes, and they are indicated in the music by a system called modal notation. Leonin used only one mode, while his successor, Perotin, expanded the structure into its final form of six individual modes.

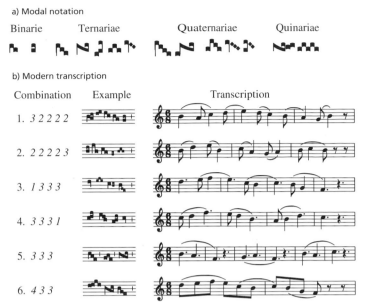

a) Modal notation

Binarie   Ternariae   Quaternariae   Quinariae

b) Modern transcription

Combination	Example	Transcription
1. *3 2 2 2 2*		
2. *2 2 2 2 3*		
3. *1 3 3 3*		
4. *3 3 3 1*		
5. *3 3 3*		
6. *4 3 3*		

126 The common ligatures of modal notation are shown in this example (*a*), together with a transcription into modern notation (*b*). As may be observed in the transcription, the time values of the notes depended upon their positions in the patterns. The vertical stroke at the end of each example, and after the first and second ligatures in Combination 5, indicates a rest.

OPPOSITE **128 and 129** This facsimile of a thirteenth-century manuscript (*top*) shows the first part of a three-part motet based on the Gregorian chant melody *Mors* (*Death*). The tenor voice appears at the bottom of each page, with the upper voices above. A modern transcription of the work appears beneath the manuscript folios.

Modal notation was first described by the Englishman John of Garland, often called Johannes de Garlandia (*c.* 1195–*c.* 1272) in the treatise *De musica mensurabili* (*Concerning Measured Music*). This method used a few simple **ligatures** (a series of notes written as one symbol). **Fig. 126a** illustrates the more common ligatures of modal notation, which are combinations of **longas** and **breves**. Their time value depends on the context, that is, on their position in the pattern. This procedure meant that a *breve* could have the value of either a modern eighth note (quaver) or quarter note (crotchet), and a *longa* could be either a quarter note or a dotted quarter note, depending on the ligature. By grouping the ligatures into fixed patterns, the composer was able to establish the desired rhythm. Patterns of ligatures were used to indicate the rhythmic modes, which are shown in **fig. 126b** with transcriptions into modern notation.

As may be seen in the transcriptions, the actual time values, *longa* (♩ or ♩.) and *brevis* (♪ or ♩), were arranged within the framework of a **perfectio** (♩.)—a "perfection," or sometimes two "perfections."

Mode 1: *longa–brevis* (♩♪)   Mode 4: 2 *breves–longa* (♪♩♩.)
Mode 2: *brevis–longa* (♪♩)   Mode 5: 2 *longae* (♩.♩.)
Mode 3: *longa–2 breves* (♩.♪♩) Mode 6: 3 *breves* (♪♪♪)

Thus, it can be seen that the basis of the system of rhythmic modes was the three-fold unit of measure referred to by subsequent music theorists as a *perfectio*—a "perfection." Franco of Cologne (fl. 1240–1280), described the perfectio in the following way in his treatise *Ars cantus mensurabilis* (*The Art of Measurable Song*):

The perfect long is called first and principal, for in it all the others are included, to it also all the others are reducible. It is called perfect because it is measured by three "tempora," the ternary number being the most perfect number because it takes its name from the Holy Trinity, which is true and pure perfection.

In modal notation, the *perfectio* is the equivalent of a dotted quarter note in modern notation (♩.), and the other values (♩), and (♪), could be contained in the *perfectio* in various combinations, as everything can be contained in the Holy Trinity, which was seen as "true and perfect perfection." The result of the system was that all medieval polyphony until the fourteenth century, insofar as it was in measured rhythm at all, was dominated by the ternary division of the "beat," although innovations occurred that expanded the vocabulary of note shapes to make clearer distinctions between

them. It has been suggested by some scholars that the "modular" technique of composition during the thirteenth century parallels the "modular" methodology of the medieval architect, in which, as we saw above, complicated structures were created through the repetition of a given module.

The rhythmic innovations of Leonin were developed and expanded by his successor Perotin. Perotin's advances, which one scholar has viewed as a manifestation of the passion for order so characteristic of the Gothic world, are documented in his revision of the *Magnus liber*. This work contains many new sections, or *clausulae*, which were written separately at the end of the manuscripts, providing optional "substitutions" for the original compositions. These *clausulae* are important because their creation provided the opportunity for the full exploration of the possibilities of modal rhythm. In addition, they are viewed as the "birthplace" of an important new musical form, the **motet**.

In the late twelfth century, poets began to add words to the upper voices of *organum*. This activity, literary rather than musical, created the new musical genre, the motet. (The name is derived from the French *mot*, meaning "word.") Generally speaking, the upper voices were given a Latin text which was a paraphrase or expansion of the meaning of the text given in the Gregorian chant sung by the lowest voice (the tenor, meaning the voice "holding" the others). **Fig. 128** presents a three-part motet from a folio in a thirteenth-century codex, with a modern transcription at **fig. 129**. The text of the Gregorian chant in the tenor voice, *Mors* (Death), is drawn from the alleluia sung during the Easter service.

Obviously, since the voices were singing different words at the same time, the projection of textual intelligibility was not an important concern for medieval composers. The practice of multiple texting became even more complicated as the motet evolved. Poets and composers began to mix languages in the same work, sometimes using French in one upper voice and Latin in another. The result was a total lack of aural clarity, although the singers were able to speculate on the meaning of the texts as they sang from the manuscript. Some motet texts were taken from love songs of the era, demonstrating an interesting cross-fertilization between secular and sacred musical composition.

An important early thirteenth-century secular form was the *rondellus* (rondeau [pl. rondeaux]). These were musical accompaniments to round dances in which lines performed by the full group alternated with lines sung by the leader. The form of the piece was extremely flexible, though a common element is the recurring refrain. The pattern of the earliest rondeaux was generally *a A a b A B*, with the capital letters indicating a repetition of both text and music and the lowercase letters indicating a phrase in which the music was repeated but the text was different; in the fourteenth century the two-line refrain was also used to begin the piece, with the resulting pattern *A B a A a b A B*. **Fig. 130**, a rondeau by the French composer Guillaume d'Amiens (*c.* 1250–1300), shows the poetic form clearly.

130 A rondeau by Guillaume d'Amiens shows the refrain (1, 4, 7), the repeating phrase (2, 8), and the independent phrases (3, 5, and 6), resulting in the rhyme pattern *A B a A a b A B*. (Capital letters signify the repetition of both text and music, with small letters indicating only the repetition of the music.)

	a				b						
1,4,7. De	ma	da	-	me	vient	2,8. La	grant	joi	-	e	que	j'ai;
3. De	li	me	sou	-	vient;						
5. N'en	par	-	ti	-	rai	nient,	6. Mais	tous	jours	l'a	-	mo	-	rai;

Dances such as these were undoubtedly accompanied by instruments, but there is little manuscript evidence documenting instrumental music in the thirteenth century. However, literary references, theoretical treatises, manuscript illustration, and cathedral sculptures indicate that instruments were widely used, frequently providing the musical setting for singing and dancing. *Trouvères* and troubadours sang to instrumental accompaniment, *jongleurs* were expected to be proficient on a minimum of ten instruments, and peasants played instruments to accompany their rustic dances. Thus, information does exist indicating that instrumental music was a feature of life at every level of society, although very few actual pieces remain. This may have been because most music was performed by professional musicians, who probably improvised their compositions, rather than writing them down. Furthermore, music among rural peasants was undoubtedly passed from generation to generation by oral tradition.

Literature

One of the most important vernacular literary works of the thirteenth century was the *Roman de la Rose* (*Romance of the Rose*), which proved to be exceptionally popular among medieval readers. Its fame is confirmed by the fact that the work exists in more than 200 manuscripts, many of which contain sumptuous illustrations (**fig. 131**). Long recognized by scholars as a significant work in the French literary tradition, by the end of the fourteenth century the *Roman* was translated into Italian, Dutch, and English.

The *Roman* contains two portions of unequal length, written by two authors at an interval of about forty years. The first 4,058 lines were composed by Guillaume de Lorris, and the longer portion (lines 4,059–21,780) by Jean de Meun (or Meung). According to information given in the second part of the work, Guillaume began the *Roman*, but died before completing it. Other internal evidence suggests a thirteenth-century date for the work; the poem refers to the struggle between Charles of Anjou and Manfred for the Kingdom of Sicily (see Chapter 11), and it assumes in line 6,643 (Charles "is now king of Sicily") that Charles is still living. Hence, the poem must have been completed between 1268, the year of the conflict, and 1285, the year of Charles's death.

Both authors were originally from the area of Orléans, which during the first half of the thirteenth century was known for humanistic studies. Jean evidently migrated to Paris, the most important intellectual center in France during his lifetime, when interest in literary studies declined in the city of his birth. Scholars believe that he was associated in some way with the University of Paris, and that he lived close to the house where Robert de Sorbon had established a residence for poor theological students—an institution that eventually developed into the Sorbonne; today it contains the university's Faculties of Letters and Sciences.

131 The Lover performs the *immixtio manuum* (mixing of hands) in an act of homage to the God of Love in this illumination from a manuscript of the popular *Roman de la Rose*, thereby becoming his vassal: "with clasped hands I became his man." This poem by Guillaume de Lorris and Jean de Meun focuses on courtly as well as Christian love in an elaborate vision of medieval life.

Over the centuries an obvious question has arisen concerning the artistic unity of the two parts of the *Roman*. Charles W. Dunn has compared the process of composition to the building of a great French cathedral, saying it was "conceived by its first architect in early Gothic, temporarily enclosed by a modest apprentice, and then extended on a grandiose plan and executed in an advanced and ornate style." Some critics have seen the first part of the work as a lyrical celebration of courtly love (see Chapter 10), while the second part is often interpreted as a denunciation of the ideals of courtly love and an elevation of naturalistic doctrine. These features have led to the observation that, like a Gothic cathedral, the poem comprises both the grotesque and the sublime, the sacred and the profane. Its individual details may be enjoyed by the unsophisticated, while the erudite can appreciate its complex architectonics. Hence, in spite of its varied workmanship, the whole is controlled by the same Gothic instinct for order underlying diversity that was characteristic of the cathedral builders, the scholars, and the composers. Recent interpretations have further defined the controlling device that unifies the two parts as allegorical method—a hallmark of both sacred and secular literature in the Middle Ages. Critics also point to irony as a basic literary technique throughout the entire work.

Medieval readers were familiar with the subject matter of the poem, since, by the end of the twelfth century, the works of Chrétien de Troyes and Marie de France were well known, and had established a standard pattern for French literature (see Chapter 10). Their focus on courtly love was adopted by Guillaume de Lorris, who translated the experiences of the lover into the realm of dreams. In the poem, typical human actions are personified by the forces that influence behavior: the Lover wishes to woo his Lady (the Rose); her initial responsiveness is represented by Fair Welcome, who encourages him; however, her modesty (Shame) repulses him; her dominance over him is represented by Danger (a French form of the Latin word *dominarium*, which means domination), who "blocks his advance." The first part of the poem describes the Lover's reactions to these various characters.

As may be seen in the poetic translation by Harry W. Robbins, which renders the French poetry into blank verse with five-beat lines, the *Roman* is introduced as a dream:

When I the age of twenty had attained—
The age when Love controls a young man's heart—
As I was wont, one night I went to bed
And soundly slept. But then there came a dream
Which much delighted me, it was so sweet.
No single thing which in that dream appeared
Has failed to find fulfillment in my life,
With which the vision well may be compared.
Now I'll recount this dream in verse, to make
Your hearts more gay, as Love commands and wills;
And if a man or maid shall ever ask
By what name I would christen the romance
Which now I start, I will this answer make:

"The *Roman de la Rose* it is, and it enfolds
Within its compass all the Art of Love."
The subject is both good and new. God grant
That she for whom I write with favor look
Upon my work, for she so worthy is
Of love that well may she be called the Rose.

Both authors—Guillaume de Loris and Jean de Meun—are explicit about the centrality of the theme of love in the *Roman*. Indeed, the work exemplifies the doctrine of Christian love as well as the amorous content of much medieval poetry. There are also overtones of vassalage and the feudal society, as may be seen in the following quote. In this passage, the hero has been wounded by five arrows from the bow of the God of Love; although he pulls out the shafts, the arrowheads remain imbedded in him:

Straightway with rapid step the God of Love
Approached me, and the while he came he cried:
"Vassal, you now are seized; there's nothing here
To aid you in defense or toward escape.
In giving yourself up make no delay;
For the more willingly you abdicate
That much more quickly will you mercy gain.
He is a fool who with refusal thwarts
The one whom he should coax and supplicate.
Against my power no striving will avail.
Be well advised by me that foolish pride
Will gain you nothing; cede yourself as thrall
Calmly and with good grace, as I desire."

The Lover submits to the God of Love, who tells him:

For your advantage, it is my desire
That you should pay me homage, press my lips
Which no infamous man has ever touched.
No churl or villain did I ever kiss;
Rather he must be courteous and frank
That I thus make my man; though, without fail,
He must sore burdens bear in serving me.
At that, with clasped hands I became his man.
Most proud was I when his lips touched my mouth;
That was the act which gave me greatest joy.

This small segment demonstrates only one aspect of the vast mirror of medieval life and thought contained in the poem. The *Roman* remained popular for centuries, and had a significant influence on fourteenth-century writers, including Dante, Chaucer, and the unknown author of *Sir Gawain and the Green Knight*.

Summary

One of the most important developments of the thirteenth century was the rise of the medieval university, which established, in its structure and traditions, the basis for our modern institutions of higher learning. Beginning in Italy and France, these associations of masters and students soon became a significant facet of life in England and eventually throughout Europe. The universities provided education for men seeking careers in government, and generated an atmosphere in which its professors had the intellectual stimulation and freedom to create vast syntheses of thought, known as *summae*.

Cities were also the birthplace of the Gothic cathedral, which has been compared to the great philosophical masterpieces in terms of the comprehensive nature of its artistic expression. Functioning as "bibles in stone and stained glass" for illiterate laypeople, these magnificent structures told the traditional legends of the Christian religion; in addition, the buildings themselves presented awe-inspiring environments for worship.

The development of polyphonic musical compositions exhibited similar features. Composers working at the cathedral of Notre-Dame in Paris invented a system known as the rhythmic modes, which enabled the creation of "cathedrals in sound" by subjecting musical expression to principles of rational order.

The architectural metaphor can also be extended to literary works such as *The Roman de la Rose*, which told fascinating tales drawn from ancient as well as earlier medieval sources. Functioning as a mirror of courtly love, and making use of the popular allegorical technique, this vernacular poem was widely read in the following centuries. Like the cathedral, it was a comprehensive expression of the sacred and the profane. Thus, in essence, an analysis of the spectacular monuments of Gothic culture leads us to see a common theme, or thread, of encyclopedic detail and rational order which determines the structure and style of these architectural, philosophical, musical, and literary monuments.

Suggestions for Further Reading

Primary sources

University Records and Life in the Middle Ages, by Lynn Thorndike (New York: Columbia University Press, 1944), remains a useful collection of materials from medieval universities.

Three important works of Bonaventure are printed in *Bonaventure: The Soul's Journey into God, The Tree of Life, The Life of St. Francis*, edited by Ewert Cousins (New York: Paulist Press, 1978). *Basic Writings of St. Thomas Aquinas*, 2 vols., edited by Anton Pegis (New York: Random House, 1944), is a fine edition of the works of the great philosopher.

Gothic Art: 1140–c. 1450, by Teresa G. Frisch (reprint ed., Toronto: University of Toronto Press, 1987), provides an extensive collection of documents that concern art within the social milieu of the High Middle Ages.

The most accessible prose translation of the *Roman de la Rose*, by Guillaume de Lorris and Jean de Meun, is by Charles Dahlberg (reprint ed., Hanover, NH: University Press of New England, 1983). The work has been translated into English verse by Harry W. Robbins in *The Romance of the Rose*, by Guillaume de Lorris and Jean de Meun (New York: E.P. Dutton & Co., Inc., 1962).

Secondary sources

The classic work on the medieval university is *The Universities of Europe in the Middle Ages*, by

Hastings Rashdall, 3 vols., new edition by F.M. Powicke and A.B. Emden (Oxford: Oxford University Press, 1936). *The Medieval Universities: Their Development and Organization*, by Alan B. Cobban (London: Methuen & Co., 1975), is a thorough study of specific European universities. *The Rise of Universities*, by Charles Homer Haskins (reprint ed., Ithaca, NY: Cornell University Press, 1957), remains a valuable brief introduction to the topic.

An excellent study of the development of medieval thought is *Medieval Foundations of the Western Intellectual Tradition, 400–1400*, by Marcia L. Colish (New Haven: Yale University Press, 1997). Another recent survey of medieval philosophy is David Luscombe's *Medieval Thought* (Oxford: Oxford University Press, 1997). *The Evolution of Medieval Thought*, by David Knowles (2nd ed., by D.E. Luscombe and C.N.L. Brooke, London: Longman, 1988), is a fine introduction to the study of medieval philosophy.

A recent work that offers new ways of viewing the art of the thirteenth and fourteenth centuries is *Gothic Art: Visions and Revelations of the Medieval World*, by Michael Camille (reprint ed., London: Orion Publishing Group, 1996). Another fine study by Camille is *The Gothic Idol: Ideology and Image-making in Medieval Art* (Cambridge: Cambridge University Press, 1989). Two studies, which are older but still useful are: *Gothic*, by George Henderson (reprint ed., Harmondsworth, UK: Penguin Books, 1978), and *Gothic Art: From the Twelfth to the Fifteenth Century*, by Andrew Martindale (New York: Praeger Publishers, 1967).

The Gothic Cathedral: The Architecture of the Great Church: 1130–1530, by Christopher Wilson (London: Thames and Hudson, 1990) is a clear explication of the principles and development of the Gothic cathedral. A specific study of French Gothic style is given in Jean Bony's *French Gothic Architecture of the 12th and 13th Centuries* (Berkeley: University of California Press, 1983). *Technology and Resource Use in Medieval Europe: Cathedrals, Mills and Mines*, edited by Elizabeth Bradford Smith and Michael Wolfe (Aldershot, UK: Ashgate, 1997), contains several interesting articles dealing with technological innovations in cathedral building.

Madeline Harrison Caviness has provided a brilliant study in *The Early Stained Glass of Canterbury Cathedral* (Princeton: Princeton University Press, 1977); see also her volume in the series *Corpus Vitrearum Medii Aevi: Christ Church Cathedral Canterbury* (London: Oxford University Press, 1981). *The Narratives of Gothic Stained Glass*, by Wolfgang Kemp, translated by Caroline Dobson Saltzwedel (Cambridge: Cambridge University Press, 1997), discusses in detail the structure, legends, narrators, and donors of Gothic windows. A provocative study of the "trade windows" at Chartres may be found in *Bread, Wine, and Money: The Windows of the Trades at Chartres Cathedral*, by Jane Welch Williams (Chicago: University of Chicago Press, 1993). *The Gothic: Literary Sources and Interpretations through Eight Centuries*, by Paul Frankl (Princeton: Princeton University Press, 1960), provides an interesting collection of commentaries on Gothic style, both contemporaneous and in the following centuries.

Music and Ceremony at Notre-Dame of Paris, 500–1550, by Craig Wright (Cambridge: Cambridge University Press, 1989), is a fascinating study of the interaction between architecture and the development of music and liturgy. Another work that explores the connections between architecture and liturgy is *The Service Books of the Royal Abbey of St.-Denis: Images of Ritual and Music in the Middle Ages* (Oxford: Clarendon Press, 1991), by Anne Walters Robertson. Chapters 9, 10, and 14 of *Medieval Music*, by Richard Hoppin (New York: W.W. Norton & Co., 1978), provide a detailed discussion of the Notre-Dame school, the rhythmic modes, and the development of polyphonic practice.

A helpful collection of articles is contained in *Rethinking the Romance of the Rose: Text, Image, Reception*, edited by Kevin Brownlee and Sylvia Huot (Philadelphia: University of Pennsylvania Press, 1992). Two works by John V. Fleming, *The "Roman de la Rose": A Study in Allegory and Iconography* (Princeton: Princeton University Press, 1969) and *Reason and the Lover* (Princeton: Princeton University Press, 1984), are essential to any detailed study of the work.

14 THE TRAUMATIC FOURTEENTH CENTURY

T HE FOURTEENTH CENTURY is often referred to as calamitous, catastrophic, or cataclysmic, and it was, indeed, a time of dreadful disaster—both natural and man-made. The century began with periods of famine that caused widespread starvation throughout western Europe. Further, those people who survived were physically weakened and prone to infectious disease. Their condition made them obvious victims of the next calamity—the Black Death.

Often called the "plague," the Black Death struck Europe in the middle of the century, killing between one-third and one-half of the population. The psychological and emotional effect on the survivors was devastating, with many people turning away from the Church because of its inability to offer satisfactory consolation or to provide answers concerning the cause of the epidemic.

The plague also caused a severe labor shortage, which enabled the lower classes to bargain for higher wages, rather than accepting what was offered. The peasants were able to leave the manor to seek employment elsewhere, resulting in what has been called "the disintegration of the manor."

A further crisis in confidence afflicted the Church when the papacy moved to Avignon, in southern France, where it remained for some seventy years. At one point there were two popes, one in Avignon and one in Rome (a crisis known as the "Great Schism"), but the situation was finally resolved in 1417 by the decree of a church council.

In the latter part of the fourteenth century, expectations for a better life, as well as dissatisfaction with labor laws, led to a series of peasant revolts throughout northwestern Europe. Although several centuries would pass before the peasants were able to achieve their goals concerning conditions of employment, these early riots were evidence of a growing assertiveness among working people.

The final blow to strike the people of fourteenth-century Europe was the Hundred Years War, fought between England and France. The ultimate result was the removal of English authority from all of France except Calais, but the French people had suffered dreadfully during much of the century.

Reactions to these calamities were varied, provoking a change in almost every aspect of human existence—political, social, moral, religious, artistic, and intellectual. The era was thus one of transition, ultimately resulting in a new and expansive vision of life.

Famine

During most of the High Middle Ages, the population of Europe increased dramatically, tripling in the years between 1000 and 1300. This was the result, in part, of several centuries of favorable weather and the adoption of various agricultural innovations (see Chapter 5). Although life expectancy was modest by modern standards, a generally abundant food supply contributed to a low childhood mortality rate, which compensated for the deaths occurring in what we would consider middle age.

The increase in population, however, naturally meant there were more mouths to feed. By the late thirteenth century, Europe was overpopulated in terms of its ability to provide sufficient food for all of its citizens, and by 1300 the exploitation of arable land had been pushed to the limit. Marginal lands that had been cultivated although they had rocky soil or poor natural drainage provided an uncertain harvest, and fields that had formerly been fertile were becoming eroded or impoverished from lack of nutrients. Many farmers disregarded the productive custom of allowing land to lie fallow for a certain period of time, and there was inadequate crop rotation. The practice of monoculture—the growing of one crop, such as grapes for wine—had been economically profitable during the previous centuries, but it resulted in devastation when a climatic change affected the crops, or when the soil was impoverished. As yet there was no scientific seed production, nor any radical technological breakthrough that would produce a higher yield on a limited acreage. Furthermore, local famines were an inevitable result of poor transportation.

These conditions were further aggravated by climate change in the early fourteenth century, when average temperatures in Europe dropped by about 20 degrees. The Mediterranean countries were affected more sporadically than those further north, but it is clear that famine in the south was no less dire than that in the area of northern Europe. Sicily, for example, forbade the export of grain in order to protect the supply for its own citizens. In the north, herring, a protein staple, migrated away from the Baltic Sea, which froze over during several winters. Grain rotted in the fields, and some crops could no longer be raised in marginal areas. Recent scholars have estimated that the food shortages affected an area of approximately 400,000 square miles (1,036,000 square km) in Europe during the bad seasons, which increased after 1300; terrible famines struck various countries between 1309 and 1315. A chronicler in Alsace reported that starving people cut down the corpses of executed criminals from the gibbet and ate them. In the great famine in the Low Countries between 1315 and 1317, the leading Flemish textile and trading centers lost between 5 and 10 percent of their populations, and the rest were seriously weakened.

According to Jean de Venette, a priest and master of theology at the University of Paris:

> Yet you must know that I, at the age of seven or eight, saw this great and mighty famine begin the very year [which had been] foretold, 1315. It was so severe in France that most of the population died of hunger and want. And this famine lasted two years and more, for it began in 1315 and ceased in 1318.

Conditions were equally dreadful in England. As the chronicler Johannes de Trokelowe, a monk at St. Albans, reported in his *Annales*:

> [In 1315] the land was so oppressed with want that when the king came to St. Albans on the feast of St. Laurence [August 10], it was hardly possible to find bread on sale to supply his immediate household . . .
>
> The dearth began in the month of May and lasted until the feast of the nativity of the Virgin [September 8]. The summer rains were so heavy that grain could not ripen. It could hardly be gathered and used to bake bread down to the said feast day unless it was first put in vessels to dry. Around the end of autumn the dearth was mitigated in part, but towards Christmas it became as bad as before. Bread did not have its usual nourishing power and strength because the grain was not nourished by the warmth of summer sunshine. Hence those who ate it, even in large quantities, were hungry again after a little while. There can be no doubt that the poor wasted away when even the rich were constantly hungry . . .
>
> Four pennies worth of coarse bread was not enough to feed a common man for one day. The usual kinds of meat, suitable for eating, were too scarce; horse meat was precious; plump dogs were stolen. And, according to many reports, men and women in many places secretly ate their own children.

Although scholars have debated whether demographics and climatic change were truly significant factors in the events of the fourteenth century, they generally agree that subsistence at the starvation level in many areas of Europe produced a weakened population, with many people unable to survive illness and disease, or to cope with the next calamity that befell them—the Black Death.

The Black Death

The Black Death, or plague, is a disease usually carried by fleas living on rodents. It can be passed to humans when they are bitten by fleas, which are parasites of the rat population. The symptoms of the illness are high fever, aching in the arms and legs, and swellings (buboes) in the lymph nodes. This form of the disease is known as bubonic plague, and is not always fatal, although it tends to seriously deplete populations already debilitated by malnutrition. Two other forms of the plague are usually fatal: septicemic plague, which infects the bloodstream, and pneumonic plague, which attacks the lungs. This latter type of plague is virulently contagious, and accounts of the epidemic of plague in the fourteenth century indicate that both the bubonic and pneumonic varieties were widespread.

The primitive conditions of hygiene present in the urban areas of medieval Europe encouraged the dissemination of plague germs. The crowded cities, surrounded by heavy walls and with sewage flowing in the streets, created perfect conditions for the development of epidemics. Furthermore, medical care was neither readily available nor effective. Doctors were quick to flee when they encountered the symptoms of contagion, or else, when they did stay, they often administered remedies that further weakened the victims of disease.

In October 1347, a ship from Genoa, Italy, arrived in the port of Messina, in Sicily. It was filled with grain from the region of the Black Sea, and carried, in addition, hundreds of black rats infested with fleas. It was obvious that the crew was deathly ill, but before they could be turned back to sea, the rats ran down the ropes and into the city. As the rat population died, the fleas, seeking a ready host, attached themselves to humans.

The disease spread northward rapidly, as may be seen in **Map 23.** Moving in waves, it reached northern France by 1348, England by early 1349, and into Scandinavia by

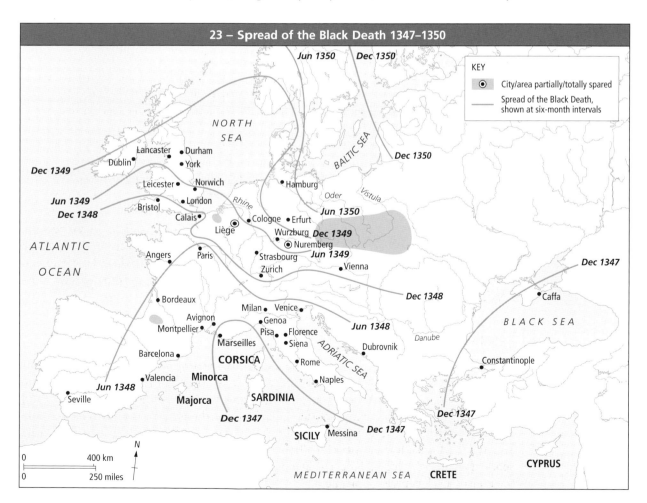

23 – Spread of the Black Death 1347–1350

KEY

◉ City/area partially/totally spared

— Spread of the Black Death, shown at six-month intervals

the end of that year. Some small areas were spared, probably because they were at a distance from the main trade routes. The devastation of the European population, in which at least one-third of the people died, occurred most often in children and the very old, as well as adults with low resistance because of malnutrition.

Reports of the plague and its effects exist in sources from all areas of Europe. For example, the French chronicler and master of theology Jean de Venette described in his *Chronicle* the effects of the plague, which he defined as the second of the great calamities of the fourteenth century:

> All this year [1348] and the next, the mortality of men and women, of the young even more than of the old, in Paris and in the kingdom of France, and also, it is said, in other parts of the world, was so great that it was almost impossible to bury the dead. People lay ill little more than two or three days and died suddenly . . . He who was well one day was dead the next and being carried to his grave. Swellings appeared suddenly in the armpit or in the groin—in many cases both—and they were infallible signs of death . . .
>
> Some said that this pestilence was caused by infection of the air and waters, since there was at this time no famine nor lack of food supplies, but on the contrary great abundance. As a result of this theory of infected water and air as the source of the plague, the Jews were suddenly and violently charged with infecting wells and water and corrupting the air. The whole world rose up against them cruelly on this account. In Germany and other parts of the world where Jews lived, they were massacred and slaughtered by Christians, and many thousands were burned everywhere, indiscriminately.

In Siena, Italy, the plague was equally virulent and destructive. The writer Agnolo di Tura del Grasso described the effect thus in his *Cronica maggiore* (*Great Chronicle*):

> The mortality began in Siena in May (1348). It was a cruel and horrible thing; and I do not know where to begin to tell of the cruelty and the pitiless ways. It seemed to almost everyone that one became stupefied by seeing the pain. And it is impossible for the human tongue to recount the awful thing. Indeed one who did not see such horribleness can be called blessed. And the victims died almost immediately. They would swell beneath their armpits and in their groins, and fall over dead while talking. Father abandoned child, wife husband, one brother another; for this illness seemed to strike through the breath and sight. And so they died. And none could be found to bury the dead for money or friendship. Members of a household brought their dead to a ditch as best they could, without priest, without divine offices. Nor did the death bell sound. And in many places in Siena great pits were dug and piled deep with the multitude of dead. And they died by the hundreds both day and night, and all were thrown in those ditches and covered over with earth. And as soon as those ditches were filled more were dug . . . And there were also those who were so sparsely covered with earth that the dogs dragged them forth and devoured many bodies throughout the city.

The plague was also described by the famous Italian author Giovanni Boccaccio in his *Decameron* (1351). This work consists of a collection of tales told by friends who had traveled away from Florence to spend time in the countryside, hoping to avoid the epidemic. In the Introduction, Boccaccio describes the ravages of the plague in the city:

> The condition of the lower, and, perhaps, in great measure of the middle ranks, of the people was even worse and more deplorable; for, deluded by hope or constrained by poverty, they stayed in their quarters, in their houses, where they sickened by thousands a day, and, being without service or help of any kind, were, so to speak, irredeemably devoted to the death which overtook them. Many died daily or nightly in the public street; of many others, who died at home, the departure was hardly observed by their neighbors, until the stench of their putrefying bodies carried the tidings; and what with their corpses and the corpses of others who died on every hand the whole place was a sepulcher . . . Nor, for all their number, were their obsequies honored by either tears or lights or crowds of mourners; rather, it was come to this, that a dead man was then of no more account than a dead goat would be today.

132 A grimacing, skeletal image of Death rises from a tomb, reminding viewers of the inescapable reality of the end of life. Grim artworks such as this proliferated after the devastation of the Black Death, as people confronted the profound social dislocation and psychological stress caused by the epidemic. This example is taken from the *Book of Hours of Anne of France*.

The psychological effects of social dislocation among survivors were devastating. Some individuals experienced profound pessimism and renounced life. Others adopted an "eat, drink, and be merry" attitude towards existence. As Boccaccio remarked, again in the Introduction to the *Decameron*, "[Some] maintained free living to be a better preservative, and would baulk no passion or appetite they wished to gratify, drinking and revelling incessantly from tavern to tavern, or in private houses (which were frequently found deserted by the owners, and therefore common to every one)." Some turned towards God, seeking answers in religious belief, while others eschewed their former religious affiliations. Many believed that God was punishing humanity for its sins, or viewed the plague as one manifestation of the struggle between God and the Devil, in which the Devil was winning (**fig. 132** and **fig. 133**).

One of the most dramatic responses was the formation of a new religious sect known as the **flagellants**. These individuals trudged the roads of Europe, chanting and beating themselves and one another with barbed whips. The German chronicler Hugo von Reutlingen described the phenomenon in his country:

> At that time the flagellants were wandering about the country in crowds on all the roads and

133 In this woodcut, *Imago mortis* (*Image of Death*), from a Nuremberg printed book of 1493, skeletons dance with gruesome glee on an open grave. The figure on the left plays a *shawn* to provide musical accompaniment for the dance, while the streaming viscera of the skeleton on the right provide a grisly reminder of the inevitable.

paths, cruelly martyrizing their bodies themselves with blows of the cruel knots which they had tied in their scourges, for in every scourge the knots were tied threefold; such was the order . . . Two pieces of iron, with sharpened upper end passing through the knots, beat the backs of the penitents and caused a ring of four-cornered wounds . . . Once during the night and twice in the daytime they tortured themselves with cruel blows, while the singing of hymns sounded with astonishing cadence and, marching in a circle, they threw themselves down to the ground and in such a manner as to form a cross. This they used to do six times a day, and they remained so long as one might say a few paternosters . . . It was strictly forbidden to the brethren to ask for a bath at any time or to wash their heads. No one was allowed to speak to a woman, and just as little to have his beard shorn, except in special cases when the master gave permission to some brother. Nor would anyone have dared to wear freshly washed clothes before the time for changing had duly come.

As they performed their rituals, the flagellants begged for God's mercy, singing chants such as this:

> Your hands above your heads uplift
> That God the plague may from us shift,
> And now raise up your arms withal
> That God's own mercy on us fall.
> Now beat you sore
> God to adore.
> For God all pride abandon now
> And he His mercy us will show.

Many explanations were given for the occurrence of the plague which did not depend upon a purely religious response. The faculty of medicine at the University of Paris, for example, declared that the epidemic of 1348 was caused by the unusual planetary conjunction of Saturn, Jupiter, and Mars in the sign of Aquarius. This event had created hot, moist conditions, which, in turn, caused the earth to exhale the poisonous vapors that produced the plague.

Other authorities were inclined to place blame elsewhere. As earlier and later in history, the Jews, accused of poisoning wells, were blamed for the crisis. In France, there is evidence of supposed "confessions" of the Jews, supporting this claim. According to trial records from the prison in the castle of Chillon in 1348, there were "Confessions of the Jews . . . who had been arrested in the New Town concerning the poisoning of which they were accused, of wells and springs here and elsewhere, also of food and other things with the purpose of killing and extermining the whole of Christendom."

The German city of Cologne was more moderate in its response to the crisis. In a letter from magistrates in that city to the municipality of Strasbourg (1349), caution and restraint were advocated:

> If now in the large towns prosecutions and executions of the Jews were to be
> instituted (which in our town we would not permit so long as we are able to prevent
> them, as long as we are convinced that the Jews are innocent of the atrocious deeds
> brought up against them), this procedure might give rise to great trouble and entail
> serious consequences. And if we are called upon to express our opinion in regard
> to this great plague, we must confess that we consider it to be a scourge of God, and
> consequently we shall permit of no prosecutions of Jews in our town on account
> of these rumors, but we shall protect them, as they were faithfully protected by our
> forefathers. We therefore urgently and amicably beseech you that, as in all matters
> you are accustomed to proceed with wisdom and caution, you will in this matter
> of the Jews be guided by justice and moderation.

As people searched for causes and cures, Europe was devastated by economic and social chaos, inflation, and a lack of morality that was evident in greedy and avaricious monetary practices as well as debauchery. One obvious result of the plague was a severe shortage of labor, which led to a phenomenon sometimes called "the disintegration of the manor." The reality of the epidemic had ended the willingness of the peasants to accept their hard, monotonous lives. Their decreased numbers allowed them to bargain with employers for better wages, and to increase their opportunities for mobility. Increased demands and expectations soon led to insurrection. Furthermore, in many countries, the peasants were angry at being taxed to pay for war (see below), and at the frequent pillaging of their property by bands of mercenary soldiers.

Peasant Unrest

One of the most violent uprisings of the fourteenth century was the *Jacquerie*—"Jacques" was a nickname for a French peasant—in France (1358), which was described thus by the French court historian Jean Froissart in his *Chronicles*:

> Some of the inhabitants of the country towns assembled together in Beauvoisin,
> without any leader: they were not at first more than one hundred men. They said,
> that the nobles of the kingdom of France, knights, and squires, were a disgrace to it,
> and that it would be a very meritorious act to destroy them all: to which proposition
> every one assented, as a truth, and added, shame befall him that should be the

means of preventing the gentlemen from being wholly destroyed. They then, without further council, collected themselves in a body, and with no other arms than the staves shod with iron, which some had, and others with knives, marched to the house of a knight who lived near, and breaking it open, murdered the knight, his lady, and all the children, both great and small; they then burnt the house.

Froissart goes on to describe the extent of the rioting, and the growing numbers of peasants and townsmen involved. The lords sent for help from the surrounding countries, and soon were able to retaliate. According to Froissart, "They began therefore to kill and destroy these wretches wherever they met them, and hung them up by troops on the nearest trees." Ultimately, the *Jacquerie* was crushed. A mob of poorly equipped, untrained peasants proved no match for knights armed with swords, lances, and axes. The *Jacquerie* is usually viewed as a vicious riot by unruly and disorganized peasants, and some scholars have suggested that it cannot be properly identified as a true "peasant rebellion."

Peasants in England undertook similar action some decades later (1381), but this time their uprising was relatively disciplined, and sought true social reform. Their activities created a crisis that led Froissart to observe: "Never was a country in such jeopardy as this was at that period." In his discussion of the revolt, Froissart provided contextual information about the English situation, describing the condition of peasants there:

> It is customary in England, as well as in several other countries, for the nobility to have great privileges over the commonalty, whom they keep in bondage; that is to say, they are bound by law and custom to plow the lands of gentlemen, to harvest the grain, to carry it home to the barn, to thrash and winnow it; they are also bound to harvest the hay and carry it home. All these services they are obliged to perform for their lords, and many more in England than in other countries.
>
> The evil-disposed in these districts began to rise, saying, they were too severely oppressed; that at the beginning of the world there were no slaves, and that no one ought to be treated as such, unless he had committed treason against his lord, as Lucifer had done against God; but they had done no such thing, for they were neither angels nor spirits, but men formed after the same likeness with their lords, who treated them as beasts. This they would not longer bear, but had determined to be free, and if they labored or did any other works for their lords, they would be paid for it.

In addition to these traditional conditions of serfdom, the common people in England were subject to a piece of legislation called the Statute of Laborers (1380), which attempted to keep peasants tied to the land, to freeze wages and prices, and to impose new taxes, including a poll tax on everyone over the age of fifteen. The new legislation was enforced by commissioners who were sent into the country to make certain that everyone was paying the tax. According to chroniclers, this led to gross abuse and misconduct on the part of the officials, who sometimes took the liberty of inspecting girls to ascertain whether or not they were virgins, and exacting taxes from them as adults if they were not.

Froissart described in his *Chronicles* how the oppressed lower classes were incited to action by a "crazy priest" named John Ball, who vehemently pointed out the differences between the nobility and the common people (**fig. 134**). Advocating a leveling of social classes, Ball claimed that "things cannot go on well in England, nor ever will until every thing shall be in common; when there shall neither be vassal nor lord, and all distinctions leveled; when the lords shall be no more masters than ourselves." Word of Ball's harangues reached London, where they influenced the urban workers, who "began to assemble and to rebel." They gathered peasants from the surrounding agricultural areas, and, under the leadership of a man called Wat Tyler, marched on London in June of 1381, demanding to see

the king. They professed loyalty to King Richard II, who was age fourteen at the time, but wanted to protest the unpopular regency government which was directed by the king's uncle, John of Gaunt, duke of Lancaster. The mob frightened the government into meeting their demands and repealing the hated legislation, but once the situation had stabilized, Wat Tyler was killed, the peasants scattered, and the king revoked all the concessions he had granted.

Similar revolts spread throughout Europe, and an analysis of the events shows certain common features. The uprisings tended to be associated with a rising level of expectation. The plagues, famines, and wars had reduced the available manpower and placed the peasants and laborers in a good bargaining position. They were impatient with the rate of improvement in their status, and feared a forced return to their previous condition. The fact that the most important uprisings took place near urban centers suggests that city growth and the relative freedom of the artisans may have raised the aspirations of the peasants in the surrounding countryside.

The revolts were bloody and shocking, but they had little real effect on economic trends. Serfdom was doomed by economic forces that ran deeply. The manorial system proved to be less productive than a freer system in which tenants paid rent and participated in the benefits of increased production; they were no longer living as serfs. However, the logic of this transformation became evident very slowly. The emancipation of the serfs spread gradually eastward, and was not realized in Russia, for example, until a proclamation by Tsar Alexander II in 1861.

Although most of the riots were a product of discontent among the rural peasantry, urban life in western Europe suffered stress as well. There was an oversupply of goods, coupled with a drop in demand, and the resulting unrest led to riots by workers in many cities and towns.

134 In this manuscript illumination, John Ball (identified by the name on his cloak, but sometimes known as the "crazy priest") is seated on horseback as he speaks to crowds of people. The leader of the Peasants' Revolt, Wat Tyler, is shown at the left. Ball advocated a leveling of social classes in England, insisting that all property should be held in common. His ideas contributed to the revolt, influencing both agricultural and urban workers.

As if famine, plague, and riots were not more than enough to bear, the citizens of Europe in the fourteenth century were, in addition, subjected to almost constant warfare. Indeed, it has been suggested that the amount and duration of war in that century has been equaled in history only by the conflicts of the twentieth. Armed aggression was evident in all of the European states, including Germany, Italy, Bohemia, and Hungary. The Angevin rulers of the kingdom of Naples continued their struggle with Sicily, while the Sicilians sent armies to conquer Greece, and in Spain the Reconquista was still in progress. The French fought the Flemish and the Burgundians, and the English struggled with the Scots, the Welsh, and the Irish before the two nations became embroiled in a lengthy and bloody conflict with each other.

The Hundred Years War

The Hundred Years War, fought between England and France between 1337 and 1453, bears the dubious distinction of being the longest war in western history. As scholars have observed, however, it was not the conflict itself that was most significant to the future of Europe, but rather, the changes in modes of warfare brought on by technological advances and methods of waging war.

As noted earlier, the relationship between England and France had been a problematic one, characterized by constant struggle in the areas of France held by the Angevin monarchs (see Chapters 9 and 11). Difficulties between the states were aggravated when Edward III became king of England in 1327. He inherited the English monarchy from his father, Edward II, and through his mother, Isabelle of France (daughter of Philip IV, "the Fair"), he held a legitimate right to the throne of France. When the French king, Charles IV, died without an heir in 1328, the Capetian dynasty which had ruled France since 987 ceased with him. Edward III, the English king, put forward a claim based on his lineage through his mother. He was indeed the closest relative to the Capetian line, and the throne was rightfully his.

The idea of an English king on the throne was abhorrent to the French, however, and the Estates General (see Chapter 11) rapidly identified a preferred successor to Charles: Philip VI (r. 1328–1350), a cousin of the last Capetian kings, who founded the Valois dynasty. Philip moved quickly to preserve the throne and traditions of France for the French. The Hundred Years War was, in large measure, an outgrowth of the dispute that occurred as a result of this dynastic struggle. There were, of course, other factors involved, including economic competition to control the wool and wine trades. Ultimately, the chance to end the centuries of dispute between the countries proved irresistible, and war began.

Initially, both England and France relied on traditional feudal military strength, with the aristocratic armed cavalry providing the most significant force. But the English knights found themselves greatly outnumbered by the French army, and turned to the new weapons and techniques they had encountered in their earlier battles with the Scots, Welsh, and Irish. These Celtic fighters had opposed the mounted English knights with effective new weapons such as the longbow, the crossbow, and the pike (**fig. 135**). The longbows, in particular, were enormously powerful: the arrows they shot could penetrate a suit of armor at a distance of 600 feet (180 m). Furthermore, continuous volleys of arrows, launched by many bowmen, could rapidly repulse a large number of mounted knights. The French chronicler Jean Froissart described the use of the longbow by the English at the Battle of Poitiers in 1356:

> To say the truth, the English archers were of infinite service to their army, for they shot so thickly and so well, that the French did not know which way to turn themselves to avoid their arrows . . . In that part the battle was very hot, and greatly crowded; many a one was unhorsed, and you must know that whenever any one fell, he had but little chance of getting up again . . . The English archers shot so well that none cared to come within reach of their arrows, and they put to death many who could not ransom themselves.

The crossbow was even more effective, shooting metal bolts called *quarrels*, which could pierce the thickest armor and shatter the bones behind the metal. In fact, these were the first weapons to be officially condemned by the Church because of their destructive capabilities.

Crossbows had been made in various forms since antiquity, but they were not used frequently in the Middle Ages before the eleventh century. Byzantine Anna Comnena, in the *Alexiad* (see Chapter 7), described the crossbow as a novelty:

> In order to stretch it, one does not pull the string with the right hand while pushing the bow with the left away from the body; this instrument of war, which fires weapons to an enormous distance, has to be stretched by lying almost on one's back; each foot is pressed forcibly against the half-circles of the bow and the two hands tug at the bow, pulling it with all one's strength towards the body. At the mid-point of the string is a groove, shaped like a cylinder cut in half and fitted to the string itself; it is about the length of a fair-sized arrow, extending from the string to the center of the bow. Along this groove, arrows of all kinds are fired. They are very short but extremely thick, with a heavy iron tip. In the firing the string exerts tremendous violence and force, so that the missiles wherever they strike do not rebound; in fact they transfix a shield, cut through a heavy iron breastplate and resume their flight on the far side . . . Such is the crossbow, a truly diabolical machine.

People were frightened by the power of the crossbows, but the social implications of the weapon were even more dramatic. By using these weapons, any peasant would be able to cut down a knight, thereby shattering the concept of feudal order and chivalry that provided the structure and boundaries of their society.

Another widely employed weapon was the pike, which was a long spear. Groups of men armed with pikes (pikemen) formed dense, phalanx-like formations that were effective in both offensive and defensive actions. For example, in a battle at Morat (Murten) in Switzerland (1476), there were four rows of pikemen assembled on the outside of a wedge formation consisting of 10,000 men. It was the duty of the attacking pikemen, whose pikes were about 16 ft. 6 ins. (5 m) long , to break up the opposing battle charge so that the men with shorter weapons (only 5 ft. 5 ins. [1.6 m] in length) could rush forward. Alternatively, when defending against a cavalry charge, the pikemen could turn to form a "hedgehog," with pikes facing outward.

Although gunpowder had been known in Europe since the late twelfth century, it was not used extensively in the first part of the Hundred Years War. Even though gunpowder itself was relatively inexpensive to obtain, the weaponry that employed it was not. Cannons and handheld guns were costly, and were not used regularly until the sixteenth century. However, the French king did use cannons in central France and Aquitaine during the final phases of the war. Although these weapons were not particularly mobile, their immense firepower was able to penetrate previously unimpregnable fortress walls with relative ease.

In the initial phase of the war, the English proved victorious. Since they were severely outnumbered, they employed what we would recognize as guerrilla tactics: they attacked the French with small bands of warriors, led by nobles, but relying on common infantrymen who used the new weapons. They plundered villages and vineyards, burned bridges, and managed to disrupt trade, retreating before the French could amass their armies to retaliate. There were few pitched battles during the first part of the war. However, the English proved victorious when they assailed the French army with arrows dispatched from longbows at the first major confrontation, which took place at Crécy in 1346.

The English continued their harassing techniques for several years under the leadership of the heir to the throne, Edward, "The Black Prince." In 1356, at the Battle of Poitiers, the English were again victorious, this time capturing the French king and taking him to be held for ransom in London.

Following this action, there were several temporary truces, and the final phase of the war began in 1415, when a new English king, Henry V (r. 1413–1422), decided to invade France and settle matters once and for all. Later that year, a bloody battle at Agincourt opened the way for the English to conquer all of northern France.

As the English prepared to march south to complete their conquest, three things occurred to turn the balance of power to the French. First, Henry V died of dysentery in 1422, removing the most powerful English leader of the entire war. Second, although the weak French king Charles VII (r. 1422–1461) was not able to take advantage of the opportunity, a miracle occurred. An illiterate peasant girl, Joan of Arc, heard mysterious voices telling her to go to the king to ask him to place her at the head of the French army; she would lead the forces to victory over the English. King Charles agreed, and Joan, with shorn hair and wearing armor, rode into battle. She was surprisingly successful, and the victories that occurred under her leadership infused the French with a new sense of power. They began to believe that they could defeat the English, after all.

Joan was captured by the Burgundians in 1430 and sold to their allies the English, who charged her with witchcraft, and turned her over to the Inquisition. The inquisitors closely examined her claims of hearing mystical voices, and inquired into her "unusual" habit of wearing men's clothing. She was ultimately condemned as a heretic, and was burned at the stake in 1431. Although she was executed before the war ended, her role in bolstering French confidence was probably crucial to their final success.

The war was finally brought to a close when a third significant event happened and the Burgundians decided to break their alliance with the English and support Charles VII instead. The French forces could now concentrate on defeating the English and driving them from Paris, Rouen, and Guienne. The English were exhausted by this time, and were willing to sign a peace treaty. Thus, the war ended in 1453, with the English retaining only Calais, and with the victorious French united at last.

The results of the Hundred Years War were profound, and not simply because the English no longer had control of vast areas of France. Most important was the demise of feudalism. The new military tactics had made the medieval knight obsolete, and with him the notion of an ordered hierarchy in society. Now the king could hire and equip an army with inexpensive and uncomplicated weaponry, and any infantryman could fell a knight with one good shot. The army had thus been revolutionized, along with the civil administration. Furthermore, peasants no longer viewed themselves as powerless. They began to ask why 90 percent of the population should work to support a wealthy caste of 5 to 10 percent. As discussed above, outbreaks of violence such as the *Jacquerie* in France and the Peasants' Revolt in England demonstrated that both the rural and the urban commoners were willing to challenge the idea of privilege.

As might have been expected, the Church was not immune to these changes. In fact, the events of the fourteenth century produced a religious crisis of profound proportions.

Crisis in the Church

The religious difficulties of the fourteenth century had their roots in the struggle between Philip IV ("the Fair") of France and Pope Boniface VIII (see Chapter 11). Following the death of Boniface in 1303, and then the short pontificate of Benedict XI (r. 1303–1304), a Frenchman was elected pope, and it was rumored that the French king had controlled the decision. The protests against the new pope, Clement V (r. 1305–1314), became violent, and he was forced to flee from Rome with the cardinals who had voted for him. Philip IV granted them residence at Avignon, in southern France, initiating a seventy-year period referred to by the Italian poet Petrarch as the "Babylonian Captivity" of the Church.

The next eight popes were in residence at Avignon, and were looked on by much of Christendom with great suspicion. Although for the most part well-intentioned and pious, they were generally regarded as mere functionaries of the French king. A massive papal palace was built at Avignon in southern France, and the entire bureaucracy of the papacy was in residence in the city. Even a strong and well-regarded papacy would have been unable to solve the enormous problems caused by the plague, the Hundred Years War, various popular revolts, a declining economy, and the vast social changes that resulted from these events. But the Avignon popes did little to enhance their images as leaders of the Church. They appeared to be obsessed with money, and were perceived as being indifferent to the severe social problems.

One of the most vocal of their critics was St. Catherine of Siena (*c.* 1347–1380), a mystic associated with the Dominican order. In a letter to Pope Gregory XI (r. 1370–1378), she urged the return of the papacy to Rome and begged him to use his power to solve the problems facing the Church:

> Alas, sweet father, with such gentleness I beg you, nay I say to you from Christ crucified, to come and overthrow our enemies. Put no faith in the Devil's counselors who may try to block your good and holy resolution. Show the manliness I expect from you—no more cowardice! Answer God's call to you to come and take possession of the place of the glorious shepherd St. Peter, whose vicar you still are, and then to raise the standard of the holy cross for, as by the cross we were delivered . . . so when this standard—which I see as the solace and refuge of Christians—is raised, we shall be delivered from war, disputes and iniquities and the infidel people from their infidelity. In this way you will come, and then you will see holy Church reformed through the appointment of good pastors.

Pope Gregory did move the papacy back to Rome, but died in the following year. When the Italian people rioted in the streets, demanding the election of an Italian, the College of Cardinals accommodated them by electing Urban VI (r. 1378–1389); but a majority of cardinals returned to Avignon, declared Urban's election invalid, and elected another Frenchman, who took the name Clement VII (r. 1378–1394). This action initiated the period in church history known as the Great Schism. Between 1378 and 1417, there were two papacies—one at Rome and one at Avignon, each with its own College of Cardinals, its own bureaucratic network, and its own treasury. As may be imagined, there was constant conflict between the two, with each competing for the support of secular rulers and each regularly anathematizing the other.

Healing the Great Schism was a complicated matter, since no clear authority existed to determine which was the authentic papacy. By the early fifteenth century, people were advocating the convening of a church council to settle the dispute. In 1409 over 500 prelates met at the Council of Pisa. They declared that both popes were "notorious schismatics," and elected yet another pope, Alexander V. However, the other two popes refused to abdicate their positions, and the Church was left in the embarrassing situation of having three popes. The predicament was resolved by the convening of yet another council, which met at Constance, in Germany, in 1414. The Council of Constance deposed all three popes and elected Martin V (r. 1417–1431), thus ending the schism. Furthermore, the council took action to declare conciliar supremacy. In a decree entitled *Haec sancta* the council stipulated:

> First, it [the council] declares that being lawfully assembled in the Holy Spirit, constituting a general council and representing the Catholic Church Militant, it has its power directly from Christ, and that all persons of whatever rank or dignity, even a pope, are bound to obey it in matters relating to faith and the end of the Schism and the general reformation of the Church of God in head and members.
>
> Further, it declares that any person of whatever position, rank, or dignity, even a pope, who contumaciously refuses to obey the mandates, statutes, ordinance,

or regulations enacted or to be enacted by this holy synod, or by any other general council lawfully assembled, relating to the matters aforesaid or to other matters involved with them, shall, unless he repents, be subject to condign penalty and duly punished, with recourse if necessary, to other aids of the law.

Thus, the Great Schism was effectively ended. The century of turmoil had, however, greatly increased disgust and dissatisfaction with the practices of the Church. Movements of pious laymen and women, such as the Beguines and the Brethren of the Common Life (see Chapter 12) gained many new followers, and the Franciscan order was split by an argument over ecclesiastical wealth. The most radical members of the order called for a return to "apostolic poverty," and denounced the wealth of the Church. Heresy reappeared, along with radical ideas promulgated by the followers of intellectuals such as the Bohemian reformer Jan Hus (c. 1369–1415) and the English theologian John Wycliffe (c. 1330–1384). Criticism of the Church and institutional religious values also emerged in art, music, and literature.

Cultural Reaction

The reaction to the vicissitudes of the fourteenth century on the part of writers, artists, and musicians was dramatic. As a result of the decline in ecclesiastical authority following the Avignon papacy and the ensuing Great Schism, music, as well as the other arts, took on a flourishing secularism. Furthermore, the aristocracy began to rival the Church as patrons of art and music. The resulting works reflected the social and intellectual values of the elite, and were characterized by extraordinary complexity and sophistication. Furthermore, musical expression made a great technical advance.

Music

The music of the fourteenth century is generally referred to as the *Ars nova* ("The New Art"), a phrase borrowed from the title of a treatise by the composer and music theorist Philippe de Vitry (1291–1361). It was the product of a self-consciously "modern" movement, which, first and foremost, proclaimed a new concept of rhythm and musical time.

As discussed in Chapter 13, music in the thirteenth century was characterized by a triple division of the beat. The composers and theorists of the fourteenth-century *Ars nova* developed a theory of dividing the beat in a less rigid and more flexible manner, allowing, for example, a division into two parts, instead of three. This gave composers the possibility of creating music that was much more fluid and subtle. According to the theorist Jean de Muris, writing in 1319:

That all perfection does in fact lie in the ternary number is clear from a hundred comparisons. In God, who is perfection itself, there is singleness in substance, but threeness in persons; He is three in one and one in three. There is, therefore, an extraordinary congruity between one and three . . . Since the ternary number is to be found everywhere, there is no reason to wonder any further whether it is in fact perfect. The binary number must, by comparison, be called imperfect, even though it may thus fall into ill-repute. But unity, since it is continuous, is divisible not only into three parts, but into many more, ad infinitum.

Thus, de Muris provided a philosophical justification for the division of the beat into two or four parts, in addition to three.

The avant-garde composers and theorists provoked a furious reaction from those writers who believed in maintaining the status quo—"perfect time," with its division of the beat into three parts. One of the most vocal was Jacques de Liège, who wrote in his *Speculum musicae* (*Mirror of Music*, c. 1330) of the relative merits of the new system and the old, which he refers to as *Ars antiqua*:

> The *Ars nova* permits imperfect time [the division of the beat into two parts]; the *Ars antiqua* never permitted such a thing . . . if, however, [the composers] were content merely to talk about the imperfections in question, to treat them only theoretically, that would be more acceptable. Unfortunately, that is not the case. They put their theories into practice, and not seldom at that . . .
>
> If, then, the *Ars nova* is said to be more subtle than the *Ars antiqua*—and so much may in fact be granted—it cannot be said on that account to be also more perfect. Not every subtlety is an improvement; more subtle is not necessarily more perfect. Subtlety is not among the degrees or kinds of perfection—so much is clear from the fourth book of [Aristotle's] *Metaphysics*. Nor has it even been sufficiently proven that the *Ars nova* is in fact subtler than the *Ars antiqua*.
>
> It is said, moreover, that the *Ars nova* is more difficult than the *Ars antiqua*. It is not, however, on that account alone to be judged more perfect . . . art, though it is sometimes said to have essentially to do with what is difficult, has in fact to do essentially with what is good and useful. Art is a virtue that perfects the soul by means of reason.

Ignoring such criticism, the composers of the new music were eager to make use of their new developments. They soon began to cause problems for the Church because of their abandonment of musical tradition. One of the most famous diatribes against the *Ars nova* came in a bull, *Docta sanctorum Patrum*, issued by Pope John XXII (r. 1316–1334) in 1323:

> Certain disciples of the new school, much occupying themselves with the measured dividing of beats, display their rhythm in notes new to us, preferring to devise new methods of their own rather than to continue singing in the old way. Therefore the Divine Office is disturbed with these notes of quick duration . . . The result is that they often seem to be losing sight of the fundamental sources of our melodies in the **antiphoner** and **gradual**, and forget what it is that they are burying under such superstructures . . . The voices incessantly rock to and fro, intoxicating rather than soothing the ear, while the singers themselves try to convey the emotion of the music by their gestures. The consequence of all this is that devotion, the true aim of all worship, is neglected, and wantonness, which ought to be eschewed, increases.

The criticisms of the new music were even embedded in the texts of motets:

Certain merchants are now arising amongst the populace. They turn fine gold into lead, and exchange sweet-smelling flowers for foul odors. These men are called, if I am not mistaken, professional singers. When they see some great man in public, they look for their best song, one that they really like. Then they sing it with a great proliferation of little notes, and boast of their singing. They sing not, I think, for the love of God, but for the love of that great man. You are such hypocrites! Have you never looked at the Holy Gospel, where you may read the work of the Lord concerning such matters? So be it then; you have received your price.

Virtuoso performance, rhythmic complexity, and increasing secularism became accepted features of music as the fourteenth century progressed. All of these qualities may be found in the works of two of the most famous composers of this era: Francesco Landini and Guillaume de Machaut.

Francesco Landini

Francesco Landini was born in Tuscany about 1325, and lived until 1397 (**fig. 1356**). He was a victim of smallpox in childhood, and went blind at an early age. His first biographer, Filippo Villani, speculated that this disability was responsible for his turning to music as a profession:

136 Francesco Landini's tomb rests in the Cappella Ginori of the Church of San Lorenzo, Florence. The poignant inscription reads: "Francesco, deprived of sight but with a mind skilled in instrumental music, whom alone Music has set above all others, has left his ashes here, his soul above the stars. Taken from mankind on September 2, 1397."

Francesco was hardly past the middle of his childhood when disaster struck him blind with the smallpox. Music, however, compensated him for his loss with the bright lights of fame and renown. A harsh mischance took away his bodily sight, but his mind's eye was as sharp and acute as an eagle's . . . When [he] had lived for a while in blindness, and was no longer a child, and could understand how miserable it was to be blind, and wanted some solace for the horrors of his everlasting night, he began, as adolescents will, to make up songs—this by the kindness of heaven, I think, which was preparing in its mercy a consolation for so great a misfortune. When he was a little older still, and had come to perceive music's charm and sweetness, he began to compose, first for voices, then for strings and organ. He made astonishing progress. And then, to everyone's amazement, he took up a number of musical instruments—remember, he had never seen them—as readily as if he could still see. In particular, he began to play the organ, with such great dexterity—always accurately, however—and with such expressiveness that he far surpassed any organist in living memory . . . What is more, he played superbly on the fiddle, the lute, all the strings and winds, and every other sort of instrument. And imitating by voice all those instruments that give a pleasant sound in their various ways, and mingling them with the ordinary sounds of human voices, he invented a third species of music, a combination of both of the other two and a source of great charm and delight.

Landini's skill as a performer was notable, as was his talent for musical composition. His output was prolific, consisting of 154 polyphonic songs: eleven **madrigals**, two *cacce*, and 141 *ballate*. The extant works, because of their sheer number and fine quality, provide the most complete picture of musical developments in late fourteenth-century Italy. However, unlike his famous French contemporary Guillaume de Machaut, Landini composed neither Mass movements nor other kinds of liturgical music. His musical output was devoted to the standard forms of secular polyphony.

Guillaume de Machaut

Machaut was born about 1300, and lived until 1377. In his youth, he was employed in the household of John, count of Luxembourg and king of Bohemia, who granted him various church benefices. Later in life he was awarded a position as a canon at Reims by Pope Benedict XII (r. 1334–1342). His duties consisted of singing in liturgical services, and, although he was required to participate in a certain number of masses each year, he was otherwise free to travel.

Following John's death, Machaut had many other royal patrons, and his association with them is described in several of his poems. He was prolific as both a poet and musician, and his poetry gives much information about his life at Reims, telling of his experiences during the plague and the Hundred Years War. It also reveals personal interests, such as horseback-riding and falconry, as well as his love of the French countryside. According to such evidence, he seems to have led a rather worldly life. His extant works consist of seventeen poems of various lengths, and many musical compositions, including both secular and sacred pieces.

Machaut's most famous work is his *Messe de Nostre Dame* (*Mass of Notre-Dame*), which is also his largest musical composition. It contains polyphonic settings for all sections of the Mass, and is the first complete setting of the **Ordinary** known to have been written by one composer as a unified structure. Machaut's Mass was the only one of its kind written in the fourteenth century. It was not until midway through the century following his death that early Renaissance composers began to create complete masses.

137 The cloister of Gloucester Cathedral (constructed 1351–1412) is the earliest surviving example of the ornate fan vaulting and elaborate tracery that became popular in English cathedrals and spread to the Continent. The fan vaults were created by using curved half-cone-shaped corbels set in horizontal rows which support a series of flat panels at the top of the vault. The elegant ribs are not structural, but consist of tracery formed by carving the solid corbels.

Architecture

The intricacy that characterized the music of the fourteenth century was also a feature of the new stylistic developments in architecture. English cathedrals began to use **fan vaulting** and elaborate tracery in the ceilings of the naves and cloisters (**fig. 137**) and modifications of this style were used by architects in eastern Europe, most notably in Bohemia. At Prague, the capital city of Bohemia, and of the Holy Roman Empire after the coronation of

Charles IV of Bohemia in 1349, the architecture was patronized by the emperor, and developed a unique style. Charles IV probably viewed the cathedral at Prague as a personal monument in the tradition of French monarchs, and saw the brilliance of the architecture as a reflection of his glory and importance. He had many of his ancestors buried in the eastern chapels, and, like kings such as Louis IX (St. Louis), he spent a great deal of money providing the church with sumptuous liturgical vessels, jewels, and relics.

The Cathedral of St. Vitus at Prague was constructed with an elevation featuring a glazed triforium and large clerestory windows. The sculptor and architect, Peter Parler (1330–1399), made use of an innovative vaulting system to create a mesh-like design of intersecting diagonal ribs. This **net vault**, as it is known, emphasizes the ornamental unity of the ceiling through the length of the nave (**fig. 137**). The style, which was used initially at Prague, became more complex in the fifteenth century as it spread throughout Germany and eastern Europe.

Literature

Like the music of the period, the literature of the fourteenth century made a radical departure from the past, reflecting a new concern with naturalism and human expression. This preoccupation may be seen in the works of the most famous Italian authors of the time (known in Italian as the *Trecento*, or 1300s)—Dante, Petrarch, and Boccaccio. All three were born in Tuscany, and all were influenced by the same cultural climate. The time frame of their lives coincided for a brief period; Dante, the oldest, died in 1321, when Boccaccio, the youngest, was eight years old. There are also personal links among the three; as a child, Petrarch met Dante, and Boccaccio became a close friend of Petrarch in his later years. Their works also exhibit certain common features, most notably the expression of love for three adored women. Dante wrote in sublime terms of his love for Beatrice, a woman he met when he was eight, and who became, in his masterpiece *The Divine Comedy*, his spiritual guide in the third part, *Paradiso*. Petrarch composed many sonnets for his love, Laura, and Boccaccio dedicated many of his works to his adored Fiammetta, his "exalted and noble love."

Boccaccio's irreverent tone and keen human observation were a strong influence on the greatest English writer of the fourteenth century, Geoffrey Chaucer. In France, Christine de Pizan was also breaking with convention and showing a female perspective on the world.

Dante

The works of Dante Alighieri (1265–1321) have been analyzed by scholars as both the culmination of medieval literary culture and the beginning of Renaissance literature.

138 In 1344, the French architect Matthew of Arras designed the splendid choir of St. Vitus Cathedral in Prague (constructed 1347–1385). His work was continued by the German Peter Parler, who combined English and French building techniques with his own design for large clerestory windows on either side of the supporting piers, and devised a new and highly decorative system of vaulting. His net vaults create a fascinating geometrical web of diagonal ribs which form intersecting diamond-shaped patterns.

Certainly, the subject matter of *The Divine Comedy* is typical of medieval religious expression, though many scholars have also pointed to the fusion of religion and theology with the tradition of courtly love in Dante's great masterpiece. The work also exemplifies the numerological structures so admired by medieval people, and it has frequently been compared to the creations of medieval architects. Scholars who see the work as indicative of the coming Renaissance have discussed Dante's use of Classical sources and his glorification of human, in addition to divine, love as a pathway to salvation. Further, it was written in Italian, a vernacular language, rather than the customary Latin.

The work is divided into three parts: *Inferno* (Hell), *Purgatorio* (Purgatory), and *Paradiso* ("Paradise"). The best-known of the three is the first part, in which Dante describes the levels of Hell, and places many of his political enemies among the sinners. His guide in exploring the nether regions is the Classical Roman poet Vergil. Dante and his companion encounter the souls of the wrathful and gloomy as they reach the fifth circle or level:

> But let us now descend to greater misery; already every star is falling, that was ascending when I set out, and to stay too long is not permitted.
>
> We crossed the circle, to the other bank, near a fount, that boils and pours down through a cleft, which it has formed.
>
> The water was darker far than perse [grayish-blue]; and we, accompanying the dusky waves, entered down by a strange path.
>
> This dreary streamlet makes a Marsh, that is named Styx, when it has descended to the foot of the gray malignant shores.
>
> And I, who stood intent on looking, saw muddy people in that bog, all naked and with a look of anger.
>
> They were smiting each other, not with hands only, but with head, and with chest, and with feet; maiming one another with their teeth, piece by piece.
>
> The king Master said: "Son, now see the souls of those whom anger overcame, and also I would have thee to believe for certain,
>
> that there are people underneath the water, who sob, and make it bubble at the surface; as thy eye may tell thee whichever way it turns.
>
> Fixed in the slime, they say: 'Sullen were we in the sweet air, that is gladdened by the Sun, carrying lazy smoke within our hearts;
>
> now lie we sullen here in the black mire.' This hymn they gurgle in their throats, for they cannot speak it in full words." Thus, between the dry bank and the putrid fen, we compassed a large arc of that loathly slough, with eyes turned towards those that swallow of its filth; we came to the foot of a tower at last.

Because the poet Vergil was not a Christian (he died in 19 BC), he could not accompany Dante to Paradise. Instead, Beatrice became his guide, functioning as a literary exemplar of the salvific power of human love.

Many of the works of Petrarch, though not as lengthy and complex as the *Divine Comedy*, also reflect the long tradition of courtly adoration for an unattainable woman.

Petrarch

Francesco Petrarch (1304–1374) was raised in Avignon, where his father was a notary, and, like many other bright young men of his time, he studied law. Finding that he was not satisfied by training for this profession, he joined a monastic order, which gave him the necessary time for writing and studying the Classics.

Petrarch devoted his life to the recovery, editing, and copying of Latin manuscripts, and to corresponding with scholars with similar interests. His works concerning Latin writers, especially Cicero, did much to encourage the retrieval and revival of Classical culture.

Petrarch was not, however, immune to the charms of women and the tradition of courtly love. His affection for a married Florentine woman named Laura de Sade is memorialized in a large collection of poems which make up the *Canzoniere* (*Songbook*). The poetic form most often used by Petrarch was the sonnet, a fourteen-line lyric poem usually divided into two parts—eight lines (often set 4 + 4), followed by six lines (3 + 3). This form was influenced by earlier Italian poets, as well as by the tradition of troubadour poetry and Islamic verse.

Petrarch's expression tends to be contemplative and self-reflective, often exploring contrasting emotional states, as in the following example, which dwells on the emotions provoked by his unrequited love for Laura:

> I find no peace, and I am not at war,
> I fear and hope, and burn and I am ice;
> I fly above the heavens, and lie on earth,
> and I grasp nothing and embrace the world.
> One keeps me jailed who neither locks nor opens,
> nor keeps me for her own nor frees the noose;
> Love does not kill, nor does he loose my chains;
> he wants me lifeless but won't loosen me.
> I see with no eyes, shout without a tongue;
> I yearn to perish, and I beg for help;
> I hate myself and love somebody else.
> I thrive on pain and laugh with all my tears;
> I dislike death as much as I do life:
> because of you, lady, I am this way.

Petrarch was a great influence on Boccaccio, especially in later life. Indeed, the younger man said he would probably not have published the bawdy tales of *The Decameron* if his friendship with Petrarch had begun earlier.

Boccaccio

Giovanni Boccaccio (1313–1375) was the illegitimate son of a merchant, Boccaccino di Chelino, and a woman who was probably from Florence or Cetaldo. He was acknowledged by his father soon after his birth, and seems to have been well treated by him during his childhood. He received a good education, which was probably focused on the rudiments of accounting, because Boccaccio's father wanted him to be a functionary in a bank. He was not happy in the business world, however, and his father permitted him to leave the counting house to study canon law at the University of Naples. Though this career was not congenial either, Boccaccio's studies there introduced him to the worlds of scholarship and literature.

In the 1340s Boccaccio worked in Florence and other Tuscan towns, acting as a diplomatic functionary of the communes, and serving on various boards and agencies. The most important experience of his later years was the development of his friendship with Petrarch. The two men visited one another and carried on an extensive correspondence. It is evident from the development of Boccaccio's works that Petrarch strengthened his disciple's devotion to poetry.

The stories contained in Boccaccio's famous *Decameron* are entertaining, comic, and bawdy. Some scholars have seen this mood as a reaction to the reality of the dreadful contagion of the plague (the *Decameron* was completed in 1351). The tales are recounted by people from Florence who have gone to the countryside in hopes of avoiding the epidemic. Many of them are highly irreverent, making fun of members of the clergy and monastic orders. One of the stories concerns a convent, "very famous for its sanctity and religious spirit." A novice in the order, Isabetta, has fallen in love with a young man whom she met when he accompanied one of her relatives on a visit:

> Finally, since each desired the other, the young man devised a means of being able to visit his nun secretly . . . As this went on for some time, it happened one night that he was seen by one of the nuns as he was leaving Isabetta's cell, without either of them being aware of this.

The nun tells her colleagues, and they decide to keep watch over the young novice in order to catch her with her lover:

> Now Isabetta knew nothing about any of this, and one night she had her lover come to her; this was immediately noted by the nuns who were keeping watch. When it appeared that the time was ripe, a goodly part of the night already having passed, they divided themselves into two groups: one stood guard outside the entrance to Isabetta's cell; the other ran to the bedroom of the abbess. When their knocks were answered with a reply, they said: "Get up, Mother Superior, get up immediately! We've discovered that Isabetta has a young man in her cell!"
>
> That night the abbess was in the company of a priest whom she often had brought into her bedroom in a chest, and when she heard the noise, fearing that the nuns, in their excessive haste and zeal, might beat down her door, she got up quickly and dressed in the dark as best she could; and thinking that she had picked up her folded nun's veil of the sort which is called "psalters," she picked up the priest's pants instead; and she was in such a hurry that, without realizing it, she threw his pants over her head in place of her "psalters," left her bedroom, and quickly locked it behind her, saying: "Where is this cursed woman?"
>
> The other nuns were so anxious and eager to catch Isabetta in the act that they did not notice what the abbess had on her head; she reached the door of the cell and, with the help of the other nuns, forced open the door. They rushed in and found the two

lovers in each other's arms; taken by this sudden surprise, not knowing what to do, they lay motionless.

The young girl was immediately led off by the other nuns to the convent's meeting hall. The young man remained there; he dressed, and then waited to see how the affair might end . . .

Having taken her seat in the meeting hall in the presence of all the nuns, who were looking only at the guilty girl, the abbess began to vilify the young nun in terms never before used of a woman, telling her how her indecent, her depraved actions, had they ever become known outside the convent, would ruin the sanctity, the honesty, and the good name of the convent; and to her verbal abuse, she added the most serious of threats.

The young girl, in her timidity and shame, knowing she was guilty, did not know how to reply, hoping with her silence to arouse a feeling of compassion in the others. And as the scolding of the abbess continued, the young girl happened to look up and see what the abbess was wearing on her head, with suspenders dangling on either side. Realizing what the abbess had been doing and regaining her self-confidence, she said:

"God save you, Mother Superior; tie up your bonnet and then tell me what you will."

The Abbess, who did not understand what she meant, replied: "What bonnet, you slut? Even now you have the nerve to be clever? Do you think what you have done is a joking matter?"

Then, a second time, the young girl said: "Mother Superior, I beg you to tie up your bonnet; then say anything you please to me."

At this, many of the nuns glanced up at the abbess's head, and she put her hands to her veil—then, they all saw why Isabetta had spoken as she had. When she realized that she was equally guilty and that there was no way to cover up her sin from the others, the abbess changed her tone and began to speak in a completely different manner, concluding that it was impossible for anyone to defend oneself from the desires of the flesh. And she said that everyone should enjoy herself as best she could, provided that it be done discreetly as it had been until that day.

And after Isabetta had been set free, the abbess returned to sleep with her priest, and Isabetta with her lover. And, in spite of all the other nuns that envied her, Isabetta had him come to her many times; the other nuns, without lovers, sought their solace secretly in the best way they knew how.

The irreverent tone regarding the clergy conveyed in stories such as this was also a feature of the works of the Englishman Geoffrey Chaucer, though his literary portraits are much more subtle.

Geoffrey Chaucer

Geoffrey Chaucer was one of the finest poets in the English language. He was born about 1342, the son of a merchant in the wine trade who had associations with the royal court. Chaucer was educated in London, and became a page at about age fifteen in the household of the countess of Ulster, who was married to the third son of King Edward III. In 1359, he was sent to France as a soldier in one of the forays during the Hundred Years War. He was captured near Reims and was ransomed with funds contributed by the king, among others. Literary scholars believe that his interest in writing was sparked when he encountered, in France, the *Roman de la Rose*, which he began to translate.

After his return to England, Chaucer became a courtier in attendance to the king, and was patronized by John of Gaunt, Duke of Lancaster. He was a prodigious reader in several languages, including Latin, French, Anglo-Norman, and Italian, and he was also interested in science; he seems to have become an expert in astronomy, medicine, physics, and alchemy. The king used his linguistic expertise by sending him on diplomatic missions to various countries in Europe, where he came into contact with the works of Boccaccio, among others. His experiences, together with his wide-ranging education, furnished him with a vast fund of material from which to draw the plots and characters for his writing.

Chaucer's works, especially *The Canterbury Tales*, exemplify the new trait of naturalism that emerged in art and literature in the period following the Black Death. This collection of stories, told by an imaginary group of pilgrims on their way to visit the shrine of Thomas Becket in Canterbury Cathedral, includes tales drawn from all over Europe, as well as the ancient world and the Orient; they explore the entire range of human emotion and experience. In addition to providing entertainment, most of the stories have a moral point, and end with a proverbial maxim, though these are drawn from life experience, rather than theological prescription.

The "Prologue" to *The Canterbury Tales* contains a concise portrait of each of the pilgrims, who represent people from all walks of life, all professions, all social classes, and both genders. Although the constraints of space limit this discussion, it is possible to obtain a sense of Chaucerian style in two brief excerpts from the "Prologue." The first describes a squire—the son of a knight—who is traveling with his father on the pilgrimage. Chaucer's image of the young man encapsulates many of the qualities and virtues attributed to a young male participant in the game of courtly love:

He had his son with him, a fine young Squire,
A lover and a cadet, a lad of fire
With locks as curly as if they had been pressed.
He was some twenty years of age, I guessed.
In stature he was of a moderate length,
With wonderful agility and strength.
He'd seen some service with the cavalry
In Flanders and Artois and Picardy
And had done valiantly in little space
Of time, in hope to win his lady's grace.
He was embroidered like a meadow bright
And full of freshest flowers, red and white.
Singing he was, or fluting all the day;
He was as fresh as is the month of May.
Short was his gown, the sleeves were long and wide;
He knew the way to sit a horse and ride.
He could make songs and poems and recite,
Knew how to joust and dance, to draw and write.
He loved so hotly that till dawn grew pale
He slept as little as a nightingale.
Courteous he was, lowly and serviceable,
And carved to serve his father at the table.

The second excerpt portrays a cleric from Oxford, still a student, who is more dedicated to buying books and studying Aristotle than he is to eating or finding a lucrative profession:

An Oxford Cleric, still a student though,
One who had taken logic long ago,
Was there; his horse was thinner than a rake,
And he was not too fat, I undertake,
But had a hollow look, a sober stare;
The thread upon his overcoat was bare.
He had found no preferment in the Church
And he was too unworldly to make search
For secular employment. By his bed
He preferred having twenty books in red
And black, of Aristotle's philosophy,
Than costly clothes, fiddle or psaltery.
Though a philosopher, as I have told,

He had not found the stone for making gold.
Whatever money from his friends he took
He spent on learning or another book
And prayed for them most earnestly, returning
Thanks to them thus for paying for his learning.
His only care was study, and indeed
He never spoke a word more than was need,
Formal at that, respectful in the extreme,
Short, to the point, and lofty in his theme.
A tone of moral virtue filled his speech
And gladly would he learn, and gladly teach.

As may be seen from these brief snippets, Chaucer was fascinated by humanity, in all of its various manifestations. Rather than writing didactic tales that focus on salvation and religious obligation, he sought to portray the human qualities of a variety of characters, each of whom exemplifies his or her social class, profession, and experience in life.

Although during the Middle Ages the writing of poetry and essays was largely the province of males, an accomplished woman, often cited as the first female professional writer in Europe, joined their ranks in the fourteenth century. Her name was Christine de Pizan.

Christine de Pizan

Christine de Pizan (c. 1364–1430) was born in Italy, the daughter of a famous physician and astrologer who took a post at the court of the French king Charles V while she was an infant. The rest of the family joined him in Paris in 1368. Christine's education was fostered by her father, and she was able to take advantage of the cultural and intellectual opportunities available at the court. About 1379 she married Etienne de Castel, a royal secretary. Their marriage appears, unlike typical unions of the Middle Ages, to have been a love match, one described with passion and affection in Christine's poetry. The couple had three children, two sons and a daughter, born between 1381 and 1385.

In 1389, Etienne died in an epidemic, and Christine was left a widow. Rather than following the usual path available to women in her situation, which was either to remarry or enter a convent, she was determined to support her children with her pen. She began to write and to look for patrons, initially composing love poetry in the courtly style. She wrote many poems in this genre; one of the most admired was a long narrative entitled *Le Livre du Duc des Vrais Amants* (*The Book of the Duke of True Lovers*). In addition, she composed many verses expressing the sorrows of widowhood, a new topic for lyric poetry.

Christine was especially vocal about her perceptions of misogyny, and wrote many diatribes in defense of women. Some of her strongest statements were made when she participated in an intellectual debate concerning the worth of the popular thirteenth-century work *Roman de la Rose* (see Chapter 13). Her primary arguments against the work were that it spoke of women in a derogatory tone, and that it was immoral and useless. In a letter to Pierre Col, a canon of Paris and Tournay, Christine storms:

> I can only be surprised how someone dares to praise this book in which there are so many things that horrify the human heart and lead it to damnation.
>
> You say that as far as you are concerned you "prefer to be blamed for appreciating and loving a book rather than be one of those subtle blamers." You resemble Heloise . . . who said that she would rather be called "whore" by Master Abelard than be a crowned queen. This shows very well that those wishes that please most are not always the most reasonable.
>
> You say that everyone knows "that there are still seven thousand people . . . who are more than ready to defend it." Answer: it is a general rule that bad sects grow easily, just like weeds, but there are cases where greater numbers do not mean that their cause is better. And may it please God that there will never be such a group assembled; it is not an article of faith: may everyone have his own opinion.

139 The work of Giotto (1266–1337) demonstrated a new realism and concentration on human emotion. Here, in the *Lamentation*—a fresco in the Arena Chapel in Padua—the figures in the foreground possess substance and volume reminiscent of Classical sculpture, and their emotional reactions upon viewing the dead Christ are heart-rending.

Christine strikes out against the literary treatment of women in the *Roman de la Rose* in another work, *The God of Love's Letter*:

Why then if women are weak and flighty, and easily manipulated, silly and lacking self-control, as some clerkly authors say, why do those who pursue them have any need of ruse? And why do women not give in at once, without requiring that strategies and tricks be used to catch them? For it is not necessary to go to war for a castle that is already captured. And even a poet as subtle as Ovid, who was later exiled, and Jean de Meun in *The Roman de la Rose*: What great exertion! What an elaborate enterprise! And what great learning, both accessible and obscure, what adventures he described there! And how many people are entreated and begged, and how much effort and trickery is there in order to accomplish nothing more than the deception of a maid through fraud and cunning, for that is the ultimate goal! Does a weakly fortified place require such an assault? How can one try so hard for so easy a prize? I do not understand or believe that such great effort is needed to capture a weakly fortified place, nor scheming, nor ingenuity, nor great subtlety. It is necessary to conclude that, since scheming, great ingenuity, and great effort are required to deceive a noble or a low-born woman, they are not so fickle as is said, nor is their behavior so changeable.

Painting

Like the literature of the period, accomplishments of the visual arts in the fourteenth century emphasized naturalism. The foremost artist of the era, the Itaian painter Giotto di Bondone (*c.* 1266–1337), was a transitional figure like Dante, with many scholars seeing his work as part of the early Renaissance. However, it is also possible to view him as a late-medieval artist, and to examine his work within the context of the fourteenth century.

Little is known about Giotto's education and the early part of his career. There is evidence, however, that he was in Florence by 1301, and by 1303 he was working in Padua, initially at the Church of St. Anthony. In 1305, still in Padua, he was commissioned by the wealthy banker Enrico Scrovegni to decorate the walls of the family chapel, known as the Arena Chapel.

Giotto transformed this unimpressive building into a monument in honor of the Virgin Mary. By using ornamental bands to divide the walls and vault, he created panels on which he painted various scenes from the life of the Virgin and Christ. Giotto's special talent was his ability to distill a complex narrative into one highly charged emotional image. For example, in the *Lamentation* (**fig. 139**), the attention of the viewer is focused on the mother and son, while accompanying figures heighten the heart-rending effect through their obvious mourning. The angels floating in the sky also exhibit powerful emotions of grief, adding intensity to the images of the mourners below.

Technical details in the painting reveal several aspects of Giotto's art that were revolutionary. In comparison to his predecessors, whose paintings were virtually two-dimensional, Giotto deepened space through the use of **foreshortening** in the painting of the figures in the front, and through architectural details such as the receding rocky hillock with the barren tree in the background. He also broke with the tradition of using gold as a principal color, incorporating much more variety in his paintings. The most intense color was used in the darkest areas, although these shades contain subtle highlights of white, so that the result is one of brightness, even in a somber scene such as this. The emotional and intellectual effect of the work was radically different from the art of the High Gothic period. Like Chaucer and Boccaccio, who were fascinated by the human aspects of experience, Giotto sought to replicate nature and humanity in his art. This led him to search for technical solutions to problems of depth and dimension, and to find ways of expressing human emotion in painted images. As Boccaccio remarked in the introduction to one of the tales in the *Decameron*, which he dedicated to Giotto:

> Giotto, had such a prodigious fancy, that there was nothing in Nature, the parent of all things, but he could imitate it with his pencil so well, and draw it so like, as to deceive our very senses, imagining that to be the very thing itself which was only his painting.

Summary

The fourteenth century was one of calamity and disaster, with famine, revolt, plague, and war changing the face of European society forever. The results of population loss, economic disruption, and a loss of confidence in the ability of the Church to deal with the problems of humanity caused a radical shift in religious, political, and cultural life. The system of vassalage, which had provided the political framework for much of the Middle Ages, was destroyed by the loss of population during the plague, and in addition, the technological advances in warfare made the feudal aristocracy obsolete. The Church suffered through the Avignon papacy and the Great Schism, emerging in a weakened position.

Artists, musicians, and writers responded to the changing circumstances by focusing on the experience of human life in all its richness, as opposed to a life directed solely towards the salvation of the human soul. The works of Chaucer and Boccaccio told entertaining stories about real people, just as the paintings of Giotto encapsulated true human emotion. All of these developments pointed towards radical changes in cultural, religious, and political life—changes that would be embodied in the movements known as the Renaissance and Reformation, to be discussed in the Epilogue.

Suggestions for Further Reading

Primary sources

Many chronicles exist that describe the plague and its effect in various countries. One of the most powerful is *The Chronicle of Jean de Venette*, edited by Richard A. Newhall and translated by Jean Birdsall (New York: Columbia University Press, 1953). See also *The Black Death: A Chronicle of the Plague*, by Johannes Nohl (London: George Allen & Unwin, Ltd., 1926), an old, but still useful, compilation of sources concerning the epidemic.

The finest chronicle of the Hundred Years War is by Jean Froissart: *The Chronicles of England, France, and Spain* (New York: Dutton, 1961).

There are many editions of Dante's *Divine Comedy*. An excellent translation is the one by John Aitken Carlyle, Thomas Okey, and Philip H. Wicksteed (New York: Vintage Books, 1959). Another is by John Ciardi (New York: W.W. Norton, 1970). Several of Petrarch's works are contained in *Selected Sonnets, Odes and Letters*, translated by T.G. Bergin (New York: Appleton-Century-Crofts, 1966). A convenient selection of twenty-one of the tales in *The Decameron*, with critical articles, may be found in *The Decameron*, by Giovanni Boccaccio, translated and edition by Mark Musa and Peter Bondanella (New York: W.W. Norton, 1977).

The best edition of Chaucer's works is the *Riverside Chaucer*, edited by Larry D. Benson (Boston: Houghton Mifflin, 1987), which includes an extensive glossary and bibliography. A critical edition of nine of the tales is contained in *The Canterbury Tales: Nine Tales and the General Prologue*, by Geoffrey Chaucer, edited by V.A. Kolve and Glending Olson (New York: W.W. Norton, 1989). Both of these editions are in Middle English. A version in modern English is *The Canterbury Tales*, translated by Nevill Coghill (Harmondsworth: Penguin Books, reprint ed., 1986).

The Selected Writings of Christine de Pizan, translated and edited by Renate Blumenfeld-Kosinski and Kevin Brownlee (New York: W. W. Norton, 1997) provides a graceful translation, as well as relevant scholarly articles.

Secondary sources

The Black Death: Natural and Human Disaster in Medieval Europe, by Robert S. Gottfried (New York: Free Press, 1983, is a fine analysis of the plague and its effects on European society. See also Philip Ziegler's *The Black Death* (New York: John Day Co., 1969) and Rosemary Horrox, ed., *The Black Death* (New York: Manchester University Press, 1994). Another excellent account of the plague is *King Death: The Black Death and its Aftermath in Late Medieval England*, by Colin Platt (Toronto:

University of Toronto Press, 1996).

The Great Famine: Northern Europe in the Early Fourteenth Century, by William Chester Jordan (Princeton: Princeton University Press, 1996), provides a good discussion of the starvation conditions in northern Europe.

David Nirenberg's fascinating study *Communities of Violence: Persecution of Minorities in the Middle Ages* (Princeton: Princeton University Press, 1996) examines the violent interactions of Christians, Muslims, and Jews in fourteenth-century Aragón.

The Hundred Years War: England and France at War c. 1300–c. 1450, by Christopher Allmand (Cambridge: Cambridge University Press, 1988), is a clear and succinct presentation of the conflict between France and England. A more comprehensive study of the war may found in Jonathan Sumption's massive work *The Hundred Years War*, 2 vols. (Philadelphia: University of Pennsylvania Press, 1999). Warfare in the era covered in this chapter is discussed in *War in the Middle Ages*, by Philippe Contamine, translated by Michael Jones (London: Basil Blackwell, 1984), especially Chapter 4.

Two works by Donald R. Howard, *The Idea of the Canterbury Tales* (Berkeley: University of California Press, 1976) and *Chaucer: His Life, His Works, His World* (New York: E.P. Dutton, 1987), present interesting and informative accounts of Chaucer's life and works. An interesting collection of articles concerning Chaucer's *Canterbury Tales* is contained in *Chaucer and the*

Craft of Fiction, edited by Leigh A. Arrathoon (Rochester, MI: Scolaris Press, Inc., 1986). The first section of *The Cambridge History of Italian Literature*, edited by Peter Brand and Lino Pertile (Cambridge: Cambridge University Press, 1996) contains fine articles concerning Petrarch, Dante, and Boccaccio. *Dante's Vision and the Circle of Knowledge* by Giuseppe Mazzotta (Princeton: Princeton University Press, 1994), provides an excellent introduction to the study of Dante.

Fourteenth-century music is thoroughly described in *Medieval Music* by Richard Hoppin (New York: W.W. Norton, 1978), chapters 15–18. A fascinating study that contains material concerning the effects of the plague on artistic expression is Paul Binksi's *Medieval Death: Ritual and Representation* (Ithaca, NY: Cornell University Press, 1996).

A classic work, still valuable, is Johan Huizinga's *The Waning of the Middle Ages: A Study of the Forms of Life, Thought, and Art in France and the Netherlands in the Dawn of the Renaissance* (London: E. Arnold & Co., 1924). The most recent translation of this work, by Rodney J. Payton and Ulrich Mammitzsch is titled *The Autumn of the Middle Ages* (Chicago: University of Chicago Press, 1996).

Bruce Cole's *Giotto: The Scrovegni Chapel, Padua* (New York: Braziller, 1993) provides a fine analysis of Giotto's work. Another excellent study of the artist is *Giotto as a Historical and Literary Figure*, edited by Andrew Ladis (New York: Garland Publishers, 1998).

EPILOGUE

This book has traced the development of civilization in western Europe and its neighboring areas from the collapse of the Roman Empire in the fourth century to the flowering of medieval culture in the thirteenth—an era brought to a close by the struggles of the fourteenth. Along the way we have studied the consolidation of strong monarchies in several countries, the evolution of the church under the direction of an increasingly influential papacy, and the expansion of western Europeans toward the eastern Mediterranean resulting from pilgrimages and crusades. As we have seen, the medieval era was characterized by vibrant and enduring cultural achievements, including the foundation of universities and the development of scholastic philosophy. Medieval architects and builders created awe-inspiring Romanesque and Gothic cathedrals and the magnificent sculptures and stained-glass windows that adorn them. Musicians in the Middle Ages were able to devise a system of musical notation that enabled them to pass their compositions from generation to generation in a clearly defined form. Medieval writers continued the tradition of the epic poem, producing several literary monuments that encapsulated the values of people in the Middle Ages. Looking ahead, it is possible to see that all of these accomplishments provided the foundation for the brilliant cultural developments that occurred during the historical era known as the Renaissance.

In a sense, the disasters of the fourteenth century—famine, the Black Death, and the Hundred Years War—made way for the burgeoning economic life of the Renaissance. The dissolution of the manor provided opportunities for a larger portion of the population to improve their lives, and many people moved to urban environments; the growth of cities offered a wide variety of professions, including many positions in new civic bureaucratic administrations; increased wealth led to the patronage of artists and musicians by non-noble magnates; and the Europeans continued to expand their horizons through exploration, often sponsored by monarchs such as Ferdinand and Isabella of Spain and Elizabeth I of England.

Following the Great Schism, the church was governed by a series of popes chosen for their bureaucratic skills and fiscal expertise, rather than for spiritual reasons. Their worldly lifestyles and moral abuses led to widespread criticism, and this condemnation became one factor in the emergence of a religious movement known as the Protestant Reformation.

The monarchies of France, Spain, England, and the Holy Roman Empire continued to solidify their power, exemplified by kings such as Francis I, Henry VIII, and Philip II. In Italy, the city-states of the north developed individual governments administered by the citizens, but controlled by wealthy magnates such as the Medici in Florence and the Sforza family in Milan.

Renaissance artists followed the trend begun by Giotto and his contemporaries toward a more natural representation of humans—both physically and emotionally. The painters conquered the problem of creating images that appeared to be three-dimensional, although they were actually produced on flat surfaces. Architects of the fifteenth and sixteenth centuries led the way in recovering the artistic styles of the Greco-Roman world, and began covering churches and chapels with domes, rather than Gothic vaulted naves.

As literacy became more prevalent, much literature was written for pure entertainment, rather than moral and religious instruction. Following the realistic style of Boccaccio and Chaucer, writers continued to portray individuals as they actually behaved, rather than presenting a didactic moral image.

In the realm of music, the *Ars nova* had opened the possibility for complex rhythmic expression, and composers of the fifteenth and sixteenth centuries continued to explore these innovations, while they began to experiment with clearly defined harmonic structures. The church continued to be a major patron of musicians during the Renaissance, but kings and wealthy magnates sponsored much music for court ceremonies and entertainment.

In summary, it is clear that the people of the Middle Ages provided a foundation for the culture of the Renaissance, and indeed, for the culture of the modern world. The brilliant and fascinating medieval era is not only an engrossing subject for historical analysis—it remains a permanent and vital aspect of our lives and institutions.

Kay Slocum, 2004

LIST OF MEDIEVAL POPES

Sylvester I (314–335)
Marcus (336)
Julius I (337–352)
Liberius (352–365)
Damasus I (366–384)
Siricius (384–399)
Anastasius I (399–401)
Innocent I (401–417)
Zosimus (417–418)
Boniface I (418–422)
Celestine I (422–432)
Sixtus III (432–440)
Leo I (the Great) (440–461)
Hilarius (461–468)
Simplicius (468–483)
Felix III (II) (483–492)
Gelasius I (492–496)
Anastasius II (496–498)
Symmachus (498–514)
Hormisdas (514–523)
John I (523–526)
Felix IV (526–530)
Boniface II (530–532)
John II (533–535)
Agapitus I (535–536)
Silverius (536–537)
Vigilius (537–555)
Pelagius I (556–561)
John III (561–574)
Benedict I (575–579)
Pelagius II (579–590)
Gregory I (the Great) (590–604)
Sabinianus (604–606)
Boniface III (607)
Boniface IV (608–615)
Deusdedit (615–618)
Boniface V (619–625)
Honorius I (625–638)
Severinus (640)
John IV (640–642)
Theodore I (642–649)
Martin I (649–655)
Eugenius I (655–657)
Vitalian (657–672)
Adeodatus (672–676)
Donus (676–678)
Agatho (678–681)
Leo II (682–683)

Benedict II (684–685)
John V (685–686)
Conon (686–687)
Sergius I (687–701)
John VI (701–705)
John VII (705–707)
Sisinnius (708)
Constantine (708–715)
Gregory II (715–731)
Gregory III (731–741)
Zacharias (741–752)
Stephen II (752–757)
Paul I (757–767)
Stephen III (768–772)
Adrian I (772–795)
Leo III (795–816)
Stephen IV (816–817)
Paschal I (817–824)
Eugenius II (824–827)
Valentine (827)
Gregory IV (827–844)
Sergius II (844–847)
Leo IV (847–855)
Benedict III (855–858)
Nicholas I (the Great) (858–867)
Adrian II (867–872)
John VIII (872–882)
Marinus I (882–884)
Adrian III (884–885)
Stephen V (885–891)
Formosus (891–896)
Boniface VI (896)
Stephen VI (896–897)
Romanus (897)
Theodore II (897)
John IX (898–900)
Benedict IV (900–903)
Leo V (903)
Sergius III (904–911)
Anastasius III (911–913)
Lando (913–914)
John X (914–928)
Leo VI (928)
Stephen VII (928–931)
John XI (931–935)
Leo VII (936–939)
Stephen VIII (939–942)
Marinus II (942–946)

Agapetus II (946–955)
John XII (955–963)
Leo VIII (963–964)
Benedict V (964–965)
John XIII (965–972)
Benedict VI (973–974)
Benedict VII (974–983)
John XIV (983–984)
John XV (985–996)
Gregory V (996–999)
Sylvester II (999–1003)
John XVII (1003)
John XVIII (1004–1009)
Sergius IV (1009–1012)
Benedict VIII (1012–1024)
John XIX (1024–1032)
Benedict IX (1032–1044)
Sylvester III (1045)
Benedict IX (1045) [for the second time]
Gregory VI (1045–1046)
Clement II (1046–1047)
Benedict IX (1047–1048) [for the third time]
Damasus II (1048)
Leo IX (1049–1054)
Victor II (1055–1057)
Stephen IX (1057–1058)
Nicholas II (1059–1061)
Alexander II (1061–1073)
Gregory VII (1073–1085)
Victor III (1086–1087)
Urban II (1088–1099)
Paschal II (1099–1118)
Gelasius II (1118–1119)
Calixtus II (1119–1124)
Honorius II (1124–1130)
Innocent II (1130–1143)
Celestine II (1143–1144)
Lucius II (1144–1145)
Eugenius III (1145–1153)
Anastasius IV (1153–1154)
Adrian IV (1154–1159)
Alexander III (1159–1181)
Lucius III (1181–1185)
Urban III (1185–1187)
Gregory VIII (1187)
Clement III (1187–1191)
Celestine III (1191–1198)

Innocent III (1198–1216)
Honorius III (1216–1227)
Gregory IX (1227–1241)
Celestine IV (1241)
Innocent IV (1243–1254)
Alexander IV (1254–1261)
Urban IV (1261–1264)
Clement IV (1265–1268)
Gregory X (1271–1276)
Innocent V (1276)
John XXI (1276–1277) [so-called; error in numbering, since there was no John XX]
Nicholas III (1277–1280)
Martin IV (1281–1285)
Honorius IV (1285–1287)
Nicholas IV (1288–1292)
Celestine V (1294)
Boniface VIII (1294–1303)
Benedict XI (1303–1304)
Clement V (1305–1314)
John XXII (1316–1334)
Benedict XII (1334–1342)
Clement VI (1342–1352)
Innocent VI (1352–1362)
Urban V (1362–1370)
Gregory XI (1370–1378)
Urban VI (1378–1389)
*Clement VII (1378–1394)
Boniface IX (1389–1404)
*Benedict XIII (1394–1423)
Innocent VII (1404–1406)
Gregory XII (1406–1415)
**Alexander V (1409–1410)
**John XXIII (1410–1415)
Martin V (1417–1431)
Eugenius IV (1431–1447)
Nicholas V (1447–1455)
Calixtus III (1455–1458)
Pius II (1458–1464)
Paul II (1464–1471)
Sixtus IV (1471–1484)
Innocent VIII (1484–1492)
Alexander VI (1492–1503)

* = Avignon pope
** = Pisa pope

GLOSSARY

Alids Supporters of the third **caliph**, Ali, who eventually became known as **Shi'a**.

allodial land Land held directly and absolutely, rather than as **fiefs** from another lord.

ambulatory The walkway around the apse of a church that allows access to the chapels.

anchoress A woman who lived a completely isolated and enclosed religious life, rather than participating in a monastic community.

ansar The followers, or "helpers" of Muhammad, who were inhabitants of Medina; they became converts to Islam during the *hijra*, in contrast to the *muhajirin*, who emigrated to Medina with the Prophet.

antiphoner A medieval chantbook containing the music and liturgy for the Mass. The term was later applied, in addition, to books that comprised the materials for the Office.

apostolic life The pattern of living established by the early Christian apostles. It was itinerant and entailed poverty and the preaching of the Gospel.

apostolic succession A part of the **Petrine theory** that claims that the pope is a direct successor of St. Peter.

apostolic tradition A concept that refers to the era of Christ's life and the period immediately following, when his apostles were disseminating his teachings.

apse A semicircular polygonal space at one or both ends of the **nave** in a Roman **basilica**; in a Christian church, usually placed at the east end of the nave, but sometimes at the end of the transept arms.

apsidal chapel A chapel that extends from the **apse**.

asceticism A lifestyle based upon self-denial practiced by some early Christians. It became a prominent feature of monasticism in the Middle Ages.

assize A court convened and conducted by the *missi dominici*.

atrium The entrance to a **basilica**. Also an open court, sometimes colonnaded or arcaded, in the form of a church.

aya (pl. *ayat*) A verse in the **Qur'an**.

bailli A rank of French royal official drawn from the middle and lower classes of society. These officials were given a salary to administer justice and collect the revenues due the king in defined geographical areas known as bailiwicks.

ballata (pl. *ballate*) A **monophonic** secular song in which a three-line refrain is sung both before and after a seven-line stanza in the form *A b b a A*.

banalities Utilities such as the mill, oven, and wine press, located on a **manor**. They were used by the **serfs**, who gave a portion of their produce in payment.

barrel vault A semicircular, tunnel-shaped vault that covers the **nave** in a Romanesque church or cathedral.

basileus Greek for "hereditary king" and the title given to the Byzantine emperor.

basilica A Roman building consisting of a rectangular structure with an **atrium** at its narrower end. This form provided the basic ground plan for many medieval cathedrals.

Beghard The male counterpart of a **Beguine**.

Beguinage A home or small area inhabited by **Beguines**.

Beguine A female member of a lay religious group dedicated to poverty, who lived communally in urban areas, and supported themselves by weaving and sewing.

bema A raised platform behind the chancel rail where the clergy sat during ceremonies.

bonnier A bonnier was equivalent to 1,080 square feet (100 square metres); 6 bonniers = 6,480 square feet (600 square metres).

bordar A **villein** of the lowest rank who rendered menial service for a cottage held at the will of his lord (from the French *borde*, meaning plank). See also **cottager**.

breve (pl. *breves*) A medieval term referring to a note that may generally be transcribed as an eighth note ($\flat$). Its exact value depended upon its position in the ligature, and in the pattern of ligatures which determined the mode.

caccia (pl. *cacce*) A three-part secular composition in which the two upper voices form a vocal canon with words; the lowest voice, or tenor, is usually non-canonic and untexted. It is generally assumed that this part was played by an instrument.

caliph (or *khalifa*) The title of the successor to Muhammad as leader of the Islamic community.

canon An ecclesiastical official connected with a cathedral.

catacomb An underground cemetery with recessed areas for tombs.

catastrophae Latin for "sensational acts."

cathedra The bishop's chair or throne in the cathedral.

cenobitic monasticism A monastic movement in which the monks lived together in a common establishment.

champlevé A metalworking technique in which the background is scraped away before being filled with molten glass.

Chancery The royal (and papal) department of government responsible for drafting documents and writing letters.

chartulary A collection of charters, as for an estate; also a manuscript volume or roll containing copies of original documents relating to the foundation, privileges, and customs of monasteries, convents, municipal corporations, educational establishments, and other such institutions.

chasse The French name for a **reliquary**, generally of French origin, and made in the shape of a **sarcophagus**.

ciborium or **baldacchino** An elaborate canopy placed over the altar.

civilitas Governance according to civil law.

civitas (pl. **civitates**) A Roman designation for a city.

clausula (pl. **clausulae**) A section of **organum** in syllabic, or "group" style.

clerestory The row of windows on the second level of a **basilica**, above the columns that bordered the **nave**.

colée (or **paumée**) The blow delivered to the candidate for knighthood by the sponsoring lord during the dubbing ceremony.

colonettes Piers attached to columns that are decorative supports for the vault of a Romanesque or Gothic church.

colonus (pl. **coloni**) Roman tenant farmers who did not own their land, but could not leave it.

comes A count in Merovingian society.

comitatus A group of warriors led by a common chieftain.

consanguinity A term used to indicate that marital partners (or potential partners) were too closely related to be married, according to canon law. It was often used in the Middle Ages to justify the annulment of a marriage.

consolamentum The "spiritual baptism" received when a Cathar became a **perfectus**, symbolized by the laying-on of hands by an established *perfectus*. The initiate became spotless and without sin.

conversus (pl. **conversi**) Lay brothers who were accepted into Cistercian monasteries, where they did manual work such as farming, building, and herding sheep.

cope A full-length semicircular cloak worn as a liturgical vestment.

cottager A **villein** of the lowest rank; sometimes known as a **bordar**.

count palatine A feudal lord or nobleman with sovereign power over his holdings or lands.

cruciform The cross shape on which the design of a medieval church or cathedral was based.

cupola A small dome.

curial class The aristocratic men of Rome, who traditionally served in the government.

Danelaw That part of England conquered by the Danes in the ninth century. It comprised East Anglia, eastern Mercia, and the region of the present-day counties of Lincolnshire and Yorkshire.

demesne That portion of a **manor** that was cultivated for the direct benefit of the lord.

denarius (pl. **denarii**) A coin made from silver; forty *denarii* made a **solidus**.

diet An assembly of secular and ecclesiastical dignitaries.

dineros Thirty *dineros* made up the fee paid by Jews in thirteenth-century Spain, recalling the thirty pieces of silver paid to Judas in exchange for Jesus.

discant A style of **organum** in which a newly composed melody is added to an existing Gregorian chant melody.

Divine Office A continuous cycle of daily prayer sung or recited at specific hours: Matins (2 a.m.), Lauds (daybreak), Prime (6 a.m.), Terce (9 a.m.), Sext (noon), None (3 p.m.), Vespers (about 5:30 p.m.), Compline (before retiring).

ell A measure of length that varied in different countries. The English ell was 45 inches (114 cm), the Scotch ell was 37 inches (94 cm), and the Flemish ell was 27 inches (68 cm).

emir An Arabic title that literally means "commander," but is often translated as "prince." The title was used by important military officers, governors of provinces, and by the virtually independent rulers of many provinces of the Islamic Empire, who nominally held power under the **caliph**.

emirate An independent state ruled by a provincial governor known as an **emir**.

Epicureanism A philosophy that advocated the pursuit of happiness through an avoidance of pain and strife and the cultivation of quiet enjoyment.

enquêtuer Emissaries of the king of France, established by Louis IX, similar in function to the Carolingian **missi dominici**.

eremitic monasticism An early form of highly ascetic monasticism; from the Greek *erêmia*, "desert."

escheat If a **vassal** failed to fulfill his responsibilities according to the feudal contract, or if he died without an heir, the **fief** would escheat (revert) to the lord.

Exchequer Royal office responsible for the collection of taxes and the supervision of the accounts of local officials.

Exchequer Rolls The oldest English public records that compiled judicial fees, feudal dues, and other financial transactions.

fan vault A vault decorated with cone-like shapes that are ornamented with patterns of ribs and tracery.

fealty The part of the ceremony establishing **vassalage** that required swearing loyalty to the lord on the Bible or a casket of holy relics.

feudal aids Occasional responsibilities required of a **vassal**. These were usually financial, such as a contribution for the knighting of the lord's eldest son, the marriage of his eldest daughter, or ransom if he were captured.

fiedel The German term for the **vielle**—a bowed instrument with five strings.

fief A grant of land to a **vassal** in exchange for military and judicial services.

fiqh Religious law or Islamic jurisprudence.

fisc The public treasury in the kingdom of the Franks.

flagellant A member of a religious group that developed in response to the Black Death. The adherents beat themselves and one another with barbed whips in hopes of avoiding the plague and receiving forgiveness for sinful behavior.

flying buttress A masonry arch that springs from a pier and extends to the ground, thereby supporting and strengthening the vaults and allowing Gothic architects to build cathedrals with higher elevations.

foreshortening Reducing or distorting parts of a represented object to make it seem three-dimensional.

forum The central square of a Roman city, where temples, government buildings, and businesses were situated.

freeman One who is not a **serf** but who may have been bound to his lord by payment of rents.

friar A member of the Franciscan or Dominican order who existed as a **mendicant**, espousing poverty and providing for daily needs through manual labor or begging.

frith Under Salic Law, the fine for an offense such as abduction.

fyrd An Old English term for the Anglo-Saxon army.

Gallican chant The most important form of liturgical chant in the kingdom of the Franks from the time of Clovis (d. 511) until its suppression by Pepin and Charlemagne.

geld The general land tax in Anglo-Saxon and Norman England.

glebe land That portion of a **manor** cultivated for the benefit of the church.

Gnosticism A religious sect whose members believed that all other religions were merely preparatory to their revelation of truth, which they revealed only to their own adherents.

goliard A cleric who had generally given up the religious life, or a wandering student who traveled around Europe telling tales and singing songs. These were often critical of the religious establishment.

gradual A book that contains music and liturgy for the Mass.

Grafen (counts) Noblemen of the Carolingian Empire who

maintained peace in the inner areas. They functioned as military commanders, judges, provincial governors, and royal representatives.

griffin A fantasy creature with the body and legs of a lion and the head and wings of an eagle.

groin vault A construction formed by two barrel vaults, intersecting at right angles.

guild An association of craftsmen or merchants that set guidelines for the conduct of trade or production, and that provided social benefits to its members.

hagiography Biographical literature concerning the lives and actions of the saints.

hajj The Muslim pilgrimage to Mecca, expected of all believers at least once during a lifetime.

halberget A kind of cloth, possibly hemp.

haram A sacred area, such as that surrounding the Ka'ba in Mecca.

hauberks The coat of chain mail worn by warriors of the eleventh and twelfth centuries.

hides Units of taxable land assessed to the *geld*.

Hijaz A province in Arabia, containing Mecca and Medina and bordered by the Red Sea.

hijra (or *hegira*) Muhammad's exodus from Mecca to Medina in 622.

homage The ceremony in which a **vassal** pledged himself to a lord.

icon A painting or mosaic image of the Virgin Mary, Christ, or the saints.

imam The spiritual leader of the Muslim community.

immixtio manuum The action

in which a **vassal** placed his hands between the hands of his lord during the **homage** ceremony.

jihad Holy war, generally referring to the struggle of the Muslim believer to obey the will of Allah, but also, to some factions, including physical war against the enemies of Islam.

jongleurs Itinerant musicians, jugglers, dancers, and animal trainers who traveled from court to court in medieval Europe.

judería An isolated Jewish community living in an urban area.

justiciar The chief political and judicial offices of the Norman and later kings of England until the thirteenth century.

Ka'ba The sacred shrine at Mecca that is the goal of Muslim pilgrimage.

khandaq A Persian word meaning "trench," used to describe the gulch dug to protect Medina from the Meccan assault (627).

lancet A tall, pointed window without tracery.

lay investiture The choosing and consecrating of ecclesiastical officials by the king.

leat A man-made water trench that feeds a mill.

lete Under the Salic Law of the Franks, a person whose status was between a free man and a slave. *Letes* may have been descendants of conquered people who had been assimilated into the tribe; they were not landowners, but cultivated the land of others, paying rent in produce and services.

liege lord The lord to whom primary military responsibility

was pledged by a **vassal**.

ligature A symbol incorporating a series of musical pitches.

longa (pl. *longas*) A note that may be transcribed into modern notation as (♩) or (♩.).

lute A plucked string instrument brought into Spain before the ninth century by the Muslim conquerors.

madrigal In the fourteenth century, the Italian madrigal was a work for two voices. The texts are eleven-syllable lines arranged in two or three three-line groups and a two-line refrain with the form *a a b* or *a a a b*.

mandorla An almond-shaped structure that often encased images of Christ and the Virgin Mary in medieval iconography.

Manicheanism A religion based on the teachings of the Persian prophet Mani, who taught that the universe was created by two gods—one good and one evil.

manor A self-contained agricultural settlement that provided sustenance for a community of peasants and their lord and his family.

Markgrafen (margraves) Carolingian noblemen with more military authority than *Grafen*, who governed the border regions of the empire.

mawali A term used to describe non-Arab Muslims in early Islamic history.

mendicant A term applied to those (especially in religious orders) who lived entirely on alms.

metropolitan An alternative term for archbishop or archbishopric.

mihrab A niche in the wall of a

mosque, indicating the direction of Mecca.

minaret The tower of a mosque from which the *muezzin* chants the call to prayer.

missi dominici "Messengers of the Lord" who traveled around the Carolingian empire, inspecting the activities of the officials and transmitting the orders of the emperor.

miter Part of the insignia of a bishop—a tall cap, deeply cleft at the top, wht outline of the front and back having the shape of a pointed arch.

monophony Music that features a single melodic line.

mosque A building where Muslims pray.

motet A musical form in which one, two, or three voice parts, with texts, are added to Gregorian chant.

mudéjar A Muslim living in Christian Spain.

muezzin A man who chants the call to Muslim prayer five times during the day.

muhajirin The original converts to Islam, who emigrated to Medina with the Prophet.

nave The congregational area of a church, usually its western limb, flanked by aisles.

Neoplatonism A philosophical system based on the teachings of Plato, which advocated belief in a transcendent, eternal being identified as "the One" or "the Good." Later Christian philosophers synthesized Neoplatonism with the doctrines of Christianity.

net vault A vaulting system that creates a mesh-like design of diagonal ribs.

neumes Signs written above the texts of chantbooks to indicate the rise and fall of the melody.

oblation A process whereby children, known as **oblates**, were "given" to a monastery, where they remained committed to the religious vocation for their entire lives.

oliphant An ivory horn, often decorated with carvings.

Ordinary Sections of the Mass that use the same text in every celebration: *Kyrie, Gloria, Credo, Sanctus,* and *Agnus Dei.* The parts that change from day to day are known as the Proper of the Mass.

organum Music consisting of intervals that simultaneously duplicate a chant melody.

organistrum A string instrument played by turning a crank attached to a wheel.

pallium A liturgical vestment worn over the chasuble (a sleeveless mantle) by the pope, archbishops, and some bishops of the Roman Catholic Church.

papal legate A representative of the pope who delivered papal directives and convened courts of inquiry.

paumée See *colée.*

Peace of God A decree proclaimed by church councils that prohibited violence against women, peasants, merchants, and members of the clergy.

perfectus (pl. *perfecti*) The higher level, or elect, to which—the Cathars taught— all should aspire.

perfectio A unit of rhythmic measure codified by medieval musical theorists, generally transcribed as a dotted-quarter note ($\downarrow$.).

pericopes Selected passages, usually from the Scriptures, to be read at liturgical ceremonies.

Petrine theory A doctrine that established the bishop of Rome as the head of the Church Universal.

pilgrimage choir A unit formed by the **ambulatory**, **apse**, and adjoining chapels in a Romanesque church.

plenary indulgence Complete remission granted by the church for the punishment due to an individual's sins.

polyphony Music consisting of more than one melody sung or sounded simultaneously.

preux "Valliant." The military prowess and strength expected of a knight.

primogeniture The policy by which the oldest son inherits his father's title and property.

prosa A form of chant that resulted when new words were composed to a preexisting chant.

psaltery A kind of zither played either by plucking or striking the strings.

qibla The indication of Mecca as the direction for prayer.

Quadrivium The grouping of arithmetic, geometry, astronomy, and music in the Roman educational curriculum.

quintaine A dummy dressed as a knight in chain mail that was set up on a post. Toppling it was the test whereby a newly knighted man proved his valor.

Qur'an The holy book of Islam, containing 114 *suwar.*

Ramadhan The month during which Muslims maintain a fast from sunrise to sunset.

rebec A gourd-shaped bowed instrument with three strings.

relief The fee paid for inheritance of a **fief**.

reliquary A container for the relics of saints.

Ridda Apostasy from Islam. The wars that occurred in Arabia following Muhammad's death are known as the *Ridda* wars.

romance A literary genre begun in the twelfth century, the plot of which often concerns an adulterous love affair between a married noblewoman and a knight of lower social status.

russet A coarse, homespun cloth commonly used in peasants' clothing.

sacrament A formal religious act or rite, such as the Eucharist.

sacramentary The liturgical book used by the officiating bishop or priest; it generally contained only the texts that changed according to the liturgical calendar.

salat The Islamic practice of ritual prayer, which takes place five times daily: at daybreak, noon, mid-afternoon, after sunset, and in the early part of the night.

Salian The name, meaning "salty," given by the Roman emperor Julian to a tribe of Franks who lived close to the North Sea; it was later used to describe an eleventh- and twelfth-century German dynasty.

Salic Law The law code of the Salian Franks.

sarcophagus (pl. **sarcophagi**) A freestanding tomb in wide use during the Roman and early Christian eras. Its shape resembled an elongated tent.

scriptorium (pl. *scriptoria*) The area of a monastery where the copying of manuscripts took place.

scutage A fee paid by a **vassal**

to a lord in lieu of military service.

selvedge The edge of a fabric, tightly woven so that it will not fray.

seneschal A royal official in France who administered areas close to hostile territory. Seneschals were able to command the necessary strong military force, and to direct localized battles. Otherwise, their duties were the same as the **baillis**.

sequence A melody added to the chant, particularly as an extension to the "Alleluia;" it was often furnished with a prose text, generally composed with rhyming pairs.

sequence A religious poem with pairs of rhyming lines, set to music.

serf An unfree peasant (**villein**), who was not allowed to leave the **manor** where he was born. He held a plot of land on the manor, and had to give the lord a share of the produce he raised, as well as providing labor for cultivating the lord's **demesne**.

sharia The religious law of Islam.

shawm A double-reed wind instrument with a piercing sound, often played outdoors.

Shi'a Muslims who believe that all **caliphs** should be direct descendants of Muhammad.

socman A peasant, below the status of a **freeman**, but above the rank of a **villein**, who was bound to his lord by a payment of money rent and some jurisdictional dependence.

solidus (pl. **solidi**) The basic unit of currency under the Salic Law of the Franks. It was made up of 40 **denarii**.

solmization The practice of providing a syllable to be sung for each pitch, thereby aiding the memorization of melodies.

Stoicism A philosophy that maintained there was a single rational principle controlling the universe and establishing universal harmony. Stoics cultivated self-control, courage, and devotion to duty.

studium generale A term closely corresponding to the modern concept of a university. In the thirteenth century it seems to have indicated an institution with organized facilities for study and the ability to attract students from a broad geographical area.

subinfeudation A term that refers to the dividing of a **fief** by one lord and the granting of portions of it to other lords, thereby establishing a relationship of **vassalage** with them.

suit to court The responsibility of a **vassal** to attend the court of his lord and to offer advice and judicial opinion.

summa (pl. **summae**) A philosophical treatise that presented knowledge as an integrated system.

sunna The actions and sayings of Muhammad used in determining legal precedent.

Sunni Muslims who believe that the actions of Muhammad (**sunna**) are of primary importance in guiding the community.

sura (pl. **suwar**) A chapter in the Qur'an.

syllogism A logical construction that presents two statements from which a conclusion can be drawn. (a = b; c = a; therefore, c = b)

tertiary A lay affiliate of a religious order.

thegn A warrior or attendant in Anglo-Saxon England.

tithe The 10 percent of a person's income that was given to the church.

transept The transverse arms of a cross-plan church.

tributarius A man in Merovingian Gaul who cultivated the land of another at a fixed rent. He was of lower status than a free man.

triforium The space between the **nave** arcade and the **clerestory**.

Trivium The grouping of logic, rhetoric, and grammar in the Roman educational curriculum.

trobairitz A female **troubadour**.

troubadour A poet/musician of southern France. The name came from the Provencal verb *trobar*, meaning "to find" or "to compose in verse."

trouvère The northern French counterpart of the **troubadour**.

Truce of God A measure stipulating that men should abstain from warfare and violence from Wednesday night to Monday morning of each week.

tympanum A semicircular area above the main doors of a church. It was frequently sculpted with scenes from the Bible or the lives of Christ, the Virgin Mary, or the saints.

ulama Muslim clergy or religious scholars.

umma The community of believers in Islam.

universitas (pl. **universitates**) A word used in the twelfth, thirteenth, and fourteenth centuries to denote a group of persons with common interests and independent legal status, such as a guild or a municipal corporation.

usury The practice of charging interest on loans, viewed as a sin by the medieval church.

vassal A nobleman who pledged his loyalty and fidelity to a lord by vows of **homage** and **fealty** established himself as a vassal, thus becoming a partner in the relationship known as **vassalage**.

vassalage A political system based on bonds of loyalty between men of the aristocratic warrior class.

vassi dominici Men who have obligated themselves to a lord, promising military service.

vielle A bowed instrument with five strings. It was made in a variety of shapes.

villein A free-born peasant, who was subject to labor services. He held a share of land in the open fields of his **manor**.

virgate A measure of land between 20 and 40 acres.

volo That part of the pledge given during the **homage** ceremony in which the **vassal** indicates that he is willing to "be the man" of his lord.

voussoirs Wedge-shaped insertions in the supporting arches of a **barrel vault**.

wattle and daub Woven branches (wattle) plastered with mud or clay (daub); a technique used in the construction of walls.

wiches Salt mines.

Witan The council of Anglo-Saxon nobles that elected the king and advised him on matters such as legislation.

PICTURE CREDITS

Frontispiece: © 2001, Photo Scala, Florence
1. © Cameraphoto Arte, Venice
3. © Vincenzo Pirozzi, Rome
6. Kunsthistorisches Museum Vienna
8. © Vincenzo Pirozzi, Rome
9. by permission of the Syndics of Cambridge University Library
11. AKG Images/Erich Lessing
12. © Cameraphoto Arte, Venice
14. British Museum, London
15. British Library, London
16. © The Cleveland Museum of Art, Purchase from the J.H. Wade Fund, 1930.504
17. © The Trustees of the Chester Beatty Library, Dublin
18. Robert Harding Picture Library/Mohammed Amin
20. Spectrum Picture Library
23. © Metropolitan Museum of Art, Harris Brisbane Dick Fund, 1939 (39.20)
24. Germanisches National Museum
25. Stiftsbibliothek St. Gallen
26. Bodleian Library, Oxford
27. Bayerische Staatsbibliothek
28. British Library, London
29. © Domkapitel Aachen
30. © Paul M.R. Maeyaert
35. Staatarchiv Zurich
36. Bibliothèque Nationale de France
41. University of Cambridge Unit for Landscape Modelling
42. Royal Library, The Hague

43. University Library of Heidelberg
44. The British Museum
45. University Library of Heidelberg
46. British Library, London
49. Musee de la Tapisserie, Bayeux, France/ Bridgeman Art Library. With special authorisation of the City of Bayeux
50. © A.F. Kersting
51. © 1990, Photo Scala, Florence
52. Bayerische Staatsbibliothek
53. © Domkapitel Aachen. Photo: Ann Münchow
54. Biblioteca Apostolica Vaticana
55. Bibiliothèque Nationale de Paris # Mc. Coislin 79, fol 2
58. The Bridgeman Art Library
59. The Art Archive/Dagli Orti
57. Jean Dieuzaide
65. Photo: Alison Frantz
67. Snider/The Image Works
68. © Paul M.R. Maeyaert
69. © Angelo Hornak
71. © Angelo Hornak. Courtesy of the Dean and Chapter of Durham Cathedral
73. © Paul M.R. Maeyaert
75. © Paul M.R. Maeyaert
76. Bildarchiv Foto Marburg
77. Musée Rolin, Autun
78. © Paul M.R. Maeyaert
79. © V&A Picture Library
80. © V&A Picture Library
81. © Bayerisches National Museum

82. British Library, London
83. By special permission of the City of Bayeux
85. © Biblioteca Ambrosiana. Auth no. 020/04
86. University Library of Heidelberg
90. The Bridgeman Art Library
91. © 1990, Photo Scala, Florence
92. © 1990, Photo Scala, Florence
93. The Art Archive/Cathedral of Monreale City/Dagli Orti
94. © Photo Scala, Florence/ Art Resource, New York
95. © Paul M.R. Maeyaert
97. Bibliothèque Nationale de France
98. University Library of Heidelberg
99. Biblioteca Governativa, Lucca
100. The Society of the Antiquaries of London
101. Cadw.Crown Copyright
102. © 2001, Photo Scala, Florence
103. Ciccione/Photo Researchers Inc.
104. The Art Archive/Real Biblioteca de lo Escorial/Dagli Orti
106. Biblioteca Apostolica Vaticana
107. Staatliche Kunsthalle Karlsruhe
108. © Bayerisches National Museum
109. National Library of the

Czech Republic
110. Bibliothèque Nationale de France
111. New College, Oxford/World Microfilms
112. Bildarchiv Preussischer Kulturbesitz
115. © Angelo Hornak
116. © Angelo Hornak. Courtesy of the Dean and Chapter of Canterbury Cathedral
119. © Angelo Hornak
120. © Angelo Hornak. Courtesy of the Dean and Chapter of Canterbury Cathedral
121. © Angelo Hornak
122. © Hirmer Verlag
123. Bildarchiv Foto Marburg
124. © Photo RMN – J.G. Berizzi
125. © 2004 Foto Pierpont Morgan Library/Art Resource/Scala, Florence
126. © Domkapitel Aachen. Photo: Ann Münchow
128. The British Library
131. Bibliothèque Nationale de France
132. © 2004 Foto Pierpont Morgan Library/Art Resource/Scala, Florence
133. Wellcome Trust Medical Photographic Library
134. The British Library, London
135. The British Library, London (detail)
136. Archivi Alinari, Florence
137. The Bridgeman Art Library
138. © Barry Lewis/Corbis
139. © Quattrone, Florence

TEXT CREDITS

Every effort has been made to trace or contact copyright holders, but Laurence King Publishing would be pleased to rectify any errors or omissions brought to their notice at the earliest opportunity.

Ams Press: from *A Source Book for Medieval History: Selected Documents Illustrating the History of Europe in the Middle Age*, edited by Oliver J. Thatcher and E. H. McNeal (Ams Press, 1971).

Ashgate Publishing: from *The History of Saladin*, by Baha al-din Shaddad, translated by D. S. Richards (Ashgate, 2001).

Cambridge University Press: from *Life in the Middle Ages*, vol. 4, by G. G. Coulton (Cambridge University Press, 1954); from "Confrerie, Bruderschaft, and Guild: The Formation of Musicians' Fraternal Organisations in Thirteenth- and

Fourteenth-Century Europe", by Kay Brainerd Slocum, in *Early Music History*, 14 (1995).

Columbia University Press: from *Heresies of the High Middle Ages*, by Walter L. Wakefield and Austin P. Evans (Columbia University Press, 1969); from *University Records and Life in the Middle Ages*, by Lynn Thorndike (Columbia University Press, 1944); from *The Chronicle of Jean*

de Venette, translated by Jean Birdsall, edited by Richard A. Newhall (Columbia University Press, 1953).

Constable & Robinson Ltd.: from *A Medieval Garner*, by G. G. Coulton (Constable, 1910).

Cornell University Press: from *A History of Medieval Spain*, by Joseph O'Callaghan (Cornell University Press, 1975).

The Dorsey Press: from *Medieval History: A Source Book*, edited by Donald White (The Dorsey Press, 1965).

Dover Publications: from *On Divers Arts*, by Theophilus, translated by John G. Hawthorne and Cyril Stanley Smith (Dover Publications, 1979).

Dreyers Forlag: from *From the Sagas of the Norse Kings*, by Snorri Sturluson, translated by Erling Monsen and A. H. Smith (Dreyers Forlag, 1967).

Harcourt Inc.: from *The Black Death: A Turning Point in History?*, edited by William M. Bowsky (Holt, Rinehart & Winston, 1971).

HarperCollins Publishers: from *The Black Death: A Chronicle of the Plague*, by Johannes Nohl (George Allen & Unwin, 1926).

HarperCollins Publishers Inc.: from *Life in a Medieval Castle*, by Joseph Gies and Frances Gies (Harper & Row, 1974).

Hispanic Society: from *Hispano-Arabic Poetry and Its Relations with the Old Provencal Troubadours*, by A. R. Nykl (Joseph Furst, 1946; Hispanic Society, Baltimore, 1986).

Peter Lang Publishing Inc.: from *Troubadour Lyrics: A Bilingual Anthology*, by Frede Jensen (Peter Lang, 1998).

Macmillan Publishers: from *Spain in the Middle Ages*, by Angus MacKay (Palgrave Macmillan, 1977).

Nelson Thornes: from *The Chronicle of Jocelin of Brakelond, Concerning the Acts of Samson, Abbot of the Monastery of St. Edmund*, translated by H. E. Butler (Thomas Nelson, 1949).

W. W. Norton & Company: from *The Decameron*, by Boccaccio, translated and edited by Mark Musa and Peter I. Bondanella (W. W. Norton, 1977); from *The Selected Writings of Christine de Pizan*, translated and edited by Renate Blumenfeld-Kosinski and Kevin Brownlee (W. W. Norton, 1997).

Oxford University Press: from *Acts of the Christian Martyrs*, translated by Herbert Musurillo (Oxford University Press, 1971); from *History of the Franks*, by St. Gregory of Tours, translated by O. M. Dalton (Clarendon Press, 1927).

Oxford University Press Inc.: from *Islam: From the Prophet Muhammed to the Capture of Constantinople*, 2 vols., by Bernard Lewis (Oxford University Press, 1987); from *Letters of Hildegard of Bingen*, vol. 1, edited by Joseph L. Baird and Radd K. Ehrman (Oxford University Press, 1998).

Paulist Press: from *The Life of Saint Anthony*, by Athanasius of Alexandria, translated by Robert T. Meyer (Newman Press, 1950); from *Bonaventure: The Soul's Journey Into God, The Tree of Life, The Life of St. Francis*, edited by Ewert Cousins (Paulist Press, 1978).

Pegasus Press: from *The Vezelay Chronicle*, by Hugh of Poitiers, translated by John Scott and John O. Ward. Medieval & Renaissance Texts & Studies (Pegasus Press, 1992).

Penguin Books Group (UK): from *The Koran*, translated by N. J. Dawood (Penguin Classics, 1999); from *Two Lives of Charlemagne*, by Einhard and Notker the Stammerer, translated by Lewis Thorpe (Penguin Classics, 1999), translation © Professor Lewis Thorpe, 1999; from *The Alexiad of Anna Comnena*, translated by E. R. A. Sewter (Penguin Classics, 1969); from *The Song of Roland*, translated by Dorothy L. Sayers (Penguin Books, 1957); from *The Letters of Abelard and Heloise*, translated by Betty Radice (Penguin Books, 1974); from *The Canterbury Tales*, by Geoffrey Chaucer, translated by Nevill Coghill (Penguin Classics, 1951)

Penguin Putnam Inc.: from *The Lais of Marie de France*, translated by Robert Hanning and Joan Ferante (E. P. Dutton, 1978); from *The Romance of the Rose*, by Guillaume de Loris and Jean de Meun, translated by Harry W. Robbins (E. P. Dutton, 1962).

Prentice-Hall Inc.: from *The Crisis of Church and State, 1050–1300*, by Brian Tierney (Prentice-Hall, 1964); from *Selected Sonnets, Odes and Letters*, by Petrarch, translated by T. G. Bergin (Appleton-Century-Crofts, 1966).

Princeton University Press: from *Abbot Suger: On the Abbey Church of St.-Denis and its Art Treasures*, edited and translated by Edwin Panofsky (2nd edition by Gerda Panofsky-Soergel) (Princeton University Press, 1979).

The Random House Group (UK): *from English Historical Documents, vol. II, 1042–1189*, edited by David Douglas and G. W. Greenaway (Eyre & Spottiswoode, 1953); from *English Historical Documents, vol. III, 1189–1327*, edited by Harry Rothwell (Eyre & Spottiswoode, 1975).

Random House Inc.: from *The Records of Medieval Europe*, edited by Carolly Erickson (Anchor Books/Doubleday & Co., 1971); from *Basic Writings of Saint Thomas Aquinas*, vol. 2, edited by Anton C. Pegis (Random House, 1945); from *The Divine Comedy*, by Dante Alighieri, translated by John Aitken Carlyle, Thomas Okey and Philip H. Wicksteed (Random House, 1962, 1950).

Simon & Schuster Inc.: from *Music in the Western World: A History in Documents*, edited by Piero Weiss and Richard Taruskin (Schirmer Books, 1984).

Margaret E. Taylor: from *Recueil de texts relatifs a l'histoire de l'architecture et a la conditions des architects en France au moyen age* (Editions Auguste Picard, 1929). Translated from the Latin by Professor Margaret E. Taylor, Wellesley College.

University of California Press: from *The Early Medieval Sequence*, translated by Richard Crocker (University of California Press, 1977).

University of Pennsylvania Press: from *The Capture of Constantinople: The "Hysteria of Constantinopolitana" of Gunther of Pairis*, edited by Alfred J. Andrea (University of Pennsylvania Press, 1997); from *Witchcraft in Europe: 400–1700, A Documentary History*, 2nd edition, by Alan Charles Kors and Edward Peters (University of Pennsylvania Press, 2001).

University of Toronto Press: from *Liturgies in Honour of Thomas Becket*, by Kay Brainerd Slocum (University of Toronto Press, 2003).

INDEX

Aachen 116, 120
Abbasid dynasty 91, 95–6
Abbey Church, Fulda 122–3
Abbey Church, St.-Denis 297
Abd-al-Rahman I 93–4
Abelard, Peter 311–15, 377
Abu al-Abbas 95–6
Abu Bakr 84–5
Adelaide, of Sicily 278–9
administration, government
   Carolingian 108
   English 325–6
   French 327–8
Adrian IV 274
agricultural revolution 136–63
agriculture 140–4, 407
Albigensians see Cathars
Alcuin 115, 116, 119, 124
Alexander III 274
Alfonso I 282
Alfonso VI 217, 218, 281–2
Alfonso X (the Wise) 337–8
Alfonso Henriques 283
Alfred the Great 166
Ali (cousin of Muhammad) 87
allodial lands 179
Almohades 283, 284
Ambrose 26
Amiens Cathedral 394–5
Angevin empire 264–8
Anglo-Saxons 63–7, 130
Antony, St. 32–3
Aquinas, Thomas 369, 384–6
Arabic 79, 98
Arabization 98
arches 232, 388, 389
architects 390–1
architecture
   14th century 424–5
   Carolingian 120–4
   Classical legacy 20–2
   Gothic 296–9
   Merovingian 61
   Romanesque 232–41
Arianism 26, 71, 92
aristocracy
   Carolingian 111–14
   domestic life 157–60
   education 300

liege lords 148
   rights 322
   vassalage 145
   women 157
Aristotle 382
Arius 25, 26
Ars nova 421–3
art
   Early Christian 35–6
   Carolingian 245–7
   Romanesque 395–6
   Gothic 395-6
   Late Middle Ages 433
Arthurian legend 300–1
Athanasian Christianity 26, 56, 71
Athanasius of Alexandria 25, 26
Augustine 27–8
Autun Cathedral (St.-Lazare) 241–4
Avars 107
Averroës (Ibn Rushd) 283–4
Avignon 419

Baghdad 91
Baldwin of Flanders 211, 212, 213
Balkans 192
Ball, John 414–15
Baltic territories 340
Basil I 186
Basil II 187
basilicas 20–2
bathing 160
Bayeux Tapestry 252–3
Becket, Thomas 205, 265–6
   martyrdom commemorated 246–9
Bede 69
Bedouins 75
Beguines 351–2
Benedict of Aniane, St. 218
Benedict of Nursia, St. 34
Benedictine monasteries 34–5, 215, 218–20
Bernard of Clairvaux 222–3, 224, 245, 314–15, 340
Bible 29
bishops 25, 30

Black Death 406, 408–13
Blanche of Castile 329
Boccaccio, Giovanni 425–9
Boethius, Anicius Manlius Severinus 44–6
Bohemia 189, 340
Bohemond of Otranto 211, 213
Boleslav the Great 188
Bologna, university at 375–6
Bonaventure 369, 383
Boniface VIII 332–3
books, production of 353
Brethren of the Common Life 352–3
British Isles 63–71, 137, 166
   see also England
Bulgaria 192
buttresses 388
Byzantine empire 47–54
   11th century 207
   13th century 341–5
   culture 187
   golden age 185–8

calligraphy 99
Cambridge University 380
cannons 418
Canterbury 205–6
Canterbury Tales, The (Chaucer) 430–1
Canute the Great 167
Capetian dynasty 173
Carolingian Empire 102–32, 145
Carolingian minuscule 117
Carolingian Renaissance 115–26
Carthusians 222
Cassiodorus 46–7
castles 158–60, 170, 215, 326
Cathars 353–5
cathedral schools 299
cathedrals 237–40, 386–95, 424–5
Catherine of Siena, St. 420
Celtic church 69
Celtic culture 63–71
cenobitic monasticism 34
chant singing 30, 124–5, 254
Charlemagne
   Aachen 120

Carolingian Renaissance 115–17
   coronation 102
   death 126
   Holy Roman Empire 104–11
   Spain 249
Charles IV 416
Charles VII 418
Charles of Anjou 335
Chartres Cathedral 392, 393, 394
Chaucer, Geoffrey 429–31
children 161, 220, 300
chivalry 305
choir monks 224
Chrétien de Troyes 301–2
Christ, humanization of 364–5
Christianity
   Arianism 26, 71, 92
   Athanasian 26, 56, 71
   conversion to see conversion to Christianity
   early Church 25–6
   Fathers of the Church 26–30
   missionaries 68, 69, 192
   monasticism 31–5
   origins 22–4
   Orthodox 185, 192
   papacy 30–1
   Roman Empire 16
   Scandinavia 192–4
   Spain 94, 203–5
   women 24, 35, 113–14, 360–1, 363–4
Christianization see conversion to Christianity
Christians, Spain 93
Christine de Pizan 431–3
Church 162, 175, 176, 349, 419–21
churches 230, 232–7
Cistercians 222–5
cities 292, 349
Clare of Assisi 360–1
Classical legacy 12–22
Classical Roman culture 42
Clement V 333, 419
clerical reform 180
climate 137, 407